# AUTHENTIC DECOR

# PETER THORNTON

# AUTHENTIC DECOR

## THE DOMESTIC INTERIOR

## 1620-1920

FOR MY THREE DAUGHTERS

EMMA,
MINNA
AND DORA

First published in the United Kingdom in 1984 by
George Weidenfeld & Nicolson

Reprinted in 1985
First published in paperback in 1993

This paperback edition published in 2000 by
Seven Dials, Cassell & Co
Wellington House, 125 Strand
London, WC2R 0BB

Distributed in the United States of America by
Sterling Publishing Co., Inc.
387 Park Avenue South,
New York, NY 10016-8810

A CIP catalogue record for this book is available
from the British Library

ISBN 1 84188 109 0

Designed by Trevor Vincent
Colour separations by Newsele Litho Limited.
Filmset by Keyspools Limited, Golborne, Warrington, Lancs.
Printed and bound in Italy by L.E.G.O., Vicenza

Facing Title Page:
The Study of Crown Princess Marie of Bavaria at the Residenz, Bamberg, 1844
*Wittelsbacher Ausgleichsfonds Inventarverwaltung, Munich*

# CONTENTS

# AUTHOR'S NOTE TO THE SEVEN DIALS EDITION OF 2000

For this re-issue I would like to draw attention to an article published in *Oud Holland* in 1998 (112Nr.2) by my friend and colleague Professor Willemijn Fock of Leiden University. She took my Plate 45 here as an example of the way Dutch artisits of the 1650s, 60s and 70s sometimes portrayed most convincingly features in middle class interiors which were not actually present – they were too grand for such a setting. The artists did this in order to flatter their patrons and/or to demonstrate their virtuosity in the handling of perspective and the depiction of different materials, surfaces or patterns.

For example, Oriental carpets were not to be seen on floors in such settings until the very end of the century whereas matting, which was increasingly used as the century wore on, even in important rooms, is rarely depicted because the rendering of it offered no great challenge. Only in aristocratic houses might carpets occasionally be found on floors, Professor Fock says, and she speaks with great authority having studied hundreds of Dutch inventories, notably from houses in Leiden but also from Amsterdam and The Hague. Nevertheless, a difficulty I find about this (not an insuperable one, of course) is how so many Dutch artists were able to find carpets on floors to depict so accurately – and carpets of different patterns – so there must have been quite a few somewhere. Were they perhaps to be seen in dealers' shops? Of course

the study of interiors requires both prongs of attack – the archival and the pictorial – but I do maintain that we have no better eveidence of how rooms looked in the past than pictures of the sort reproduced here, and Professor Fock agrees with me on this point.

I also want to say that the emphasis I placed on the importance of Madame de Rambouillet in the 1620s may have been excessive but made the point about the strong links with Italy. I also suspect that a few more rooms than I imagined were being decorated with grotesques (*arabesques*) in Paris during the 1760s. Much more has been discovered about Chiswick House since this book came out. Indeed, the presentation of historic rooms has come forward amazingly since 1984 in much of the Western world. And the 'period eye' I wrote about in my original Introduction (top of page 9) has indeed moved on; people today can tolerate greater density in the furnishing of rooms along with far more complicated patterns than we could back in 1983. And the young are now capable of taking in images with amazing rapidity.

At the end of the Notes on page 397 I have added a short bibliography of works brought out since 1984 which I have found helpful and that carry our subject on a good deal further.

## ERRATA

p.48, lines 20 & 21, *for* envelope *read* enveloppe

p. 104, plate 119: The date of the original painting from which this print was made is 1736.

p.105, plate 120: The date of this painting is 1736.

p.143, line 2, Piranesi produced a set of designs for Egyptian motifs in 1769.

p.187, plate 240, line 3, *for* Coffinet *read* Coffinel

p.263, plate 348: *The title should read* A young Swedish officer's room in Stockholm, *c.* 1837–38

*In order to assemble the large group of illustrations reproduced in this book photographers all over Europe and America have assisted by providing photographs, many of which had to be taken under conditions that were far from ideal. No one could regret this more than the photographers concerned. In some cases, therefore, less than perfect photographs have been reproduced here because it was considered essential to include them, the aim of this survey being as far as possible to comprise images that were not already well known.*

# ACKNOWLEDGEMENTS

This book was written at home in my spare time. Only someone who has lived alongside that often irritable, generally pre-occupied and mostly rather unhelpful being, the author in his own home, can have any idea of what burdens the other members of his household have to bear. It is to my wife, therefore, that I owe by far the greatest debt since she remained remarkably cheerful all along, even when faced with these additional shortcomings of mine. Moreover, during the many months involved she gave me much excellent advice and not infrequent encouragement.

It was Mark Boxer who conceived the idea of publishing this book and who nursed it through its infancy. Before he left Weidenfeld, he and I had established the outlines which were later developed by myself in collaboration with Tristram Holland and Linden Lawson. No doubt many other people were involved but these were my principal contacts and my debt to all three is immense.

I work at the Victoria and Albert Museum in London. It would have been virtually impossible to compile the information encompassed in this work without the facilities which that institution can provide – access to its Art Library and its Print Room, with their helpful staff, the presence of knowledgeable colleagues to advise one within their specialities, excellent photographers, and much else. I am of course particularly grateful to the members of my own Department, that of Furniture and Woodwork, for the help and advice they have so freely given me. I should like particularly to thank Simon Jervis and Clive Wainwright for their generosity in always being prepared to discuss problems and for drawing my attention to numerous works with which I was unfamiliar. My thanks also go to John Hardy, Frances Collard and Catherine Norman for their kindness on many occasions. I am exceptionally grateful, however, to Stephen Astley, who ferreted out much information for me from obscure corners of various libraries and helped me secure a great amount of material. The many photographs of objects in the Museum's collections, incidentally, were taken by Ken Jackson and Philip de Bey.

Friends and colleagues all over the world also helped me but some deserve especial mention. I am particularly grateful to Elisabet Hidemark of Nordiska Museet in Stockholm for wide-ranging help over many years. I am also much indebted to Sam Dornsife, the specialist in nineteenth-century decoration, for throwing open his library to me and making many illustrations available for my studies. I have been much helped by Florence Montgomery, Elaine Dee, Roger Moss, Gail Winkler, Janet Byrne, Ellie Reichlin, Edgar Mayhew, Christopher Monkhouse and Kathryn Hiesinger in the United States; Pierre Verlet and Jacqueline Viaux in France; Hans Ottomeyer, Lorenz Seelig, Burkard von Roda and Helmut Börsch-Supan in Germany; Dyveke Helsted, Inge Meier Antonsen and Tove Clemmensen in Denmark; Barbro Hovstadius and Suzanne Bennet in Sweden; Christian Witt-Dörring in Austria; Daniela Di Castro and Alvar Gonzalez-Palacios in Italy; Hedwig Szabolcsi in Hungary; Kees Burgers and Wies Erkolens in Holland; Bozenna Majewska-Maszkowska in Poland; and John Harris, Jill Lever, Jane Preger, Robin Middleton, Lisa Clinton (Lady White) and Jack Baer in my own country.

The private individuals and the institutions who own the originals of the images reproduced in this book are gratefully acknowledged in the relevant captions. I apologise if in some cases credit has not been given in the proper manner. Artists' names are given where appropriate.

For especial help with procuring certain photographs and for information about specific illustrations I am also greatly indebted to the following: Ferenc Batàri, Francis Burne, Andrew Ciechanowiecki, Charlotte Christensen, Jonathan Fairbanks, Stig Fogelmarck, Wilhelmijn Fock, the Knight of Glin, Ian Gow, Bredo Grandjean, Elma Hernmarck, Françoise Jestaz, Sanne Jolles, Alistair Laing, Olivier Lefuel, Giles Mandelbrote, Pauline Metcalf, Friedrich Oswald, Jane Nylander, Anne Parsons, Cristina Piacenti, Peter Pröschel, William Rieder, Cordelia Rose, Theo Lunsingh Scheurleer, Marie-Anne Simons, Tamara Rappé, Michael Snodin, Anna Somers-Cocks, Michael Stürmer, Natalie Stutchbury, Renée van der Vloodt, Roger Ward, Gillian Wilson and Ole Woldbye.

The remarkable pictures from the Jagiellonian University, Cracow, were provided by the Royal Castle, Warsaw.

Last but by no means least I would like to record my gratitude to Louisa Lawson, my assistant, whose interest in this project, patient handling of the typing, and efficient organisation of the correspondence provided the vital support without which it would have been almost impossible for me to have accomplished this task.

Peter Thornton  London, 1984

# INTRODUCTION

To write about the history of interior decoration no longer needs justifying, but to do so in anything like a serious vein may still require an apology. I was therefore grateful when my youngest daughter drew my attention to a passage in Macaulay's *History of England* (1848), where he maintains that 'Readers who take an interest in the progress of civilisation and of the useful arts will be grateful to the humble topographer who has recorded these facts [about the meanness of the lodgings of those taking the waters at Bath, early in the eighteenth century], and will perhaps wish that historians of far higher pretensions had sometimes spared a few pages from military evolutions and political intrigues, for the purpose of letting us know how the parlours and bedchambers of our ancestors looked.'[1]

Taking courage from this episode, I started to write the present book which surveys the decoration and arrangement of the domestic interior in the Western world between 1620 and 1920. I have not included public rooms, although it must be admitted that the reception rooms of especially grand people have from time to time taken on something of a public character.

The subject is illustrated with a large number of pictures of rooms, all made at the time, when the decoration in each case was new or virtually so. These illustrations show rooms as they actually were – if we allow for a certain amount of editing, as will be explained. Not a single modern view has been included for the simple reason that such views are always misleading; no surviving room can possibly have come down to us unchanged in some respect (and often in many) and no restoration, however skilful, can be anything other than an attempt of a given date to recreate something the restorer can never have seen.

The main illustrations, the views of rooms, are supplemented by a number of coeval designs which throw light on contemporary intentions and aspirations.

Whenever the opportunity arose I chose the most charming picture available. I did so not merely for the pleasure such images give us today but because they also convey some of the delight that people of the time found in the style which was in favour at the time concerned. Such pictures help to remind us that styles we find unattractive were thought enchanting when new – by many people, at any rate.

Some of the captions are rather long. This is because I have found that not everyone finds it easy to take in at a glance many of the features and details which are to be seen in pictures like those reproduced in this book. Sometimes they need a little guidance so as not to miss significant points.

It was Mario Praz who first drew widespread attention to this subject as a whole in his *An Illustrated History of Interior Decoration* (London, 1964).[2] Praz, who was Professor of English Literature at the University of Rome, was in fact not all that interested in the history of interior decoration, as Hugh Honour has pointed out.[3] The 'true subject' of this 'conversationally discursive' book, Honour insists, 'is not interior decoration but the ruminations and memories, the visions and fancies prompted by paintings of interiors'. Praz did however open up for a wide public the delights that could be found in contemporary illustrations of decorated interiors, and since his book came out the interest which this subject has attracted has increased enormously. Some people find such pictures interesting for their own sake; others seek information about past practices from them. All must find them fascinating for what they tell us about the kind of space with which our ancestors surrounded themselves indoors. If this present book is therefore seen as complementing Praz's work I shall be well satisfied. This fresh offering brings forward a further large number of illustrations which are not at all well known (indeed, many have never been published before). Moreover in the text I have tried to draw attention to some aspects of the subject that Praz hardly touched upon.

It is often claimed that illustrations like those included in Praz's book and in this work cannot be trusted. I believe this is a gross exaggeration. Of course all works of art, however humble, have to some extent been edited by the artist for one reason or another, and one has to try and take into account the artist's purpose in making the picture.[4] Nevertheless the degree of licence is never all that large and, as Harold Peterson has so pertinently observed, so long as the artist was portraying a scene in the *milieu* in which 'he and his potential viewers lived, one can normally accept his depictions as accurate. If he portrayed a detail that everyone would know was wrong or impossible, he would be destroying the effectiveness of his picture. Under normal circumstances he would be careful not to do it.'[5] Such pictures, therefore, must constitute the best evidence we have got for how rooms looked at the time concerned.

In order to make the selection of pictures used in this book, it should be added, about three times as many were assembled and many more surveyed. When scanning such a wide spectrum the idiosyncracies of individual artists, and the peculiarities of a particular representation, assume far less significance and it becomes possible, or so it would seem, to get quite a good idea of what was the norm at each stage. I believe, therefore, one should look at such pictures for what they *do* tell us, and that the more pictures one looks at the easier it becomes to recognize what was characteristic during each phase.

If we consider the rooms in which our own personal friends and acquaintances live, it is obvious that there are many different ways of arranging and decorating a house, and this was always so. Nevertheless, each period of history has its own way of seeing things – its own 'period eye', as it were – which, by some strange process, seems to affect pretty well everyone. This in effect means that people in circles that react to fashion, even when it is only to quite a limited extent, possess a common way of viewing rooms – and, indeed, much else. It means that a certain degree of density in the arrangement of the furniture is regarded as generally acceptable at that moment. It means that at some periods a larger number of objects can be tolerated *en masse* in a room than at others. It means that there are variations in how much pattern the eye can assimilate: in the late Victorian period it was a great deal while in the 1930s it was very little. As I write, in 1983, it seems that the contemporary eye can tolerate rather more fussy patterns and arrangements than could that of between, say, 1930 and 1970. Although there will always be exceptions, therefore, what characterizes a period in the field of interior decoration is the density of pattern and arrangement that prevails at that time. The change is more rapid than one might suppose (for example, it is not a question of each generation having a fixed sense of these matters) and I expect it will eventually be possible to recognize the characteristics of a decade quite easily with practice. It will be understood that the characteristics in question are not simply a question of how the walls are decorated, of what furniture is present, and of the pattern of the carpet. It is something much more subtle and I can at present only define it as a matter of density.

In surveying such a large body of illustrations I have also been struck by the speed with which ideas about fashionable decoration must have spread. In the nineteenth century especially (for which of course there is plenty of pictorial evidence), it is amazing to see the same novel feature appearing in scenes of the same date from places that are widely separated geographically. This suggests that information about such matters could swiftly be obtained almost anywhere in the Western world from the centres where fashion was created. Naturally a person had to *want* to obtain such information in order to take trouble to secure it quickly but, when this was the case, the process could be very rapid indeed: we should reckon in weeks, not in years, as is generally supposed. Count Tessin, the Swedish Court Architect, sitting in Stockholm in the late seventeenth century and eagerly awaiting news of fresh fashions from Paris, could expect to receive it in about three weeks,[6] and I understand that the Princess Lubomirska, whose magnificent residences in Poland and elsewhere in Central Europe leave us in no doubt that she cared about these matters, could obtain books from Paris in about a fortnight at the end of the eighteenth century.[7]

Fashions in interior decoration caught on so quickly that it is not unreasonable to view this subject as an international phenomenon, for it cut across all borders. Moreover, it seems to me that it is only when we have plotted the international development that we can safely turn to local variants and peculiarities. Indeed, what seems to have happened right through the three centuries covered by this book was that new fashions spread very quickly among people who cared, and that it was only then that these same fashions percolated down through the social strata in the places to which they had first so speedily spread – and it did so at very different rates in the different localities. This last process could indeed take years. It is because fashions spread rapidly among those who, for lack of a better term, one may call 'top people' that our studies must inevitably be concentrated primarily on the kinds of décor with which they chose to surround themselves. For our purposes it is the main line that matters. However, a number of illustrations of what are clearly not 'main-line interiors' have been included as a reminder that the process of percolation was always taking place, everywhere, and quite erratically.

These are big questions which cannot be gone into at all deeply here but a word must be said about the principle of the 'false start'. New fashions are quite often introduced as radical innovations, in an effort to break with the prevailing mode and not infrequently as an almost conscious affront to those who espouse the latter. At any rate the new fashions are not at first accepted outside a quite narrow circle, even among people who are interested in these matters. A more moderate, less shocking, version of the new style is then gradually developed which eventually commends itself to a wider public. It is after this long delay – it can take twenty years – that something like the original and erstwhile shocking style is generally adopted. Two well-known instances of the 'false start' principle are the introduction of Neo-Classicism in Paris in the mid-eighteenth

century[8] and the manner in which an uncompromising 'modernist' style appeared in Vienna around 1900 almost overnight. In both cases a much more moderate style was evolved after the rather startling arrival of the style in its first form, and in both cases it was not until some twenty years later that a substantial number of people gradually became accustomed to the new lines.

Given that there is a *Zeitgeist*, or 'period eye' as I called it for lack of a better term, and that this governs the general appearance of rooms at each stage in some subtle way, what can we helpfully say about the way 'interiors' are created?

The client obviously has a large say in the matter in most cases, and his role needs no defining here. In the seventeenth century, when the co-ordinating and dominant role of the architect had not yet been properly established except in certain court circles, a well-educated client would quite often direct the building of his own house, if only because he tended to know more about the newest forms of building than the master-builder who was to erect the house. The latter was an artisan working in an ancient tradition with only a limited knowledge of recent developments in his own field. The client-architect, on the other hand, had usually travelled abroad and often had access to books (including handbooks on building and architecture) which he could read and for the most part understand. What has been said, incidentally, applies equally well where the client was a woman, and it hardly needs to be added that women have always had an important influence on the planning and appearance of the interior of houses. A striking example of this was Mme de Rambouillet, who makes her appearance at the beginning of our story (see p. 14). Women's importance in this field has been recognized by writers on architecture from an early date, although it was only in the second half of the nineteenth century that books on the subject actually began to be addressed directly at women. Among the earliest was that by the novelist Harriet Beecher Stowe, written in collaboration with her sister Catherine Beecher, entitled *The American Woman's Home* (New York, 1864), but the epitome of the genre was Jacob von Falke's *Art in the House* (Vienna, 1871; Boston, 1878) in which a whole chapter is devoted to 'woman's aesthetic mission'.

In the eighteenth century the professional architect gradually became more firmly entrenched as a knowledgeable leader of a team of craftsmen (bricklayers, carpenters, paviours, plumbers, etc.) and tended to produce proposals to which the client could react, so that a compromise was eventually reached between the client's requirements and the architect's idea of how the building should look, inside and out.

Architects steeped in the Renaissance tradition, in which a unified and therefore harmonious scheme was the highest ideal, needed to pay attention also to the interior (and even sometimes to the most prominent pieces of furniture) if they were to achieve the desired effect. Not all architects recognized the need, however, and others found themselves unable to exercise the necessary control over the craftsmen who had to carry out the scheme, as we shall see.

Architects were anyway not usually called in unless there was actual building to do, and since it is unusual for fundamental changes to be made to a house more than once in a generation, less extensive changes were more commonly carried out with the aid of other agents. If one simply wanted to 'do over' a room, one called in an upholsterer who could in fact almost totally alter its appearance without changing the basic interior architectural structure at all. He did this mostly with the aid of textile confections – upholstery, in the stict sense of the term – but, during the late seventeenth and eighteenth centuries he was very happy to provide a complete decorating service, engaging and co-ordinating the efforts of sub-contractors of many kinds.

Even when an architect was involved, because the alteration was more

9

1, 2] THE SAME ROOM IN 1819 AND 1821
Sir John Leicester's Picture Gallery in Hill Street, London. Only minor changes were made in the three years that separate these views. The furniture, which had originally been placed against the walls in the eighteenth-century manner, had crept out on to the floor by 1821. A table has been introduced to stand out in front of the ottoman in the draped alcove. (From William Carey's *Descriptive Catalogue* of the collection, 1819, and John Young's more elaborate catalogue of 1821.)
*Victoria and Albert Museum, London*

fundamental or an extension was being undertaken, an upholsterer would be brought in to complete the task and it was often the work of the upholsterer that was most evident as one surveyed a newly finished room. This could be infuriating for the architect if he was displeased with the final effect, whether this was due to his having failed to control the furnishing or because he had had no say in the matter whatsoever. It was in fact a bold architect who ventured to control an upholsterer of standing. There was anyway plenty of opportunity for friction. It is not therefore surprising that the architects levelled a great deal of criticism at this influential and often rather powerful class of tradesman.

Such criticisms were no doubt being expressed by architects already by the end of the seventeenth century, but the first reference to the problem is probably that made by Le Camus de Mézieres in 1780.[9] He insists that the furniture of an important bedchamber should be designed by the architect 'and not by the upholsterer who should confine himself to executing the designs'. It happens all too often, Le Camus says, that the upholsterer determines how the entire furnishings should look but he does so without regard to the principles of architecture, his own interests being the only guide. As a result what he creates is faulty. It is up to the architect to pay attention to all such details, Le Camus insists.

Those great architects of the Napoleonic era, Percier and Fontaine, took the same line: furnishing, they state, is so closely associated with the decoration of the interior that no architect can afford to ignore it.[10] This message does not seem to have got through to many English architects by the 1820s, however, for John Britton tells us that the British architect 'rarely exhibits in his designs anything beyond the bare walls of his rooms' whereas he ought, Britton believes, 'to exercise his judgment on furniture [by which he means furnishings], which so much affect interior decoration ... we contend he ought not to leave a house ... till he sees and approves all the furnishings and fittings ...'.[11]

William Mitford goes further and wants the architect and the upholsterer to work together 'like Rubens and Snyders in painting'.[12] He believes this was how it used to be 'in Paris, under the last Bourbons' (i.e. when Le Camus was writing). He then goes on to say that 'furnishing is generally reckoned the lady's business', adopting a rather patronizing tone about female talents in this direction. He describes what happens when a lady seeks the help of an upholsterer for whom 'Beyond all others his spirits of Novelty and Variety are objects of ... worship'. The upholsterer 'is versed in the ways of leading her' and knows 'the weak points in human nature'. 'Nothing is so advantageous for him as to gain prevalence for a new fashion of very bad taste' because then he will soon be asked to change it, or so Mitford insists, 'for of all things change is most beneficial to him. ... The upholsterer's interest ... is in direct opposition to the architect's credit.'

The battle between the architects and the upholsterers raged right through the nineteenth century. The sharpness of Mitford's attack suggests that the upholsterers were in the ascendant during the early decades of the century. The architects seem to have regained a certain degree of control by the middle of the century but one senses a note of resignation in Robert Kerr's comments, made in the 1860s, when he writes that 'the architect must not venture to reckon without in the first place his client, and in the second place his client's upholsterer', although he hopes the architect and upholsterer 'can be made to work together intelligently and artistically', in which case 'very charming effects can be realised'.[13]

Jacob von Falke was less polite, however. Writing around 1870, he refers to the upholsterer's 'usual insipid routine' but he does admit that 'there are upholsterers and decorative artists who can both understand and carry out artistic intentions'.[14] Charles Eastlake was even more outspoken: 'I have never

## 3, 4] TWO VIEWS OF A ROOM IN COPENHAGEN
### 1866–7 and 1908–10

The Blue Saloon in the royal residence at Amalienborg. The drawing shows the new unified Neo-*Louis* XV-cum-XVI décor introduced in the 1860s (although the building dates from the mid-eighteenth century the ceiling is known to be Neo-Rococo). In the photograph of 1908–10 (below) much of this décor survives but the hangings have all been replaced and additional items of furniture introduced, probably when the large mirror-fronted stove was installed in 1888. The much increased weight of ornament of the late-nineteenth-century arrangement shown in the photograph is very evident. The two princesses at the piano are the sisters of Alexandra, the consort of the future King Edward VII. (These two plates, and the two which follow, appear in T. Clemmensen and M. Mackeprang, *Christian IX's Palae paa Amalienborg*, Copenhagen, 1956 – a pioneering work in the field of historic room-arrangement and furnishing.)
*Danish Royal Collection, and National Museum, Copenhagen*

met with a class of men who were so hopelessly confirmed in artistic error as ordinary decorators ... [he] is absolutely recognized as an authority, and will have everything his own way, or you had better not have employed him at all.'[15]

It will be noted that Eastlake refers to 'decorators', not to upholsterers. Already in the second quarter of the nineteenth century some upholsterers were seeing themselves as 'decorators',[16] presumably as a reflection of the fact that people were now speaking of 'interior decoration' as a concept, Percier and Fontaine's *Recueils de Décorations intérieures* (Paris, 1808–12; see note 10) being the earliest important title to embody the term, followed shortly afterwards by Thomas Hope's *Household Furniture and Interior Decoration* (London, 1807), Santi's *Modèles de Meubles et Décorations intérieures ...* (Paris, 1828), and also Richard Bridgens' *Furniture with Candelabra and Interior Decoration* which probably first appeared in London before 1833 and perhaps as early as 1820 (see Pl.327).

By the late nineteenth century, however, a distinction began to make its appearance between the upholsterer and the decorator, and the latter tended to regard himself (or herself, for this was an activity in which women already in the early 1900s found they could profitably take part) as a cut above the ordinary upholsterer. This distinction is implied when Edith Wharton and Ogden Codman wrote, in their *The Decoration of Houses* (New York, 1897), that 'house-decoration has come to be regarded as a black art by those who have seen their rooms subject to the manifestations of the modern upholsterer. Now, in the hands of decorators who understand the fundamental principles of their art, the surest effects are produced. . . .' Nevertheless two other Americans, H. W. Desmond and H. Croly were still not happy, according to their *Stately Homes in America* (London and New York, published in 1903). In their estimation 'the worst danger is the excessive influence exerted by certain firms of professional decorators. This influence is wholly different from that of the architects.' On another page they refer to 'professional interior decorators'. This must be one of the first times this new class of practitioner in the field is positively identified by the title that is now familiar to us all.[17]

This running fight between the architects and the upholsterers was rather unseemly. No doubt most upholsterers were uneducated and had no training in architectural principles, but the architects really had only themselves to blame if, in completing a project, the upholsterers were largely left to their own devices. An architect's training tended to set him apart and encouraged him to think it beneath his dignity to worry about such a mundane matter as furnishing and decoration which was, after all, largely ephemeral – it was rarely left untouched for more than twenty years or so and was often changed much sooner. Nevertheless the most successful schemes of interior decoration have usually been those where an architect collaborated closely with a skilful upholsterer, guiding the latter and respecting his skills. Moreover, a truly skilful upholsterer could produce miracles on his own and often did so. Indeed, on all those occasions when a change was contemplated but no architect was called in, the upholsterer worked on his own and the results could be absolutely delightful. Many of the rooms shown in our illustrations must have been re-decorated by an upholsterer who has left the basic interior architecture untouched. As has already been said, he could transform a room so that it was virtually unrecognizable to those who had known it before.

The occupants of rooms also change things all the time. They move furniture around, they add items and remove others. This is a continual process, yet most people are not aware of how frequently they make such changes in their own surroundings. It is for this reason, at any rate, that the main illustrations in this book, which are arranged more or less chronologically, are inserted in the sequence according to the date of the picture itself and not of the décor depicted,

5, 6] ANOTHER ROOM IN THE ROYAL RESIDENCE AT AMALIENBORG 1888 and 1908–10

The Danish Queen Louise is seen in the earlier photograph (above) in her Chinese Room, in which were several pieces of Chinese furniture including the card-table on the left and the large cabinet on the right. Note the elaborate *portière*. In the later view (opposite) the Chinese cabinet has been replaced by a Netherlandish piece from the seventeenth century and the card-table has retired under a cloth. The *portière* has been replaced by a shawl, and a carpet lying on felt takes the place of the fitted carpeting. The candelabra in their vases have been electrified. The two Rococo mirror-fronted pieces have remained in position throughout. By 1908–10 the density of ornament had been somewhat reduced, compared with the state in 1888.
*Danish Royal Collection, and National Museum, Copenhagen*

even when this can be established accurately. By the same token the reason for including so many architects' and upholsterers' designs is that these do actually provide a sure indication of taste at the moment they were executed; they are not overlaid with later accretions.

Very little has been said in this book about iconography, not because it was of no importance but because it always pertained to a given situation, usually reflecting favourably on the qualities or career of the owner of the house concerned. Nothing helpful can be said about general principles in a survey such as this, and the allegorical significance of the most important schemes executed as paintings or sculpture has usually been the province of art historians.

This survey is divided into six sections, each covering fifty years. The material in each section has in turn been grouped under four headings:

GENERAL SURVEY. Here an attempt is made to survey the general architectural and artistic development in so far as it affected the interior.

PLANNING AND ARRANGEMENT. Something needs to be said at each stage about the disposition of rooms in a house and the purposes they fulfil, in order to understand how they are decorated and furnished.

THE ARCHITECTURAL SHELL. This deals with the interior architecture and fixed decoration – ceilings, walls, chimneypieces, windows, floors, and furniture designed for specific positions.

LOOSE FURNISHINGS. This deals with all the other items that one could expect to find in the various rooms.

# 1620-1670

THE YEAR 1620 has no particular significance for the history of interior decoration in Europe. The early 1620s, however, saw the completion of the Luxembourg Palace and the remodelling of Mme de Rambouillet's house in Paris – two events that had an important influence on taste in this field. By this time it was also evident that people of an intellectual cast of mind in most European countries had acquired some knowledge of the pattern evolved in Renaissance Italy for civilized life indoors. Many understood its essential principles and applied them as best they could.

One of the principal aims of Renaissance architecture, whether applied to the exterior of a building or indoors, was to produce harmony. Harmonious effects could be contrived in several ways, but one important requirement was that the architectural and ornamental features of a building, or of a room, should possess *regularity*. In so far as the decoration of the interior is concerned, this involved treating the various decorative elements in a consistent, unified manner. One way of charting the assimilation of Renaissance principles across Europe, therefore, is to study inventories and note where unified schemes of decoration make their appearance. Since inventories mention loose furnishings rather than fixed ornament which is part of the room, it is to the textile components – the upholstery, in its widest sense – that attention should be directed. The French used the term '*emmeublement*' (today spelt '*ameublement*') to denote a unified suite of upholstery made for a specific room, and it is noteworthy that this word first makes its appearance in the late sixteenth century. References to such unified effects become increasingly common during the first quarter of the century, and by the 1630s they were the norm in fashionable interiors in France, Holland and England – and probably in other countries as well.

Unified schemes of decoration contrived by means of upholstery may be seen in the Dutch interior of *c*.1630 shown in Pl.16 and in the Parisian room illustrated in Pl.34. Inventories offer parallel evidence. For example, a smart French bedchamber was described in 1625 as having a fine embroidered bed 'with the furnishings of the room to match'.[1] The Princess of Orange's luxurious closet at The Hague (it had a Rubens set into the chimneypiece) was all done up in green velvet trimmed with silver and gold lace, according to an inventory of 1632.[2] The wall-hangings, the day-bed, the chairs and the table-carpet were all *en suite*; only the window-curtain was of a different material (taffeta) but even this was green. When the State Rooms at Ham House were re-decorated in the late 1630s; the North Drawing Room was provided with a complete *ameublement* of white satin embroidered almost certainly with gold (although this is not actually stated), in order to echo the white and gold decoration of the panelling.[3] Indeed, in this last example, if this surmise is correct, the whole room must have been unified in one scheme of white and gold, with both paintwork and textiles matched. Mme de Rambouillet's famous 'Chambre bleue', where she held daily salons, must have had a character somewhat similar to the room at Ham, for we know that her room was painted

## 7] MODERN PLANNING IN 1647: A NEW FRENCH CHATEAU

From Pierre Le Muet, *Manière de bien bastir . . .* , 2nd edn. of 1647; supplementary volume of buildings designed and built by the author; the Château de Pont (Pont-sur-Seine, Aube) was built about 1640. The front range contains two apartments disposed symmetrically on either side of the central entrance vestibule. Each has an antechamber, a bedchamber (the positions of the beds are shown), and a closet and/or a *garderobe*. That on the left has a room less and may have been for the husband, the other being for his wife – the bed in the adjoining *garderobe* indicating this was either a private bedchamber or that of a lady-in-waiting. The plan is awkward because one had to traverse an antechamber to reach the main stairs. Beyond, on that side, is a dining-room (so designated) and a further apartment with a bed in an alcove backed by a *garderobe*. A subsidiary apartment with an alcove-bedchamber lies at the corner. *Victoria and Albert Museum, London*

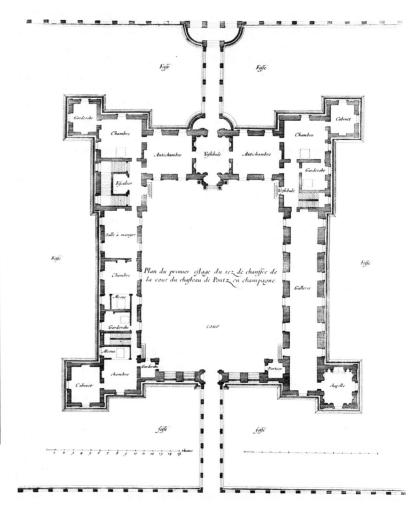

blue, that the hangings were of blue velvet with a pattern executed in gold, and that all the chairs and the table-carpet were *en suite*.[4]

The changes made by the Marquise when she did over her Parisian house caused a sensation and, although we do not know precisely why, reference was made by a contemporary observer to the '*regularité*' of its interior. The fact that she had spent her childhood and youth in Rome (her father was the French Ambassador and her mother was a Roman princess) meant that she must have been familiar with arrangements in elegant Italian houses around the year 1600 and it is probable that, when she came to live as a newly-wed in Paris, she saw to it that the latest Italian ideas were incorporated in her house which she began to re-model in 1619. At any rate the innovations to be seen there were noted by the influential people who attended her salons, with the result that soon her ideas were being copied, as a contemporary stated, 'in all well-ordered and splendid houses' in the French capital.

It is said that even the Queen sent her decorators to see if they could pick up a tip or two from Mme de Rambouillet's new arrangements. At that time the Luxembourg Palace was being built as a residence for the Queen, the widow of Henri IV and currently Regent of France. Marie de' Medici was of course Italian by birth and, like Mme de Rambouillet, she cannot have been ignorant about Italian arrangements indoors. Moreover, while her architect was French, Italian decorators and craftsmen were brought in to work on this important project. Once finished, in the mid-1620s, the Luxembourg became probably the most influential building in the whole of Europe. Visitors to Paris often made a point of going to see it and many recorded their impressions of its amazing splendours. Even its ground-plan was studied and sometimes copied for other buildings, while elements of its sumptuous decoration remained a potent source of inspiration for the best part of half a century.

Two useful books were published in Paris at this period, both aimed at helping people who were about to build a house. Pierre Le Muet's *Manière de bien bastir pour toutes sortes de personnes* came out in 1623 and provided a series of ground-plans for houses of different sizes together with guidance concerning the proportion of rooms, where to site the fireplace, and so forth. A fresh edition was brought out in 1647 together with a supplement giving most enlightening plans of some of the newest buildings in France. With these to hand there was no excuse for not understanding how an apartment should be organized (Pl.7). For those interested in the interior of houses, Louis Savot's *L'Architecture françoise des Bastimens particuliers* was even more helpful. This handbook was published in 1624, but the important architect François Blondel thought it worth re-issuing, with a few comments, as late as 1673. Savot provides information about such things as paving materials and timber, but he also comments on planning and on the distribution of rooms. For instance, recognizing that grand people habitually received visitors in their bedchambers, he insisted that such rooms should be provided with an escape route – a back-passage, in fact – so that the owner of the room could get away from unwelcome callers without having to pass through the front rooms. He suggests that a day-bed (a '*couchette*', he calls it) should be placed in a corner opposite the bed. Interestingly, Savot claims that it was the French who invented the gallery and he states that these long rooms should always have a 'closet' – a small room – at one end. If the arrangements at Ham House are anything to go by, large portraits were hung in the gallery and miniature portraits in the adjacent closet which was a sort of treasury. This was certainly the case by the 1670s, but the two rooms were done over in the 1630s and they were probably already then organized in this way.[5]

At this same period pattern-books with series of engravings devoted to specific ornamental features of interior architecture began to be published in Paris. It is no accident that the earliest were for chimneypieces, since the chimneypiece was the dominant architectural feature of a room. This was not only because the fireplace tended to be a large feature; it was also the source of warmth and was the main source of light after darkness had fallen, except on gala occasions in wealthy households where they could afford lots of candles. Moreover the hood over the fire which collected the smoke tended to protrude into the room and was difficult to disguise. Architects therefore took considerable trouble from an early date to integrate this important feature into their schemes for interiors, and many people must have welcomed the guidance which pattern-books provided. The most notable of these was Jean Barbet's *Livre d'Architecture* which appeared in 1632 and was re-issued in both Paris and Amsterdam in 1641 (Pl.25). In 1633 there also appeared Pierre Collot's series for '*plusieurs sortes de cheminées*' (Pl.21). Designs for ceilings were also welcome, and in about 1640 there appeared a series of designs by Jean Cotelle for the decoration of this other principal feature (Pl.10).

Barbet's volume was dedicated to Cardinal Richelieu and purported to show 'what there is that is handsome in Paris'. Presumably some of the chimneypieces he illustrates resembled those in Richelieu's own mansion, the Palais Cardinal, which later became the Palais Royal – a building that was to contain influential schemes of interior decoration at several periods in its long history, and did so from the outset under Richelieu himself. Particularly noteworthy was his *grand cabinet*, essentially a small but luxurious reception room, which was long regarded as 'the marvel and the miracle of Paris' as Sauval put it, writing in the middle of the century.[6] By then Sauval could also write with admiration of Cardinal Mazarin's even more sumptuous palace which was decorated between 1645 and 1647. Once again there was an Italian connection, for Mazarin was a native of that country. A report written in 1649, just after the palace had been completed, claimed that 'all the Nations of the Earth' had been constrained to contribute to the furnishing of the famous Gallery of Antiquities, but one of its chief ornaments was a large table with a top of *pietre dure* which must have been Italian, while most of the Classical statues very likely also came from Italy.[7] So did many of the artists who decorated the interior, but most notably G.F. Romanelli who painted the ceiling of the Gallery. The Palais Mazarin seems also to have been remarkable for its planning, for there were no less than four principal apartments, according to Sauval, each with a *salle* or principal reception room, an antechamber, a bedchamber, and an alcove bedchamber which was reserved for state or ceremonial purposes, together with the requisite allocation of closets, dressing-rooms and the like.[8]

Anne d'Autriche, the widow of Louis XIII (d.1643), ruled France as Regent during the minority of her son Louis XIV, with Mazarin as her Minister and confidant. She too set herself up in great style and luxury, first at the Louvre and then at the Palais Royal, the mansion built by Richelieu. Anne's apartments were regarded as especially remarkable; Christopher Wren claimed that he went many times to see 'the glorious Appartment of the Queen Mother at the Louvre' during his visit to Paris in 1665.[9] A marquetry floor laid in her other apartment at the Palais Royal by the highly capable joiner Jean Macé apparently astonished all beholders, and the mural decoration of the Queen's closet at the Louvre, which consisted of numerous small landscapes, was described as 'highly admirable'.[10] Some of the artists who decorated the Queen's rooms may well have been Italian but, as we shall see, from about this time on the principal artists working on advanced decorative schemes in or near Paris were French. So competent had French artists and craftsmen now become that there was no longer any need to call in the leading figures from Italy.

Only some of the most important buildings with significant interior decoration erected in the French capital between about 1620 and the middle of the century have been mentioned, but of the host of lesser buildings that were constructed many were fitted out with a refined elegance and a degree of comfort hitherto unknown anywhere in Europe. The excitement all this generated in France acted as a spur to French architects, designers of ornament, and the craftsmen engaged in trades that contributed to high-class interior decoration; and this in turn gave such people increasing confidence in their own taste and capabilities. This was to stand them in good stead during the next phase, which opened around 1660 and was to produce the supreme glories of Versailles and its many dependencies. It also attracted the attention of foreigners. Indeed, by 1660, there was no longer any doubt that it was now the French, not the Italians, who set the pattern for civilized life indoors in all its aspects, and not least in the field of interior decoration.

In certain advanced circles outside France this had already been recognized earlier, but it is still very difficult for us to plot the spread of French fashion in this particular field because the information required is by no means readily available. It is not sufficient to survey the principal building projects during this period because it takes some years to plan and then erect an important building, or even to alter it in any significant way; and it can only be decorated and furnished when the building is largely completed. However, new ideas about interior decoration can be transmitted quite rapidly and, if understood by those who have to carry out the task, can be put into practice in existing buildings with no great delay. It is therefore possible that decoration based on the French model was to be seen in many places some while before the study of architectural history indicates.

The illustrations from a book published in Copenhagen in 1645 suggest that this indeed was the case (Pls.38–41). In the scene reproduced in Pl.40 the interior architecture and windows are old-fashioned but the bed and chairs would not have been out of fashion in Paris in 1640 (cf. Pls.26 and 27). The artist would hardly have included such features if they had not been recognizable to the readers of the book which, incidentally, was a Danish version of a famous romance published in Paris about twenty years before. In the same way the fact that the engraving shown in Pl.33 could appear in London in about 1640, illustrating a sophisticated décor closely similar to what was smart in Paris at the same date, indicates that there were quite a few people in England by that time who could appreciate the French ideal. However, the spread of French ideas in this field was in no way consistent or even-paced. In many parts of Europe, especially in the less elevated strata of society, it took a good deal longer to make its mark (see, for example, Pl.31).

At the English court it is probable that rooms decorated and furnished on the new French pattern were in existence by the mid-1630s and perhaps before. It is well known that already by 1620 Inigo Jones was introducing into England a new style of building based on Italian precepts, principally those of Palladio and Scamozzi, and he may have introduced furnishings to match, either imported directly from Italy or made to his own designs. His versatility as a designer was more than equal to the task, but there is no evidence that the domestic interiors for which he was responsible were decked out in an Italian manner (the picture and sculpture galleries created for the Earl of Arundel, which are the only Jones interiors of which we have contemporary illustrations, cannot be classed as domestic). On the other hand it is known that in 1636 he took *French* designs for chimneypieces and modified them when decorating some rooms for Queen Henrietta Maria. The Queen was herself French, the daughter of Marie de' Medici who had built the Luxembourg, and she would have been familiar with the arrangements to be seen in her mother's residences in the early 1620s before she herself came to England at the age of sixteen to marry Charles I. Moreover, the Queen seems to have employed a French designer herself although it is not

clear whether, like André Mollet who was dealing with the royal gardens at Wimbledon, he was brought over to England to carry out her wishes or whether he sent drawings over to her from Paris.[11] The style of interior decoration evolved in London under Henrietta Maria seems to have been adopted within a narrow court circle, but its spread was smothered by the Civil War.

At the court of the Prince of Orange at The Hague, French influence also seems to have been evident indoors rather earlier than elsewhere. The unified scheme of decoration in the Princess of Orange's closet in the Stadholder's Residence at The Hague is known from an inventory taken in 1632 (see p. 14). Frequent reference is made in that same inventory to 'French chairs' which, if they were not actual importations from France, were presumably of a French type and therefore most probably of the sort in England then called a 'back-stool'. Mention is also made to a '*lit à l'ange*', which was the French term for a bed with a flying tester (i.e. without posts).[12] These facts betray a knowledge of French fashions but they hardly prove that the complete décor was French in taste. However, this was probably the case for the Prince, Frederik Hendrik,

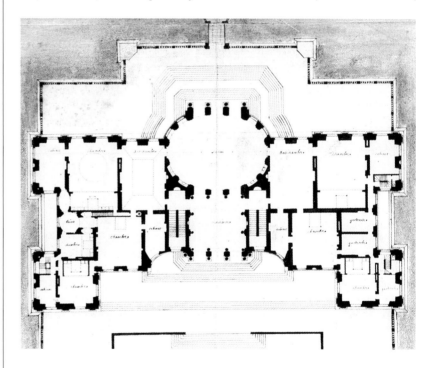

8] THE ORIGINAL PLAN OF VAUX-LE-VICOMTE   1657

Louis Le Vau's plan of the principal floor, showing two chief apartments disposed on either side of the great oval *salon*, each comprising an antechamber, bedchamber, and closet (*cabinet*) with escape-routes behind. The more important bedchamber is that on the left with the domed ceiling. It has a bathroom with twin baths behind. This was the apartment destined to receive Louis XIV when he visited this dazzling country residence of his Minister of Finance, Nicolas Fouquet (see p. 17). The secondary bedchambers will have been for more private use either by the occupants of the ceremonial apartments or by their closest entourage – a wife, a mistress, a gentleman of the bedchamber or a lady-in-waiting. The position of the beds and the placing of the chairs are shown, as is the location of two *garderobes* – houses of office.
*French private collection*

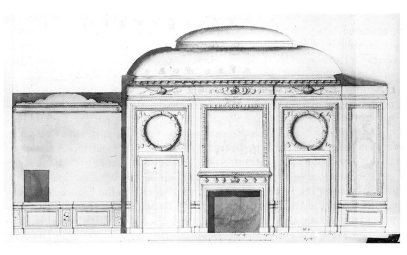

9] FRENCH ROYAL DECOR IN THE 1650s

Apart from the evidence provided by the crowns, sceptres and fleurs-de-lis, the
signature of Antoine Ratabon on the reverse indicates that this design was for a royal
commission, since he was Intendant et Ordonnateur des Bâtiments du Roi during the
first years of Louis XIV's reign. It is also signed Petit, probably for Louis Petit who was
Contrôleur des Bâtiments at Versailles and Fontainebleau. This, therefore, shows the
style favoured just before Le Brun wrought a revolution in taste in fashionable circles.
A comparison between this neat but rather pedestrian design and that illustrated in
Pl.42 makes the difference clear. (By Jean Cotelle (see Pl.23); dated 1654.)
*Ashmolean Museum, Oxford*

had strong French inclinations. His mother was French, Henri IV was his
godfather, he had lived in Paris as a child and he later made a special visit to the
French capital to study its new buildings. As early as 1620 he started to rebuild
along French lines the little palace of Honselersdijk, not far from The Hague.
Some of its features are supposed to have been inspired by the Luxembourg.
Later, in the 1630, he re-developed the centre of The Hague, and he engaged a
French architect, Simon de la Vallée, whose father had been Master of Works at
the Luxembourg. It can hardly be supposed that the interior of the buildings
erected within Frederik Hendrik's orbit were anything but French in style.
Already by 1634 an English visitor to The Hague could write that 'The ladies
and gentlemen here [are] all Frenchified in French fashion'.[13]

It is also noteworthy that Parisian engravings of ornamental features
connected with the interior were being copied and offered for sale in Amsterdam
by 1641,[14] which shows there was a demand for information on such matters in
Holland by that time. The fact that some of the Dutch engravings were
simplified versions of the Parisian originals only goes to show that French
models were also being sought by the middle class, who wanted something less
elaborate and less ostentatiously fashionable. Indeed, the middle class
throughout Europe probably found the Dutch version of French taste in these
matters very much more acceptable right through the middle decades of the
century: the French style in its pure form, with its strongly aristocratic
overtones, would only have appealed readily to courtiers and other people with
rather grand ideas about their own station in life. Direct French influence was, it
seems, only brought to bear generally during the last third of the century.

In the meantime important new buildings continued to go up in France and

by far the most famous, both then and now, was the château of Vaux-le-
Vicomte, built for the wealthy minister Nicolas Fouquet and completed in
1661 (Pl.8). It was planned on the most advanced lines and was decorated in the
most sumptuous manner. What is more, those who worked on its interior were
Frenchmen all working to the design of one co-ordinator, Charles Le Brun, also
a Frenchman. Fouquet entertained his king, Louis XIV, and the court at Vaux in
the summer of 1661, and shortly afterwards the King had him accused of
embezzlement and arrested. For the history of interior decoration, what is
important in this incident is that Louis took on to his own payroll Le Brun and
the whole team of decorators who had worked with him at Vaux and put them to
work on projects which were to provide the King with a setting worthy of his
standing as a monarch of a great nation, appointed by Divine Right.

As a young man Louis had seen and noted the splendours of Cardinal
Mazarin's *palais* and he was familiar with those created more recently for his
mother at the Louvre and in the Palais Royal. He now set about re-decorating
parts of the Louvre for himself, employing for the purpose Le Brun and his
many skilful assistants. The Galerie d'Apollon still bears witness (albeit now
rather muted) to the new glories they contrived. It was begun in 1663. At about
the same time he did up his father's hunting-lodge (it was scarcely more) out at
Versailles. Christopher Wren, who was in Paris in 1665, wrote of 'The Palace, or
if you please, the Cabinet of Versailles', in reference to its diminutive size, and
stated that he had visited it twice.[15] He spoke of its pretty exterior of stone and
red brick with blue tiles partly gilded, and of its rooms 'crouded with little
Curiosities of Ornaments'. The Louvre he regarded as 'a School of Architecture, the best probably, at this Day in Europe'. He went there daily, studying
the building works, the design of the cranes, and the craftsmen engaged in
'Carving, Inlaying of Marbles, Plaistering, Painting, Gilding etc.'. And when he
came back to England he brought with him engravings 'that [he] might not lose
the Impressions' of what he had seen. Indeed he was able to bring 'almost all
France in Paper' and one can be fairly sure that among these many engravings
were some by Jean Le Pautre, several examples of which are reproduced here
(Pls.42 and 46–49). Le Pautre's delightful illustrations of interior architecture
and furnishings vividly convey to the beholder what was admired in this field in
and around Paris in the 1660s: the style of Charles Le Brun.

The transformation of Versailles into the vast palace which was to become so
famous did not begin until 1669, but before then Louis arranged many
entertainments in the park there, including a particularly famous one in 1668.
Elaborate structures were devised by his designers for these festivities and it was
probably in these ephemeral buildings that were first seen some of the most
delightful effects that were to be embodied in more permanent form in the
enlarged château. A more solid structure was the Pavillon de la Ménagerie, a
miniature château forming the centre of the royal zoo, built in 1663 and 1664.
Here too, novel features were tried out, probably for the first time. Most notable
in this case was the new type of chimneypiece with an opening of low
proportions.[16]

When in 1624 Sir Henry Wotton, who was familiar with Italian architecture
and had no great admiration for French building, published his handbook
entitled *The Elements of Architecture*, he explained at the outset that 'Well
building hath three Conditions – Commoditie, Firmness and Delight'. It is
noteworthy that the first condition (or aim, as we would call it) was
'commodity'. The word comes from the French '*commodité*', which means
convenience but carries an implication of comfort. Creating *commodité* was
indeed an important aim of leading French architects in the second half of the
seventeenth century. One might even say that comfort as we understand it was
invented by them during that period.

## Planning and arrangement

A great house of the Baroque period was usually divided into three distinct areas: one where the family lived, one which served the purposes of ceremonial, and one for the services. As Francis Bacon explained in his essay on building (1625), 'You cannot have a Perfect Pallace except you have severall sides . . . One for Feasts and Triumphs and the Other for Dwelling.'[17] In fact the two distinct parts of the house he mentions (he took the service areas for granted) were more commonly on different floors than on different sides. The rooms set aside for ceremonial functions were usually organized as an apartment of state, while in the family's area there would usually be an apartment for the husband and another for his wife. There were normally further apartments of less imposing character tucked away in wings or in the inferior rooms upstairs for the junior members of the family and the senior staff. Servants lived in attics, over the stables, or in what were often little more than cubby-holes fitted in wherever there was space. Personal servants often lived somewhere within the apartment of their master or mistress.

During this period an apartment comprised the personal living quarters of an individual. Even the ceremonial 'state apartment', which did not normally have an occupant, stood ready to receive an individual: the monarch, a monarch's representative, or some other very exalted person, if such a person came to stay. At its most basic, an apartment could consist merely of a room with a bed in it, together with an associated closet. Grand people, on the other hand, might have apartments comprising a whole string of rooms, yet the innermost, the most private rooms in this complex would always consist of a bedchamber and one or more closets. An apartment of this grander sort may be likened to a tube closed at one end. Visitors to the apartment entered at the open end and penetrated the tube as far as they were permitted by the staff who were always in evidence to control such matters. The degree of a visitor's penetration was recognized by everyone as an indication of that visitor's standing with the owner of the apartment. The outer rooms (those near the mouth of the tube) were thus the most public in the sequence. The innermost rooms were not actually sealed off, because there were normally several private ways of entering or leaving the apartment, known only to the owner and the staff who used these back-passages or *dégagements* to evade notice or for domestic purposes.

Much attention was paid throughout the seventeenth century to distributing the rooms in such a way as to impress the visitor while at the same time procuring the maximum of convenience and comfort for the owner, his family, and his friends. In *The Elements of Architecture* Henry Wotton insisted that 'a gracefull and usefull distribution' could be achieved by organizing the rooms with an eye on 'their apt Coherence' so that they could be viewed 'without distraction, without confusion'. One commonly adopted means of achieving coherence was to line up all the doors of an apartment *en enfilade* so one could see along the whole sequence of rooms. The layout of these rooms was thus very evident; their impact was greater and the apartment could seem even more spacious than it really was. 'The doors ought to be all on a row, close to the windows, to gain room,' wrote Sir Balthazar Gerbier in his *Counsel to Builders*, a book published in 1664 and apparently based on Louis Savot's *L'Architecture francoise*. One of the comments made in praise of Mme de Rambouillet's arrangements (see p. 14) was that after climbing the graceful stairs one entered a large and bright *salle* which 'gave on to a long suite of chambers and antechambers, the doors of which were in correspondence, forming a very beautiful perspective'.[18] Wotton disapproved of this solution, however, claiming that it was 'merely grounded upon the fond ambition of displaying all our Furniture at one Sight'. It was nevertheless the favourite arrangement and

remained so in England for much of the eighteenth century. The French, on the other hand, began to work out rather more subtle solutions during the course of the century (Pls.8 and 53), and were to develop *distribution*, as they termed it, to a fine art by about 1730.

A cleverly organized plan ensured that the visitor came up the stairs and was presented with a sequence of sumptuous or delightful effects as he or she proceeded through the rooms. It was also the aim to provide privacy for the occupant of the apartment. This was achieved by having several small rooms – closets, dressing-rooms, *garderobes*, etc. – behind the bedchamber to which the occupant could retire, and by ensuring that there was a means of leaving the apartment without being seen by visitors who were in the more public outer rooms. In one of these small rooms would be placed the close-stool, and very occasionally there would be a bathroom but this was more often set apart in the basement or in a wing. Savot (1624), who did not really approve of baths so long as one changed one's linen frequently, in fact suggested that a grandee who wanted to have a bathroom 'for some other reason' (e.g. for show) should place it in the basement rather than upstairs, because this facilitated the carrying of water to the bath and because vaulting offered a better ceiling for such damp and steamy places than did one of timber.

On ceremonial occasions one dined in the Great Chamber (by 1620 usually called the 'Dining Chamber'), or in the *salle* in France. South of the Alps great houses usually had a *loggia* where one could dine of a summer evening, perhaps under an awning. In more northerly climes one might dine in a Banqueting House which was a separate building in the garden. The *salle* or Great Chamber could be cleared after the meal for the company to dance or otherwise be entertained (Pls.19 and 25).

On less formal occasions the family dined in a parlour, sometimes called a '*salette*' in France or '*saletta*' in Italy. It is often stated that special rooms for dining were not provided in France, but one has to dine somewhere and inventories usually show which were the rooms in which meals were habitually taken by the presence there of a buffet (essentially a sideboard but then often called a 'cup-board' because cups and other plate were commonly displayed on it; Pls.19 and 13), as well as of a dining-table. In fact the term '*salle à manger*' does occur on plans of French buildings from at least the 1640s onwards (Pl.7) but it was more common in France for dining facilities to be provided for the family in a *salette* and later in an antechamber. A small number of people could of course dine together anywhere, even in a bedchamber. All that was required was one of the several types of folding table which the servants could bring in and later remove. Until the middle of the century, the dining-table proper was a massive piece of furniture which could not easily be moved; it commonly had draw-leaves which provided extra surface area when needed. When dining-parlours became smaller and more intimate later in the century, circular or oval tables were introduced. This facilitated circulation by the servants and was more convivial. Such tables usually folded and were either carried out after the meal to stand in some passageway, or stood folded against the wall, leaving the floor clear. The dining-room thus could serve other purposes between meals – which is perhaps why the French rarely called it a dining-room. To them it was an antechamber (or some other room) where one also ate.

Chairs also stood against the walls except when pulled forward for use. The outside backs of upholstered chairs were therefore frequently left uncovered; there was no point in wasting money on a surface that was not normally seen (Pls.44 and 51). Quite often seat-furniture was lined up along a wall in close array and must then have formed a striking band of decoration in a room (Pl.34). Its arrangement thus was all part of the striving for *regularité* and coherence.

In bedchambers where an aristocratic pattern of life was adopted, the bed stood projecting into the room with its head against the wall, so there was equal space on either side. Especially important beds might stand on a raised *parquet*, as the French called it, and might in addition have a balustrade to prevent anyone other than the most exalted from approaching too close to the bed (Pl.136). This was normally only the case with a state bed, the culminating feature of a state apartment. Such beds possessed a potent symbolism reflecting the high estate of the owner, or of the exalted person who, he hoped, would come on a visit and sleep in the state bed. Unless a monarch or an ambassador came to stay, the state bed therefore tended to remain unused. The *lit de parade*, as it was called in France, was 'a magnificent bed set up in the principal chamber of the apartment, where ordinarily no one would ever sleep', explained the *Dictionnaire de Trévoux* (1704). Quite frequently the grand bed in the owner's apartment was not used regularly either; a less ostentatious bedchamber somewhere behind the scenes was obviously more private, more snug and more convenient. It was probably also safer, for security was a constant consideration in an age where to a large extent a household had to provide its own protection. For this reason alone, the innermost rooms of an apartment were the most secure. If the porter at the front door let a stranger in, there were plenty of staff about who would have noticed any visitor who was doing something suspicious. At night servants might be found sleeping on bed-rolls or simple camp-beds, dragged out of some cupboard and placed to cover strategic points. It would thus have been difficult for anyone to move about unnoticed.

## The architectural shell

An architect or a master mason responsible for designing and erecting a building in the seventeenth century fundamentally influenced the appearance of its rooms just as he does today, if only in the way he handled the proportions of each room and the manner in which he disposed the openings – the windows and the doorways. He might go further and design the chimneypiece, the door-cases, the window-surrounds and other fixed features, but in most cases he left each of these tasks to the independent contractors who each had their own traditions and their own book of patterns based either on what they had seen in their field elsewhere or on published designs which were not necessarily entirely up to date. Where a notable measure of unity was achieved through such collaboration, it was usually due to the fact that the various contractors all worked in the same general stylistic tradition. It was only rarely the case that an architect was able to impose his will on these contractors and insist that they follow designs provided by himself and intended to bring a measure of cohesion to the main features of the interior architecture. The concept of the architect as a person of a superior intellect and status who could co-ordinate an enterprise to produce stylistic unity was still in its infancy, and this was particularly so with regard to the interior. Certain Italian architects had apparently achieved such a dominant position already in the sixteenth century but it was uncommon north of the Alps before 1670.

If the architect did concern himself with the decorative features of a room, the item to which he would be most likely to pay attention was the chimneypiece, the source of heat, light, and therefore seemingly of life itself – a symbolic focus as well as a feature in its own right. During the sixteenth century the Italians had devised formulae for fireplaces that have remained in favour ever since. The principal form comprised a projecting chimney-breast with a surround to the opening. The area above the opening, on the front of the chimney-breast, was an obvious site for ornament which could either be architectural in character or sculptural, or both. The typical grand chimney-piece produced in Europe around 1620 was massive, with a large opening of tall

proportions, above which was heaped a wealth of ornament. French architects set about making this salient feature of the room more compact, the ornament gradually becoming better integrated with the structure (cf. Pls.21 and 47). As François Blondel said in his *Cours d'Architecture* of 1683, 'Formerly one spent much on the building and decoration of chimneypieces which were excessively loaded with ornament; but today they are far less massive and, with their simple lines, seem far more graceful.' Because it was such an eye-catching part of the decoration, architects and builders were eager for guidance in how to form chimneypieces and, already from the 1630s onwards, sets of engravings were being published in Paris to answer the demand (see p. 15 and Pls.21, 25 and 34). Apart from tidying up the architectural and carved ornament, another way of making the edifice seem less massive was to set a picture into the chimney-breast (Pls.23, 35 and 49). If the picture was to fit well in terms of size and proportion, it had to be painted specially for that actual position.

In the Netherlands the chimney-breast was cut back at the fire-opening so that it essentially formed a hood which was then often supported on columns or brackets (Pls.16 and 37). There was little or no ornament above a heavy cornice or mantel-shelf. Since the smoke had to rise quite high before it was trapped within the hood, it was the practice to hang a sort of pelmet round the underside of the overhang. The linings of these *tours de cheminées* seem to have been of a white material, possibly linen, and may well have been detachable so that they could be washed. On either side of the hearth, within the hooded space, it was common to face the wall with delftware tiles, either plain white or with blue figures. Sir William Brereton acquired sufficient tiles for two fireplaces when he visited Amsterdam in 1634–5, and he sent home with them explicit instructions as to how they were to be arranged when installed. One set was decorated with soldiers; the infantry were to flank the fireplace facing each other (he had purchased half facing left and half right) while the cavalry were for the hearth.[19]

Fireplaces with such large openings were apt to be draughty in summer when the fire was not lit. With the French form of opening, it was possible to fill it from the front with a chimney-board which could be made of timber (which made it heavy and awkward) or of sheet metal, but more frequently it was of canvas stretched on a frame like a picture and painted in the same way. Some of the published designs for chimneypieces of the 1660s show chimney-boards in position (Pl.48 shows a version with two panels; the design in Pl.47 could serve as a pattern for one).

An important fireplace would have a cast-iron fire-back, decorated in relief with the family's coat of arms or some figurative design. Where wood was burned, the fire-back had to be wide and large, but for coal it could be narrow and tall in proportion. With logs one needed a fork and a 'billet hook'; for coal one needed a poker and tongs. The most striking feature of a wood-burning fireplace, however, was the pair of fire-dogs or 'andirons' (from the French '*landier*') which supported the billets or logs. Fire-dogs had become large and ornamental by 1620, to such an extent that some fireplaces were provided with a smaller pair called 'creepers' which actually supported the logs so the larger pair became purely decorative (Pl.26). Ordinary fire-dogs were of iron but the most handsome were of brass which reflected the firelight pleasingly. The size gradually decreased, presumably in relation to the lower openings of fireplaces, and fairly simple forms became fashionable – balusters, finial-like shapes, and huge globes (cf. Pl.15 with 26 and 33). As the carved masks and other ornaments of chimneypieces in the French style, or the polished marble columns of the Dutch variety, caught the firelight and the fire-dogs shimmered, a seventeenth-century fireplace at night cannot have seemed massive or overpowering. The effect must in fact have been delightful, especially as there was rarely much other light in the room after dark.

Not every room had a fireplace but one could bring in a brazier, very much as one might an electric heater today. Braziers varied greatly in form but were essentially metal containers for burning charcoal, which burns very hot.[20] For safety they were often fitted with a pierced lid. They mostly had stands but, with a long handle, such a heater served as a bed-warmer. Open versions were the 'chafing dish' on which one could *réchauffer* food, and the smaller edition which was useful for warming curling-tongs. A miniature form of brazier had an earthenware container that was placed in a wooden housing and was useful as a foot-warmer (Pl.50; also 51).

The other eye-catching feature of an important room in a grand house was likely to be its ceiling and, once again, engraved proposals for ceilings were widely welcomed when they began to be published in Paris during the second quarter of the century. One important set of engravings was Jean Cotelle's *Livre des divers ornemens pour Plafonds* of about 1640 (Pl.10); they were for ceilings

10] DESIGN FOR A CEILING, PARIS   *c.*1640

After the chimneypiece the ceiling tended to be the most eye-catching architectural feature of a room, so it likewise often became the object of special attention from architects. This design by Jean Cotelle, who designed the chimneypiece shown in Pl.23, is for an important ceiling, presumably in Paris where he was active as a designer of interior ornament from 1633 and through the middle years of the century. He in fact published a whole series of designs for ceilings in the 1640s.
*National Gallery of Canada, Ottawa*

executed in relief in plasterwork.[21] It is evident from some original designs by Cotelle in the Ashmolean Museum that such ceilings were by no means always left plain white. Some have details picked out in gold; others have coloured grounds (Pl.24). To what extent the Parisian example was followed elsewhere is not at present known but it seems improbable that such plasterwork was invariably left just white.[22] Other types of ceiling were undoubtedly coloured, often boldly. This was certainly the case with timbered ceilings, where the beams were still being picked out in the mediaeval manner. As for flat ceilings, there is a vast literature on the colourful compositions that artists, often of wide renown, have painted on them. At a period when the walls were often decorated in a riot of colours (look at the chimneypiece by Cotelle himself shown in Pl.23) it seems unlikely that the ceilings were not brought into the scheme. If the walls were white with gilded detailing, however, as in some of Cotelle's mural designs, then the ceiling may well have been white as well.

The fixed decoration of walls in the seventeenth century is not easy to describe helpfully here, but some aspects of the subject have been dealt with elsewhere. Excellent essays on plasterwork exist, for instance,[23] while a vast literature is devoted to the study of painting on walls, although the art historians who concern themselves with this matter understandably concentrate on those exercises that have great artistic merit and thus tend to give their readers a rather false view of the subject as a whole. Figurative painting was in fact executed only in quite exceptionally important rooms. Most painting on walls was of a far less ambitious character; in many cases it consisted merely of a colour wash, and it was only in rather special rooms that the more elaborate schemes composed of formal ornament were to be seen. Most of this more ordinary painted decoration has long since disappeared.

Painted decoration of the more ambitious kind was, like plasterwork, mostly confined to the frieze of the wall – the part below the cornice and above the main wall area – for the post-Renaissance architect has always regarded this band along the upper part of the wall as the principal site for adornment and, if he concerned himself at all with mural decoration, this would be where he concentrated his efforts, or those of the craftsmen working under him. Having spent what we today tend to think an inordinate amount of time studying the Classical column, its form, proportions and ornament, the post-Renaissance architect tended to view a wall rather like a column rolled out flat. Thus, just as the capital and entablature at the top of the column were the chief decorative components, so the upper part of a wall merited special attention in terms of decoration. And just as the shaft of the column was normally left undecorated, so the architect tended to pay little attention to the main wall area, technically known as the 'filling'. This was left for the upholsterer to decorate (see p. 22). Most seventeenth-century walls in rooms of any importance had dados, and these were left undecorated or with their surface area simply divided up into panels. In the analogy with the Classical column, a dado is a plinth on which the shaft or filling rests, and it therefore merits no more ornament than does a plinth.

Although architects rarely concerned themselves with the decoration of the main wall area, they tended to do so if the wall of an important room was to be panelled (Pls.9 and 42). Among the designs by Jean Cotelle,[24] who was active in Paris during the 1640s and who can probably be regarded as a specialist in interior architecture, are several designs for panelling consisting of plain rectangles with bold mouldings which were apparently to be gilded. It is likely that other conscientious architects engaged on important exercises provided similar designs or at least checked designs submitted by the master joiner concerned, to ensure that the format blended happily with the overall décor of the interior architecture for which he was responsible.

Much seventeenth-century panelling was painted, sometimes with complicated schemes. Pine and other softwood panelling was almost invariably painted, although oak was also sometimes used for high-class panelling that was to be painted – that in the best rooms at Vaux, for instance, is of this much more expensive timber. Oak, walnut, chestnut and certain other woods were more usually left bare when used for panelling or for other interior work, and a favourite seventeenth-century treatment of woodwork was to disguise a softwood with 'graining' that simulated the appearance of one of these more expensive timbers. Related to graining was marbling, by means of which the various types of marble or other expensive stones were imitated in paintwork. Actual facing with marble was a form of wall-decoration reserved only for very special rooms indeed. Such a cold and unyielding surface was not agreeable in a domestic setting; its use was confined to adorning exceptionally splendid reception rooms, such as *salons*, or very luxurious bathrooms. Marble simulated in paintwork on wood, on the other hand, was warm to the touch and therefore acceptable throughout the house. As it also produced an air of grandeur, it was doubly welcome as a form of decoration in an age when grand effects were very much admired.

In the middle of the century certain other effects came into favour for the decoration of walls. One of these was to simulate other costly materials in paintwork. At Rosenborg Castle in Copenhagen is a room decorated with a painted imitation of tortoiseshell, executed in the late 1660s.[25] Lapis lazuli and other materials were likewise imitated. A particularly astonishing effect was that created for the Princess of Orange, before the middle of the century, by cannibalizing some Oriental lacquer screens and fitting the resulting panels to the walls of her closet.[26] This exotic form of wall-decoration was to be imitated, first in other residences of the House of Orange, and then elsewhere. Where genuine Oriental lacquer was unobtainable, or where there was insufficient for the room concerned, chinoiseries could be produced by European painters, working with ordinary paints and varnishes, which were charming and not too unlike the genuine article. The imitation of Oriental lacquer was called 'japanning' and the term is today used to distinguish the European product from the original.

If it is difficult for us to imagine the wonder with which our mid-seventeenth-century ancestors regarded lacquer from the Far East, it is perhaps even harder for us to imagine the awe and delight that plates of mirror-glass inspired. It was not possible to make what we would regard as a large sheet of glass until late in the century[27] but larger areas could be contrived by juxtaposing several plates, and several small rooms were being decorated with such composite panels in France by the 1660s.[28] A striking enough effect could of course be achieved simply by hanging a looking-glass on the wall, especially if it was a large one. Better still was to have more than one! The Archbishop of Sens gave a ball in 1651 in a room where 'Fifty of the richest and most beautiful Venetain mirrors serve as delightful pictures displaying the faces, the expressions and poses, the smiles, the graces, the charms, the hands and arms of all the fine company that is entertained in this room', as a contemporary verse put it.[29] On 19 February 1633 the *Gazette de France* carried a report of a ballet put on at the Hôtel de Chevreuse, noting particularly the way mirrors with silver frames were suspended in front of the exquisite tapestries.[30]

Windows form an important feature of a wall. Their proper disposition has always been a major preoccupation for the architect, affecting not merely the proportions of the room but the way daylight falls in it. Leaded lights were beginning to go out of fashion by 1620; they were clumsy, easily broken and tiresome to repair. They were usually made to open inwards so that they might not be buffeted by winds, and they thus took up space. Windows with wooden glazing-bars represented a great advance: they were more robust and could open outwards. Windows with wooden framing could also be made to slide up and down. Such sliding sashes (from the French *châssis*, a frame) were apparently being used in fashionable Parisian rooms by 1640 or so, as the engraving reproduced in Pl.34 shows. It was only the lower half of the window that moved in the early forms of sash-window because they were not counterbalanced with weights until late in the century, and it would have been virtually impossible to move a sash in the upper half without this refinement. Early sliding sashes were held up in the open position by catches at the sides.[31]

Although a few windows had been fitted with curtains during the Middle Ages, these were by no means common until late in the seventeenth century. Instead, interior shutters were used, which excluded light and provided insulation. From 1620 onwards shutters in many respectable rooms were fitted in pairs meeting in the middle of the window, each side usually composed of two hinged leaves (Pls.28, and 29, 35). They were also mostly arranged in two or more tiers, and in the Netherlands shutters were often not fitted to the top section of the window. Shutters could be used to exclude strong sunlight, and various effects of light and shade could be achieved by closing some of them while leaving others open (Pl.29). When curtains *were* fitted, it was usually to exclude sunlight rather than cold. Another means of excluding strong light was to fit a 'sash', which was a simple frame fixed inside the glazed window, forming a stretcher on to which was tacked paper or a thin linen or silk material which was then soaked with oil or turpentine to make it more translucent. Sashes could be tinted green or some other dark colour; two seem to be fitted to the windows in the Dutch room illustrated in Pl.44.

In the main ground-floor rooms of Dutch houses of the grander sort floors were often paved with black and white marble quarries but these were by no means always laid in a simple chequer-board pattern (Pl.37). Lesser ground-floor rooms had lead-glazed tiles (black, green or yellow) or quarries of less costly stone, while upstairs floors were of timber boards. Surprisingly, the nails were often left visible (Pl.30), although by 1660 or so Roger Pratt was explaining how one could hide the nailing by using headless nails which were 'much the neatest'.[32] The boards could be laid in fancy patterns (Pl.34) but truly elaborate wooden floors (*parquet marqueté*) were only to be found in palatial buildings. The floor in Marie de' Medici's closet at the Luxembourg (1620s; see p. 15) was particularly remarkable and was said to have been executed in a technique brought from Italy.[33] A fine example of such marquetry floors is to be seen in Pl.11; this shows the state of this art-form in the 1660s in Paris. It must however be admitted that such very complicated floors were not practical and were evidently in need of constant repair. In Italy quite elaborate patterns were executed in bricks of several colours, sometimes specially shaped to fit the pattern. Faience or majolica tiles, decorated with delightful patterns in colour, were fairly thick and could therefore also be used for flooring, although this does not seem to have been at all common, probably because they were expensive. The technically similar but much thinner delftware tiles did not lend themselves to the facing of floors except in the front of hearths.

Certain pieces of furniture which were intended to occupy a prominent position in an important scheme of interior decoration might claim the attention of the architect to such an extent that he might even provide a design for them. For instance, the large cabinet on a tall stand usually composed of six rather slender legs, which seems first to have made its appearance in the 1620s and went out of favour about 1680, presented a façade particularly well suited for an architectural form of decoration, and a few surviving drawings suggest that architects were responsible for the design of certain no doubt very special commissions of this class.[34] The same applies to state beds which formed the

**11] THE FLOOR OF A LUXURIOUS FRENCH CLOSET**  *c.*1668

This astonishing floor is faced with marquetry composed of several kinds of wood outlined with pewter (*parquet marqueté*). This is likely to be a very early example of such decoration. This shows that famous general, the Great Condé, at the height of his career. He was a man of culture, associating much with Racine, Bossuet, La Bruyère and Molière, for instance, and he is seen here in a book-lined study or closet. On the richly decorated reading-desk lies a book which was published in 1667 or 1668. The throne-like gilded chair would seem to confirm his notorious reputation for arrogance. The seat is furnished with a cushion that has elaborate gold tassels at the corners. The table-carpet is of silk brocaded with gold thread. He has a foot-stool. The splendour of Condé's surroundings foreshadows those soon to be created at Versailles under Le Brun. The old palace there was extended at about the time this miniature was painted.
*Victoria and Albert Museum, London, Jones Collection*

tops of such tables that merited a special design if they were to match the general décor of the room.[36]

The next generation of architects was going to pay much more attention to designing components that featured notably in their schemes, but there can be little doubt that architects and other prominent designers were thinking about such problems before the middle of the century. If it really mattered that the décor should have a unified appearance, as it did to quite a few people by 1630, someone had to try to co-ordinate the designs; it cannot have been sufficient to trust to luck and convention by leaving the designing of each component to the individual contractors concerned.

## Loose furnishings

The decoration that has been described so far was fixed and therefore difficult to alter. The loose or easily replaceable furnishings that were introduced once the architectural shell had been completed could be changed as frequently as the owner decided this should be done. A rich owner might make alterations to the replaceable furnishings of his room every few years, but he would be unlikely to alter the fixed fabric more than once in a generation. It was the upholsterer who provided the most noticeable parts of the replaceable décor; indeed, with his assistance, an owner could totally transform the appearance of most rooms so that only the most discerning would recognize that the architecture was more old-fashioned than its new adornment.

The upholsterer dealt primarily with furnishings made of textile materials of various kinds, but his chief contribution to the appearance of a room was in most cases the hangings he supplied and fixed on the walls, if only because they covered so extensive an area. At this period, unless a room was panelled, it had to be a very insignificant or humble room indeed not to have wall-hangings of some kind. The simplest wall-hangings were of plain cloth while the richest were so valuable that special enveloping loose covers were provided for them to protect them when the room was not actually in use.[37]

Hangings were usually made to fit a particular wall. They were made up from widths which, in the case of materials of silk, were about 20–21 in. (51–53 cm) while woollen or worsted materials were rather wider – but in any event they were all far narrower than materials generally are today. If the widths were juxtaposed, the vertical seams might be disguised with applied trimming – a galloon, or a lace made of silk or of metal thread (Pls.32 and 87). A more striking effect could be achieved by using alternating widths of two different materials or two materials of different colours. Round the whole hanging there would frequently be a wide border: half a width was obviously convenient as it avoided wastage. If the border material was also used for bands alternating with the main material, the latter came to have its widths completely framed or 'paned' by the bordering material. These 'impaned' panels were much in favour during the seventeenth century. Such flexible arrangements made it possible to fit a hanging to walls of any size. The same system was adopted for gilt-leather hangings. Here too, the main field was of one pattern which was normally surrounded by a separate border; strips like pilasters were also available for inserting between panels of the main pattern. All gilt-leather hangings were composed of rectangular skins joined to make up the area required (Pls.15 and 37). Tapestries form rather an exceptional class because they mostly had large scenes on them, worked from an existing design or 'cartoon'. If one ordered a hanging to be woven from such a cartoon and one had a particular wall in mind, adjustments could be made; but most tapestries seem to have been sold ready-made and so might not fit the walls on which they came to hang. For this reason tapestries were not infrequently taken on round the corner of a room and,

focal point of the state bedchamber. Although these confections were essentially the preserve of the upholsterer (see p. 23), so important was the role played by this impressive and expensive piece of furniture that architects must on occasion have furnished special designs for them (Pl.60).[35] Another class of furniture for which architects may have provided designs was the decorative table which might constitute an important feature of a room. The tops of such tables were meant to be seen, unlike those of ordinary tables which were hidden by a table-carpet (see p. 24), though they were carefully protected when not 'on show'. They might either consist of a fine slab of marble or of an intricate example of inlay or marquetry work. However, it was the stands rather than the

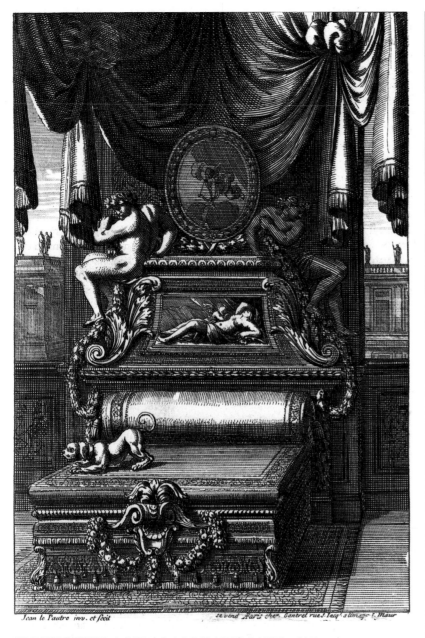

12] DESIGN FOR A *LIT A LA ROMAINE*, PARIS   1660s

This is by Jean Le Pautre (see Pl.42) and comes from a series devoted to beds of this class which had no posts. Instead, the hangings were suspended from the ceiling, usually in the form of a tent-like pavilion. There is evidence that suggests such beds were regarded as being not suitable for stately use. Indeed, the presence of the lap-dog, the scene of Cupid and Psyche, and the Cupid with bow and arrow above, point to an altogether more light-hearted purpose. If this assumption is correct, one could expect to find this bed in the bedchamber of a great man's mistress, not in his state apartment. Note the rigidly dressed counterpane, the cylindrical bolster, and the carpet under the bed.

*Victoria and Albert Museum, London*

where they came to obscure a doorway, some arrangement had to be made so that they could be pulled to one side when the door was open (Pl.25).

Tapestries came in several qualities and even the coarse weaves were quite expensive, but other types of hanging could also be very expensive indeed. This was especially so of those executed with elaborate professional embroidery, or in a specially rich silk velvet. Gilt leather was not cheap; nor was silk damask; nor brocatelle, a silk material specially suitable for wall-hangings since it was strengthened with linen threads. Only slightly less expensive were the finest worsted materials; the range of worsted and woollen stuffs available in the seventeenth century (and also right up to 1900) was far greater than anything we know today. There was a whole class of coarser, more robust stuffs with bold repetitive patterns of widely differing scale; the general name for these in England seems to have been 'dornix'. They were well suited for wall-hangings.[38] A type of material with especially large patterns was called '*tapisserie de Bergame*' (or '*de Rouen*' because that is where much of it was made), but whether this too would have been called 'dornix' in England is not certain.[39] It was no longer fashionable by 1670. Hangings of linen or cotton materials hardly come into the picture at this stage. Painted hangings existed as well. They had been very popular in the sixteenth century but seem to have gone out of fashion by the mid-seventeenth, except for very grand exercises with large painted scenes on them derived from, or similar to, those on tapestries. Few specimens survive and very little is known about them at present.

Most of the materials used for wall-hangings were equally suitable for the hangings on beds but, since bed-curtains had to be pulled back, the material could not be stiff. This excluded gilt leather, brocatelle and tapestry. Bed-hangings were usually lined with a material of lighter weight than that of the main material used for the exterior; the lining material was scarcely less important as it was visible on the back faces of the curtains and was normally also used for the front of the head-cloth and the counterpane or coverlet. The main valances (i.e. the strips of hanging that depended from the edges of the tester) were, together with the counterpane, the most richly trimmed components of a grand bed.[40]

Important beds came accompanied by a set of seat-furniture decorated *en suite*. The Countess of Leicester noticed this was the fashion in Paris in 1640 when she wrote home explaining that '6 chears of on sorte, 6 of on other, and 6 stooles ... is just the number that is used hear to all good beds'.[41] The wall-hangings might also be *en suite*, but already by the middle of the century it was common to hang tapestries in a smart bedchamber. If there was a table-carpet in the bedchamber, it too might be *en suite* with the rest of the *ameublement*. In other rooms the chair-covers, wall-hangings and other textile items would likewise often match to produce the unity which was so admired.

Window-curtains, however, had not by 1670 assumed the decorative role they were later to play; they were still entirely utilitarian (although they might be of the same colour as the *ameublement*) and were not disguised or made into pleasing features. Unlike bed-hangings, they did not as yet have valances (what we call pelmets) and they were rarely divided to form a pair which could be pulled to opposite sides of the window so as to present a symmetrical effect. Heavy, lined bed-hangings made a bed into a warm and snug box; but window-curtains, which were rarely fitted for warmth, were mostly of thin materials like sarsnet (a silk taffeta) or linen; they must have acted mainly as sun-blinds. They pulled neatly to one side and were therefore fairly unobtrusive (Pls.34 and 44). There were some paired curtains at Ham House in the 1650s which may have been there already by 1640,[42] and a few other early instances can be cited, but such symmetrical treatment was uncommon before 1670, and many windows did not have curtains at all until well into the eighteenth century.

Curtains, both for beds and windows, had rings of iron or horn running on iron rods that had loops at each end. These loops dropped on to right-angled hooks hammered into the wall or bed-post.[43] The rings were mostly fixed along the top edge of the curtain, but sometimes loops of tape were threaded through them so that the curtain would hang some 4–6 in. (10–15 cm) below the rod. This was presumably thought to ease curtain-drawing, which in other cases could also be facilitated by attaching a cord to the top corner of the hanging.

Table-carpets might be *en suite* with the *ameublement* of a room but could be of any material. Like wall-hangings, they could simply consist of a plain piece of cloth, untrimmed, while the most costly were very sumptuous indeed (Pls.34 and 11). Many were embroidered, sometimes with exceptional delicacy; others were tapestry-woven specially for the purpose (Pl.16). At Tournai a special class of table-carpet with a woollen pile was woven. Pile rugs woven in Turkey and Persia were also used as table-carpets, as numerous Dutch and Flemish pictures show (Pls.15, 37 and 50). Those who could afford a large Oriental carpet might well lay it on the floor, but the smaller rugs could best be displayed on a table – and if one owned such an exotic object one usually wanted to show it to advantage. Imitations of Turkish rugs were made in Europe (in England they were described as 'turkeywork'),[44] but they were not very common. They were used on tables and on the floor. The importation of Oriental rugs had increased so much by the middle of the century that they were no longer treated with exceptional reverence and were therefore more frequently placed on the floor.

Between 1620 and 1670 chairs with fixed upholstery were mostly variants of the so-called 'farthingale' chair which, if given any special designation at all, was often called a 'back-stool'. It had a simple and characteristic form with a rectangular back-rest that did not reach down to the seat (Pls.27, 40, 43 and 44).[45] It came in every degree of richness, both in the decoration of its visible wooden members (with turning on a lathe, for instance, or painting or gilding) and in the quality of the covering material and elaboration of the trimming and nailing. Many were covered with plain cloth, many more had seats and back-rests of leather, and great numbers were made with seats and back-rests covered in turkeywork specially woven for the purpose in rectangular panels.[46] A very splendid set of about 1625 is to be seen at Knole near Sevenoaks, covered in red silk velvet trimmed with gold fringe, and with the woodwork decorated to match with gilding and a red glaze. Slightly larger versions of the back-stool, but fitted with arms, were also produced to serve as 'great chairs', that is, as the seat of honour among a set of chairs. Wide seats of the same general conformation but suitable for two people were also made.

The other common form of chair at this period was that with turned members, which was produced in most countries with local variations. It had a rush seat which was sometimes furnished with a cushion (Pl.95; a version with arms appears in Pl.39). 'Dutch chairs', 'Dutch matted chairs' and 'Dutch flagg-chairs' (i.e. of rushes) are mentioned in not a few English inventories of the third quarter of the century, suggesting that there was a notable export trade in such chairs, extending, as with Dutch delftware tiles and other wares, to all those areas which could be conveniently reached by Dutch coastal shipping. Some 'Dutch chairs' are specified as being green, while contemporary paintings show that many were black.

Back-stools and their variants with arms were the fashionable seat-furniture of the period, but the turned 'Dutch chair' seems to have been acceptable in quite smart surroundings. Few examples of either class have survived, however.

Such chairs as have survived in large numbers from this period are of a massive type, made of oak and embellished with bold carving; this is simply because they are more robust. Seat-furniture of this kind represents a survival of an older style: although it continued to be made in country districts until well into the eighteenth century, by 1620 it was already considered provincial and one never sees such chairs in fashionable portraits. Incidentally, while they were not upholstered they must always have been furnished with a fat down cushion which, like most ornamental cushions of the time, would have had large tassels at the corners.

The person to whom most honour was due on any given occasion indoors would occupy the 'seat of honour'. On most occasions the person of the highest status would be the master of the household himself and so he would have the most imposing seat (Pls.18 and 19) which, at the beginning of our period, was often called the 'great chaire' and had arms whereas lesser chairs did not. If a person of higher status was present, however, that person would 'take the chair' instead. Degrees of respect were indicated by literally raising the person being honoured above other people. Thus the seats of 'great chairs' were rather higher than those of other chairs, and they often required a foot-stool which also raised the person's feet above those of others present. Placing the seat of honour on a raised platform or dais[47] conveyed a sense of respect even more obviously, while raising a canopy over the seat was a further signal of the presence of someone of high estate. The practice varied in each country: in England anyone of the rank

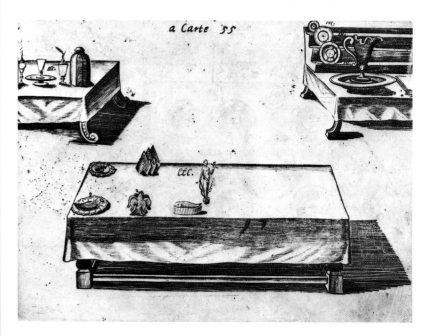

**13] DINING-ROOM ARRANGEMENTS    1621**

The dining-table is covered with a table-cloth on which stand examples of the items that should be used for dressing the table: a fancily folded napkin, a figure and various dishes. Reference is made in the text to figures of wax and sugar-paste, some of them no less than three *palmi* tall (about 31 in., 78 cm). Above are the side-tables, one for serving wine, the other a buffet or 'cup-board' with three stages at the back for the display of plate, all covered with a cloth. In front, on the buffet, stand the ewer and basin for rinsing the hands before and after the meal. On the side-board (left) are a flask of water, covered drinking-cups, and a glass standing on a salver in which wine was served to any guest who called for drink. (From Mattia Geigher's *Lo Scalco* which was published in Padua; Geigher (Jäger?) came from Mosburg in Bavaria, so his treatise probably had something of an international flavour.)
*British Library, London*

of earl and upwards might sport a canopy on ceremonial occasions; while in Sweden almost anyone could put up a canopy, to the extent that a visiting French diplomat, writing in 1634, suggested they raised them merely to prevent spiders falling in the soup.[48] Whatever the case, canopies were a striking feature in the state apartments of grand houses during the period. In form they were like the tester of a fashionable bed, with valances and a head-cloth. As there were no bed-posts, the canopy had to be suspended with chains from the ceiling or back wall. The curtains were not functional, so there were only two and they remained permanently tied back to the wall. A canopy (or 'estate' as it was sometimes called) would normally be *en suite* with the covering of the chair of state that accompanied it. Such seats of honour usually had a matching foot-stool and sometimes (perhaps only in royal contexts) also a pair of taller stools which stood flanking the main seat.

Rush matting of a robust kind was still being laid on floors in fashionable houses in the more northerly European countries in 1620 but the practice seems to have fallen from favour by the middle of the century, probably because floors were now more pleasing to look at and carpets of various kinds were increasingly being laid on the floor. The northern type of matting was thick and insulating (it was also used to block draughty windows and doors during very cold weather), and it had the advantage that, being light in colour, it reflected daylight off the floor which produced a pleasing effect. Such thick matting was woven in strips which could be sewn together to make a floor-covering of any size, and it might even be 'planned to the room', in which case it came to be the earliest form of fitted carpet. This type of matting had the drawback that it needed replacing every few years; moreover, it tended to retain dirt, and cleaning under it was difficult because it was heavy. A thinner and much harder form of matting existed which resisted wear more successfully, did not hold dirt, and could be more easily lifted because it was light in weight. It was apparently produced in North Africa but may also have come from the Iberian Peninsula; Pepys saw 'a very fine African mat' in London in 1666, the Duchess of Ormonde had a 'Tangier mat' under her bed at Kilkenny Castle in 1684, there was a strip of Spanish matting at the Nassau residence in Brussels in 1618, and 'Portugal mats' are mentioned frequently in the grandest bedchambers from the 1670s until into the early eighteenth century.[49] These mats came in widths, like cloth, and could be used as runners or sewn together; it seems that some had black or coloured patterns.

Pile carpets were being laid on the floor in grand houses in some quantity by the middle of the century (Pls.50 and 45). Persian carpets (often so designated at the time) were the most expensive but 'Turkey carpets' were by no means cheap. Reference is also made in inventories to carpets from Cairo (Cairine, Kerrein, Querin) and to 'musketta carpets' (or '*mosquets*' in France) which may simply indicate they were prayer-rugs originally intended for use in mosques.[50] Pile carpets were made at Cuenca in Spain for local consumption, and in England floor-coverings of 'turkeywork' were produced, but the output was probably not very great (see p. 24). Some very sumptuous carpets were also made at the Savonnerie factory on the outskirts of Paris but, at this stage, they were all for royal use. Technically they were similar to Turkish carpets, but their patterns were all entirely European in character. A striking series was made for the floor of the Galerie d'Apollon at the Louvre, one of the first major enterprises undertaken by Le Brun for Louis XIV (see p. 17; the carpets were paid for in 1666).[51]

Pile carpeting woven in widths which could be sewn together to form a large carpet (as a rectangle or fitted to the room) did not apparently exist before the eighteenth century, but various types of velvet with a worsted pile existed and some were sufficiently robust to be used on the floor. Cardinal Mazarin had a carpet made up with three widths of moquette to produce a covering roughly $4\frac{3}{4} \times 1\frac{1}{2}$ yd $(4.3 \times 1.4\,\text{m})$, which would have been large for a table and may therefore have been for the floor.[52]

The principal types of bed in use between 1620 and 1670 can be seen in the illustrations. It was fashionable to hang tapestries in bedchambers, although in countries with a warm climate these rather stuffy hangings were probably replaced by something that had a cooler appearance in summer. Summer and winter sets of hangings for beds and walls were provided for smart rooms right through the century, and a Parisian theatre audience in the 1670s would certainly have understood the joke when one character mocked another because, he said, 'Your bed-curtains are for summer and your valances for winter.'[53] Special bedside tables or 'pot-cupboards' were unknown but a chair was often placed alongside the head of a bed to serve the same purpose (Pls.17, 51, 68 and 75). Occasionally contemporary illustrations show a chamberpot standing on the chair. If there were other chairs in the room they would usually be set against the wall in the conventional manner (Pls.27 and 33). There would normally be a table in a bedchamber on which could be placed the chamber-candlestick and something to drink (Pl.41). The table might also serve as a dressing-table. Dressing-tables are first mentioned in the middle of the century and could stand in the bedchamber (Pls.28, 40 and 64) or in special dressing-rooms (Pl.72). They were entirely hidden by their table-carpets, which were in turn protected by a '*toilette*', a small linen cloth which might be richly trimmed.

Dining-rooms were distinguished principally by the 'cup-board' or 'buffet' on which plate could be displayed or from which wine was dispensed (Pls.13, 15 and 31). When 'dressed with plate' such a cupboard was very impressive – as was the intention. Near such a buffet would be placed a wine-cooler, which was a large vessel of copper or marble (occasionally of silver) in which bottles or flagons of wine and flasks of water could be kept cool (Pls.74, 87 and 108). These vessels also made handsome containers for flower-arrangements.

Closets and other small private rooms attached to bedchambers fell into various categories. There were the luxurious *cabinets*, as they were called by the French – although Francis Bacon, in his essay 'Of building' of about 1625, shows that the term was not unknown in this country – where sumptuous effects were wanted for one's private pleasure and to dazzle one's friends. Here, moreover, new and sometimes rather bizarre effects could be tried out because convention could be ignored. It was therefore here that the Princess of Orange had the walls faced with Japanese lacquer for the first time (see p. 21). Mme de Rohan's closet, with its hangings of moquette (woollen velvet), also fired the imagination, and the Parisian coterie that habitually met there called themselves 'La Moquette' after these hangings.[54] Other closets served as dressing-rooms or places for the close-stool. Personal servants might have their beds there.

Some small rooms also served as studies, in which case there would be a desk on which to read and write, and bookshelves. Until the 1660s, bookshelves were open but might be protected by a curtain; the glass-fronted bookcase only came into fashion at the end of the century (Pl.92). A fringe might be nailed along the edges of the shelves to flick dust off the tops of books when they were withdrawn (Pl.11). A sturdy table was useful in a study or library for handling large volumes but might equally serve as a desk, covered with a cloth (often green which was known to be kind to the eyes) on which could be placed an actual desk – a small piece of furniture with a sloping top (Pl.11).

Latrines were built into houses, sometimes sluiced down with rain-water from the roof, but it seems that these smelly arrangements were intended particularly for the staff and were situated well away from the principal rooms. Grander people had a close-stool standing somewhere in the private areas of their apartment. These could take the form of an armchair with a ring-seat

**14] LACK OF LIGHT AFTER DARK** *c.*1625

After dark there was very little light in rooms until the introduction of gas lighting, except on very special occasions. Here we see a single oil-lamp which can be suspended from a wire (see Pl.18). Psyche probably unhooked it and carried it to the bed in order to see Cupid, whose bow lies on the table. This striking painting by Simon Vouet was painted either in Rome before his return to Paris in 1627 or immediately afterwards. The bed is not characteristically French but may be Italian. The tester has no cornice or valances, but cup-like finials are fitted above the posts.
*Musée des Beaux-Arts, Lyon*

(literally a *chaise percée*) under which was housed a basin which a servant would empty after use. A refinement was the box-like close-stool which had a lid 'trunk fashion'.[55] Usually close-stools were discreetly hidden either in a niche masked by curtains, or in a specially contrived 'stool house' or 'house of office' furnished with a door (Pl.64). Chamber-pots, incidentally, were brought into the bedchamber in the evening and removed again in the morning (Pl.64).

Bathrooms were rare before 1670, but this does not mean that everyone was dirty. Bath-tubs could be brought into a person's apartment and filled with hot water. The normal procedure was to place a linen cloth inside the tub, so that one did not touch the clammy wooden sides, and on this a wooden stool (Pl.70). If possible the whole was then enveloped in a tent which trapped the steam and formed a sweat-bath (Pl.138). Francis Bacon describes how one should lie on a bed after such a bath, wrapped in warm cloth and with ointments well rubbed in, for no less than twenty-four hours afterwards.[56] He was no doubt referring to a rather special performance; simpler ablutions could be achieved with the aid of a basin (Pls.73 and 43). Louis XIV is said to have washed himself daily with 'spirit', presumably a preparation like eau-de-cologne or after-shave. Moreover, hands were rinsed before and after meals (Pls.13 and 26). People were probably not much dirtier than we would be if we did not have hot and cold piped water readily available at the turn of a tap.[57]

There were still only two means of lighting a room after dark: with candles or with a simple oil-lamp.[58] Examples of the latter may be seen in Pls.18 and 14. They consisted of a shallow vessel of metal containing the oil in which lay a wick. The vessel was suspended by a stout wire which could be hooked on to a convenient ledge or nail. They did not give an especially good light and were

rarely used in grander settings. There one used candles. Wax candles were comparatively expensive; those of tallow, however, were quickly consumed and very smelly. 'Base and unlustrous as the smoky light that's fed with stinking tallow' is how Shakespeare described them in *Cymbeline*. In 1664 Pepys experimented with candles of beeswax in his office at the Admiralty to discover how expensive this form of lighting would be 'and to see whether the smoke offends like that of tallow candles'. White candles of refined wax were particularly admired, but some candles were coloured yellow.[59]

Holders for candles took many forms. Everyone is familiar with simple candlesticks which could be placed on a table or a candle-stand (Pls.19 and 28). The commonest form used in polite circles was of brass. All other forms (except lanterns, used in corridors and other draughty places) might be classed as 'branches' because the nozzle was at the end of an arm or branch. The branch could project from a plaque hanging on the wall (what we would call a sconce) and when the plaque was in the form of a brass dish or plate with repoussé decoration, it was called a 'plate candlestick' (Pl.28). The plates were usually of brass, but Mazarin in 1653 had some of tinplate[60] and Fouquet in 1661 had sconces with back-plates each formed with five pieces of mirror-glass[61] which reflected the light better than brass or tin. At Hardwick Hall there are two branches in the form of human arms made of papier mâché which are similar to some that were at Fontainebleau in the 1640s, and Mazarin also had some '*bras*' of this sort.[62] 'Branches' could also project from a central body suspended from the ceiling to form a chandelier (called a *lustre* in France where the word *chandelier* means any candle-holder). Chandeliers are by no means common in French and English inventories before 1670 but contemporary paintings show that brass chandeliers were to be seen in most Dutch rooms of any pretensions (Pls.35 and 45). Beautiful chandeliers composed of beads of rock-crystal mounted on wire armatures (like the later glass chandeliers) were suspended in a number of splendid rooms in France during this period, but they were very expensive objects (Pl.74). Charles II owned one for which he had a protective 'case of taffeter with ribbons' made in 1667.[63]

Candle-stands on which one could place candlesticks with one or more holders were still unusual in England in 1641, when it was necessary to describe one belonging to the Countess of Arundel as 'a standard . . . for a candlestick to rest on';[64] (but see Pl.33). By 1650 or so, however, elaborate stands were being made in Paris. Quite a few were in the form of black boys and were called '*guéridons*' because at about that time a black vaudeville actor of this name was very popular in Paris. The Queen Mother (d.1666) owned a pair of blackamoor stands, and she attended a party given in her honour in 1651 where there were around the room and at equal distances Moors in the form of *guéridons*.[65]

No very rigid conventions seem to have governed the hanging of pictures at this period, as a glance at the plates will show. They were often hung in front of tapestries, with the nail driven through the hanging (Pls.20, 27, 33 and 34), while the Dutch, at any rate, sometimes hung large pictures close up under the ceiling. Maps were a favourite form of decoration and framed engravings were also popular. A writer in 1658 gave some guidance on these matters.[66] '[Do not] Clutter the Room with too many Pieces,' he advised; and 'If they hang high above reach, set them somewhat bending forward at the Top from the Wall' (the same applied to the way looking-glasses were suspended; see Pl.44). For the Great Chamber he recommended landscapes, history paintings or scenes of hunting. For the Dining Room, portraits of the King and Queen, together with 'two or three of their own [the owner's] bloud: Or of chiefe Nobility to waite upon their princely Persons'. There should be more portraits in the Withdrawing Room. In the Bedchamber the owner should hang his wife's portrait but it should not be too prominent lest 'an Italian minded guest gaze too long' on it.

## 15 ▷
## An elegant dining-parlour in Antwerp
### 1620

This shows a room in Rubens' house. The presence of a buffet and draw-leaf table indicates that this room was habitually used for dining. So do the rather tall chairs standing against the walls, one of which is an armchair which would have been used by Rubens himself, as head of the household, or by any guest of superior rank whom he wanted to honour. The draw-leaf table has its leaves pushed in and is covered with a Turkish carpet. The buffet or 'cup-board' has a two-stage stand for the display of cups and other rich plate. The top surfaces would be covered with a linen 'cupboard cloth' when the cupboard was dressed. Note the bare floor, the windows with interior shutters to the two lower tiers, the displayed tapestry-woven cushions on the black leather chairs, the splendid brass fire-dogs, and the wall-hangings which are almost certainly of gilt leather that came in panels with separate borders which are here clearly visible. Paintings by Rubens hang on the walls. (By Frans Francken II.)

*National Museum, Stockholm*

## 16 ▷
## A bedchamber in a rich burgher's house, Holland
### c. 1630

A good example of unity achieved by means of textile furnishings, in this case of Dutch tapestry-woven items including (left to right) the hangings of the box bed panelled *en suite* with the walls, the cushion on the X-frame chair, the *tour de cheminée* or valance under the characteristic Dutch form of projecting chimney-hood, the table-carpet made for the purpose, and two cushions displayed on the fixed seating. On the hearth stands a brass 'curfew' (from '*couvre feu*'), which prevented sparks flying out at night. Flanking this is a pair of very tall brass fire-dogs. The back of the fireplace is blackened but alongside are areas faced with blue and white delftware tiles on which hang a shovel and tongs. The panelling is typically Netherlandish, with inlaid ornaments of a black wood – perhaps ebony but more likely stained pear-wood. Note the display of Chinese blue and white porcelain, which was still far from cheap at that time, and what looks like a small plaster-cast of the Farnese Hercules. Set into the window-glass is a small panel of stained glass. (By Gonzales Coques.)

*Musée d'Art et d'Histoire, Geneva*

17 △
## A bedchamber in Amsterdam
### 1632

The posted bed is of the massive type with a carved headboard. The tester is hipped like a roof, a form common in Holland and Germany but not, it seems, in France or England. This bed no doubt had five finials, one at the apex and one above each post. Note the iron-bound coffer at the foot-end and the chair alongside the bed with a chamber-pot beneath. The pictures are set high and against the ill-fitting hangings. Since the woman's clothes are on the table, presumably she is in her nightgown. She sits at her dressing-table which has a small cloth over it (a *toilette*); on it stands a dressing-mirror. (From Jacob Cats, *Spiegel van den Ouden en de Nieuwen Tydt.*)

*British Library, London*

18 △
## Feeding the baby. Antwerp
### c.1625

Although this fireplace is fitted with an adjustable pot-hook which is in use, this does not seem to be a kitchen. Plate, including candlesticks and porringers, is ranged on shelves ready for use in the dining-parlour next door. The father sits in a 'great chair' and his wife is seated in a '*bakermat*', a wickerwork nursing-seat used in Holland throughout the seventeenth century. It supported the back and one could stretch out one's legs to form a trough in which it was easy to turn the baby round as one swaddled it (the rolled-up swaddling band is on the floor), head toward's one's feet, resting on the pillow. The older child has its own chair, a simple affair, no doubt with a rush seat. An oil-lamp is suspended by a wire from the overhanging chimney-breast. (By Magdalena van de Passe.)

*Rijksmuseum, Amsterdam*

## 19 ▷
## Dancing in a Great Chamber, the Netherlands
### *c*.1620

This scene is probably set in the Great Chamber of a fairly large house, after a banquet, the dining-table having been cleared away. The dressed 'cupboard' or buffet, with its display of plate, remains in position. The owner of the house is probably the old man seated in a 'great chair' by the buffet. One can imagine him having clapped his hands and said, not half an hour before, as Capulet does in *Romeo and Juliet* after his banquet:

> *Come, musicians, play.*
> *A hall, a hall! give room! and foot it, girls.*
> *More light, you knaves; and turn the tables up,*
> *And quench the fire, the room is grown too hot.*

The sketchily rendered wall-hangings could be intended to look like dornix or one of the other worsted and linen materials made for the purpose. The virginals are of the characteristic Flemish type. Note the three-legged turned stool with cushion, the interior porch with a *portière*, the chandelier, and the single candlestick on the buffet. (By Crispin de Passe, presumably the Elder (d.1637), who was a member of the Antwerp Guild but worked from 1612 at Utrecht.)
*Gemeente Museum, The Hague*

## 20 ▷
## A Dutch dining-parlour
### *c*.1620

The table is set for a sumptuous meal for a small party. The linen cloth has a worked border and seems to be laid over a fringed table-carpet. Napkins cover the individual bread-rolls which lie on trencher-plates. The flower on the central pie is artificial. There are knives but no forks. Chairs with leather backs (and seats, not visible) are pulled up to the table. The girl sits on a chair with arms, the seat of honour. There is a stool in front. The cloth on the buffet on the left is of linen-diaper; on it stands a wine-jug and fruit bowls. The wall-hangings are in panels with intervening borders and one is taken round the corner of the room. Between the pictures, which hang on a central ring from a nail driven through the hangings, is an octagonal looking-glass. (By David Vinckeboons.)
*British Museum, London*

**21, 22, 23**

# French chimneypieces
## 1620s and 1630s

Because the chimneypiece was the principal feature of interior architecture and could set the tone for the rest of the décor, this was the first indoor component on which architects bestowed their talents for design to any great extent.

◁ 21

Sets of engravings of chimneypiece designs began to be published in Paris in the 1630s. (From a series by the architect Pierre Collot of *Pièces d'Architecture où sont comprises plusieurs sortes de cheminées*, published in 1633.)

*Victoria and Albert Museum, London*

22 △

This handsome design of the 1620s, based on a late-sixteenth-century Italian formula, has been attributed to Simon Guillain, a Parisian architect who was also a sculptor and worked on the decoration of various royal buildings including the Château at Blois.

*Kupferstichkabinett und Sammlung der Zeichnungen, Staatliche Museen, Berlin*

23 △

This vividly painted composition dating from the 1630s is a reminder of how colourful interiors could be at this period. It is by Jean Cotelle, an architect and decorative painter who had a royal appointment and was employed on many important commissions in Richelieu's Paris. It is decorated with a coronet. The blank space must be intended to hold an overmantel painting.

*Ashmolean Museum, Oxford*

24 △

# Parisian ceiling design
## 1630s

Another design by Jean Cotelle (see Pl.23), this time for a rich stucco ceiling, no doubt for a grand Parisian room. After the chimneypiece the ceiling was the most eye-catching feature of a room and some architects therefore paid attention to the decoration of this part of the interior architecture. Here the architect has offered alternative ground colours, one being blue, the other the more usual white. Perhaps there was to be a painting in the centre. (Signed 'J. Cotelle'.)

*Ashmolean Museum, Oxford*

◁ 25

## Dancing in a Parisian *salle*
### 1630s

Abraham Bosse, who drew and engraved this scene, had also engraved a series of designs for chimneypieces by the architect Jean Barbet in 1632 (cf. Collot's series of the same time; Pl.21). The chimneypiece illustrated here is based on Barbet's work and shows how this feature dominated the interior. The walls are fitted with tapestry hangings, one of which is roughly pulled back so that the door can open. The interior shutters are arranged in three tiers, and there are two types of seating. Note the frame round the whole composition; this was incidentally instructive to those seeking guidance on picture-framing.

*Victoria and Albert Museum, London*

26 ▷

## The bedchamber as reception room, Paris
### late 1630s

This engraving by Abraham Bosse is one of his many delightful scenes of life indoors in fashionable Parisian houses during the 1630s and 40s (see Pls.28 and 34). As in Pl.25 he has introduced a chimneypiece in the Barbet style. Note the imposing fire-dogs, which were purely decorative, and the smaller, functional set known as 'creepers' which actually supported the logs. A pair of bellows hangs inside the fireplace. The bed is of the standard type favoured during the two middle quarters of the century (in England and elsewhere often called a 'French bed') which presented a box-like form when the curtains were drawn, and had no woodwork visible. On a side-table stand a ewer and basin for rinsing the hands after the meal, with a towel to dry them afterwards. The ladies are dining together, the text explains, because their husbands are all away doing business or hunting. One of them is holding a fork – at that date still not all that common a practice.

*Victoria and Albert Museum, London*

◁ 27
## A smart Parisian bedchamber
### 1630

Here we see a surgeon about to bleed the lady; he is applying a tourniquet. The maid brings in a ewer and basin for washing after the operation. Behind is a bed of the type known as '*lit à housse*' (literally a 'loose-cover bed' because it resembled the protective loose covers put over splendid beds to protect the hangings). It has ribbons for closing the gap at the foot end. A lute lies on top of the bed: its pegbox is visible. The seat-furniture is ranged against the walls and comprises the standard 'back-stool', X-frame '*pliants*' (folding stools) and an upholstered form. The nails on which the pictures and looking-glass hang must be driven straight through the tapestries, which are fitted to the walls. (By Abraham Bosse.)

*British Museum, London*

28 ▷
## The effects of candlelight, Paris
### 1630s

This shows an important occasion in a rich bourgeois house in Paris – the return from the marriage ceremony of the newly-weds and their guests – yet the only illumination in this rather smart bedchamber seems to come from the sconce on the wall (with its brass reflector-plate) and a pair of candlesticks on the dressing-table. On normal occasions there may well have been only one candle in a room. The couple, while grateful for the fine presents to be seen on or by the table, are urging their friends to leave them alone together. A *lit à housse* stands in the corner – an arrangement that would not be found in a grand nobleman's bedchamber. Note the cords with tassels for tying the curtains (see Pl.41). The painted shutters are closed. (By Abraham Bosse, from the suite *Mariage à la Ville*.)

*Bibliothèque Nationale, Paris*

◁ 29

## A patrician cabinet of paintings in Antwerp

### c.1635

A scene in the Burgomaster of Antwerp's house. Nicholaas Rockox was a wealthy humanist and collector, as well as an astute politician. He enjoyed an international reputation as an antiquary. We see here some of his Classical busts, and there is a small figure on the mantel-shelf. Even in this rather splendid house the boards are bare and have their nails showing. However, the hearth is tiled. The pair of leather-backed chairs has gilded tooling. There are interior shutters on the two lower tiers of window. Interesting is the way the pictures are hung, and the looking-glass on the right which is suspended by a cord and tassels from a ring through the 'paned' textile wall-hangings. The circular tables both have table-carpets, the one being used for the meal being also covered with a linen cloth. One woman is eating with a fork. (By Frans Francken.)

*Bayerische Staatsgemäldesammlungen, Munich; photograph from Jürgen Hinrichs, Artothek, Planegg*

30 ▷

## A Dutch interior

### 1631

The most striking feature of this room is the set of wall-hangings of gilt leather. Such a large pattern could only have been composed with several skins for each repeat. This picture gives some idea of how brilliant was the effect produced by hangings of this type, which was particularly favoured by the Dutch. The 'great chair' in which the master of the household is seated is taller and more imposing than the chair being used by his wife. A Turkish carpet lies on the table. No attempt has been made to disguise the nailing of the floor-boards. (*Portrait of Antoine Renniers and his wife*, by Cornelis de Vos.)

*Museum of Art, Philadelphia; W.P. Wilstack Collection*

## 31
## A dining-parlour
## in a castle near Zürich
### 1643

There is nothing advanced about this scene: as far as the style is concerned, it could have been set in the previous century; but the household is a rich one, that of the Provincial Governor (*Landvogt*), Hans Bodmer, who lived at Greifenzee Castle some 15 miles (24 km) north of Zürich. He and his wife, with their numerous children, sit at a large table covered with an elaborate linen cloth. The parents sit in 'great chairs', the children on backed stools characteristic of the Alpine region. No one has a fork, but beakers for drink stand in front of each diner. A wine-flagon and cooler are on a stand at the back. To the right is a painted faience stove. The buffet dressed with its set of 'cupboard-cloths' has a small display of plate including a vase of flowers. To the left is a niche with a cistern and basin for rinsing the hands. A small collection of books is on a shelf; below is an hour-glass. There are panels of stained glass in the leaded windows. Between the windows hangs a looking-glass that can be covered by a cloth; it was thought necessary thus to preserve a mirror's reflective properties, which still seemed rather magical. To the right is a comb-case with combs and other toilet requisites, a hand-mirror and a clothes-brush. Note the stags' heads.

*Private collection; photograph obtained through* Du *magazine and with the help of Dr Eva-Maria Lösel*

Je donne aux bons esprits la premiere teinture
Je polis le discours & le rends plus correct
Des langages divers j'enseigne le secret
Tant par doctes leçons que par bonne lecture.

*LA GRAMMAIRE*

Je suis de tous les arts la baze & le degré
Je verrou du palais ou preside la gloire
L'entrée du Parquet aux muses consacrée
Et le portail doré du temple de memoire.

### 32 △
## A Parisian bedchamber
### 1630

This room is simplified, but instructive. The wall-hangings are 'paned', loom-widths of material being 'impaned' with another, in this case an elaborate border of galloon. The two forms are upholstered; they have a fringe all round and decorative nails at the corners. When the curtains were drawn round this type of bed it would have had a box-like appearance with no woodwork showing. The hangings on the bed seem to be *en suite* with those on the walls, which would have produced the unified effect then fashionable. The finial on top of the post is also covered *en suite*. One

of the groups of four 'buttons and loops' at each end of the valances is visible; they ensured that there were no draughty gaps. Note how the curtain is wrapped out of the way during the day. The text explains that grammar is the basis of all culture, allowing one to enter the 'Parquet of the Muses'. The *parquet* was the raised area, often enclosed by a balustrade, that was soon to lend its name to the composite patterns of wood which were increasingly used for flooring such areas. The balustrade would have run behind the form on the right (the original drawing has probably been mis-rendered by the engraver, who has understood the balustrade to be associated with an outside staircase). (By Grégoire Huret.)

*Bibliothèque Nationale, Paris*

### 33 △
## An English lady's bedchamber
### *c.*1640

Scenes of English interiors of the seventeenth century are rare and this is one of the earliest. This scene represents the sense of Sight and is one of five engravings that belonged to Samuel Pepys. They were labelled by one of his clerks 'The Genteel Habits of England about the year 1640'. It shows a most advanced taste, closely modelled on fashionable practice in Paris. Only circles close to the court of Charles I and his French wife lived in such surroundings, and we probably see here the kind of furnishing that was to be found in interiors designed by Inigo Jones and his assistants. The bed is of the fashionable, box-like type with a flat tester and four finials (not visible). The fire-dog with its huge brass sphere is just like that shown in Pl.34. Note the characteristic Charles I frames round the portraits hanging against the tapestry, and the 'back-stools' placed against the wall. Most striking is the dressing-table flanked by a pair of candle-stands. The table is covered with a fringed 'carpet' and a *toilette* of linen with a lace border. On this lies a dressing-box which must have a looking-glass in its lid. (Signed 'Edmond Marmion invent et fecit'.)

*Pepys Library, Magdalene College, Cambridge; by kind permission of the Master and Fellows*

LES VIERGES FOLLES.

*Tu vois comme ces Vierges foles*
*S'amusent inutilement*
*Apres des actions friuoles,*
*Dont Elles font leur Element.*

Bosse inu. et fe.

*Les Ieux, les Festins, la Musique,*
*La Dance, et les liures d'Amour ;*
*C'est à quoy leur Esprit s'aplque,*
*Y passant la nuict, et le jour.*

A Paris, Chez le Blond, rue S. Denys, au Pauillion Royal. Auec Priuilege du Roy.

*O que ces Ames insensées*
*Cherissent les Mondanitès !*
*Leurs parolles, et leurs pensées*
*Ne s'attachent qu'aux Vanités.*

*D'vn faux lustre leur vie esclatte;*
*Elles aiment ce qui leur nuit*
*Et lors que le Monde les flatte,*
*Il les enchante et les destruit.*

## 34
## The parlour in an elegant Parisian house
### 1640s

Another charming scene by Bosse with a chimney-piece in Barbet's style (see Pls.25 and 26). Note the great brass fire-dogs, which reflect the flames so strikingly. The windows are of the early sliding-sash variety, in which only the bottom section moved and there were not yet any counterbalancing weights. Each window is fitted with a single curtain against sunlight. A picture and looking-glass are hung on nails driven through the neatly fitted verdure tapestry. The closely set row of chairs must have formed a noteworthy decorative band of colour. They are covered *en suite* with the fitted table-carpet. The floor has boards arranged almost like parquet. On the table is a globe, which in those days was a far more decorative object than those made today. The lap-dog has its own cushion. The only sign that these girls are in fact meant to be 'foolish virgins', as the legend calls them, is the pile of unfilled oil-lamps in the front right-hand corner, but these young women look as if they had plenty of servants to fill the lamps when they were needed.

*British Museum, London*

## 35
## A Dutch parlour
*c.*1650

The formula is much the same as that used in Pl.36, the intention in both cases being to show the family in suitably impressive surroundings. In this case the handsome cabinet is of the sort which relied for its effect on tortoiseshell backed with red pigment, with gilt copper mounts. On top are three vessels arranged formally as ornaments. The widths of material (a brocatelle or worsted material of the dornix class?) that went to make up the wall-hangings are clearly distinguishable. The window has no less than four tiers, the lower three being fitted with pairs of two-leaf interior shutters. A Persian carpet covers the table. Note the three sizes of chair: a superior one for the mistress of the household, a child's chair for her small daughter who is learning to make pillow-lace, and a middling one for the old woman. Low chairs like the last are sometimes specified as being for women in contemporary inventories. There are no candles in the chandelier, which is of the type made in great numbers in the Low Countries, notably at Dinant, and exported in some quantity. The picture over the fireplace seems to have been made for that position. Note the entirely bare wooden floor of rather wide boards. (By Gillis van Tilborch.)

*Museum Boymans-van Beuningen, Rotterdam*

## 36 ▷
# A party in a Dutch house
### 1647

The scene is set in what was presumably the principal room in the house of a wealthy citizen. Perhaps a wedding is being celebrated. The room is quite expensively furnished. The black cabinet with the flower-arrangement on top is of the type made in Antwerp and probably also in Amsterdam. When the doors are opened numerous small brightly coloured paintings are usually revealed. A black-framed looking-glass is suspended between the windows. Its lower edge rests on hooked supports set in the wall and the frame is held canted forward by a double system of cords ending in tassels. There is a silk bow at the top. The buffet (oak or walnut) at the back is not dressed with plate. Note the way that a series of landscape paintings is hung like a frieze above the main wall-decoration, the precise nature of which is indistinct. (By Hieronymus Janssens.)

*Alan Jacobs Gallery, London*

## ◁ 37
# A Dutch parlour
### c.1660

This well-to-do couple wear the unostentatious clothes favoured by the Dutch bourgeoisie in the middle of the century, but their surroundings are all costly. Note the marble columns supporting the hood of the projecting chimneypiece, the splendid Turkish carpet on the table, the wall-hangings of gilt leather with their striking gold and blue pattern, and the black and white marble floor. The overmantel painting must have been commissioned specially for that position, since it fits so perfectly. (By E.H. van der Neer.)

*Museum of Fine Arts, Boston*

## 38, 39, 40, 41
# Four Danish bedchambers
## 1645

Illustrations from a book which was a Danish version of Honoré d'Urfé's pastoral romance about the shepherdess Astrée (1610–27), which has been called the first French novel.

**38** (*below, top left*)

The massive form of bed of the kind seen here was in favour from the late sixteenth until the mid-seventeenth century. The Germanic version often had a roof-like hipped tester with finials (cf. Pl.17; a variant is seen in Pl.67). Like other beds they invariably had curtains, with valances hiding the rods and rings although these components are rarely present on surviving beds of this class. A handsome covered cup and a covered beaker stand on the table. A clock and a looking-glass hang on the wall. The floor is tiled. There is a chandelier.

**39** (*below, top right*)

A variant of the massive type of bed, with a flat-topped wooden tester. Note how the bed-curtains

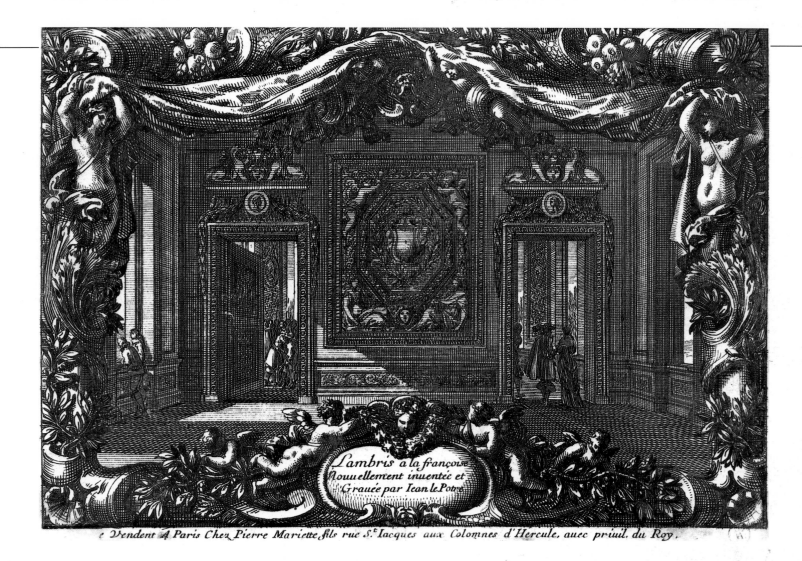

*Lambris a la françoise Nouuellement inuentée et Grauée par Iean le Potre.*

*e Vendent A Paris Chez Pierre Mariette fils rue S.t Iacques aux Colomnes d'Hercule, auec priuil. du Roy.*

are tied together with ribbons at the corner to exclude draughts. There is a bed-step. A glass and a comb-case hang on the wall. Below is a turned chair.

### 40 (*opposite, below left*)

The box-like bed shown here is rather like that shown in Pl.27 and suggests that Parisian fashions were already being transmitted rapidly by the 1640s. The chairs are also of a form that would have been perfectly acceptable in a smart Parisian house, although the French version would perhaps have had turned legs. A chest stands near the bed. On the table stands a dressing-mirror along with a brazier for warming the curling-tongs that will enable the woman to create the side-curls that were then the rage.

### 41 (*opposite, below right*)

This bed is probably of the same type as that shown in Pl.28, but the details are indistinct or may have been misunderstood by the draughtsman. Were the cords purely decorative or did they hang loose, with matching cords inside forming pairs that enabled one to reef up the curtains when they were not needed? Note the festooned wall-hangings and the local variant of the back-stool. (All from *Den Hyrdinde Astrea*, Copenhagen, 1645.)

*Royal Library, Copenhagen*

### 42 △
# Title-page of a Parisian pattern-book
## 1660s

This shows examples of the latest forms of wall-panelling 'newly invented', as it says in the cartouche. From this design alone one can learn much about the new style in door-cases, about the proportions between dado and the main wall surface, and about the newest fashion in framing. The repertoire of ornament which evolved at and around the French court under the direction of Charles Le Brun was disseminated throughout Europe by patterns like this. Such engravings were available singly or in sets from print-sellers in Paris. The draughtsman here responsible was Jean Le Pautre who was considered one of the most able artists working in this propagandist genre.

*Victoria and Albert Museum, London*

## 43 ▷
## A Dutch lady Dressing
### 1665

She has presumably only risen a short time ago from the bed in the background. The ewer and basin on the floor were probably used for washing her face and hands. On the dressing-table is her toilet-set comprising, amongst other things, a looking-glass, a pin-cushion, a clothes-brush and the case for it, all covered in red silk trimmed with silver braid. The table-carpet is of some material with a pile, but it does not seem to be a Turkish or Persian rug. Could it be an example of the pile table-carpets woven at Tournai at this period? The painting above the doorway has a carved frame which seems to be silvered. Note the use of a large map as decoration. (By Jacob Ochtervelt.)

*Museum of Art, Carnegie Institute, Pittsburgh, Pennsylvania; Henry Lee Mason Memorial Fund, 1954*

## 44 (*below, left*)
## A Dutch interior
### 1660s

Probably a bedroom seen from the bed end of the room. The woman sits at her dressing-table with its looking-glass above, canted so she may see herself when seated. There would normally be plenty of light in that position for dressing the hair and making up, but the lower part of the window is obscured, apparently with 'sashes' (see p. 21) but just possibly by the outside shutters being closed. Simple curtains are also fitted. It is evidently a very sunny room. The chairs are of the standard type. One can see how the outside back of the nearest is not covered because chairs stood against the wall when not in use. The proportions have gone awry; the door is too low and the seated woman is too small, while the window-catches are too high up to reach conveniently. (By Pieter Janssens, d. 1672.)

*Städelsches Galerie, Frankfurt-am-Main; photograph from Jürgen Hinrichs, Artothek, Planegg*

## 45 ▷
## An enfilade of rooms in a Dutch house
### 1665

This delightful scene probably shows the principal bedchamber, entrance hall and dining-parlour of a Dutch middle-class villa, a small country retreat outside one of the large cities. Since the maid is busy sweeping out the dining-room it is probably morning, which may explain why the man is still in bed. His wife is playing on her Flemish-style spinet. The tall windows are in a new style without transoms and let in more light, as this scene demonstrates; but it was therefore even more necessary to fit sun-curtains to the windows. Those seen here are of a thin red material, probably sarsnet, a thin taffeta. There is a Persian carpet on the floor, evidence of considerable wealth, as is the splendid gilded looking-glass of Dutch manufacture hanging canted forward on the wall. There are two handsome brass chandeliers: one at least is suspended on a bare wire, and neither has candles in its holders. Note also how low the chandeliers are hanging; this was normal throughout the seventeenth century. (By Emanuel de Witte.)

*Museum Boymans-van Beuningen, Rotterdam*

46, 47, 48, 49
## Designs for chimneypieces
### mid seventeenth century

The tendency was towards more compact forms with smaller openings. Jean Le Pautre issued several sets of engravings for chimneypieces in the latest Parisian style during the 1660s, most of them undated. So great was the demand for such patterns that several sets were copied and sold by print-sellers in Amsterdam.

◁ 46
From *Cheminées à la moderne*, Paris, 1661. Note the fire-back and the generally low proportions.
*Victoria and Albert Museum, London*

47 △
A Dutch copy of another design from the same set. The copy is undeniably less well drawn than the original.
*Metropolitan Museum of Art, New York; Harris Brisbane Dick Fund, 1935*

48 △
From *Cheminées à l'italienne*, undated. Note the
chimney-board that enables one to close off the
opening when the fireplace is not in use.
*Victoria and Albert Museum, London*

49 △
From *Nouveaux dessins de Cheminées à l'italienne*,
after 1665. It was evidently important to show to
what extent this imposing chimneypiece projected
into the room, so a plan is given underneath and a
profile appears on the right. By introducing a
human figure, Le Pautre has given a sense of scale
(the fire-dogs are thus seen to be enormous) and he
demonstrates how such a fireplace should blend
with the rest of the interior architecture.
*Victoria and Albert Museum, London*

## 50 △
## A grand Dutch bedchamber
### 1661

The young mother and her husband are receiving visitors who have come to see the new baby. The mother is seated formally in an armchair that stands on a Persian carpet; she faces the door through which a friend has just entered. Beside the mother is a table covered with a second Persian carpet on which are displayed a splendid ewer and basin. The bed is a rich variant of the standard box-like form. Its finials are of an unusual shape. A maid brings forward a chair for the visitor, and also a foot-warmer in its wooden housing. The wall-hanging is pulled aside as the door is open. The marble floor has an intricate pattern. (By Gabriel Metsu.)

*Metropolitan Museum of Art, New York; Gift of Pierpont Morgan, 1917*

## 51 ▷
## A more modest Dutch bedchamber
### 1660s

The bed is of the box type much favoured in the Netherlands. It has curtains and a valance across the opening, apparently of a fine, plain worsted material. The same material is used as a *tour de cheminée* (note its lining of white material, which was probably detachable for washing) and perhaps also for covering the chairs. Once again the outside back of the chair is not covered. The arrangement of the fringe is clearly shown. Both the chairs are of an old-fashioned pattern. The table has a draw-leaf and is covered with a Turkish rug. On the floor are a foot-warmer and a pair of bellows. Tiles flank the fireplace, and a cittern hangs on the panel. (By Cornelis de Man.)

*Museum of Fine Arts, Budapest; photograph from Corvina Archives by Károly Szelényi*

# 1670-1720

MANY of the subjects chosen to illustrate this section have to do with French royal interiors. This is no accident, for the enormous energy, the high degree of talent, and the sheer scale of the activity that was brought to bear on planning and decorating the French royal buildings in this period make it inevitable that their influence should be paramount. But, paradoxically, although their effect was to reach so far into the future, Louis XIV, the monarch who presided over these immense enterprises and who took a very personal interest in them, was old-fashioned when it came to court ceremonial. He imposed on his courtiers highly formal and complicated rituals which were all intended to underline his position as monarch by Divine Right; but even Louis, himself almost indefatigible, needed to be able to retire to a less oppressive atmosphere where he could relax with his family and closest entourage. In the French royal buildings, therefore, were forged at this time two patterns which still have significance today: on the one hand, a pattern for what a palace should be like; and on the other one that provided a background for comfortable and civilized relaxation.

The buildings which were to have these parallel, profound effects were erected in the 1670s and early 1680s. By far the largest enterprise was the building of the Château Neuf de Versailles which consisted of a magnificent 'envelope' that was wrapped round three sides of the relatively small château at Versailles (see p. 17). Work on the envelope was started in 1669 and was not entirely completed by the time the court moved out there from Paris in 1682. The sumptuous décor of the Grands Appartements in this huge building is legendary, and many are the descriptions that have come down to us from over-awed visitors to this impressive setting for the ceremonies of state. At the other end of the scale and representing the reverse of the medal, as it were, was the Trianon de Porcelaine; a small maison de plaisance built in the park at Versailles in 1670.[1] Little more than a pavilion, with only two bedchambers (Pls.61 and 62) and a décor that was entirely blue and white, it was considered enchanting at the time. It had been put up by the King to please his new mistress, Mme de Montespan, and the speed with which the work had been carried out was regarded as almost miraculous; it seemed as if it had been brought there by fairies. Rather more substantial was the small palace he built for her at the village of Clagny, outside the park a stone's throw from the huge Château Neuf.[2] This 'maison de délices' was completed by 1680 and also had many pleasing features including a very beautiful gallery, a sumptuous bathroom and a long, low silhouette which was to be much imitated. In a treatise on architecture published 100 years later, Clagny was still mentioned as being especially remarkable.[3] By the end of the 1670s, however, Louis was still not satisfied and sought relaxation further afield. He discovered a site some miles away at a place called Marly where he started, in 1679, to plan the famous little château of that name. 'The King never allowed ceremony at all at Marly,' wrote the Princess Palatine. 'No ambassadors or envoys were permitted to come there;

## 52] DOORS IN THE GRAND TRIANON (TRIANON DE MARBRE), VERSAILLES 1686–8

From a suite of engravings by Pierre Le Pautre, son of Jean, showing doorways and panelling in the French royal palaces set up during the 1680s under Jules Hardouin Mansart who was appointed the King's *Premier Architecte* in 1683. Mansart had a large drawing-office staffed by many highly talented architects and draughtsmen, and did probably not design these distinguished elements himself, but they were clearly thought sufficiently noteworthy to merit a special publication. The doors are in pairs – a device that had been introduced by the 1650s and was used, for example, throughout the main rooms at Vaux (see Pl.8). It produced a symmetrical effect that contributed greatly to the measured rhythms of a panelled interior. (From *Portes à Placard et Lambris desinés par le Sr. Mansard et nouvellement executez dans quelques Maisons Roiales, etc.*, said by Fiske Kimball to have been published 'after 1691'.) *Victoria and Albert Museum, London*

PORTES Des Appartemens de Triannon

A Paris chez I. Mariette ruë St. Iacq à la Victoire Avec Privilege du Roi.

3

there was no etiquette . . . , in the *salon* everyone . . . was allowed to sit down.'[4] It was regarded as an immense honour to be allowed to follow the King when he went to stay at this small retreat. It should be added that in the palace of Versailles itself the members of the royal family each had their private apartment to which they could retire. Particularly noteworthy was that of the Dauphin on the ground floor.

A fresh round of royal building came at the end of the century, starting in 1687 with the building of the Trianon de Marbre on the site of the Trianon de Porcelaine (which had not properly stood up to the weather), and continuing at the turn of the century with the revamping of the Ménagerie (see p.17) and extensive re-decoration at Marly. The new, lower fireplace-openings were now to be seen everywhere, the panels of mirror-glass above were reaching up to the ceiling, panelling was breaking out of the old rectangular forms, and a whole much less formal repertoire of decoration was being evolved. It was of some proposed ornaments for the little *maison de plaisance* at the Ménagerie that Louis commented to his architect in 1699 that 'something more youthful would surely be appropriate'. He was not discussing the décor of a palace, of course, but this remark reflects the fact that, as far as French royal buildings were concerned, a generally more relaxed atmosphere was now considered appropriate in all but the most stately settings. The seeds from which sprang the light-heartedness of the Rococo were sown at this period.[5]

By this time it was no longer solely in the royal buildings that advanced ideas were being tried out. Novel features combining elegance with comfort were to be seen in a number of Parisian mansions (Pls.77, 81–83, 113 and 114), and impetus was given to the spread of these new ideas by the publication in 1691 of Augustin Charles D'Aviler's *Cours d'Architecture* which was a far more practical and less academic work than that of the great François Blondel which had come out in five volumes between 1675 and 1683 (Pls.53 and 58). D'Aviler's book was revised several times and was found helpful well into the eighteenth century.[6]

After the death of Louis XIV in 1715 the focus of attention moved back to Paris where the Regent, the Duke of Orléans, had his residence at the Palais Royal – the building erected by Richelieu and subsequently lived in by Anne d'Autriche. Now, for the third time in less than a century, this building was to be the scene of important innovation in the field of interior decoration. The work was carried out under the brilliant direction of Gilles-Marie Oppenord. Pl.106 shows his style clearly, with its irregular shapes that have replaced the rectilinear, its curving forms that work three-dimensionally, and the tall glasses dominating the whole composition. The conventional framework seemed to be breaking up; a whole new style was being born. The gallery decorated by François-Antoine Vassé for the Comte de Toulouse around 1717 was equally impressive and was talked of with great admiration long afterwards (Pl.105).

By 1670 it was widely recognized that the French had a special talent for contriving elegant and comfortable settings for a civilized existence, and by the end of the century French supremacy in this field was even more evident. In 1694 the Swedish Court Architect, who knew a great deal about developments in France, insisted that 'all that concerns the interior of apartments . . . is improved upon daily in France and it is there they achieve such great success'.[7] The Swedish Crown was in fact quick to imitate the latest French fashions and others did so as best they could. It was not only the wish that had to be present; one also needed to have the artistic and technical skills. The spread across Europe of French taste in these matters was therefore uneven; but France had no rival in this field and it was merely a matter of time before pretty well everyone was following the French lead.

Magnificent arrangements certainly existed elsewhere. Lady Mary Wortley Montagu, for example, noted how luxuriously appointed were the palaces of Vienna when she was there in 1716, and the same could be said of those of Rome. No doubt comfort was not unknown in these places either; but tastes there were conservative. The future did not lie that way. Fresh ideas mainly came from France and it was the French style that prevailed, as subsequent developments show.

The only alternative style was that offered by Holland and then by England, and this was essentially a simplified version of the French idiom which appealed more readily to middle-class patrons. For the French style was unashamedly aristocratic, and abroad it was first taken up at the courts, whence it gradually percolated through the social strata.

The Dutch and the English contribution to the interior decoration during this period lay in goods rather than ideas. The Dutch produced enormous quantities of delftware in the form of tiles – brightly coloured and easy to clean – and pottery that was highly decorative. They also imported most of the Chinese and Japanese porcelain that came to Europe, and because it was available in Holland in greater quantities than elsewhere, they set a fashion for displaying it massed in formal arrangements (Pl.98). They also imported lacquer and likewise showed how this could be used for decoration, either unaltered or cut up and made into panels (see p.21). The principal English contribution was the chair with a caned seat and back. Large numbers were exported and became so popular on the Continent (not so much in France but almost everywhere else) that imitations were soon made in most countries. In some countries the makers of such imitations acknowledged their debt by calling themselves 'English chairmakers'.[8]

An important variation of the French pattern emerged in Holland at the end of the seventeenth century under the pencil of Daniel Marot. This talented French architect had worked in the French royal drawing-offices as a young man but had had to go into exile in 1684 on account of his religion. This Huguenot refugee settled in Holland and was soon working for the ruling family there, the House of Orange. He brought with him an intimate knowledge of Parisian design and decoration in its most advanced form. However, the Parisian style of which he had such deep knowledge was that of the 1670s and early 1680s. After that his personal experience of the originals ceased and he had to rely on whatever fresh information came his way. The result was that, by the end of the century, some of Marot's designs were rather old-fashioned and in some aspects were even a little bizarre – but, because of his genius and training, his compositions were always beautifully integrated and consistent. At any rate the many suites of engravings of his designs that were published in Holland had an enormous influence on fashionable decoration outside France during the 1690s and the first decades of the eighteenth century (Pls.97–100, and cf. 101 with 136).

Perhaps his principal contribution, however, lay in that he demonstrated, through his views of a complete interior, how unity of design could be applied to the decoration of a room as a whole (Pl.99), making it amply evident what pleasing effect such unity could produce. Architects before Marot had had to design furnishings for important rooms but it is unlikely that anyone previously can have paid quite so much attention, in such detail, to every aspect of interior furnishing and decoration, and certainly no one previously had ever published such a wide range of designs for all these various components. Marot worked for the Stadholder who became King of England as William III. The Marot style came to England with him, and here too it had a profound effect. The style also influenced taste at some of the German courts, while in Holland itself it remained dominant until well into the second quarter of the eighteenth century, gradually becoming acceptable to the middle classes. At any moment during its long run, however, the countries where Marot's style prevailed could, and often did, also come under direct French influence. For example some of the leading upholsterers in London at the turn of the century were Frenchmen, and so apparently was the principal upholsterer at The Hague.[9]

Partly because the Stadholder was also King of England, but also because the commercial feud between the Dutch and the English had finally come out in England's favour, the Dutch influence on England waned and the flow in fact came to be reversed around 1700. Evidence of this comes from the new regulations issued to the cabinetmaker's guild at The Hague in 1711 which, among other things, stipulated that those seeking to become masters should build as their 'masterpiece', proving their competence, 'an English cabinet six feet high . . . with drawers below . . . veneered with walnut', which must be what we would call a bureau-bookcase. In that same year, a German visiting Amsterdam noted the many shops selling fine cabinetmaking but added that what was to be seen there was 'nothing like as good and delicate as that to be seen in England'.[10]

## Planning and arrangement

Jean Courtonne published a treatise on perspective in 1725 and added a '*digression*' on the question of '*distribution*', by which he meant 'the use an architect should make of the space on which one seeks to erect a building', a skill which should be regarded as 'the principal and most essential' of an architect's tasks to which 'all others . . . should be subordinated'. He added that 'we French' had carried the art of distribution much further than any other nation.[11] However, the advance made in this art was fairly recent. In the first edition of his *Cours d'Architecture* of 1691, all D'Aviler said was that 'The least apartment in order to be complete must have four rooms: i.e. an antechamber, a bedchamber, a closet, and a *garderobe* which should always lead to a small staircase.' The 1710 edition, revised by the architect Le Blond, includes about a dozen pages headed '*De la nouvelle Manière de distribuer les Plans*'.[12]

Le Blond explains that the state rooms (*appartements de parade*) ought to be at the front of the house; the private apartments (*de commodité*) at the back. Some people prefer to spend their day in the main apartment but to retire to a small apartment on a mezzanine floor for the night. A state apartment should comprise a vestibule; two antechambers, the first for servants to wait in, the other where people of distinction can gather and which also serves as a dining-room; a *salon* where people of quality are received and one may dine on special occasions; a bedchamber for summer use (in winter one retired to a small bedchamber on a mezzanine); a *grand cabinet* where one received people on business; a closet serving as a study or office; a gallery which is the most magnificent room in the house where the most splendid furniture and works of art are displayed; an '*arrière-cabinet*' or back-closet where documents are kept in safety; and three *garderobes*, one serving as a dressing-room, one as a store for clothes where a personal servant also sleeps, and one where the close-stool used to stand although one now has a water-closet. He does not use an explicit term for this amenity and is indeed a bit vague about it, explaining that 'the manner of building this sort of place is entirely new'. However, he mentions water with pipes and a tap, as well as a valve.

Much ingenuity was brought to the question of distribution by the French, as Courtonne claimed and as a study of plans of the period makes very evident. The arrangements always seem clear and neatly calculated to promote a pleasant way of living. This is evident on paper: it must also have been apparent to the visitor to such new buildings, in so far as the reception rooms were concerned; the visitor was not meant to be aware of the private rooms. There was, at any rate, a great deal to be learned from the French plans of buildings that began to

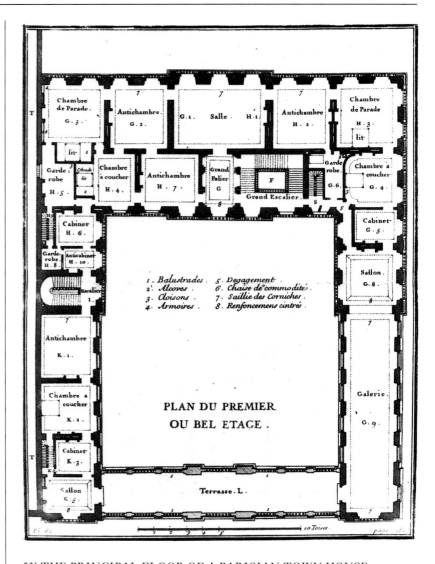

**53] THE PRINCIPAL FLOOR OF A PARISIAN TOWN HOUSE** *c.* 1690

From Augustin Charles D'Aviler's important *Cours d'Architecture* of 1691. This and another plan, which shows the ground floor, are the only plans in the book and must have been included to convey some idea of modern French ideas on planning. The visitor, having come up the main stairs from the central vestibule below, would have entered the great central *salle* overlooking the garden. On either side is an important apartment, each with its antechamber, *chambre de parade*, private bedchamber, closet and *garderobe*. The apartment on the right was probably the most important as it is associated with a *salon* and a gallery; furthermore its secondary bedchamber is larger and has rounded corners which was something of an innovation at this time. The other apartment may have been for a lady; its beds stand in an alcove and it has both a closet and an *anti-cabinet*, as well as two *garderobes*, one of which was probably a dressing-room. Each apartment has a 'house of office' tucked away next to its *garderobe*, one at least of which would have housed a bed for a personal servant. A third apartment is in the left-hand wing. Note the back-stairs which could serve either as access for the staff or as escape-routes for the occupants of the apartments.
*Victoria and Albert Museum, London*

appear at the end of the seventeenth century, and an intelligent architect who had sight of such engravings could profit greatly, especially if he could lay hands on a copy of the 1710 edition of D'Aviler, with its helpful explanations about distribution. In the 1720 and 1730s even more helpful publications became available.

Le Blond (1710) noted that the second antechamber in a French house often served as a dining-room. He used the term '*salle à manger*', which is also to be seen on a design for Clagny of the 1670s although it has been claimed it was not employed before the 1780s. For more formal meals with fairly large numbers, one might use the *salon* – a room that often, but not always, occupied a central position on a plan. Something like the same distinction was made in England where the family and friends would by this time habitually eat in a 'dining parlour' but a large house might still have a 'Great Dining Room'. The latter went out of fashion during the second half of the century, after which the English – and no doubt other nations – followed the French practice and on formal occasions dined in the 'saloon'. People no longer sat down to interminable meals with endless courses and carousing. Moreover, society had become more exclusive towards the end of the seventeenth century. It was no longer a mark of favour to be entertained amongst as many guests as possible; now, the smaller the company, the greater the honour. Huge dining-rooms were therefore no longer needed.

Meals could also be taken at occasional tables set up in a bedchamber or elsewhere. Those fashionable new beverages, tea, coffee and chocolate, were also normally enjoyed round some small table carried in (or forward from the wall) for the occasion, which was usually presided over by the lady of the house (Pls.94 and 95). Tea-drinking would often take place in a closet, it seems.

In France the bedchamber was undoubtedly a room of reception; it was the innermost of such rooms, but this does not mean it was in any sense a drawing-room where one could relax. No one really relaxed in society at that period except in the privacy of a closet or a *petit appartement* (Pl.84). Mark Girouard, whose *Life in the English Country House* (New Haven and London, 1978) is so entertainingly informative about these matters, has suggested that English bedchambers were more private than French ones, but the evidence is difficult to obtain. One might receive people in one's bedchamber if anticipating congratulations or compliments (Pls.50 and 68). Saint-Simon bragged about his wife having received 'the whole of France' on the morning of their wedding, and he mentions that she did so reclining on her bed. When the pretty Mlle de Fontanges was made a duchess and granted a huge pension by the ageing Louis XIV in 1680, she accepted everyone's compliments in the same position.[13] If anyone saw the irony, they were not so ill-mannered as to say so. A royal bed, incidentally, was treated with the utmost reverence, even when unoccupied. Princes of the blood bowed to it if they had to pass through the room; ladies made a deep curtsey. Not only was there a protective balustrade; a royal bed might in addition be warded by a *valet de chambre* who made sure that no one too closely approached this symbol of near-divinity.

The rigid formality of court life, and indeed of most social intercourse, during this period made it imperative to have places of retreat in which one could relax. This led to the development of entire private apartments behind the scenes in great establishments, and also of the closet as a delightful and comfortable little room where one could get away from the irksome demands of etiquette. Le Blond (1710) speaks of a '*grand cabinet*', by which he means a large-sized closet, but he says it is for receiving people on business. In fact *grands cabinets* in important houses were very glamorous reception rooms of moderate size, larger than most ordinary closets, where one could expect to find select company not at all devoted to 'business'. Catherine of Braganza's closet at

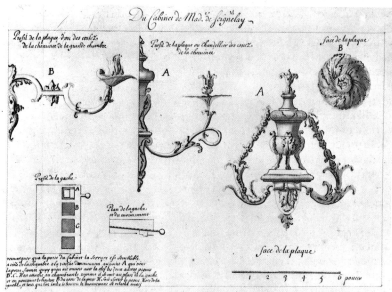

**54, 55] CHIMNEYPIECE IN A FASHIONABLE CLOSET, PARIS** 1693

Mme de Seignelay had done up her house in an exceptionally elegant manner. These two drawings were sent from Paris to Nicodemus Tessin, the Swedish Court Architect, who took such pains to discover every detail about the latest French fashions in decoration. Apart from the large plate of mirror-glass set into the chimney-breast, what was considered remarkable about this room was its metalwork, which was not of gilt bronze but of cut steel executed by the most skilled locksmith in Paris and of 'a neatness that surpasses anything ever seen before', as Tessin's correspondent wrote in a letter of 11 September 1693 when forwarding these drawings to Sweden. The writer also sent four specimens of the locksmith's work. The delicately chased sconces (A) must be those on the chimney-breast; the others (B) were in her '*grand chambre*'. *National Museum, Stockholm; Tessin-Hårleman Collection*

Whitehall was clearly quite large, for she would sit there in the evening conversing 'with the ladies who happen to be there, who form a circle round Her Majesty', while several gentlemen were present including ambassadors and any important foreigners who happened to be visiting London, as well as Charles II himself and the Duke of York who were both 'seeking relief from more mighty cares, and divesting themselves awhile of the restraint of royalty'.[14] The room was hung with sky-blue damask with gold lace disguising the seams. The decoration of a very spectacular French *grand cabinet* at the end of the century may be seen in Pl.78. It is largely panelled with mirror-glass, which was an exceptionally expensive way of decorating a room at the time. Indeed, during this period it was even more the case than before that closets, being rooms where informality reigned, were places where unconventional and even rather daring or crazy forms of decoration could be adopted. There were closets entirely decorated with Chinese porcelain vases and dishes (Pl.98), and with walls painted with arabesques dotted with monkeys or scenes from the Italian Comedy. Such fanciful ornament would not have been suitable in a state room, one can be fairly sure. The unconventional decoration of Mme de Seignelay's closet was probably not echoed by that in her *salon* or antechamber (Pls.54 and 55).

Both men and women had dressing-tables and these were sometimes placed in the bedchamber (Pls.64 and 75); but grand people tended by this time to have an additional small room (in fact, another closet) at the back of the bedchamber where they dressed, and very fashionable people might receive callers there as they dressed in the mornings. When that was the intention, the dressing-room would of course be decorated with style (Pl.72).[15] Studies were also small rooms which could either belong to an apartment or might be joined to a library, for books were now sufficiently common for it to be normal for any respectable large house to have a room set aside for them. Most studies were businesslike and scarcely decorated at all, but some were as glamorous as any smart closet (Pl.11).

Day-beds, which were now the appurtenance of any fashionable lady, seem usually to have stood in her closet and could be very spectacular objects indeed (Pls.66, 73 and 83). By the 1670s extremely comfortable 'easy chairs' (*fauteuils de commodité*) were being developed; they were armchairs with much padding, usually with cheeks or wings, and sometimes at first with adjustable backs. By the end of the century the various elements had blended into the integrated form of winged chair with which everyone is familiar. However, such seat-furniture was to be found in the closet or the bedchamber, not in the drawing-room. The same probably at first applied to the sofa which was essentially a widened easy chair; indeed the Dauphin had a sofa *en suite* with some easy chairs in his closet at Versailles.[16] In 1692 it was still necessary to explain that 'the sopha is a form of day-bed like those used by the Turks' but they were to be seen in many of the smartest houses by 1700, wherever French taste was being closely followed.[17] The French frequently called this piece of furniture a '*canapé*', as they still do. It may well be that the earliest *canapés* were derived from a form of ceremonial couch with double ends which eventually acquired a back. A ceremonial couch was a seat of state and would have had a canopy suspended above it, which could account for the name although no firm evidence can be put forward for this theory.[18]

Chairs and other seat-furniture continued to stand against the wall at this period. It was sometimes necessary to protect the walls, as at one English house where there were some 'large pictures with guilded frames sett within the wainscott' which had 'iron rods to defend them from chairs'.[19] Chair-backs grew taller from the 1680s onwards and upholstered furniture became commoner, so the ranks of seat-furniture must have constituted an even more

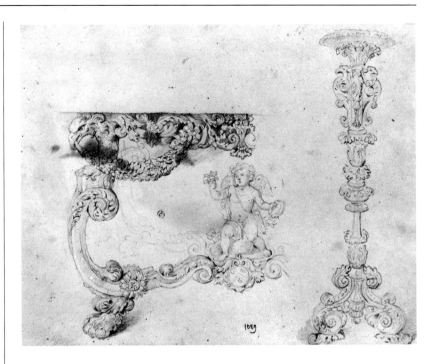

56] DESIGN FOR A CONSOLE TABLE AND CANDLE-STANDS, FRANCE *c.*1680

Probably drawn by Nicodemus Tessin when he visited Paris in 1687. He acquainted himself with the latest fashions in the French capital and kept abreast of developments after his return to Stockholm (see Pls.54 and 55). The table will have been flanked by a pair of stands, with a looking-glass hung above. Such highly decorative ensembles were normally positioned between windows, against a pier. The feet of the single stand shown are of a form favoured in Paris in about 1680.
*National Museum, Stockholm; Tessin-Hårleman Collection*

eye-catching feature of the decoration (Pls.96 and 99).

Another very striking decorative ensemble was the 'triad'. This recently coined word describes the suite of table, looking-glass and pair of candle-stands (Pls.56, 75 and 66 where no stands are shown). Designed as a group, it was a favourite ornamental feature in elegant rooms from the 1670s until early in the eighteenth century. It was normal but not mandatory to set up this group against a pier (i.e. between two windows) with the candle-stands flanking the table. The stands, with their candelabra perched on top, got in the way of the window-curtains and this very probably explains why the pull-up curtain was evolved during the last two decades of the century. Candle-stands also tended to get knocked over and damaged. Perhaps they were even a fire hazard. At any rate they went out of fashion in the early eighteenth century as a component of the triad, and the candelabra were placed on the table instead, which not only had the advantage of greater safety but meant that the candle-light was charmingly reflected in the glass above.

The next move was to integrate the glass in the panelling to form a 'pier glass' and to fix the table to the wall below, tucking in its legs so that it came to form the characteristic eighteenth-century console table (Pl.105). The triad was particularly well suited to serve as a dressing-table since the light from either the windows or the flanking candles fell helpfully on the face of someone seated in front of such a table. At first the table had rather slender legs but a new, more

57] A CANDLE-STAND IN THE GRANDS APPARTEMENTS AT VERSAILLES   1670s

The furniture in the State Apartment at Versailles (built in the second half of the 1670s) was mostly of silver but this was melted down in 1689, and furniture of wood, carved and gilded, was made to replace it. This is the original drawing for a suite of engravings by Jean Bérain, who was probably just recording what he saw for Louis XIV, whose official draughtsman he was at the time. This stand may have been one of those made by the Parisian silversmith Delaunay.

*National Museum, Stockholm; Tessin-Hårleman Collection*

sturdy type '*en forme de bureau*' (like a writing-desk with drawers) was evolved in the late seventeenth century (Pls.85 and 78) with quite short legs that made the whole thing much steadier. From there it was a logical development to remove the legs and fill the space entirely with drawers – whereupon you had a 'commode'. This new class of furniture was to be seen in Paris by the first decade of the eighteenth century (Pl.83) but not, it would seem, much earlier. The Princess Palatine, writing to her half-sister in Germany in 1718, still felt it necessary to explain that 'a commode is a large table with large drawers',[20] and it is unlikely that commodes were to be seen outside Paris and its environs much before 1730 or even later. Bearing their ancestry in mind, it is not suprising that until well into the eighteenth century, commodes were normally associated with a looking-glass, the two items being considered as an entity.

Candle-stands (or *guéridons*; see p.26) could be placed anywhere, but it was preferable to have them close to the wall where they were less likely to get knocked over. Even when they had been banned from the triad-suite standing at the pier, they were to be found in other parts of the room but most commonly, it seems, in the corners. One amusing piece of evidence for this is the masked ball given in 1706 where four young French noblemen dressed up 'in gold with golden masks and silver sashes like carved gilt *guéridons*. They wore candelabra on their heads and stationed themselves at the four corners of the room.'[21]

## The architectural shell

French architects and their clients became increasingly fascinated by the idea of facing walls with large areas of mirror-glass. By 1670 they had achieved some striking effects in relatively small rooms by abutting plates of mirror-glass to form larger panels, and this system continued to be used although strenuous efforts were at the same time being made to increase the size of the individual plates. So great was demand for mirror-glass in France that a factory was set up in 1665 to produce it, under royal patronage, using the Venetian method of blowing; but this limited the size severely, and even then the new factory was not able to fulfil orders until 1670. It was not until the French had developed a method of casting glass that much larger plates could be made. That occurred in the 1680s, but the first four unblemished mirrors of this sort could only be presented to Louis XIV in 1691, and the production was attended by so much breakage (the silvering was especially difficult) that only eleven mirrors of a substantial size, 80 × 45 *pouces* (85 × 48 in., 216 × 122 cm), were produced between 1688 and 1699! Nevertheless the French claimed to be able to make plates of 100 × 60 *pouces* (106 × 64 in., 269 × 163 cm) by 1700 and the Venetians conceded that the French were their masters in this field when, already in 1697, they decided henceforth to confine their own production to plates of 45 × 20 *pouces* (48 × 21 in., 122 × 53 cm) or less.[22] No other country was in fact able to rival the French in this activity until late in the eighteenth century.

Therefore most of the glamorous effects achieved with mirror-glass before the mid-1690s, including the famous Galerie des Glaces at Versailles (early 1680s), were created with blown '*glace de Venise*' produced either in Venice or in France. However, the availability of the larger sheets began to affect the design of mural decoration in and around Paris at the very end of the century, and completely transformed the appearance of fashionable rooms early in the next. The designers at first concentrated on the chimneypiece (as always) and then on the pier-glasses which were now becoming a fixture.

At first small panels of mirror-glass were set into the chimney-breast, above the opening which was becoming lower and smaller, and below an inset painting or some other form of ornament. The first published design showing this dates from 1691 (Pl.58). The glass panels then increased in size (Pl.54) and quite soon were stretching up towards the ceiling, whereupon they were given frames that were no longer rectangular (Pls.79 and 82). With the more lively outline of the frames went fireplace-openings of a correspondingly fanciful shape, and not long afterwards the shape of the surround (of marble or stone) also began to project and recede to produce curves in three dimensions (Pls.106 and 119). By 1720 panels in a few rooms had reached up the full height from the mantel-shelf or dado to the cornice. Much larger free-hanging looking-glasses could now also be made. It is clear that people were excited by the effects produced by all this glass. To be able to see oneself in a glass from head to toe was regarded as amazing.[23] Besides, the glass reflected candle-light prettily.

Many suites of engravings appeared in Paris between 1685 and 1720 showing the new forms of chimneypiece and other elements of mural decoration. Unfortunately not many are dated. Most notable are the suites by Pierre Le Pautre who worked in the royal drawing-office, and who was almost as prolific as his father, Jean. The titles of Pierre's suites are revealing: 'Doors and panelling ... executed in some of the royal palaces'. 'A book of chimneypieces in the apartments at Versailles...'. 'Chimneypieces at Marly...'. 'Chimneypieces *à la Royalle* with large mirror-plates...'. 'Fashionable panelling in new buildings in Paris'.[24] Two other draughtsmen-designers working in the royal drawing-

A. *Contrecœurs chantournés*
B. *Lambris d'Apui*
C. *Chambranle*
D. *Gorge en balustre*
E. *Gorge en Cloche*
F. *Buste*
G. *Corniches des manteaux*
H. *Montant*
I. *Chute de feston*
K. *Miroir*
L. *Vase*
M. *Corniches des Chambres*
N. *Poutre*

Pl.58.                                      Page.169.

**MOYENNES CHEMINÉES POUR LES CHAMBRES.**

58] CHIMNEYPIECE IN A FRENCH BEDCHAMBER  1691

This engraving, showing two complete chimneypieces of medium size 'for bedchambers', was published in D'Aviler's *Cours d'Architecture*. This is probably the earliest published illustration of the novel form of chimneypiece with a plate of mirror-glass (K) set into the attic of the chimney-breast. Note also the low dado (B) and the fire-backs (A). (Engraved by Pierre Le Pautre.)
*Victoria and Albert Museum, London*

offices, Jean Bérain and François Francard, also provided suites of chimney-piece designs in the new fashion.[25] Add to these the numerous designs for other classes of decorative art (vases, tables, candle-stands, door-furniture, silver-ware, arabesque wall-decoration, etc.), and the books on architecture with plans of buildings newly erected in or near the French capital, and it will be seen that an enormous amount of information was available by the early eighteenth century about developments on this front in France. No other country produced anything approaching this quantity. It reflects the excitement and the pride with which the French viewed their achievements. What is equally noteworthy is that the greatest innovations, the most impressive advances, were made within the royal drawing-offices, spurred on by the drive, personal interest and good judgement of the King himself – thus refuting the common view that anything civil servants set their hand to must inevitably be mediocre.

The news about glazed walls travelled quickly. In 1687 Tessin, the Swedish architect, saw the closet of the Princess of Orange (Mary, about to become Queen of England) at the little Dutch pleasure-palace at Honselersdijk, and this had a ceiling of mirror-glass. The walls were of Oriental lacquer, as had been those of her predecessor. This House of Orange passion for lacquer associated with massed porcelain and now also with mirror-glass was spread by the princesses. One married the Stadholder of Friesland; she had a closet faced with lacquer panels cut from Chinese screens. Another married the Elector of Brandenburg; she had a Porcelain Room built in the mid-1690s at Oranienburg (note the name) outside Berlin on House of Orange principles, and a few years later a 'small Mirror and Porcelain Closet' at Schloss Lützenburg, now Charlottenburg, in Berlin itself. It had red panels with glass and gilt carving. By 1700 she also had a 'Glazed Bedchamber' where the glass panels alternated with panels of green damask.[26] Pl.98 shows a closet of slightly later date in Berlin with such a décor. Queen Mary (the Orange connection again) brought the fashion to England. The accent in these Dutch exercises was usually on the exotic – the lacquer, the massed array of porcelain – but the style was nevertheless essentially French, as one of Daniel Marot's suites of engravings reminds us, for it was entitled 'Novel chimneypieces with panels of glass in the French manner', and even those designs that have a strongly Dutch character still owe much to French practice.[27]

Fire-dogs had become much smaller, which presumably explains why the French now called them *chenets* (from *chienette*). Towards the end of the seventeenth century each *chenet* became linked with its 'creeper' (a smaller fire-dog that actually carried the log), and the fire-bars stretched out at right angles to meet in the centre of the fireplace. Eventually the pair became linked so that a grid was formed, making a single unit of the whole structure (Pls.78 and 86). A grate for coals could replace the bars for wood. Fire-screens became decorative and no longer purely functional during the last decades of the century (Pl.99). They mostly had tripod stands with a leaf that was adjustable in height. A new form with a decorated leaf that could slide up or down (a 'cheval screen' or '*écran à coulisse*') was invented. Fire-irons were stood upright against hooks set into the cheeks of the fireplace (Pls.54 and 78). At Ham House, and probably elsewhere, one could gauge the status of a room by the richness of the fire-irons allocated to it, the best rooms being furnished with silver-handled irons[28].

The striving for unity in the décor remained a paramount consideration, but in some places this was carried through more consistently than in others. As far as mural decoration was concerned, the pattern was as usual set by the chimneypiece. This governed the height of the dado, which was normally slightly lower than the mantel-shelf; and if there was a panel above the fireplace (either glazed or containing a painting) its height would govern that of the other panels, if there were any. Their outline would likewise echo that over the fireplace. Panels generally grew larger during the period but most remained rectangular.[29]

Panelling[30] was usually painted during this period and the colours were often strong. Polychromy was in favour during the second half of the seventeenth century. The stunning effects that could be contrived with various-coloured facings of marble could also be reproduced here by means of marbled paintwork. At the end of the century, it became fashionable in the French palaces to have the walls white with gilded mouldings and carvings.

The sliding sash window had by the 1670s acquired a counterbalancing system of weights and cords running over pulleys, and it was in widespread use in England and Holland by 1700. The French, and no doubt other nations, knew about it but did not generally adopt it. Shutters were to be seen in most grand houses, now reaching the full height of the windows, and each pair folding in half lengthwise so as to fold away neatly into the window embrasure. The panel-face that remained visible began to be decorated *en suite* with the rest of the décor towards the end of the century. Double windows were fitted to some rooms against the cold.

Wooden floors now became general. Floors of stone or marble were mostly confined to halls, landings, and great saloons. Parquet with regular patterns, the pieces within squares set square or diagonally, was now to be seen in important French houses but it took some while for this neat form of flooring to be more widely adopted (Pl.66). In the 1680s some extremely elaborate floors of '*parquet marqueté*' were laid in various closets in the French royal palaces but these gave a lot of trouble and were soon taken up again (Pl.76).[31]

## ▽ 60] DECOR DESIGNED BY AN ARCHITECT   *c.*1699

This drawing by William Talman is a project for a 'Trianon', a retreat for King William III which was to have been on the Thames opposite Hampton Court. It shows clearly which elements Talman considered 'architectural features'. There would have been other furnishings, but these would be standard items obtainable commercially and not specially designed. A little more than half the drawing is reproduced here, the centre being the domed vestibule under the lantern. On the right (not shown) is a large room, rather severely decorated, which is probably the Great Dining Room. Shown here is the principal apartment with a richly appointed Withdrawing Room that serves as Antechamber to the Bedchamber. The latter is curious because it has a corner-fireplace tucked away alongside the head of the bed, which would probably not have met with approval among French academic architects. It also has a rather low ceiling to leave space for a subsidiary bedchamber above. Did this smaller room serve as the owner's private bedchamber, the other being for show? Beyond the State Bedchamber is a splendid closet, the chimneypiece of which has an oval plate of glass inset.
*Royal Institute of British Architects, London, Drawings Collection*

## △ 59] PARISIAN MURAL DECORATION   *c.*1685

The original drawing for the engraved title-page of a suite of designs by the famous cabinetmaker André Charles Boulle. He was a most capable draughtsman and presumably himself designed the sumptuous works of art that emanated from his workshops at the Louvre. As this illustration shows, his creations included furniture, bronzes and complete schemes of mural ornament. Thus the four pedestals were probably supposed to be executed in ebony, tortoiseshell, brass and pewter, and the numerous vases were no doubt of gilt bronze. The panelling in the same style is the kind of background against which 'boullework' furniture (see p. 157) was meant to be seen. (For *Nouveaux Desseins de Meubles et Ouvrages de Bronze et de Marqueterie. Inventés et gravés par André Charles Boulle.*)
*Kupferstichkabinett und Sammlung der Zeichnungen, Staatliche Museen, Berlin*

Pls.81–83 show three sides of a room designed by 'Sr. Blondel', presumably Jean-François Blondel (b.1681), where he has indicated how all the elements should look, including the bed in a niche (a novel idea at this date, with the bed set parallel to the back wall) and a commode (also then an entirely new type of furniture). He has applied his skill consistently to produce a unified decorative scheme. Daniel Marot, in achieving similar results in Holland (Pls.99 and 100), also provided designs for a wide range of furnishings. Presumably the Dutch craftsmen with whom he had to work once he had arrived in Holland, capable as they were, did not possess the talents for design that Marot could have expected of their counterparts working in the service of the French Crown, and he therefore felt it necessary himself to provide the designs that these craftsmen required in order to achieve the unity of design he knew was essential for his schemes.

Marot is a notable example of the architect paying attention to detail, but any architect wishing to achieve a unified décor in a room would have had to keep an eye on these matters. Known examples are few: Nicodemus Tessin's interest in every conceivable detail of French interior decoration may have been extreme but is probably symptomatic. Pls.102–104 show Nicolas Pineau, no mean architect, providing designs for bed-hangings. Jean Bérain, a designer who turned his hand to interior architecture (notably for the Dauphin), composed the mural-scheme shown in Pl.80, with its sliding shutters. And when Oppenord drew a proposal for the Regent's bedchamber at the Palais Royal in 1716, he showed very clearly how he wanted the state bed to look. It was essential he should do so because it was the principal feature of the composition.[32] Pls.60 and 98 suggest that William Talman in London and Eosander von Göthe in Berlin took much the same sort of interest in the details that they considered important for their schemes, and which therefore can be regarded as part of the architecture.

## Loose furnishings

Wall-hangings changed little during this period from their form in 1670. Hangings made up with widths of two materials alternating to form vertical stripes were still in favour, although most hangings were made with a single material. All but the meanest were trimmed, and the convention was now firmly established whereby fringe was produced in two lengths so that a fringe of normal length could be attached along the bottom edge of a hanging, so as to hang downwards in the ordinary manner, but a shorter fringe, which could not droop, was used for the vertical edges. Along the top edge one could attach either a long fringe hanging downwards or a short fringe mounted upwards. In Pl.97 one can see the two lengths on a panel which also has a capping in the form of a fixed festoon at the top. Cappings were fashionable during the last decade of the seventeenth century and the early eighteenth century. The effect of a capping could be produced by attaching a fringe horizontally, some distance down from the top, as in the Italian picture reproduced in Pl.89. Cappings were particularly popular in Italy during the Baroque period. Some very elaborate wall-hangings with cappings, furbelows and ruffles may also be seen in the Marot view of a room shown in Pl.99. *Portières* were now often made *en suite* with the wall-hangings so as to produce yet greater unity in the décor.

Straight fringe is familiar to everyone; another form, very fashionable between 1680 and 1710, was what the English called 'campaign fringe' (from the French *campane*, a bell), the hangers of which ended in bell-like tufts. This gave a very rich look to an edging. The headings of fringes could also be elaborate. Netted fringes, on which the heading consisted of a deep openwork net that ended in separate little tassels, were going out of fashion by 1670. Developed from this was an extremely elaborate form of trimming, used on the most expensive types of furniture, which had an openwork lace heavily adorned with metal wire and creamy strips of parchment, and tufts of coloured silk, all of which produced a three-dimensional bordering. For a while in the 1690s it became fashionable to trim upholstery, including that on seat-furniture, with a ruffled pie-crust effect (Pls.84 and 86).

Tapestries were still popular but there was a tendency to treat them as if they were rigid panels fitted to the walls, which meant that their principal character as a textile material was largely nullified. Great scenes in perspective were now fast going out of favour; two-dimensional designs (notably grotesques) were in greater demand, as were verdure tapestries which had a limited sense of depth (Pl.94). Even where scenes with figures were rendered in this medium, the figures were usually small and thus the sense of depth was rarely overpowering. On the whole three-dimensional effects were played down in tapestry from this period onwards, although there were to be exceptions. Tapestries had been devised during the Middle Ages to suit the mobile way of life then practised by the seigneurial classes who moved from castle to castle with all their furnishings and hangings, which therefore needed to be both robust and quick to erect and dismantle. (This is the origin of the words *meubles, mobili, Möbel,* meaning loose furniture.) By the late seventeenth century there was no need for such versatility, and there was really no point in hanging a wall with this expensive material except that it carried prestige – this was what our heroic forefathers had had, was the implication – and of course it also indicated that one's purse was rather deep. For all practical purposes, therefore, tapestries had long been an anachronism. If you wanted a picture on the wall, after all, you could do better with a proper painting.

Daniel Cronström, writing from Paris to Nicodemus Tessin in Stockholm at the end of the seventeenth century, makes a number of observations on what was fashionable for wall-hangings in France. For instance he says that hangings of silk damask were more fashionable than those of brocatelle. He advocates having hangings of flame-red camlet (a worsted material) alternating with brocatelle that could be pink with green, blue or violet – or white instead of pink. Or you could have hangings of Turin satin with appliqué pilasters designed by Jean Bérain. All this, he says, is in the new taste. A closet looks good with green damask from Genoa which also has appliqué pilasters. He also mentions cappings, which he calls *campanes* (because the gathering could produce a bell-like flute; nothing to do with the fringe of that name) and says they are now to be seen almost everywhere in Paris.[33] He implies that one could not use velvet in summer in Paris although in Sweden it might be acceptable, with the cooler climate. At this period the most fashionable colour for damask was crimson, partly because it looked so splendid, especially with gold trimmings, but no doubt also partly because it was more expensive than damasks of other colours owing to the cost of the dye which produced crimson.

Cronström also maintains that gilt leather was no good in Paris,[34] and indeed it seems to have been seldom used now in fashionable houses although it remained popular in Holland, Germany, and Scandinavia until the 1720s.

It may seem strange that camlet, a worsted material, could be used in the smartest settings, but such woollen materials could evidently be very decorative although few specimens have survived. Damask made with worsted instead of silk became fashionable for hangings on walls and beds in the late seventeenth century. Some worsted materials, notably paragon (a kind of camlet), could be printed with patterns, and there were materials like 'Kidderminster stuff' which had simple patterns in their weave. 'Scotch pladd' was also used occasionally for hangings at the turn of the century and Pl.109 shows a plain striped material which is probably a worsted. Altogether grander was mohair, which at this time was a silk material, watered or *moiré*, as the French call the result of the *moirage* treatment.[35]

Printed linens, which were mostly of a fawn colour with block-printed patterns in red and black, were probably used sometimes for lining small closets, but the printed cottons that were to become such a feature of late-eighteenth-century decoration had scarcely made their appearance by 1720. *Chintes*, which were cotton materials with painted patterns made in India (also called 'painted calico'), were beginning to invade Europe in quantity during the last decades of the previous century, despite unsuccessful attempts at prohibition. They were chiefly made into clothing, but some rooms were gaily decorated with these brightly coloured materials. Wallpaper existed but was still hardly used at this period.

Cronström also stated that one should avoid having textile hangings in the dining-room. Panelling was better, he said, because it did not retain the odour of food. Gilt leather had the same advantage, which explains why it is more frequently listed in inventories of rooms where meals were often taken.[36]

Window-curtains suddenly came into their own in the 1670s as an intentionally decorative element of rooms. A balanced, symmetrical look had already been achieved by dividing each curtain so the two halves could be drawn to opposite sides of the window. The next move was to mask the rods and rings with a pelmet, and here long experience of curtain-heads masked by valances on beds suggested how these details should be arranged. In a bedchamber such resemblance had the added advantage of producing yet further unity of design. Some time not long before 1690 a new form of window-curtain made its appearance in elegant surroundings and was soon to be seen in all the smartest houses. It could be pulled up or lowered by means of cords running over pulleys at the window-head, either inset in the embrasure or set into a projecting pulley-board mounted on brackets above the opening. This board also formed a convenient mounting for a pelmet. At this early stage this form of curtain was pulled straight up. Some very rudimentary pull-up curtains may be seen in Pls.90 and 91. The purpose of most window-curtains at this period was still to cut down the amount of sunlight; what are clearly sun-curtains may be seen in Pls.66 and 85.

Since the bedchamber might be used as a reception room in a grand apartment, the bed itself was here a formal piece of furniture which, in a really important room, might be designed by the architect to match its surroundings (Pl.99). The architectural bed during this period retained the traditional box-like form, topped by four finials (Pl.75). It had no other excrescence breaking this block-like mass except that, from about 1680, testers usually had a shallow doming[37] which might be visible from the outside although beds grew so tall at this period (and remained very tall until about 1715) that the outside of the dome was usually hidden from anyone standing in front of the bed – the position from which it was meant to be seen. An unobtrusive moulding might also be permitted along the top edge of the valances. All the ornament was otherwise concentrated in the hangings, and especially in the valances which could have outlines that were very intricate – but only in two dimensions. This was the form favoured in France for all beds that were to stand in formal settings, and it was adopted elsewhere as well. The bed that a *grand seigneur* placed in his private bedchamber would no doubt often be of much the same form as the bed or beds in the grand rooms although it would be rather less lavish.

There was a class of bed that was completely unlike the formal type; it had a flamboyant tester or canopy with fantastic hangings to match. Such beds cannot have stood in formal surroundings; they must have been intended for use in settings that were essentially un-serious where such frivolous confections would not have been inappropriate. The two beds shown in Pls.61 and 62, with their

61, 62] THE TWO BEDS IN THAT ROYAL LOVE-NEST, THE TRIANON DE PORCELAINE, IN THE PARK AT VERSAILLES
early 1670s

Each is carefully described in the royal accounts and was considered exceptional at the time (*un lit extraordinaire*). A mirror was set into the head-boards. The cupids were of papier mâché. The beds with all their accompanying seat-furniture and the decoration of the rooms themselves were all in blue and white, like Chinese porcelain. These two sketches must have been made by the Swedish architect Nicodemus Tessin, who was in Paris between 1677 and 1680 when the décor of the Trianon was still one of the marvels of the French capital. He has noted how the undersides of the testers were arranged, and has sketched the pattern of the plasterwork ceiling of the Chambre d'Amour (the other bed stood in the Chambre de Diane and was presumably for Mme de Montespan). At the foot of the beds are shown *porte-carreaux* with their pairs of *carreaux* or squabs.
*National Museum, Stockholm; Tessin-Hårleman Collection*

astonishing flying testers (what the French called an 'impériale'), stood in the Trianon de Porcelaine, that light-hearted fairy palace which Louis XIV created for Mme de Montespan (see p. 48). The day-bed shown in Pl.66 also has an amazing tester with hangings hitched up in a most complicated manner. This, too, as the scene shows, was not standing in any room of ceremonial.

Many of Daniel Marot's designs for beds, published in Holland, show testers of great complexity with scrolled cresting and festooned valances, and with the hangings caught up in fanciful arrangements (Pls.101 and 99). It may be that Marot got his inspiration for such designs from the beds in the Trianon de Porcelaine, and perhaps equally crazy beds installed in *maisons de plaisance* elsewhere in and around Paris. The bed shown in Pl.66 suggests that there were others and that they were not unfamiliar to those who would see this engraving. Marot did after all work in the royal drawing-offices before he left France to go into exile in 1684. At any rate, beds with complicated testers, based on Marot's designs and quite unlike the formal beds to be seen in France, were being placed in state bedchambers and other formal bedchambers in Holland and England by the end of the century, and Pl.136 shows that this type of bed also enjoyed favour in Germany. In France, to place such a bed in a formal bedchamber would surely have seemed an apalling solecism. As William III's ambassador reported to his royal master in 1698 from Paris, 'the beds ... that are made here ... are all square outside right to the top ...; at the top ... they are no wider than at the base.'[38] It is evident that he was familiar with the Marot type of bed and found the French formula very different.

The beds in the Trianon had 'flying testers' and several of Marot's designs were also for beds without posts, but it must not be thought that a '*lit d'ange*', as such a bed was called, was invariably a frivolous affair because Louis XIV himself had a bed with a such a tester in his bedchamber at Versailles. The tester was suspended at the foot end by cords made with silver-gilt thread, attached to hooks in the ceiling.[39] Most beds of this class, however, were for less impressive settings and it was said in 1692 that the mark of a true courtier was that he was a connoisseur of 'that great art, the tying up of the curtains on a *lit d'ange*'.[40] When one sees a picture like that shown in Pl.66, one can understand the point of this remark.

A state bed was normally by far the most expensive piece of furniture in the house, and it was not unusual on the occasion of important marriages for splendid beds to be given as wedding presents. There are many descriptions of the beds which were given to high-born ladies in France in the seventeenth century, some of these rich confections having cost several thousand *livres*. Such figures are thrown into some sort of perspective if one recalls that the services of a good cook could be procured for 300 *livres* per annum and those of a serving-girl for 30. Even quite a modest bed might cost about 90 *livres*, seven-eighths of which was the cost of the textile hangings while the rest was for the woodwork which was not visible and was therefore undecorated and roughly made.

Beds with domed testers of various shapes were favoured in Germany and to some extent in Holland and Scandinavia (Pl.67). There were various types of bed used by less exalted people: some of these were simple versions of the grand beds, but a type which had one or both ends of the tester sloping enjoyed widespread popularity.

Before 1670 the upholstering of chairs had been a very primitive business. The padding was piled in a heap on top of a canvas base nailed across the seat-frame, and a cover was then nailed over it which tended to produce a domed shape. Gradually means were contrived to keep the padding in position with techniques borrowed from saddle-makers,[41] and one can discern in contemporary illustrations systems of quilting and more substantial stitching introduced with this aim in mind. During the last quarter of the seventeenth century,

however, the craft of upholstering seat-furniture evolved very rapidly. All the techniques in use up to 1920, with the important exception of springing, had been devised by 1700. Having said this, it also needs to be recorded that the upholsterer's entry into this area was new (he had been a dealer in second-hand goods in the previous century) and at first he had no great craft tradition that maintained high standards of technique and finish. Upholstery in all its branches was therefore a fairly crude trade in which splendid effects were contrived principally by using expensive covering-materials fancily trimmed with intricate fringes and galloon. The workmanship was really rather poor but, as it was not visible, this did not seem to matter. It was only as expertise showed that padding needed to be better secured, and that various weaknesses could be avoided if care were taken, that the skills introduced to correct these faults were forged into a tradition which then was refined until it was to reach a high point of competence, combined with great artistry and good judgement, in France around 1770.

In the decoration of interiors it was obviously the upholstered types of seat-furniture which made the greatest impact. Most eye-catching were the sofas or *canapés* which made their appearance towards the turn of the century (Pl.78). The related '*fauteuils de commodité*' or 'easy chairs', designed to provide the utmost comfort, in this period usually had seats comprising one or more large cushions filled with down lying in a well which had a padded rim. Their backs were also padded, much use now being made of horsehair which was springy but could also be kept in place quite easily.

The so-called 'farthingale chair' (see p. 24) had grown a taller back by the 1680s and the gap between its padded back-rest and seat gradually became narrower. This stage is represented by the chair in Pl.72. Around 1700 the gap disappeared entirely both in France and England (and perhaps elsewhere) on some very fashionable chairs (Pl.93). The 'gap-less' form remained in favour in England but was apparently less used in France. In England this form was called a 'back-stool', which was a reminder of its origins. In the 1660s and 1670s the 'armed farthingale' had for a while had its arms covered with the same material as the back and seat, but soon the arms were left bare. The bare-armed chair with a gap below its padded back remained the standard form of armed chair, as opposed to easy chair, until well into the next century (Pl.86). Eventually it acquired padded arm-rests although the arm-supports remained uncovered.

Unlike the Dutch and the English, the French had not taken greatly to the caned chair in the seventeenth century; but they adopted it with zeal around 1720. The French changed its proportions: it grew wider, more accommodating, and curvilinear.[42] The gap below the caned panel of the back was retained, and both armed and unarmed versions were produced. Such chairs were often furnished with shaped squabs that could be tied to the seat and the back with tapes. These squabs were like small mattresses, squared and with tufting – the precursor of buttoning, in which the thread that kept the tightly packed stuffing in place was looped round a bunch of unspun filaments of linen, forming a tuft that prevented the thread pulling back into the padding. The technique was essentially a form of quilting suited to very thick padding. Squabs or mattresses made in the same way were used on day-beds, benches and the like, such as the day-bed shown in Pl.93. The Dutch and English form of caned chair may be seen in Pls.65 and 92. By 1720, however, such chairs had gone out of fashion in Holland and England.

On the other hand, a form that was to make a powerful impact on the history of European furniture was introduced in Holland and England around 1700, although it did not become at all common until after 1720; this was the back with a splat. No one seems sure which nation adopted it first but both had strong links with China, stronger than any other nation at the time, and this form had been used in China since the Middle Ages. The splat stretched from the seat-rail to the cresting and could by its very nature not be upholstered. As everyone who has studied furniture knows, the Anglo-Dutch chair-back with a splat was to become immensely popular, and because the wooden splat was shaped and lent itself particularly well to carving, such chairs could be made to blend with carved or modelled stucco ornament on the walls. Their seats offered little scope for the upholsterer, and in grand houses where the seat-furniture was integrated with the rest of the décor, this form of chair looked to the mural decoration and to the larger items of wooden furniture (cabinets, sideboards, beds, etc.), whereas the more fully upholstered types tended to relate to the hangings on walls, beds and windows.

From the 1680s until 1730 or so, the coverings of rich material on grand chairs were detachable. They were made in two parts which slipped over the backs and the seats and were held in place with hooks and eyes at the corners and, at a later stage, with tabs with eyelets that hooked on to studs under the seat-rail. These slip-over covers could be removed and placed in store when the house was not dressed. The system was later replaced by providing protective loose covers over the grand upholstery, which was then fixed. Between about 1685 and 1710 slip-over covers in some palatial settings had deep skirts which gave the chair a totally different silhouette to that with which we are familiar (Pls.71, 99 and 136).

The rush-bottomed 'Dutch chair' or its local variants still remained popular all over Europe (Pl.95), but it was sometimes fitted with a detachable squab in the same way as the caned chair. Some very elegant versions of this class of chair, painted black and decorated with chinoiseries in gold (and perhaps decorated in other ways as well) were used in the French palaces, probably for occasional use since they were light and easily movable.[43]

Although seat-furniture in grand rooms might be covered *en suite* with the rest of an *ameublement*, in less exalted circles chairs might be covered in a wide variety of materials which did not necessarily match anything in the room, often because they were bought ready-made, off-the-peg. In England standard 'farthingale-type' chairs covered with turkeywork were produced in large quantities during the second half of the century and were probably exported in considerable numbers.[44] Turkeywork was popular for dining-rooms, probably because its pile surface was comfortable, but it cannot have been all that practical as it was difficult to clean. In particularly sumptuous surroundings in the French palaces, some seat-furniture was covered with Savonnerie carpeting but this was exceptional. Similar in effect but rather less expensive were the various types of woollen velvet (*moquette*, mockado, *trippe, caffa*, caffoy, etc.) which could also be seen in very respectable houses. Tapestry-woven covers were never common but were to be seen in France in fashionable circles from the 1690s and right on through the eighteenth century. Chairs of the 'farthingale' type often had seats and backs covered with leather. The plainer sorts of such chairs must have been produced in series like most of those covered in turkeywork. At the beginning of the eighteenth century many chairs in Scandinavia and Central Europe seem to have been covered with gilt leather (not a few chairs of the period have been so covered much more recently, however) but this fashion never caught on in France or England where such covers were very rare. In Italy, from the early eighteenth century at any rate, upholstered chairs were often covered in 'damask leather', which was leather stamped with a scorched pattern achieved with the aid of a wood block and a hot iron plate applied under pressure. As for covers of silk or worsted, most of the types of material used for hangings could be used for chairs.[45] In the seventeenth century, people did not mind having chair-seats of silk em-broidered with gold or silver thread; but such coverings were none too comfortable and went entirely out of fashion after 1710 or so.

In order to cover a chair with the narrow materials available at the time, one had to join widths together; this produced a seam which was not easy to disguise and gave rise to weakness in the covering. A cord might be stitched along the join. A more effective cover was provided by a lace or a galloon which then tended to produce a striped effect. Towards the end of the century some Parisian upholsterers were making a virtue of necessity and stressing the linear divisions, and would even make panels of a width of material and surround it with a border, perhaps mitred at the corners, all trimmed with galloon forming a bold rectangle set in the middle of the back and again on the seat. Most smart seat-furniture was trimmed with fringe in the seventeenth century but after 1700 fringes were exceptional.

Carpets were coming off tables and being placed on the floor increasingly during the third quarter of the seventeenth century but even in 1723, when Savary des Bruslons published his informative *Dictionnaire de Commerce*, it was still possible to state that '*un tapis*' was a covering which one laid 'on tables, platforms [which implies a dais or the parquet in an alcove], prayer-stools, trunks, coffers, etc.', no mention being made of floors as such. The English word 'carpet' carried the same definition as *tapis* and one would have described a carpet in much the same way in England at this date. An inventory of Petworth drawn up in 1670 indicates that there were no carpets on the floor permanently in that house. Not a few carpets are listed as being in store, on the other hand, and were presumably only brought out when and where needed. The list includes six Persian carpets, one of them 7 yds (6.4 m) long, some Turkey carpets (i.e. from Turkey), several 'foote carpetts' of turkeywork, a carpet of needlework and six plain cloth carpets bordered with gilt leather. The last items must have been table carpets and the huge Persian can only have gone on the floor, but it was still necessary at this date to specify that a carpet was for use on the floor, if it was not of such a great size that its purpose was evident.[46]

Information about floor-coverings in this period is indeed not easy to discover, but some light is shed on the matter by Savary even though he does not specifically mention floors. He lists the various classes of carpet (*tapis*) which were available in France in the period just before his book came out. First he mentions the carpets made at the royal factory at the Savonnerie. Next come the '*tapis de tapisserie*' which must refer to tapestry-woven carpets. Today, we would call this class of carpet an 'Aubusson'. In an English inventory of 1679 mention is made of an 'arras foot-cloth' which could well refer to such a carpet.[47] Savary states that these carpets came from Rouen, Arras and Felletin. He then mentions '*tapis de moucade*' from Tournai which must be carpets made of moquette, presumably in widths sewn together. Turning to imported carpets, he refers to Persian and Turkish carpets which he says could be with a pile or flat (*ras*); the latter were presumably tapestry-woven *kelims*. All of them came through the port of Smyrna, he says. The best Eastern carpets are the '*Musquets*' (see p. 25); there were also types known as '*tapis de pic*' which were the largest sort, while the smallest type were called '*cadenes*'. Next he lists the '*tapis d'Angleterre*', evidently turkeywork as this material could be used on chairs as well as on the floor. And finally there were 'German carpets' which were of wool like serge, some of which were called '*tapis quarrez*'. This sounds like a tartan effect but there may be a connection with this and the 'Scotch carpeting' which came to be used extensively during the middle of the eighteenth century.[48] As if he did not mean it too seriously, he says there were also carpets of dog's hair! A duty of one *sou* was payable on these; by contrast, the duty on a Persian carpet was seven *livres*.

To complete Savary's survey one should turn to his entry on mats and matting (*nattes*). He says that mats were hardly used at all in Paris any longer (1723), although they were still to be seen in the provinces, and they were much used abroad – presumably he meant in warm climates. He refers in glowing terms to the mats made in the Levant, some of which were expensive but made with 'much art both in their bright colours and in their patterns'. Such were probably the Tangier and Portugal mats which contemporary documents show were to be seen in England, Ireland and Holland – and probably elsewhere – from the 1670s until about 1720, usually placed under beds.

Several general changes took place in the furnishings of rooms in the grander houses during this period. In the first place the quality of objects increased and they became generally more expensive, both in the materials of which they were made and the intricacy of their ornament. Much attention was now paid to achieving a high degree of comfort and convenience – *commodité*. It is no accident that the names of two new forms of furniture evolved during this period acquired names reflecting this – the *fauteuil de commodité*, which we noted was the French name for an easy chair, and the *commode*, a term that is less of a mouthful than our 'chest-of-drawers' and neatly reminds us that this new class of furniture was so much more convenient to use than the old chest or coffer, with its heavy lid and the fact that you had to unpack all the items at the top in order to reach things stored at the bottom.

In bedrooms there were still no bedside tables[49] and people still placed chairs next to the bed, but the massive livery-cupboard was now finally ousted and, if it was replaced by anything, this would be by a neat cabinet or, at the end of the century, a chest-of-drawers or *commode* (Pl.83). The *Mercure Galant*, a Parisian journal which commented on the latest fashions, noted in December 1673 that 'People of quality no longer have foot-carpets in their alcoves [i.e. on the raised floor in which stood the bed] because they collect dust. This is why they now face their alcoves with *parquet*. . . .'[50] It must have been for the same reason that the thin African matting or 'Portugal mats' became such a favourite material for placing under beds.

Now that the dining-room was quite small, the circular or oval table, with gate-legs and falling leaves, was especially favoured, notably in England and Holland (Pl.65). The caned chair also became the most acceptable form for dining-rooms, except in France. The massive 'cup-board' or buffet, with its tiered stages for the display of plate, had also gone out of fashion, although temporary arrangements were made for such displays on important occasions (Pl.87). Sideboards now took the place of the great cupboard and, towards the end of the century, these were often furnished with a top of a slab of marble or some other stone – the slab constituting the most expensive component in many cases. Such slabs were of course easy to wipe clean – obviously an advantage in a dining-room. At the end of the century elegant dining-rooms, specially designed for the purpose, were sometimes provided with a fixed buffet which was part of the architecture. Pl.80 shows one such scheme in Paris, designed by Bérain. It had niches that could be closed off with sliding panels. Presumably the plate was kept permanently on the shelves and was protected by the shutters when not displayed. In Holland, and to some extent in England and elsewhere, apsidal niches with shelves forming a fixed buffet were fashionable from the 1690s until the 1740s (Pl.108). Plate and glass could be ranged on show on the higher shelves, above the arrangements for dispensing wine and rinsing glasses.

A piece of furniture which made its appearance during the last third of the seventeenth century was the glazed bookcase, designed to protect books more effectively than could shelves furnished merely with a curtain (Pl.92). As the number of books in libraries increased, it became necessary to have steps in places where one could not reach the upper shelves. A hanging-shelf of the kind

seen in Pl.95 also frequently served as a bookshelf in closets.

Ornamental objects of many kinds were to be found in houses at this period. Porcelain objects were not only used in massed arrays (see p. 49); for example one might place a vase or jar of porcelain or faience (delftware) on the hearth to hide the empty fireplace when the fire was not lit, perhaps with an arrangement of flowers in the vase. Garnitures (i.e. sets of three, five or even seven vessels *en suite*) were placed on mantel-shelves and over door-cases (Pls.72 and 73). *Jardinières* with flowers (cut or growing) were placed on the floor, and small ones were sometimes stood on ledges formed by projecting cornices (Pl.73). Figures of various sorts were available; plaster-of-Paris statues were exported from Holland, some of them gilded. There were wax figures, and alabaster ones in the round or in relief. Artificial flowers of silk, paper, straw or even glass were to be seen, especially in those parts of Europe where flowers could not be brought to bloom all the year round.[51] Vases of real flowers, never arranged very carefully, it seems, were also placed about the house, but not as an obligatory piece of decoration. It is as if the vase of flowers was a casual, informal after-thought. Very different were the great formal arrangements of festooned foliage and tubs with shrubs which were used to decorate special festivities. Indeed, such shrubs are a formal class of ornament, trimmed stiffly and dragooned so as to continue, as it were, the formal arrangements to be seen in the gardens outside.

As for pictures on the walls, oil-paintings sometimes had curtains to protect them from strong sunlight; the Dauphin even had roller-blinds on some of his pictures at Meudon. Frames of oil-paintings and engravings might be gilded but many were black. Some were silvered, others were blue, red or a combination of these colours with gilding. Delicate items were put under glass. Celia Fiennes saw a closet at Lady Donegal's house in which were 'many pictures under glass of tent stitch, sattin stitch [,] gumm and straw-work, also India flowers [,] birds, etc'.[52] Robert Boyle, the famous scientist, advocated the use of papier mâché for decorating picture-frames 'and other Curious Movables' in 1672.[53]

No new development seems to have taken place in lighting between 1670 and 1720, as far as we know, except that in parallel with the general increase in luxury more candles were burned so there must have been better illumination in most rooms of consequence after dark. Multiple candlesticks with the nozzles arranged in a circle (*girandoles* or candelabra) were favoured for placing on candle-stands and on tables backed by a looking-glass in which the lights would be reflected, thus further increasing the illumination. Chandeliers of glass became rather more numerous towards the end of the seventeenth century. These and the *girandoles* were furnished with drops and chains of glass which caught the light in a delightful manner. Chandeliers were never hung very high up (until the nineteenth century, probably): La Bruyère tells a nice story of how a man passing under one caught his wig on it.[54] This was in 1688, when wigs were tall but not amazingly so.

The box-like close-stool was now the common form. It was sometimes made of cedarwood, for its pleasant smell. Some close-stools were decorated most splendidly, with velvet or leather, handsomely trimmed, or with painted ornament. In England experiments were being carried out to improve the water-closet. Celia Fiennes saw such an arrangement at the turn of the century at Burfield Lodge, a house used by Queen Anne, which she describes as 'a little place with a seate of easement of marble with sluices of water to wash it all down'.[55] The English must have earned a reputation, at least among the French, for having invented a workable contraption in this line, for water-closets were known in France as '*lieux à l'anglaise*' – English places.

## 63 ▷
## A Dutch bedchamber
### 1669

From an album of sketches by Gesina Terborch of her own family and surroundings executed around 1670. Alongside the bed stands the close-stool. A map hangs on the wall as decoration. A fringed velvet table-carpet covers what is probably a draw-table which could, if necessary, be used for meals. On it stands a single candlestick and a standish with writing implements. The door has a simple latch. Note the brightly painted child's chair with its chamber-pot in the cubbyhole below. The artist has depicted herself in what looks like special finery.

*The Rijksprentenkabinett, Amsterdam*

## 64 ▷
## A Dutch lady at
## her dressing-table
### *c.*1670

It is morning and this lady has only recently got up. The maid was sweeping out the room and had not yet had time to remove the chamber-pot and chamber-candlestick when her mistress asked her to dress her hair. A *toilette* lies over the velvet or fine cloth table-carpet which completely hides a circular table. On it stands a wash-basin and ewer. The bed is of the standard pattern. Behind is a 'house of office' with its door open so that the close-stool is visible. (Anon., Utrecht School.)

*The Minneapolis Institute of Arts*

### 65 ▷
## An English bedchamber
### *c*.1685

An illustration at the head of a sheet of music with a song called 'A Curtain Lecture', the words 'by Mr. Durfey'. The husband prefers strong drink to the charms of his wife who complains that she 'Must hug my Pillow wanting you/And whilst you tope all the day/Regale in cups of harmless Tea' – which throws light on how the word 'tea' was then pronounced. It was at this time a highly fashionable beverage. The bed has the greater height favoured during the late seventeenth century. Note the double line of fringe at the bottom of the curtains (or rather the 'bone-graces' and 'cantoons', the narrow curtains at the corners; the main curtains in this scene are hitched up). There is a bolster and pillow. Behind is the decorative bedhead, above which is a curious star, which may be purely decorative or some form of night-light. In a Swedish inventory of 1694 mention was made of some lamps 'made like a star'. A chamber-pot is visible under the bed. Behind the bed is a folding gate-leg table suitable for taking a meal in the bedchamber. Chairs with caned seats and backs like that standing against the wall were the standard seat of the period 1680–1710 in England but they were mostly used with a cushion or squab. The way the high-hanging paintings are canted forward is noteworthy. There is no floor-covering.

*The Print Collection, Lewis Walpole Library, Yale University*

### 66 ▷
## An elegant Parisian day-bed
### 1686

A French drawing of a bed very like this is in the Tessin-Hårleman Collection in Stockholm, so this is no mere fantasy. It is very like the amazing beds in the Trianon de Porcelaine (see Pls.61 and 62). Above the elaborate head-board (with an oval mirror-plate?) rises a canopy which is purely decorative. The lady resting on this amazing confection has undone her corsage and her admirer fans her. He sits on a *tabouret* (stool) and holds back the fringed sun-curtain. An imposing table and looking-glass (canted forward) are set against the pier. Such a set normally also comprised a pair of candle-stands at this date. The parquet floor is noteworthy. (By Jean de St-Jean.)

*Bibliothèque Nationale, Paris*

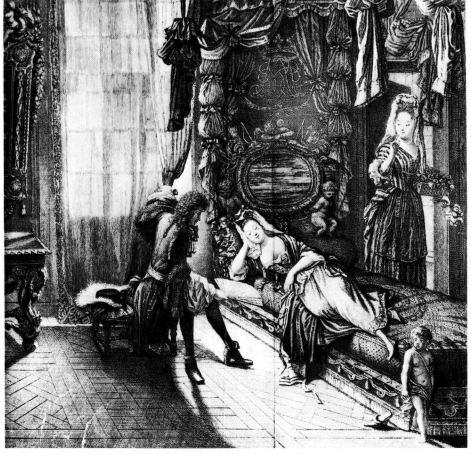

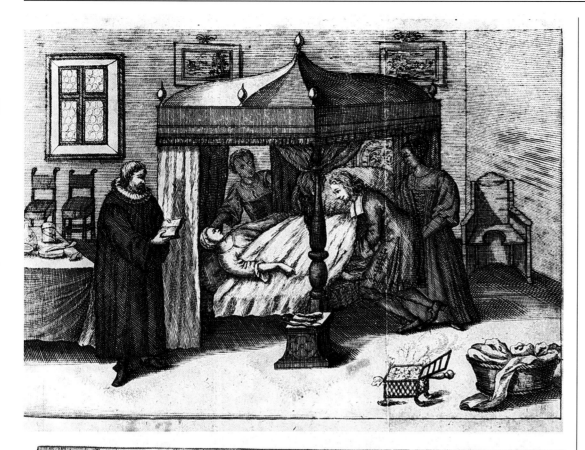

◁ 67

## A provincial German bedchamber
### *c.*1679

From a book on obstetrics first published in 1679. The furnishings seem rather old-fashioned for that date, but the average reader of the book would probably not have been unduly worried by any apparent anachronism and there must anyway still have been numerous rooms looking like this in the provinces. The bed has the domed tester popular in Germany throughout the century. The bed-head appears to be of carved wood. Note the bows hiding the nails on which the two pictures are suspended. The scene is of a stillbirth, so the parson has been called in. On the box-stool lie surgical instruments; there are others on the table. A brazier stands on the floor. In the background is a delivery-chair. Some local variants of the back-stool stand against the wall. (From Christian Völter, *Neu eröffnete Hebammenschuhl*, Stuttgart, 1687 edition.)

*Württembergische Landesbibliothek, Stuttgart*

◁ 68

## Another German bedchamber
### late seventeenth century

Although this scene was published in 1705, the hairstyles suggest that it probably dates from the 1680s. It comes from a history of the city of Fürth, not far from Nuremberg. The bed is of the standard mid-century form in use all over Europe. A chair stands alongside. The new-born baby is securely strapped into its cradle and a maid brings a bowl of soup for the happy mother. The large structure on the right may at first be taken for a tiled stove but is in fact a distorted view of a tiered 'cup-board' or buffet of a sort which would surely have seemed old-fashioned in any major European city by this date. (From Johann Alexander Baener, *Kurzer Bericht von den Altherthum und Freyheiten des freyen Hof-Markts Fürth samt denen Prospecten ... der vornehmsten Gebäue ...*, 1705.)

*Victoria and Albert Museum, London*

◁ 69
## A luxurious dressing-room
### c.1680

This painting retains its original brass frame; it is executed behind glass and backed with foil (*verre eglomisé*). It shows the penitent Magdalene but the setting is a sumptuously decorated room in some Catholic country – perhaps Italy, possibly France. The wash-basin has a tripod stand and a handsome ewer. The dressing-table is covered with a closely fitted table-carpet with no protective *toilette* of linen. The red and gold wall-hangings are of a textile and are fringed at top and bottom. A looking-glass hangs on the wall. The pendulum clock has a long case to disguise the weights. The floor is tiled, suggesting a warm climate.

*Victoria and Albert Museum, London*

71 ▷
## A French scientific salon
### 1680s

Painted on a fan-leaf like Pl.70, and of about the same date, this shows a room in which ladies and gentlemen are taking an interest in scientific matters. One man is using a telescope, several people are consulting globes and maps, there are numerous heavy tomes (including some in a tray in the foreground), and instruments of various kinds can be seen everywhere. The bookcase on the left has a protective curtain. Each window has a single sun-curtain of a thin white material with red stripes. The chair on the left has deeply quilted upholstery which may be tufted. By the man with the telescope are three chairs in a row with seat-covers that have deep valances reaching to the floor forming a box-like silhouette. At the far end is a table against a pier with flanking candle-stands (only one is visible). A handsome cabinet on a tall stand is on the right. On the floor is a European carpet with fringe.

*Messrs Kugel, Paris*

### ◁ 70
## A sumptuous French bathroom
### 1680

The bath is a huge circular vessel of marble which has been lined with a lace-trimmed cloth. Above it hangs a rich canopy. Alongside stands a day-bed with its own canopy. Both canopies have gilded, carved wooden domes. Statues stand on huge pedestals. The marble chimneypiece has a fine garniture of nine pieces. There is a two-manual harpsichord with a stand characteristic of Parisian instruments of about 1680; the player sits on a stool. There is a silver brazier in front and a silver case in which stands an orange-tree. The floor has a fancy pattern perhaps intended to resemble *parquet marqueté*. With its many cupids, this scene painted on a fan has amorous overtones.

*Victoria and Albert Museum, London*

*Femme de qualitez a sa Toillette.*

*Femme de qualité déshabillée pour le bain.*

## 72 △
## The levée of a grand lady, Paris
### late 1680s

It is presumably wintertime and the central feature of this lady's room is the fireplace at which a maid is warming the lady's gown before its owner puts it on. The other maid dresses the hair of the lady, who has a lace-trimmed cloth over her shoulders to protect her clothes from powder and loose hairs. On the table is a splendid toilet-set, probably of silver. A case for combs (one put the combs in the pockets and wrapped it around them) lies on the magnificent *toilette* which covers the whole dressing-table. The man sits on a highly fashionable chair with the new, higher back. Behind him is a *porte-carreaux* with two fat *carreaux* lying on it. Note the garniture on the mantel-shelf. The scene is probably set in a bedchamber; the chimneypiece seems too large for a dressing-room, which was never a large chamber.

*Bibliothèque Nationale, Paris*

## 73 (*right*)
## A lady washing her feet, Paris
### 1685

She sits on a fashionable day-bed which is furnished with a 'tufted' mattress and bolster (see p. 58). The vertical bed-head bears a royal crown and the Apollo-emblem of the Sun King, Louis XIV. The reason for this is not clear; nor is the significance of the monogram (AM?) in the frieze. Such a basin would today be called a wine-cooler, but here it serves as a footbath. On the left is a perfume-burner. On the projecting cornice stands a garniture of vases of the sort more often to be seen on mantel-shelves (Pls.72 and 99), and a large covered vase and two big bowls of flowers. The half-glazed door has a *portière* outside; its lock and bolt do not seem to have been effective and the man has come upon the lady who wears only her shift. (By Jean de St-Jean.)

*Bibliothèque Nationale, Paris*

## 74 ▷
## A royal ball in Paris
### 1682

The ball was held to celebrate the King and Queen's return from Strasbourg in 1682; the scene decorates an almanack for that year. The setting does not look imaginary and could be at Versailles. The splendid chandeliers are probably early examples of those composed with glass, instead of rock-crystal, beads and drops. The two-branched sconces are backed with mirror-glass. The elaborate floor is probably of wood rather than marble. On the mantel-shelf is a *garniture de cheminée*. The table laid for a collation has a diaper cloth laid over the table-carpet. On the trencher-plates lie folded napkins with knives and forks alongside. What looks like a massive silver wine-cooler stands in front.

*Bibliothèque Nationale, Paris*

## 76 ▷
# Patterns for elaborate parquetry, France
### *c.*1700

From the same collection of drawings as Pls.77 and 78, these presumably show the patterns to be seen on floors in grand houses in Paris or nearby in the 1690s. The narrow pattern at the bottom left is not unlike one laid in the Queen's bedchamber at Ham House in 1673, so these patterns were not necessarily ultra-modern at the time this drawing was made.

*Bibliothèque de la Conservation, Versailles*

◁ 75

## A French bedchamber
### *c.*1690

The tall bed indicates a date late in the seventeenth century, as do the tall backs of the chairs; the form of their feet suggests that the scene is set in the early 1690s. The bed is of the characteristic French shape, simple in outline. The seat-furniture and table-carpet are *en suite* with the bed-hangings, all of red velvet with gold fringe. The window-curtains are also red and are pulled by a tasselled cord. Note the large forward-canted looking-glass. Flanking the dressing-table is one candle-stand; its pair is not shown. Note the floor of parquet set diagonally within squares in the new French fashion. (Artist unknown.)
*Victoria and Albert Museum, London*

77 ▷

## French mural decoration
### *c.*1700

On the left a wall in the Duc d'Uzès' house which has panels and pilasters of mirror-glass with gilt ornaments. Note the vases above the doorway on the right. What on the left is essentially an inset looking-glass, complete with glass frame, is of a shape which would have been ultra-fashionable in 1699. This drawing belongs to a series which cannot be later than 1701 (see also Pls.76 and 78).
*Bibliothèque de la Conservation, Versailles*

78 ▷

## An elegant French closet
### *c.*1700

Pl.77 helps to date this drawing, which shows a '*grand cabinet*' (a small reception room) with panels entirely composed of plates of mirror-glass. As if this were not enough, a large looking-glass (with a glass frame?) and a mirror-backed sconce have been hung against the glazed walls. The low fireplace-opening is very evident; so are the *chenets* now linked to fire-bars that support the logs. There are hooks for the fire-irons. A desk with an inlaid top, and an upholstered sofa, stand against the wall. The latter has a valance with lappets (*lambrequins*), each hung with large tassels.
*Bibliothèque de la Conservation, Versailles*

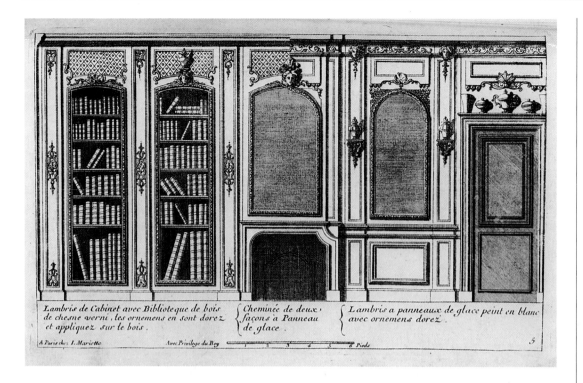

*Lambris de Cabinet avec Biblioteque de bois de chesne verni, les ornemens en sont dorez et appliquez sur le bois.* {*Cheminée de deux façons à Panneau de glace.* {*Lambris a panneaux de glace peint en blanc avec ornemens dorez.*

*A Paris chez I. Mariette*     *Avec Privilege du Roy*     .5

## Parisian proposals for mural decoration
### *c.* 1700

The new, taller panels of mirror-glass that came into fashion during the very last years of the seventeenth century may be seen here. On the left is a scheme for a library with inset bookshelves forming decorative panels, all of varnished oak with gilt ornaments, sometimes called '*à la capucine*'. On the right the panelling is treated in the fashionable manner, painted white with gilt mouldings and carved decoration. (From J. B. Le Roux, *Nouveaux Lambris de Galeries, Chambres et Cabinets*, Paris, undated.)

*Metropolitan Museum of Art, New York; Harris Brisbane Dick Fund, 1930*

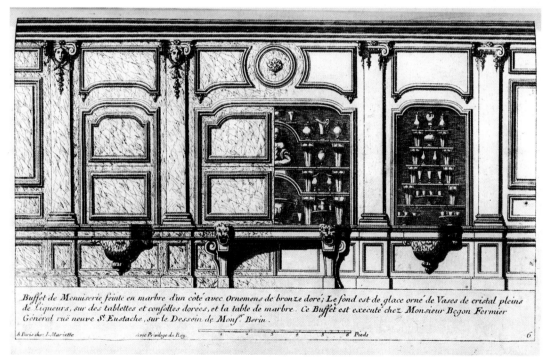

*Buffet de Menuiserie feinte en marbre d'un côté avec Ornemens de bronze doré; Le fond est de glace orné de Vases de cristal pleins de Liqueurs, sur des tablettes et consolles dorées, et la table de marbre. Ce Buffet est executé chez Monsieur Begon Fermier Général ruë neuve St Eustache, sur le Dessein de Monsr Berin.*

*A Paris chez I. Mariette*     *Avec Privilege du Roy*     6

## A luxurious Parisian dining-room
### *c.* 1700

From the same source as Pl.79, but this room certainly existed whereas the other engraving showed proposals. The built-in buffet in this room was designed by Jean Bérain for the *Intendant* of the French Navy, Michel Bégon, who built himself a house in the rue neuve St-Eustache. The panelling was marbled (*menuiserie feinte en marbre*) with gilded ornament. The niches could be enclosed with doors (shown on the left half), which were counterbalanced and must have slid into recesses behind the panelling. A copy of this engraving was sent to Tessin in Stockholm (see Pl.54) in November 1700.

*Metropolitan Museum of Art, New York; Harris Brisbane Dick Fund, 1930*

81, 82, 83

# A new design for a bedchamber with the bed in a niche, Paris
### c.1710(?)

Three views of the same room designed by 'Sr. Blondel', presumably Jean-François Blondel. The bed is certainly 'en niche' and almost certainly has a 'bed-head' or 'chevet' at each end, for the sake of symmetry; if so, this must be an extremely early manifestation of what was to become a favourite form of bed in France (i.e. sideways on). Also entirely novel is the commode (perhaps this is the earliest illustration of such a piece of furniture) which serves as a console beneath the very tall pier-glass. Both form part of the architecture. Here already is to be seen the conformation that was to become so common in the second half of the eighteenth century. Note also the deep 'French' windows and the tall glass over the fireplace.

*Metropolitan Museum of Art, New York; Harris Brisbane Dick Fund, 1930*

84 △
## A French lady entertaining friends in her closet
### 1703

She relaxes on her luxurious day-bed which has a mattress, cushion and base-valance with ruffled edges, a form of trimming that was fashionable at this date. The curtain may be part of a canopy, an up-to-date version of that to be seen in Pl.66. The figures of two friends are lightly sketched in at the back. (By Bernard Picart.)

*By gracious permission of Her Majesty the Queen; Windsor Castle Library*

a Paris chez Duchange avec P. du R.

B. Picart fecit

◁ 85
## A large looking-glass, Paris
1690s

Looking-glasses were frequently hung against the pier between windows. Instead of the rather rickety tables that had at first accompanied them a new and more sturdy form was now sometimes adopted, as here. It could serve as a dressing-table or could support a candelabrum, in which case one could dispense with the unstable candle-stands that had previously flanked such groups. Note the sliding sash of the window which may be counterbalanced. This is really a fashion-plate. (By Jean de St-Jean.)

*Victoria and Albert Museum, London*

86 △
## An elegant bedchamber, Paris
*c.*1698–1700

The curious trimming of the armchairs with a ruffled edge and valance was fashionable for a few years just around the turn of the century. Pl.99 shows Daniel Marot using it in Holland a few years later. The bolster lying in front of the shaped head-board of the bed has a similar frill. Note the chimney garniture, the linked fire-dogs with pyramids, and the fire-back with a coat of arms. (By Bernard Picart, who returned from Holland to Paris in 1698 and left again in 1710.)

*Bibliothèque Nationale, Paris*

### 87, 88 △ ▷
## Setting for a feast in Bologna
### 1693

The room was top-lit but also had windows at each end with old-fashioned round glass *occhi*. Paintings decorate the frieze; below are green damask wall-hangings with the individual widths masked by a gold galloon and with a gold fringe forming a sort of capping. Note the several canted looking-glasses and the *portières* at the doors. The huge chimney-piece has been turned into a multi-stage buffet for the display of plate. More plate is set out on small

'cup-boards' alongside. In the corners at one end stand shaped tables dressed with a cloth made ragged to resemble stalactites, with plate and vessels of glass set on pedestals and brackets likewise disguised (Pl.88). Large wine-coolers stand below. The central table is set for sixty-six diners. The sculptures on the table are executed in sugar-paste. This feast was given at the Palazzo Vizzani by the Gonfalonier Francesco Ratta, whose device was a palm-tree. The griffins were gilded. (Engravings by Giacomo Giovannini after drawings by Marco Antonio Chiarini.)
*Archivio di Stato, Bologna*

## 89
## A banquet in Bologna
### 1701

The table in the centre of the room is of a fancy shape with four lobed corners. There is a centre-piece with two large grottoes from which a rainbow arches. The whole fanciful arrangement comprises numerous figures, probably of sugar-paste – the first porcelain figures, most of which served a similar purpose, had not yet been made. Behind the table is the buffet of plate with lesser buffets at the sides. This banquet was given by Count Alamano Isolani to celebrate his election as Gonfalonier of Bologna in November 1701. It was held in the courtyard of his *palazzo*, a velarium having been stretched across the opening to enclose the space while the walls, as we see, were covered with huge silk hangings. (Engraving by Francesco Antonio Meloni.)

*Archivio di Stato, Bologna*

## ◁ 90, 91
## A Dutch study
### 1690s

These two views are in fact of the same room, although the proportions have been distorted; the early bureau-bookcase provides a point of reference, but the armchair has been removed from the window-wall and placed next to the fireplace in the second view (below). This chair has a squab, but the other chairs do not although they too are caned. Note the looking-glass hanging on one pier; it has a cresting. Under it a small gate-leg table has been parked against the wall. The windows have simple pull-up curtains with pelmet-boxes.

*Messrs Sotheby, London*

## 92 ▽
## Samuel Pepys's Library, London
### *c.*1693

This and its companion drawing showing the opposite end of the room are well-known, but one is included here because views of English seventeenth-century interiors are so rare. Between the windows that look out across the Thames is a table with a handsome looking-glass above. In the centre is Pepys's desk covered with a close-fitting carpet on which lies a small reading-desk. He had a chair with a caned back and (presumably) seat which, as the other drawing shows, had squabs laid on the seat and tied to the back for comfort. The other chair has a caned seat and no squab or cushion. Near the window on the left are some steps for reaching the upper shelves of the bookcases. Pepys had twelve such bookcases made between 1666 and the time of his death in 1703; they differed only in minor details. Bookcases with glazed doors must have been something of an innovation when the first batch were made. Note the large map of Paris on the wall, hung on ribbons with ornamental bows.

*Reproduced by courtesy of the Master and Fellows of Magdalene College, Cambridge*

◁ 93

## A French drawing-room
### *c.*1705

This sketch by Sébastien Le Clerc shows a fashionable Parisian drawing-room in use. Two tables have been set up for gaming with dice. The chairs, with the fashionable high backs of the time, have been pulled up round the tables from their regular positions at the walls. The parquet is square-set. The mural ornament is well shown; note the candle-branches.

*Ecole Nationale Supérieure des Beaux-Arts, Paris*

### 94 (*below, left*)
## Tea-party
### *c.*1700

This delightful little scene is painted on a fan-leaf. It is set in a fashionably furnished middle-class room which could be anywhere in Europe north of the Alps, but is perhaps in Holland. It has charming verdure tapestries actually fitted to the walls. The window has divided curtains. A garniture stands on top of the cabinet; there is apparently another on the mantel-shelf. The folding table is noteworthy. This setting is considerably grander, and perhaps later, than that shown in Pl.95.

*By courtesy of Mr Cyril Staal*

◁ 95

## A Dutch tea-party
*c.*1700

The company sits round a small oval table of the sort much favoured in Holland in this period. It had a painted top which was hinged on a tripod pillar so that, when not in use, it could be placed close to the wall where it provided colourful decoration. Note the kettle-stand, presumably of wood. The chairs are of the turned variety with rush seats which, as this picture shows, were acceptable in quite smart surroundings. Behind is a hanging-shelf or '*tablette*' which in Holland was sometimes called a '*theeraak*' because, as here, the tea-set was often stacked on it. The cockatoo's perch can be lowered by a cord running over a pulley in the ceiling. There is a window-curtain to the old-fashioned inward-opening leaded window. (By Pieter van den Berge, entitled '*Namiddag*' or '*L'Apresdinee*'.)

*Museum Boymans-van Beuningen, Rotterdam*

96 △

## The Picture Collection in the Castle at Prague
1702

The height of the doors suggests that this room was perhaps not all that large, but the numerous tiers of pictures show this was more than a closet or picture cabinet. The seat-furniture stands close-set against the wall in the usual manner for that period. On a central table covered with a Near-Eastern carpet stands a fine globe. (By Johann Bretschneider.)

*Germanisches Nationalmuseum, Nuremberg*

◁ 97

## A Dutch chimneypiece in the French taste
*c.*1700

One could see this and similar chimneypieces in the new style 'in several places in Holland and the other Provinces', as the inscription indicates. They had all been made to the designs of Daniel Marot (see p. 49) who styled himself 'Architect to His Britannic Majesty' in reference to William III, King of England (note the royal arms and crown on the fire-back) and Stadholder of the United Provinces of the Netherlands, who died in 1702. Although forced to live in exile on account of his religion, Marot kept a close eye on artistic developments in his mother country and his designs were strongly French in flavour, if rather old-fashioned by Parisian standards. Setting a plate of mirror-glass into the chimney-breast just above the opening of the fireplace was a novelty that Marot must have seen in Parisian engravings of the 1690s (e.g. Pl.58). He may have learned about wall-hangings with festooned cappings like those shown here from the same source. (From *Nouvelles Cheminées faittes en plusieur en droits de la Hollande et autres Provinces du Dessein de D. Marot....*)
*Victoria and Albert Museum, London*

◁ 98

## Massed porcelain as decoration, Berlin
1703

A view of the Porcelain Cabinet at Schloss Charlottenburg, Berlin, designed by the architect to the Court of Brandenburg, Eosander von Göthe, in 1703 and completed by 1706. Much use is made of mirror-glass but the principal decoration was formed with numerous pieces of Chinese porcelain arranged in formal patterns. Rows of small vases set on brackets form borders to the glass panels, dishes decorate the frieze, vases stand in ranks on the cornices, and huge jars occupy strategic places. So great was the need for porcelain vessels to accomplish such schemes in Germany at this period that japanning workshops turned out wooden vessels painted to look like 'chinaware'. When these were executed by a good artist, one could probably not tell the difference from across the room. (From the *Theatrum Europeaum* (Vol. XVII, which dealt with the year 1703), 1716; engraved from von Göthe's own drawing.)
*The Royal Danish Library, Copenhagen*

*Dessein des rahret Porcelain Cabinets. in Charlottenburg, Anderer Seiten.*

Livre dappartement Inventé par Marot Architecte du Roy.

Bibliotheque inventée et gravée par D. Marot avec preuillege des Etats Generaux des prouincei Vnie et d'hollande et West Frise.

## A state bedchamber in Holland
### *c.*1703

This unified scheme of decoration has been achieved entirely with upholstery. The pattern is set by the bed, the focal point of the scheme. The furbelows on the tester are echoed by those forming a pelmet-like capping along the top edge of the wall-hangings, the festoons on the head-cloth appear again as pilaster-like ornaments on the walls, and flounced edging of the bed-curtains is repeated on the *portières*. Note the chairs, close-set against the walls; note also the carpet. In the fireplace is a tub with a bush (orange or myrtle?) and two large porcelain or delftware jars. The chimneypiece has a glass panel and garniture above. Sconces with mirror-backs hang against the walls on tasselled cords. The iron rod round the outside of the tester is for a curtain that protected the rich bed-hangings from dust. This splendid composition by Daniel Marot characterizes the sumptuous settings he created in Holland and in England for William III and his courtiers; see Pl.97. (From Marot's *Second Livre Dappartement*, published in The Hague in 1703.)

*Victoria and Albert Museum, London*

## A library, Holland
### *c.*1700

The bookcases are carefully integrated with the architecture and are themselves of architectural form. The shelves have dust-fringes at their front edge. Note the busts and globes placed on top. By the window, which is fitted with pull-up curtains, is a barometer. The placing of the stools in the window-embrasure is noteworthy. There is a sturdy desk and a comfortable easy chair with wings. The chimneypiece, which has a small piece of glass inset, includes a pendulum clock which bears a royal crown. This composition by Daniel Marot presumably gives a good impression of the appearance of elegant libraries in the residences of William III and his courtiers in Holland and England. (From the *Nouveaux livre de Paramens inventée et gravée par D. Marot, architecte de sa Majesté Britannique.*)

*Victoria and Albert Museum, London*

*profile du Ciel de Lit*

*Ciel du Lit*

*Lict de S.A.S. Madame la Duchesse de Mecklenbourg a de Nassau 1708 Sur le Desien de D. Marot*

◁ 101

## The Duchess of Mecklenburg's bed
### 1708

This bed was executed to the designs of Daniel Marot for the Dutch princess Sophia Hedwig of Nassau-Dietz who married Karl Leopold, Duke of Mecklenburg-Schwerin in 1708. Marot continued to serve the House of Orange long after his royal master, William III, had died in 1702. The bed is a *lit d'ange* (i.e. it has a flying tester supported by chains from the ceiling or back wall and has no bed-posts) and the curtains pull round to meet at the foot end. The underside of the tester is shown separately with part of its inner valance, and the head-board for another bed is shown at the top. Note how rigidly flat is the top surface of the 'counterpoint' (counterpane), the sides of which are tucked in behind a heavy moulding that is partly covered with the same material as that used for the hangings. (From P. Jessen, *Das Ornamentwerk des Daniel Marot*, Berlin, 1892.)
*Victoria and Albert Museum, London*

102, 103, 104 ▷
## Bed-hangings, Paris
### *c.*1730

From a book of patterns for beds by no less a designer than Nicolas Pineau which must have been welcomed by upholsterers seeking guidance in the interpretation of the new style. These three sheets are for one bed which had a flying tester, or '*impériale*' as it was called in France, like that shown in Pl.101. Pl.102 shows the head-cloth (B. *Dossier*) behind the headboard (A. *Chantourné*). Pl.103 shows the tester with its interior and exterior valances (*Pentes*). Pl.104 shows the counterpoint (A. *Courtepointe*) with two of its three falling sides (C. *Pentes*), and two of the three base-valances (B. *Soubassements*) which went between the legs of the bed-frame. The key-letters B and C have mistakenly been reversed on this sheet. (From *Nouveaux desseins de Lits inventés par Le Sieur Pineau*.)
*Metropolitan Museum of Art, New York;*
*Harris Brisbane Dick Fund, 1930*

A. Chantourné  Nouveaux desseins de Lits inventés par le Sieur Pineau.  B. Dossier.
à Paris chez Mariette rue S. Jacques aux colonnes d'Hercules.

102

A. Courtepointe B. Soubassement C. Pante.  Mariette excud.

104

103

## 106 ▷
# Chimneypieces for the Palais Royal Paris
### 1715–20

Proposals for the re-decoration of the Palais Royal, residence of the Duke of Orléans, the Regent during the minority of Louis xv. By the Duke's Chief Architect, Gilles-Marie Oppenord. Note the irregularity of the openings and frames above. The marble fireplace-surrounds were also to be irregular in plan, as the sketches at the bottom show. Two of the chimneypieces are for closets (or studies; note the attributes of learning) while the third is for an 'Indian drawing-room' – however, the only indication that this is the case is the Indian with a feathered head-dress at the top.

*The Cooper-Hewitt Museum, New York; the Smithsonian Institution's National Museum of Design*

## 105 ▽
# An important French console table
### c.1715–20

This superb drawing may have been executed by Carl Hårleman when he visited Paris in the 1720s, at which time this table must have been quite new. The crowned lilies of France on the stretcher show this table stood in a royal building. It has been suggested that it was by the architect Gilles-Marie Oppenord (see Pl.106), but the exuberant style brings to mind the name of the sculptor and decorator François-Antoine Vassé whose principal achievement was the magnificent carved panelling in the Gallery of the Hôtel de Toulouse, in Paris, completed in about 1718.

*National Museum, Stockholm; Tessin-Hårleman Collection*

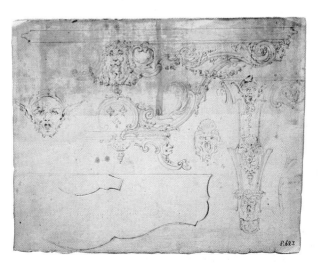

## 107 ▽
## Panelling in Paris
### c.1710–15

Executed in ink on tracing-paper, such drawings were probably copies of important designs made for sale to people wanting information about new fashions in the French capital. They could presumably be made available more speedily than engravings. This is one of several in the collection of French designs formed by the Swedish royal architects during the late seventeenth century and first decades of the eighteenth century; they were extremely well informed about the latest developments in French decoration of their own times. This particular drawing belonged to the Swedish Court Architect Carl Hårleman. In the present state of published knowledge it does not seem possible to attribute this design firmly to any particular architect, but one can be fairly certain that it was for an important scheme of decoration. It may be by François-Antoine Vassé; see Pl.105.

*National Museum, Stockholm; Tessin-Hårleman Collection*

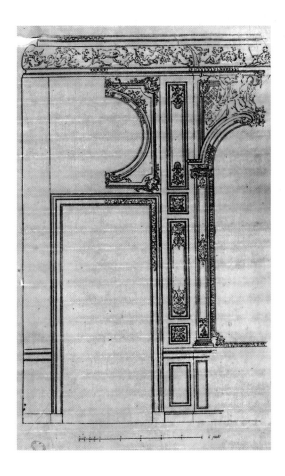

## 108 ▽
## An early Neo-Palladian interior, England
### 1719

This scene of a supper-party is set in a grand interior couched in that curious variant of Baroque, the English Neo-Palladian style. Characteristic are terminal figures like those seen in profile on the door-frame, and the Atlas-figure supporting the arch above the niche containing the buffet.

Eagles with wings spread were also a popular motif with Neo-Palladian designers. The sconces, probably of silver, flanking the doorway are of a type especially favoured in England; they seem to be surmounted by ducal coronets. (This drawing by Marcellus Laroon is inscribed 'Presented to King George 1st a picture I painted in 1725' and '*Premiere pensee*', so this is the sketch of 1719 for a picture now in the Royal Collection.)

*By courtesy of Messrs P.D. Matthiesen, London*

⊲ 109

## A middle-class parlour in Antwerp
### 1716

There are many old-fashioned features in this room, most notably the seat-furniture but also the chimneypiece. The striped wall-hangings are probably of worsted and were a common form of wall-decoration in less grand rooms in many parts of Europe, such materials being exported in considerable quantities from northern France. The window-curtains are of a thin white material and act as sun-blinds. The pair of hanging shelves is also noteworthy. A black cabinet, probably made locally, is in the background. Through the doors, which are half glazed, is a bed which looks rather up-to-date. Its green hangings are probably of a worsted cloth. (By Jan Joseph Horemans.)

*By courtesy of Kunsthandel Schlichte Bergen, Amsterdam*

110 △

## An evening with friends, France
### 1720s

The high-backed armchairs date from early in the century, but the chimney-glass and clock suggest a date in the 1720s. This gathering may be in a *grand cabinet*; it seems too comfortable to be an ante-chamber and one presumably did not hold card-parties in the bedchamber. The way candlelight was reflected in the glass is nicely shown here, as is the general effect of light from some six candles and the fire – on which the black servant is laying a log. One *chenet* is clearly shown. A small pair of bellows lies on the mantel-shelf. Note the parquet floor, the pictures with ribbons hiding their cords, and the close-covered 'outside backs' of the chairs. Beside the fireplace is a sofa. (By Pierre-Louis Dumesnil the Younger.)

*Metropolitan Museum of Art, New York; Bequest of Harry G. Sperling, 1971*

# 1720-1770

THE YEARS between 1720 and 1770 saw the budding Rococo style unfold, come to full flower, and then wither in the cool winds of Neo-Classicism. Evolved in France in the 1720s and 1730s, the Rococo style was eagerly taken up all over mainland Europe, a particularly happy variant being developed in Bavaria and Franconia. Although many excellent scholars have tried to determine at precisely what moment the style made its appearance, it really grew out of the style that was fashionable in Paris during the first quarter of the century and all one can say is that, around 1730, ornaments in this new taste acquired a spiralling, spinning character which, when handled well, has a tension that holds the forms together; but handled by less talented artists it allows the forms to disintegrate in a graceless manner, as if the centrifugal force had taken over. Far from being an easy idiom to master, it required immense skill to handle with success.

The Rococo style affected the interior in every direction – in the decoration of panelling, of stucco ceilings, of candle-branches, of furnishing textiles and wallpapers, of much furniture, and of almost all small ornaments. A room completely decorated in this style – and by now such unified schemes were common – was a far cry from the solid, often rectilinear and always clear-cut forms of the seventeenth century. When the fashion was at its height, rooms sometimes had rounded corners, ceilings were often coved, walls might be broken up with recesses, and panelling commonly had extremely fanciful outlines – all of which gave the room an almost organic aspect, an effect which was much enhanced when such rooms were seen by candlelight. The flickering light rarely came from a central chandelier; the candles were mostly held in 'branches' set close to the walls. The light therefore raked the mouldings, producing highlights on the near side of them (they were often elaborately carved) and dancing dark shadows beyond. If the ornaments were gilded, moreover, the decoration could seem almost liquid and quivering. Add to this the fact that the fashion was now to inset large plates of mirror-glass into the panelling, often placed opposite each other to produce endless reflections, and it will be understood why the total effect could border on the psychedelic. There seemed to be no fixed points; all was in movement.

While late Baroque was turning into Rococo on the Continent, something rather different was happening in England. The options obviously open to English architects were either to adopt the new style that had been developed in France during the late years of Louis XIV's reign, or to continue following a rather provincial version of the Franco-Dutch taste which had so readily appealed in the second half of the seventeenth century. In fact to some extent they did both; but they also looked back with surprisingly strong admiration to the style which had prevailed in the north of Italy a century and a half before, and especially to the buildings of Andrea Palladio whose works on architecture had been published in Venice in 1570, and which now became the bible of this Neo-Palladian school.[1] The fact that Inigo Jones, England's first great post-

Gothic architect, had himself worked in a style largely derived from Palladio, was seen as evident sanction for so whole-heartedly espousing, even at this late date, the teachings of the Italian master. Indeed, Inigo Jones joined Palladio as the twin deities of the Neo-Palladian movement. Some remarkably faithful imitations of villas erected long before in the sun-baked countryside near Venice were now, in the late 1720s and 1730s, set down in wind-swept and rain-soaked English shires. As Lady Mary Wortley Montagu wrote in 1753, when the English Palladian style had largely run its course, 'Vistas are laid open over barren heaths, and apartments contrived for a coolness agreeable in Italy but killing in the north of Britain.' The Palladian taste did not in fact remain pure: an amalgam of the three styles – French Baroque, Franco-Dutch Baroque, and Neo-Palladian – was soon evolved; but it was far more strongly Classical than the style currently admired in France, and therefore elsewhere in Europe. It established a characteristic English tradition for the building of grand houses, large and small. This tradition made little or no impression on the Continent but was adopted in the British colonies on the East Coast of North America, and thus was to have a powerful influence on the buildings of that continent.

The time when American taste could affect Europe was still a long way off, but America now began to be a major consumer of European fashions, at first largely those coming from England but later those coming from France as well. Moving goods (and ideas) half-way across the world from the British capital did not take much longer than moving them to the furthest parts of Britain, and one should view the principal cities of the East Coast of North America as scarcely more provincial than Norwich, Exeter, York, Dublin or Edinburgh – if at all. Of the Bostonians, at any rate, a commentator could claim in 1720 that 'Their customs and manners are the same with the English. . . . In the concerns of civil [civilized] life, their dress, [dining] tables, and conversations, they affect to be as English as possible; there is no fashion in London but in three or four months is to be seen in Boston.'[2]

When it comes to interior decoration, it would be interesting to know more about that of Wanstead House which was being decorated about 1720. It was the first large house built in the Neo-Palladian style and judging from the single known view of its interior (Pl.120), together with the fact that it was greatly admired at the time, it set the pattern for the grand English Palladian interior, a formula that remained in favour well into the 1750s (Pl.167).[3] It was built for the banker Sir Richard Child by the architect Colen Campbell. Information is coming to light about the furnishings of Chiswick House, the villa outside London built by Lord Burlington for his own use and to his own plans (based firmly on Palladio), with the help of William Kent, in the late 1720s and completed about 1736. Chiswick also exerted a powerful influence on English taste, as is well known, and that influence was probably not confined to the exterior. Now largely empty, this delightful small building should be envisaged with a full complement of furniture (two of the rooms were bedchambers) designed for precise locations in the main rooms. In 1727 William Kent, who was specially interested in interior architecture, was engaged to complete the great house at Houghton, built by Colen Campbell for Sir Robert Walpole. Some of the smaller rooms that he decorated, with dark panelling and gilt carving, show how pleasing a Neo-Palladian interior could be. Plans, elevations and sometimes also sections of these and other great Neo-Palladian houses were published primarily in *Vitruvius Britannicus*, the successive volumes of which came out in 1715, 1717 and 1725.[4] The decoration of the principal rooms is sometimes shown in the sections.

When faced with providing the key pieces of furniture required to complete the grand Neo-Palladian rooms he was creating, Kent could find nothing ready to hand, so he had to attend to the designs himself. Palladio was of no help, as the great north Italian architect did not illustrate any furniture designs in his treatise. Kent had perforce to look elsewhere for examples of furniture that seemed suitable for interiors in the Italian style of the late sixteenth century, which is what he and Burlington were essentially trying to recreate. Kent had only paid a fleeting visit to Venice and Vicenza, Palladio's home territory, whereas he had spent several years in Rome and Florence, so it is hardly surprising that it was mainly to Roman and Florentine furnishings of the sixteenth and seventeenth centuries that he turned for inspiration. The furniture he eventually created, while borrowing some of its basic forms from earlier Italian furniture, was nevertheless imbued with the vigorous, ebullient spirit of the Baroque, that is, of its own time. He was probably responsible for the fact that a simple version of the Italian Renaissance *sgabello* became the standard type of hall-seat in England for the next century or so. Moreover, the massive, boldly architectural carcass-furniture he devised was to influence the design of English (and therefore American) furniture in that branch profoundly. Considerable impetus at a high social level must have been given to the spread of his concepts through the publication by his follower John Vardy entitled *Some Designs of Mr. Inigo Jones and Mr. William Kent* in 1744 which included a number of furniture designs. Slightly less grand were the designs in William Jones' *The Gentlemens or Builders Companion containing a variety of useful designs for doors, . . . chimney-pieces, slab tables, pier glasses . . . ceiling-pieces . . .*, published in London in 1739, and *The City and Country Builder's and Workman's Treasury of Designs; or the art of drawing and working the ornamental parts of architecture . . . By Batty Langley*, of 1740 (Pl.134). Fresh editions of the latter came out in 1741, 1750 and 1756. It was evidently extremely useful to those who needed information about these matters.

The springs from which the mainstream of European interior decoration flowed were, however, to be found in France and it was widely recognized – even more so than in the seventeenth century – that the French were extremely skilful in this whole area of activity, in the devising of ornaments and in creating settings for an extremely pleasant way of life where convenience was regarded no less highly than decoration. 'Their houses are in general excellent; no people have ever studied so much or succeeded so well in enjoying all the conveniences of life as the French do', wrote Lady Holland in 1765,[5] while the author of an essay on silk-design, published in 1756, insisted that 'The French designers of ornaments have been and are at present esteemed the most happy in their inventions. . . . No wonder that all the rest of the European nations take the French patterns of ornaments for their rule and pattern to imitate.'[6] He went on to say this applied particularly to the design of fashionable silk materials, in which field Lyon set the tone each year, but there is evidence in plenty to confirm that what he claimed was a general truth.

A central figure in the history of French taste during this period was Jacques-François Blondel, professor of architecture in Paris who trained, at his private

school and his rooms at the Louvre, many of the leading architects of the third quarter of the century. These included, for instance, C.N. Ledoux, one of the most original of the early Neo-Classicists in France, the influential C.L. Clérisseau who instructed Robert Adam and others, and Sir William Chambers, architect to George III, who executed some of the best work done in Britain during the 1760s and 1770s. Blondel was also enormously influential through his many publications which betray astonishing industry, a sure eye, and a seemingly complete mastery of the subject in all its branches. The most entertaining of his works was that *De la Distribution des Maisons de Plaisance et de la Décoration des Edifices en general*, which came out in two volumes in 1737/8. The numerous plates were drawn and engraved by Blondel himself (Pls.116 and 117) and the book explains clearly and in a practical manner how to plan a modern building and how it should be decorated. It is *par excellence* the book that sets out the aims of advanced architects working in the Rococo style, and the accent was on the smaller buildings, the *maisons de plaisance*, in which the French so greatly excelled throughout the eighteenth century.[7] Blondel produced a *Traité d'Architecture dans le goût moderne* in the same years which was a treatise not unlike D'Aviler's of 1691 (see pp. 49–51). He also continued an earlier great publication, the publisher Mariette's *Architecture française* (Paris, 1727–38), with his own work in four huge volumes with 600 plates under the same title, published between 1752 and 1756. He then contributed the articles dealing with architecture in Diderot's famous *Encyclopédie* of the 1750s and early 1760s. And finally he prepared a *Cours d'Architecture civile* which was based on the course he gave in his own school; this was completed by Pierre Patte and brought out in three volumes between 1771 and 1777 (i.e. partly after Blondel's death in 1774). During all this period he was lecturing, teaching and pronouncing judgement upon architecture and interior decoration, both modern and ancient. His versatility was enormous.

Not only was Blondel extremely well informed about French architecture, he was also immensely proud of its achievements, and this particularly applied to the enormous strides that had been made by the way of advancing during his lifetime the art of decorating the interior. 'French architects excel in this genre of decoration,' he insisted, and he added that, for an architect of his day, 'interior decoration' embraced the design of 'panelling, but also doors, windows, chimneypieces, cornices, ceilings, floors, and also the principal pieces of furniture, the location, shape and purpose of which should be taken into consideration when the distribution of the plan is being worked out'. Distribution was always one of Blondel's chief concerns – it should be 'the first goal of the architect', he claimed, and it will have been noted that the word is included in the title of his seminal publication of 1737–8. He insisted that designing the decoration of an interior is fascinating work but, important as this aspect certainly is, it will not suffice if convenience and comfort have been ignored. One cannot praise too greatly, he writes, some of our French architects for the way they bring uniformity to the design of a room and its furnishings, an extremely interesting part of architecture which, along with the question of distribution, has 'aroused the curiosity of foreigners'.[8]

While it was interiors at the Palais Royal and at the Hôtel de Toulouse which made a deep impression on Parisians shortly before 1720 (p. 49), in the mid 1720s the houses which attracted particular attention were the Hôtel de Lassay and the Hôtel de Roquelaure, the latter being the work of J.B. Le Roux who, during the 1730s, often collaborated with Nicolas Pineau who had returned from Russia some time between 1727 and 1731. Together they designed the Hôtel de Mazarin (*c.*1735), which quickly came to enjoy enormous esteem. Pineau's mural decorations in the Rococo taste were of especial refinement and subtlety. Blondel spoke of them as being of 'great beauty, executed in the most

**111] LIVING IN A RUIN; THE ULTIMATE IN ROMANTIC DREAMS OF ANTIQUITY, ROME 1760s**

This charming sketch by J.L. Clérisseau shows the Ruin Room which he designed, and which still survives, at the convent of S Trinità dei Monti near the top of the Spanish Steps. It was really more of a *loggia*, as part of the roof was left out to produce a truly ruined aspect. The furniture was all designed to look like Classical fragments – the desk in the form of a damaged sarcophagus, a piece of cornice serving as a table, a capital providing a seat, and an antique niche a basket for the dog. The great German art historian Winckelmann wrote a letter in 1767 enthusiastically praising this amazing illusionist exercise.

*Reproduced by permission of the Syndics of the Fitzwilliam Museum, Cambridge*

modern taste; the curious should visit it …'.[9] But probably the most magnificent interiors created during the 1730s were those at the Hôtel de Soubise (Pls. 126–129), the architect for which was Germain Boffrand. These rooms were immensely influential; indeed, they still today seem to exemplify the most magnificent side of Parisian High Rococo. One delightful building, the principal room of which owes much to the inspiration provided by the Princesse de Rohan's oval *salon* at the Hôtel de Soubise, is the Amalienburg outside Munich, completed by 1739, and built by Cuvilliès who had received his training in Paris. Many French architects of this period went to work abroad – sometimes men of the first rank like Pineau who spent some years in Russia, Boffrand who visited Würzburg, and Cuvilliès who worked in Munich.

In many parts of Germany the French lead was taken up and developed, often with most happy results. The same cannot really be said of England, where the Rococo never took proper root. In interior architecture, even in the most famous English expressions of the genre, like Chesterfield House and Norfolk House, it remained a veneer laid over a traditional English Neo-Palladian background.[10] The disjointed, attenuated forms, and the lack of integration to which this style is prone, are too often present in English Rococo interiors (e.g. Pl.168), showing that the style did not really suit the English temperament. At its best – and it can then be charming – it is an enlivening of the Neo-Palladian Baroque idiom (Pl.167). The principal English architect to whom it fell to have to handle the Rococo idiom was Isaac Ware, but as his *Complete Body of Architecture* (London, 1756) so clearly demonstrates, he was much more at home when working within his 'native' Neo-Palladian tradition. Pl.135 shows a subject from that influential work.

Already in 1737, in his *De la Distribution des Maisons de Plaisance*, Blondel had criticized the tendency in Rococo decoration to load schemes down with a 'ridiculous jumble of shells, dragons, reeds, palm-trees, and plants', and as the Rococo became increasingly extravagant, not to say wild, during the 1740s, criticisms became ever more common. The reaction against Rococo was not far behind, and in the early 1750s the first manifestations of Neo-Classicism were appearing in Paris.[11] One of the difficulties faced by students of this style lies in establishing what was new about the Classicism that became fashionable in Paris in the late 1750s. There were a few motifs which may be instantly recognized, but otherwise it can be difficult to distinguish from earlier work in this tradition. Indeed, the French, even during the height of the Rococo phase, had never fully abandoned Classicism. It was the accepted style where sober formality was required. It was therefore normal not merely for dignified civic buildings but also for dining-rooms where a degree of formality was considered appropriate. Moreover, when seeking a style that might serve as an antidote to Rococo exaggeration, French architects and designers needed to look no further than the Classicism of their own great and glorious age, that of Louis XIV. Even at the time, some French writers commented on resemblances between the new style and that of the late seventeenth century; and Englishmen visiting Paris immediately after the Seven Years' War had ended in 1763 felt that what the French were now beginning to do was nothing new. To them it seemed simply Classical, as was their own native Neo-Palladianism.

Yet a change did take place. A new, uncompromising, almost brutal, form of Classicism made its appearance. The celebrated furnishings of the court official and art collector Lalive de Jully (1756) were in this style, and so were the engravings in J.F. Neufforge's important *Recueil élémentaire d'Architecture* which eventually comprised nine volumes (with no less than 900 plates), the first of which were available in 1757 while volume five was at the printers in 1761.[12] Delafosse's designs were couched in the same idiom (Pl.112). Not everyone espoused this severe style, and a milder version became the accepted form for fashionable interiors and furnishings from the mid 1760s onwards. In the meantime exercises in the Rococo taste also reflected the reaction. Symmetry was re-imposed, ornaments were bridled, stiffness pervades the flowing lineaments.

An important expression of this late, stiffened form of Rococo was the re-decoration in about 1755–7 of an apartment for the Duchesse d'Orléans at the Palais Royal (yet again the centre of attention) to the designs of the architect Contant d'Ivry (Pl.171). Blondel considered these schemes near-perfect. The frivolities of the Rococo had been banned but the 'male style' so enthusiastically advocated by some of the modern young architects (like Neufforge, he presumably meant) had not taken their place – a *'juste milieu entre ces deux excès'* had been struck and he thought it admirable.

It should be added that Mme de Pompadour, who is so often regarded as the

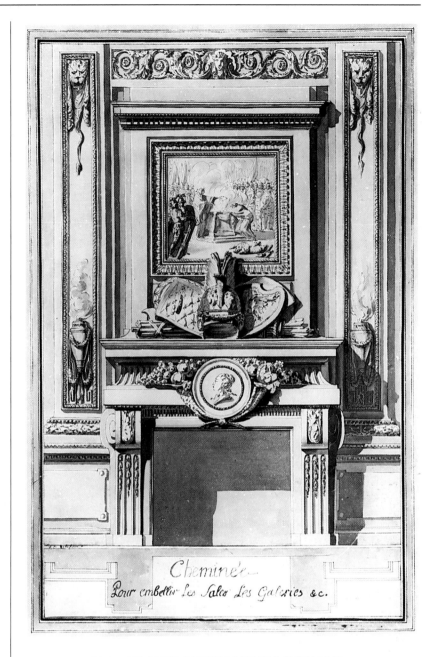

**112] THE MORE UNCOMPROMISING FORM OF EARLY NEO-CLASSICISM** 1760s

By the Parisian designer and architect Jean-Charles Delafosse, and presumably intended for publication, this composition shows a chimneypiece suitable for 'embellishing large reception rooms [*salles*] and galleries'. But while the scale may be large, the overpowering style is very different from that of the Rococo. Delafosse published numerous suites of engravings of ornament and furnishings in this uncompromising vein from 1767 onwards. Note also the decoration of the flanking pilasters, the frieze above, and the dado, all in a quite new taste. Delafosse was a teacher of drawing; the qualities of his admirable draughtsmanship are well demonstrated in this bold composition.
*Staatliche Museen, Berlin*

Rococo's presiding genius, in fact showed considerable appreciation of Classical art. There seem to have been Classical features at some of her small buildings – 'love-nests' would not be an inappropriate term since they were primarily places in which to welcome the King – perhaps already at the Château de Crécy-Couvé (1756) and certainly at the Saint-Hubert hunting-lodge completed in 1758. Moreover, the famous and delightful Petit Trianon, which was built for her to the designs of the Court Architect Gabriel, is in a fully-fledged Neo-Classical style. Mme de Pompadour, who died in 1764, did not live to see it completed and the interior was not decorated until after the building was otherwise finished, in 1766 or 1767, but it may be that she saw sketches for some of the interior embellishments. Whatever the case, her judgement in these matters was excellent and her influence on French taste at this period immense, not merely because she occupied a powerful position as the King's mistress but because she took such a personal interest in the huge number of commissions for furnishings and decoration that were given during her 'reign' in connection with the royal buildings that concerned her.

Her brother, the Marquis de Marigny, her junior by six years, came to disapprove of the Rococo style and, by 1756, was recommending that the Académie should hold competitions in 'the interior decoration of grand residences, in order to correct the poor taste in ornamental design which prevails today'.[13] Since he occupied the post that *de facto* made him Minister for the Arts in an age when such a post effectively influenced artistic output, his views were of considerable importance.

The buried Classical buildings at Pompeii and Herculaneum were being excavated in the middle of the century. Those who braved the then hazardous descent into the rooms were amazed and excited by the wall-paintings in particular, and these discoveries certainly affected contemporary interests and taste. But Classical antiquities were not in themselves novelties; there had been extensive collections in Rome since the sixteenth century and, by the mid-eighteenth century, such assemblages existed in many parts of Europe. One important collection was that of the Comte de Caylus which he published in seven volumes between 1752 and 1767. These made available to designers and architects an immense repertory of entirely new motifs.[14] What had changed, however, was the approach to Classical art and architecture, which now became much more strictly archaeological in character. Learned societies sent out architects to survey ancient monuments: two important publications that resulted from such activities were Le Roy's *Ruines des plus beaux Monuments de la Grèce* (1758) and Stuart and Revett's *Antiquities of Athens* (1762). Such works increased the interest in Classical buildings and provided accurate information about proportion, scale and ornamental detail. Further impetus was given by Winckelmann's authoritative *Geschichte der Kunst des Altertums* which appeared in 1764 in Rome and was published in English and in French two years later. Winckelmann was a learned enthusiast who was interested primarily in theoretical matters, in the *spirit* of Classical art rather then its archaeological aspects. But his insistence that the only way for contemporary civilization to become truly great was through imitating the Ancients provided scholarly sanction and a powerful stimulus to those who believed that correct taste must lie somewhere in the realms of Classicism.

French Neo-Classicism gradually spread across Europe during the 1760s. Paradoxically, it hardly affected Italy until later in the century although that country, and Rome especially, had provided the chief stimulus from the outset. In the hands of William Chambers, it reached England already in the second half of the 1750s, for not only was he familiar with the Roman monuments but his studies in Paris had led to friendship with several of the most advanced French architects. Some of his early interiors had a veneer of Rococo detailing, or embodied Neo-Palladian motifs, but Chambers went on to produce fastidious schemes in a measured version of Neo-Classicism reflecting his learned approach to the subject: for instance at Lord Bessborough's house at Roehampton in the early 1760s, and at the Queen's House (the former Buckingham House) which he largely re-built in the mid-1760s and which very much caught the public's attention. To many English people there probably did not seem to be all that much difference, nevertheless, between the rooms Chambers produced in the 1760s and those designed by William Kent and John Vardy in the 1730s and 1740s. The whole thing was now a bit lighter and there were fewer ornaments, but both were evidently Classical and not Rococo.

On the other hand, the few interiors designed by James Stuart after his study of the antiquities of Athens were quite different in character, much more akin to the work of the 'brutal' school in Paris. Stuart's chief work of this date was the decoration of the State Rooms at Spencer House, the designs for which were conceived around 1759. They were a conscious attempt by Stuart and a group of *cognoscenti* to devise a formula for interior decoration which was truly based on that of the Ancients. The decorations at Spencer House were much ahead of their time and had no direct successors. However, the style had a certain influence on Robert Adam, who returned from Rome in 1758 and shortly afterwards took over the decoration of Kedleston, for which Stuart had already produced some designs in an early version of the 'Spencer House style'. Adam had spent some three years in Rome studying the monuments with Clérisseau as his tutor (again the French connection), and he brought back to England a detailed knowledge of Classical ornament which stood him in good stead when faced with the many projects for interior decoration that it was his good fortune to receive in the following years. These included Croome Court for the Earl of Coventry in the early 1760s, Syon House for the Duke of Northumberland in the later 1760s, and Lansdowne House in Berkeley Square for the Earl of Shelburne shortly before 1770. His style, now so well known,[15] was enormously influential at the time. Also important was Chambers' *A Treatise on Civil Architecture*, published already in 1759. Among other early publications of Neo-Classical ornament, mention should be made of Matthew Darly's *The Ornamental Architect*, the plates of which are dated 1770. This book was intended to assist not only architects but also painters, carvers, stucco-workers, embroiderers, tapestry-weavers and cabinetmakers, as its title-page proclaims. It is sometimes not realized today that the schemes of interior decoration by architects such as Chambers, Stuart and Adam were very colourful, particularly during the early phase of Neo-Classicism before 1770. Later, more muted colour schemes came into favour.

To the Parisians, and no doubt to many Londoners as well (not to speak of the citizens of Copenhagen, Philadelphia, Munich and many other places), novelty was important. In the mid-1760s, everything in Paris had to be '*à la grecque*', in the Greek taste. The term does not seem to have had any special significance, but many objects said at the time to be decorated in this taste had ornaments taken from the Classical repertoire. The approach in such cases was no different from that which borrowed motifs from imported Chinese wares – or invented them if necessary. The same is true of the Gothic forms which began to enjoy popularity in England in the middle of the century. For all the underpinnings of archaeology and talk of the 'Classical virtues', the Classical world was a remote concept around which one might weave romantic fantasies. A man like Chippendale was perfectly happy to raid the repertoires of Chinese, Classical or Gothic forms indiscriminately when composing designs for furniture,[16] and he was not unique in this.

Goods from the Far East continued to pour into Europe. These included silk materials, porcelain, lacquerwork, screens and fans, as before, but now also painted silks and wallpaper which were specially suitable for interior decoration. Imitations of all these things were of course made in Europe (the Parisian imitations of lacquer were particularly skilful at this stage) and so extensive was the fashion for Oriental wares, both genuine and imitation, that a fresh category had to be created in the French royal inventories for these '*Divers ouvrages de la Chine*'. Entirely fantastic chinoiseries had commonly been incorporated in Rococo schemes of decoration during the 1730s and 1740s in France, and continued to be so in the 1750s elsewhere. There was no place for such frivolities alongside Classical forms when the latter were being taken seriously, as they were by the Neo-Classicists, and chinoiseries tend to disappear from the scene after 1760 or so, only to reappear at the end of the century. The tendency in the middle of the century was anyway towards rather more accurate renderings of Oriental subjects – a development much stimulated by William Chambers' publication in 1757 of *Designs of Chinese Buildings, Furniture, Dresses, Machines and Utensils*, based on drawings he had made in China during the 1740s. He expressed the hope that the designs 'might be of use in putting a stop to the extravagancies that daily appear under the name of Chinese'.[17] However, his offerings were only really to bear fruit in the late 1780s.

Unlike Chinese, Gothic forms could be seen without difficulty in old buildings all over Europe. Students of history were familiar with mediaeval manuscripts and their illuminations. Antiquaries collected relics, genuine or spurious, of famous historical figures of the Middle Ages. Architects and builders had to prop up or restore mediaeval structures, and others (notably at Oxford and Cambridge) had to build new wings and quadrangles in the old style. Many people, therefore, were familiar with Gothic forms although no systematic study had at that time been carried out. For some reason that is not easy to explain, however, the English began well before the middle of the eighteenth century to erect the occasional building in a style that embodied pastiche elements of mediaeval ornament. Vanbrugh and William Kent both built houses with unmistakable Gothic features. Kent's Esher Place of the early 1730s had an interior with Gothic details, and he built a strange underground house with furniture to match called 'Merlin's Cave', an illustration of which was published in 1744. Sham Gothic ruins, admired for the romantic atmosphere they created, sprang up in many a country-house park during the 1740s.[18] Batty Langley published his *Gothic Architecture Improved* in 1742, suggesting that the style was suitable 'for all parts of private buildings'. Furniture to go in such settings was being produced in the 1750s while, at Twickenham on the Thames, Horace Walpole was busy transforming a villa called Strawberry Hill into the first major Neo-Gothic building.[19] The famous 'Holbein Chamber' of 1759, for instance, had a ceiling (of papier mâché) based on the so-called Queen's Dressing Room at Windsor Castle, while the chimneypiece was inspired by that of the tomb of Archbishop Warham at Canterbury Cathedral, and the screen was copied from the choir in Rouen (Pl.220). It will be seen that a new and far more serious approach was here being forged. But Walpole and his friends were in advance of their times. A glance at William Pain's *The Builder's Companion and Workman's General Assistant ... All the principal rules of Architecture, from the Plan to the Ornamental finish ...*, published in London in 1765, and showing 'Gothick frontispieces for the inside of Rooms' and 'Gothick Chimneypieces', reveals such ornament grafted on to Classical, indeed late Neo-Palladian, structures much in the same way as Rococo motifs had been a few years earlier.

Not only ideas for interior decoration, but actual goods required for furnishing, moved from one country to another. The French had the monopoly when it came to luxury wares – furniture, carpets, soft-paste porcelain, tapestries – and when any other country entered the luxury field, it was almost always French wares that were imitated. The only important exception was true porcelain which was exported in quantity from various factories in Germany but principally from Meissen; it was mostly in styles devised at Meissen and was imitated even by the French on occasion. There was also a considerable export of glassware from Bohemia, comprising drinking-vessels and looking-glasses. The Italian glass industry was still active but had lost the supremacy it had enjoyed in the sixteenth and seventeenth centuries. The French still retained the monopoly in making large sheets of plate-glass (see Pl.128) for the simple reason that no other nation was able to master the techniques involved.[20] Italy still provided the bulk of furnishing silks – silk damasks and silk velvets – the best of which still came from Genoa. Italy also was the source of most of the marble slabs that were to lie on pier-tables, sideboards and commodes. For the same purposes were produced slabs of *scagliola* (imitation inlaid marble of coloured stucco) which was much in demand among the wealthier English patrons. England did not seriously attempt to compete with the French in the luxury market abroad but was enormously successful in meeting the requirements of middle-class customers at home and all over the rest of Europe, producing large quantities of practical and unfussy wares of all sorts, from furniture to pottery. English tea-tables, writing-desks, and dining-tables were eagerly sought. The English open-back chair was in great favour and widely imitated. Woollen goods (worsteds) were a major English export, much of them being used for furnishing; and English carpeting also found a market. English flock wallpapers were the rage, even in France. Apart from this, the only other export of any consequence was that of delftware tiles from Holland – although such wares were now produced in other countries as well.

The cost of decorating a smart house in Paris was now prodigious. 'When a house has been built nothing is yet accomplished; one has not yet laid out a quarter of the cost; then come the joiner, the upholsterer, the painter, the gilder, the carver, and the cabinetmaker, etc.' Even a fairly modest English gentleman could say in 1749 that 'Surely ye inside expenses of a House shou'd always be reckon'd at as much as the Shell'.[21]

## Planning and arrangement

In 1725 Courtonne could write of the 'new art of distribution' (see p. 50) and J.F. Blondel stated in 1754 that this important part of architecture had been brought to a high state of perfection in France during the previous thirty years or so.[22] You can pile column on column, he said, your profiles can be 'more regular and delicate even than those of Palladio and the most famous architects of our own day', you can bring in the most skilled sculptors to work on the decoration of your building, but what success will attend your efforts if your ground-plan is badly distributed?[23]

The old distinction between the state apartment (*appartement de parade*) and the private apartment (*de commodité*) still very much obtained, as Blondel explains,[24] but he shows that a third type of apartment had now been introduced, the *appartement de société* which was intended for receiving friends and family, and could be joined to the more formal state apartment if the company to be entertained was large. There was still a state bed in a French state bedchamber even though few people (mostly mothers who were lying-in; see Pl.170) now received company while in bed. In England by the middle of the century, state bedchambers had largely gone out of fashion; few were now built and most of those that existed were either hived off or had had their beds removed. What was now needed was a string of reception rooms for entertaining, with dancing, cards, collations, billiards, etc. The days when entertaining consisted of great sit-down banquets were now well and truly over.

In a new French house of this period there could be up to three antechambers but the first might serve as a vestibule or, more often, as a dining-room if there was no separate *salle à manger* specially designed for the purpose. The third might be called a *salle d'assemblée* in cases where it lay in the state-room sequence. The first antechamber-cum-dining-room[25] should have a sober character contrived with an '*architecture mâle*' – a masculine form of décor. A stove was appropriate in such rooms. The second antechamber was for receiving more distinguished guests; it was appropriate to decorate this with carved panelling and large plates of mirror-glass which produced an air of grandeur.

The modern *salon* does not rise through two storeys, Blondel says, except in country houses. *Salons* are for receiving people of distinction, for concerts, dances and similar festivities. Here it is convenient to place sofas (designed *en suite* with the panelling, which produces a harmonious whole) which save one from having to bring in extra chairs when there are many people present, and so disfiguring a room. Chairs seating two people may be placed against the piers. A *salle de compagnie* was a smaller reception room, a withdrawing-room, within the *appartement de société*; it might be next to the dining-room.

Pl.137 shows the view of a dining-room published by Blondel in 1737–8.[26] A plan accompanies the illustration and indicates that this is the wall opposite the windows, between which stands a marble-topped table that thus faces the large marble buffet shown in the view. On the buffet one set out the dessert, he explains, and adds that while such buffets constitute 'one of the principal beauties of dining rooms in country houses', such features should never be installed in really grand houses – presumably he means in Paris. Note that sofas, shaped carefully to follow the contours of the panelling, are placed in a dining-room. A number of mid-eighteenth-century dining-rooms have what Blondel calls '*fontaines*' from which water ran into basins where the servants could rinse glasses, etc. These usually very decorative features were developed from the cisterns and basins of the Baroque period (still much used in many parts of Europe at this date); in England the facility was built into ornamental urns with a lead-lined drawer in the pedestal serving as the basin (Pl.213). Blondel, anyway, does not recommend installing this feature in the dining-room as it gives rise to dampness, and the ministrations of the servants are disturbing. *Fontaines* should be set up in some adjacent room, he suggests. In fact he liked to have a special room next to the dining-room where food could if necessary be warmed on small stoves before being served.

Husbands and wives still tended to have separate apartments and therefore also bedchambers. It was considered exceptional that a couple living in Bordeaux should have had twin beds, as the inventory drawn up on the husband's death in 1755 reveals.[27] The fashionable pattern by the middle of the century was for the lady of the house to occupy the grand apartment where she could 'hold court' if she felt so inclined, and for the husband to occupy a private suite behind the scenes. Her bed would be sumptuous, his less so. The bedchamber (*chambre de parade*) should be as splendid as possible. Some grand bedchambers still had alcoves formed by balustrades or columns, with a raised area of parquet (Pls.129 and 172). The alcove should be hung with a textile material, tapestry still being thought especially appropriate (Pl.127). *Chambres en niche*, in which the bed was enclosd in a niche, were only to be found in private apartments (Pls.159 and 152). Sometimes the back wall of the niche could slide open so that the servant could more easily make the bed. Elsewhere the back of the niche might be faced with mirror-glass but grand people should avoid doing this, Blondel insists; this is only suitable for very private apartments. The beds in a niche have two heads (*chevets*) because they are seen from one side and therefore have to present a symmetrical aspect to the room.

*Cabinets* (i.e. closets, although the French term always seems to carry a grander connotation) are small rooms which, according to Blondel, fall into two categories. The first comprises rooms where one deals with one's private business affairs, those which serve as studies, and those which are repositories for books and treasured objects. The last kind should have top-lighting so as to leave all the wall area free for bookcases. If the room is a picture-cabinet, it is important that the paintings be arranged carefully and with taste – and here Blondel, in 1752, urges his readers to visit the picture cabinets of the Duc d'Orléans (presumably at the Palais Royal), Monsieur de Julienne, and Monsieur la Boissière who, we happen to know, had built a small house up on

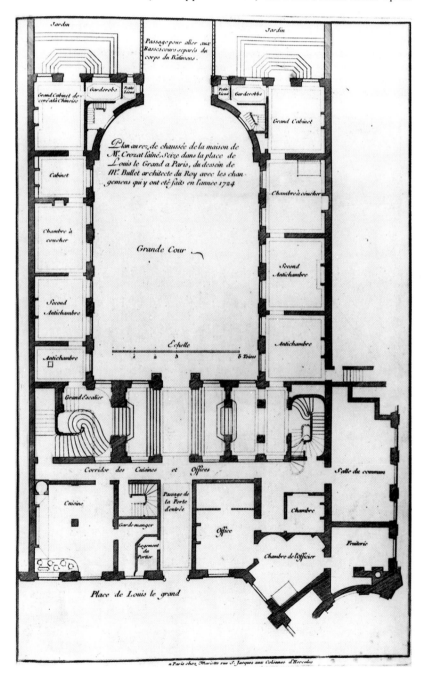

## 113, 114] THE GROUND AND FIRST FLOOR OF THE HOUSE OF THE RICH FINANCIER, CROZAT, IN THE PLACE VENDOME, PARIS
early eighteenth century

Designed by Pierre Bullet, architect to the King, the house was completed in 1702 but altered in 1724. The variety of shapes given to the rooms is noteworthy. In the wings are two small apartments, each ending in a *grand cabinet* with French windows opening onto the garden. That on the left is decorated *à la chinoise*. After ascending the main stairs, a visitor would have turned right to enter the great antechamber which preceded the *salon*. Beyond is the principal bedchamber with the fashionable rounded corners, and a large closet. A *garderobe* and *petits lieux* (perhaps sluiced) lie beyond. An oval vestibule opens on to a terrace and forms a link with the other apartment (presumably that of Crozat's wife) and the gallery in a wing. In the opposite wing is another apartment. The family presumably dined in the Great Antechamber which lies above the kitchen, or possibly, when truly *en famille*, in the other antechamber at the top of the stairs. (From Mariette's *Architecture françoise ou Recueil des plans, elevations, coups et profils des eglises, hôtels & maisons particulières de Paris, etc.*, Paris 1727.)
*Victoria and Albert Museum, London*

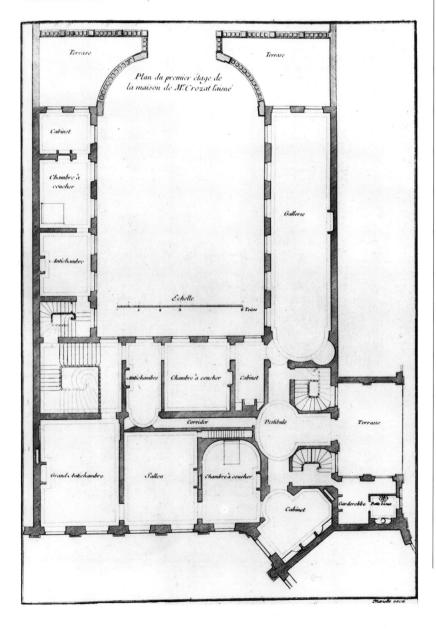

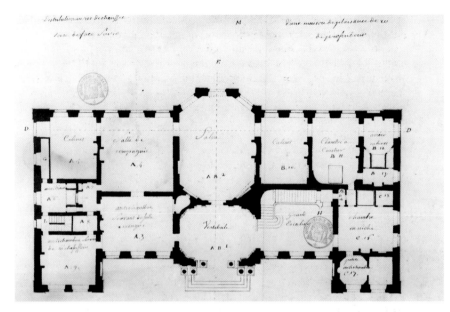

△ 115] AN IDEAL BUILDING, FRANCE   *c.*1740

Apartment A, the *appartement de société*, is for entertaining friends in the afternoon and includes the entrance vestibule, a large *salon*, a drawing-room (*salle de compagnie*), closet, a private closet with a day-bed in a niche called the *méridienne*, an antechamber serving as a dining-room, and a serving-room for warming the food. Apartment B is the state apartment (*appartement de parade*) which is more formal. It can be used for morning business visits centred round the *levée*. For parties it and the *appartement de société* can be used together, forming a string of reception rooms. It has a *grand cabinet* or small drawing-room in front of the main bedchamber. The *arrière-cabinet* or more private closet has a day-bed in a niche. There is, however, also a private bedchamber with attendant closets forming Apartment C which is the *appartement de commodité* – of comfort or relaxation; in fact a private retreat. Upstairs are further reception rooms and several more apartments. (From an unpublished manuscript by J.F. Blondel entitled 'Abrégé d'Architecture concernant la distribution, la décoration, et la construction des bâtiments civils', Paris, about 1740.)
*Bibliothèque Nationale, Paris.*

Montmartre the year before Blondel's *Architecture françoise* appeared. It was a house which may have embodied a number of original features.[28] The second type of closet includes dressing-rooms, oratories, water-closets and what he calls a 'méridienne' which, from plans, one knows had a day-bed in it and was presumably a lady's retiring-room.

Briseux, in 1743, refers to the small private rooms behind a bedchamber as normally consisting of an 'arrière-cabinet' (or back-closet) and two *garderobes*, but 'one may add a third small closet which contains a day-bed, and to which one gives the name *Boudoir*'. The Marquis de Mirabeau considered the boudoir an essential appendage to a grand house: 'A palace should contain an apartment for winter and another for summer, you need an *appartement des bains* [i.e. a group of rooms serving the bathroom], mezzanines, closets, *garderobes* and *boudoirs*.'[29] The décor of these small rooms could be delightful, as was the boudoir of Mme de Pompadour at Bellevue (*c.*1748–50) with its embroidered silk hangings and over-doors with chinoiseries by Boucher. The Duc de Menars wanted his boudoir 'very small and very warm' and it was to be decorated with nothing but 'nudities'. Indeed, there tended to be an implication

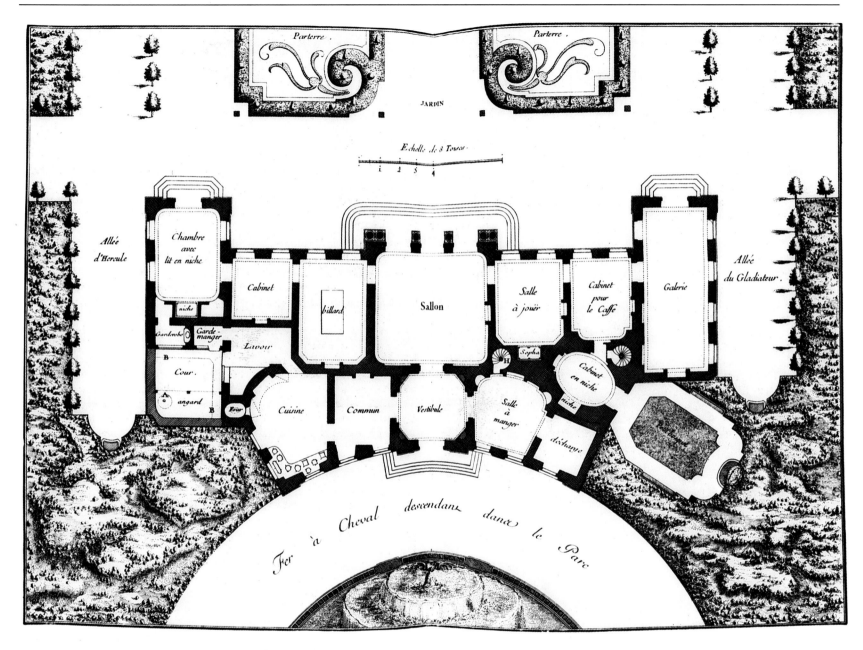

**116] PLAN FOR A 'TRIANON', FRANCE    1738**

A Trianon was a small building in the park, not far from the main building, to which one could escape to get away from the cares of official life – a place where one could entertain a few friends or which one could lend to a favoured guest. It was a complete little house with one bedchamber and a suite of rooms for enjoying oneself. The bed here is set in a niche, itself an indication of relaxation, not to say *volupté*. The bedchamber was protected from the main rooms by a closet serving as a sort of antechamber. The main rooms centred on a *salon* and included a billiard-room, a room for card-games, a room 'for taking coffee', and a gallery. Behind the coffee-room lies a seemingly very private oval closet, with a day-bed in a niche, which opens on to a small private garden. There is a room specially designed as a dining-room. With a few discreet servants and the means to maintain such an establishment, one could surely have an exceedingly pleasant time in such a building. (From J.F. Blondel, *De la Distribution des Maisons de Plaisance et de la Décoration des Edifices en general*, Vol. II, Paris, 1738.)
*Victoria and Albert Museum, London*

of licentiousness about boudoirs from the outset and already by 1727 an enterprising Parisian publisher had brought out a *Manuel des boudoirs* which contained what he pretended were scandalous stories about the young ladies of Athens.[30] No doubt the targets of his wit were a good deal nearer than Athens.

The decoration of closets 'is not really susceptible to gravity', maintains Blondel, and it was even more true now than in the seventeenth century that it was in these highly informal rooms that were first to be seen some of the most imaginative innovations in terms of décor. But although these intimate rooms were private retreats, many were described and sometimes even illustrated at the time, which suggests that their owners showed them off with some pride to favoured acquaintances.

The accent on private and intimate rooms became increasingly noticeable as the eighteenth century wore on. In line with Blondel's recommendation that all well-appointed houses should have private apartments with low ceilings, small rooms tucked up on mezzanines (*entresols*) were in favour (Pl.123) and '*petits appartements*' were to be found in all the French palaces. Some of these small rooms could be very luxurious, and the idea gradually spread. The London architect Isaac Ware, in his *Complete Body of Architecture* of 1754, had something of this sort in mind when he stated that 'A dressing-room in the house of a person of fashion is a room of consequence'. The English naturally also gave thought to these matters, and the distribution of their ground-plans can be quite clever, but they display none of the subtlety of the French solutions (e.g. Pls.113, 114, 115 and 116) and no space is devoted to the question of distribution in the English architectural treatises of the period (but see p. 145).

By this period servants were having to go about their business behind the scenes. Blondel did not want to see them fussing around the buffet; small rooms where one could dine in private without servants were devised, and ground-plans show numerous small linking passageways by which servants could move about the house largely unseen. And, with the invention of the bell operated by wires, the day came when servants could be summoned; they no longer needed to hang around their masters awaiting instructions. The *Daily Advertiser* of London carried a notice on 5 March 1744 that 'John Westbrook . . . performs all manner of Smith's Work, also hangs small Bells in Gentleman's Houses to call their Servants'.

An *appartement des bains* comprised not merely a bathroom with one or more baths (Pl.138) but also an antechamber where the servants foregathered, a bedchamber with as many beds as there were baths next door, a *garderobe* where one could change, and a '*Cabinet d'aisance à soupape*' – a 'place of easement', the outlet of which was closed by means of a valve. As Blondel explains, these places have 'for some years come to be much used in France in houses of consequence[31]; they are known by the name of *lieux à l'angloise*'. These English *lieux* (today corrupted to 'loos') are said to have been invented in England but 'several people of that country tell me they had not heard of their being used in London'. Nevertheless, Celia Fiennes had seen one at the turn of the century, made for Queen Anne (p. 60), and no less than ten water-closets were installed at Chatsworth in the early 1690s. In Blondel's scheme a boiler behind the bathroom supplied hot water to the taps of the bath through the walls. Baths still frequently had a canopy-like tent over them, so that one could retain the steam and make it into a kind of sauna.

It was at a ball given in August 1739 that for the first time there were separate *garderobes* for the ladies and for the gentlemen. The two doors were marked and, as a commentator pointed out, this innovation 'brought infinite credit to Monsieur Turgot', Provost of the Merchants of Paris, who gave the party.[32]

## The architectural shell

While the chimneypiece continued to form the focal point of a room,[33] it was no longer quite so obtrusive a feature – at least in France, or where French features were being followed, for there the openings were now smaller and the proportions were lower. There was no longer a great ornamental composition above, either, because this position was now usually occupied by a large area of mirror-glass which, in shape and framing, formed part of the integrated mural decoration of the room as a whole. Separate designs for chimneypieces were now rarely published in France; the feature is usually shown as part of a view of the whole wall (Pl.126). In England and Germany the old tradition of publishing separate designs for chimneypieces was maintained, however (Pls.134 and 133). Moreover, there tended to be a striking ornamental feature on the chimney-breast, which, in England, usually consisted of a bold architectural composition in which mirror-glass sometimes played a part but where more often a painting or (especially beloved of the Neo-Palladians) a sculptured relief was to be found. The surrounds of English fireplaces were also almost invariably of architectural form. Much in evidence were Classical features which often included the human figure in the form of caryatids or mythological scenes – the latter also commonly appearing in the reliefs above. Isaac Ware felt it necessary to warn his readers about the embarrassment that 'nudities' could cause. 'In a chimney-piece they would be abominable,' he insists; 'some drapery is always to be allowed: the question is how much and in what manner.' Pl.135 shows the illustration that he included to exemplify his assertion that 'shewing a thigh is contrary to . . . modesty', whereas if 'drapery be executed well, and the limbs will be seen through it; there will be at once elegance and decency'.

Little change took place at this period in the form of fire-irons or the other equipment usually associated with fireplaces. Grates for burning coal were becoming decorative in England where the burning of this fuel was now widespread, even in the most exclusive circles where hitherto it had been thought rather vulgar to burn anything but logs of wood. Chimney-boards continued in use, to fill the opening during the summer when the fire was not needed. However, one new accessory, introduced in the middle of the century in England, was the pierced metal fender which prevented red-hot coals from rolling off the hearth-stone on to the wooden floor or the carpet.

Stoves had long been acceptable in the best rooms in Germany, Central Europe and Scandinavia (Pls.151 and 175). They might be made of glazed earthenware including faience, or of cast-iron plates. Iron stoves were taken to America and were much favoured by the Pennsylvania Dutch (*Deutsch*) immigrants. It was presumably from these 'closed' stoves (i.e. the fire was not visible except when the door was opened) that were developed the open stoves of Benjamin Franklin which, he later stated, he had invented in 1742. These had a double metal skin, so that they not only transmitted radiant heat but also circulated warm air from vents in the surrounding jacket. The idea was known in England, and a catalogue was published by some smiths in 1765 with designs for various sorts of cast-iron stoves including models described as 'Philadelphia', 'Venetian' and 'French'[34]. However, it does not seem that such stoves gained much popularity in polite society in England even though Lady Mary Wortley Montagu had written from Germany to her sister about the English 'obstinacy in shaking with cold six months in the year rather than make use of stoves, which are certainly one of the great conveniences of life . . .'. She vowed to install one in her chamber at home 'in defiance to the fashion' but there is no evidence that she ever did.[35] In 1737 Blondel considered it acceptable to have a stove (presumably of faience) in the dining-room but not in any other important room because 'they could not but produce much dirtiness'. Some forty years

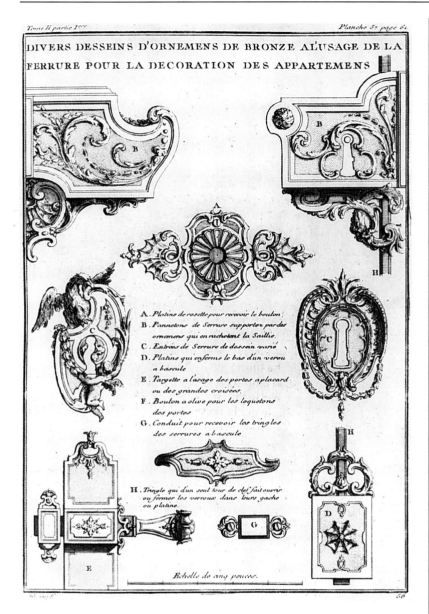

Tome II partie 1ere · · · · · · · · · · · · · · · · · · · Planche 57 page 61

DIVERS DESSEINS D'ORNEMENS DE BRONZE A L'USAGE DE LA
FERRURE POUR LA DECORATION DES APPARTEMENS

A . Platine de rosette pour recevoir le bouton.
B . Pannetons de Serrure supportez par des
ornemens qui en rachetent la Saillie.
C . Entrées de Serrure de dessein varié.
D . Platine qui enferme le bas d'un verou
a bascule.
E . Targette a l'usage des portes aplacard
ou des grandes croisées.
F . Bouton a olive pour les loquetons
des portes.
G . Conduit pour recevoir les tringles
des serrures a bascule.

H . Tringle qui d'un seul tour de clef fait ouvrir
ou fermer les verroux dans leurs gache
ou platine.

Echelle de cinq pouces.

**117] FRENCH ROCOCO DOOR-FURNITURE   1738**

From *De la Distribution des Maisons de Plaisance et de la Décoration des Edifices en general*, Paris 1738. Blondel seems himself to have drawn the many delightful illustrations in his treatise. It is interesting to compare this plate with that of similar subjects which he also drew for his monumental *Cours d'Architecture* of 1777. In the later versions the freshness has been lost; the forms are stiff and banal.
*Victoria and Albert Museum, London*

later, Mercier was claiming that stoves made him feel depressed; with their 'insipid, weak and invisible heat' suitable only 'for antechambers, places where one dines, and cafés'.[36] French stoves could be highly decorative, and were often architectural in form. For instance at a sale in Paris in 1769 there were two 'in the form of pyramids'.[37] A French stove of about that date is shown in Pl.189.

The mural decoration of the period is best shown by the plates; more thorough discussions may be found in various works.[38] Some contemporary comments are of interest. Isaac Ware (1756) explained that rooms with stucco walls tend to be cool while those that are 'wainscoted are naturally warmer' (obviously because the panelling insulates the room), and rooms furnished with wall-hangings are the warmest of all. However, when you heat the room 'The stucco room ... becomes hottest of all; and the wainscot hotter than the hung'.[39]

Carved wall-panelling, Blondel writes (1737–8), may be treated simply with clear varnish, which he considered far more attractive than coloured paintwork. He states that some people have started to paint panelling shades of yellow (he mentions *jonquille* and *citron*) and other colours (in 1752 he mentions blue, green and yellow), but such treatment is in his view only suitable for small rooms and never for the state rooms. However, where there are wall-hangings one may paint adjacent woodwork to match. State bedchambers are often painted white with gilded ornaments but he feels white is too striking; it looks like stone or marble and is not conducive to sleep. It is best for rooms used in daytime or in summer on account of its fresh appearance. In 1752, by which time the most riotous Rococo confections had already been created (and were being criticized by Blondel and others), he insisted that gilding should be used sparingly – too much does not produce a beautiful effect. Beyond these few remarks of Blondel's about colours, not much is known at present about colour-schemes, and serious research has been devoted to these matters only quite recently.[40] While in France white and gold schemes were considered appropriate for grand rooms and coloured schemes were mostly to be found in smaller rooms, apparently a rather darker and richer colour-scale was favoured in the English-speaking world and in Holland and Germany, and the lighter schemes only began to appear after 1750. Even the earliest Neo-Classical colour-schemes were a good deal more full-blooded than is generally supposed. Architects who had studied in Rome had after all not merely looked at ancient ruins; they could not have avoided seeing modern or recent Roman decoration which was exceedingly colourful, and this certainly made a powerful impression on them as the work they did on their return shows.

While the carving of the panelling in the grandest rooms was executed by people called '*sculpteurs*' in France, in England by the middle of the century much ornament of his sort was being rendered with papier mâché. Isaac Ware (1756) deplores the fact that 'Paper has, in a great measure, taken the place of sculpture' in 'the decoration for the sides of rooms'. William Shenstone, doing up his house in 1752, records that he has seen 'a small specimen of the chew'd Paper for Ceilings. 'Tis pretty, but I think them unreasonably dear....'[41] He seems to have bought them all the same, and notes that the 'Ornament of the Middle, and four Spandrells for the Corners' should be painted 'with Flake White and thin Starch'. The cove, he says, should be 'washed over Oker'.

Savary des Bruslons, in his *Dictionnaire de Commerce* of 1723, states that 'paper wall-hangings' (*cette espèce de tapisserie de papier*) have been so perfected and are so pleasing that there is scarcely a house in Paris where there is not some place which is decorated in this way 'be it garderobes or places even more private' (*lieux encore plus secrets*). This suggests that wallpaper had not yet moved into rooms of any importance, but by the 1730s papering was becoming common in England, and in the 1740s it could be found in large and elegant rooms.[42] At this time it came in large sheets rather than rolls.

The popularity of English flock papers in France in the 1740s and 1750s is shown by that barometer of mid-century fashionable taste, Mme de Pompadour: she had 'English paper' in her bathroom at the Château de Champs in the late 1750s. (The term 'bathroom' has a vaguely antiseptic implication today but her '*cabinet de bain*' was anything but that, we can be sure.)[43] The flourishing English export trade in flocked papers led to imitation: in 1755 a Parisian engraver was claiming he could make flocked papers as good as those from England and that he could provide patterns 'suitable for the largest apartments'.[44] The Seven Years' War curtailed the import of English products into France and, when it was over, the French imposed a customs duty which was so effective that the indigenous industry was able to catch up and successfully meet the local demand.[45] During the 1760s Jean-Baptiste Réveillon became the most successful manufacturer of wallpapers in France. Not only was he an astute businessman but he paid his designers well, and French wallpapers soon became justly famous and widely sought. Eventually, Réveillon's enterprise became a *Manufacture Royale* (1784). This was a mixed blessing for he had his house ransacked and burnt down by the mob during the first days of the Revolution.

Most wallpapers produced during the period under review imitated textile materials in their patterns – velvets, damask and other figured silks, printed cottons, chintzes and even needlework. One London manufacturer in 1737 advertised that he could provide 'fine hangings made to match any Needlework, shaded in a most beautiful manner'.[46] Hand-painted papers usually with bushes and birds but sometimes with human figures in landscapes, were imported from China in some quantities from about 1720 onwards, and made a colourful wall-decoration that enjoyed great favour among those who could afford them. Imitations that were presumably less expensive were reproduced in Europe.

Wallpapers might be used, as today, as a fixed wall-decoration, usually pasted onto a canvas lining. They could also be pasted onto canvas fixed to battens in the same way as wall-hangings, and were thus removable. This is made clear by several advertisements in Parisian newspapers offering 'rooms' of such hangings for sale. Whether mounted on battens or pasted direct onto the walls, the canvas might first be faced with a lining paper in addition. The technique of printing with distemper, still used today, was perfected during the third quarter of the century.

One could also obtain sheets of printed frames, garlands and ornaments of various kinds that could be cut out and pasted on the wall in an almost endless variety of combinations. Chippendale charged for putting up ornaments of this sort at Mersham-le-Hatch in Kent in 1767.[47] Engravings were also sometimes pasted on walls as decoration, with similar cut-out frames and ornaments linking them into a unified scheme. Such 'print rooms' were popular in England and Ireland – and, apparently, in South Carolina, if a local merchant's advertisement of 1765 refers to such decoration. 'The expense of papering a room', he claims, 'does not amount to more than a middling set of Prints.'[48]

The most astonishing schemes of decoration created in Paris around 1720 depended to a great extent on the brilliant effects produced by large plates of mirror-glass. The plates that could now be made increased in size as the century wore on. When the effects of Mme Hérault were sold in 1759 a great curiosity was a mirror 65 *pouces* (70 in.) high and 50 *pouces* (53 in.) wide (1.78 × 1.27 m). The cost of these huge plates was enormous, and several illustrious ladies in 1727 petitioned Louis XV for permission to buy plate-glass at the same rate as the King, who obtained what he required from the royal factory at Saint-

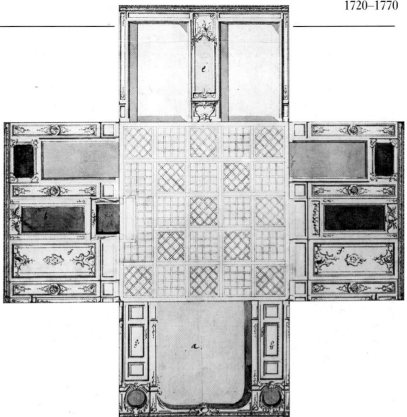

**118] PARQUET IN THE FRENCH STYLE**  *c.*1725

A proposal for the Margrave's bedchamber at Ansbach which was completed with minor changes in 1731. Couched in a fairly advanced taste betraying considerable knowledge of recent developments in France, this design is for an alcove-bedchamber for the Margrave and his wife. The chimneypiece is in fact described as being in the French style but instead of having mirror-glass set into the chimney-breast, there was to be a portrait. A glass is set into the panelling between the windows, with a console table fitted against the wall below. The alternating pattern of the parquet also follows the new French formula. (From the archives of Schloss Ansbach.)
*Bayerischer Verwaltung der staatlichen Schlösser, Gärten und Seen, Munich*

Gobain at a special discount.[49]

The forms of parquet evolved at Versailles and the other French royal palaces at the end of the seventeenth century were generally adopted all over Europe during the next fifty years (Pl.118). For a while the French gave up making elaborate *parquet marqueté* floors although such floors continued to be made in Germany, often to extremely complex designs.[50] However, when Classicism returned to France some very splendid floors with regular patterns began to make their appearance in and around Paris (Pl.200). The famous views of the Duc de Choiseul's new house, painted in miniature on a snuff-box, show several such floors.[51] Some English patterns for parquetry borders are shown in Pl.130, but Isaac Ware claimed in 1754 that 'the use of carpeting at this time has set aside the ornamenting of floors in a great measure'.[52] We tend to think of floors of wood or of marble or some other stone, but Ware reminds us that 'in elegant houses the floors . . . are of stucco. . . . This may be coloured any hue.' What he says applies not merely to England: stucco floors were common all over Europe. They could be elaborately patterned (in Italy and Germany) and took a high polish.

Germain Boffrand, the famous architect who had been responsible, among other things, for the rooms at the Hôtel de Soubise (mid-1730s) that attracted so much attention, published drawings of his buildings in a *Livre d'Architecture* in 1745 (Pls.126–129). One chapter is devoted to '*Des décorations intérieures et des ameublements*' ('interior decoration and suites of furnishings'). The first sentence states that 'At present the interior decoration of apartments constitutes a major part of architecture in Paris' (i.e. of the architect's business). He was not particularly happy about this development because he felt it had been brought about at the expense of the exterior, which was not receiving sufficient attention. He has nothing very startling to say about interior decoration but ends by stressing that 'Furniture [he uses the word in its wide sense] contributes much to the beauty of an apartment, and especially when hangings, tables, sofas, chairs and other furnishings seem to have been made for positions in which they harmonise with the design and lineaments [of the rooms].'

## Loose furnishings

Boffrand, in his *Livre d'Architecture* of 1745, also makes some observations on wall-hangings. The walls of bedchambers, he states, are usually hung with tapestries (*tapisseries*). He mentions 'histories, landscapes or other subjects', which just about covers the repertoire of tapestry design, but indicated that he is speaking of proper tapestry-woven hangings: the French word '*tapisseries*' can also be used less specifically to mean wall-hangings in general, the creations of a *tapissier* or upholsterer. He says that really beautiful tapestries are rare, but when they are 'well-drawn' one should not hang paintings on them. He then goes on to say that one may sometimes make wall-hangings of 'velvet or other materials of different colours' for use in winter, while for summer one may have hangings of taffeta 'which lend an air of freshness'. It is all right to hang pictures on hangings of this sort, he adds. Blondel (1752) more or less repeats what Boffrand had said, stressing that tapestries and other hangings are particularly suitable for bedchambers. He, too, refers to changing the hangings in summer and winter 'which produces novelty twice a year; moreover, when the rest of the furniture [upholstery] is of the same material, [this] forms an ensemble the uniformity of which is pleasing'.

For the most part the classes of materials which one could hang on walls were not technically different from those used from 1670 to 1720, though patterns changed with the fashions. These changes were naturally less rapid than those which affected dress-materials where, with silks, the fashion was being deliberately modified by the Lyons silk-designers every six months and had altered unmistakably within a few years. The Lyons weavers assigned the copyright for a design of dress-materials for six years; for furnishing silks the period was twenty-five years.[53] Bimont, who wrote an important manual on the upholsterer's business, published in 1770, lists the various materials used and their special properties. Silk damask comes first; it could be in two or even three colours, and there were less expensive qualities mixed with linen and/or cotton, suitable for use in the country or for servants' beds. He then mentions various silk materials (*gros de Tours*, velvet, *moiré*, *siamoises*) and says of brocatelle that it is used 'for cabinets of paintings and libraries' by which he must mean small rooms, in fact rather luxurious closets. Of the worsted materials, he mentions camlet which came plain, striped and with a *moiré* effect.

'*Toiles peintes*', Bimont says, are only used in the country: he is presumably referring to Indian painted cottons or European printed imitations. But the Chinese painted silk taffetas known as *Pékins*[54] were by no means to be found merely in rustic surroundings. These were now much used, he said, and it is evident that these ravishing materials were to be seen in the very best houses in town. A notable example was Mme de Pompadour's small château, Bellevue, where 'all the furnishings were of *pékins* of various colours'. Mlle Dechamps, a dancer at the comic opera with many rich admirers including the Duc d'Orléans, had the whole of her drawing-room (*salon de compagnie*) done up in this material, '*tendu d'un péquin d'un grand goût, avec le meuble pareil*' – the chair-covers *en suite*.[55] See also Pl.163.

Wall-hangings in the eighteenth century were usually nailed to a framework of battens fixed to the walls, and the nails were masked by some kind of border, or 'fillet' as it was called. At first these were of wood, carved and gilded, or perhaps painted. In the middle of the century it became fashionable in England (and no doubt elsewhere) to fit fillets of papier mâché or composition instead. These might have a lace-like appearance or could resemble carved mouldings (Pl.168 may show such a fillet). Gilt leather, which had gone out of fashion for wall-hangings, was also sold in narrow strips for bordering. A prominent Virginian visited the Governor's Palace at Williamsburg in 1771 and observed that the room was hung 'with plain blue paper & border'd ... with a narrow stripe of Gilt Leather wch. I thought had a very pretty effect'.[56]

The windows in most rooms of any importance were furnished with curtains by 1720. Divided curtains were still common but the pull-up type was considered smarter. After 1720 windows with curtains normally had pelmets. The 'festoon' curtain was a single hanging which was drawn straight up to the pelmet-board to form a billowing and not always very tidy horizontal mass below the pelmet (Pls.147 and 149). This was a common form all over Europe. In the English-speaking world another form was greatly favoured from the middle until the end of the century. It was divided and each half was pulled up diagonally towards the outer corners of the window. This formed draped festoons with 'tails' at the side and was sometimes referred to as 'draped' or 'in drapery' (Pl.233).[57] A transitional form seems to have existed comprising a pull-up curtain of the straightforward festooned kind, but with fixed tails at the sides. Bimont, writing in France in the late 1760s, describes both types of pull-up curtains as being 'à l'italienne' but says the divided kind is much more decorative. It is therefore curious that it is so rarely to be seen in French illustrations. Pl.207 shows some, while German curtains of this sort, perhaps provided by a French upholsterer, may be seen in Pl.187. There is a reference in a London newspaper to 'Roman drapery curtains',[58] and the term 'Venetian curtains' is also sometimes found in English inventories although precisely what this meant is unclear.

Curtains were made of the same material as the wall-hangings and bed-hangings, if there were any, to produce the desired unity, but one gets the impression that curtains were still not installed for the sake of warmth: it was bed-hangings that kept you warm at night. Curtains were provided more in order to soften the outlines of the windows and to exclude strong light. Many window-curtains during the middle of the century were made of lightweight materials, and these were apparently preferred when there was no need to match a heavy material elsewhere in the room. One material, a thin taffeta known as '*quinze-seize*' because it was 15/16ths of a French ell wide, was made specially for window-curtaining. The half-silk known as *siamoise* was also fashionable in France for window-curtains, according to Bimont (1770) who insisted that it must be pulled by means of cords as it was likely to tear, showing that it was a thin material. Among the less common materials mentioned in mid-century French documents are 'Italian gauze painted in the Indian taste', and satin painted with Chinese figures. Curtains of muslin first appear in France in a Marseilles inventory of 1745,[59] but these may have served as mosquito-curtains; in Italy gauze had been used for bed-curtains at least since the sixteenth century. Indeed, the word 'canopy' comes from the ancient Greek word for a mosquito-net (kōnōps = a gnat).

Sashes (see p. 21) were still being inserted in windows to exclude strong light in the 1720s and even later. The 'skreens to the windows' at Cannons, in Middlesex, in the mid 1720s were presumably sashes; as this was one of the most splendidly furnished houses in England, there can be no question of these fittings being unfashionable. Many were painted. One tradesman announced (1735) that he produced 'Blinds for Windows, painted on Canvas, Silk or Wire [gauze] ... N.B. He kept the first shop for that Business in London, and hath made it his constant practise ever since ...'. Another (1741) spoke of 'Spring Curtains and Blinds for Windows ... of a new Invention, Convenient to keep the Sun off in Summer, or the cold winds from coming in between the Sashes in Winter, and particularly necessary in Rooms up Stairs in narrow Streets, where the opposite Windows overlook each other'.[60] In France blinds were called 'stores' (from stora, the term used in Italy where blinds were common, as they have long been in all hot countries). Once again Mme de Pompadour provides an early example: in 1755 her boudoir at Bellevue was furnished with 'A blind of Italian taffeta, painted with bouquets of flowers and garlands that are transparent'; it seems to have had a copper or brass roller and 'a silk and gold cord ending in an elaborate tassel'.[61] Venetian blinds certainly existed in England by the 1770s; in France they were called 'jalousies à la persienne', a term that occurs in a document of 1769.[62] 'Glass-curtains' – small pieces of material fitted inside the window-panes to screen the room from people outside – existed already in the seventeenth century and are occasionally mentioned in eighteenth-century documents. A lady-in-waiting in the French royal household was provided with four such 'rideaux de vitrage' in 1751; they were each 'half a width wide and two and a half feet high'.[63]

Isaac Ware stated that floors were no longer decorated in England by the 1750s because carpeting had become so widespread – in the better sort of houses, he should have said. In saying that 'it is the custom almost universally to cover a room entirely', he is clearly referring not to separate carpets, Oriental or European, but to fitted carpet of the style in use today, with floors completely covered with widths of carpeting, sewn together; at this time there was a separate border. Benjamin Franklin sent some carpeting from London back to his wife in Philadelphia in 1758 and explained to her that 'it is to be sow'd together, the Edges being first fell'd down, and Care taken to make the Figures meet exactly: there is Bordering for the same' (Pls.196, 213 and 224).[64] Carpeting with a cut-pile surface was woven at Wilton in widths, and it is probable that the best rooms were furnished with this material. 'Wilton is famous for the manufacturing of carpets like those of Turkey but narrow, about ¾ yards wide', wrote Bishop Pococke in 1754.[65] The material was in fact a kind of woollen velvet, a moquette, and it was under this last name that it was known in France, whence the original weavers who settled at Wilton had come, and where it enjoyed a certain amount of fashionable esteem. An upholsterer in Paris, for example, could advertise in 1778 that he had for sale 'a large and beautiful carpet of English moquette which has never been used, with a handsome border', knowing that his customers would understand what was on offer.[66] The fact that he mentions the border indicates that he was referring to a made-up carpet.

Much less grand than Wilton carpet and therefore commoner was 'Scotch Carpett', which had no pile: it was of what is technically known as 'double-weave', and was reversible. According to an American visitor in 1767, it was made at Edinburgh, Hawick, Kidderminster and also at Wilton – and, he should have added, Kilmarnock.[67] Also frequently mentioned in English mid-century documents are 'listed carpets' which were the same as the French 'tapis de lizières' which, as was explained in an announcement in a Parisian journal of

1770, were 'composed of small strips of cloth [lizières de drap] of various colours woven on a loom ... They are inexpensive. One can buy them at the [shop of the] Brothers Jumeaux....'[68] The fact that this term needed explanation suggests these 'rag-carpets', as we would call them, were new in France at the time but, in England, references to them occur earlier: for example, the London Evening Post carried an advertisement for 'listed carpets' in its issue of 29 January–1 February 1737; and three years later on 24 May, 1740, we learn that 'William Crompton ... Turner to his Royal Highness the Prince of Wales [makes] on a new invented Machine, Carpet of Cloth List, which for Beauty, Strength and Service far exceed anything of that kind hitherto made' – this suggests that such materials were not unattractive and could be found in quite smart establishments. Clearly these were also in the form of strips which could no doubt be sewn together but were more probably used as runners – in which form this material was still being used in Sweden around 1900 (see Pl.467). 'List carpeting' was being made at a factory in Leeds in 1767, and the South Carolina Gazette noted that list carpets were being imported into Charleston in 1762 and again in 1767.[69]

Carpets proper, in the sense of a large pile-surfaced floor-covering woven in one piece, were of course a good deal more expensive than any of the made-up coverings. Apart from the Oriental carpets, which were now being imported in great quantities and were generally being used on the floor, European products were also becoming more widely available in the middle of the century. Superior to all others were still the products of the Savonnerie factory at Chaillot, on the edge of Paris, but they had long ceased to be reserved for royal use. An advertisement in The New York Gazetteer of 23 September 1774 refers to 'Carpets of the Royal Manufactory at Chaillot which exceed every other kind of carpets for beauty, strength, and duration of colours'.[70] The Savonnerie works also produced chair-covers and screens of hand-woven pile carpet, but these were rather exceptional side-lines. Attempts were made in England to rival the French factory in the 1750s, and by 1770 the Moorfields and Axminster factories were producing impressive carpets for important commissions.[71] The designs were mostly European in taste, and Robert Adam produced some Neo-Classical designs that were woven at these two factories for rooms he was decorating, the designs usually echoing that of the ceiling – a relationship that obviously did much to enhance the unity of the décor (Pl.208). These carpets were very expensive, but some Axminster carpets were reaching New York and probably other cities on the East Coast of America by the 1770s.[72]

Although imitations of Oriental carpets were certainly made in Europe during this period it was probably cheaper to buy the genuine article. An advertisement in a London newspaper of 1740 gives us a picture of this trade. 'Just imported and to be sold at Carpenters Hall ... a Large and fine Parcel of Smyrna, Segiadiya, and other choice Turkey-Carpets: Consisting of a great Variety of Sizes of lively colours and divers curious new-fashioned Patterns. Many fine Carpets from three to four Yards square, and others from six to seven Yards long and proportional Weadths, extremely useful for Dining-Rooms, & with Hearth and Bed-side Carpets of excellent Patterns and Fineness.'[73]

A good deal less grand but to be found in many respectable houses throughout the English-speaking world from the 1720s onwards was floor-cloth, which was essentially a width of canvas painted with thick pigment. It served as a moderately inexpensive and serviceable floor-covering until eventually, late in the nineteenth century, it was superseded by linoleum. What seems to be the earliest recorded reference comes from the inventory of the Governor of New York and Massachusetts who died in 1728, in which is listed 'Two old checkered canvas' to lay under a table'.[74] (The use of such floor-coverings under tables as 'crumb-cloths' was evidently common in the

American colonies, and may well have been quite usual in England.) Imported English floor-cloths were being advertised in Charleston in 1736, and references to them become common in England and America in the middle of the century. While most bore simple patterns of squares and diamonds, very elaborate designs were also executed, 'with the most beautiful Carpet Colours and other very curious Figures done to the greatest Perfection', as an advertisement in the *London Evening Post* for 29 January 1737 put it. The best floor-cloths were made in factories, where the tall frames required (the cloths were prepared vertically) could be set up, but such cloths could also be made by amateurs. There were also many people engaged in re-painting worn floor-cloth.

An alternative to floor-cloth was matting. An advertisement in the *London Evening Advertiser* for 29 October 1741 offered 'Barbary, Dutch and English matting'. Barbary mats will have been the thin sort which had been imported from North Africa for some time (see pp. 25 and 60). Both Dutch and English mats are referred to in contemporary French inventories of the period. Pl.221 shows matting on a floor. Some matting had coloured patterns.

Caned chairs had gone out of fashion in England by 1720, but the French had adopted them in a different form (Pl.141), and these remained acceptable in polite circles until after the middle of the century; they were usually padded with tie-on squabs. Armchairs with turned members, a relatively cheap form of seat, could be seen in many highly respectable houses; they were likewise softened with squabs and sometimes even with fixed upholstery (Pl.152). However, in smart surroundings it was the comfortable *fauteuil* which reigned supreme. In its 'Louis Quinze' form, with its curvaceous and accommodating shape, and well-rounded padding on its seat, back and arms, it was one of the most satisfactory forms of seat-furniture ever devised, pleasing both the eye and the human frame (Pl.119). The 'French Chairs' for which designs appeared in English furniture pattern-books in the 1750s and 1760s were attempts to imitate the form, although the English versions never quite match the originals for elegance. The French form was imitated in every other European country as well, but again never entirely satisfactorily. When the squared forms and straight legs were introduced under the influence of Neo-Classicism, the magic evaporated; the stuffing was then also squared and the whole was immediately less accommodating, and seemed less comfortable. Chairs with straight legs had come in already in the late 1750s and were common by 1770, but it is noteworthy that Louis xv (d. 1774) never acquired a straight-legged chair for use in his personal apartments during his lifetime, and chairs of Rococo form and merely with Classical ornament were still being turned out as late as the 1780s.[75]

Classicism apart, many English mid-century chairs, including comfortable armchairs, had squared straight legs often braced with stretchers simply because this was a sturdy conformation, an instance of the practical character of English furniture that was coming to be so widely admired on the Continent – although not greatly in France. The squared legs went with squared backs (at most with a bowed top edge) and arms and supports of square section, so the stuffing of seat and back had of necessity to be squared as well (Pl.166). Thus the shape came to be entirely different from the contemporary standard French form which had domed stuffing with rounded edges (Pl.165). In order that the stuffing should maintain its squared shape, English upholsterers had perforce to develop sturdy edges, which were contrived by compacting the stuffing with lines of stitching that retained the shape. This was all hidden by the canvas cover and the superimposed top cover; but the English also needed to locate and retain in position the padding of their thinner backs and seats (much thinner than the domed forms on French chairs), so they secured the stuffing with bold stitching looped over 'tufts' (see p. 58). The tufts went through the top-covers

as well and were therefore disposed with care (see Pl.166). They broke up rather plain surfaces, producing a more lively effect. This important detail is usually omitted when chairs of the period are being re-upholstered today. The French did not adopt tufting before 1770, it seems, except for squabs and mattresses which, like English chair-backs and -seats, were squared and of equal thickness all over.

Especially comfortable chairs had fat cushions filled with down (Pls.119, 139 and 173), but considerable comfort was achieved with horsehair, tow and other materials. Springs were not a normal feature of comfortable seat-furniture until the 1840s (see p. 155), but pioneering attempts do seem to have been made using metal springs of some sort in the third quarter of the century. In Berlin the 'English Chair-maker' Funke (the term only meant that he made chairs in an English style) was reported in a local newspaper of 7 October 1769 to have made 'a pearl-coloured stuffed sofa [*Kanapee*] with carving, springs and gilding'; and in 1772 a bill for a chair of some sort includes an item for springs.[76] Louis xv's daughter Mme Victoire also seems to have had a sprung chair of some kind (it was described as a *bergère à ressorts*) which she obviously loved dearly. When her sister Mme Louise decided to retire to a convent in 1770, Mme Victoire was implored by her friend Mlle Campan not to follow suit: 'Have no fear, my child,' said the great lady as she lay stretched out in her beloved chair, 'I would never have Louise's courage. I love life's comforts too much. Without this chair here, I'd be lost [*Voici un fauteuil qui me perd*].'

Bimont, who published a most informative manual for upholsterers in 1770, states that gilt nails in rows, which form a neat decoration to the edges of upholstery (though the actual fixture of the covering is achieved with tacks which have to be disguised either by the gilt nails or with braid), should be positioned with a small gap between each head, a hole for the nails being made with an awl before they are finally hammered into place. On English and American chairs the nailing sometimes forms decorative patterns and may even serve to protect corners (Pl.166).

Some bills for furniture at Temple Newsam House, Leeds, provide information on several points.[27] There is mention of 'crimson silk lace to trim' some chairs in 1735, and to some damask chairs having a 'cord soed round' as trimming. There were also some protective 'scarves' for the backs – primitive antimacassars. Something of the kind is to be seen on Madame Geoffrin's chair shown in Pl.173. Some of the Temple Newsam chairs had their outside backs covered with harateen, a worsted material, watered and with a stamped vermicular pattern as well. This would have been less expensive than the material on the front which was visible; for chairs still normally stood with their backs to the wall. 'When a person comes into his chamber, and finds the chairs all standing in the middle of the room, he is angry with his servant, and rather than see them continue in that disorder, perhaps takes the trouble himself to set them all in their places with their backs to the wall. The whole propriety of this new situation arises from its superior conveniency in leaving the floor free and disengaged.'[78] The practice in France was the same, but the French quite often did not even bother to cover the outside backs of their chairs, leaving a neat, usually checked, canvas showing – when there was a chance to see it at all.

Chairs with expensive covers now almost invariably had separate protective loose covers of checked or striped linen material. These could be quite decorative, but were of course removed when there was company. However, quite a few English people allowed themselves to be portrayed sitting in chairs that were still fitted with their loose covers (Pl.196). Rather grander loose covers of taffeta, embroidered linen or some other light material were sometimes fitted to chairs in summer, especially on the Continent. Such covers might have fringes. Otherwise smart chairs in France and England were never fringed during the period under review, though in Italy and in some parts of America the Baroque tradition of fringing lived on, it seems (Pl.155). On really expensive French chairs the exchanging of summer and winter coverings was facilitated by having detachable inner frames to seat and back, and detachable arm-pads. The top cover could then be removed and the replacement nailed on in its place, after which the re-covered frame was slipped back into position. Blondel describes such features in his *Architecture françoise* of 1752, as if they were rather new ideas.

The term 'four-poster' is modern and is misleading because posted beds rarely had four posts; there were usually two posts at the foot end and a tall headboard which rose to support the head end of the tester. Whatever its correct name, however, this form of bed remained popular. Elaborately decorated, it was the form used for ceremonial beds (Pls.169 and 171) while, at the other end of the social scale, it was used by relatively humble people, the hangings then being of an inexpensive material on a simple framework. In France a bed of this shape was sometimes termed '*à la duchesse*'. The variant with a flying tester was said to be '*à l'impériale*', and indeed beds of this form were often very splendid (Pl.172). The difference in shape already existing at the end of the seventeenth century between French and English beds (see p. 58) still existed eighty years later – the French favouring a squared shape with what one might describe as 'two-dimensional' valances (Pl.161), while the English liked bold cornices above, either architectural in character or pierced with Rococo scrollwork. To counterbalance the projecting corners of these cornices, the valances below were likewise made to project at 45 degrees at the corners. (Pl.143 shows a Dutch version of the standard English grand bed of about 1740, but the nearest corner is badly drawn.) Thus what one saw of an English tester was a bold cornice with balancing valance below, whereas the French form presented a flat valance which, however, often had top and bottom edges of fancy outline.

Less formal but often still very splendid was the form that stood sideways against the wall and therefore had to have two head ends (*chevets*). The testers of such beds usually comprised some form of dome (Pl.217). Bimont (1770) called this form '*lit à la romaine*'; a variant was known as '*lit à la turque*' while a particularly fashionable version was the '*lit à la polonaise*'. This last had a small dome supported by iron rods curving up from the corners of the *chevets* to the dome. These S-shaped rods were hidden by the hangings. A domed tester (or rather, half of such a component) was sometimes fixed to the wall above the bed instead of being supported by posts or irons (Pl.217). There were various other forms in use, including the 'slope bed' or *lit en tombeau* which, if it had two sloping ends, might be called a *lit à double tombeau*.

Illustrations such as Pls.127, 136, 171 and 172 show that bed-hangings could be of enormous complexity, with elaborate valances, the curtains often drawing on rods but now frequently drawing up intricately 'in drapery' (Pl.169). The development of the upholsterer's art, especially in France, was very rapid after the middle of the century and was to prepare this craftsman for the *tours de force* that were to be required of him in the next century. This applied especially to drapery and the cut of curtains , but the skills involved with the stuffing and covering of chairs also advanced strikingly at this period.

According to Bimont (1770), looking-glasses should be hung vertically, rather than canted forward as had been the practice in the seventeenth century. As we have seen, great use was made of large plates of mirror-glass set into the panelling, especially in France (p. 99). Boffrand stressed that care should be taken when disposing such features in an interior, but the commonest positions were always above the fireplace and on the piers between windows. The built-in pier-glass was an accepted and important feature of elegant rooms all over Europe by the middle of the century. Beneath the glass was usually placed a pier-table designed *en suite*; an alternative was to have a commode in that position. When in November 1727 a Berlin newspaper referred to a 'so-called Parisian commode', it was necessary to explain that this new kind of furniture was a sort of '*bureau* [or rather] a table beneath the glass'.

When the looking-glass in Louis XV's study at Versailles had to be re-positioned because the panelling was being re-adjusted on account of some alterations that were being carried out, the commode (which was in this case a jewel-cabinet) was moved at the same time.[79] An English upholsterer pointed out in 1768, with reference to some fine commodes he was about to supply for the State Bedchamber at Hopetoun, outside Edinburgh, that 'These in grand appartments are more intended to furnish & adorn than for real use.'[80]

The pair of candle-stands which had originally accompanied a pier-table and its looking-glass had long since been discarded,[81] but the English retained the tall candle-stand, precarious as it was, for use in elegant rooms right through the eighteenth century, placing it in the corners of the room. The French, if they needed to support a candelabrum and it could not stand on a console-table or the like, introduced sturdy pedestals which were much more practical and safe.

No great advance took place in the field of lighting during the period under review. People seem to have used candles more freely, so there must have been generally more light after dark than hitherto, in houses of any consequence. In 1749 an oil-lamp '*à réverbère*' was invented in Paris; it presumably had a reflector that increased the amount of light. When there was no other light in a room, a candle could be dazzling, so small screens that clipped on to candlesticks were often used in studies and closets. There was also a style of twin-branched candlestick which had a lampshade no different from those used today, known as a '*garde-vue*' and made of paper or sheet metal. Many people liked to keep a night-light (a 'morter') burning so that the bedchamber was not entirely dark at night, and various devices were introduced to make such lights safe and simple. One which can hardly have been either was that invented in 1762 by a mechanic named Musy as an aid for the sick. He claimed that it warmed a bowl of soup; rang a bell to warn the owner that it was time to take another dose of medicine; produced a gentle light that would not tire the eyesight or disturb a sleeper; and had a screen on which the hours were projected, presumably by shadows from the candle.[82]

Lanterns, which had hitherto been seen only in halls and passages or on staircases, became much more elegant during this period and might now be seen in the very smartest surroundings (e.g. Pl.215).

### 119 ▽
## The return from the ball, France
### 1730s

This charming picture shows, among other things, how much light came from the fire after dark. The candles in the branches on the chimney-glass are not lit but two candlesticks have been brought in (as they always were; they did not normally remain standing in a room) by the servants, one of whom is helping her mistress remove her outer garments. Note the fire-tongs cradled in a metal hook set into the side of the fireplace. The *chenets* have sphinxes as fire-dogs and the billet-bars reach back to form supports for the logs. An occasional table has been pulled forward and the armchairs are scattered around, very much in use, but a sofa stands against the wall beyond the chimneypiece. The chairs are in the *Régence* style, and are early versions of those shown in Pls.140 and 160. Note their thick stuffing, the huge and very comfortable down cushion, and the way the outside back is not disguised (the chequered base-canvas of the back of the chair on the right at the back can just be seen). The palm-leaf framing of the chimney-glass suggests that the scene is taking place in a bedchamber, palm-leaves being emblematic of sleep. One can see a carved wall-panel on the left, then the window-curtains which are drawn, and a pier-glass in which the room is mirrored. (After a painting by Jean-François de Troy; engraved by Beauvarlet.)
*Bibliothèque Nationale, Cabinet des Estampes, Paris*

### 120 ▷
## A reception room at Wanstead House, England
### c.1730

Wanstead had been built for the banker Sir Richard Child (seen seated on the right) by Colen Campbell around 1720. It was in the Neo-Palladian style and the interior was remarkable for its splendour. It set a pattern for the decoration of grand English houses for several decades. This view, painted between 1729 and 1731, shows admirably the general style of the décor; rather similar features may be seen in Pl.108. Striking ornaments of this room were the chandeliers and the handsome carpet which was perhaps of needle-work: no large pile carpets were being woven in England at that time and the pattern does not seem to be in the Savonnerie style. The tea-table seems to be of silver. Note the divided window-curtains with their heads not hidden by pelmets. This picture is said to show the ballroom but it seems too small, and one would scarcely have taken tea in the ballroom. That room at Wanstead is known to have been large, created in the 1720s by joining two rooms together. (By William Hogarth.)
*Museum of Art, Philadelphia; The John H. McFadden Collection*

## 121
## The main rooms at Houghton, England
### 1735

Another of Colen Campbell's Neo-Palladian creations (see Pl.120); but the interior was largely decorated by William Kent. Building started in 1722; Kent was on the scene by 1727 and this section was first published in 1735. (From the 1760 edition of *The Plans, Elevations and Sections, Chimney-Pieces and Ceilings of Houghton in Norfolk; Built by the Rt. Honorable Sr. Robert Walpole ... Delineated by Isaac Ware and William Kent Esqrs.*)

*Victoria and Albert Museum, London*

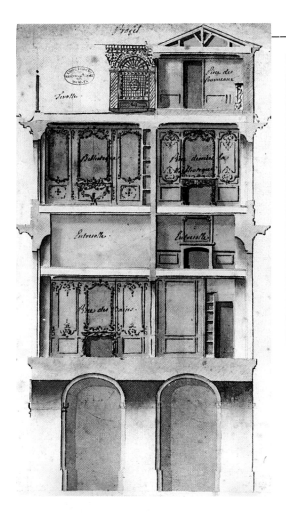

## Section through a house in Bayonne
### 1733

The house is organized in a conventional manner for the period, but the mural decoration is imbued with a lively plasticity that was exceptional in France. The house was in fact designed by Juste-Aurèle Meissonnier who originally came from Turin, and there is a strong dash of Italian Baroque in the ornaments, notably in the broken pediment over the chimneypiece of the main *salon* on the first floor. Meissonnier had a royal appointment as a draughtsman under Louis XIV and the rich provincial, le Sieur Brethous, who commissioned the artist to decorate his grand house in Bayonne, no doubt thought he was securing a scheme in the main line of Parisian fashion, whereas in fact he got something rather strange and unconventional. Meissonnier was proud of it, however, and had this section published along with the plans of the house. Note the arrangement against the walls of the still rather high-backed chairs.

*Victoria and Albert Museum, London*

123 △

## The Petits Appartements at Versailles
### 1732

This private suite created for Louis XV shows the small scale of these intimate and charming rooms. The bathroom and its antechamber with a bed are on the solid ground floor. A mezzanine (*entresol*) has been fitted in but it has to share a window with the room below, with the result that its share of the window is at floor-level. Above is a small library with panels of mirror-glass and a console table, and with a small room next door. On the roof is a room for a furnace which presumably heated the bath-water, while alongside is a terrace with trelliswork and aviaries. By 1742, at any rate, there was a lift (*chaise volante*) serving this apartment. This building lay between two small courtyards tucked away behind the main parts of the Palace. It was in small, intimate rooms like this that the Rococo style first made its appearance.

*Archives Nationales, Paris*

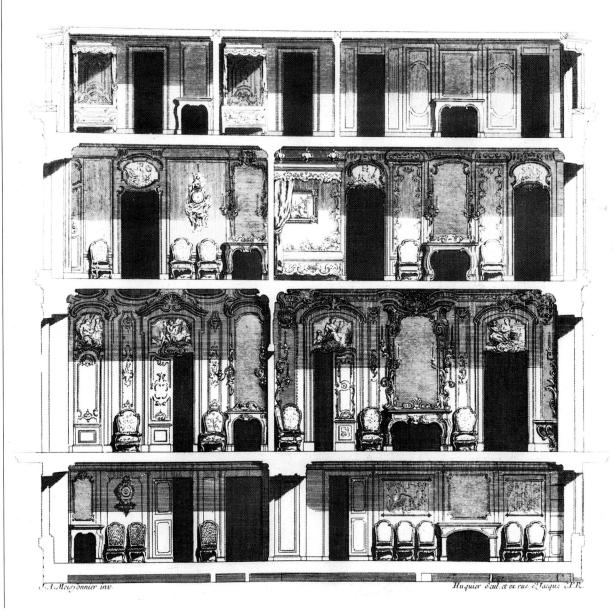

◁ 124
## Fixing the bow, France
### 1727(?)

The sofa on which the young couple is seated fits the carved and gilded wall-panelling precisely, as in the design reproduced in Pl.137. The sofa is covered in a brilliant sea-blue damask; one can see the seams joining the widths. The walls are painted and in the central panel is a very fine bronze-cased clock supported on a bracket. The effect of the grain in the wooden sections of the parquet, laid at 45 and 90 degrees to each other, shows clearly. (By Jean-François de Troy; dated either 1722 or 1727. This and the painting shown in Pl.125 were in a sale together in 1762 and are probably of the same date.)

*Nelson–Atkins Museum of Art, Kansas City, Missouri*

125 ▷
## At the dressing-table, France
### 1727(?)

The lady is being helped into her gown. She shows her bracelet to a seated admirer. The dressing-table is covered with flowered muslin with a flounced top which seems to be placed over a red or pink silk material. The toilet equipment is partly of silver and partly of red japanned work. In the background is a corner-cupboard with shelves above, on which stand a ewer and basin for washing the hands and perhaps also the face. Alongside is a panel with gilt carving and, to the right, a fixed panel of mirror-glass which reflects the opposite side of the room and shows a door with a *portière* and a painting over the door. On the 'pilaster' between the panel and the mirror is a bracket supporting an ornamental vase. A sofa covered with tapestry stands below. (By Jean-François de Troy.)

*Nelson–Atkins Museum of Art, Kansas City, Missouri*

Pl. LXI.

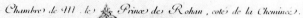
Chambre de M. le Prince de Rohan, coté de la Cheminée.

Pl. LXII.

Chambre de M. le Prince de Rohan, coté de l'alcove.

## 126, 127 (*opposite page*)
## The Prince de Rohan's bedchamber at the Hôtel de Soubise, Paris
### *c.*1736

The decorating of the magnificent town residence of the Prince after his marriage in 1732 was one of the chief undertakings in this line during the mid-1730s. The architect was Germain Boffrand who published these two views (and those shown in Pls.128 and 129) in a retrospective volume of his works which appeared in 1745. The second plate shows the front view of the state bed in its alcove which is hung with a tapestry by Boucher. Note how the pictures are suspended with cords and huge tassels. (From Boffrand's *Livre d'Architecture*, Paris, 1745.)

*Victoria and Albert Museum, London*

## 128, 129 (*this page*)
## The Princesse de Rohan's bedchamber at the Hôtel de Soubise, Paris
### *c.*1737

The Princess's apartment lay immediately above that of her husband (see Pls.126 and 127) and was decorated in a particularly sumptuous manner. Here we see her state bed, with its flying tester, standing behind a balustrade that is serpentine in plan. The suspension of the paintings is curious. The well-mannered, controlled character of this superb example of Parisian Rococo is noteworthy. These two plates were engraved by Pierre Edmé Babel, who also engraved compositions by Meissonnier (see Pl.122) and himself went on to publish some fairly extreme expressions of the Rococo style. (From Boffrand's *Livre d'Architecture*, Paris, 1745.)

*Victoria and Albert Museum, London*

## Ceiling-designs, England
### 1740s

131, 132 ▷

Executed by Andien de Clermont who came to England about 1716, bringing with him a close knowledge of the style of arabesques or *singeries* practised at the turn of the century by artists such as Claude Audran, Gillot and Watteau. He must have been responsible for the designs of a whole range of tapestries woven in London (Soho) during the 1720s: but he continued to work in this style throughout the Rococo period, although he finally turned (without much enthusiasm, it would seem) to a Neo-Classical idiom. The first design has been dated 'about 1750' by one great authority, and both the present designs were probably composed during the 1740s when this style had long been out of fashion in Paris. The first design is for Lady Beauchamp-Proctor's dressing-room at Langley Park in Norfolk, a house designed by Matthew Brettingham. The other is for the drawing-room at the Earl of Baltimore's Woodcote Park in Surrey, the architect of which was Isaac Ware (see p. 91). The wall-panels were also painted by Clermont.

*Victoria and Albert Museum, London*

## Floor-patterns, England
### 1739

◁ 130

There are four patterns for key-frets, and a central pattern. Such designs were suitable for floors of parquetry or marble, or for borders in ceilings and on chimneypieces, and also for many other forms of ornament. The manual from which this comes contains six such plates. There are patterns for paving, borders, balustrades, chimneypieces, etc. (From Batty Langley, *The City and Country Builder's and Workman's Treasury of Designs ... the ornamental parts of architecture*, London, 1740 (most plates dated 1739); revised edition, 1750.)

*Victoria and Albert Museum, London*

## A German design for a chimneypiece
### 1744

133 ▷

The overmantel decoration is in the style that would have been novel in Paris in the 1690s. The central panel might be of mirror-glass or, more likely, filled with a painting. Note the fire-back and fire-dogs. The details show tiled roofing and various forms of balustrade, since this is a plate from a dictionary of architectural terms. (From Johann Friedrich Penther, *Lexicon Architectonicum*, Augsburg, 1744, which has a text in both German and Italian. Did the work have an influence on Italian architecture? It seems improbable.)

*Victoria and Albert Museum, London*

## 134 ▷
### English designs for chimneypieces
#### 1739

Although characteristically English of the period, these forms are based on Italian antecedents of the late sixteenth and early seventeenth century, notably one in the Palazzo Farnese of the 1560s, published by Vignola in Rome later in that century and in Paris by D'Aviler in 1691 (see p. 49; also in later editions). This is a clear reminder of how dependent English architecture and interior decoration could be on long outmoded Italian formulae during this, the Neo-Palladian phase. This page is one of several showing such designs. (From Batty Langley, *The City and Country Builder's and Workman's Treasury of Designs ... the ornamental parts of architecture*, London, first published in 1740 (plates mostly dated 1739); but this is from the 1750 edition which included some extra plates.)

*Victoria and Albert Museum, London*

## 135 ▷
### Chimneypiece in the
### Classical taste, London
#### 1754

From Isaac Ware's *A Complete Body of Architecture ... from original designs*. This illustration accompanies a chapter on drapery as applied to statues. Ware explains that 'Modern sculptors are fond of nudities; but in a chimney-piece they would be abominable'. He therefore asks that statues in 'the parlour of a polite gentleman' should be clothed with drapery in the manner so admirably achieved by 'the Greeks and Romans, which it would be glorious to imitate'. The caryatids shown here demonstrate on the one hand 'a caryatick figure perfectly clothed, and on the other, one according to the present licentiousness of sculpture, in great part naked ...'. (Drawn by Charles Grignion.)

*Victoria and Albert Museum, London*

## 136 ▽
## German design for a bed
### 1720s

This is one of the designs for 'newly invented and very curious French beds' that were published in Augsburg by the architect Johan Schübler about 1730 or perhaps slightly earlier. No beds like this had been seen in France, it would seem, for forty years and it is probable that Schübler derived much inspiration from the published designs of Daniel Marot (e.g. Pl.101), who was of course

French although he spent most of his active life in Holland. Schübler's designs were influential in Central and Northern Europe, so his engravings should be studied with care. This design shows the kind of decoration he considered suitable to go with such a bed, which is in a style poised ready to launch into the Rococo. Note the hangings, perhaps of appliqué work; the *portière*; the chair with its skirted seat-cover; the candle-stand; and the candlestick on the curving balustrade which follows the edge of the raised floor of the alcove, on which lies a carpet or mat. (From Johann Jacob

Schübler's Works '*zu innerer Ausziehrung Fürstlicher Palläste und anderer schöner Zimmer in vornehmen Häusern … Neu inventiert zehr curieusen Frantzösischen Betten*, Augsburg, n.d.; this work was published by the heirs of Jeremias Wolff, print-seller in Augsburg, who died in 1724; the engravings for the Works came out in series, probably over a period of some years, and were reissued many times.)
*Victoria and Albert Museum, London*

## 137 ▷
## One end of a country-house dining-room, France
### *c.*1738

This shows a *buffet* or sideboard of marble that was presumably white because the walls were white. The ornaments were gilded. The display of plate arranged on the buffet would blend with the picture above which shows costly vessels – but arranged in an asymmetrical composition that would have been unthinkable a decade earlier. However, the buffet was intended principally for setting out the dessert, according to the explanatory text. It is built into a niche or bay which has doors disguised in the panelling. Note that sofas are now thought suitable furniture for a dining-room, and also how they are designed to fit the panelling precisely. (From Jacques-François Blondel, *De la Distribution des Maisons de Plaisance et de la Décoration des Edifices en general*, Paris, 1738.)
*Victoria and Albert Museum, London*

## 138 ▷
## A bathroom and lavatory, France
### *c.*1738

From the same work as Pl.137. The twin baths with their enveloping canopies were furnished with hot and cold water, as a diagram in Blondel's treatise shows. The vases on brackets were purely decorative. On the left is the lavatory – the *lieu à soupape* or place with a valve; such rooms were also known as '*lieux à l'anglaise*', English places. A diagram made its mode of operation clear. One tap was for sluicing the bowl but, with the other hand, the user also had to lift a handle to open the valve that otherwise closed the drain-hole. There was a second tap which controlled an upward-directed jet which enabled the contraption also to serve as a bidet.
*Victoria and Albert Museum, London*

## DECORATION D'UNE SALLE A MANGER VÜE DU CÔTÉ DU BUFFET ET DONT LES ORNEMENS SONT DOREZ SUR UN FOND BLANC

1.er Volume Planche 85 partie 9.e

A . Table de marbre pour recevoir des desserts
B . Groupe d'enfans de bronze portantes des girandolles
C . Grand tableau coloré et posé entre des pilastres de menuiserie
D . Porte de dégagement pratiquée dans des portions circulaires

E . Grand trumeau de glace formant avant corps.
F . Sopha dont la forme est assujettie à la traverse d'en bas des glaces
G . Petit dessus de porte point ou camaïeu rehaussé d'or.
H . Partie de la corniche qui doit couronner cette pièce

## LIEUX A SOUPAPE VÛS DU CÔTÉ DU SIEGE.          DECORATION D'UNE SALLE DE BAIN VÜE DU CÔTÉ DES BAIGNOIRES.

A . Niche dans laquelle est pratiqué le Siege
B . Elevation du Siege dont l'on trouve le plan et la Coupe, planche 86, N.° 3.
D . D'acier revêtu de maroquin
E . Toilette sur laquelle sont ajustées les mains qui font agir la bonde et ajustoir
E . Glace en forme de panneau à dessein d'éclairer les gardrobes placées derriere
F . Panneaux de menuiserie servans de voleaux de porte a des armoires de la
     profondeur de la niche, pour serrer les ustanciles nécessaires a l'usage de cette pièce.

A . Elevation des baignoires
B . Niches dans lesquelles sont enclavées les baignoires
C . Imperiales enclavées dans les culs de four qui forment les niches
D . Rideaux qui vont et viennent sur des tringles tournantes et qui meublent le fond de ces niches
E . Rideaux attachés sur les extremités des niches, et qui se tirent lorsque l'on met les baignoires
     en usage
F* . Corniche en forme de vaussure pour racheter la hauteur des planchers.

### 139 ▷
# The reading from Molière, Paris
### c.1728

This famous painting is included here because it beautifully conveys some of the most delightful aspects of Parisian life indoors on the eve of the Rococo period. It is believed to show the drawing-room of a cultivated banker. The room is furnished in the very latest taste. The low easy chairs are in a new style, perfectly designed for genuine relaxation. Three are covered in silk damask matching that on the walls, but two are covered in a different material which may be tapestry-woven or of needlework. Maybe these two chairs have been brought in from the room next door. The silk on the walls is surrounded by a gilded fillet or moulding. Below stands a low, glazed bookcase with a handsome bronze clock standing on it. The carved door has a *portière*. In front is a painted screen set up to protect the company from draughts; the French call this a '*paravent*' (an anti-draught) to distinguish it from a fire-screen, '*écran*'. The screen is decorated with arabesques copied from a suite of engravings by Antoine Watteau that was published in 1728. The brocaded silk of the dress worn by the woman on the left can also be dated fairly narrowly. Such patterns were in fashion in the late 1720s. (By Jean-François de Troy.)

*By kind permission of the Dowager Marchioness of Cholmondeley*

### 140 ▷
# 'La Toilette', Paris
### 1742

This probably shows the corner of the woman's bedchamber. Her dressing-table is on the right. There is a scarf over the dressing-glass. The chairs (*fauteuils*) are of the ultra-comfortable form evolved in France during the second quarter of the century. They are covered with silk damask. Note the close-nailing. There is a nine-leaf screen faced with Chinese painted paper, a highly decorative object. The equipment of the fireplace is clearly shown. The cheval fire-screen has a shelf that folds away and articulated candle-arms. The occasional table in the corner is a much less grand affair than that shown in Pl.141. (By François Boucher.)

*Thyssen-Bornemisza Collection, Lugano, Switzerland*

## 141 ▷
# Coffee in the closet, Paris
### 1739

This well-known painting by François Boucher
shows a small room in a middle-class house. The
furnishings are tasteful but not luxurious. The
caned chairs will have been bought ready-made,
but the carved console table on the left was
presumably provided when the panelling was
installed, probably not long before this scene was
painted. The japanned tea-table is a fashionable
piece, the sort of thing one purchased from a
*marchand-mercier*, a dealer in elegant furnishing
accessories and trifles. The woodwork of the room
is japanned in sea-green and has gilded mouldings
and ornaments. The wall-hangings are of a textile
material, perhaps a woollen damask. In the glass is
reflected a door which has a divided *portière* with
rather larger rings than was normal at this period.
Note the dark colour of the glazing-bars of the
window.

*Musée du Louvre, Paris*

## Taking a bath, France
### 1740s

The bath is probably of copper. It stands on a marble floor. The walls, with their massive Rococo reliefs, are presumably of stucco. There seem to be long stools and a sofa against the wall, and there is a dressing-table standing out in the middle of the floor. It has a lace-trimmed *toilette* and a scarf over the dressing-glass. The curtains are divided. (Engraved by L. Surugue in 1744 after a painting by J.B. Pater.)

*Bibliothèque Nationale, Paris*

144 ▽

## Lying-in in somewhat grander style, Holland
### late 1730s(?)

The painter Cornelis Troost has used the same composition for this as for the painting shown in Pl.142, but the furnishings are much more expensive. The trimming of the bed is more elaborate, for example, and the chairs are rather smart. The chimneypiece is in the style promulgated by the ageing Daniel Marot during the second quarter of the century.

*Library of the Wellcome Institute for the History of Medicine, London*

142 △

## Lying-in, Holland
### 1737

The young mother sits up in bed sipping broth from a porringer. She has a reticule conveniently hooked on to the board forming the side of the bed. The hangings are of green worsted trimmed with red braid. The room is not very grand, but there is a highly decorative leather screen painted with a landscape. The window has only a single curtain; the lower section has a shutter which is closed to keep out the strong light. A characteristic Dutch wall-clock hangs beyond. Note the layette-basket and the wicker cradle with its cord which can be threaded through the holes to secure the baby. On the old-fashioned candle-stand is a small brazier or chafing-dish for warming the baby's feed. Another brazier will be in the wooden foot-warmer. The armchair is an up-to-date model of the traditional turned chair with a ladder back and rush seat. (By Cornelis Troost.)

*Museum Boymans-van Beuningen, Rotterdam*

## 145 ▽
## A French bourgeois bedchamber
### 1730s

Dining *à deux* in the bedchamber, with an occasional table placed by the fire. A wine-cooler stands on the floor. By Parisian standards the furnishings of this room are in the style that was fashionable about 1715 but, while a considerable measure of comfort pertains, nothing speaks of great luxury. The outside back of the simple chair is not covered. Note the glass set into the chimneypiece in the manner which had first been introduced back in the 1690s. The bed has a simple flying tester which must be supported from hooks in the ceiling. The head-cloth is gathered but otherwise unadorned; there is a decorated head-board below. A chair stands by the bed. On the left is a dressing-table with rather a smart stool. The floor is of parquet and the wall-hangings have a capping. (Engraving by P. Surugue after a painting by J. B. Pater said to date from 1735; published 1753.)

*Bibliothèque Nationale, Paris*

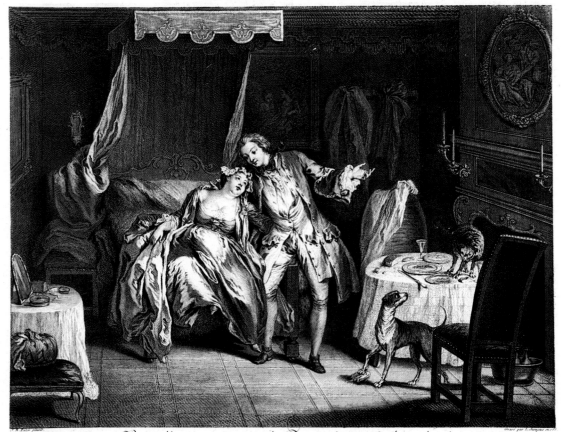

*Madame Bouvillon pour tenter le Destin le prie de luy chercher une puce*
Roman comique Tome 2 Chap XI

119

## 146
## Reception rooms of
## an English country house
### 1747

The height of the dado (at this period it would be waist-high) shows that this room was not as large as it seems in this picture, so the figures are rather too small. The interior is typical of elegant but not especially grand English houses built in the Neo-Palladian tradition at the point when it is yielding rather uncertainly to the Rococo. The overmantel has Rococo features but lacks the *brio* associated with the genuine article. It is copied from a design in de la Cour's *5th Book of Ornaments* which appeared in London in 1743. Note the busts on brackets, which were a favourite English Palladian motif, the array of Oriental porcelain on the mantel-shelf (it cannot be called a garniture in the sense that it was designed as a set), and the Turkey carpet. The chairs are covered with silk damask and have stylish, unbraced cabriole legs. Note the plain top of the tea-table, which was a practical piece of occasional furniture. Such houses were probably rather bare, but they cannot have been quite as bare as the artist would have us believe. He must have done a bit of editing. (*Mr and Mrs Richard Bull in their house at Ongar in Essex*, by Arthur Devis.)

*New York University, Institute of Fine Arts*

## 147 ▷
## An English country-house drawing-room
### 1741

A reticent form of décor like this must have been common in the houses of well-to-do English families, for many paintings show rather similar interiors where ostentation was obviously not admired. Yet there are several expensive items in the room, notably the bureau-bookcase with its glazed doors. The windows are fitted with elegant pull-up curtains that have tassels on the extremities of their shaped pelmets. Note the plain tea-table which has been brought in for the occasion, as has the kettle-stand with its pie-crust edge. On the table is a tea-chest containing tea-caddies, and a tea-set on a tray. The open-back chairs are typical of English seat-furniture of the 1730s; they have carved cabriole legs and drop-in upholstered seats. Remarkable is the large carpet which appears not to be Oriental. If so, it may have been made at Axminster. (*Sir Henry Gough and his family*, by William Verelst.)

*English private collection; photograph from the Victoria and Albert Museum, London*

## 148 ▷
## A middle-class bedchamber(?), Western Germany (perhaps Kassel)
### 1752

The room is panelled in a manner obviously inspired by French examples. The window has shutters but no curtains. The floor is of two sorts of wood. This is likely to be a bedchamber, as suggested by the presence of a dressing-table in the corner. On it stands a vase of flowers, a feature not often seen in eighteenth-century views of interiors. The table-cover (under the muslin *toilette*) and the chair-covers are *en suite*. The chairs are in the English style. Similar chairs are to be seen in the room beyond, which apparently has blue damask wall-hangings. The walls of the room beyond that have what is probably a *chinoiserie* wallpaper modelled on Indian chintz patterns. (By Johann Valentin Tischbein, Court Painter to the Landgrave Wilhelm of Hesse whose residence was at Kassel.)

*Kunstmuseum, Düsseldorf*

149 △
# Tea and cards, Leipzig
## 1744

Here elegant company is being entertained in a reception room, perhaps a *salon*. The proportions are misleading. The height of the door-handle shows that the figures have been drawn too small (as is often the case) and that the room was therefore not as large as it seems here. Note the pull-up curtains, the sconces and chandeliers (none of which hold any candles), and the stove in a niche in the background. The tables are apparently of the easily-removable variety with tilting tops. The caned chairs are examples of the ubiquitous 'englische Stühle', German versions of the characteristic English form of chair which enjoyed great favour all over Central Europe in the middle of the century. (Illustration by A. Vernarin from the German translation by Luise Gottsched of Alexander Pope's *Rape of the Lock*.)
*British Library, London*

151 ▷
## Drawing-office in the Royal Naval Dockyard, Copenhagen
### 1752

This shows Captain-Commander Diderik de Thurah, architect to the Danish Navy, in his drawing-office where he also made accurate models of the ships that were to be built in the dockyard outside. The work-bench with the lathe and other tools that he needed for this activity is on the right. Some uncompleted men-o'-war may be seen through the window. De Thurah, whose younger brother was Court Architect, was welcomed in court circles; he taught the King how to operate a lathe and he designed an elegant little lathe for the Queen. One of his ship-models is preserved in the Danish Royal Collection. He was eventually ennobled. It is perhaps not surprising, therefore, that his drawing-office should be rather grandly appointed with draperies (apparently fixed) at the window-heads, a fine pier-glass, smart chairs, stucco ornaments on the ceiling, and a floor decorated with elaborate parquetry. An iron stove is on the left. (Engraved by O.H. de Lode.)

*Royal Library, Copenhagen*

Langt mindre end faren belönningen er
Had fölger de troefastes Möye
Men Verden forsvinder; Had Verden har kier
Jeg derför fravender mit öye
Og blot eet nödvendigt vil tragte at faae
At ieg ved Dommedags komme
For Dommeren kand med ære bestaae
Som lönner af Naade de fromme.
Kiobenhavn A° 1752 D. de Thurah.

◁ 150
## An elegant bedchamber, Leipzig
### 1744

The fireplace has proportions not unlike that shown in Pl.133. The bed is of a French pattern (sideways on with a canopy fixed to the wall) which must have been highly fashionable at the time. There is a clock in the corner alongside window-curtains, the main set of which pulls up against simple disguised pulley-boards while the set of net curtains below is of the divided kind. A Bohemian(?) looking-glass hangs against the pier. In front is a dressing-table with the usual *toilette* and dressing-glass with scarf. A bird-cage stands on a tripod table. The object hanging on the fire-surround must be a hand-screen, for protecting the face when the fire is hot. (By A. Vernarin, from the same source as Pl.149.)

*British Library, London*

152 ▷
## A corner of a Parisian apartment
### 1746

Although said to be the *Salon* in Mme du Deffand's house, this would in fact seem to show a *chambre en niche*, a closet with a day-bed in a niche. Under the corner-shelves there is some other piece of corner-furniture which may be a washstand. The chair is far from grand, being of the simple turned type to which upholstery has been nailed. Under it lies a squab with a checked cover. On the mantel-shelf stand a pair of ordinary candlesticks, and a chamber-candlestick – all without candles, so this is a daytime scene. Mme du Deffand's literary circle was famous; among her friends was Horace Walpole. (Drawn by Charles-Nicolas Cochin, whose role in French cultural life was paramount at this period.)

*Bibliothèque Nationale, Paris*

### 153
# A dance in Northern Italy
*c.*1740

This scene is certainly set in Italy, probably in the north and quite possibly in Venice. The small mirror-backed sconces hanging from ribbons are typically North Italian, and bold cappings to the wall-hangings were much favoured in Italy during the late Baroque period. The chimneypiece is characteristic of the Veneto; note the painted chimney-board inserted in the opening, suggesting it is summertime. A row of porcelain bowls serves as a garniture. (Attributed to Jean Barbault, a French painter who spent many years in Italy and died in Rome in 1766.)

*Swiss private collection; photograph from Aeschimann, Geneva, through Galerie Pardo, Paris*

◁ 154

## A dining-room in the Veneto
*c*.1750

While people might dine in any of the larger rooms in the house, one room (often called the *saletta* in Italy) was habitually used for dining. That this was such a room is indicated by the presence of a large open-shelved buffet and four tables that act as sideboards. The chairs are of a type that show English influence. The small sconces with mirror-backs are characteristically North Italian, as is the manner in which they are suspended with cords from hooks set just below the cornice. Note also the curious way the paintings are suspended. The cords of the pull-up curtains are clearly visible; there are tassels attached to the lower edges of the curtains at the points at which the cords are fitted (at the back of the curtains, running through rings). Note the carved cornices. The windows are old-fashioned with leaded lights opening inwards.
*Museo Correr, Venice*

◁ 155

## A collector's house in Rome
1744

An English *milord*'s residence in Rome, presumably a house or an apartment he has rented. All around stand and lie evidence of his intellectual and antiquarian tastes – maps, a drawing of St Peter's, a globe, urns, busts and reliefs. However, the interior is that of a Roman late Baroque palace with console tables, a huge pier-glass in the adjoining room (not fixed but tilted in the seventeenth-century manner), sets of chairs ranged against the wall, and fine marble floors. The walls are hung with material. A handsome pull-up curtain with carved cornice is on the left. On the right is a curious bookcase with caryatids that look Egyptian. The chairs are trimmed with metal lace and with fringe; the latter had gone out of fashion north of the Alps early in the century. (*William Drake of Shardeloes and his tutors*, by James Russell.)
*By kind permission of Captain F. Tyrwhitt-Drake*

### 156–161
# Parisian interiors
### 1760s

Six scenes from J.F. Marmontel's *Contes Moraux*, first published in Paris in 1765 (these are taken from a Dutch edition of 1779).
*Victoria and Albert Museum, London*

◁ 156
The shelves have a fringe nailed along their front edge. On top of the bookcases and scattered about are objects reflecting intellectual pursuits. The table is Classical in taste.

157 (*opposite, top left*)
The divided curtains seem to be lightweight, for excluding strong sunlight. Note the decorative vase on a bracket and the small panel of glass inset below an ornamental overmantel. On the floor is a carpet from the Savonnerie or some other French factory.

158 (*opposite, top right*)
Note the dining-chairs, the arrangement of the candlesticks, and the carpet under the table.

159 (*opposite, below left*)
The light in this scene comes from the fire. Note how the occasional table has been moved to where it is required. A pug dog sits on its cushion.

160 (*opposite, centre*)
The bed is of the domed kind, and is perhaps a *lit à la polonaise*. Its inside valance is visible. A chair seems to serve the purpose of bedside table, but what may actually be a 'night-table' has been moved away from the bed. On it stands a covered bowl, perhaps of broth.

161 (*opposite, below right*)
The more conventional form of bed current in mid-century France, with a simple tester and rather shallow valances. There is a chair by the bed but an occasional table that could serve as a night-table is again present. Such tables would soon oust the chair from that position alongside the bed.

## An intellectual couple in a Library, France
### late 1760s

Several elements of the décor in this room are Classical, although the chairs and the writing-table are still in the Rococo taste. Note particularly the scene of a Classical sacrifice (probably a painting) on the panel above the bookcase, which itself has Classical ornaments. The ink-stand is also in this Antique vein. Note the curtains fitted inside the glazed doors of the bookcase to protect the bindings from light. (Attributed to François Guérin, who exhibited a painting of a 'young man conversing with a young lady on scientific matters' at the Paris Salon of 1769.)

*National Trust; Waddesdon Manor*

◁ 163

## A French closet in Sweden
### *c.* 1760

The wife of Count Carl Gustaf Tessin, son of Nicodemus (see Pls.54 and 56), who had been Swedish Ambassador in Paris and was no less francophile than his father. His country house, Åkerö, built to Carl Hårleman's designs in the late 1750s, was planned on French principles and decorated in a French manner. The Countess' closet, shown here, has a Parisian-style desk, a French chair covered with Beauvais tapestry, and a Parisian wall-clock. The walls are hung with painted Chinese silk (what the French called *pékin*) and the fitted corner-cupboard is painted *en trompe l'oeil* with a pagod sitting on a red lacquer cabinet that is based on an engraving by Boucher, and with a putto peeping from behind a curtain after Coypel. The bureau-cabinet and tea-table may be English, however. The brilliantly coloured carpet is Turkish. The dining-room at Åkerö is famous for being decorated in an exceptionally early form of Neo-Classicism after drawings supplied by Le Lorrain. (By Olof Fridsberg.)

*National Museum, Stockholm*

## 164 ▷
# Mural decoration, France
### early 1750s

A French architect's proposal for a room which was to have rounded corners at one end. The Rococo forms are here beginning to stiffen, as the first reactions against the style make their mark. Panelling with similar features was installed at Mme de Pompadour's little Château de Bellevue. The panels of this room were to be decorated with 'feuilles de Chinois', which probably meant chinoiserie compositions. The triple-dragon supports of the console table beneath the inset panel of mirror-glass were no doubt intended to enhance the exotic character of the room, which may have been conceived as a 'Chinese closet' although there is nothing very Chinese about the rest of the decoration. Christopher Huet was a notable painter of chinoiseries at this period, and it is perhaps worth noting that he decorated a room with such subjects for Mme de Pompadour at another of her small châteaux, that at Champs-en-Brie, which was done over for her in the late 1740s. This drawing was in the collection of the Swedish Court Architect, Carl Johan Cronstedt. He could have acquired it in many ways, but one possibility is that he received it from Jean Erik Rehn, a designer in the royal service, who was in Paris in 1755–6, collecting important drawings to inspire his colleagues back in Stockholm.

*National Museum, Stockholm*

Chaise à la Reine

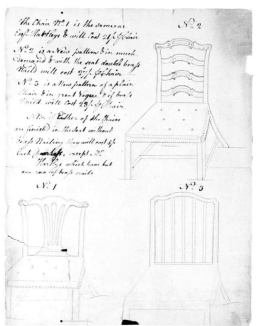

## ◁ 165, 166
# The French and English forms of seat-stuffing
### mid eighteenth century

The French stuffing (far left) was heaped to form a domed effect (here also on the back), the rounded forms blending well with the curves of the standard Rococo-period frames. The English mid-century chair (near left) had a rectilinear frame so the seat-stuffing was shaped to match – with squared edges. The stuffing on such English chairs was commonly secured with visible tufting which relieved the severe lines somewhat. Nailing could be ornamental but could also provide a measure of protection for the corners of the seat. Chair no. 2 was a 'New Pattern & in much demand' when the upholsterer sent these sketches to a client; no. 3 was also new and 'in great Vogue'.

*The Metropolitan Museum of Art, New York;*
*Harris Brisbane Dick Fund, 1933; and National*
*Trust, from the Dyrham Park Archives*

## 167
## Dining-room in an English country house
*c.1750*

A design by the architect James Paine for the dining-room at Felbrigg in Norfolk. The room, which survives, was executed closely after this drawing, although, as the inscription says, 'instead of the ornament over the centre Door there is pictures intended' and 'the Glass frame that is in the Right hand pier is to be executed' (i.e. of two proposals for the pier-glasses that on the right was selected). Both ends of the room were to be identical, so there are eight oval glasses set into stucco frames while there are family portraits in the rectangular frames. The delicate stucco-work (there is also a very fine ceiling) was executed by the famous stuccoist Joseph Rose who arrived to supervise the work in April 1752. The basic structure of the decoration remains Neo-Palladian and Rose's genteel ornaments trail discreetly around the Classical forms. Note the busts on brackets, a favourite device with the English Palladians.

*National Trust; Felbrigg*

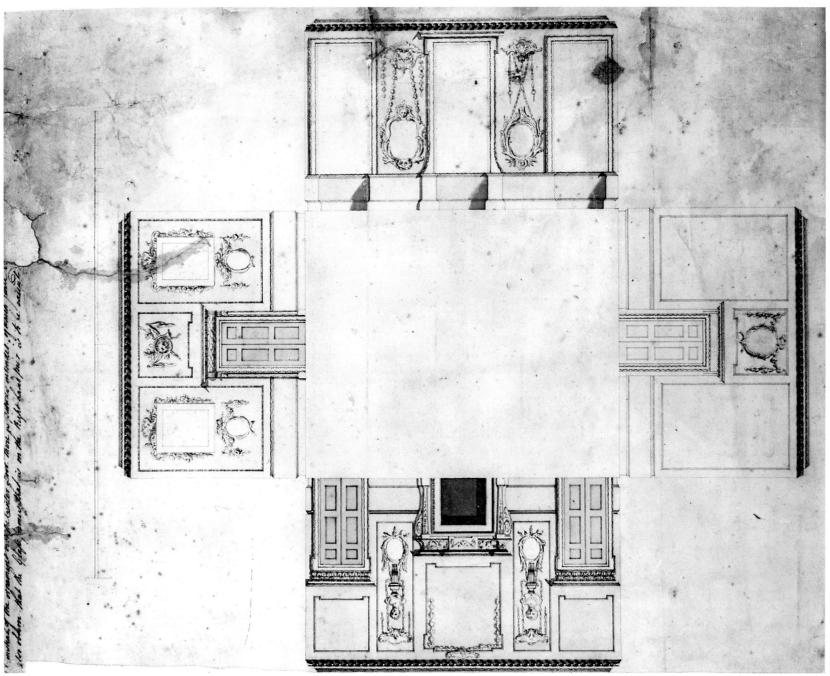

### 168 ▽
## Proposal for a drawing-room, England
### 1755–60

The disintegrating character of the Rococo elements in this composition may partly be due to the fact that the draughtsman, John Linnell, was a young man when he executed the drawing. However, this characteristic is also typical of much English decoration in the Rococo style (see p. 91). As it happens, Linnell went on to master the style with greater success than most of his countrymen. The chimneypiece has the proportions of the standard English Palladian form but is kitted out with Rococo ornaments in which a measure of asymmetry is apparent. The asymmetry may seem greater here than would have been the case when the scheme had been carried out (if it ever was),

when the pair to the sofa illustrated would have been placed on the right of the chimney-breast. Presumably a balancing and equally crazy confection would also have been above the other sofa, but it might have housed a barometer instead of a clock. The walls, which may have paper hangings, seem to be trimmed with an applied paper or papier mâché border of Rococo scrollwork. Linnell's father was a prominent London upholsterer with premises in Berkeley Square. The accuracy with which the son depicts the sofa shows that he had an intimate knowledge of the family's business, which he continued after his father's death. Note the rigidly cylindrical bolsters. Another drawing by Linnell is reproduced in Pl.169.

*Victoria and Albert Museum, London*

### 169 △
## English design for a grand bed
### *c.1760*

Drawn by the upholsterer John Linnell (see Pl.168) and perhaps associated with the work he carried out at Kedleston from 1759 and over many years. Several motifs may derive from designs by James 'Athenian' Stuart, who worked at Kedleston in 1757 and was replaced by Robert Adam in 1759. Although the spirit of this composition is that of the Rococo, several elements are Classical (the medallion, the baluster bases to the columnar bed-posts, the moulding of bay-leaves), and a certain stiffness pervades the whole conception. The bed-curtains were designed to be pulled up 'in drapery' in the same way as contemporary window-curtains.

*Victoria and Albert Museum, London*

V. A. M.

## 170
## A luxurious bedchamber, Paris
### *c.*1764

Painted on a Sèvres porcelain plaque, the scene shows a mother lying-in and receiving the congratulations of her friends on the arrival of the new baby. On the floor lie packages of *dragées*, the traditional French gift for the occasion. The little girl (with padded protection for the head) offers some to the parrakeet which surprisingly seems tempted to try one. The furniture in this room is all *en suite*, the woodwork being painted white while the upholstery is in a purple and white striped silk. Note the tie-backs for the bed-curtains. The lace-trimmed counterpane lies on the bed even though it is occupied; two huge pillows accompany the bolster. There is no carpet on the parquet floor, even by the bed. The chimney-glass has a frame carved to represent palm-fronds, an emblem of sleep. A sconce with two very contorted branches hangs alongside the glass; its pair would of course have been hanging on the other side. On the mantel-shelf has been placed a candlestick, which would seem superfluous; and what must be an artificial flower in a small, square vessel. A pair of bellows hangs at the side of the chimneypiece. An old label on the reverse explains that this plaque was presented in 1765 to Monsieur de Courteille, Director of the Sèvres porcelain factory. His daughter Mme de Rocheouart is the proud mother. (Painted by the leading Sèvres painter, Dodin.)
*Victoria and Albert Museum, London*

PLANS ET ELEVATIONS D'UNE CHAMBRE A COUCHER DE PARADE.

### 171 △
## The State Bed at the Palais Royal, Paris
### 1755–7

The focal point of the Duchesse d'Orléans' apartment decorated by Contant d'Ivry in the late 1750s. The Rococo style has now stiffened, being again on a tight rein. The architectural critic J.F. Blondel thought these rooms solved the problem of how to replace the excessive frivolity of the Rococo without returning to the oppressive heaviness of the style of Louis XIV. Here he says, a '*juste milieu entre ces deux excès*', a 'golden mean', has been achieved; and of this bedchamber he claimed (in 1762) that it is 'one of the best decorations of the kind which has been seen up till now in the interior of our suites of apartments'. (From J.F. Blondel, *Cours d'Architecture*, Paris, 1777. According to Blondel, this is a truer representation than that given in Diderot's *Encyclopédie* of 1762, where the relevant text was also by Blondel.)
*Victoria and Albert Museum, London*

### 172 (*above, right*)
## A French state bed
### 1760s

This was published in 1769 in the first volume of Roubo's *L'Art du Menuisier*, a lengthy treatise which came out between 1768 and 1775 on the craft of joinery and cabinetmaking. Roubo had attended classes at J.F. Blondel's school of architecture and was still a journeyman when this part of the book appeared, although he had become a master joiner before the work was completed. The precision with which this bed and its surroundings are depicted may be due to Roubo's training under Blondel, but it is probable that the bed actually existed and that Roubo had had something to do with its creation. It may be relevant that he was patronized by the Duc de Chaulnes. Perhaps this bed was set up in the bedchamber of the Duke's wife. With all those cherubs and floral garlands, it can hardly have been intended for a man! Anyway, a grand bedchamber in France by this time tended to be used by the wife as a state room, with all that the term implied (it is here called '*une chambre à coucher de parade*'); but probably with a reduction in the degree of pompous ceremonial so that this was now a reception room with a bed in it (still symbolizing high rank) rather than a bedchamber in which one received. The balustrade is shown in two forms for, even if the bed had actually been made, Roubo here wanted to provide as many designs as possible, and in this way he could offer two formulae for balustrades while he was about it. Note that tapestry hangings are still deemed suitable for a bedchamber at this period.
*Victoria and Albert Museum, London*

## 173 ▷
# Mme Geoffrin's bedchamber, Paris
### *c.*1770

This and Pl.174 show rooms occupied by this famous hostess. Her rather old-fashioned bed, possibly dating from the 1740s, stands in a sort of alcove that has actually been formed out of a separate room. A window beside the bed has been blanked off, and the embrasure contains bookshelves with a picture above. Curtains can be pulled across the opening. By the time this picture was made Mme Geoffrin was old and no doubt felt the cold – hence, presumably, all the curtains, and the multi-leaf screen. However, it is not clear how one could untie the upper set of tapes round the window-curtains when one wanted to draw them; maybe they were not intended ever to be drawn. Her comfortable chair is caned but has loose squabs and what looks like a 'scarf' – an early antimacassar. The bed not only has bed-curtains but is protected by a set of case-curtains running on a rod fitted outside the tester. (By Hubert Robert.)

*Musée de Valence; photograph by courtesy of Monsieur Moulin*

## 174 ▷
# The setting for Mme Geoffrin's famous salons, Paris
### *c.*1770

Wife of the manager and part-owner of the French Royal Glassworks at Saint-Gobain, Mme Geoffrin had set up already in the 1740s as hostess of a salon for writers, men of learning and artists. Distinguished foreigners also tended to drop in on these cosmopolitan gatherings, through which Mme Geoffrin exerted considerable influence on cultural life in the French capital. As far as interior decoration was concerned, however, her tastes were simple, as this and Pl.173 show. Most of the furnishings are in the Rococo style and probably date from the 1740s and 1750s, but two tables in the room stand out on account of their strong Classical forms. The frames round her pictures are also plain and rectilinear, quite unlike the typical frames of the Rococo period. Many of her pictures were by artists who habitually painted in a Neo-Classical manner; but she also greatly admired the work of Boucher, which epitomizes the spirit of High Rococo. Note the pull-up curtains and the rather spiky arrangement of flowers (perhaps dried) in the vases. (By Hubert Robert.)

*Musée du Louvre, Paris*

## 175 ▽
## A senior customs official's drawing-room in Elsinore, Denmark
### 1765

The calm simplicity of this room has much charm. The general character is not unlike that of Samuel Pepys's room, back in the late seventeenth century (Pl.92). It has very little in common with that of the smart London or Parisian rooms such as those shown in some of the preceeding illustrations. This is the room of a respectable man who was not too concerned with fashion. The writing-chair is a Danish version of an English mid-century model. It seems strange that he did not use it at his desk. He may have found it more comfortable when he sat by the stove, in preference to those rather stiff caned chairs, which presumably date from the first two decades of the century. The simple chest-of-drawers is from about 1730. The desk is formed of a trestle table with a case of pigeon-holes standing on it. Captain Lütken seems to have valued his books, if that is what the glass-fronted cupboard contains. Between the windows is a small Baroque

looking-glass. The curtains are simple and functional; one can see the hooks on to which the rods drop. Note the curious arrangement of the maps and the pictures (mostly of ships in frames of gilt lead, as a document reveals). The cast-iron stove is of a model first made in 1698, as the date on its side proclaims, but such stoves were made from the same moulds over a long period afterwards. It stands on four stone quarries. Note the bare floor. There is no dado, but a deep skirting runs round the room except behind the stove. The candle on the desk has a green shade clipped on to it. Apparently this room cannot have been arranged thus before 1752. (Drawn by Captain Lütken himself.)

*Danish private collection; photograph from the National Museum, Copenhagen*

◁▽ 176, 177

# A Milord's room in Naples

### c.1770

Two views of one of the rooms rented by Lord Fortrose while staying in Naples on the Grand Tour. The man playing the violin on the left is Sir William Hamilton, British Ambassador at Naples from 1764 until 1800, during which time he joined in numerous antiquarian enterprises including the excavations at Herculaneum and Pompeii. The basic décor of the rooms is couched in a late version of the Rococo style, the decoration of the walls being executed entirely with paintwork. The opening of the fireplace is filled with a chimney-board painted *en suite* with the décor of the room. Above is a rather narrow overmantel-glass, which must be a local product, in common with the various tables and the chest-of-drawers. Some of the furniture, however, must have been brought from England, notably the mahogany bureau and the set of open-backed chairs. Note the small Rococo brackets supporting spear-heads and figurines. It is suggested that the superimposed over-door paintings are by David Allan who did much work for Sir William.

*Jocelyn Fielding Fine Art Ltd*

# 1770-1820

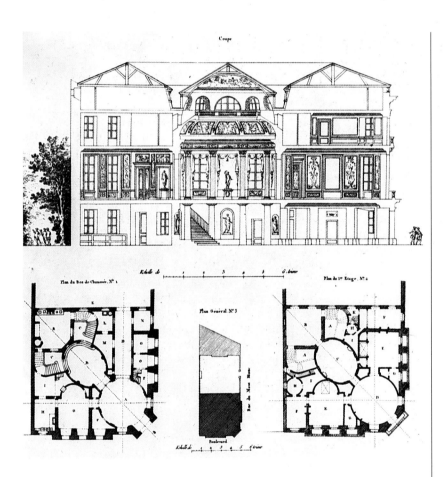

**178] AN EXCELLENT EXAMPLE OF INGENIOUS FRENCH PLANNING: THE MAISON MONTMORENCY, PARIS 1772**

In this 'charming *maison de boulevard* where there are new ideas', C.N. Ledoux had to cope with a corner site and laid his plan with a diagonal axis as indicated in this plate, which was published in 1802 by Krafft and Ransonette in their book on 'the most beautiful houses built in Paris and its surroundings' – i.e. in recent years. On the left is the ground floor with the entrance, vestibule and staircase (A, B and C). The principal floor is on the right. The stairs lead to an antechamber (B) that opened into an oval dining-room (C), with a circular '*salon de compagnie*' or drawing-room beyond. There is a bedchamber (E) to each side of this axial sequence; each has a closet, a dressing-room, a *garderobe* leading to a back-stairs and a '*lieu à l'anglaise*' or 'loo' (F, G. H and I).

*Victoria and Albert Museum, London*

CLASSICISM in one form or another was the dominant style during these fifty years. By 1770 the Rococo style had more or less been driven from the fashionable interior in France and England, and was not to be found in the better sort of house anywhere in the Western world by 1780. In that year appeared Le Camus de Mézieres' important treatise *Le Génie de l'Architecture*. This Parisian architect refers with evident satisfaction to the current good taste, so different from that which had admired 'the mass of vague, baroque ornaments which one cannot describe but which we call chicory; let us avoid all such gothic extravagances'. Critics of the Rococo had used the term 'chicory' from the outset, back in the 1750s, in describing its fantastic forms, and both 'baroque' and 'gothic' here simply mean bizarre; at this point Neo-Gothic was hardly a style to reckon with – certainly not in France. It is interesting in passing to note that he blames Nicolas Pineau for introducing the Rococo taste, but was sufficiently discerning to add that 'This artist had however plenty of talent and great facility as a draughtsman' (see p. 89); it was just a pity that he had taken up this 'singular genre that rested entirely on caprice'.

Le Camus speaks of the 'infinity of new buildings' which were then going up in the suburbs of the French capital, which 'seem to promise further delights and pleasures'. We are on the right track now, he is saying, with our Neo-Classical taste. Many of the houses he will have admired were to be published by Krafft and Ransonette in 1802 when they brought out their *Plans, Coups, Elévations des plus belles Maisons et Hôtels construits à Paris et dans les Environs*, a publication which also dwelt lovingly on the details of significant interiors. One such house which caused a sensation for the luxurious way it was appointed as well as its elegant exterior was that built for Mlle Guimard who was *première danseuse* at the Opéra (Pl.207).[1] Started in 1770, it was paid for by one of her many lovers and built to the designs of Claude Nicolas Ledoux. The same architect was responsible for the famous *Pavillon* erected shortly afterwards on the King's orders for the Comtesse du Barry at Louveciennes, just outside Paris. This jewel of a house was one of the first examples of fully integrated and unadulterated Neo-Classicism. The advanced taste of its decoration and furnishings impressed all who saw it. Towards the end of the 1770s, Ledoux built the Hôtel de Thélusson for a rich banker's widow. With its gigantic entrance-archway and its wonderful garden, it was 'one of the greatest attractions of Paris', according to one observer of the time, and it became necessary to issue admission tickets. Among the other houses noteworthy on account of their décor was that built for Mlle Dervieux by A.T. Brongiart in the late 1770s but which was extended for her a decade later by that excellent architect and designer, François Joseph Bélanger (Pl.234). Like Mlle Guimard, Mlle Dervieux was also a celebrated dancer with rich admirers. In the end, however, she married her architect! The house of Vigée-Lebrun, the well-known portrait painter,[2] was designed for her and her husband in the

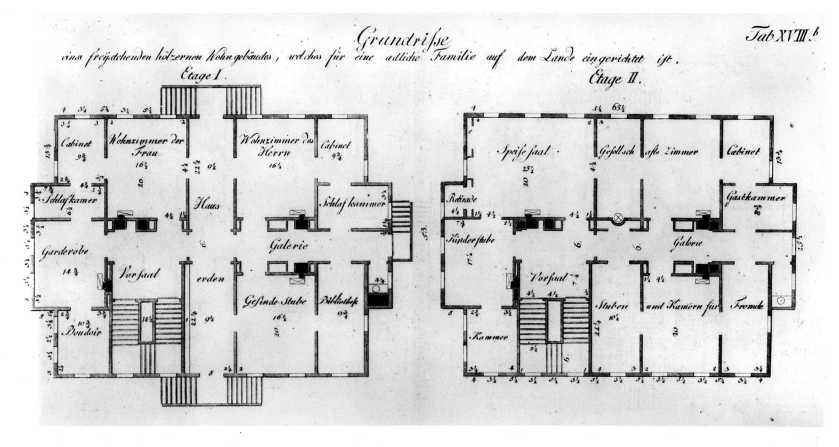

*Grundrisse*

*eines freijstehenden hölzernen Wohngebäudes, welches für eine adliche Familie auf dem Lande eingerichtet ist.*

Etage I.          Tab XVIII.b

Etage II.

mid-1780s by the architect J. A. Raymond; it comprised elegant rooms for the two of them, as well as a top-lit gallery above for the display of paintings with a smart sale-room alongside (he was a dealer in pictures). It was noteworthy also for the ingenious distribution of its rooms on an irregular plan.

The French excellence in 'distribution', which had been acknowledged for some time, in no way diminished towards the end of the century. Giacomo Quarenghi, the Bergamot architect who made such a successful career in Russia, said in 1785 that he had 'sought as far as possible to make myself familiar with the distribution of rooms in the houses of the French, a skill which still appears to be entirely theirs'. If one compares French plans of this period with those made in other countries, the subtlety of the former is frequently evident. Quite obviously Robert Adam found planning to such refinement a challenge which he did not feel he had quite met. When publishing his plans for Derby House (1779) he stated that they 'exhibit an attempt to arrange the apartments in the French style, which, as hath been observed in the first part of this work, is best calculated for the convenience and elegance of life'. In Volume I of his *Works* (1773–8) he had indeed admitted that 'A proper arrangement . . . of apartments [is a branch of] architecture in which the French have excelled all other nations: these have united magnificence with utility in the hotels of their nobility, and have rendered them objects of universal admiration.'[3] Ledoux's plan of the Maison Montmorency, with its diagonal axis, is an excellent example of the brilliant handling of such problems (Pl.178).

Although Rome remained the principal source of inspiration for those with inclinations towards a Classical idiom, it now became increasingly common for architects (and many of their patrons) to visit Paris to see what was new. While

**179] GERMAN PLAN FOR A SMALL FREE-STANDING WOODEN HOUSE IN THE COUNTRY FOR AN ARISTOCRATIC FAMILY**   1794

Entering from the outside steps at the bottom, one could turn left to the antechamber containing the only staircase in the house. On this side lay the wife's drawing-room (*Wohnzimmer der Frau*), closet, minute bedchamber, *garderobe*, and a boudoir. On the other side lay the husband's rooms: a drawing-room, closet, bedchamber and (across the passage) library (*Bibliothek*). The big room next door is presumably a family dining-room. Upstairs was a grander dining-room which must have been awkward to use, a nursery (*Kinderstube*) and a large number of rooms for guests. Although it is not quite fair to compare this proposal with contemporary French schemes, one cannot claim that the distribution of this house was very convenient. (From Friedrich Schmidt's *Der Bürgerliche Baumeister*, II, Gotha, 1794.)
*Victoria and Albert Museum, London*

there they could buy copies of the latest books of designs. Previous generations had been able to do the same, but now the choice was wider. Jacques-François Blondel's *Cours d'Architecture* (see p. 89) became available in the 1770s, the last two volumes having been completed by Pierre Patte after the master's death and published in 1777. The last of the 900 plates of Jean-François Neufforge's *Recueil élémentaire d'Architecture* were brought out in 1772 and provided a wide selection of motifs for those interested in the new style. It is noteworthy that he had intended to state in the title that the designs were 'for interior decoration' (see p. 91, note 12). Jean-Charles Delafosse's engravings were appearing in batches right up to 1785 (Pl.112), and there were the engravings of Juste-

François Boucher (Pl.203) and Johann Thomas Hauer as well. Roubo's extensive work on joinery of the superior sort, *L'Art du Menuisier en meubles* (1772–5), provided detailed information on panelling, floors, balustrades, furniture and much else (Pl.172). And although not illustrated, Bimont's *Principes de l'Art du Tapissier* (1770) helped one to understand the mysteries of intricate upholstery; while J.F. Watin's handbook on gilding and decorative paintwork, the third edition of which appeared in 1776, was also useful to those who knew something about the matter already and especially if they could also study some high-class Parisian work of this sort.

Although the lead in the field of interior decoration had been held by the French since the 1620s now, after the middle of the eighteenth century, England began to exert an influence on other countries which increased rapidly as the century wore on. French interest in England concentrated primarily on her political ideas and on scientific discoveries; the French were not particularly impressed by English arrangements indoors, although they had admired English wallpapers until they had learned how to make better ones themselves (see p.99), and they appreciated English carpeting (see p.101).[4] The one important example of the French imitating the English in matters affecting interior decoration is that of making fine furniture of solid mahogany. The English had been doing this commonly since the 1740s, but it was only in the 1780s that the French adopted the timber for fashionable use to any great extent. But while otherwise English influence was hardly evident in France at this period, it was to be seen elsewhere, sometimes quite strikingly, particularly in those countries with which England had strong trading connections.

The British colonies in America were a captive market for English goods and ideas, and English influence there remained paramount even after the Revolution and the securing of independence. In America this influence was evident at all social levels, not only because the colonists for the most part turned automatically to England but also because nothing much else was on offer – at least, not until late in the century when American contacts with France increased. By this time a considerable number of people in America were rich and could afford expensive furnishings in the newest taste. Through pattern-books or with the assistance of English architects and builders, they could erect splendid houses in the English style, and they could deck them out with English furniture or excellent imitations.

In East Coast America English influence was consistent and universal. In other countries, it was essentially to a middle-class clientèle that English goods and patterns appealed, and it was therefore largely the less grand, more down-to-earth English offerings that interested them. Those who wanted to be grand or luxurious looked to France. England, on the other hand, was the home of sturdy common sense. An editorial in the *Journal des Luxus und der Moden*, which began to appear at Weimar in 1786, explained to its readers, for example, that 'English furniture is almost without exception solid and practical; French furniture is less solid, more contrived and more ostentatious'. The article added that 'England will undoubtedly maintain its position of dictating taste in this sphere for a long time to come.'[5] Such claims might have been made equally well about English pottery from Staffordshire, which was being exported in enormous quantities by the 1770s, and about much of the metalware coming from Birmingham and Sheffield. The Weimar journal was widely read in Central Europe and, through its commentaries and the patterns that it published, it helped to spread further a taste for the English style which also manifested itself in those other areas where English trade was significant – Scandinavia and the Iberian Peninsula. All these areas, however, had their own strong traditions in the field of building and, even if the aristocracy mostly looked to France for inspiration, the middle classes tended *not* to adopt English

models for their houses, inside or out. It was only English furnishings that caught their fancy.

The authors of several English publications providing information about English fashions in this realm put some of their text into French, not because they hoped to reach a French public but because French was the lingua franca, the language understood by all educated people everywhere. Thus Robert and James Adam's *Works in Architecture* (1773–9; Pls.185 and 208) had captions in French as well as English. George Richardson's *New Designs in Architecture* (1792; Pl.181) included a full French translation. Ince and Mayhew's *The Universal System of Household Furniture*, which brought its readers 'above 300 designs in the most elegant taste, both useful and ornamental' in the 1760s, had its title-page and part of its text in French as well. And Thomas Chippendale brought out a complete French edition of his influential *The Gentleman and Cabinet-Maker's Director* in 1762.

The British did apparently make one important contribution of more general application at this point, around 1770. It lay in their having adopted with greater enthusiasm than anyone else, and at an early date, the painted grotesque which became the basis for much wall-decoration all over Europe at the end of the century and well into the next. It comprised well-separated medallions and rectangular-framed panels in relief (or painted to seem so), arranged on a vertical axis surrounded by a symmetrical system of scrollwork and Classical motifs. Infinitely variable, the formula enabled decorators to cover almost any area, of whatever shape, with two-dimensional embellishment that carried with it a convincing Classical air. Although the formula was primarily used for walls, permutations of it could in fact be applied to virtually any object (Pls.208, 236 and 237).

Grotesque ornament had been popular in Europe on and off since the sixteenth century, and notably in the late seventeenth century in France. The French called all such ornament '*arabesques*', although it derived from the sort of thing one could see in the excavations of Antique Classical ruins (i.e. grottoes, hence *grottesci*) principally in Rome and nearby. One could go and see these ruins and excavations for oneself and make sketches of them, as Robert Adam did in the 1750s; but until illustrations of them became widely available, the best impression one could obtain of how such ornament looked when new was provided by Italian Renaissance interpretations. These may not have been archaeologically correct but they caught the spirit of the style and they were more or less complete; even if in disrepair they were at least not in ruins. And they were accessible. Moreover, artists and architects of the eighteenth century believed, probably correctly, that their sixteenth-century predecessors had had many more and better opportunities of studying Classical ruins, so many of which had been swept away in the intervening two centuries.

The French were not ignorant of the grotesque style, but English architects first took it up again and applied it widely. What is more, they published their designs in handsome volumes that gained respect even in France. First off the mark was William Chambers, who in 1759 brought out *A Treatise on the Decorative Part of Civil Architecture* which included illustrations of such ornaments. By the early 1760s Chambers was having important rooms decorated with grotesques (e.g. a room for Queen Charlotte at Buckingham House, and one at Moor Park which survives). However, much more extensive use was made of grotesque ornament by Robert Adam, and by the early 1770s there were quite a few rooms in Britain decorated in this manner, most of them the work of this energetic and ambitious Scottish architect. While Adam had taken great pains to study original Classical decoration he obviously derived much inspiration from Renaissance exercises in this vein like, for example, the Villa Madama, conceived by Raphael and decorated by Giovanni da Udine and

Giulio Romano in the early 1520s, which is decorated with a colourful network of grotesque embellishment that is echoed in schemes like that for Derby House (Pl.208). Adam published the latter and other schemes of decoration that he had already carried out in his *Works in Architecture* which began to appear in 1773, with five instalments being published as a volume in 1778 and a second coming out in 1779. This had a profound influence in England and America; it may also have had some in France.[6]

A few rooms in Paris were probably being decorated with *arabesques* in the late 1760s, and an important room in which the formula was employed was the salon at the Hôtel Grimod de la Reynière which was decorated by Charles-Louis Clérisseau in the early 1770s.[7] Clérisseau had been Adam's friend, guide and drawing-master in Rome in the 1750s, so he may well have been a prime mover in the revival of the grotesque or *arabesque* style both in France and in England.[8] In any case, by 1780 the style was well established in France as well as in Britain. Clérisseau's delight in *grottesche* is reflected in Pl.111.

A variant of the grotesque formula was the so-called 'Etruscan style' which tended to embody a different colour-combination, inspired by Greek vase-decoration, in which terracotta predominated (Pl.243). It was introduced by Adam for a dressing-room or closet at Derby House about 1775 and again at Osterley, also for a closet. In its initial form the style should be regarded as a playful variant of grotesque, suitable for the embellishment of a closet, and therefore somewhat different in character from the basic grotesque formula which was thought appropriate for grander and more formal rooms.

Although scholars had studied the Classical remains with great interest since the Middle Ages, it was almost impossible to obtain accurate information about them before the 1770s unless one had visited them oneself. But then books with plates providing accurate representations began to appear; among them were many which offered inspiration for painters of grotesque ornament. For example, two monographs on the Baths of Titus were published in 1776. Two years later came one on the Villa Negroni. The Baths of Constantine were the subject of yet another, in 1780, while the last of the eight volumes on the finds at Herculaneum, *Le Antichità de Ercolano*, only appeared in 1792 – the first having come out in 1757. All this gave yet further impetus to the new fashion for such decoration, and fresh delights in this revived idiom were soon to be seen in Paris. Bélanger's pavilion for Mlle Dervieux was one of the most original and charming (1789; Pl.234), and his brother-in-law Dugourc was responsible for other important exercises in this vein. The most brilliant painter of such decoration was Rousseau de la Rottière; his work may be studied in the closet made for Mme de Sérilly, now in the Victoria and Albert Museum. One of the chief sources of *Empire* mural decoration, as expressed by Percier and Fontaine (see below), is to be found in such Parisian schemes of the late 1780s. The Pompeian style of mural ornament, so beloved by the architects of the Greek Revival, was also merely a late variant of this formula.

Painted decoration had now become the chief vehicle for embellishing the interior. Simple paintwork has always been required and there had been periods before when painted ornament and painted effects had been of importance, but the Rococo had not been one of them. The period which saw Neo-Classicism in full flower was, on the other hand, one of those during which painters of such decoration enjoyed discriminating patronage.

Grotesque ornament was not the only form of painted decoration, although it was the most important. In the 1780s a fashion sprang up for painting rooms to look as if they were out of doors; a very early expression of this must have been that in Mlle Guimard's house of the early 1770s (Pl.207). By the 1790s it was widespread (see p. 150). Graining, marbling and similar effects simulated with cunning paintwork were also a striking feature of the period.

Apart from making interiors more colourful, these forms of mural decoration had the effect of suppressing interior architectural features. Walls now became flat with only shallow chair-rails, friezes etc. (Pls.224, 229 and 246). Chimney-pieces became insignificant surrounds to the aperture of the fireplace. The breaking-up of the surfaces was now largely contrived with paintwork – or with wallpaper which began to imitate a wide range of coverings, less expensive than the real thing (and a reminder that the French name for wallpaper is '*papier peint*'). Apart from repeating patterns, one could buy borders, complete pictorial schemes, and simulations of marbling, stucco-work, friezes and other architectural features.

French architects and decorators could be found working in every part of Europe at the end of the eighteenth century. Many were there by invitation and were acknowledged masters of their business. The influence that such people brought to bear on the foreigners with whom they worked could be of considerable importance; but nowhere did it have quite such a profound influence as in England, where the architect Henry Holland, working for the Prince of Wales (the future George IV), was building Carlton House, conceived in 1783 and largely finished by 1787. The interior of this important building was largely decorated by Frenchmen,[9] even if the architect and the managers of the firms involved were English. Indoors Carlton House, therefore, was an almost pure expression of Parisian taste of the 1780s. Sheraton illustrated its Chinese Drawing Room in his *Cabinet-Maker and Upholsterer's Drawing-Book* of 1793, and admitted that he had also based his conception of a main drawing-room on that at Carlton House (Pls.232 and 233). Sheraton's book was immensely influential, not only throughout the British Isles but also in America and on the Continent – notably in Scandinavia, Germany and Central Europe. A German edition which appeared in Leipzig in 1794 spread even further the anglicized form of the Parisian taste of the 1780s that Sheraton's work encapsulated.[10]

As a result of the turmoil caused by the French Revolution and the subsequent wars, very little building of relevance here was carried out in France in the 1790s and, except for its grand projects, this remained the case during the rule of Napoleon and until after his defeat in 1815. But indoors, matters were quite different. One of the great stylistic changes in interior decoration took place in the 1790s in Paris, the new style being what we now call '*Empire*', using the French term for the Imperial phase of Napoleon's career which in fact lasted only from 1804 to 1815. The *Empire* style, on the other hand, remained popular in many parts of Europe and America for much longer. Pattern-books with illustrations of ornament in this style were still being published in the 1840s, notably in Italy.[11]

The first important manifestation of this new style was the re-decoration carried out in 1798 at the house of the banker Récamier. This was supervised by the architect Louis-Martin Berthault, but the designs for the enterprise were supplied by the architect Charles Percier. The house was done up in a most luxurious manner, which was in itself a surprise in these years of upheaval, but it was the style displayed there which caused such a sensation. The bedchamber of Mme Récamier, especially, became one of the sights of Paris; the watercolour reproduced in Pl.241 is an example of the interest the decoration of this room aroused.

Charles Percier and his partner Pierre-François-Léonard Fontaine (who seems to have been more the business head in the partnership) created the new style, the primary effect of which was to be seen indoors. Indeed it is noteworthy that the important series of designs that they started to publish in 1801 and completed in 1812 has the title *Recueil de Décorations intérieures comprenant tout ce qui a rapport à l'ameublement*.[12] This book was of seminal importance, but its rather dry illustrations with no shading or indication of relief make it difficult for us to see quite why it generated such excitement (Pl.237). A glance at Pl.243, however, shows how such schemes looked in colour. Apart from the academically accurate illustrations in P.N. Beauvallet and Charles Normand's *Fragmens d'Ornemens dans le Style Antique* (1804–20; Pl.239) which supplemented Percier and Fontaine's publication,[13] a host of popularizations of the style soon appeared – notably Pierre de la Mésangère's *Meubles et Objets de Goût* (Pls.267 and 268), which was a journal first published in 1802 and surviving until 1835,[14] but including the seemingly influential upholstery designs by d'Hallevant and his successor Osmont (Pls.269, 270, 271). The style was further spread by fashion journals in Germany and England which reached a yet more widespread public.[15]

When Napoleon in 1800 asked who were the best architects in France, he was told that Percier and Fontaine 'have charming ideas', that what they do 'is extremely elegant', and that they have had much success in the field 'of interior decoration and in the design of furniture'.[16] Soon they were receiving 'royal' commissions from the Consul and later Emperor, and after 1802 they were working exclusively for him. Their style was transmitted by the Napoleonic court and the Imperial nobility (not to speak of ambassadors and allied monarchs) all over Europe – Milan, Rome, Florence, Naples, Amsterdam, Madrid, Kassel, Würzburg, Munich and elsewhere.

While the French were busy creating and developing the *Empire* style, the English and the Germans were embarking on what is called the Greek Revival, a late variant of the Neo-Classical vein embodying simple, chunky forms. It was a style that primarily affected the exterior, making an impression indoors chiefly in monumental buildings. In domestic settings the Grecian taste for the most part found expression in plainer surfaces, and a reduction or suppression of relief ornament. This in turn made architects more reliant on painted decoration to produce articulation in such interiors. The architect C.R. Cockerell observed in 1821 that 'We stick a slice of anc[ien]t Greek Temple to a Barn which is called breadth & simplicity, than which nothing can be more absurd ... I am sure that the grave & solemn arch[itectur]e of Temples were never adopted to Houses, but a much lighter style, as we may judge by the vases, the object being space & commodiousness'.[17] Carried indoors, this 'lighter style' led to a plain and chaste form of décor (Pl.246), echoing the sentiments of Robert Smirke, one of the best architects working in this style, who insisted that 'As the moral character is corrupted by luxury, so is art vitiated by the exuberance of its ornaments.... An excess of ornament is ... the symptom of a vulgar and degenerate taste.'[18] Advocates of Classical revival from the seventeenth century onwards had tended to harp on the moral virtues of the Classical Age that Classical forms were believed to evoke. This was never stronger than in post-Revolutionary Republican France (think of J.L. David's painting of the *Horatii* or that of Juliette Récamier, vestal white, reclining on her Grecian couch) which saw close parallels between itself and Republican Rome; but such sentiments were by no means confined to France at this period.

A wish to reform taste and impose a strong measure of Classical purity lay behind the publication in 1807 of *Household Furniture and Interior Decoration executed from designs by Thomas Hope*. Hope was a rich banker with a profound interest in Classical and Egyptian archaeology. He thought the current English taste in furnishing deplorable, and set about trying to improve it personally. He did so first by doing up to his own designs his London house in Duchess Street (*c.*1800–4) which he then readily allowed people to visit. Then, in his book, he published views and descriptions of the rooms along with illustrations of furnishings that he recommended as being acceptable. Hope's style owed much to Percier and Fontaine's *Recueil*, over half the plates of which had appeared by 1805; indeed he knew Percier personally and admired him greatly, as the foreword to *Household Furniture* makes clear. His furnishing schemes were somewhat arid and were by no means to win universal approval, but his detail designs and motifs were a potent source of inspiration for English and American designers. A more agreeable and imposing form of Regency Classicism was that shown in the plates to C.H. Tatham's *The Gallery at Castle Howard*, a monograph published in 1811. The plates both in Tatham's and in Hope's volumes were drawn by Henry Moses, a talented and knowledgeable draughtsman who seems to have done much to spread the most pleasing aspects of Grecian taste in its purest form. Hope's tastes subsequently veered away from the austere style of his published work; the schemes he devised for his country house in Surrey, The Deepdene, may actually be described as florid (Pls.278 and 279).

One of the rooms in Hope's London house, and therefore illustrated in *Household Furniture*, was in the Egyptian style, as were a number of the other subjects he included. He warned that this style should not be adopted lightly, it was not a frivolous idiom; but it must be admitted that it was usually handled in a rather playful manner by *Empire* and Regency designers, who seem to have regarded it as no more serious a style than chinoiserie (Pl.180).[19] It is often claimed that the style came into favour after Napoleon's invasion of Egypt in 1798 and the subsequent publication of Vivant Denon's *Voyage dans le Basse et la Haute Egypte* (1802). No doubt these events aroused further interest in

180] CHIMNEYPIECE IN THE EGYPTIAN TASTE, MILAN 1811

One of the more curious offerings in that small and evidently inexpensive book, Pietro Ruga's *Invenzioni diverse di mobili ed utensigli ... per usi comuni della vita* which appeared in Milan in 1811 and seems to have had a certain influence. This style enjoyed considerable popularity at this period, along with Chinese and 'frivolous' Gothic. *Victoria and Albert Museum, London*

Egyptian culture, but designers in Paris and various places in Italy had in fact flirted with Egyptian motifs since the 1780s at least.

As for the Chinese taste, this enjoyed one last great phase of fashionable enthusiasm in England which began in the mid-1780s and had exhausted itself by 1820, not to rise again to any great extent until the 1930s.[20] Sheraton's illustrating the Chinese Drawing Room at Carlton House (see p. 141 and Pl.232) helped greatly to spread the fashion in England, and this is probably sufficient to explain the style's popularity right through the Regency period for interiors in a light-hearted vein. The Prince of Wales's 'Marine Pavilion' at Brighton (rebuilt by John Nash in 1816), with which most people today are so familiar, was in fact a late expression of the style, where the scale has become somewhat overpowering and the handling a little on the heavy side. Something of the same character may be seen in the Chinese drawing-room shown in that curious book of *Original Designs ... drawn by and under the direction of G. Landi, architectural painter ...*, published in London in 1810 (Pl.254). The delicate, fairy-like make-believe of Rococo chinoiserie no longer seems to have been attainable; maybe it was not even thought desirable any longer.

While much Regency architecture and décor was light and graceful, there was a tendency to swagger, which was no doubt the result of England having finally been victorious over the French after more than a century of war and global competition. This less than attractive characteristic is, however, amply balanced by the arrogance that a great deal of French *Empire* art betrays! One can only be thankful that the two great nations have lived more or less in harmony ever since – for each still had much to offer the other.

How much England contributed to the early development of Neo-Classicism, back in the mid eighteenth century, is open to debate (see p. 92); but there can be no doubt that England was the cradle of one concept that emerged to run parallel to Classicism and was to affect fundamentally architecture, planning, and the way life was lived indoors. The concept in question was the Picturesque. At first this sprang from a romantic way of looking at landscape and then at buildings in landscapes: they had to look natural, not contrived. The Classical rectilinear, box-like house encompassing all the necessary rooms was no longer in favour. Asymmetry and irregular shapes came to be admired (Pl.182). John B. Papworth, in his *Rural Residences ... of 1818* refers to the 'bare and bald style ... in building' and of the 'vapid and monotonous character' which was the norm and was so different from 'elegantly varied and picturesque forms in harmony with the surrounding scenery'. He insists that with 'houses that have been built piecemeal, from the time of James I to the present day, the more unaccommodating the parts are to each other, the more suitable for the style proposed, and if the several rooms have no other connection but by stairs or passages, the design is then approaching to perfection'. In fact a rambling assemblage of buildings 'forming a picturesque whole ... pleases principally from the curious manner in which they are combined'. Edmund Bartell, the author of *Hints for Picturesque Improvements in Ornamental Cottages* (London 1804), likewise claimed that 'A cottage [which in this context meant a small-scale house in the country for middle-class habitation or upper-class retreat] or any other building, is rendered more picturesque where parts have been added at different times'. If buildings of this character were not to be found, moreover, the tendency was now to build them where they were needed. In that case excellent advice was to be found in works like Bartell's and in James Malton's *An Essay on Cottage Architecture* (London 1798) which had the telling sub-title 'Being an Attempt to Perpetuate on Principle that Peculiar Mode of Building which was originally the Effect of Chance ...'.

Asymmetry and irregularity seemed to be the hallmarks of Gothic, Tudor or Elizabethan buildings, and Picturesque ideals thus gave enormous impetus to

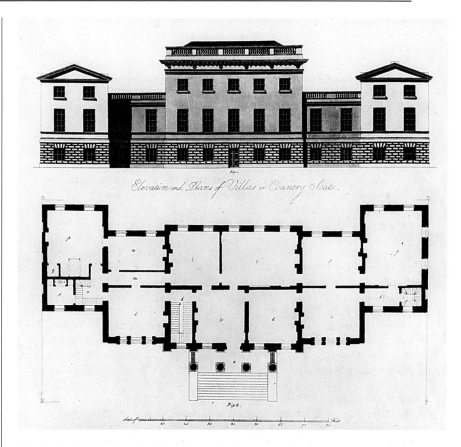

**181] PLAN OF AN ENGLISH COUNTRY VILLA OF THE CLASSICAL TYPE 1791**

Entirely regular in its conformations, such a building epitomizes the Classical tradition in architecture and should be contrasted with buildings designed on Picturesque lines like that shown in Pls.182–184. The façade is that of the garden front. Husband and wife share a bedchamber; the bed is outlined. Behind is a water-closet in a 'Powdering Room'. Outside this 'inner area', on either side of the passage, lie the lady's and the gentleman's two dressing-rooms (N & O). To one side of the Hall lies a staircase; facing are two doors, the left-hand leading to the family dining-room (Breakfasting Room: L), and the other to the main dining-room (C). To the right lie the 'First Drawing Room' and the 'Music Room or Best Drawing Room' (F & G). To the right of the Hall is a 'Common Parlour' and Library which one suspects were rather private. This is quite a convenient scheme, but displays no great subtlety. (From G. Richardson, *New Designs in Architecture ...*, London, 1792.)
*Victoria and Albert Museum, London*

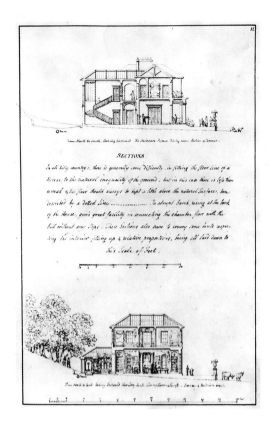

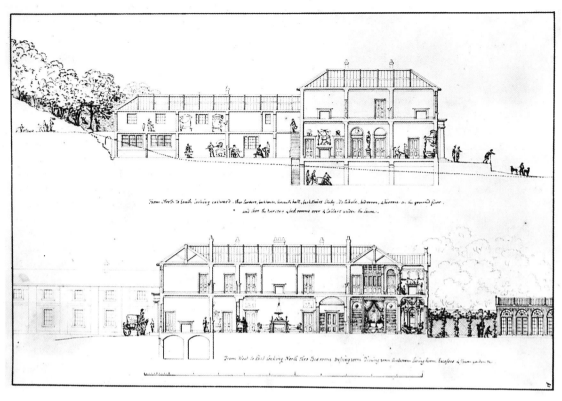

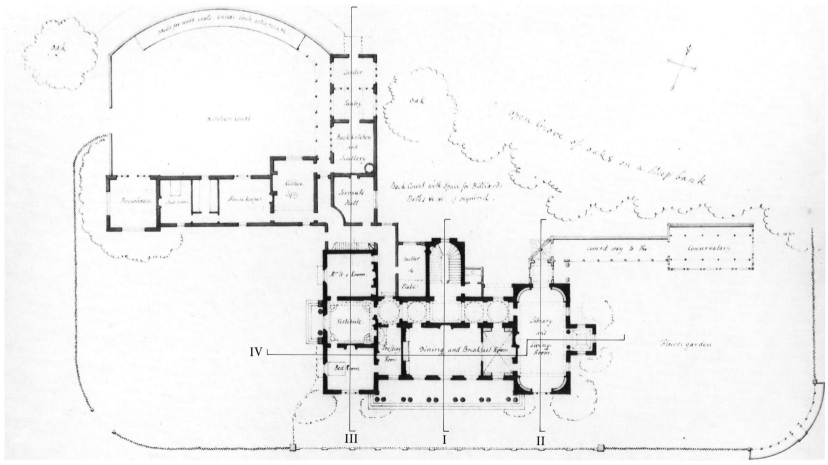

the interest in these styles. Neo-Gothic had already made its appearance, and there were many instances of building in variations of this style during the later decades of the eighteenth century in England and Scotland. In the 1790s Neo-Gothic began to spread across Europe in the wake of Romanticism (Pl.240), an important agency of its dissemination being J.G. Grohmann and F.G. Baumgärtner's *Ideen Magazin für Liebhaber von Gärten, Englischen Anlagen und für Besitzer von Landgütern* ('Ideas for lovers of gardens, [and] English garden-design and [for] the owners of country-houses'), which came out in Leipzig with texts in German and French and was obtainable through agents in St Petersburg, Moscow, Pest, Florence and Paris. The celebrated Berlin architect Carl Friedrich Schinkel, who was a great admirer of Gothic buildings as a young man although he became an arch-priest of the Greek Revival, contrasted them with those cast in a Classical mould. 'Antique architecture', he wrote in 1810, 'has its effects, scale and solidarity in its material masses, Gothic architecture affects us by its spirit.'[21] Unfortunately it was not always quite so sublime, for as Edward James Willson wrote in *Specimens of Gothic Architecture* (1823–5), 'we see ... city merchants inhabiting castles', while the 'ignorance of artificers' often produced buildings of 'an insipid character'. What is more, 'the refinements of modern interior demands' could not really be satisfied in such imitations of the Gothic.[22]

The Picturesque appealed to those whose approach to nature was romantic and whose view of history was idealized. It also appealed to the many people who, towards the end of the eighteenth century, felt the need for a more relaxed and informal way of life. This need was felt particularly strongly by the British, who increasingly abandoned irksome conventions except in the most formal circumstances. Since the upper classes in England had especially deep roots in the country, moreover, it was the manners principally associated with upper-class life in the country that were gradually adopted by polite society everywhere, even in the cities; for this was a period of great 'anglomania'. Thus the Englishman's riding-coat became standard wear for gentlemen all over Europe – hence *redingote*, the French for a man's coat. Englishmen, moreover, were not ashamed to be portrayed sitting on chairs still hidden by their inexpensive loose covers (Pl.196). And the English were the first to move fine furniture out from its habitual place against the wall, bringing it out round the fireplace and *then leaving it there* (Pls.186 and 188; see also p. 147). The French way of achieving a greater degree of informality lay rather in providing further privacy in the way of comfortable boudoirs and closets where people could be at their ease – French social talent resting, as it so largely does, on a wish to put other people at their ease. As Robert Adam remarked early in the 1770s, the

French are a 'social and conversible people'. For the French, relaxation was to be found in rooms that were pleasing and conducive to good conversation, rather than in side-stepping conventions.

## Planning and arrangement

In Robert Adam's commentary to the plans of Syon House, which he had remodelled in the early 1760s,[23] he explained the function of the various rooms and in so doing followed fairly closely the sequence Blondel had adopted in his discussion of distribution (see p. 93). Adam will certainly have been familiar with the great French theoretician's works, most probably with his *Cours d'Architecture* (1771–7). While the explanation Adam gives concerns Syon, what he has to say obviously had general application. He tells us that 'The hall ... is a spacious apartment, intended as a room of access where servants in livery attend'; it is finished in stucco. 'The anti-rooms on each side, are for the attendance of servants out of livery....' Next come the 'public and private eating-rooms', the second of which also has walls of stucco 'that they may not retain the smell of victuals.... Next to the great eating-room, lies a splendid with-drawing room, for the ladies, or *salle de compagnie*, as it is called in French'; it has a ceiling 'painted in compartments' which, as the room survives, we can see means in the Classical style based on his study of Roman Renaissance and Antique decoration. Next to this lies the Gallery, which is 'finished in a style to afford great variety and amusement; and is ... an admirable room for the reception of company after dinner, or for the ladies to retire to after it'.

There is a closet at each end, 'the one circular for [the display of] china, and the other square for miniatures.... The great circular saloon ... is a room of general rendezvous, and for public entertainments....' Of the private apartments he says less, for they comprise 'the Dutches's bed-chamber, an anti-room for the attendance of her maids, her toilet or dressing-room, her powdering-room, water-closet ...'. The Duke has a dressing-room, powdering-room, writing-room, and water-closet. Since no second bedchamber is mentioned the Duke and Duchess must have shared the same bed. In grand English houses married couples quite often had separate apartments at this period but shared a single bedchamber; in France each tended to have separate bedchambers as well.

Adam apologizes for dwelling at such length on this matter of how the rooms were distributed but explains that 'this is one of those branches of our art [i.e. architecture], which has not hitherto been treated of with any accuracy, or studied with any care; though of all others the most essential, both to the splendour and to the convenience of life'. In this last he was right; English architects did not make pronouncements about distribution until the nineteenth century, although they had always had to take it into consideration when planning a house and adjusting the plan to the wishes of the owner. Adam furthermore recognizes that 'the French style ... is best calculated for the convenience and elegance of life'.[24] Nevertheless he himself evidently found it difficult to reconcile the various requirements (see the caption to Pl.185).

Le Camus de Mézières, the Parisian author of *Le Génie de l'Architecture* of 1780, was in no doubt that his countrymen displayed enormous talent when it came to the cunning distribution of rooms. He devotes much of his book to the subject, but most of what he says merely builds on Blondel's recommendations. He does, however, confirm that the mistress of the house occupied the main apartment, with its bedchamber which serves mainly for state; she used the private bedchamber behind the scenes otherwise. What is noteworthy about Le Camus' work is that he gives a large amount of space to a discussion of the small rooms that are not for ceremony. This is yet another reflection of the longing for

182, 183, 184] SECTIONS THROUGH AN ENGLISH PICTURESQUE COUNTRY HOUSE 1812

These delightful sketches are from Humphrey Repton's 'Red Book' for a house at Sherringham in Norfolk. It will be seen that the plan has been conceived on Picturesque lines, irregular and with straggling wings (cf. Pl.181). Lines showing where the sections were taken have been added to the plan to make them readily intelligible. The first section shows the main staircase, hall, and a bedroom above. The second cuts through the principal living-rooms – the drawing-room with exit to the conservatory – and the two main bedchambers above. The third shows the kitchen and nursery wing, the owner's study and a ground-floor bedroom. The fourth (which runs the length of the house behind the main façade) shows the same bedroom, the dining-room, antechamber, drawing-room and a 'recess' or closet. Upstairs on the right is the boudoir leading off the main bedrooms.
*Royal Institute of British Architects, London, Drawings Collection*

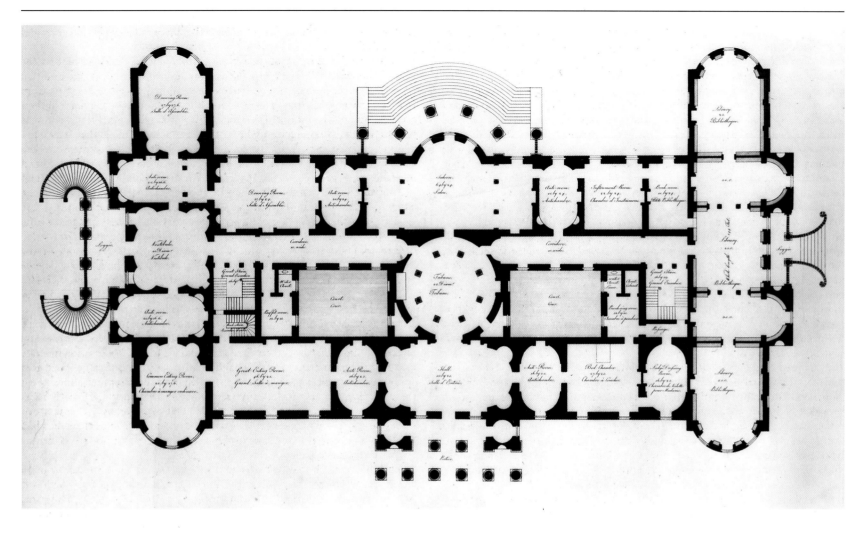

185] PROPOSED PLAN FOR THE PRINCIPAL FLOOR OF LORD
BUTE'S HOUSE AT LUTON, BEDFORDSHIRE   1771

This ground-plan by Robert Adam provides a chain of associated reception rooms
which make it possible to entertain a large number of guests who can circulate through
the rooms, eventually ending up where they started. The sequence starts from the
central Saloon and leads off to the left through an anteroom, the main Drawing Room
or *salle d'assemblée* (note that the terms are given in both English and French), a further
anteroom where there is a choice of going into a second Drawing Room in the
projecting bay or of continuing round a vestibule, another anteroom, and into the
Common Eating Room (presumably used normally by the family), the Great Dining
Room and on back through the hall and central Tribune. The corridor with the Great
Stairs provides a short-cut back to the Tribune as well. The rooms on the right are for
the family. The Library is extensive and it is hardly surprising that the ladies of the
next generation invaded this area which, when this plan was drawn, was still the
preserve of the gentlemen in the family. The lady of the house presumably occupied
the wing opposite the Library when it was not being used for receptions. Although
Adam had to fit all this into the conventional elongated formula for a mid-eighteenth-
century English country house, one can hardly claim that he has been especially subtle
about the planning. A Frenchman would probably say that the spaces were too
repetitious. (From R. and J. Adam, *The Works in Architecture*, Vol. 1, London, 1773.)
*Victoria and Albert Museum, London*

privacy and relaxation away from the cares of the world which characterizes the
period just prior to the Revolution.

He dwells especially on the boudoir, which he calls '*le séjour de la volupté*', a
place where there should be '*l'air de galanterie*'. The boudoir was always the
personal room of a woman. It could be done up in a most luxurious manner and,
at this period, the term still carried with it the implication that this was a setting
for dalliance and erotic pursuits, whether real or imagined. Mme de Genlis, an
old lady writing in 1818, after the restoration of the monarchy, about pre-
Revolutionary times, remarked on how surprising it was now to hear young
ladies 'calling their closet a boudoir, as this bizarre term was not formerly used
except by *courtisanes*'.[25] However, the stunning decoration that was to be seen
in the boudoirs of *demi-mondaines* in the pre-Revolutionary period had a
profound influence on fashion. Antoine Caillot went to see the charming house
of Mlle Dervieux in 1788 (i.e. before she built the extension shown in Pl.234),
and after having described the sumptuous décor of the boudoir, with its ceiling,
walls and floor completely faced with mirror-glass, and its cushions strewn
about ready for 'amorous combats', as he put it, went on to point out how 'Mlle
Dervieux and the other nymphs of the theatre set the tone of the boudoir
for young ladies of quality and bourgeois women of the better sort'.[26] So
one should probably pay attention to the decoration of the boudoirs of

*demi-mondaines*. Having once influenced the décor of boudoirs in more respectable houses, modified and less extreme versions of such new fashions were soon spreading to other rooms.

Le Camus did not share Mlle Dervieux's love of mirror-glass: 'Its multiplicity produces a sad and monotonous effect'. There ought, he says, always to be twice as much space between each panel of glass as the glass is wide. These intervals should be hung with rich materials, framed and each with a picture 'artistically hung with large tassels and cords of silk mixed with gold thread'. He mentions all this when discussing the decoration of an elegant boudoir and goes on to explain that in a niche should be a day-bed or *ottomane* (Pls.215 and 216), and in a deeper alcove should stand the bed which he suggests ought to be *à la polonaise* (see p.156 and Pl.217). The mouth of the alcove should be furnished with carefully arranged curtains to control the lighting. As for the colour of the furnishings, he says red is too fierce, yellow produces an unpleasant reflection, green can seem too sombre; he concludes that blue and white are really the only colours one can use in a boudoir. The carved woodwork throughout should be gilt with a white background; this makes it seem less heavy. Le Camus suggests the ceiling should be painted 'blue with clouds, perhaps with a couple of doves'. A carpet should be laid on the fine parquet floor in winter. He has much else to say, his section on the boudoir being one of the longest in the book. How different from the early years of the century, when it would have been the décor of the main bedchamber or the *salon* that received such attention.

A curious statement is made in the Weimar magazine, the *Journal des Luxus und der Moden* for September 1807: 'The latest form of artistic room-decoration demands that the bedchamber of a young and beautiful woman be no longer regarded as an unapproachable private place in the house, but that it should now rather be opened together with the rest of the [reception] rooms (with which it should belong) when there are social gatherings.' For this reason the bed had to be one of splendour, as in France, the article insists, and the accompanying illustration shows a bed which is evidently based on Parisian upholsterers' patterns of *lits à la polonaise*. Presumably the French fashion of receiving in the bedchamber was strange to many Germans, whose bedchambers therefore needed bringing up to standard! This was perhaps rather late in the day, for the French were about to make *their* bedchambers a good deal more private, on the English pattern.

A Danish book, *Fashions in Copenhagen for both Sexes, and the Furnishing of Rooms after the Fashion*, the second edition of which appeared in 1777,[27] has some interesting observations to make on décor. Speaking of bedchambers, it tells us that in Copenhagen 'night-tables are old fashioned'. This seems strange, for bedside tables, known as 'night-tables' in England and made in pairs, were a comparatively new invention (see Pl.160) and few English bedrooms had them before 1760. The Danes can hardly have given them up so soon; the reference must be to ordinary tables placed near the bed being unfashionable, which indeed was so. Before the introduction of the bedside table it had been customary to place a chair alongside (see Pl.161). Other points made by the Danish handbook are that it was the height of fashion to have very few pieces of furniture in a room, that large cupboards were banned from the drawing-room, that under the pier-glasses should stand tables for playing cards, and that console tables with marble tops were no longer in fashion. As for commodes, these should now be of mahogany with simple mounts; if one owns a commode of the inlaid sort (i.e. with marquetry) with a marble slab, one retains it – presumably because it had been a very expensive acquisition – but 'otherwise these are beginning to go out of fashion'. The Danes were here expressing a preference for the English type of commode – of mahogany with a wooden top –

and turning away from the French fashion that favoured parquetry veneers and marble tops.

In his brief discussion of distribution, Robert Adam had stated that the English followed the French formula (as best they could, he should have said) in all respects except that 'In one particular ... our manners prevent us from imitating them. Their eating rooms seldom or never constitute a piece in their great apartments, but lie out of the suite, and in fitting them up, little attention is paid to beauty.' The French would say that the antechambers they habitually used as dining-rooms tended to be decorated in a simple but none the less elegant fashion. 'The reason for this is obvious', Adam tells us. 'The French meet there only at meals, when they trust to the display of the table for show and magnificence, not to the decoration of the apartment; and as soon as the entertainment is over, they immediately retire to the rooms of company.' He then explains that 'It is not so with us. Accustomed by habit, or induced by the nature of our climate, we indulge more largely in the enjoyment of the bottle.' Moreover, because 'every person of rank here is either a member of the legislation, or entitled by his condition to take part in the political arrangements of his country', the men like to discuss these matters after dinner and therefore 'The eating rooms are considered as the apartments of conversation, in which we [i.e. the men] are to pass a great part of our time.' This explains why 'Soon after dinner the ladies retire. ... Left alone, they [the men, again] resume their seats, evidently more at ease, and the conversation takes a different turn – less reserved – and either graver, or more licentious.' This last observation was also made by a Frenchman visiting England in 1810/11.[28] Although he noted that politics were a subject of general interest in England, both for men and women, the latter 'do not speak much in numerous and mixed company'. The writer was incidentally much shocked by the English habit of installing a chamber-pot somewhere in the dining-room, which the men could use once the ladies had withdrawn – and did so freely, he says, 'as a matter of course, and [it] occasions no interruption of the conversation.'[29]

The same writer visited Osterley Park, the important house outside London which Robert Adam had re-decorated in the 1760s and 1770s and which still presents much of its Adam décor and furnishing to the visitor today. However, the new craving for a more relaxed way of life and less formal arrangements indoors had led to the furniture being pulled out from its intended positions against the walls. 'Tables, sofas, and chairs, were studiously derangés [sic] about the fireplaces, and in the middle of the rooms, as if the family had just left them, although the house had not been inhabited for several years.' So, by the time of the Frenchman's visit, the fashion was well established, it seems. 'Such is the modern fashion of placing furniture carried to an extreme, as fashions always are, but the apartments of a fashionable house [now] look like an Upholsterer's or cabinet-maker's Shop.' As he remarked of the English elsewhere in the book, 'the height of fashion is, to banish everything like *géne* and ceremony'.

The new fashion of placing furniture out on the floor, and especially round the fireplace, is neatly exemplified by the proposal for a drawing-room made in 1800 by a young English architect (Pl.186) where we see the pair of sofas placed at right-angles to the fireplace instead of alongside, flanking it, against the wall. A Frenchman's proposal of the year before for a room in Munich (Pl.187) clearly shows the difference. The latter scheme represents the conventional eighteenth-century formula; the English scheme is heralding the new century with its characteristic scatter of furniture. At first, of course, such *dérangé* schemes were far from scattered or in any sense random – and, as we shall see, the apparent clutter of a typical late-Victorian room was also a good deal less haphazard than it looks to us now. A charming drawing of an English *dérangé* drawing-room in use is reproduced in Pl.188. It was drawn in 1805 and shows a

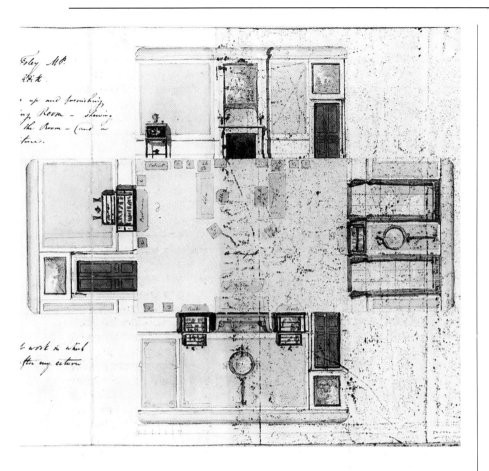

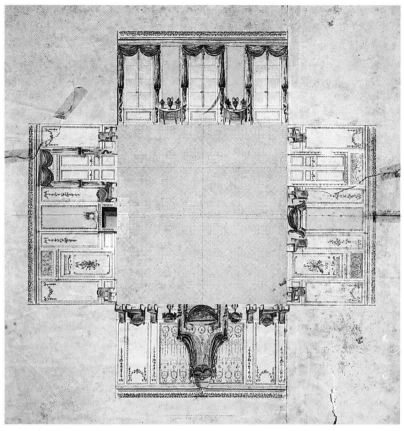

◁ △ 186, 187] THE ARRIVAL OF INFORMALITY
IN ROOM ARRANGEMENT

The plan above dates from about 1799 and is for a *salon* arranged in the traditional
manner with all the furniture standing against the walls. The plan on its left is an
English proposal for a drawing-room dated 1800, showing a pair of sofas placed at right
angles to the fireplace, with tables in front of each sofa (the third sofa, opposite, also has
its table). Out on the floor beyond the pair of sofas are seats called '*tête-à-têtes*'. All will
have produced an air of comfort and ease round the fireplace. The design above is for
the *salon* of the future Queen Karoline of Bavaria in the Munich Residenz, probably
drawn by Charles-Pierre Puille and representative of the best in French formal
conventions of the period. The English design is by Charles Heathcote Tatham and
bears a note that it was 'the first work in which I was engaged after my return from
Rome'. It was for the West Drawing Room at Stoke Edith, the seat of the Rt Hon.
Edward Foley, MP.
*Royal Institute of British Architects, London, Drawings Collection; Bayerische
Schlossverwaltung Planarchiv, Munich*

◁ 188] AN ENGLISH MIDDLE-CLASS DRAWING-ROOM,
CUMBERLAND   1805

The ladies sit on the sofa, which has been pulled out at right-angles to the wall in the
manner which now became fashionable. The way occasional tables were moved about
where needed is well demonstrated by this sketch, one of many made by John Harden,
an amateur artist of comfortable means who leased a house in the Lake District not far
from the home of William Wordsworth and his sister Dorothy, with whom the Harden
family became friends. Two candlesticks stand on one table: presumably it will soon
be dark.
*Abbott Hall Museum, Kendal*

room deep in the country. It is evident that the fashion spread rapidly in England, and it no doubt also passed quickly to the new United States of America, but it does not seem to have been taken up on the Continent until after 1810 or even later.

The same illustration shows two occasional tables placed conveniently within reach of the ladies sitting on the sofa. Such light, removable pieces of furniture had been used since the seventeenth century and even earlier but it had not been fashionable, throughout the Baroque and Rococo periods, to have other pieces of furniture standing permanently out in the middle of the floor – except for massive dining-tables, which were too heavy to move all the time; writing-desks of various kinds, and certain very splendid tables which were there solely on account of their decoration. Otherwise furniture almost always stood with one of its sides against the wall.

Around 1800, however, a need sprang up to have a table standing permanently by the sofa, in front of it. This may partly have arisen because people no longer felt constrained by the convention that had required all furniture to be wall-bound, and this would explain why the 'sofa-table' was introduced in England before anywhere else. It was of course highly convenient; one could put books on it, one could have tea on it or do one's sewing there (Pl.186). But it was not only the rectangular-topped sofa-table that appeared on the floor at this stage; round tables also began to occupy such a position, often with chairs set round – or, at least, pulled up when needed (Pls.250 and 263). The invention of more efficient lamps (see p.157) encouraged people to cluster round such tables, of an evening, where they could all benefit from the strong illumination (Pl.275). Such an arrangement had been widely adopted throughout Europe by 1815 (see e.g. Pls.260, 264, 277 and 279), and Queen Hortense, writing in her memoirs about her life in Paris between 1810 and 1812, claimed that she had been the first person in France to place a round table in the *salon* at which one could work (at needlework, that is) or otherwise occupy oneself. From remarks that follow this statement it is clear that she engaged in these occupations while company was present, as is already implicit in the remark that she did this in her *salon*.[30] She also throws in the comment that the practice of working at a table in the drawing-room was something one did in the country. Presumably she meant that this had previously been the practice in the country, where greater informality has always reigned. Maybe the English, with their sofa-tables, were also bringing into the city a practice first established in their estates in the country, as was the case with so many English fashions at this period (see p.145). Wartime privations also encouraged the greater domesticity that both sofa-tables and round tables betokened. The Viennese fashion journal, *Zeitung für die elegante Welt*, explained in 1807 that 'There are very few balls [these days] and people try to avoid expense and meeting strangers . . . and therefore prefer sitting in a small circle by the stove or fireplace, or at the cosy round table . . . domestic life has become much pleasanter.'

Before Queen Hortense presided over her salon, sitting at her new round table, in about 1810, as she explains in the same passage of her memoirs, the mistress of the house had taken up a controlling position seated beside the fireplace with all the other ladies who were present sitting 'in a circle', while the men stood around in the centre 'making sparkling conversation'. The same thing is described in another memoir of 1812 concerning the Tuesday *salons* at the Duchesse de Bassano's house in Paris where 'Huge armchairs *meublants* [see below], their backs to the wall, were occupied by the ladies who came and went all the time. The men stood in the middle, and a woman might come in, sit down behind them, speak to no one, and see only backs.'[31] The armchairs here described as *meublants* were those designed to blend with the décor of the

particular room; they were part of the architecture and were never to be pulled forward or otherwise disarranged – *dérangé*. Sofas (*canapés*) and armchairs (*fauteuils*) of this architectural sort 'were nothing but *meublan[t]s*', says Mme de Genlis (in 1818, writing of the past) and were 'placed [*rangés*] round the panelling where they always remained (Pls.187, 205, 226, 232 and 187). Mme de Genlis was speaking particularly of royal residences, but what she says seems to have applied to all important houses in Paris up to the time of the Revolution. What is more, the implication must be that such formal arrangements were no longer fashionable in Paris in 1818.

While the mistress of the house occupied the seat next to the chimneypiece (then still the principal feature of the room), no one used the other *meublant* armchairs. Instead they sat on chairs of a lighter kind which were introduced when required. They were set in an inner circle,[32] the 'circle' being that to which Queen Hortense referred in her statement about how a *salon* had been used before she introduced her round table. However, by 1812, if we can trust the description of the Duchesse de Bassano's *salon*, the ladies were sitting in the *chaises meublantes*, which was something new (Pl.250). The lightweight chairs, incidentally, were called '*chaises courantes*' because they could be moved. Sometimes they were fitted with casters to facilitate their 'running'.

As Mark Girouard has pointed out in his fascinating analysis of English social life and its affect on the planning and furnishing of English country houses,[33] Fanny Burney shows how, already by 1782, some people in England were trying to get rid of 'the circle', which many thought had a stultifying effect on conversation. In December of that year Miss Burney visited a smart London house where the hostess said, 'My whole care is to prevent a circle'. Rising hastily, the lady then 'pulled about the chairs, and planted the people in groups with as dexterous disorder as you would desire to see'.[34] When Humphrey Repton in 1816 contrasted the old-fashioned 'Cedar Parlour' with a modern 'Living Room', he illustrated a late-Baroque room with the chairs standing in a circle in the middle of the floor, and a modern room with groups of people engaged in various activities (talking, reading, playing the harp, and so on), seated on a miscellaneous selection of chairs, 'scattered in groups', as he called it.[35] The mixed styles of the chairs in Repton's illustration may be the reflection of a curious phenomenon revealed by an advertisement concerning the sale of the stock of a Liverpool upholsterer in 1814. 'The fashion now is with many Gentlemen', we are informed, 'to have every chair of a different pattern, in the same apartment.'[36] This fashion does not seem to have taken a firm hold of the public's imagination at this stage; plenty of unified schemes of decoration, with chairs *en suite*, were being created until much later. But it was a sign of what was to come. And in the 'antiquarian interior' (see p.150) such mixed styles were to be perfectly acceptable.

Acceptance of the Picturesque concept of irregularity and asymmetry in the plan of a house soon affected the way people looked at its furnishings, which in turn led to the furniture being disposed in a similarly irregular manner. If your house was no longer symmetrical, there was no longer any reason why your furniture should be arranged with formal regularity. Sentiment therefore joined with the craving for informality and comfort to form a yet more powerful stimulus to the devising of a new pattern of living indoors, and therefore of new conventions for the furnishing of rooms. The process began with the arrival of the sofa-table, and of the round table out in the centre of the room, and continued with 'mixed sets' of chairs. Once the formal arrangements had started to break up, the process was fairly rapid, but it took place principally in drawing-rooms and *salons*. The dining-room, which was always a more formal venue, resisted the change for much longer (see Pls.393 and 473).

Admirers of the Picturesque derived especial delight from buildings in mixed styles: these symbolized organic growth, something that had not been created in one single bout of activity. This inevitably led to a fresh evaluation of Gothic building. Indeed, if you wanted to create a new building that was truly Picturesque you could not go far wrong if you couched it in the Gothic style, making it look as if parts had been added at various times. As for furnishing such buildings, one could have furniture made that was ornamented with Gothic motifs, just as one could get 'Grecian' or 'Chinese' furniture. But some people of an antiquarian frame of mind wanted actual Gothic furniture in their Gothic houses, and this was much less easy to obtain although a trade in such goods was well established in England by the early nineteenth century. The fact that Christie's, the London auctioneers, found it worth holding a sale of ancient wooden carvings, old panelling and antique furniture in 1825 indicates that there was by then a substantial demand for such material to deck out 'antiquarian' interiors or create furniture in a fairly plausible Gothic style.[37] Gothic antiques, however, do not by and large come in sets, so one had to make do with disparate pieces, and the 'antiquarian interior' therefore came to comprise a mixture of styles: Gothic (both genuine and contrived), Tudor, Elizabethan and even Baroque. This accustomed the eye to rooms of unmatching furniture, which was to become of immediate importance when, in the second half of the nineteenth century, people who were not especially antiquarian in their approach but who liked 'antiques' began to furnish their own perfectly ordinary houses with such bric-à-brac.

The days had long since passed when the whole of a gentleman's library could be contained in one book-cupboard and now, in houses of any standing, the library was an extensive room with ranges of volume-filled shelves along the walls. The bookcases were often designed as an element of the architecture. Such rooms had formed part of the private apartment of the gentleman-owner of the house but increasingly, as the eighteenth century came to a close, the library was invaded by the women in the family who gradually turned it into a family drawing-room, introducing all kinds of additional comforts (Pl.245). This development at first took place primarily in England. It was as if the English womenfolk, by taking over this gentleman's sanctum during the day, were taking their revenge for being sent off to the drawing-room after dinner. This annexing of the library into the rooms of company reflected the generally more relaxed pattern of behaviour coming in at that period, the breaking of conventions, as well as the changing status of women in the upper classes. It must, incidentally, have enabled girls of a studious turn of mind to improve their education very considerably.

No notable changes seem to have taken place in the realm of sanitation, it is surprising to note, except that water-closets became general in English houses of the grander sort and in many French houses as well, as published plans reveal. Bathrooms, on the other hand, were still fairly rare although, as the description of the Italian bathroom furnishings shown in Pl.242 indicates, they were becoming more common at the end of the eighteenth century. The aged Mme de Genlis, who never let slip an opportunity of criticizing the upstart society – as she saw it – of post-Napoleonic France, not only stated that baths were now, in 1818, much commoner than hitherto, but also insisted that 'Sloth and idleness have greatly contributed to their establishment [in such large numbers] and their maintenance. The unoccupied have found the forenoons so drawn out since one has started to dine at six o'clock.'

## The architectural shell

The general tendency during the period was towards suppressing architectural features indoors. Although many architects of the time introduced segmental vaults and domes whenever the opportunity arose (Pls.241 and 246), the characteristic room of this strongly Classical period was box-like and plain. Mouldings and relief ornament were kept shallow. Chimneypieces were made plain and simple. Flues were built deeply into the wall so one could do away with chimney-breasts. In fact, fireplaces could be completely unobtrusive apertures in the wall, with a minimal surround, to which no attention whatsoever was drawn (Pls.229 and 246).

With the playing-down of the chimneypiece, attention now switched to the ceiling. Already in the 1770s Robert Adam, when commissioned to design a room, would usually address himself to the ceiling first (Pl.208). In a grand room, this would in turn dictate the pattern of the carpet which Adam (and no doubt other architects) often designed so as to reflect that of the ceiling. The character of the decoration on the ceiling also determined how the walls should be treated.

Having banished bold effects of relief and mass, however, articulation of the surfaces now had to be achieved by means of painted decoration, and striking effects were executed in this medium. Wallpapers played a similar role. Brilliant yet subtle effects were achieved with paints and glazes in this period; indeed, the art of simulating marble, grained wood and bronze has probably never reached greater heights. French decorators excelled in this realm, and it was said by the next generation that it had been French experts in these techniques, brought over to work on the decoration of Carlton House in the 1780s, who had introduced these skills to England and by their example brought this form of decoration into such favour during the Regency period.

Elaborately decorated ceilings remained in fashion in England from the late 1760s until about 1800. At first they relied on bold architectural ornament, but gradually this grew less obtrusive as paintwork came to the fore. The colours were mostly a good deal stronger in tone than is generally realized because the architects responsible were familiar with the striking colour-schemes to be seen on ceilings in Rome – some of which were quite modern, while many dated from the Renaissance and some even from Classical times – and the artists who executed the best work for such schemes in England were mostly immigrant Italians. Numerous illustrations of English Neo-Classical ceilings have been published.[38] It was the practice to paint the inset panels on canvas or paper first, and to fix them in position on the ceiling afterwards. This was not only easier, it also meant that the mouldings and other elements in relief could be painted or gilded first without damaging the more artistic compositions that were to be pasted in position afterwards.

It is much less easy to find illustrations of the contemporary French ceilings. Such evidence as comes readily to hand suggests that the development was fairly similar, as one might reasonably expect. It was apparently not uncommon for French ceilings of the second half of the century to be painted to resemble a sky with clouds, but some elaborately decorated rooms had the illusion carried on down the walls, with trees or landscapes and sometimes figures as well (Pls.199 and 207). Panoramic wall-decoration had been known in Classical times and was not uncommon, it would seem, in Renaissance Italy. It had not been much in favour during the seventeenth and eighteenth centuries but now, around 1770, it was revived, particularly in France. An early expression of the fashion was to be seen in the *salon* at Mlle Guimard's house, which was decorated about 1771 (Pl.207). In England a room at Norbury Park, Surrey, was painted, early in the 1780s, to look as if it were a pergola in a wooded landscape, and a room from Drakelow Hall in Derbyshire painted in 1793 with a landscape 'viewed' over a real trellis fence may now be seen at the Victoria and Albert Museum.[39] Parallels may be seen all over Europe, for example at Schloss Paretz near Berlin where David Gilly created two rooms that seem to be set in landscapes, executed in the mid-1790s, and the slightly earlier exotic landscape with trelliswork and monkeys at Liselund in Denmark. The style was inevitably spread yet further afield when the widely read Leipzig *Magazin für Freunde des guten Geschmacks* in 1789 illustrated a design for a room with a simple version of such decoration.

By about 1800, however, the enthusiasm for illusionistic scenic effects seems to have been on the wane in really fashionable circles. With the 'Grecian' and 'Pompeian' tastes now in the ascendant, schemes of flat, two-dimensional decoration were especially in favour. These relied on extensive areas of flat colour, usually plain, with bold borders. If there were any other ornament it usually took the form of a discreet repeated pattern executed in paintwork, free-hand or stencilled. Stencils helped the painter to produce repeating patterns speedily and with precision. The best work, however, was still done entirely free-hand, without such aids, and was naturally more costly. These effects could also be contrived with wallpaper.

The walls and ceilings of elaborate schemes were frequently conceived together. 'When the profiles [i.e. the relief decoration and mouldings on the walls] of rooms are gilt, the ceilings ought likewise to be gilt,' Sheraton tells us and adds that 'The usual method is to gild the ornaments, and leave the ground white, pearl-colour, light blue, or any other that may be proper to set off the gilding to advantage.'[40]

Both ceilings and walls might have ornaments of papier mâché and other moulded substances. British architects like Adam made great use of small repeating motifs moulded in composition or cast in pewter which, painted over, looked deceptively like carved ornament on chimneypieces, walls, and so on. The fillets used for edging wall-hangings (Pl.196) could also be of composition or papier mâché. And papier-mâché ornaments of all kinds could be purchased for embellishing walls and ceilings in complete schemes (Pls.220 and 221). Such decoration was widely used in England during the second half of the eighteenth century, and also in America, but it was not apparently much seen on the Continent until around 1800. By 1812, at any rate, there was a showroom in Paris where one could buy ornaments of all kinds, including sets for complete rooms in the fashionable *Empire* style, moulded of a special composition at the factory of a certain J. Beunat at Sarrebourg (Saarbrücken). In his catalogue, Beunat offered to produce ornaments in this medium to any design that architects cared to provide. A revised and extended catalogue was produced some while later by Beunat's successor, J.J. Heiligenthal, who seems to have moved the works to Strasbourg. In 1813 the Weimar *Journal für Luxus, Mode und Gegenstände der Kunst* mentioned Beunat's enterprise, which presumably means these ready-made ornaments were also available in Germany. The article explains that the '*mastic pierre*', as Heiligenthal called their composition, was made of gypsum, clay and mastic, and that one simply glued the moulded slips in the desired positions. Mme de Genlis (1818) praised the Beunat manufacture as one of the triumphs of French industry, so this method of decoration was perhaps more widespread than has hitherto been supposed.[41]

The real triumph of French industry at this period, however, lay in the making of wallpaper.[42] Not only were the French technically skilful – for so were the English – but the artistry which they brought to the design of their papers was much greater than others could or were prepared to muster. The names of the best manufacturers, such as Réveillon, Zuber and Dufour, are still renowned and rightly so. Because such firms took such care in the production of their papers, and because they paid their designers well, the best papers were not cheap and they were therefore to be seen on the walls of the best houses. There were of course inferior qualities for more ordinary settings as well. Some idea of how greatly wallpaper was valued can be obtained from advertisements

for flats in Paris during the 1780s, when the fact that the walls were papered was often specified.

Brilliant imitations of Lyon furnishing silks with Neo-Classical patterns were produced in wallpaper in about 1780. Simulations of chintz were common. Strips like the silk furnishing-borders were obtainable for pasting round walls that were otherwise plain – to rather striking effect. One could buy papers with *trompe l'œil* representations of stucco ornament, or of Gothic tracery, or of Classical statues in niches. Scenes for covering entire walls were available, and some were the work of excellent artists. One could, as today, buy papers bearing patterns identical to those of a given textile material so that window-curtains and chair-covers could be made to match. Something of the kind seems to be shown in Pl.276. At the beginning of the nineteenth century a fashion sprang up for simulating draped silk materials; these papers looked absolutely astonishing when put up on the walls. Pl.337 probably shows such a paper, but one cannot be sure because the resemblance to the real thing is so close.

Yet more expensive than fine wallpapers were furnishing materials of woven silk. Even the renowned French silk industry at Lyon was declining during the last two decades of the eighteenth century, faced with the slump in demand brought about by the switch in fashion from silk to printed cotton and muslin. Various efforts were made to revive the industry, and Napoleon placed huge orders for furnishing silks with the chief weaving establishments at Lyon, notably that of Camille Pernon. These *Empire* confections lacked the full subtlety of silks woven a generation before, but they were striking and one should try and imagine the interiors of Percier and Fontaine executed with such materials, coupled with white muslin. Satin was in particular favour, plain or with spaced-out, repeated motifs often rendered in a golden yellow. In this material a particularly brilliant green was much favoured, as was a sharp crimson and a very bright yellow. White was also much loved, no doubt for its connotation of purity and Classical virtue. Mme de Genlis remarks on the bizarre modern fashion – as she called it in 1818 – of hanging walls with materials that were pleated instead of stretched.[43]

George Smith, who published a somewhat pedestrian *Collection of Designs for Household Furniture and Interior Decoration* in London in 1808,[44] surveys briefly in his introduction the materials he felt were appropriate to the different kinds of room. After claiming that 'the pleasantest materials are silk and fine cloth', by which he means woollen or worsted materials, he goes on to explain that 'superfine cloth, or cassimere, will ever be the best' for 'Eating Rooms' and libraries where 'a material of more substance is requisite than for Rooms of a lighter cast'. By this last he means more 'feminine' rooms such as drawing-rooms. He insists that crimson and scarlet are best, but if one uses calico it must be of one colour 'in shades of moroon or scarlet'. 'In elegant Drawing Rooms', on the other hand, one should use 'plain coloured satin or figured damask' if one wants richness but 'lustring and tabarays' will do. Lustring was a glazed taffeta while tabouret was a half-silk of a single colour, often striped with alternating satin and ribbed effects. He also allows calico, if much draping of the upholstery is required, but it should be 'glazed mellow', and one should go for the small patterns, he advises.

One should proceed in quite a different manner if faced with doing up an ornamental cottage in a truly Picturesque manner. Here Edmund Bartell (1804) can offer advice.[45] After having discussed the propriety of fitting the Gothic windows of such a cottage with stained glass (he was for it), he maintains that oak 'cannot be excelled' if one wants to complete the romantic look. 'Doors, window-frames, floors, skirting, chimney-pieces, etc., should correspond with the chairs and tables, and be left as from the hands of the carpenter [i.e. untreated].' He mentions particularly the Gothic Library of 1752 at Felbrigg

Hall in Norfolk 'where all the bookcases, window-shutters, doors, etc., are [of oak] left entirely without paint'. The plastered walls of such rooms should otherwise be white or 'tinged with a wash of some modest, pleasing colour'. He advocates the use of 'milk paint' and explains how it was made.

The interior walls in rooms of this period still normally had a dado topped with a moulding or 'chair-rail'. Even in rooms painted or papered with panoramic scenes there tended to be at least some kind of dado in the form of a simulated fence or parapet. In the case of rooms dressed to resemble the inside of a tent, on the other hand, where the ceiling too was hung with material, the wall-hangings were taken all the way down to the floor to complete the illusion. While it was perhaps not the first 'tent-room', one of the earliest of importance was that at the Comte d'Artois' little château at Bagatelle, outside Paris, a mere pavilion created in a matter of weeks during the autumn of 1777. Tent-rooms became much more common during the *Empire* period and, while formerly they had usually been made for men with a military background, women now also began to live in rooms draped like tents – but then the allusion was to Turkey and the East and not to an army encampment. Percier and Fontaine seem to have devised a number of such settings; perhaps the most famous was the boudoir of the Princesse de Courlande of 1802. But they then also began to hang other kinds of room right to the floor, without a dado, although they did so only with a loose hanging, not one stretched out on the wall (Pl.241).

A curious form of wall-decoration may be seen in Pl.227, which is from a German work of 1799. It consists of framed panels bearing decoration, and the caption states that they are 'lacquered panels of tinplate from the English manufactories'. Matthew Boulton, the famous Birmingham engineer and manufacturer of metalwork, produced colour-printed metal plates in the late 1770s, finished by hand presumably with oil-paint. Boulton's 'mechanical paintings' were used at Mrs Montagu's London house in Portman Square, and were inset in some ceilings in Bedford Square. It may well be that this was what the compiler of the German book had in mind and, although it has not been thought that Boulton's line in room decoration was much of a success, it may be that it was welcomed more widely than is currently supposed. It is possible that the plates were of japanned iron sheet of the class that is often called 'Pontypool' – because ware of this type was made there, although much of it came from Birmingham and London.

The French still held the monopoly in producing large sheets of glass with the casting method that no other nation had entirely mastered until late in the eighteenth century.[46] The sizes of the plates they were able to produce had continued to increase and, during the middle of the century, many French architects had yielded to the temptation to face walls extensively with mirror-glass. By 1780, however, a reaction had set in, when Le Camus de Mézières was claiming that 'Mirrors in too great numbers and badly positioned render a room sad and bring on melancholy' (see p. 147). Le Camus advises placing mirror-glass with plenty of wall-panelling between; he also specially warns his readers against fitting glass that is curved in plan into rooms that are circular or oval, because such glass distorts the image – as anyone who has been to an old-fashioned funfair will know. He also has much to say about blemishes in glass, about the necessity of matching the colour of plain mirror-glass, which varies considerably, and about the sharp practice of some *miroitiers* who place defective glass between the windows where its faults are not easy to see at first glance.

About 1780 there first appeared in Paris trick chimneypieces where, instead of having a large plate of mirror-glass above the fireplace reflecting the room, a similar plate was installed of clear glass that one could look through. There was thus a window which required a pleasing view, and the siting of such a feature

189] A FRENCH STOVE   *c.*1770(?)

From a catalogue of faience stoves made at the factory of a certain Sieur Ollivier. They were signed 'Taraval', who is probably identical with the Inspector of the Royal Buildings (see Pl.219), and probably show the sort of heating apparatus Blondel thought acceptable in fairly grand dining-rooms. Some of the stoves in the catalogue are rather bizarre, but most adhere to the Classical tradition.
*Victoria and Albert Museum, London*

had to be carefully planned. A glass used in this way, but not over a fireplace, may be seen in Pl.237, which shows the wall of a luxurious boudoir created in about 1801 when the use of such effects was at its height. What intrigued people was how the smoke was led away from the fire since the wall seemed to be all glass, but it was of course not too difficult to devise a system of flues hidden in the piers framing the glass. Chimneypieces fitted between windows were to be seen in a number of fashionable rooms in Paris after 1800 (Pl.250). How far this fashion spread is not clear, although presumably it did to some extent. In such an arrangement the fireplace came to form a console to the pier-glass or chimneypiece above. Although there was a general tendency to play down the fireplace at this period, making little of its surround, chimney-ornaments became very showy and were often so elaborate that they had to be furnished with glass hoods or domes to protect them from dust. This was particularly necessary with clocks, but domes now became almost a standard feature of the mantelshelf.

Fireplace-openings were best filled with a chimney-board in summer or when the fire was unlit; this hindered draughts and held back soot falling down the flue. The common pattern comprised a canvas stretched on a frame and painted. These boards were sometimes decorated *en suite* with the room, and some of those that survive now provide evidence of how the original décor looked. 'Bough pots' with flowers or shrubs were also placed in the fireplace in summer, just as they had been in the seventeenth century. Even the ancient *feuillage* was still being placed in fireplaces in provincial towns; for instance, at the town of Boscawen in Massachusetts, it was reported as late as in 1800 that 'In summer, green pine boughs adorn the fireplace, and fill the room with odor.'[47] A flower-arrangement may be seen in the hob-grate in Pl.229.

In France or wherever logs were commonly burned, fire-dogs were retained in the fireplace, and those produced in the reign of Louis XVI could be exquisite (Pl.205). In England, where coal was now being burned even in elegant houses, grates of some kind were fitted into the fireplace. In order to narrow down the width of a standard opening, a hob-grate was fitted, with a hob on each side and a grate between; it was formed with specially designed plates of cast iron (Pl.224). The design of these grates had become extremely elegant by 1770. Some grates at Schloss Paretz outside Berlin, dating from about 1800, seem to derive from English patterns.[48] Their fireplaces in the wall are hemispherical and present a circular opening to the viewer, the bottom half of the opening being spanned by a grate. The architect responsible was David Gilly whose brilliant but short-lived son Friedrich had been in England in 1797–8.

Heating in Germany, and throughout Scandinavia and Central Europe, was normally achieved with a stove, either of cast-iron or of faience (Pls.225, 248, 264 and 266), and this form of heating was to be found even in rather grand rooms. It was certainly not confined to antechambers and lesser rooms, as in France at this period. Stoves of faience were often huge structures, and for this reason were made as attractive as possible. The inventor Sir Benjamin Thompson (Count Rumford; see Pl.224) devised an improved fireplace with angled cheeks and a choked throat to the flue which was a good deal more efficient than anything hitherto seen, but this hardly affected the appearance of fireplaces until after 1820.

In windows the panes of glass tended to become larger. The English finally adopted the double-doored 'French window' at the end of the century. The incentive to do so was that the main reception and living-rooms in grand houses had now usually come down from the first to the ground floor, and one wanted to be able to walk out into the garden. French windows also opened onto balconies. Not everyone was equally enthusiastic about this novel feature. James Malton in 1798 called them 'the new fashioned windows of Italy opening

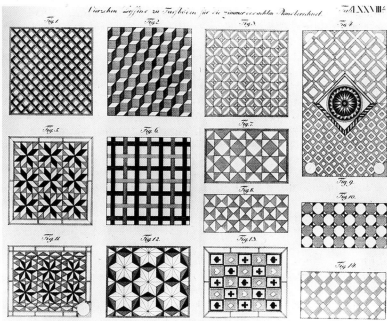

190, 191] PATTERNS FOR PARQUET FLOORS   1799

The top plate shows (top, from left to right) patterns for the bedroom of the sons of the family and a guest-room – all in the attic; and (below, left to right) ones for the young lady's room and the closet on the ground floor, and for the antechamber, main bedchamber and library on the first floor (*Beletage*, sic). The lower plate shows further patterns. (From Schmidt's *Der Bürgerliche Baumeister*, 1799.)
*Victoria and Albert Museum, London*

to the floor' which he claimed were 'originally intended to survey the lawns, the vistas, and the groves of Claude, in their summer attire, or the canal of Venice [but] are now to be seen in every confounded street of London, that a clear survey may be enjoyed of muddy streets, and to inhale the full fragrance of the effluvia, or dust of scavengers, from below'.[49]

In order to conjure up a truly romantic atmosphere in a Neo-Gothic room, nothing was so effective as a window of stained glass. The art of making this had never entirely died out, if only because ancient windows sometimes needed mending; a modest revival in the craft seems to have taken place in the mid eighteenth century in England, although it was not until shortly before 1800 that projects of any size were undertaken. Before that anyone wanting to install stained glass had usually had to obtain some ancient panels. Already by 1761 a Londoner named Paterson was holding auctions of stained glass at an address in the Strand, and old glass was apparently being imported from Flanders and elsewhere at that period.[50] Stained glass is pigmented on one side only, but much use was made of coloured glass from the late eighteenth century onwards. One could also paint glass with oil colours, or one could paste transparencies against a plain-glass window-pane, the transparencies consisting of paper painted in oils with suitable subjects and varnished to make it translucent. Some stained or painted glass is to be seen in the Duchesse de Berry's room (Pl.296), which suggests that the art was being practised with some skill in France by 1820, and there is also evidence that interest in this form of decoration was reviving in Germany at this time.

The French were still constructing elaborate floors of wood in their most splendid dwellings and their example was followed in more modest fashion elsewhere. Some fairly complicated parquetry patterns from a German architectural work are reproduced in Pls.190 and 191, and it seems that the best work outside France was probably executed in Germany, where there had long been a tradition of superior craftsmanship in wood that had often been bestowed on intricately decorated floors. In England carpeting was much more widespread, and bare floors were not common in houses of the better sort. When a carpet was provided, however, it was usual to leave a width of floor free round the edge. It was not usual to have a parquetry border round the edge until well into the nineteenth century in especially grand rooms.

## Loose furnishings

The upholsterer's art reached new heights after 1770, especially in Paris. The cutting of material became more subtle; amazing confections were contrived with drapery, often using combinations of materials; and trimmings became even more eye-catching than before.

In the 1790s there was a tendency to attach festoons of drapery in every possible position: between the legs of seat-furniture, across their backs, everywhere on beds, all round the room, and at the heads of windows (Pls.187, 231, 250, 246 and 248). Upholsterers of the *Empire* phase went even further, flinging lengths of material over curtain-poles, smothering rooms with muslin veils and turning beds into veritable Niagaras of textiles (Pls.252, 241 and 269–271). Since the *Empire* fashion for tumbling drapery swept across the whole of Europe and the United States, it was evidently adored by the customers, although traditionalists like Mme de Genlis found it absurd. In the same way as we have banished symmetry from our gardens, she says (by introducing the *jardin anglais*, she meant), so it is thought that 'one ought to exclude it from our apartments, one ought to dispose the draperies haphazardly. This affected disorder makes all the *salons* look ridiculous; it is as if one had stepped into a room where the upholsterer had not had time to finish his task.'[51]

She speaks of the considerable extra yardage of material that such schemes required. This conspicuous expenditure may have been encouraged by official efforts to persuade people to 'buy French' and support the Lyon silk industry; but it was also rather a brave effort to indulge in such lavish display in time of war – for these schemes were at their most outrageous during the height of the Napoleonic era. It may well be that the most extreme confections were rigged up for war-profiteers with *nouveau riche* tastes; but this flamboyant style was taken up by people of fashion everywhere. It was therapeutic, and it counterbalanced the severe lines of contemporary furniture.

Of the two forms of window-curtains that were in use around 1770, those which pulled up *à l'italienne* began to fall from favour while the divided type had regained its old ascendancy by 1800. Many divided curtains were not furnished with pelmets at all from the 1770s onwards, even in very smart surroundings (Pl.200), so it became necessary to make the rods and rings looks presentable. By 1820 rods had become striking and bold features, and by 1830 they had acquired elaborate finials and fancy brackets (Pls.311 and 314).

Both forms of curtain, however, were usually furnished with pelmets that masked the rods and rings. Pelmets at the end of the century mostly took the form of festoons with bows or rosettes at their tie-points and with tails which could be short or very long (Pl.207). They were a development of the fixed and purely decorative curtains provided for window-openings and niches from about 1780 and on through the *Empire* period (Pls.219 and 215). Festooned pelmets could also be purely decorative and not necessarily accompanied by curtains (Pl.265) but in that case they often had a roller-blind instead, it seems. It was ornament of this kind that Thomas Jefferson ordered in 1808 for his house, Monticello, when he specified there should be 'Drapery for the tops of 4 windows ... no curtains being desired'.[52] By 1800 or so the festooned pelmet had become a striking feature of the fashionable interior (Pls.247, 246, 248, 261 and 245). It was often supplied with curtains of muslin to soften the light (Pl.268), as well as with a blind. George Smith (1808) explained how some curtains had drapery of silk (i.e. festoons, now of some complexity) with muslin curtains 'to draw on rods as usual', and that 'Curtains thus constructed require spring blinds of the same colour as the principal Draperies, to drop behind the muslin, and the Drapery to remain fixed.'[53]

The standard formula for window-curtains (and for many beds) during the late *Empire* and Restoration periods in France, whatever its apparent intricacies, rested on the combination of two weights of materials, a heavy one for the drapery and a lighter one for the secondaries (Pls.269–271). Two materials of different colours often formed the primary component, and drapery was frequently arranged so that a lining of a further colour showed to advantage. The astonishing inventiveness of Parisian upholsterers at this period may be sensed from studying their designs, large numbers of which were published.[54] As George Smith commented, 'In France the first-rate painters do not think themselves degraded by providing Designs for the Cabinet-maker or for the Upholsterer'. He regretted this was not the case in England, but it was probably not the case anywhere else either – which explains why the French patterns were so much in demand and why French fashions in this field were therefore spread so effectively.

When there were two or more windows in one wall, such complicated draperies, with their poles projecting sideways, soon came to seem like a single composition and designers quickly evolved the so-called 'continued drapery', a term which Smith uses already in 1808. A good example of this is shown in Pl.268, but far more complicated confections were to be created, the fashion remaining popular until around 1830. It was never totally dropped in the nineteenth century, and was to come back into favour at its end.

Towards the end of the eighteenth century the 'French rod' was invented: it had two pulleys at one end and one at the other. Cords operated from one side could thus be made to draw a pair of divided curtains back or forth along the rod. This ingenious device remained in use until well into the present century. Other hardware associated with window-curtains now became of importance – rods, finials, brackets, hold-backs (*embrasses*), rings and cleats. The trimmings used at the time were very complex; the illustrations here give some idea of their richness. The heavy tie-back of looped cord ending in a large tassel which was to become a feature of much drapery after 1820 seems to have its origins in the eighteenth century. Several are listed in an inventory of Marie Antoinette's effects at Versailles in 1792.

One problem which had to be faced by upholsterers at this stage was that of curtaining pointed Gothic windows. One solution is shown in Pl.256 where a splendid roller-blind, painted like stained glass, may be seen partly pulled down. Blinds with painted decoration were now fairly common. *An Essay on Transparent Prints*, published by Edward Orme in London in 1807, gave details of how to decorate blinds of silk, linen or wire gauze with oil paints, and with varnish 'front and back but only where you want the light to shine through'. Blinds of metal gauze were apparently not uncommon in the late eighteenth century; a shop selling such wares opened in Paris in 1787, for instance.[55] Orme describes some roller-blinds which pulled upwards out of a box at the bottom of the window. Presumably the 'paper curtains' in General Salem Towne's house in Massachusetts in 1799 were paper blinds, and it is clear from reading Orme's slight work that a 'blind' could also be of paper stretched on a frame like the 'sashes' of the seventeenth century (see p. 21).

In the field of floor-covering no very great change took place during the period with which we are now concerned. Carpeting became much commoner but the types that were available were no different technically to those which had existed before (see p. 101), except that 'Brussels carpeting' now joined the repertoire. This was not very different from the cut-pile carpeting of the Wilton type, but the pile was left uncut so that it consisted of loops. Looped pile carpeting was being woven on no less than 1,000 looms at Kidderminster by 1838. Proper hand-knotted carpets woven in one piece (as opposed to strips of carpeting that could be sewn together to make up areas of floor-covering) continued to be made at the Savonnerie, at Aubusson, at Axminster and at Moorfields. The last was still active in the 1780s when William Bingham bought in London for his house in Philadelphia 'everything which the taste and luxury of the time had invented' including a Moorfields carpet decorated with one of the 'most expensive patterns', but weaving seems to have ceased in 1792.[56] A man named William Sprague set up a factory at Philadelphia in the 1790s to make hand-knotted pile carpets which were remarkable for being woven in strips that were subsequently sewn together, rather than in one piece as was usual for hand-knotted weaves. Sprague's carpets were very expensive, but 'Scotch carpeting' (often called 'ingrain' in America) was being woven at various small establishments on the East Coast by 1800. For instance, at an auction of an artist's effects at Lexington, Kentucky in 1812, there was offered for sale 'a large Kentucky Scotch carpet'.[57]

Floor-cloth was used even more widely than before in the English-speaking countries (see p. 101 and Pl.228). At Appuldurcombe, a house on the Isle of Wight, an inventory of about 1780 refers to 'A floor cloth painted in Imitation of India Matt'.[58] A Bostonian was billed in 1772 for four yards of floor-cloth painted 'Turkey Fatcheon' (i.e. like a Turkey carpet), while a Boston firm charged a customer in 1788 for 'Painting a Room and Entry Floor Cloth ... with a Poosey Cat on one Cloath and a Leetil Spannel on ye other, Frenchman like', which must mean 'in the Savonnerie style' – the French being known at this stage for portraying life-like flowers and animals on their carpets.[59] Early in the nineteenth century a man in Baltimore took out a patent for making carpets of paper for use in summer.[60] The venture does not seem to have been successful, but something similar seems to have existed in England in the 1830s (see p. 228). Floor-cloths, incidentally, were 'cool in summer and most useful in winter, because they can be cleaned in long spells of rainy weather by washing them as you would the floor, whereas woolen carpets must remain wet & dirty during bad weather', as an advertisement of 1810 for a firm in Lexington states.[61] The *Charleston Courier* informed its South Carolina public in 1803 that 'a Lisbon floor matt' was now available in that city, and soon after was advertising 'India Floor Mats, Plain and Coloured', 'Alicant mats for Phizzes' ('Piazzas', the term used for porches in Charleston), and 'Summer Floor Matts of various sizes and colours'. In Virginia in 1818 'Holland rush carpets [justly celebrated for their durability] of different breadths and qualities' were being advertised.

In seeking to make beds and seat-furniture ever more comfortable, upholsterers experimented with different ways of stuffing, with various forms of springing, and even with air-cushions. In 1758 someone in Paris suggested making a mattress containing several pigs' bladders filled with air. Whether anyone actually made such a mattress is not recorded, but a contemporary newspaper in Hamburg took up the story and there was more talk of this idea in 1774. Two years later a Paris newspaper carried a report on the new 'cushions and mattresses of oiled skin [*peau huilée*] filled with air' which were 'filled via a tap or valve'.[62] Mme de Genlis mentions as something that French industry had brought to a high degree of perfection (by 1818), along with casting plate-glass and making rich silk materials, '*les lits aériens de M. \*\*\**'.[63] She does not give the maker's name but presumably she is referring to some form of pneumatic bed. Air-cushions of india-rubber were anyway being made in Berlin in 1842.[64] Early experiments had already been made with springs (p. 102) but note should be taken, as it certainly will have been by the upholsterers at the

192] EARLY SEAT-SPRINGING  *c.*1805

A 'chamber horse' for exercising with a sketch of the four tiers of spiral springs in the seat. First published by Sheraton in London in 1793, it was re-published in Leipzig between 1800 and 1810 in the journal entitled *Sammlung von Zeichnungen der neuesten Londner und Pariser Meubles*. It took a further decade or so to think of fitting such springs in furniture designed for comfort.
*Victoria and Albert Museum, London*

time, of the spiral springs used in the 'chamber-horse' or spring exercising-chair which was popular in England during the second half of the eighteenth century.[65] Sheraton illustrates the seat of such a chair and shows its springs in his widely read *Drawing-Book* of 1793, and the same illustration was included in the German edition which appeared in Leipzig the year after (see also Pl.192).

Seats were also given more comfort by making their stuffing resilient yet firm, and by making it stay in position. Badly stuffed chairs quickly go out of shape; their padding gets compressed and distorted. The English had had firm, squared edges to their chair-seats since the middle of the century, as well as tufting (see p.102). The English squared edge (see Pl.166) not only produced a technical advantage but was aesthetically more pleasing with the characteristic squared look of the standard English upholstered chair. With the rounded *fauteuil* (see Pl.165) the French had naturally preferred rounded forms for the stuffing. Once the French had also accepted the rectilinear forms of Neo-Classicism for their seat-furniture (which in general they had been very reluctant to do because the old Rococo formula was so comfortable), they too decided that they needed squared edges to the stuffing. The technique they employed may have differed in some way from that already being used by the English but, by the end of the century, chairs with such squared effects were said to be 'French stuffed' (for example, by the upholsterer George Smith in 1808). Squared stuffing was a noteworthy feature of most upholstery from the late 1780s onwards. In England squareness was imparted even to bolsters which one would expect to be rounded (Pl.247). In the caption to his illustration of a 'French State Bed', Sheraton in 1792 says that 'square bolsters are now often introduced'.

Chair-covers were still mostly matching the other main textile materials in the room where they stood, and wallpaper manufacturers were able to make their materials match chair-seats if necessary. Woven silks and printed cottons were sometimes produced with patterns specially designed to be cut out and made up as chair-coverings (Pl.232).

Chairs with expensive covers needed protecting and were therefore usually provided with loose covers. These were made to look fairly presentable, as is shown by many Englishmen and some Americans being perfectly content to be portrayed sitting on chairs from which these covers had not been removed (Pl.196). In America, where they had continued occasionally to nail fringe round their chair-seats, long after fringe had gone out of fashion for this purpose in England and France, loose covers were probably more frequently fringed than in Europe, but some European loose covers certainly had fringes too. That loose covers were thought acceptable for normal use is shown by a document of 1799 concerning some charming samples of brightly coloured striped linens which were proposed for the chairs in the Assembly Rooms in Edinburgh. These are described as 'Four patterns of Strypes ... for the Slips or Cases'. They were sent with the recommendation that they be judged by candlelight because that is how they would normally be seen. One of the patterns was presumably selected and not long afterwards a Lady Helen Hall was demanding that the Directors of the Assembly Rooms 'permit the covers of the sofas & benches ... to be given out on the nights of the Dancing school balls ... for nobody likes to sit upon dirty canvas with nails standing out, to tear their cloaths every time they move'.[66]

Since seat-furniture had normally stood against the wall until late in the eighteenth century, to be pulled forward from the walls only when needed, and therefore the outside backs of chairs had not been seen to any great extent, there had been no need to cover them with expensive material, nor to decorate the backs with carving or other form of ornament. But once chairs had begun to remain standing permanently out on the floor, in the new informal manner,

their backs could be seen and there was a tendency to decorate them so the back view was more acceptable. It took some while for chairmakers to change their ways; but some upholsterers in England, and perhaps elsewhere as well, provided a sort of apron the top edge of which they tacked to the top edge of the outside back so that it could hang down and, as it were, hide the chair's nakedness. This curious fashion was current only during the first quarter of the century.

Day-beds took many forms during this period. Some were merely single-ended couches or *chaises-longues*. If the latter were less than 5 *pieds* long (5 ft 4 in., 1.62 m) it was called a '*duchesse*' according to Bimont, writing in 1772. A high-backed version popular under the *Empire* was known as a *Paphos*. Pommier and Marcus, two leading Parisian upholsterers at that period, each gave their names to varieties with backs of different shape. Sheraton (1792) illustrated what he called a 'sofa bed' which was a lightweight, movable piece of furniture (it had casters) on which one presumably reclined (Pl.231). It had curtains depending from a domed tester fixed on the wall above, and was no doubt intended for use in a boudoir, as was the '*Pariser Causeuse*' (Parisian conversation-seat) which the Weimar *Journal für Literatur, Kunst, Luxus and Mode* in 1817 explained was 'a rest-bed for the boudoir of an elegant lady'. Resting on it she could talk to a female friend, the report added. The *causeuse* is illustrated; it resembles a French bed of the period with two 'ends', or '*chevets*' as they were called. Although day-beds were mandatory in a boudoir, this room also often contained a bed in an alcove or niche, or so it would seem. Important bedchambers also seem to have been furnished with day-beds in addition to their principal piece of furniture, and ladies sometimes received company there formally, while lying on the day-bed – notably when 'lying-in'. If they did so, they had to be sure to 'always have a *couvre-pieds*' with which to hide their feet, Mme de Genlis insisted (1818). 'Decency demands it because, stretched out like that, the smallest movement may uncover the feet and even the legs. Besides,' she added, 'a pretty *couvre-pieds* is a very decorative ornament; people make do without them these days but nothing looks so sloppy.'[67] Once again she was getting at her Post-Revolutionary, Post-Napoleonic compatriots, with their uncouth ways.

Although the form of bed with a flat tester that we call a 'four-poster' continued to be made during this period, the fashionable type of bed was now that with a dome held up by rods rising from the four corners of the bed or by brackets fixed to the wall behind. It was no longer known as a '*lit à la polonaise*' (see Pl.217); indeed, it needed no special designation because it was such a common form. Some had prow-like ends, however, and this earned them the name '*lits en bateau*'. Sheraton illustrates a variant of the double-ended, domed form which had curved ends and sides (i.e. the mattress was oval in plan). No doubt this was based on a French model, but he implies that the invention was his. 'As fancifulness seems most peculiar to the taste of females,' he claims, 'I have therefore assigned the use of this bed for a single lady'; but then he adds, 'though it will equally accommodate a single gentleman.'

In Paris people of a particularly amorous disposition sometimes had a plate of mirror-glass set into the domes of their beds but this practice was less eagerly adopted after Calonne, the Minister of Finance, was nearly cut in half when the glass fell out of the tester of his bed. The precise circumstances do not seem to be recorded but the Parisians made plenty of jokes about the event.[68] The motives which lay behind an arrangement at Friedrichsfelde, near Berlin, were very different, on the other hand. There the bed, which stood opposite the windows, was surrounded with panels of mirror-glass in such a way as to reflect the outside and make the occupant feel he was 'actually lying out in the open air'.[69] This was recorded in 1786, at about the time that the parallel taste for panoramic wall-decoration was also coming into favour.

During this period a great deal of furniture was painted, even in very splendid rooms, where it would be made to match the painted walls. Gilding was often associated with paintwork to make the effect less overpowering. People with antiquarian inclinations liked their furniture to be black since this was a colour associated with age. 'The black furniture of ancient days' is a phrase used by Bartell in describing ancient oak which, he maintained, was suitable for the Gothic interior, whether ancient or modern.[70] To such tastes old oak had to be the colour of dark molasses or actually blackened. Pseudo-Gothic furniture, made for such interiors, therefore also had to be black. This perhaps explains why antiquarians were particularly fond of the ebony furniture made in the Dutch or Portuguese colonies in the Far East. This also looked convincingly antiquated because it was made in traditional seventeenth-century forms, although it was probably not all that old when so eagerly collected by the antiquarians (see Pl.220).

Black was also equated with venerable standing. This is reflected in the admiration for Boulle furniture, the sumptuous forms of which rely greatly on ebony embellished with elaborate gilded mounts and brass inlay. Such furniture had been one of the chief glories of the age of Louis XIV, and André-Charles Boulle had been the best of several cabinetmakers working in this style. When mid-eighteenth-century scholars had started to look back fondly to the days of the *Roi Soleil*, regretting what had since been lost, as they thought, a few began to collect 'black Boulle' while others had furniture made in the Boulle technique – but always black.[71] Boulle, old or new, continued to be admired right through the late eighteenth century but enjoyed a particular vogue with George IV and his friends in England, and with the French royal family and aristocracy after the restoration of the monarchy. Boulle, and black furniture generally, carried an implication of solid virtues based on sound tradition, a re-affirmation of authority after the years of revolution and upheaval.

The invention of the Argand lamp in the 1780s had a profound effect on the way rooms looked at night and even affected the way rooms were used. The illumination which this new form of light produced was so much stronger than that given by a candle;[72] several people could therefore quite easily benefit from it together and this encouraged the use of the round table about which they could read, sew or play cards (see p. 149; Pl.275). Family life and entertaining in the evening took on a different pattern as a result. The Argand lamp was in fairly general use among the well-to-do by 1800 (Pl.250). It was effective and it was novel, but it was still not considered quite the thing in elegant society in Paris, and probably elsewhere, in the years around 1820 – at least, not in the principal rooms on grand occasions. Then wax candles were *de rigueur*. Mme de Genlis, ever critical of modern society, insisted that it was only young people who needed to wear spectacles because 'lamps are pernicious to the eyes'. Old people, who read by candlelight, had no need of glasses, she claimed. But what did it matter, she added sarcastically, if one damaged one's eyesight and the smell endangered one's nerves, so long as one believed the lamp to be more elegant than the candlestick?[73]

The Argand lamp was distinctive in form (Pls.250 and 336). It had a glass funnel to draw the air more efficiently through a vertical metal tube which was surrounded by a tubular meshed wick. It also had a font or reservoir for the oil at one side, set slightly above the oil-intake which was fed by gravity. This font unfortunately cast a shadow but the difficulty could be obviated by having twin burners, one on each side of the font, and elegant lamps could be made in this symmetrical form (Pl.307). With a hanging lamp the shadow cast by the early form of font was even more of a drawback and, short of having a multiplicity of burners round a central reservoir (an expensive solution only applicable where a large chandelier-like object was acceptable), some other answer was needed. It eventually came in the form known as an 'Astral lamp', because the principle was first used with a hanging lamp which could therefore be called 'starlike'. This was invented in France about 1809; it had a flat, annular reservoir surrounding the burner so that the shadow was at least evenly distributed (Pl.275).[74]

Ami Argand was Swiss. He patented his lamp in 1783 but the idea was stolen by a Frenchman named Quinquet (who later confessed) and this name was for a while given to this type of lamp in France. Thomas Jefferson gave an Argand lamp to the Secretary of Congress as early as 1784, but Jefferson kept an exceptionally close eye on developments of this sort in France, where Argand lamps (or rather '*lampes à la Quinquet*') were being advertised by 1785. There is no need to suppose that they were common in America until later.[75] The fact that an English handbook of 1807 on painting blinds and screens could show its readers how to make a painted shade for an Argand lamp, suggests that the form was by then familiar, on the other hand.[76]

Maintaining Argand lamps was tiresome and dirty. The viscous oil tended to block the feed, especially when the pressure had decreased as the reservoir emptied. A Frenchman named Bernard Guillaume Carcel introduced a spring-operated mechanism in 1798 to overcome this difficulty and Carcel lamps became fairly common, but their delicate mechanism was apt to break down (see p. 229). Carcel named his lamp the 'Lycnomena' – the Greek for 'steady light' – but it was usually called after its inventor.[77]

Most lighting, however, was still provided by candles of various sorts. The beeswax candle remained relatively expensive and was therefore mainly used in houses of the grander sort. Tallow candles, no less foul-smelling than they had been in the past, were burned in ordinary settings. And simple oil-lamps were used in many places, notably in the United States where, by the late eighteenth century, there was a plentiful supply of whale-oil. Safer and less messy models had been devised with a container, into the mouth of which was plugged or screwed the burner with its woven wick.[78]

Flowers came to be of great importance as a feature of interior decoration during this period. Previously the odd vase of flowers had been placed about the house, a large vessel with flowers had sometimes been placed in the fireplace when the fire was unlit, and festoons of flowers had been used in rather formal arrangements on festive occasions. But the general use of flowers everywhere was a new development. Le Camus de Mézières (1780) advised placing stands with several stages in the dining-room and decking them with banks of fresh flowers. He also suggested having glazed niches in dining-rooms filled with artificial flowers. Flowers were everywhere, arranged naturalistically with great freedom. If the real thing was out of season or unavailable, moreover, the products of the thousands of women making artificial flowers could be had – not for trifling sums, perhaps, but then these confections were exquisite and charming.

### 193 △
## A picture-cabinet in Berlin
### 1771

This shows a room in the house of the artist, Daniel Chodowiecki, who is to be seen at his desk by the window. The engraving is dedicated to his mother, who is shown here with young members of the family who are sitting at a round table – a scene that seems more characteristic of the 1820s than of the late Rococo period. However, the form of the console table and the brackets supporting small sculptures on the walls leave no doubt as to which century we are in. The chair with its curved back and caning is of the kind made in Berlin by the *englische Stuhlmacher*. The tall-backed upholstered chair is a standard form of the second quarter of the century, while the turned and rush-seated chairs are likely to be Dutch imports. Note the doll on the table and the single window-curtain.

*Victoria and Albert Museum, London*

### 194, 195 ▷
## Scenes in Danzig
### 1773

Chodowiecki visited Danzig in 1773 and made a series of charming illustrations of the houses where he called or stayed. Most of the drawings were lost during the last war, it seems.

### 194 (above)
An evening visit where the guests are received in the bedchamber. The twin beds, on the right, have their curtains closed. The windows have pull-up curtains. A looking-glass hangs on the pier; below it is a dressing-table with dressing-mirror. The chair is of the English type, presumably made locally. The floor seems to be tiled.

### 195 (below)
Along the North Sea and Baltic coasts the fashion of having large cupboards for linen and other fine household equipment standing in the living-rooms continued well into the eighteenth century. Quite often treasured vessels were displayed on top, as here. Note the faience stove. The small, curtained window probably provides the only light that enters the room beyond. The main window has a pull-up curtain of muslin. Below stands an oval folding dining-table. The chair may well be Dutch.

*Staatliche Museen zu Berlin, East Berlin*

◁ 196
## An Englishman's breakfast
*c.* 1775(?)

A perfect expression of the English country gentleman's informal way of life. The house is fairly grand, as the pier-table and glass in the room beyond indicate, but the man is depicted relaxing by the fire (note the cheval fire-screen with its strap), reading the newspaper and he is sitting on a chair which still sports its loose-cover of checked linen. He wears his riding-coat and boots. The table is of the standard mid-century form used in England – of mahogany, with gate-leg supports to large flaps – which can be removed when not required. The chairs are of the sturdy kind favoured in England in the third quarter of the century; indeed the picture could well have been painted in the 1760s and the chief reason for dating it so late is that it is attributed to Henry Walton who was born only in 1746. The narrow gold fillet trimming the plain wallpaper is noteworthy, as is the very handsome fitted carpet, made of widths of carpeting with an added border.

*Toledo Museum of Art, Ohio; gift of an anonymous donor*

197 △
## A 'salotto' in Florence
1777

The room seems to have been decorated in the previous century but the furnishings must have been deployed fairly recently, when this picture was painted, as two of the portraits are of ladies dressed in much the same fashion as the lady in the foreground. Slightly earlier in style is the carved and gilded table in the background. A Persian carpet lies on the floor, which is of tiles of two colours. The single curtain may be an artistic device, but there are certainly no carefully contrived window-curtains. On the right is Donatello's *St John* which is now in the Bargello. At that period it was in the possession of the Martelli family, members of which are seen here in this picture. (By G. Begni, a pupil of Batoni.)

*Photograph from the Marchese Leonardo Ginori*

198 △
## A collector's house in Leiden
*c.* 1775

This shows the collector Paulus van Spijk and his wife in a room containing some of their treasures and with their picture-cabinet beyond. The chairs are in the Anglo-Dutch style. The practice of having a small Turkish carpet laid on a table was retained in Holland long after it had been dropped in other countries. There seems to be fitted carpeting on the floor. (Attributed to Johannes Janson.)

*Museum de Lakenhal, Leiden; photograph by courtesy of the Kunsthistorisch Institut, Leiden University*

## 199 ▷
# A private concert in Paris
### 1773

The scene is set in an elegant oval *salon*, probably in one of those small *maisons de plaisance* built in the 1760s on the outskirts of Paris. The Classical character of the décor is very evident. Particularly striking are the pull-up curtains *à l'italienne* with their large decorative tassels and ruffled pelmets. It may be because the windows are broad and the curtains in consequence very heavy that there are cords on both sides, but one of each pair may be a dummy added for the sake of symmetry. Note the busts on pedestals against the piers. The musical trophies above the windows show that the room was built with such musical entertainment in mind. A large music-desk stands in the middle of the room. (The picture from which this engraving was made – by Augustin de Saint-Aubin, engraver to the French Royal Library – was painted by A. J. Duclos and exhibited at the Paris Salon of 1773.)

*Victoria and Albert Museum, London*

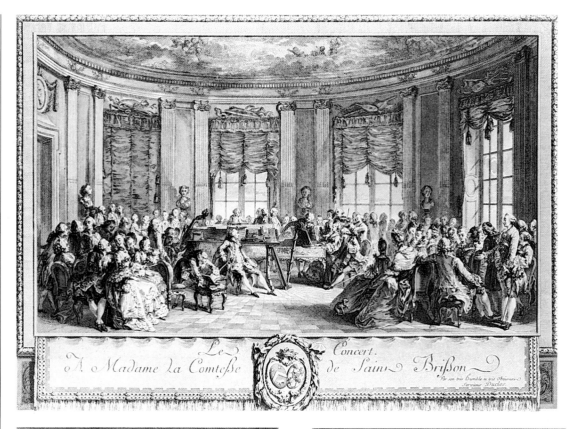

## 200 ▷
# A Parisian boudoir
### 1774

This shows one of these delightful small rooms, a lady's private retreat. She is seen dozing on her comfortable sofa (which perhaps should be called a *méridienne*), a novel in her hand. The room is done up with the utmost elegance. In plan the room is D-shaped. It has delicate ornaments on the panelling and an elaborate parquetry floor. The small console supports a vase of flowers but, when it gets dark, a servant will replace the vase with a candelabrum and the candle-light will be prettily reflected in the large plate of glass behind, which was probably flat but here looks curved (see p. 152). The divided curtains have a heading but no pelmets. The small table is easily movable but at this moment supports a bird-cage. A mandolin lies on the stool which, like the sofa, still has legs in the Rococo taste. (By S. Freudeberg.)

*Victoria and Albert Museum, London*

## 202 ▷
# A smart Parisian drawing-room
### early 1770s

Each niche contains a sofa. Above each is a canopy with curtains that are purely decorative but lend an air of importance to the room. The niches are backed with mirrors. This is an illustration from Volume V of J.F. Blondel's *Cours d'Architecture* which was published in 1777, three years after his death, having been completed by Pierre Patte who drew this composition. The 'stiffened Rococo', with introduced Classical motifs, favoured by the new generation, is here very evident. The next phase, with fully developed Classicism, is to be seen in Pl.219, where the solution to a similar problem is solved in the new idiom of around 1780.
*Victoria and Albert Museum, London*

## 203 (*right, below*)
# Dressing-room in the Classical taste, Paris
### c. 1777

A good example of the sort of engraving that spread a knowledge of Neo-Classical decoration throughout France and far beyond. Not an especially ambitious composition; it would have been relatively easy for joiners unfamiliar with the new idiom to execute. The plan showing the window-embrasures and chimney-breast makes the scheme more comprehensible. (By Juste-François Boucher, son of the famous painter, who returned from Rome in 1767 and died in 1781; from a *Recueil de Décorations intérieures*, published in Paris, 1904.)
*Victoria and Albert Museum, London*

## ◁ 201
# A Parisian bathroom
### 1774

The bath still has a tent-like canopy, but it would seem no longer to be functional as a hood forming a steam-bath (see Pl.138). A plate of mirror-glass is set into the niche behind. The bath itself is probably of copper and has a stand, making it look like a smart day-bed. Note the cloth protecting the bather from the unpleasant touch of metal, and the fact that she wears a chemise while bathing. (By S. Freudeberg.)
*Victoria and Albert Museum, London*

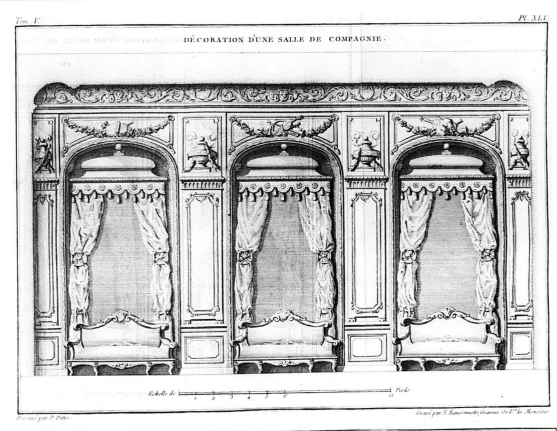

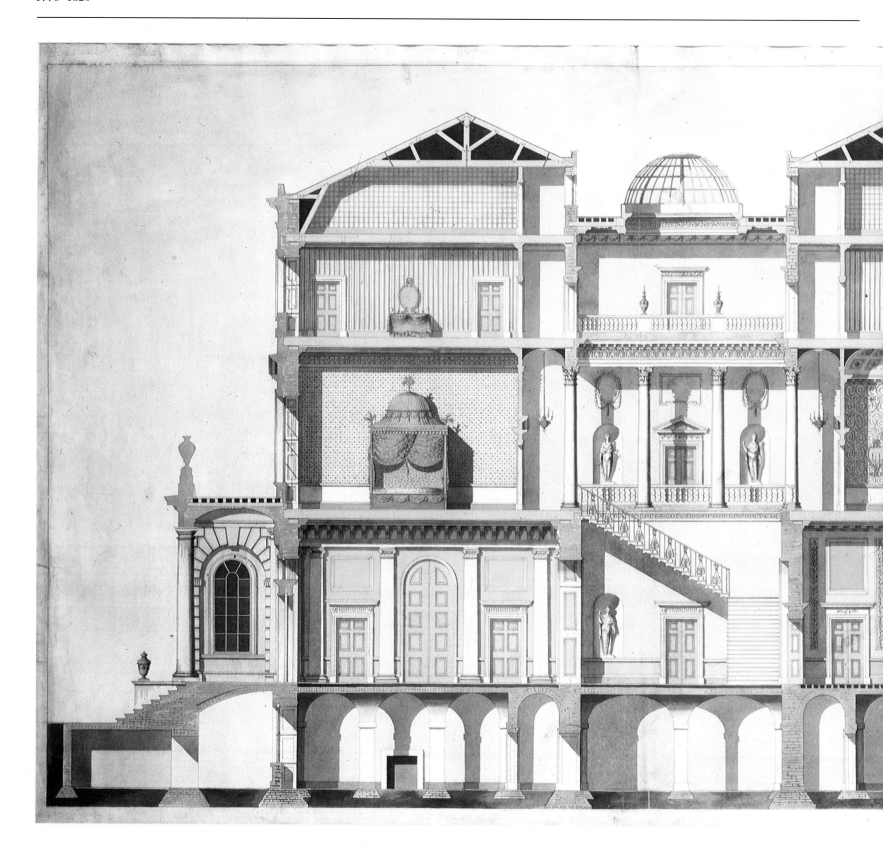

## Section through a London house
### 1774

<small>◁ 204</small>

Executed in the drawing-office of Sir William Chambers by John Yenn, and probably shown at the Royal Academy in 1774. The architect has indicated the features he regarded as worthy of his attention, the elements he would wish to control. These include a grand bed, a sofa, *girandoles*, a chandelier, a looking-glass and table, and a dressing-table. The colours of the walls and the general idea of intended patterns are also indicated. Note the bold striped effects on the second floor and the chequers in the attic.

*Royal Academy, London*

## Proposal for mural decoration, England
### 1778

<small>206 ▷</small>

This shows how such decoration might be carefully planned with a unified scheme linked by garlands of flowers. The white-painted frames were to contain paintings; the garlands of flowers (here called festoons) were to be in naturalistic colours with blue ribbons. Such ornaments could be executed in stucco or in papier mâché. (From the drawing-office of John Linnell, the important upholsterer with premises in Berkeley Square; see also Pls.168 and 169.)

*Victoria and Albert Museum, London*

## Design for the Duchesse de Mazarin's house, Paris
### c. 1777

<small>205 △</small>

The Duchesse was known to have had exceptionally good taste and the décor of her *hôtel* was greatly admired. It was decorated by the architect François Joseph Bélanger. This drawing must be associated with that commission, as it bears her name. An approximate rendering of the Duchesse's arms may be seen cast into the fire-back. Note the delicate fire-dogs. The huge panel of glass is striking. The framed green material forming the panels is presumably of silk. Chairs of this class are today usually seen bereft of their fat cushions and small bolsters which totally altered their appearance. In the Metropolitan Museum of Art, New York, there are three carpet-designs by Bélanger for this house, one of which seems to be for this room.

*Victoria and Albert Museum, London*

## A unified décor, London
### 1773

This is one of the plates from the second volume of Robert and James Adam's *The Works in Architecture* (Vol. II, London, 1779). It illustrates one of the three drawing-rooms in Lord Derby's house in Grosvenor Square, and shows the components of a room which an architect like Adam felt it proper to design himself. They include ornamental urns on pedestals, sconces, a chimney-glass, a fireplace-surround, door-cases, and a carpet which echoes the design of the ceiling. No seat-furniture or tables are shown, presumably because Adam had entrusted their design to the upholsterer or cabinetmaker (perhaps after having given him a rough sketch). The next plate in *The Works* shows details of the furnishing of other rooms in the house – doors in the Third Drawing Room and Etruscan Room, curtain-pelmets, sconces, and the commode which was to stand in the Countess' Dressing Room and which is still in the family's possession.

*Victoria and Albert Museum, London*

## Mlle Guimard's dining-room, Paris
### *c.* 1771

The house designed by C.N. Ledoux for this famous dancer, mistress of the Prince de Soubise, attracted much attention for its novel decoration. This drawing of the dining-room shows the décor of trelliswork and trees that turn the room inside out, while Venus, Mars, Fame and other deities disport themselves among the clouds surrounded by tumbling cupids. To this delightful building, called by some The Temple of Terpsichore, came all the brightest people of the day. Mlle Guimard was forced to sell it in 1786, and caused a sensation by doing so by means of a lottery which was won by a banker named Perrégaux. This drawing shows it in his time, and it could well be that the curtains shown here were replacements introduced by him. On the pedestals in the corners must have stood candelabra. Note the fireplace, to which attention is not drawn as that would spoil the out-of-doors illusion. However, space seems to have been left for some sort of overmantel mirror. If so, it was probably swathed in gauze to make it blend with the effects.

*Royal Institute of British Architects, London,*
*Drawings Collection*

### 209
## Lord Derby's garden pavilion
### 1774

This shows how Robert Adam envisaged one of his interiors being used. It shows the small pavilion designed by Adam for a *fête chempêtre* given by the Earl of Derby on 9 June 1774 at his house, The Oaks, in Surrey. The building was D-shaped in plan, with a ballroom in the centre and a horseshoe-shaped enclosed 'peristyle' containing eight dining-tables with accompanying benches, and a couple of tea-rooms at the ends. The guests seem to be in fancy dress. The servants bring food and drink from a series of sideboards. (From R. and J. Adam, *The Works in Architecture*, Vol. III, which was, however, not published until 1822.)
*Victoria and Albert Museum, London*

## 210 ▷
# A drawing-room in Naples, Italy(?)
*c.*1780

The formal arrangement of the pictures and chairs forms an essential part of the normal appearance of the room, but three chairs have been pulled forward round the tea-table, which has been brought in for the purpose. It is apparently an English table; note, incidentally, its plain top. The lady has a French-style work-table at her side, which is also a piece of furniture that can be moved about at will. The chairs seem to be Italian, and are versions of the standard French *Louis Quinze fauteuil*. The 'Nativity', top left, is by a Neapolitan painter active 1630–50.

*Private collection, Dublin*

## ◁ 211
# A drawing-room in Boston(?)
*c.* 1788

Painted by Johannes Eckstein, a German artist who emigrated to America, this shows the Samels family in their prosperous New England interior. That they were not poor is indicated by the presence of a carpet (most likely an Axminster imported from England) rather than fitted carpeting. The English porcelain figures were also costly, as must have been the mahogany furniture which was very probably made locally but in close imitation of English originals. There is a pierced brass fender. The walls may be papered in plain blue wallpaper (this is not very clear) round which a border has been pasted. For some reason there is no adornment over the fireplace: perhaps they were awaiting the arrival from England of a picture or a looking-glass.

*Museum of Fine Arts, Boston, Massachusetts*

## 212
# A German bedchamber, Dresden(?)
*c.* 1780

The bed is of the French type with 'flat' valances. The curtains are drawn to enclose the bed during the daytime. They do not match the wall-hangings, which may be of wallpaper. The divided window-curtains are of a light colour and weight, and must be to protect against sunlight. The desk is in the French style but is probably German. Note the way the pigeon-holes are used. The chair is a late German version of the French *Louis Quinze fauteuil*. The ladies are engaged in some activity such as braiding, requiring silk from several sources; the ball is held by the girl and two reels are mounted on a stand which is on the table between the windows. The dog has a cushion. Candles tend to be left in their candlesticks during the day after the middle of the century, as here (see also Pl.188). (By Johann Eleazar Schenau, who was Director of the Art School at the Meissen porcelain factory at this period; he was later Joint Director of the entire enterprise.)

*Metropolitan Museum of Art, New York; bequest of Edward Fowles, 1971*

Ifaac Taylor del. et sculp.

Published as the Act directs 1st. June 1778, by T. Cadell in the Strand.

## 213 △
### Scene in an English dining-room
1778

This shows the kind of sideboard introduced by Robert Adam and his followers in the 1760s, flanked by a pair of pedestals with urns (one is seen here). Often the urns served as cisterns for water which could be used to rinse wine-glasses. In the pedestal, which was in fact a cupboard, was a drawer lined with lead that formed a basin. In the opposite pedestal there might be an arrangement for warming plates, a metal-lined cupboard with a small heater. Note the array of plate on the sideboard, and the knife-box. On the walls may be a wallpaper. The floor has a fitted carpet. The dining-chairs are of the standard English type.

*Victoria and Albert Museum, London*

## 214 ▽
### A gentleman's dressing-room, Paris
1781

A man's dressing-table seems to be only marginally less decorated than that of a woman at this period, if this carefully detailed engraving is anything to go by. He wears a gown to protect his clothes from the powder that has to be applied to his hair. The mat on the floor is also to catch powder, hair, pins, etc. The second servant is testing a pair of curling-tongs, so the master is presumably wearing his own hair and not a wig. His tailor and an assistant have brought him a new silk coat with embroidered borders. A footman stands behind, ready to run errands or remove importunate tradesmen. Behind him is a fashionable desk with a falling writing-leaf (*à abatant*). Note the protective curtains on the two pictures. A buttoned squab for a chair lies on the floor; perhaps it is for use by the dog. (From *Le Monument de Costume*; see Pl.215.)

*Victoria and Albert Museum, London*

215 ▷
# A private supper, Paris
## 1781

This well-known engraving after a drawing by J.M. Moreau is worth close study because the details are so meticulously rendered. It would seem that these four young people are dining in a closet or small private bedchamber, because the curtained niche behind is of the form usually made to contain a bed or *méridienne* and it seems fair to assume that this is what one could see if the man on the right were to move his chair. The table has almost certainly been brought in for the occasion. The table-cloth entirely hides the legs but, since it is square, the corners have been knotted up off the ground. The two small *tables servantes* have casters and are designed for just such occasional use; their tops each contain a built-in ice-bucket. On one may be seen a vessel for cooling glasses; one can see their rims held in the slots, and their bowls resting in the cooled water. Note the elegant centre-piece topped by a pineapple. The central illumination is provided not by a chandelier but by a decorative lantern containing several candles. It has a disc above to protect the cord and tassel from heat. Presumably it can be raised and lowered to make it easy to service the candles. While the small tables still have curved legs, the oval-backed chairs are totally Classicized. The arrangements indicate that the presence of servants would be unwelcome; it was no doubt a '*souper fin*' as the title claims, but it must also have been – or so it would appear – a very private party indeed. Apart from the opened letter and a bouquet of flowers, on the floor there lies a bow which one can only suppose the man on the left has plucked from his friend's corsage. (From *Le Monument de Costume*, Paris.)

*Victoria and Albert Museum, London*

◁ 216, 217
## Walls with day-bed in a niche, Paris
### late 1770s

The military décor of the top room, above left, hardly seems very serious. The swords and vaguely Classical standards are surrounded with extremely effeminate floral ornaments with turtle-doves and wreaths. The fasces forming the legs of the day-bed seem rather a joke, and the shaped valance round the niche (which brings to mind the *lambrequins* of the 1860s – see Pl.394) seems entirely frivolous. Some *demi-mondaine* who liked entertaining young officers might have wanted such a setting for her closet. The niche is backed with mirror-glass, which Blondel had indicated should be avoided by people jealous of their reputation. The other niche, below left, contains a *lit à la polonaise*, the curving iron rods of which are formed like fronds of palm. The minimal curtains are purely decorative. (Both by Pierre Ranson (d. 1786) who published a series of engraved proposals for mural decoration in 1780(?), of which these are the original coloured designs.)

*Cooper-Hewitt Museum, The Smithsonian
Institution's National Museum of Design,
New York*

## ◁ 218
### Mural decoration in the Royal Palace, Milan
#### *c.* 1780

This distinguished engraving is one of the large plates in Giocondo Albertolli's *Alcune Decorazioni di nobili sale ed altri ornamenti* which introduced to the interested public illustrations of this architect's work for the Hapsburg Governor of Lombardy. It shows an assured handling of Classical detail. Note the treatment of the divided *portière*. The shape of the console table beneath the glass can only be deduced from its shadow, since its top has the same moulding along its edge as that of the chair-rail. The previous plate in the publication, referring to the same room, is dated 1784. (From a corpus of Albertolli's work published in 1843; *Alcune Decorazioni* was published in 1787.)

*Victoria and Albert Museum, London*

## 219 ▽
### The wall of a Parisian *salon*
#### *c.* 1785

This is one of two designs for a *salon* by Louis-Gustave Taraval, who was Inspector of Royal Buildings (see Pl.189). The sofas are set in niches that are backed with mirror-glass and framed with curtains which are non-functional and entirely decorative. It is worth comparing this with Pl.202.

*Cooper-Hewitt Museum, The Smithsonian Institution's National Museum of Design, New York*

◁ 220

## The Holbein Room at Strawberry Hill, Twickenham, Middlesex
### 1788

Horace Walpole was already altering rooms at his villa on the banks of the Thames by the early 1750s. This striking bedchamber was added to the house in 1758 and completed the year after. The room survives. The walls were hung with purple paper on which were arranged copies of the famous Holbein portraits in the English Royal Collection (then to be seen in the Queen's Closet at Kensington Palace). They had black and gold frames. The Gothic ornaments of the ceiling are of papier mâché. The bed was provided by the famous cabinetmaker William Vile, who was paid for it in 1760. It had purple and white hangings to match the rest of the décor. The ebony chairs and table were East Indian and late-seventeenth-century, and had been 'picked up at auctions'; but they were thought by Walpole and his friends to be Tudor. They set the pattern for such antiquarian exercises in interior decoration for three-quarters of a century because all the arrangements at Strawberry Hill were so widely publicized. The carpet was made by the famous actress Kitty Clive. This watercolour was executed in 1788, by John Carter. The pole fire-screen cannot be of a date much earlier than that.

*Lewis Walpole Library, Yale University*

## 221
## The Great Parlour at Strawberry Hill
### 1788

This room was in fact one of the first to be Gothicized by Horace Walpole in his Thames-side villa at Twickenham and must have looked very much as shown here by the mid-1750s. The Gothic ornaments in the frieze seem to have been of papier mâché, for in 1751 they are described as being 'a sort of stucco paper ... stamped so deep as to project considerably ... the ornaments are all detached and put on separately'. Papier mâché was certainly used in other rooms (see Pl.220). The fireplace was designed by Walpole's friend Bentley; he also designed the chairs which were then executed by a leading cabinetmaker named Hallet. They have rush seats to make them seem more mediaeval. Hallet also provided the sofas, which are of the standard English mid-century type. They have loose covers of red and white checked linen. The stained glass was added in 1774, and the famous Reynolds portrait of the three Waldegrave sisters was shown at the Royal Academy in 1781. The French bronze clock on the Chinese lacquer desk also cannot be earlier than the 1760s (Walpole visited Paris in 1765–6). It is because such changes have been made that this picture, painted by John Carter in 1788, is included here rather than earlier in the book. The matting, possibly North African, was probably introduced to add a further monastic touch. The room was also known as 'The Refectory', so presumably it served as the dining-room.

*Lewis Walpole Library, Yale University*

222 △
## Drawing-room in a Swedish country house
### 1780s

The muslin curtains are probably purely decorative; they are of the simplest kind, ruffled on a rod. There may perhaps be simple roller-blinds, operated by cords (without springs) but one cannot be sure. The looking-glass is of a characteristic Swedish form, Rococo in shape but with Classical ornaments. Below stands what is almost certainly one of those tables with a faience tray-top which is a type peculiar to Scandinavia. The chairs, with their oval *Louis Seize* backs encompassing an English splat, are typical Stockholm products of the late eighteenth century. In such a setting they are likely to have been painted (grey, pale yellow, blue or brown were the commonest colours) rather than gilded. The wall seen behind the girl (the artist's sister, Brita) is probably of canvas painted with floral garlands. She is engaged in some textile handiwork, perhaps crochet, using a work-stand. (Ribbingfors House in Västergötland, residence of the Geijer family, drawn by Frederik Adolf von Numers.)

*Swedish private collection; photograph from Nordiska Museet*

223 △
## Bedchamber in a Swedish country house
### 1783

This sketch may show a bedchamber, which it was perfectly conventional, in Sweden and elsewhere, to use also as a sitting-room. However, it is just possible that the central feature is more of a day-bed, set up in a closet. The bed is anyway set sideways-on against the wall in the French manner, and the dome of the tester may very well be fixed to the wall as it does not seem to be supported by any irons – and there are certainly no posts. Note how the hangings run on a rod outside the dome; there is no valance but the bed is none the less quite smart as it is furnished with a splendid set of plumes as a finial. The occasional table is a Swedish version of the standard English form. The chair is of the turned type. It may have a stuffed seat, but this is hidden by a checked linen loose cover. The man, Count Claes Ekeblad, who was also a General and Lord Lieutenant of a county (*län*), is engaged in making netting – one of the many handiwork pastimes acceptable in polite circles at this period. The lady is his wife, Countess Brita. (Drawn by Lars Sparrgren at the Ekeblad country residence, Stola, in Västergötland.)

*National Museum, Stockholm*

## 224 ▷
## A drawing-room in New Hampshire (?)
### c. 1783 (?)

This might be a scene in England, but it is sometimes claimed to be the home of Sir Benjamin Thompson at Concord, New Hampshire. The watercolour was discovered in New Hampshire and has associations with Thompson but, if it is of him and his family in the 1780s (the ladies are dressed in the English fashion of that date), then it has to be between 1782, when he returned to America from England, and 1784 when he left to serve the King of Bavaria and was eventually given the title of Count Rumford. In favour of this dating is the two-manual harpsichord which clearly bears the name of the well-known London maker Baker Harris, who died in 1781. Thompson was rich and would hardly have bought an old instrument to take to America. If this surmise is correct, he and his family are here shown gathered with pride round this instrument, which must have been an exceptional object in America at that date. Another indication that this may show the Thompson house in Concord is the fact that the grate is for burning coal. In America it was then unusual to burn this fuel (there was plenty of wood) but Thompson was extremely interested in heating arrangements and was later to invent the 'Rumford grate' in the 1790s. The fitted carpet is also likely to be English, perhaps Wilton; it has a narrow border attached. The walls are probably papered and painted blue, and they have a cut-out border all round. Note the dark-coloured skirting with the moulding along the upper edge painted a light colour – a feature of many English interiors at this period. The paintings behind the figures are shown set high but this could be an artistic licence, taken to avoid confusion.

*National Gallery of Art, Washington D.C.; gift of Edgar William and Bernice Chrysler Garbisch*

## 225 ▷
## An apartment in Stockholm
### c. 1790

This shows Warehouse Inspector Georg Diedrich Heimberger taking a nap, perhaps after lunch, while his daughter plays patience on a tea-table which has the usual plain top. A rather larger table of the same sort, which probably served as a dining-table when there was only the family present, stands parked in the corner with its leaf tilted. In the opposite corner is a characteristic Swedish faience stove, standing on a zinc plate, its ash-tray having been placed out on the floor. Two jars of preserves stand on the shelf. The walls are no doubt covered with canvas, painted with simulated panels in the manner often used in Sweden at this period. Note the pictures hanging from ribbons ending in bows. (Klarabergsgatan No. 68, painted by Carl Wilhelm Svedman, who married the daughter.)

*By courtesy of Herr Sten Morssing; photograph from Fotocentralen, Nora*

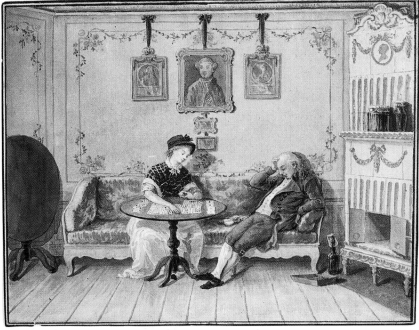

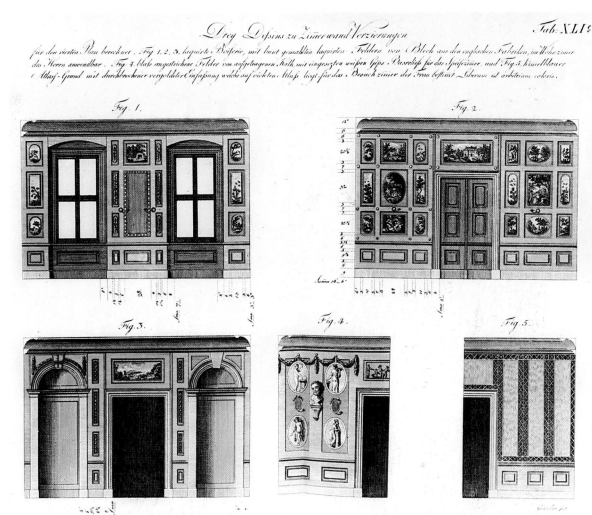

*für den vierten Plan berechnet. Fig. 1.2.3. laquirte Boiserie, mit bunt gemahlten laquirten Feldern von Blech aus den englischen Fabriken, im Wohnzimer des Herren anwendbar. Fig. 4. blaß angestrichene Felder von aufgetragenen Kalk mit eingesetzten weißen Gips Basreliefs für das Speisezimer, und Fig. 5. himelblauer Atlaß-Grund mit durchbrochener vergoldeter Einfaßung welche auf violten Atlaß liegt für das Besuch zimer der Frau bestimt. Liberam est arbitrium coloris.*

Fig. 1.     Fig. 2.

Fig. 3.     Fig. 4.     Fig. 5.

◁ 226

## Count Stroganoff's picture gallery, St Petersburg
### 1793

The Count sits reading. Servants await his commands at a respectful distance. In the central window-embrasure is a large columnar stove of faience surmounted by a bust. The room can be illuminated by candles in the chandeliers and the four candelabra on tripod stands in each corner. The parquet is French in style but the proportions are different. On the left is a small steel table, perhaps made at the imperial ordnance factory at Tula. Each picture has a label at the top of its frame. A strangely incongruous note is lent by the bird-cage by the window, and there is a ludicrous, enormously fat pugdog – or it may be an English bulldog. (By A.N. Voronikin.)

*Hermitage Museum, Leningrad*

227 △

## A plate from a German architectural manual
### 1799

Proposal for mural decoration for a gentleman's reception rooms. Figs. 1–3 have painted wooden panelling with inset 'lacquered panels of tinplate from the English factories' (*lacquirten Feldern von Blech aus den englischen Fabriken*). Fig. 4 is for the dining-room and was to be executed in distemper with inset bas-reliefs of white plaster. Fig. 5 was for the lady's drawing-room; it had sky-blue satin panels which were to be framed with violet-coloured satin over which was fixed gilded trelliswork.

*Victoria and Albert Museum, London*

228 △

## A rich New Hampshire businessman

*c.*1793

John Phillips, a graduate of Harvard, founded the Phillips Exeter Academy in 1781. His house is well appointed in a reticent vein. Note the handsome panelling and the drop-leaf mahogany table under its simple 'table carpet'. In the room beyond stands another folding table against the wall. The elaborate window-curtains pull up 'in drapery' and have a fringed pelmet. The walls were probably papered and have paper borders with a colourful floral design. Most striking are the floor-coverings which are probably of painted canvas floor-cloth but may just possibly be of some kind of carpeting 'planned to the room'. (By Joseph Steward.)

*Dartmouth College Museum, Hanover, New Hampshire*

△ 229

## A library in Scotland

late 1780s

Miss Mary Turnor Hog in the Library at Newliston, West Lothian, painted by David Allan. This probably shows a room in the old house which was replaced by that designed by Robert Adam and completed shortly after his death in 1792. The floor is fully carpeted and the walls seem to be papered and trimmed with a strip of bordering round the fireplace. It must be summer because there are flowers in the grate. The tea-table has the usual plain top. The chair and foot-stool are covered in striped loose covers. The bookcase is painted white. This would seem to be an early example of the library being used more as a family drawing-room than as a gentleman's preserve.

*Scottish private collection*

· OLOF ·      · DEN · 21 · DEC<sup>R</sup> · 1798 ·      · FAUST ·

### 230
## A middle-class drawing-room
## in Stockholm
### 1798

It is Christmastime, as the sprigs of juniper cast all over the floor indicate. This is the tail-end of the old mediaeval custom of strewing sweet-smelling greenery on floors on festive occasions. The room is in the house of Johann Rosenlind, the Master of the Stockholm Saddlers' Guild, at Lilla Nygatan No. 2. The chairs are Stockholm versions of Hepplewhite designs. Note the buttoned squabs on the settee. What looks like a wallpaper border is applied as a frieze, while the walls themselves are blue, probably painted. There are no window-curtains. The loose covers are of blue and white checks. (By Olof Faust.)

*By courtesy of Ingenjör Stig Hallberg; photograph from Kulturen, Lund*

## ◁ 231
### An English sofa-bed
### 1793

Designed by Thomas Sheraton, this is clearly based on French models for couches or *méridiennes* that would mostly have stood in elegant closets. As Sheraton explains, the drapery is 'of the French kind'. The rosettes are formed with silk cord and have hooks for the tie-backs. When unhooked 'the curtains will come forward and entirely enclose the whole bed'. The head-cloths on grand beds of this sort are pleated in 'what the upholsterers call a fluting' which is executed on a wooden frame. The tester is fixed to the wall, he states. Note the decorative festoons on the base-valance, another favourite French motif at this period. Since the tester was fixed, it is difficult to explain why the legs have casters. (From T. Sheraton, *The Cabinet-Maker and Upholsterer's Drawing-Book*, London, 1793.)

*Victoria and Albert Museum, London*

## 232 ▽
### The Chinese Drawing Room
### at Carlton House
### *c.* 1790

From Sheraton's *Drawing-Book*. Careful inspection shows that there is a screened alcove at the far end of the room which 'contains an ot[t]oman, or long seat, which extends the whole width of the room'. Only part of the divan can be seen in this view. Inside this alcove are 'two grand tripod candle-stands, with heating-urns at the top'. In front of the colonettes is a pair of incense-burners. 'The carpet is worked in one entire piece, with a border round it', which would seem to have been an amazing achievement. It is known to have been woven at Moorfields. Some of the furnishings in this room were provided by Dominique Daguerre, the celebrated Parisian dealer in luxury wares, who also had a branch in London. The chairs were actually made by the immigrant French chair-maker François Hervé, whose premises were in the Tottenham Court Road. He was probably working to designs sent over from Paris. The chairs had covers of Spitalfields silk specially woven to shape; over half the cost of the chairs was for this material.

*Victoria and Albert Museum, London*

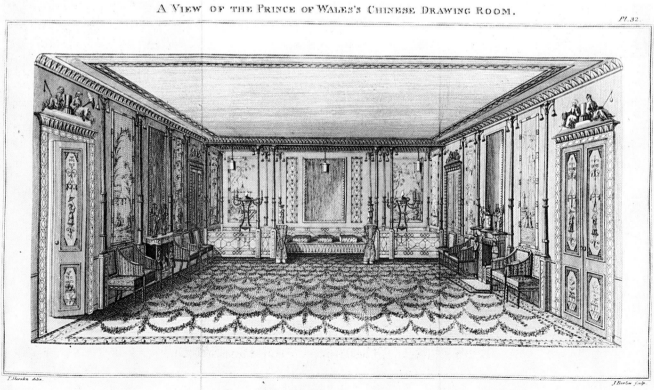

### 233
## A fashionable English drawing-room
*c.* 1790

Drawn by Thomas Sheraton, who explains that he has been to see the Prince of Wales's house (i.e. Carlton House; architect Henry Holland) as well as 'the Duke of York's, and other noblemen's drawing-rooms', but that he had 'not, however, followed any one in particular', choosing instead the features 'best suited to give a display of the present taste in fitting up such rooms'. But he then goes on to describe 'the Prince's room', saying that it has five windows instead of the four shown here, and one therefore gets the impression that this illustration shows in all essentials what the Carlton House drawing-room looked like. Note that the windows opening on to balconies are of the sliding-sash variety rather than of the French type that opened like paired doors. There are candelabra on the pier-tables. The curtains seem to consist of fixed flanking pieces, caught up with cords, and divided curtains drawn up 'in drapery', but it is possible that the whole is non-functional. The commode set under its accompanying glass opposite the fireplace is noteworthy. (From T. Sheraton, *The Cabinet-Maker and Upholsterer's Drawing-Book*, London, 1793.)
*Victoria and Albert Museum, London*

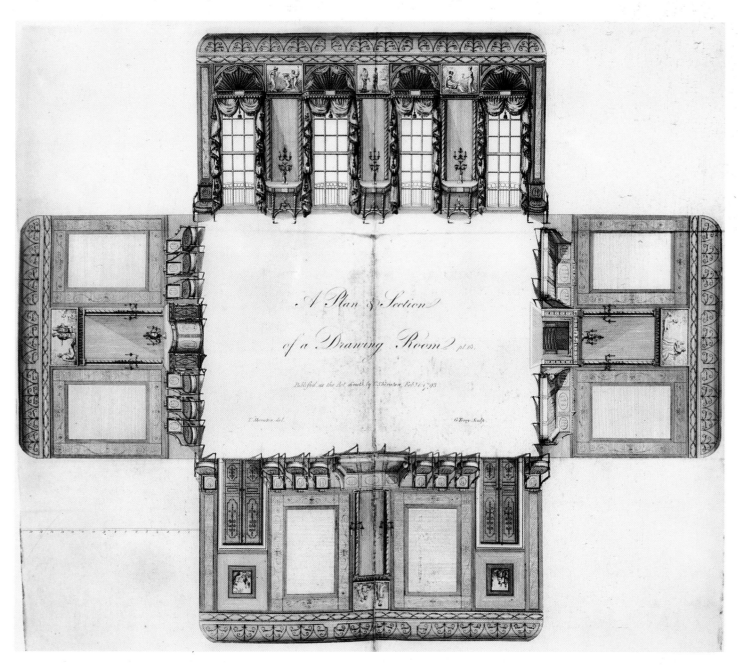

Salle des Bains de la C.<sup>nne</sup> Dervieux.

Décoration des grandes Niches.

◁ 234

## Mlle Dervieux's bathroom, Paris
### 1789

In 1789 F. J. Bélanger added on to this lady's house a dining-room and also a small wing containing a bathroom, boudoir and niche. In this delightful coloured engraving we see the bathroom with covered benches in four niches (two visible here) and its bath in the middle. Beyond is the boudoir, in which stands an armchair which was presumably furnished by the famous firm of Jacob which she is known to have patronized. The room has four apsidal niches, and on the floor lies a superb circular Beauvais carpet. Behind is a small alcove with a draped ottoman running round three sides. Off this last two small doors led – one no doubt to a *lieu* or 'loo' and the other to the back-stairs and out to a back-yard. A small garden lay to the left of the rooms shown here. Mlle Dervieux was a celebrated dancer; she liked to have musicians playing close by so that, when entertaining her friends, she could trip prettily about in the rooms shown here. Bélanger's intimate relationship with his client caused something of a scandal, but he eventually married her. When this engraving was made by Detournelle in about 1790, the Revolution was in full swing, and she is therefore here described as 'C[itoye]nne Dervieux'.
*Bibliothèque Nationale, Cabinet des Estampes, Paris*

236 ▷

## A plate from a German fashion journal
### 1795–1800

This is a proposal for a garden pavilion with painted walls. If so desired, the candelabra can be fitted with real branches, the caption informs the readers, who are here receiving news of the newly fashionable Pompeian style. From F.A. Leo's *Magazin für Freunde des guten Geschmacks*, which was published in Leipzig in the mid-1790s and had a considerable influence in Central Europe.
*Metropolitan Museum of Art, New York;*
*Harris Brisbane Dick Fund, 1930*

◁ 235
## A *salon* in Germany
*c.* 1790

By Etienne Dubois whose son wrote on the reverse that this was for a *salon* for the Prince of Hesse, drawn 'before 1792'. The painted panels presumably represent two of the seasons. The decoration on the pilasters embodies the 'pointed-oval' and cameo-ornament that were to become so common early in the next century. Note how the sofa fits the dado and panelling exactly. It has arm-rests in the form of sphinxes and a strange mixture of legs. The upholstery comprises tapestry-woven covers, it seems. The way the cushions are laid over cylindrical bolsters is noteworthy – it was a feature much employed by early-nineteenth-century designers.

*Cooper-Hewitt Museum, The Smithsonian Institution's National Museum of Design, New York*

## 238 (*opposite, top left*)
## An elaborately decorated Parisian boudoir
### 1802

A plan of the room, given in the middle on the right, shows how the day-bed stands in the niche opposite the window – both of which are shown here. The caryatid terms are in the form of pilasters standing on a shelf formed by a projecting dado. There is a dome above. The bold netted fringe ending in heavy tassels is a new form which became popular in the early nineteenth century. This room was decorated by the architect Bruneaux (Brunault?) for a Mme Cheneaux in 1802. It was extremely colourful with white figures on a blue ground, gilt framing, and lilac-coloured curtains round the blue sofa. (From J.C. Krafft and N. Ransonette, *Plans, Coups, Elévations des plus belles Maisons et Hôtels construits à Paris et dans les Environs*, Paris, 1802.)
*Victoria and Albert Museum, London*

## ◁ 237
## A window in a Parisian boudoir
### *c*. 1801

The glass which looks like a mirror was in fact unsilvered and one could look out on the statue and the foliage in the small garden beyond. Below was a clock flanked by book-niches, and in front of these was a sofa of the characteristic *Empire* form, covered with a silk with *fleurons* and stripes. Note the loose-hanging scarf forming a sort of anti-macassar, and the soft cushions that follow the graceful lines of the side-rests. The outer covers of the cushions consist of two layers of material buttoned together along their edges so that the silk covers of the cushion itself peep through – an old sixteenth-century effect that Percier revived. This design is from C. Percier and P.F.L. Fontaine's famous *Recueil de Décorations intérieures . . . executés sur leurs dessins*. The plates of this work came out in sets from 1801 and had reached No. 54 by 1805. The complete work appeared as a volume in 1812. This illustration was No. 60, so will have appeared in about 1805. The room was executed in Paris for Mme Moreau; the Moreaus' house in the rue d'Anjou was decorated by Percier and Fontaine in 1801–2.
*Victoria and Albert Museum, London*

## 239 (far right)
# Parisian upper-class decoration
### c.1815

Like Percier and Fontaine's *Recueil* (Pl.237), this is one of a series of engravings that also appeared in suites (*cahiers*), starting in 1804 until the whole sequence of twenty-four *cahiers* appeared in 1820 under the title *Fragmens d'Ornemens dans le Style Antique*. They did indeed contain numerous motifs and details in the Classical taste suitable for furnishing in rather an elaborate, if somewhat dry, style. They were 'collected or composed' by P.N. Beauvallet, who proudly claimed that he was a sculptor and member of the old Academy, and by Charles Normand, who was an architect. This plate shows two bed-alcoves in the fully developed *Empire* style. The drawings are precise and betray a deep understanding of Classical forms.

*Victoria and Albert Museum, London*

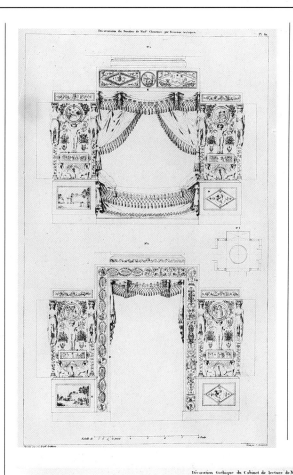

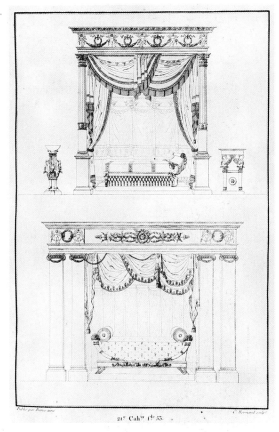

## 240 ▷
# A Neo-Gothic study, Paris
### 1801

This room was designed as a small '*cabinet de lecture*' for a Mme Vanterbergh (van der Bergh) by an architect named Coffinet. It was executed in mahogany and is an early example of the Neo-Gothic style being used in France. At this stage it was still used as a fairly light-hearted form of decoration. In England mahogany was considered entirely unsuitable for a Gothic interior; oak, preferably untreated, was thought much more appropriate. Here, however, the colour-scheme was very elaborate. For instance the spandrels were light blue with silver ornament, while the doors were light blue with red- and puce-coloured lacquer panels on which were green and silver reliefs. The arches were filled with mirror-glass, as were the roundels above. (From J.C. Krafft and N. Ransonette, *Plans, Coups, Élévations des plus belles Maisons et Hôtels construits à Paris et dans les Environs*, Paris, 1802.)

*Victoria and Albert Museum, London*

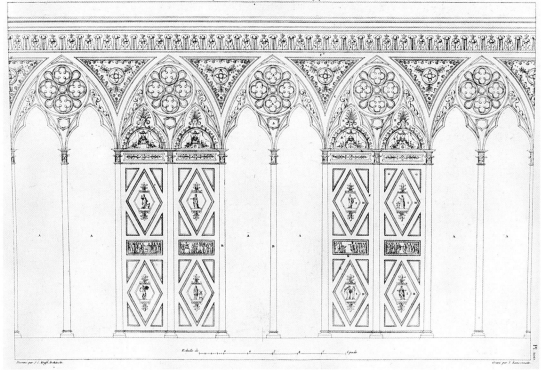

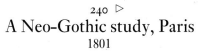

## 241 ▽
# Mme Récamier's bedchamber
### 1802

This famous room was illustrated in Krafft and Ransonette's book on 'the most beautiful houses' in Paris (see Pls.238 and 240) and was visited by everyone interested in the new fashions who had the opportunity to do so. One such student of fashion was the young Robert Smirke, who was later to build the British Museum and who visited Paris in about 1802. He made this watercolour sketch of the room which varies in detail from the

Krafft and Ransonette engraving. He shows a candelabrum on the candle-stand (which we happen to know was of marble) and includes a statue and pedestal on the left. The statue of Silence was by Chinard. There are two night-tables, one with an oil-lamp modelled on antique prototypes. The bed-hangings are of white Indian muslin with spangled gold stars and fringed. Behind the bed is a plate of mirror-glass. The wall-hangings are of violet-coloured silk with printed black border; the capping of the deep pelmet is of a buff-coloured silk with a gold border. Note the thin veil gracefully draped over the bed. The banker Récamier's

house in the Chaussée d'Antin was re-decorated by L.M. Berthault in 1798; he was apparently assisted by Percier. The furniture was provided by Jacob. The bed survives and shows that Smirke's drawing here is more accurate than Krafft's engraving.

*Royal Institute of British Architects, London, Drawings Collection*

## 242 ▷
# A Florentine bathroom
### 1798

A plate in the last issue of *Magazzino di Mobilia*, which had first appeared in Florence in 1795. This shows a bath, which can be 'of granite, or may also be of copper', and has a canopy of green silk. The hot and cold water comes from a room behind, the text explains, through pipes debouching from the lion-masks. The writer admits that 'with us [Italians] baths are not common . . . but well-to-do people are beginning to have a private bathroom' in their houses 'not merely for use in the summer season but for reasons of health'. Alongside is an upholstered chair 'which is suitable for furnishing a bathroom'; it is low with a comfortable back-rest. Underneath the seat, which is covered in the same silk as the canopy of the bath, 'is located a vessel called a bidet' (*un vaso detto Bidè*) which is used 'for baths of a special nature'. There is a decorative silk valance which hides the vessel. The stand on the left is a candelabrum of Antique Classical form.

*Studio per edizioni scelte, Florence*

## 243 ▷
# Design by Charles Percier, Paris
### 1798

The linear style of Percier and Fontaine's famous collection of designs for interior decoration (see Pl.237) is familiar to many people, but this pretty composition by Percier shows how the style they promulgated actually looked when rendered in colour and with shading. This is presumably a day-bed in a closet in the Etruscan style.

*French private collection; photograph from Studio Lourmel, Paris*

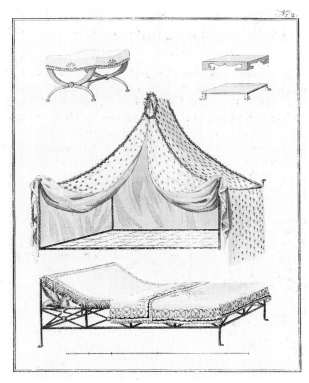

244 △

## The spread of ideas through fashion magazines
### 1790s

From F.A. Leo's *Magazin für Freunde des guten Geschmacks*, which was published in Leipzig in 1796 and had a considerable influence in Central Europe. This plate shows a bed based on Antique Classical models with colourful fitted mattress-cover and coverlet which, it says, are to be painted. Above is what one must presume to be an alternative treatment with a canopy; note that the base is of wire, which must be fairly springy. The hangings are said to be of taffeta. At the top are a stool and two foot-stools.

*The Metropolitan Museum of Art, New York; Harris Brisbane Dick Fund, 1930*

### 245 ▷
## The library as sitting-room, England
### 1815(?)

This shows the late-seventeenth-century library at Cassiobury Park after it had been re-decorated by James Wyatt in about 1800. The Baroque decoration of the overmantel has been retained, as have the cornice and the old family portraits. But the windows are of the new form and have between them narrow pier-glasses with small commodes below. The furniture throughout is in the new taste, with the exception of the spindle-back chair which dates from about 1770, and the large French *bureau plat* at which the lady sits writing which must date from the middle of the eighteenth century. Note the comfortable box formed by the ottomans flanking the sofa, and the position of the sofa-table piled with books. The lighting arrangements are interesting – a lantern, some French bronze candelabra with figures, a shaded candlestick, and two fan-type screens or *gardes-vues*. (From J. Britton, *The History and description . . . of Cassiobury Park*, London, 1837; with illustrations by A.C. Pugin. Britton, who died in 1823, first visited the house in 1800.)

*Victoria and Albert Museum, London*

### 246 ▷
## A Grecian interior, Scotland
### 1808

A design by Sir John Soane for the Drawing Room at Taymouth in Perthshire. The reticent interior architecture of the Greek Revival style is here epitomized. Note the two couches placed at right angles to the wall flanking the fireplace, the festoons between the legs of the Grecian chairs (a detail that it is surprising to find an architect including, so it must have seemed important), and the 'continued drapery' of the window-curtaining – an early example of this. The architect seems to have intended that a specially woven carpet should be provided to cover the whole floor, echoing the design of the ceiling.

*By courtesy of the Trustees of Sir John Soane's Museum, London*

⊲ 247

## An English country-house drawing-room
### 1808

A room added to Browsholme Hall, Yorkshire, in 1805 to the design of Jeffry Wyatt (later called Sir Jeffry Wyatville), this was originally intended to serve as a gallery for the fine collection of paintings amassed by Thomas Lister Parker. The latter's antiquarian interests are here reflected in the ornamental detail for, although the room is essentially Neo-Classical, the frieze is in the Neo-Elizabethan taste – one of the earliest expressions of this revival style. The curious settee may also be a Regency attempt to invent an Elizabethan sofa. Square bolsters like those to be seen on the settee were fashionable in England at this date. The windows are united by an early version of the 'continued drapery' that was soon to become so fashionable. The chairs seem to date from the 1770s. The walls have no dado and are colour-washed a pinkish orange. Note the candle-stand in the corner. Shortly after the artist recorded this room it was converted for use as a dining-room. (By John Buckler, dated 1809; a sketch for this finished drawing, made the year before, is in the British Museum.)

*Victoria and Albert Museum, London*

⊲ 248

## A Frankfurt garden-house
### c. 1811(?)

The Freiherr Anselm von Rothschild bought a house in Frankfurt in 1810 and built this small pavilion in the garden soon afterwards. At the front is an early form of conservatory with some massive stands for large flower-pots. In the room itself are ironwork stands for much smaller pots, flanking the faience stove; such stands were to become very popular in Germany right through the *Biedermeier* period. It is curious to have such an elaborate glass chandelier in such an informal room – an early example of Rothschild magnificence. The use of a foot-stool is well exemplified here. Here too is the round table in front of a sofa, a formula that was soon to be so widely adopted.

*Historisches Museum, Frankfurt-am-Main*

◁ 249
## Breakfast in an Italian *palazzo*
dated 1807

Members of the Ruspoli family at table greet two callers in a fashionably decorated room. Note the fitted carpet with a border, the wallpaper which also has a border, the new horizontal form of overmantel-glass and the elegant chairs. The skirting is marbled. The vines incorporated in the decoration of the chimneypiece confirm that this is the dining-room.

*By courtesy of Prince Alessandro Ruspoli*

250 △
## An evening at cards, Paris
*c.* 1805

The valance or capping running round the room seems to be real, rather than a simulation in printed wallpaper, as it continues above the curtains to the windows which flank the fireplace. The main hangings are probably of silk, and have woven borders of great elegance in the bold style favoured under the *Empire*. A proper carpet is on the floor; it must be a French product. On either side of the pier-glass/chimney-glass is an Argand lamp. Below are two ordinary candlesticks, and on the table is a shaded twin-branch candlestick. Note the mahogany furniture. (By Jean-François Bosio.)

*Bibliothèque Nationale, Cabinet des Estampes, Paris*

## 251 ▽
## An Italian bed
*c.* 1820

This shows how widely adopted were the general principles of French *Empire* decoration, for this splendid bed was designed for a Sienese nobleman, the Marchese Alessandro Bichi Ruspoli. Unlike most French beds of this period, however, this Italian variant has its head against the wall (note the position of the bolster), so the swans with a heavy garland are at the foot end. (Designed by Agostino Fantastici, the prominent Sienese architect.)

*Biblioteca, Siena*

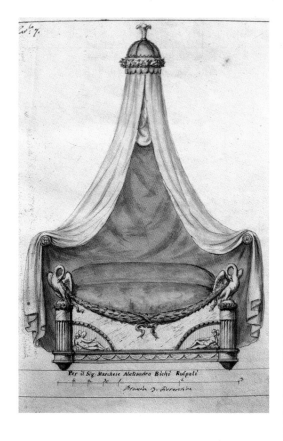

## 252 △
## The Queen of Prussia's bedchamber, Berlin
1810

An early work by Carl Friedrich Schinkel, who had joined the Prussian Department of Works in 1810 and was to become its Chief Architect five years later, this is the epitome of the draped interior so beloved of fashionable people around the turn of the century. The white hangings in fact disguise the old bed-alcove formula, for behind the columns are corner-cubicles. The bed-posts hold out a section of the hangings to form a tester. Note the capitals in the form of owls, and the genies topping the bed-posts. Two alabaster lamps are on the tables in the alcove – one can hardly call them bedside tables. The whole bed-area is slightly raised. When executed for Queen Luise, the ceiling was dark blue shading to violet at the sides.

*Verwaltung der staatlichen Schlösser und Gärten, Berlin*

## 253 ▷
## Queen Hortense's tented boudoir, Paris
1811

This shows a room in the Queen's Parisian house in the rue Cerutti (she was married to Napoleon's brother Louis who was King of Holland). Note how the drapery is carried not only across the niche but also the chimney-glass. From the ceiling hangs a lamp of alabaster. The two jewel-cabinets are now at Versailles. The handsome bookcase by Weisweiler reflected in the panel of mirror-glass behind the ottoman survives at Arenenburg in Switzerland, where the Queen was exiled after Napoleon's fall. Note the *jardinière* by the window; it is now at Malmaison. (By Auguste Garneray.)

*French private collection; photograph from Studio Lourmel, Paris*

## 254
## Drawing-room in the Chinese taste, England
### 1810

From a curious book of *Original Designs ... drawn by and under the direction of G. Landi, architectural painter and professor in the University of Bologna,* published in London in 1810 and dedicated to the Marquis of Douglas and Clydesdale. Landi is not apparently recorded at Bologna! This coloured illustration, however, represents rather well the late-chinoiserie style of the Brighton Pavilion as we can still see it today. It is a style that lacks some of the grace and lightness commonly to be seen in chinoiserie of the previous century. It is exotic but the fairy-like quality is no longer present.

*Victoria and Albert Museum, London*

## 255 ▷
## An English Neo-Gothic saloon
### 1810

From the same source as Pl.254, this shows
admirably the romantic, almost playful form of
Neo-Gothic popular in the Regency period, bereft
of the rather spooky element sought by eighteenth-
century admirers of Gothic taste. An admixture of
mediaeval motifs spanning two or three centuries is
blended with features that have only the most
tenuous links with the Middle Ages, and all are
assembled on a framework that is unmistakably of
the early nineteenth century. A detail of the
chimneypiece reproduced in the next plate of
Landi's book shows more clearly the Regency-style
clock with its Gothicized case, which is flanked by
two rather chesty Holbein ladies seated on X-frame
chairs. The fire-irons are held in stands in the form
of bishops' mitres. The fender and grate could not
possibly be of a date much earlier than the last two
decades of the eighteenth century. (From *Original
Designs ... drawn by and under the direction of G.
Landi, architectural painter and professor in the
University of Bologna*, London, 1810.)
*Victoria and Albert Museum, London*

## 256 ▷
## How to curtain a Gothic window
### 1804

A problem never easy to resolve but Sheraton, who
published this illustration in his *Encyclopaedia*
(which began to appear in 1804 but was never
completed), solved it by ignoring the awkward
shape of the window. However he proposed the
fitting of a roller-blind printed (no doubt, on
cotton) with Gothic tracery and simulations of
stained glass. Note the crescent-shaped hold-ups
through which the curtains are draped. (From T.
Sheraton, *Cabinet-Maker, Upholsterer and General
Artist's Encyclopaedia*, 1804.)
*Victoria and Albert Museum, London*

## 257, 258, 259, 260 ▽
## Domestic bliss in Frankfurt
### 1813

Even such simplified, and in places exaggerated, illustrations as these are informative. They come from a pocket-book for the year 1813, published in Frankfurt, with scenes of middle-class courtship and marriage. The first illustration shows the wedding-feast with a toast being given, to the accompaniment of a wind ensemble. Note the exceptional number of candles lit for the occasion. The chandelier seems to have multiple Argand burners. Next we see the wife lying-in, after giving birth to the couple's first child. The bed is of the French type. There is a large stove on its left. Note the tea-table. Next is shown a scene where the parents teach the child to walk, tempting it forward with a doll. An occasional table stands in front of the sofa and there is a foot-stool. On the left is a glazed bookcase. Note the Chinese figure and pair

of black 'Grecian' vases on the mantel-shelf. The fourth scene shows the couple in their drawing-room with French windows opening on to the garden. The couple now have a second child. They sit in a sofa which stands on a carpet, with an occasional table drawn in front. Behind is a small oval glass on what is presumably a wallpaper. In the centre is a square table with books, round which seat-furniture is gathered in the new fashion. The chair is of a well-known German form. (From *Taschenbuch für das Jahr 1813. Der Liebe und Freundschaft gewidmet; W. Jung invt. et fecit.*) *By courtesy of Professor Michael Stürmer*

## 261 (*opposite, above*)
## Library in a London house
### 1813

At first glance this looks like a fairly standard gentleman's house of the Regency period done up in a respectable fashion, but there are certain unusual features. Most curious is the table against the pier on the left, which is black and quite unlike the usual run of Regency furniture. Possibly it was created specially for the owner, Thomas Lister Parker, who had strong antiquarian leanings and therefore liked ancient furniture (see Pls. 247 and 262). He may have felt a black table such as this had a sort of Tudor look about it. The grey cloth covering of the floor may have appealed to the same taste. Above the table is a gilt looking-glass of about 1740. One can only guess at the date of the carved frame over the fireplace, which seems to contain a vew of a house – perhaps Browsholme, Parker's country seat? On the floor is a hearth-rug

embroidered with his crest. Note the two bell-pulls, and also the 'continued drapery' of the curtaining. It may well be that the curtains were rarely pulled, as the windows have shutters and blinds, here called 'shades' as in America. (No. 10 South Audley Street, drawn by John Buckler.)
*British Museum, London*

### 262 (right, below)
## An antiquarian's hall
### 1814

This illustration comes from the guide to Browsholme in Yorkshire (see Pl.247) which was published in 1815. It shows the hall and the assemblage of antique objects that Thomas Lister Parker introduced early in the nineteenth century; the hall had been done over in the 1750s (e.g. the doors and shutters). He had hung the walls with antlers, old armour, armorial shields and pieces of panelling. At the far end, above the massive oak cupboard which presumably comes from some farmhouse, hangs a framed piece of 'turkeywork' of which the family is still proud, dated 1450 but probably made in the seventeenth century. The chimneypiece has been made up of old oak elements from elsewhere to produce a plausible late-mediaeval or early-Renaissance look. The X-frame chairs are based on an ancient formula for ceremonial seats but must in fact be late versions, produced early in the eighteenth century. Four chairs with fancy outlines are presumably Italian *sgabelli* or hall-seats of the sixteenth or seventeenth centuries; it was clearly felt that these also lent a venerable air to a room. The two objects looking like radiator-covers that flank the massive cupboard must be the two turned chairs of about 1580 which are still in the house. They have numerous members and finials, all turned on a lathe in an intricate manner. Such chairs were much beloved by early collectors like Parker. The chandelier with antlers is also still in that position; it must have been inspired by similar confections that could, and still can, be seen in many ancient German buildings. This is one of the earliest views of a room decorated with such an 'antiquarian' arrangement. (From *Description of Browsholme Hall . . .*, 1815.)
*Victoria and Albert Museum, London*

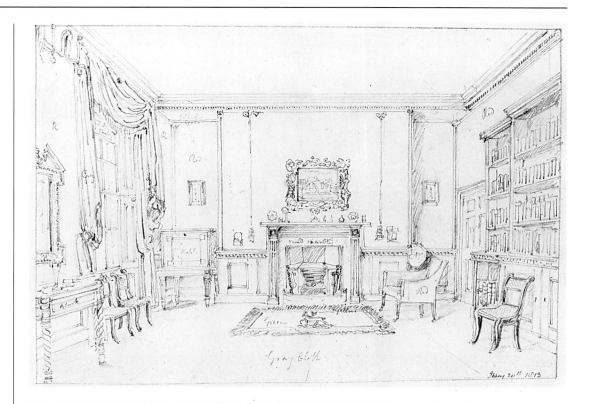

### 263
### Antechamber of a Swedish country house
### 1812

This shows the rooms on the garden front of the principal floor of a not especially large house called Löfstad, which lies near the small city of Norrköping, some 100 miles (160 km) south-west of Stockholm. Beyond is the saloon, and the *salle* lies through the door on the left. The house belonged to Countess Sophie Piper who is seen sewing on the sofa, flanked by her dogs Othello and Fidèle, while her son plays the guitar. Playing patience at what looks like a removable dining-table is the Duc de Pienne (who executed this charming watercolour), a Frenchman who was a close friend of the family but especially of the Countess's brother who was

Count Axel von Fersen (whose chief claim to fame was that he set up the abortive attempt to rescue Marie Antoinette which ended disastrously with her capture at Varennes). He was extremely fond of Löfstad and spent much time there. The house was rebuilt in 1753, but we here see it done over in the late-eighteenth-century manner reflecting French taste for a house in the country, with a blue and white *ameublement* (presumably of printed cotton) and the seat-furniture painted white and blue to match. An armchair on the right has a checked loose cover. The windows have white muslin curtains with a ball-fringe, and dark blue draped pelmets in the new taste, also trimmed with white ball-fringe. Under the round-headed pier-glasses stand Rococo gilded console tables on which are placed huge Chinese porcelain vases. The oval table probably has a tray-top and may serve both

for tea and as a work-table. The upright *secrétaire* at the end of the room (which survives) is probably by the royal cabinetmaker Georg Haupt, as may be the corner-cupboard to its left. The circular tilt-top tea-table (Stockholm-made, of English pattern) has now become a permanent feature of the room, serving as a sofa-table piled with books – the new *Biedermeier* arrangement. Note how two simple turned chairs stand in the room, painted blue and white and with blue and white squabs to match the other furnishings. The Duke sits on a chair in the Sheraton style (probably made in Stockholm but possibly an import). There is a magnificent glass chandelier which, like the Haupt desk, reminds one that this family is rather grand.

*Löfstad Castle Collection; photograph from Östergötlands Museum, Linköping*

264, 265, 266 ▷

## Three Copenhagen interiors
### *c.* 1814

From a small album which is still in the possession of a descendant of the families concerned. These charming watercolours were apparently made by a Mrs Jürgensen, whose daughter was to be married to a young man named Bruun who had however first to go on a prolonged study-tour abroad before he could marry and take up his career as a surgeon. The album was to remind him of his friends and family at home. The first shows the main room in the house of the Gyllembourg family (Mrs Gyllembourg and Mrs Jürgensen were sisters) who were living in Bredgade, a main street in an area which became fashionable in the mid eighteenth century. The house was built in 1801, and is here seen as done over in 1813 with furniture in the newest taste – a Danish version of French *Empire*. On the pedestal-like cupboard is a bowl of flowers, while a pot-plant is on the stand in the window. Note the cast-iron stove in the Classical taste in the corner. Zinc plates are fitted up the walls to protect them from the heat. There is an oval table in front of the sofa. The next picture shows the young man's own home. It has a smart wallpaper with a border, and the sofa is set into a recess. There is a Danish *Empire* looking-glass flanked by small pictures above a table with a fold-over flap and gate-leg action. The muslin curtains hang from a board that is curved in plan – a feature that seems to have been common in Denmark at the time and was no doubt to be seen in other countries as well. Note the strongly coloured rug on the bare floor; it may have been a rag-rug. The third picture shows Mrs Jürgensen's own drawing-room. She moved in as a widow in 1814, and much of her furniture was by then rather old-fashioned. Although the sofa is perhaps new, the chairs are Copenhagen versions of the Chippendale style but are covered with the now fashionable black horsehair. The mahogany commodes and their pier-glasses may date from the 1790s. The symmetrically hung and non-functional muslin curtains are noteworthy.

*Danish private collection; photographs from Thorvaldsens Museum, Copenhagen*

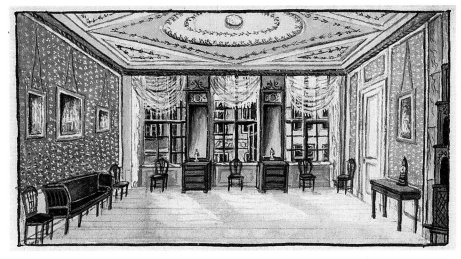

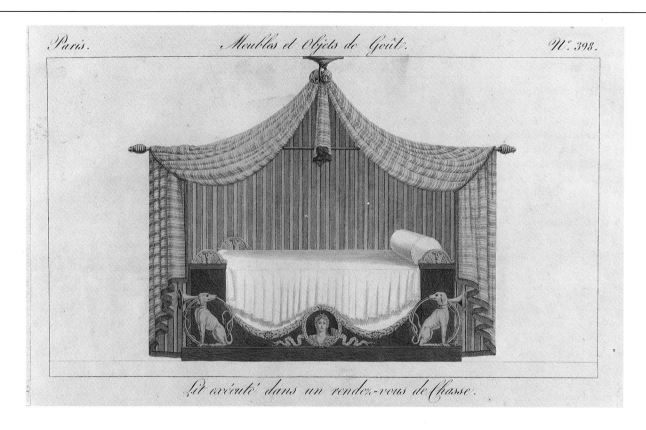

Paris.    Meubles et Objets de Goût.    N°. 398.

*Lit exécuté dans un rendez-vous de Chasse.*

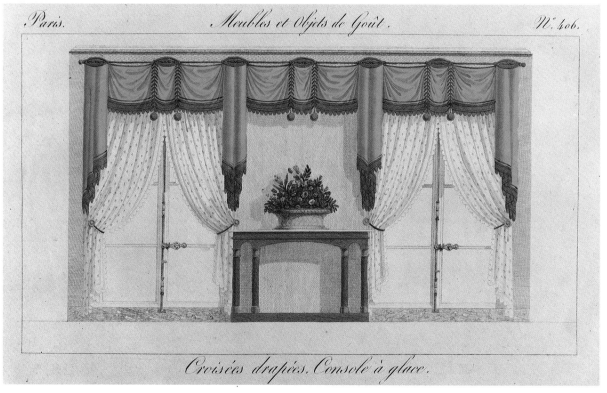

Paris.    Meubles et Objets de Goût.    N°. 406.

*Croisées drapées. Console à glace.*

◁ 267, 268

## Parisian proposals for furnishings
### c. 1814

Two plates from Pierre de la Mésangère's extremely influential magazine entitled *Meubles et Objets de Goût*, which began to appear in 1802 in *cahiers* of ten sheets at a time. The bed has been 'executed for a rendezvous of the chase' (a shooting-box); the plate bears a serial number indicating that it was published in 1814. The second illustration (for window-curtains) has a number which shows it must have appeared shortly afterwards. The bed has emblems of the chase – hunting-dogs, hunting-horns (of the French type), and a head of Diana, goddess of the chase. Its striped hangings depend from a ring fixed to the ceiling. The windows of the other plate have 'continued drapery' linking two windows across a pier furnished with a console-table and a panel of glass that reaches down to the floor. The curtaining comprises fixed silk draperies, with divided curtains of sprigged muslin held back to brass cloak-pins with cords.

*Victoria and Albert Museum, London*

269, 270, 271 ▷

## Parisian upholstery designs
### 1815–20

These small designs for soft furnishings appeared in sets and were sold principally for the use of upholsterers and their clients. They were published as a *Recueil des Draperies* by one d'Hallevant, and offered numerous variations on a few main themes. Armed with these, a skilled upholsterer could conjure up impressive schemes of decoration to deck out a new room or totally alter the appearance of an old one.

*Victoria and Albert Museum, London*

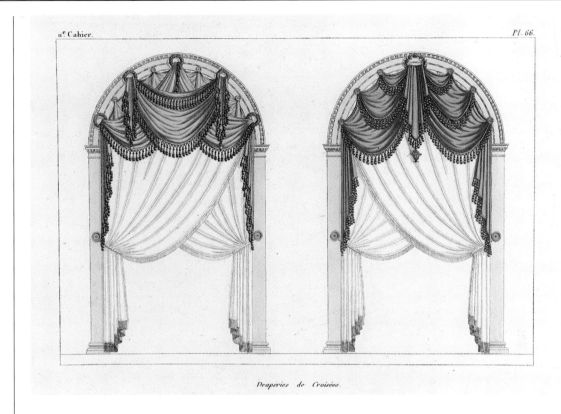

Draperies de Croisées.

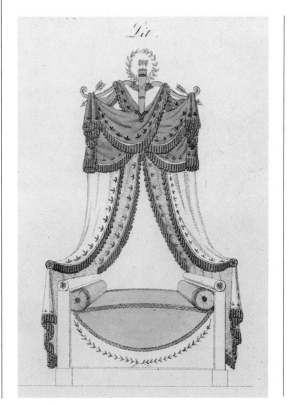

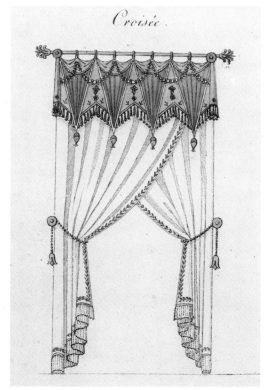

## Living-room in Southern Germany
### c. 1817

This is in a Catholic part of Germany, as may be deduced from the presence of a figure of the Virgin Mary hanging in the corner. It may be the room of the artist himself, G. F. Kersting, who lived in Dresden; there seems to be a tall easel leaning against the wall. It is curious that there is a pair of upright *secrétaires* in this small room; perhaps he and his wife had one each. Her work-table is on the left and on the commode opposite is a small Argand lamp. There is a tall looking-glass with a table below; beyond that is an ottoman with its sofa-table. By the window, with its pot-plants and hanging flower-basket, is what looks like an iron chair with Gothic features. There may be a small fortepiano with piano-stool beyond the right-hand *secrétaire*, but if so it does not seem to be of a standard pattern. Even though the room is not luxuriously furnished, it has a fitted carpet.

*Staatliche Kunstsammlungen, Dresden*

*Die Kinderstube*

### 273 (right, above)
## A South German nursery
### 1820s

There is no fear that these children will be cold at night, if the size of the iron stove is anything to go by. The arrangements seem businesslike and may well have been thought advanced. The pictures look like engravings and are probably of an improving nature. Note the wickerwork baby-carriage. (By Johann Michael Voltz, who was active in Nördlingen.)

*The City Archives, Nördlingen*

### 274 ▷
## Guest-room or garret(?), France
### c. 1818

At first one might suppose that this young lady had been given a bed in some room in the attic so she could stay the night after the ball (note the ticket tucked into the frame of the glass). She has taken great care to lay out her ball-dress on a cunning arrangement of chairs. She uses her shawl as a curtain and her band-boxes for a bedside-table. But the title seems to imply that she actually lives in this room in poverty, spending all her money on finery. Her happy smile suggests she finds this way of life perfectly acceptable. Either way, the décor looks authentic. Note the camp-bed.

*By courtesy of Mrs Stéphanie Maison*

*Luxe et Indigence.*

◁ 275

## An evening round the table, Vienna
### 1819

The relatively strong light produced by the new Astral lamp, which cast little shadow because its oil reservoir was annular and supported the glass shade, made it possible for several people to sit round it and read or sew – for which simple reason the round table standing out in the room with chairs around it soon became standard. Note the fitted cloth. This is the temporary residence at Schloss Heimburg, near Vienna, of King Jérome of Württemberg, the younger brother of Napoleon Bonaparte. His son shows him a card-house while his wife watches from a throne-like chair on the left. Friends sit around the table; a girl is playing a fortepiano and there is a billiard-table. The painted ornaments in the window-embrasures seem very modern. The curtains are exceptionally simple. (By Louis Dupré.)

*By courtesy of Galerie Carroll, Munich*

◁ 276

## A French bourgeoise reading
### 1819

The room is papered right over the ceiling to create a tent-like effect, using a striped paper matching the curtains. The paper even has a border simulating the netted fringe of the curtains; it is used to create a skirting. The sofa and two armchairs are apparently *en suite* but the rush-seated chair, set by the open work-table near the window, is of a humbler type. Note the *jardinière* with a charmingly haphazard flower-arrangement characteristic of this period. The floor paved with hexagonal tiles suggests that this is a room in the suburbs or a provincial town. (By Theodore Le Brun.)

*Metropolitan Museum of Art, New York; purchase,*
*Anne Stern Gift 1979*

### 277
## A headmaster's drawing-room, London
### 1816

This shows the room of the Reverend Dr Philip Fisher, Master of the Charter House, the famous public-school in London. The old seventeenth-century panelled room has been painted white, and he seems to have had large bookcases fitted on either side of the pedimented door-case. Most of the furniture is in the style of the 1760s, and one high-backed chair on the right looks even earlier. But the sofas sport loose covers that disguise their date, while a round table has been placed in the centre of the room – a concession to recent fashionable taste of which a woman, maybe his daughter, would seem to approve as she has drawn up a chair and is sitting at it, writing. Note the fitted carpet which is probably fairly new and the old-fashioned pull-up curtains which are perhaps of crimson morine. The black ornamental vases and ewers in the windows may be of Wedgwood 'black basaltes' and, like the busts, seemingly of Socrates and Plato, above the bookcases, help to lend the room an air of learning with a firm grounding in the Classics. (From R. Ackermann, *The History of the Colleges of Winchester, Eton and Westminster; with the Charter-House ...*, London, 1816).

*Victoria and Albert Museum, London*

## The Boudoir and a chimneypiece, The Deepdene, Surrey
### 1818

The 'Small Drawing-room' or 'Boudoir' (opposite) was apparently Thomas Hope's favourite room in the charming house in Surrey that he re-modelled and extended after buying it in 1806, employing the architect William Atkinson for the purpose. The décor shows strong French influence and is a reminder that Hope admired the Parisian architect Charles Percier (see Pls.237, 243 and 241). The temple-like baldaquin over the sofa is similar to structures that Percier had introduced into important schemes in Paris at the beginning of the century. Hope had strong ideas on the forms furniture should take, and presumably himself designed most of the items to be seen in this watercolour by W.H. Bartlett. The chimneypiece was of Mona marble from the island of Anglesey off the coast of Wales, where there was a small quarry that was owned by an important cabinetmaker and furnisher named Bullock. He undertook some of the most important furnishing schemes at this period and may well have had a hand in decorating The Deepdene. The table, which could be from his workshops in Liverpool, is now in the Victoria and Albert Museum. The chimneypiece (left) was in the Old Library, a room decorated in the 1790s (the frieze and ceiling rose), but re-decorated by Hope about 1818 when this chimneypiece would have been in extremely advanced taste; it could well have been acquired in Paris. Chimneypieces in a very similar style are illustrated in an album of *Modèles de Marbrerie* which was brought out in Paris by a publisher named Bance in 1825–6 and included many items designed by leading French architects of the time. Several are stated to be for 'M. Hope' and are by a 'M. Fedel'. The architect Achille-Jacques Fédel, trained at the Ecole des Beaux-Arts, worked for William Hope in Paris but may well have provided Thomas Hope in London either with an actual chimneypiece or at least with the design for it. The two curious lamps could be of the spring-driven variety designed by Carcel. Hope would certainly have heard of this invention. (From the unpublished album on The Deepdene compiled by John Britton in 1826 and now deposited in the Minet Library, Lambeth.)

*Lambeth Archives Department; photographs by M.D. Trace*

# 1820-1870

MANY PEOPLE still see the nineteenth century as being divided into three periods: an *Empire*/Regency phase when the dominant style was Classical and which faded out in about 1820; followed, according to this simple view, by fifty years of confusion when rooms were cluttered and every possible style was adopted, with Neo-Gothic particularly in evidence; and then the arrival of William Morris who tidied it all up – with the Modern Movement as the natural consequence.

Studies carried out in the main since 1950 have begun to show how very complicated the story actually was, but this broad analysis does provide a crude framework that serves our purpose here in dealing with interior decoration between 1820 and 1870.

In the present century Victorian arts and their foreign equivalents have until fairly recently been viewed with so much abhorrence that modern scholars who turned their attention to the nineteenth century tended to concentrate on the reformist movement that eventually swept 'Victorian art' away. Ruskin, Morris, Eastlake and their followers have therefore been the subject of a vast literature (see the next section). As for the *Empire*/Regency phase at the beginning of the century, this was usually seen as an extension of the eighteenth century when, it was averred, taste had still been pretty well infallible. So this phase was happily accepted and studied by admirers of the eighteenth century. However, the fifty years from 1820 to 1870 embraced the detested Victorian phase and have therefore hardly been studied at all – relatively speaking. Moreover, those architectural historians who have been courageous enough to make forays into this territory have looked mainly at town halls, railway stations, theatres and other public buildings which are intriguing because of their monumental scale or because they were constructed in a novel manner. Residential buildings have so far received very little attention, and virtually nothing has been said about their interiors. So it is not at all easy to decide who made the important contributions, who were the innovators, and which were the houses that were admired on account of their décor.

In fact, the Classical style of the *Empire* and Regency did not abruptly go out of fashion around 1820. A coarser, often more elaborate version remained in favour right through to 1850 or so (Pls. 302, 343, 282 and 312). Long before that time the Classical structure was often being embellished with Neo-Rococo scrollwork and even with Neo-Gothic tracery. This style is clearly embodied in *The Practical Cabinet Maker, Upholsterer and Complete Decorator* by Peter and Michael Angelo Nicholson, which was first published in London in 1826 but was re-issued as late as 1846 (Pls. 321 and 322). In Paris the designs incorporated in the *Collection des Desseins d'Ornement composés, dessinés & gravés par Jacob Petit*, which appeared in 1840, show this style at its most ungainly. In Italy the *Empire* style remained in favour perhaps even more doggedly. There the *Opera ornamentale* of Giuseppe Borsato, published in Venice in 1822, contained designs (many apparently executed) not very different from those of Ruga

dating from 1811 (see Pl. 180). In 1843 Giuseppe Zanetti produced a huge volume of designs in the late-*Empire* taste in Venice under the grandiose title *Studii architettonico-ornamentali nei quali si comprendo ... decorazioni ... suppellettili ... secondo richiedono i bisogni del secolo*, i.e. it comprised designs for decoration and furnishings 'such as the needs of the century required'. So great was the demand for these late-*Empire* designs in Italy that Borsato's work was re-issued in Milan in 1832 and a second edition of Zanetti's book came out in 1850.

Several important volumes of designs from the *Empire* period itself were also re-issued in the second quarter of the century: a third edition of Percier and Fontaine's *Recueil* (see p. 141) came out in 1827, an Italian edition was published in Venice in 1843, and it was still being cited as an indispensable mine of information in 1869.[1] Likewise the *Modèles de Meubles et Décorations intérieures, pour l'Ameublement ... dessinés par M. Santi*, which was first published in 1828, came out again (with some extra plates by Michel Jansen) in 1841. There are other examples, but it should already be clear that the *Empire* style still had validity for decorators in the middle decades of the nineteenth century.

During the eighteenth century the owners of elegant houses had been prepared to allow strangers to visit and view the more showy rooms, as long as the visitors had the right credentials. Some owners, particularly in England, had even had guide-books printed, and certain especially important houses were the subject of handsome monographs. Those published by John Britton were the most distinguished, particularly noteworthy being his *Illustrations ... of Fonthill Abbey* (1832), that on the house of Sir John Soane (1827), and his *Graphic Illustrations of Toddington* (1840). In 1826 he also prepared a monograph on Thomas Hope's house at The Deepdene (Pls. 278 and 279), 'the finest example in England of an Italian villa' as Loudon called it in 1833 (see p. 216). A Continental example of this class of publication was one dealing with the Hamburg house of Dr Abendroth, designed by A. de Châteauneuf (1839), but this also had an English connection for it was brought out by Rudolf Ackermann, the expatriate German who ran a successful publishing house in London which produced a spate of periodicals, including *The Repository of Art ...*, the principal organ for bringing news of fresh fashions in interior decoration (among much else) to Regency England. It ran from 1809 to 1828.

After 1830 or so this source of specific information gives out; Britton's *Toddington* of 1840 was one of the last. The gentleman's house ceased to be on display and became 'a temple not of taste but of the domestic virtues, its privacy only accessible to his family and friends'.[2] Henceforth published information was more general and the names of few houses are mentioned.

The position is only slightly better with regard to France. L. Normand's *Paris Moderne ou Choix de Maisons construites dans les nouveaux quartiers de la capitale et dans ses environs*, published (in Liège!) between 1837 and 1842, is of

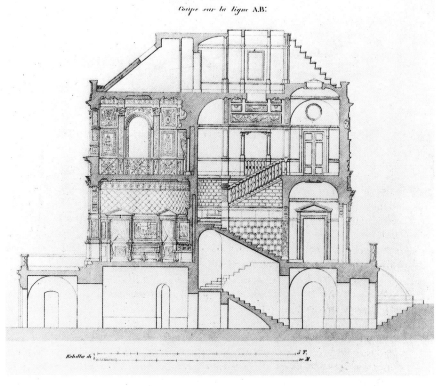

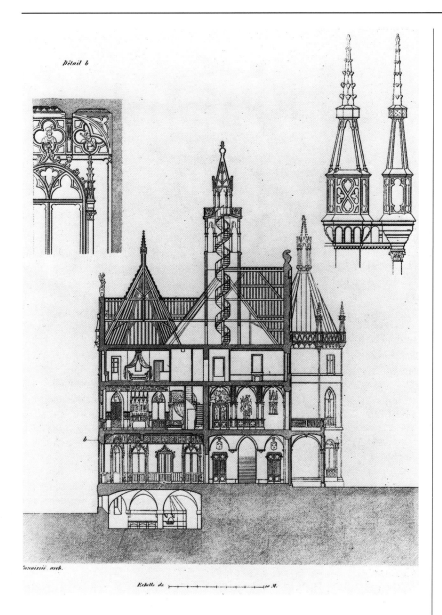

## 281] THE MAISON FRANÇOIS PREMIER IN PARIS   1823

This famous building by L.M.D. Biet was decorated in the *Style Troubadour*, some impression of which can be gleaned from this section through the two *salons*. The complete façade of a genuine house of François I's reign was moved from near Fontainebleau and incorporated in this building in the new fashionable area south of the Champs-Elysées. (From L. Normand, *Paris Moderne ...*, Liège, 1837–42.) *Victoria and Albert Museum, London*

## 280] FRENCH PICTURESQUE   1837

The Neo-Gothic Château de la Roche-de-Veau (in the Sarthe *département*) by the architect Cannissié. This Gothic is still quite playful; a room upstairs has a bed that is essentially *Empire* in concept even if the detailing may be vaguely Gothic. (From L. Normand, *Paris Moderne ou Choix de Maisons construites dans les nouveaux quartiers de la capitale et dans ses environs*, Liège, 1837–42.) *Victoria and Albert Museum, London*

some help. So is J.C. Krafft and Thiollet's *Choix des plus jolies Maisons de Paris et de ses environs* of 1838. Both include plans but a few buildings are also shown in section, presumably because their décor was thought remarkable. Normand mentions the name of the architect and the date. Krafft often mentions the architect but not the date; on the other hand he sometimes gives the name of the client. We can thus gather that the house of the actress Mlle Mars by the architect L.T.J. Visconti was decorated in a noteworthy manner, as was that erected next door by Auguste Constantin for Mlle Duchenois (Pl.328). The actor Talma's house by Charles Lelong must also have been striking inside because we are told the name of the decorators, Duponchel and Piron. The fact that a Neo-Gothic house by J.B.P Cannissié is shown in section suggests that its décor was considered significant, as certainly was that of L.M.D. Biet's 'Maison François Premier' of 1822–5, which for a while gave its name to a whole Parisian *quartier* (Pls.280 and 281).

For the 1830s through to 1864 Victor Calliat's *Parallèle des Maisons de Paris construites depuis 1830 jusqu'à nos jours . . .*, published in Paris in 1850, and *. . . depuis 1850 jusqu'à nos jours*, published in 1864, are helpful and contain a few sections of buildings that reveal the decoration of the principal rooms. A house by Lesoufaché in the rue d'Amsterdam, for instance, with rooms in a good rendering of the 'Hôtel de Soubise' style, seems noteworthy in the first volume and Félix Duban's Hôtel de Pourtalès in the second – although why this building, completed in 1839, should have been included in his second volume is not clear. It is couched in the Italianate Renaissance style which was to become a favourite within Ecole des Beaux-Arts circles. It had an impressive gallery and an 'Etruscan Room'. Sections of a few more buildings appear in *L'Architecture moderne*, which was published, be it noted, in both Paris and London, the first volume appearing in 1862.

Many French and German books appeared during the last decades of the century showing existing schemes of interior decoration: at first only incidentally, along with illustrations of exterior architecture; but later in volumes exclusively devoted to the subject. *L'Architecture moderne* was a forerunner of this genre. E. Titz's *Entwürfe zu ausgeführten öffentlichen und Privat-Gebäuden* ('Designs for executed public and private buildings'), published in Berlin in 1864, was another (Pls.401, 402, 403, 404).

While it was advisable for the fashionable decorator to scan the latest publications coming out in Paris and London,[3] it was still generally acknowledged that the French led the world in the field of decoration and especially in those aspects which were dealt with by the upholsterer. So while the English may have been innovators in the Neo-Gothic field, and seem to have brought out even more decorators' pattern-books than the French, it is still necessary to establish what was happening in Paris if one is to understand what it was that the rest of the civilized world was trying to emulate. Since so little work has yet been done on this theme and the evidence has not been marshalled, the observations that follow are only an early attempt to survey the ground, and can hardly be expected to provide an entirely balanced picture.

The outlines of the picture for the 1820s and early 1830s were provided by Normand and Krafft (see above). Thiollet and Roux's *Nouveau Recueil de Menuiserie et de Décorations intérieures et extérieures* (Paris, 1837) is also helpful, as Pls.328 and 329 show; and so is Bance's *Modèles de Marbrerie choisies parmi ce que Paris offre de plus nouveau et de meilleur goût*, which seems to have appeared in 1825–6 and includes an illustration of a chimneypiece in Mlle Mars's house. Many details can be filled in by referring to C.A. Chenavard's *Recueil des dessins de Tapisseries, Tapis et autres objets d'ameublement* of 1828, and the numerous *cahiers* of elaborate designs for upholstery published by Osmont and his successors.[4] Chenavard's designs are in the *Style Troubadour* (the equivalent of what the English called 'Elizabethan'; see p. 216) and his title-page claims that he worked 'by appointment to the Dauphine'. A fresh *Recueil* appeared in 1835. Few of Osmont's *cahiers* are dated, but the *Empire* designs seem to remain dominant well into the 1830s, a new style with Rococo scrollwork making its appearance around 1837 and a *cahier* with designs in the *Style Renaissance*, so called, coming out about 1840.

The German poet Heine visited Paris in 1836 and recorded that the Neo-Renaissance decoration of the Hôtel Rothschild was very special and that 'Here all is united that the spirit of the sixteenth century can conceive and the riches of the nineteenth century can pay for; here the Genius of Art joins with the Genius of the Rothschilds'.[5] Some details of the décor, executed about 1820, are shown in Thiollet and Roux's *Nouveau Recueil* of 1837 where, however, the style is described as being based on Greek and Pompeian decoration (Pl.329). Pl.248 shows a room at the Rothschild house in Frankfurt earlier in the century. It is still fairly modest, but later 'Le Style Rothschild' became a universal term for splendour backed by enormous wealth and a good eye for antiques. The later Rothschild palaces (e.g. Ferrières, Mentmore, Waddesdon) set the pattern for truly opulent living during the second half of the century; what Heine saw was an early expression of this lavish taste.

It is fairly certain that Félix Duban's Hôtel de Pourtalès in the rue Tronchet (1835–9) contained important interior embellishment, since he is known to have been particularly interested in interior decoration; but although the house survives, its interior was altered in the 1860s. The same architect's doing-over of some rooms for the Duc de Luynes at Dampierre (1839–41) was certainly noteworthy.[6] The Neo-Gothic architect and restorer of churches, J.B.A. Lassus, erected a polychrome brick residence in the avenue Montaigne for Prince Alexis Soltykoff (1848) which presumably had colourful interiors to match, since this architect paid great attention to ornamental detail. On the neighbouring plot was erected the famous and equally colourful '*Maison pompéienne*' for the Prince Napoleon (late 1850s). The architect was Alfred-Nicolas Normand. Apart from its much-admired painted mural decoration (based on the so-called 'Third Style' revealed by the excavations at Pompeii), this house had a delightful conservatory (*jardin d'hiver*) with a Turkish bath annexed, decorated in a mixture of Islamic and '*Néo-Grec*'. The Prince's sister, the Princesse Mathilde, seems also to have played a role in the development of the fashionable interior, not because she herself was an innovator but because her rooms were illustrated in a series of charming paintings by Charles Giraud. The Princesse's house had been re-decorated by Hector Lefuel in 1855. The Empress Eugénie, on the other hand, concerned herself a great deal with interior decoration – it was a standing joke among her entourage – and no doubt what she did was widely noted. Certainly her villa at Biarritz (1855) had an influence on the form considered fashionable for the grand seaside villa. It is probable that the décor of P.F.H. Labrouste's Villa Thouret at Neuilly (1860) was also important, as, evidently, was that of the town-house he built for the Minister of Fine Arts Achille Fould in the late 1850s. In the middle of the century the fashionable magazine *L'Illustration* began to regale its readers with articles on the way various celebrities had had their rooms decorated – some of the very first surveys of a person's arrangements indoors that are such a familiar feature of fashion journals today. One of the first to be subjected to this treatment was the famous actress Rachel, whose rooms may be seen in the engraved illustrations of the issue for 9 September 1853. Achille Fould's house was covered in the issue of 16 June 1860.

The kinds of decoration to be seen in Parisian houses of the 1840s and 1850s are exemplified by the second section of Le Bouteiller's *Journal de l'Industrie et des Arts utiles* (1840) which was devoted to '*Ameublements*' (Pl.347); by Desiré Guilmard's *Le Garde-Meuble ancien et moderne* which ran from 1838 to 1874; and by Léon Feuchère's *L'Art industriel* which comprises a *Recueil de Dispositions et de Décorations intérieures* and came out both in Paris and New York between 1829 and 1848. The *Ameublement parisien*, which seems to have been published by a man named Aubert around 1850, with designs by Beaucé, is also informative; even more so is Victor Quetin's *Le Magasin de Meubles* which ran from the 1850s right into the 1870s (Pls.395, 396 and 400).

Henry Havard, whose four-volume *Dictionnaire de l'Ameublement* (1889–90) is such a rich source of information on furnishing from mediaeval times up to about 1820, has very little to say about developments during his own lifetime. He does mention, however, that 'about twenty years ago people in Paris spoke a lot about the boudoir of Count Mnischek', and quotes the *Petite Revue* of 1864 which describes this 'little Rococo boudoir, a *chef-d'oeuvre* of its sort, entirely faced with mirrors on which gold arabesques scroll and form brackets that support a collection of Dresden china, the reflection of which doubles the magical effect. A clock and sconces of Dresden complete the harmonious image.'[7] Havard implies that for a man to have a boudoir was a bit unusual. He also draws attention to a few other rooms belonging to people in what he calls '*le monde galant*': to the boudoir of Mme de la Panouse (Virginie Heilbronn) which had been admired 'more closely' to his own time; to the actress Mme Gabrielle Elluini's Neo-Renaissance dining-room and '*Louis Seize*' salon, and Mlle Jeanne Olivier's Neo-Gothic dining-room.[8] Mme Elluini's décor was broken up by a sale in 1883 and that of Mlle Olivier in 1888, so these rooms were presumably new in the 1860s. As anyone familiar with French literature of the period will know, this was the great age of the *demi-mondaine*.

The styles of interior decoration fashionable in Paris during the 1860s are brought out clearly by *le Moniteur de l'Ameublement*, which was edited by A. Sanguineti (Pl.289). He claims that the designs he reproduces had been executed 'by the principal manufacturers or decorators in Paris', but he also undertook to provide designs himself on request for all kinds of furnishings. As the illustrations reveal, the art of upholstery reached its zenith in Paris at this time.

Apart from those styles already mentioned several more were current during this period. All were more or less faithful revivals of old styles. 'The present age is distinguished from all others in having no style which can properly be called its own', observed an English writer in 1840,[9] and it cannot be denied that this was an age of rampant eclecticism. 'It's all a game, a matter of passing fancy. If one has had enough of Grecian, one switches to the Renaissance style for the sake of change, and when opportunity offers it's back to Byzantine, before turning to the Rococo', wrote a German in 1839.[10] Which style one actually chose made less difference than one might suppose in many cases, because most of the styles were applied as an ornamental veneer to the traditional architectural shell – a shell that could with some justification be called Classical because it was developed from the Classical room-concept of the Renaissance, the Baroque and Neo-Classicism. Indeed it needs to be stressed that Classicism in one form or other remained the dominant style throughout the nineteenth century in spite of the determined attack mounted against it by advocates of Gothic.

Not only the *Empire* but also the Grecian form of Classicism remained popular right into the middle of the century. 'The Grecian or modern style', Loudon called it in 1833, adding that it was 'by far the most prevalent' style at the time.[11] In 1840 an equally well-informed authority could claim that it 'was much more consonant [than the 'French mode' – by which was meant Neo-Rococo] to the social habits and intercourse of the great mass of the British public who require a cheerful and pleasing but not a gorgeous style of decoration'.[12] There were plenty of people throughout Germany and Scandinavia, as well as in America, who would have shared this view. In these countries as well as in England, a style derived from Grecian (and also therefore obviously classifiable as Classical) was the Italian, the chief distinguishing feature of which was usually its windows and doors with rounded arches – which is why the Germans refer to their variant as the *Rundbogenstil* (rounded-arch style). 'Greek and Italian villas ... are constantly being erected in this country', claimed the writer just quoted, and the American architect A.J. Downing thought the Italian 'by far better suited to symbolize the variety of refined culture and accomplishment which belongs to modern civilization than almost any other style'.[13] No less Classical, although different in spirit and effect on account of its rich ornamentation, was the grander Italianate style now known as '*Beaux-Arts*' which, along with the related Neo-Renaissance, was to become by far the most common style for domestic (and much other) building

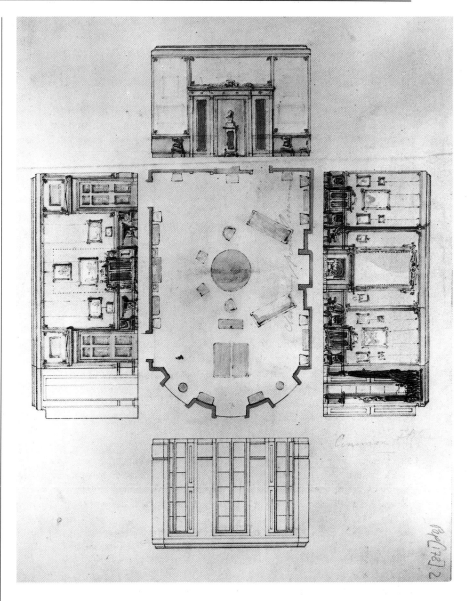

282] A GRECIAN DRAWING-ROOM IN HARLEY STREET, LONDON  *c*.1832

The colours are described as 'Cinimon & Blue', the former being confined to the panels (of silk?) which have buff-coloured surrounds, while the upholstery is dark blue. Two sofas are now splayed out from the fireplace (shown as *bergères* in the elevation). There are many interesting details in this architect's sketch. (From the drawing-office of John B. Papworth.)
*Royal Institute of British Architects, London, Drawings Collection*

283] BERLIN POMPEIAN   1830

A design by the famous architect Carl Friedrich Schinkel for the music-room in the Palais Redern, showing his proposals for the painted decoration. It also shows one of his favourite furnishing devices: a continuous ottoman or 'divan' running along a wall, in this case one of apsidal form. Flowers are much in evidence – a typical feature of the period, especially in Germany. Redern was Director of the Royal Opera in Berlin.
*Verwaltung der staatlichen Schlösser und Gärten, Berlin*

during the second half of the century (Pls.386, 284 and 287). Emanating from the Parisian Ecole des Beaux-Arts, that power-house of traditional architectural instruction that was backed by the French Académie, this style was not only adopted throughout France but was the style principally used all over Europe, and to a large extent also in America and even in England.[14] As Downing said, the French Renaissance style 'is at the present moment [1850] in high favour on the Continent', and the French 'are the best masters of it, as applied to modern uses'.[15]

There were many styles other than Classical. The increasing interest shown during the eighteenth century in the world's architectural heritage reached its culmination, appropriately enough, in 1800 with the publication in Paris of J.N.L. Durand's *Recueil et parallèle des Edifices de tout genre, anciens et modernes, remarquables par leur beauté, par leur grandeur ou par leur singularité, et dessinés sur une même échelle* in which, as the title indicates, famous buildings from all over the world were illustrated to scale. An American architect in 1829 called it 'a library in itself',[16] and although the illustrations were none too accurate and had been edited to suit Durand's thesis, the book gave considerable impetus to the study of the various historic styles. In doing so it incidentally provided fresh inspiration for the anti-Classical movement. In the introduction to that bible of the mid-nineteenth-century antiquarian, Henry Shaw's *Specimens of Ancient Furniture* (1836), Sir Samuel Rush Meyrick, himself one of the foremost antiquarians in England at the time, wrote that 'A feeling has now arisen for the ancient decorative style which it is hoped the present work will materially assist, for however beautiful the elegant simplicity of Grecian forms, these are not in themselves sufficient to produce that effect that should be given to the interior of an English residence'.[17] Durand's aim was very different from that of Meyrick, who favoured 'Mediaeval' styles; but both betoken an interest in styles of many kinds, not merely in the Classical. When H.W. and A. Arrowsmith published their book in 1840 under the title *The House Decorator's and Painter's Guide*, they added the sub-title *Containing a series of designs for decorating apartments suited to the various styles of architecture* and they listed 'Greek, Roman, Arabesque, Pompeian, Gothic, Cinque Cento, François Premier, and the more modern French' (by the last they meant the so-called '*Louis Quinze*' and '*Louis Quatorze*'; see p. 216).

Already by 1828 the possibilities had become so numerous that the German architect Heinrich Hübsch could write an essay with the title 'In welchem Style sollen wir bauen?' – 'What style should we build in?' Exactly the same question was being asked by an English architect in 1864. 'In what style of Architecture shall you build your house?' he asks his client (who is imaginary but by no means far-fetched). 'The bewildered gentleman ventures to suggest that he wants only a simple, comfortable house, in no style at all but the comfortable style, if there be one.' The architect tries to persuade him that they are all comfortable but, after he has reeled off a list of all the possibilities – by this time, more than ever – the client insists that 'I don't want any style at all ... look at myself; I am a man of very plain tastes: I am neither Classical nor Elizabethan – I believe I am not Renaissance, and I am sure I am not Mediaeval'.[18] The range of styles and their respective histories are admirably described in Simon Jervis' *High Victorian Design* (London, 1983) which, although principally about the scene in the British Isles, also throws much light on parallel developments abroad.

The chief rival of the Classical style was the Neo-Gothic, especially in its most uncompromising forms; indeed it looked for a while as if it might triumph, not least when Gothic was the style selected in 1836 for the re-building of the New Palace of Westminster, that focal point of British national pride and political life better known as the Houses of Parliament. Gothic was seen by

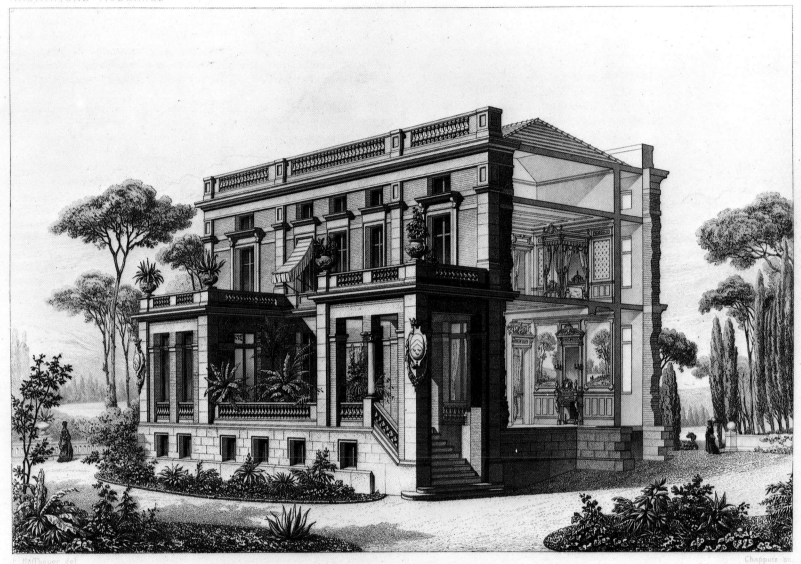

HABITATIONS MODERNES

VILLA
LAC DE GARDE _ (ITALIE)

many people as a national style with strong moral overtones, not only in England, but also by the French, the Germans and the Swedes – the last having perhaps the strongest claim since Götland (East and West) are at least parts of Sweden![19] These qualities rendered the style especially suitable for churches and public buildings generally; it was much less well suited for domestic purposes although it did find favour with the high-minded – of whom there were a considerable number.

It is possible though by no means easy to make an accommodating and pleasant dwelling in the Neo-Gothic style. It was particularly difficult when the

**284] DECOR IN THE DEVELOPED RENAISSANCE STYLE**
*c.*1870

The architect and famous restorer Eugène Viollet-le-Duc included this pleasant villa on Lake Garda in Northern Italy in his selection of *Habitations Modernes* (Paris, 1877). It was outstanding, he claimed, and very different from the many ugly buildings that spoiled that beautiful landscape. He was particularly impressed by the interior arrangements.
*Victoria and Albert Museum, London*

so-called 'reformed Gothic' came to the fore, with its uncompromising insistence on accuracy, love of 'muscularity' and especial admiration for the style of the fourteenth or early fifteenth century (Pl.369).[20] It is a style that looks marvellous in a church, but is difficult to live with in a house. For domestic purposes, therefore, those who wanted to live in Neo-Gothic surroundings tended to choose the late-Gothic style – of which the more pedantic reforming Goths disapproved (Pl.399). Although usually called 'Perpendicular', its lines are mostly horizontal while its openings are either in the form of a flattened arch or may even be actually flat-topped and so are very like 'conventional' windows, doorways and the like. As A.J. Downing (1850) put it, 'there is more domesticity in the square headed window, and we would therefore only introduce the [Gothic] arch . . . when the stronger indication of style is needed to give spirit to the composition'.[21] The 'high-pointed arch', he added, was 'only fit for churches'. It was for this reason that 'Elizabethan' (Pl.327), and its French equivalent, the *Style Troubadour* (Pl.281), enjoyed such popularity during the second quarter of the century, as this style, for all its Italianate detailing, appealed to the same sentiments that made Gothic so attractive and yet was perfectly possible to live with. The *Troubadour* style, incidentally, accustomed French eyes to Renaissance motifs and must have made it easier for the more strictly correct Neo-Renaissance style to gain acceptance so rapidly in the middle of the century.

It was, however, the Neo-Rococo that gained the widest acceptance of all for interior decoration from the 1830s until almost the end of the century (Pls.373, 374, 375, 358, 359 and 390). Its forms were rounded and comfortable, and in an age of great domesticity these were substantial virtues that mostly outweighed those associated with Classicism, Gothic, Renaissance and the rest. And yet the Neo-Rococo or 'Louis Quinze' style had started out in the late 1820s strongly associated with a more formal age, for it and the virtually indistinguishable 'Louis Quatorze' style[22] harked back to the days of the *Ancien Régime* that now seemed so attractive and stable, a time when everyone knew their place. So at first these styles carried almost political implications. Moreover, with its rich ornamentation, with much gilt carving (or, at least, moulded composition or papier mâché), it was expensive to execute; indeed, it had at first been a style taken up principally by the rich. Loudon (1833) specifically states that the style is unsuitable for the less well-off (Pl.361). There had already been a fashion for collecting old or seemingly old French furniture, notably boullework (p. 157), and this explains the remark, made in 1840, that the popularity of the 'Louis Quatorze' style 'may be in great measure traced to the anxiety for French furniture which the wealthy of this country have for some time past evinced'.[23]

Such notions, however, cannot usually have been to the fore when the Neo-Rococo was adopted in later decades. It was then to be seen in most houses, usually in the drawing-room or boudoir, for by this time, the 1840s, it was considered a 'feminine' style. It was greatly favoured by the upholsterers, as it allowed especially free scope for the use of tumbling folds of drapery, quilting, tassels, fringes and deep stuffing. The period 1845 to 1875 might well be called the 'age of the *crapaud*' – of the 'toad', the disrespectful but apt nickname given by the French to the standard, mid-nineteenth-century, heavily stuffed, deeply buttoned and elaborately trimmed easy chair (Pls.347, 373 and 374). This object, together with its sisters the sofas, *confidantes*, *ottomanes*, pouffes, and so forth, were the subject of derision among the 'Goths' and the reformers (see p. 320); but such seat-furniture embodied the true spirit of the period and was to be seen everywhere, modified *ad infinitum* by the application of different forms of embellishment to suit it to the rest of the décor.

In the 1860s the revived 'Louis Seize' style became fashionable and remained in favour until the end of the century when it enjoyed a fresh burst of popularity.

While more readily distinguishable from 'Louis Quinze' and 'Louis Quatorze', the three styles were often confused by ignorant upholsterers and commercial designers – which explains why that iconoclastic furniture historian Delves Molesworth used to refer to it as 'Le Style tous-les-Louis'. A very early instance of the *Louis Seize* revival was to be seen in a German journal of 1846, but a more significant precursor must have been the dressing-table and window-curtaining in this style exhibited by the important Parisian upholsterer Deville at the Paris Exhibition of 1855.[24]

Balzac, in his novels, describes the excitement generated by the amazing fresh opportunities for making money that offered themselves in the second quarter of the century. There were now many *nouveaux riches*, and the middle class was rapidly growing in number and influence. Balzac makes it clear that there were plenty of new rich in Paris, but they were even more numerous in England and America. These people were in particular need of guidance in many fields, not least in household management and, since the *arriviste* usually wanted to build a new house reflecting more appropriately his new standing, he needed information on how to build it, which style to chose, and how to decorate the rooms. It was to answer such questions that a spate of helpful handbooks were published – J.C. Loudon's *An Encyclopedia of Cottage, Farm and Villa Architecture and Furniture* (London, 1833; re-issued until 1867); T. Webster and F. Parkes's *Domestic Encyclopedia* (London, 1844; a trans-Atlantic edition appearing a year later); A.J. Downing's *The Architecture of Country Houses* (New York, 1850), Gervase Wheeler's *Rural Homes, or sketches of Houses suited to American Life . . .* (New York, 1851); Miss Leslie's *Lady's House Book* (Philadelphia, 1854); Robert Kerr's *The Gentleman's House* (London, 1864); and the work of the sisters Catherine and Harriet Beecher Stowe, *The American Woman's Home* (New York, 1864). Of these authors Downing and Kerr are the most literate, but all throw a great deal of light on their subjects.

One of Percier's pupils, Jakob-Ignatius Hittorff, became interested in the coloured effects with which the ancient Greeks had decorated their buildings both inside and out. As a result of a visit to ancient sites in Sicily in the 1820s, he began to publish his findings and his theories. He was not so much interested in archaeology, however; his aim was 'to find elements of use in my professional career' as an architect.[25] His ideas were to have a profound influence on the way colour was introduced in architecture during the mid nineteenth century, and this affected the interior at least as much as the exterior. As one of his friends said, 'Hittorff understood that paint, applied artistically to a building, revealed the details, set off the forms, and underlined the ideal character . . .'. Even before he had published his *L'Architecture polychrome chez les Grecs* in 1851, his ideas had long since influenced other important figures, notably the German theoretician Gottfried Semper who in the same year brought out his *Über Polychromie*, and Owen Jones whose *Grammar of Ornament* (1856), with its colour lithograph illustrations of patterns from most parts of the world, was a potent source of inspiration to designers and architects until well into the twentieth century (it remained in print until 1910). As a result of all this, colours became bolder and the juxtapositions more striking. Two less well-known pattern-books reflecting this new interest are Heinrich Asmus' *Neue Ornamente* which came out in Berlin already in 1844 (Pl.330) and Hippolyte Gruz's *Motifs de peintures décoratives pour Appartements modernes* of 1860 (Pl.288). Gruz was a *peintre décorateur* who had worked with most of the leading Parisian architects of his day, and it is significant for an understanding of the manner in which such designs were spread that his handsome and large publication was published in Paris, Liège and Berlin.

By the mid-1850s it was widely recognized that taste had somehow gone awry, and badly so. In his *Geschichte des modernen Geschmacks* ('History of modern taste') of 1866, that acute observer Jacob von Falke said that the turning-point had been the international Great Exhibition held in London in 1851. Before that event, he states, it had been impossible to get a sufficiently broad view but then, with all the world's manufactured goods on display together, '*there* lay the wretchedness in its full measure, before the very eyes of those who had the wish and the ability to see'.[26] As von Falke acknowledges, the English took energetic steps to put matters right in their own country and had so far managed to improve their products that, by the time of the 1862 International Exhibition, Falke thought they now equalled the French, and a Frenchman conceded a year later that French superiority was actually 'beginning to be disputed'.[27]

**285] REACTION AND REFORM  1860s**

The sturdy honesty advocated by Eastlake is epitomized by this illustration from his work. The construction is undisguised. There is an evident nostalgia for what were seen as the tenets that governed mediaeval craftsmanship and taste. The narrow white cloth, fringed at the ends, was to become a favourite decorative device of the reformers. (From C. Eastlake, *Hints on Household Taste in Furniture, Upholstery and other Details*, London, 1868.)
*Victoria and Albert Museum, London*

The remedy at first applied to counteract faulty taste was to study ancient art (especially that of the Renaissance) even more carefully than hitherto; but towards the end of the 1860s a more truly original style, derivative but with a novel character, began to take shape. The name of William Morris is usually mentioned first of all in this connection: but that of Charles Eastlake ought probably to be uttered in the same breath since his influence was perhaps even greater than Morris' as far as interior decoration is concerned. This was certainly so in America, where Eastlake's *Hints on Household Taste in Furniture, Upholstery and other Details* was brought out in no less than seven editions after its first publication in London in 1868.[28]

Eastlake had in fact made his reformist views public already in 1864 in an article on 'The Fashion of Furniture' which appeared in the *Cornhill Magazine*.[29] There he is already criticizing the typical Victorian sofa; for example, these pieces of furnishing 'have no more shape than a feather-bed thrown into a corner would assume, without being nearly so comfortable'. He adds, 'It is difficult to conceive anything in the whole range of upholstery more ugly than the modern settee or couch [with its] general puffy and blown-out appearance' (Pl.289). In *Hints* (1868) he calls such sofas 'a piece of ugliness which we ought not to tolerate in our houses'. This polemical tone was found vastly refreshing throughout the 1870s. Since such sofas sprang from a Rococo-Baroque, '*tous-les-Louis*' background, Eastlake was not incorrect in claiming of the 'ordinary upholsterer', who was usually responsible for these creations, that his 'notions of the beautiful are either centred in mere novelty, or derived from traditions of the Louis Quatorze period' (Pl.433).

The rugged style of mediaeval inspiration favoured by Eastlake and put forward in his *Hints* in 1868 (Pl.285) had much in common with the designs of Bruce Talbert published in his *Gothic Forms applied to Furniture, Metalwork and Decoration for Domestic Purposes*, which came out in London in 1867,[30] and with a book of furniture designs of the same date by a Warrington cabinetmaker named Richard Charles (Pl.286). It is noteworthy that Bruce Talbert also then worked in Lancashire. Simple rather than rugged forms were also the hallmark of the products of the firm which William Morris established as early as 1861. The reformers of the 1860s had one important passion in common: their use of colour, which they arranged in bold and striking combinations. In this respect they were the heirs of a development that can be traced back through Semper and Hittorff to Charles Percier at the time of Napoleon.

It was fashionable, from about 1815 to about 1840, to draw and paint views of interiors. Grand people instructed a draughtsman to make pictures of their favourite rooms; the less grand did it themselves. Thousands of such scenes exist and it was no difficult task to find illustrations for this period to go in this book (see Pls.302, 317, 318 and 334), although a special effort was of course made to find little-known pictures. By far the greatest number of such illustrations are of German and Austrian interiors and this must have encouraged the idea that there was a special Germanic style of decoration, usually called *Biedermeier*, which is the German name for that period – especially in literature.

In taking an international view of developments at this time, however, it is evident that *Biedermeier* was merely a local variant of the late-*Empire* style then current throughout the Western world. It had its origins in the Classical tradition, as did the parallel provincial *Empire* style and as did Grecian. The characteristic features of these varied expressions of late Neo-Classicism are the suppression of elaborate relief ornament and a general simplification of form. If many people in Gemany and Austria – and, indeed, in Scandinavia and much of central Europe – took this simplification further than others, it was primarily because they could not afford to do otherwise. The Napoleonic War had

**286] REFORMED SOFAS  1867**

These attempts to design a Gothic sofa must also be regarded as a reaction against the kind of design illustrated in Pl.289. Richard Charles, as yet a little-known designer working in Warrington, published these proposals in his *Cabinet-Maker's Book of Designs* already in 1867, the same year as Bruce Talbert's important *Gothic Forms applied to Furniture . . .* , and the year before Eastlake's even more influential *Hints on Household Taste*, both of which embody the same reforming spirit.
*Victoria and Albert Museum, London*

generally impoverished those countries; the Continental blockade had made expensive materials hard to procure. One had to make do with less costly timbers and textiles, for instance. If ornament was required, it was achieved by simple means.

Coupled with this shortage of money and the more luxurious materials came an actual liking for the austere which became almost self-conscious. This preference was not confined solely to the Germanic countries, however, although there it was certainly widespread; it also made its appearance in America, in Russia, in Italy, in provincial France and even in England.

Nevertheless, while the *Biedermeier* taste can be seen merely as a facet of a wider development, illustrations of rooms couched in this style exercise a peculiar fascination over us today. The atmosphere they exude delights and charms us.

## Planning and arrangement

As in gardening, there were in the planning of houses two traditions: a French one which required the plan to be regular and more or less rectangular, and the Picturesque tradition more recently evolved in England (see p. 143) where the plan straggled and had excrescences in all directions,[31] irregular and rambling in the same way as the landscaped 'English gardens' in which houses of this school were set. The French formal tradition, given a completely new lease of life under the Classicizing influence of the Ecole des Beaux-Arts, was of course to be seen everywhere including England; while Picturesque houses were erected in many places on the Continent, even in France, and also in large numbers in America. One can therefore only speak of national preferences, but these to some extent affected planning. In England the pursuit of privacy was a major preoccupation, while in France and America it was important that houses be well suited for entertaining. This is well explained by Gervase Wheeler,[32] an English architect who had an extensive practice in America and therefore well understood the national differences. For example, speaking of houses in towns, he writes that 'Even in very large houses the Americans adopt rather the Parisian than the London model, and dispose their family rooms and salons for company upon the same floor'. The English formula had the drawing-room on the first floor while on the ground floor were 'the general sitting-room, library, or dining-room'. As a result the Americans were forced to place their dining-rooms in the basement in the typical arrangement of the period; although the English pattern was being adopted in New York when Wheeler wrote, while he suggested the American formula might be 'not without useful application' in England.[33]

Both the French and the Americans preferred to have wide openings between their main reception rooms, to facilitate entertaining, and Wheeler draws attention to 'the usual American arrangement of preferring widely opening sliding doors between the rooms'. The 'English notions of privacy', on the other hand, were best satisfied by rooms which one entered and left through a door of ordinary size which separated them effectively.

The demand for greater privacy was better served by a Picturesque plan, for one could hive off into separate wings the different components of the household – the family, the servants and the service areas, the nurseries, and the guests – bachelors being in turn kept separated from the unmarried lady visitors. In any house of standing there were five indispensable rooms – a drawing-room, dining-room, library, study, and hall – but the number was commonly increased. In a large house, for example, the family might have a private suite separated from the main rooms of reception: Kerr (1864) listed these more private rooms as 'a Gentleman's Sitting-room (being a Business-

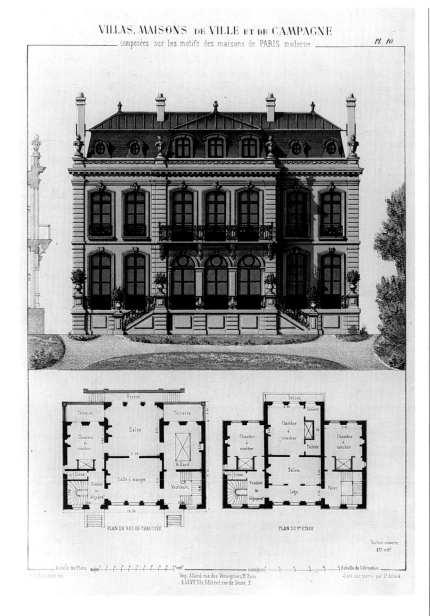

**287] A CHARACTERISTIC PARISIAN SUBURBAN HOUSE** *c.*1860

Léon Isabey, who published this illustration, was Inspecteur des Palais Impériaux. This house is described as being in the *Louis Quatorze* style, and particular attention is drawn in the text to the '*distribution*' of its *rez de chaussée* or ground floor. It will be noted that there is no bathroom, although some of the other schemes in the volume include such a feature. (From L. Isabey, *Villas, Maisons de Ville et de Campagne composées sur les motifs des habitations de Paris moderne . . .* , Paris, 1864.) *Victoria and Albert Museum, London*

room), a Lady's Sitting-room (being a Boudoir), the Bedroom, Dressing-rooms, and appurtenances of a Principal Bedchamber Suite'.

The Boudoir was 'a Private Parlour of the mistress of the house' and where there existed a private family suite there was 'no other Boudoir besides the Lady's Sitting-room', but 'In some cases . . . what is called the Boudoir is simply a secondary and smaller Drawing-room'. In the plans of American houses illustrated by Wheeler (1851) it seems to serve a purpose rather like that of the eighteenth-century French *grand cabinet* (see p. 51). Wheeler calls it 'a little gem of a room – if octagonal or oval, or quaintly cornered, so much the better – for the lady of the house; and whether boudoir, book-room, or work-room, as its fair presiding deity may determine [he advises the intending builders] let it have the sunniest aspect, the most charming prospect you can give it, for there will the taste that can best enjoy the enjoyable . . . mostly congregate'.

Also 'the Lady's Apartment essentially' was the drawing-room where, Kerr explains, 'Ladies receive calls throughout the day, and the family and their guests assemble before dinner. After dinner the ladies withdraw to it. . . . The character to be always aimed at in a Drawing-room is especial cheerfulness, refinement of elegance, and what is called lightness as opposed to massiveness . . . entirely *ladylike*' (the italics are Kerr's). Back in Loudon's time, in the early 1830s, much the same had been required, but Loudon wanted the drawing-room to be 'larger than the saloon', which he regarded as 'a sort of vestibule to the living rooms', although it might also serve as a music-room.[34] This is a far cry from the Baroque concept of a saloon, which, however, survived in France where the *salon* was still the principal reception room, there being no such thing as a drawing-room, although one could have several *salons* and they were by this time serving much the same purpose. A list of the rooms normally to be found in a French house of the period, along with an enumeration of their contents, is provided by Anastase Garnier in his *Tapissier Décorateur* (Paris, 1830). A list of the rooms that might be found in a 'complete Country House' in England, on the other hand, is given by J.C. Loudon in his informative *The Suburban Gardener and Villa Companion* (London, 1838) which has a section on 'The Arrangement and Furnishing of the House'. Loudon mentions the Elizabethan and *Louis Quatorze* styles only in connection with drawing-rooms (he does so twice, in fact) and it is true to say that the latter style, or Neo-Rococo, was the drawing-room style *par excellence* throughout this period, although, after the middle of the century, a fashionable drawing-room might also be couched in 'Louis Seize'.

In contrast to the feminine character of the drawing-room was that of the dining-room, where 'the whole appearance of the room ought to be that of masculine importance' (Kerr was only marginally less of a male chauvinist than Loudon),[35] so the décor should be 'somewhat massive and simple'. There should be a sideboard on which the owner's plate could be displayed on the occasion when he wanted to honour his guests, and in recesses flanking the fireplace should stand two 'dinner-waggons'. Although chairs in most rooms had long since come out on to the floor, away from the walls, in a dining-room 'a substantial aspect in this apartment is the unbroken *line of chairs* at the wall' (his italics again). However, 'In very superior rooms [by which he must mean 'it is now fashionable']2 it is sometimes the practice to place the chairs, or a portion of them, when not in use, not against the wall, but around the table.' Because 'no considerable traffic of dishes ought on any account to invade the main Thoroughfares' or passages etc., care should be taken when planning 'the Service-route' or 'Dinner-route' by which food came across from the kitchen. Even more care should be bestowed on 'The Drawing-room route to and from the Dining-room [which] ought to be invariably planned with an eye to facility, directness, and special importance; in as much as where there may be no other ceremoniousness whatsoever . . . there will be at least a little of that quality . . . in the act of proceeding to and from dinner' – a last vestige of Baroque ceremonial, in fact.

Garnier's list of contents in a typical Parisian dining-room of the smartest sort in 1830 includes a stove, chairs with rush-seats or covered in horsehair or *basane* (a woollen cloth), a small carpet or mats or foot-cushions to go under the table for the use especially of women (at that time women's shoes were thin and provided little insulation against contact with a cold floor), a round table of walnut or mahogany with flaps or leaves and a cloth to go over it when it was closed up and not in use (of oiled cloth, or of painted or printed worsted), some 'servantes' or side-tables with several stages, a sideboard (*buffet*), a water-filter, a *jardinière*, a clock and a bell (to call the servants). Marble slabs should be white, and it was a matter of choice whether one had window-curtains. In passing it is amusing to recall that in Trollope's *Barchester Towers* (1857) Archbishop Grantly insisted that 'there was something democratic and parvenu in a round table. He imagined that dissenters and calico prints chiefly used them.' Be that as it may, Loudon says in his *Villa Companion* of 1838, 'The dining-table may be either circular, square, or a parallelogram', and explains how a circular table may be extended 'by the addition of marginal rims', but he admits that 'where much company is kept' one needs long tables 'which not only admit of more guests, but a much greater number of dishes, in a given space'.

Loudon would not have approved of the stove to be seen in Parisian dining-rooms; he wanted a wood fire with large logs, he stated in his *Encyclopedia*. He advocated chairs covered with crimson leather with silk tufts and an easy chair placed on each side of the fire. In a closet should be the 'utensils sometimes required by gentlemen after dinner'. This closet should have thick walls and should be 'large enough for a person to stand in'. Loudon went one better than Garnier over the matter of calling the servants. Instead of a bell, he suggested in the *Villa Companion* that one should install 'a tube, or speaking-pipe'. These devices should be 'placed in a small recess in the wall, closed with a door. . . . When they are used, it is customary for the servant in waiting to ring the bell, to excite the attention of the cook to listen at one end . . . while he whispers his instructions at the other.' Incidentally, he stated that the dining-room, in middle-class houses, often also served as a library.

According to Loudon, the library 'should present a great contrast to the light elegance of the drawing-room' and he recommends that the walls be of a dark colour. There should be 'two or three large easy chairs, with movable desks', i.e. reading desks on swinging arms, and other chairs. He further observed that 'the library would be used as the family sitting-room on common occasions', which shows that the Regency invasion of this room by the women of the family had now become the norm. However, the victory was not complete, for when there was company the room 'would be the morning sitting-room for the gentlemen. . . . The ladies would occupy the drawing-room and Saloon'. Garnier, writing at about the same time as Loudon (1830 and 1833), does not include a special room called a library in his list, although there were bookcases in the boudoir and study; and libraries do not seem to feature normally in French houses at this period. On the other hand, in the *Villa Companion* Loudon claims that 'in the present day [in England] no villa, or suburban residence, having more than two sitting-rooms, can be considered complete without a library', and he recommends that the décor should be Elizabethan or Gothic. Wheeler (1851) includes a library in several of his plans for American houses, placing it usually among the reception rooms where it presumably served as an additional drawing-room on occasions. Kerr (1864) tells us that the library is not 'in the sole sense a depository for books. . . . It is primarily a sort of Morning-room for gentlemen. . . . At the same time the ladies are not entirely

excluded.' From this it would seem that women had still not consolidated their bridgehead, and that their presence in the library was only rather reluctantly condoned. If the owner is a man of learning, Kerr says, he really must cut himself off, fit double doors, and make sure the room 'becomes now essentially a private retreat'. In view of such attitudes it is hardly surprising that Disraeli makes one of his heroines hesitate before entering the library: 'It seemed too daring to go in'.[36]

Even if a grand house did not have a library, it usually had a billiard-room at this period, and the two rooms were often adjacent, perhaps with a smoking-room nearby where gentlemen could 'enjoy the pestiferous luxury of a cigar' (Kerr). This group of male rooms, which also usually included a study or business-room after the middle of the century, was normally placed well away from the rooms where the women presided. The conservatory, on the other hand, usually led off one of the 'female' rooms, although it was thought advisable to have a linking corridor or anteroom to exclude 'the warm moist air' which, Kerr was convinced, damaged the upholstery and was bad for the health. Loudon illustrates a drawing-room in the Grecian taste with a conservatory beyond forming a link to the library. 'The opening into the latter should have shutters with their backs lined with looking-glass, for effect when they are closed at night.'

A room that changed character totally during this period was the hall – or rather, a large number of halls were created which were very different from the standard vestibule by the main entrance, which had been the common pattern before and remained so throughout the present period, while the English were at the same time developing this new form of hall. It was those English architects and their clients who built large houses in the Neo-Gothic style who conceived the idea that the hall ought once again to become a central and principal feature of the house, just as it had been in the Middle Ages. During the 1830s and 1840s large numbers of imitations of mediaeval 'Great Halls' were built, mostly rising through two storeys. This huge room was at first seen through a romantic haze as the seat of 'the old English hospitality', where the owner might indeed hold a banquet for his tenants once or twice a year. Moreover, decorating it was usually rewarding. 'The English hall admits of much picturesque embellishment', says Loudon. The Neo-Gothic décor could be further enhanced with antiques: old armour, old oak, curiosities and relics of every kind. Although the character of these great halls was changing when Kerr was writing around 1864, he could still say that 'Antique furniture, by the bye, is peculiarly suitable here, – much more so than in any other part of the house'. By this time the room had taken on much of the character of the Baroque saloon, a large central space useful for functions or games, and acting as a link between the other rooms – especially on the first floor where a gallery often formed a passage off which doors led to the bedrooms. Wheeler in 1851 wanted the hall to be unobstructed by the staircase because this large space was 'very desirable if the house, as in holiday times, be filled with many dance and frolic-loving people'. Indeed, there was no longer any need for the staircase to rise directly from the hall because one did not really want ordinary visitors to go upstairs where there were no longer any reception rooms, only bedrooms with their ancillaries. By 1870 the English 'Great Hall' had become a huge living-room, sometimes top-lit (a feature unknown in the Middle Ages), and was thereafter gradually integrated with the rooms of reception and family life, generally acquiring a lower ceiling and therefore becoming easier to heat. But until then these rooms were never meant to be practical; they answered some inner spiritual need and the several attendant discomforts were evidently reckoned of little consequence. Nevertheless, it was in such huge, draughty rooms that the inglenook was developed to provide a snug and secluded corner by the fire.

Kerr (1864) makes several interesting remarks about bedrooms. He speaks of the head of the bed being 'to the wall after the English manner', while 'the French manner' had 'one side to the wall'. 'The best French arrangement (Italian also) places the bedstead in an Alcove,' he adds, but 'this is done more on sitting-room considerations than otherwise, the characteristic French bedroom of the present day being so far very much like the old English "Parlour"'. So French bedrooms were still used for reception and were a good deal less private than their English counterparts. Kerr thought the alcove worth copying as it was 'particularly suitable for the occupation of young ladies'. He recommended also that the average bedroom should be furnished with a small writing-table, a washstand, 'a pier-glass with its back to the light', a wardrobe, 'a couch, chairs, easy chairs; a chest of drawers, perhaps a cheffonier or cabinet, and so on . . .'.

In 1868 W. Jerrold's *The Epicure's Year Book* could tell us that a revolution had recently taken place in dining habits. 'The massive silver that encumbered the tables of our grandfathers, so that the diner could not see his opposite neighbour . . . has been put aside for light and graceful stands of silver, glass and porcelain, which hold flowers, and leave to every guest a full command of the table.' After describing the floral arrangements and the glass, the author explains that 'There are two, and only two, modes of serving a dinner, viz., in the pure French style, or *à la Russe*'. With the former 'the dishes appear in three services, or relays, upon the table', which is the best system if the company is small. The Russian system involved having the table 'tastefully adorned with flowers and fruits, and the triumphs of the confectioner's art; indeed, all the cold dishes. The hot dishes are served, carved apart, to the guests' (i.e. the carving was done at the sideboard, not at the table). *Cassell's Household Guide*, which must date from the early 1860s, throws further light on these matters but also describes the former practice – 'the old English way'. Forty or fifty years ago, *Cassell's* informs us, 'each successive course had to be covered with a set number of dishes, which served for ornament rather than for use, as it was impossible to taste one-third of them'. A fault of the old system had been 'the break and the disturbance caused by the removal of the cloth after cheese and the setting on the dessert' on the bare mahogany. In the French system the cloth remained on the table. This is why Eastlake, in his *Cornhill Magazine* article of 1864, could write that 'The white cloth is so seldom removed now before dessert, and the dining-table during the rest of the day is so carefully enveloped, that the festive board might as well be of deal, or at least of unpolished mahogany'.

The reformers had their own attitude to the reception rooms. B.J. Talbert in his *Gothic Forms applied to Furniture, Metalwork and Decoration for Domestic Purposes* (1867, reprinted in Boston in 1873 and 1877) had to admit that 'The greatest difficulty to deal with is the Drawing Room; there . . . the requirements are directly opposed to what is generally considered to be in the spirit of Gothic [i.e. reformed Gothic, rugged, honest, its joints showing] design'. After all, in 'the Ladies' Room lightness and grace ought to be aimed at [but] to attain this without an expression of feebleness and wanton curvature, is not easily done . . .'. Turning members on a lathe produced an effect of lightness but otherwise it was necessary to contrive soft effects with textiles; unfortunately 'there is nothing suitable to be had' at present – in 1868! Getting rid of '*Louis Quinze*' drawing-rooms was going to be a problem (Pl.358).

The water-closet was to be found in most houses of any standing by 1850, but close-stools and chamber-pots were still widely used. In 1848 some witty Parisian upholsterer disguised a close-stool as a pile of leather-bound books bearing the title '*Mystères de Paris*'; another even more arch title on such a contraption was '*Voyage aux Pays-Bas*'.

Bathrooms were familiar, but still far from common. Loudon (1833) thought such an amenity was essential in a villa, but in a cottage one could presumably do without. A smart Parisian bathroom in 1830 could still have a free-standing bath-tub of tinned copper or, failing that, of a whitewood called '*bois de cuvier*' (bath-tub wood). Garnier (1830) explains this and describes the bath-room 'hung with oiled-cloth or cotton' with percale or muslin window-curtains, a stove, a small divan, a moquette-covered platform in front of the bath, and a wickerwork dummy figure with a heater under it, over which one could air one's linen. Wheeler (1851) states that 'A bathing-room to be really useful . . . must be on the chamber floor', that is, upstairs near the bedrooms, but this of course posed problems for the plumber. Wheeler expected his clients to bathe morning and evening, and the trend in America was towards having several bathrooms in a house. When Le Grand Lockwood built his luxurious mansion at Norwalk in Connecticut in the mid-1860s he included no less than fourteen, but this was regarded as astonishing.[37]

In furnishing a room in the 1860s care still needed to be taken to achieve 'a degree of uniformity in the design', as *Cassell's Household Guide* explained. 'If there is too much diversity, the room will look as if it had been furnished piecemeal, and without due regard to the unity and completeness of the whole.' The reader was warned against 'the indiscriminate mixture of various styles', but one should not strive to reproduce 'the characteristic details again and again in the literal exactness . . . we much prefer to see uniformity . . . which arises from some similarity and congruity observable in the general character and treatment of the decoration' of a room. It was not only Eastlake and his friends who were searching for a new idiom.

Moreover, the real confusion of styles which so many people believe to be typically Victorian did not become generally acceptable until the 1880s – and even then it remained anathema both to the academically trained architect and to the reformers. By the same token, the confused clutter of furniture and knick-knacks associated in most people's minds with High Victorian also only became widely fashionable after the 1870s. There had been rooms, notably of women, filled with *bibelots*, small pictures and other ornaments since about 1820 (Pls.296 and 299), even though they were exceptional; but, if one studies illustrations of such rooms, one often finds these objects are concentrated on an *étagère* or table – they are rarely everywhere, at first. The density increases in the 1840s but many rooms were still fairly bare even in the 1850s. Really dense massing of ornaments only comes in generally around 1860 and it probably first comes in France, where ornaments were apparently less expensive than in England and perhaps than anywhere else. Fanny Trollope was already writing in the 1830s, 'It so happens that everything appertaining to decoration is to be had *à bon marché* at Paris, and we therefore find every article of the ornamental kind in profusion'. She also remarks: 'The tenth part of what would be considered necessary to dress up a common lodging in Paris, would set the fine London Lady in this respect upon an enviable elevation above her neighbours'.[38]

## The architectural shell

Rooms during this period were mostly rectangular in plan, perhaps with a projecting window-bay, but the oval and circular plans so beloved by architects of the late eighteenth century were now out of fashion. Ceilings were for the most part flat, except where the room was decorated in the Neo-Rococo style, when the typical coved ceiling of the Rococo proper was often introduced. Even Neo-Gothic ceilings were mostly flat, the Gothic elements being contrived with ribs and moulded beams to produce a 'late-Gothic' effect. As in other respects, the attributes of the many styles for which this period was noted were often applied to a simple box-like room, so that this ornament was really only skin-deep. The shape and proportion of rooms remained much the same, whatever the style. However, high ceilings were much admired, although the Victorians were not totally immune to the unease many people feel in disproportionately tall rooms, as witness their delight in the inglenook, the boudoir and the study – that 'small snuggery', as Surtees called it.

In many houses between 1820 and about 1850 it was not unusual to have no dado, so the whole wall was treated as one decoratable unit with a cornice at the top and a skirting at the bottom. Loudon (*Villa Companion*, 1838) advises that the skirting should be 10 to 12 in. (25 to 30 cm) high, 'fixed so as to project $1\frac{1}{2}$ in. [4 cm] from the wall in order to prevent the chair-backs from spoiling the paper'. Had there been a chair-rail topping a dado, this precaution would have been unnecessary. In a tall room, however, he suggests a dado be fitted but it need not be panelled; one can simply apply a chair-rail and skirting and paint or paper the wall area between as if it were a dado (a proper dado is built out from the wall). The skirting must then project so that it keeps the chair-backs clear of the wall by at least 1 in. (2.5 cm), and in order to disguise this thick skirting one fits a small projecting plinth or 'surbase'.

In the late 1830s it became fashionable to tint ceilings, white being thought too bright for many rooms. Loudon (1838) speaks of a breakfast-room tinted grey or light green with cornices either plain or tinted a slighter darker shade. In the dining-room, where 'few colours look better than a deep crimson paper in flock', the ceiling and cornice should be tinted to match. He has a great deal to say about the décor of drawing-rooms, and speaks of 'paintings of pleasing subjects, or wreaths of flowers' on the ceiling, but where the ceiling is of a plain colour 'the cornice should be relieved by other tints of the same colour, deeper and brighter than that of the ceiling'. Gilding should be used sparingly.

By the 1850s the stronger colouring associated with Hittorff and Semper's theories on polychromy was manifesting itself on ceilings, and really quite dominating (not to say oppressive), sombre yet rich colour-schemes were not uncommon by 1860, as the designs published by Gruz make clear (see Pl.288). His schemes embraced walls as well.

Ceilings and walls throughout this period could have relief decoration of mouldings in plaster-of-Paris or of papier mâché. James Arrowsmith, whose *The Paper-Hanger's and Upholsterer's Guide* of about 1830 contains a most informative appendix on upholstery including wall-hangings, states that 'every kind of cornice, borders, and other ornaments, are to be procured in paper-machee, of the most beautiful description, classical, antique, and modern', and it is probable that very many ceiling decorations that look to us like plasterwork are in fact of this material. Describing some mural decoration in the *François Premier* style in their *House Decorator's and Painter's Guide* (1840), H.W. and A. Arrowsmith (presumably sons of James) mention that 'The elegant ornaments of this style are manufactured in Paris, and a great variety of patterns may be obtained'. An interesting essay, Charles Bielefeld's *On the Use of the Improved Papier-Mâché in . . . the Interior Decoration of Buildings* (London, new edition, 1850), traces the history of its employment; the author was one of the principal English manufacturers. George Jackson & Sons' catalogues of the ornaments made in their 'Papier Mâché, Carton Piere and Patent Fibrous Plaster Works' during the 1860s show several extremely elaborate three-dimensional confections built up to give the effect of undercutting.

Colours remained light on the whole during the second quarter of the century, with darker tones in libraries and dining-rooms. James Arrowsmith, writing in about 1830 on the decoration of drawing-rooms, describes 'the walls panelled with watered silk, of pearl white, or *light* tints of pink, or lavender' (his italics) surrounded by a gilt moulding; he is referring to panels,

**288] POLYCHROMY IN THE SMOKING ROOM    1850s**

The strong and rather sombre colour schemes that came in during the 1850s are to be seen in Gruz's pattern-book of 1860, embodying the new concern with colourful effects indoors rendered in paintwork that consciously complemented the architecture. Gruz had worked for the top architects in Paris on some of the most important commissions of the mid-century – at Fontainebleau for Lefuel, at Pierrefonds for Viollet-le-Duc, for the Prince Napoléon, at the Hôtel Fould and the Hôtel Païva (which survives), and for Visconti at the Tuileries. (From H. Gruz, *Motifs de peintures décoratives pour Appartements modernes*, Paris, Berlin, Liège, 1860.)
*Victoria and Albert Museum, London*

often of Rococo outline, the field covered with material as if it were wallpaper. He then continues, 'But the improvement in paper-hangings, of late years, has caused little occasion for silk in panelling' because wallpaper is now 'equally pleasing ... to satisfy the most fastidious taste'. He also mentions walls hung with printed cotton which must have been common until 1840 but, after that, wallpaper seems to have supplanted textiles for mural decoration in all but the most sumptuous houses. H.W. and A. Arrowsmith (1840) illustrate a Neo-Rococo scheme where 'the interior of the large panels and pilasters may be finished with flock-paper or silk damask'. They, incidentally, could still write that 'strong contrast of colour' of the sort previously associated with Pompeian décor should be avoided 'as unnecessary in modern dwellings'. However, crimson still carried a lingering connotation of grandeur: Loudon (*Villa Companion*, 1838) speaks disapprovingly of 'the deep crimson colour, so frequently seen on the walls of drawing-rooms in London', which he found 'dull and gloomy', remarking that 'light, warm, sunny tints are much more suitable'. With flock papers it was usual to have gilded mouldings as borders, while with 'satin papers, a patterned border in flock ... is generally substituted'. One can also paint such a room: the surrounds a dark tint, the panels lighter and the moulding either darker still or French white – or a pale tint of the colour of the surrounds. Garnier, in his *Manuel du Tapissier* of 1830, describes the decoration of boudoirs in Paris at that time. In boudoirs of the more modest kind the hangings are of a pale material or paper with a simple pattern; light grey, blue or green with a white pattern are suitable. In more fashionable boudoirs where the upholsterer needs to have 'a fecund imagination' and cost need be no object,[39] the walls should be hung with pleated taffeta.

The woodwork of Neo-Gothic interiors, if it was not painted, was often stained dark to make it look old. The fields between Gothic ribbing and colonettes could then be treated with boldly coloured effects executed with paint or wallpaper. Thus a brightly coloured field came to have a dark Gothic framing. This was a formula adopted by A.W.N. Pugin for the decoration of important rooms in the New Palace of Westminster, the influence of which was considerable. At Westminster these schemes had been subsequently altered, the staining scraped away and the richly coloured papers removed; it was only when the original colouring was restored recently that the intended balance became evident once again.

Mass-production of wallpaper began in the 1840s. The development of printing from engraved cylinders on to rolls of paper changed the whole character of the industry. By about 1860 there were some 300 wallpaper factories in Paris alone. Papered walls were to be seen in virtually every house but there was a very wide range of qualities: from the simple patterns printed on plain paper; through the 'satin papers' which had a shiny finish executed on a finer grade of paper; to the flock papers, which could be elaborate; and, at the luxury end of the scale, the superb pictorial papers, the best of which were French, with the firms of Dauptain and later of Desfossé and Karth being conspicuous for their artistic creations. Indeed, so excellent were the best compositions of the leading factories, that such papers ousted textile wall-hangings to a very large extent, even in the houses of the most discriminating Parisians. The French papers were narrower than the English (18 compared with 20–22 in., 47 with 50–55 cm). After about 1835 wallpapers were usually applied with flour paste direct to the plaster, where necessary covered with lining-paper, instead of onto canvas. The firm of Cowtan was hanging a great deal of white and gold paper in English drawing-rooms in the 1860s;[40] this went well with the '*tous-les-Louis*' revival style of décor.

The manufacture of gilt leather with embossed patterns had never entirely ceased since it had gone out of fashion for wall-hangings early in the eighteenth century, but it came back into fashion in the 1840s and there are some rather handsome French leather panels in the Victoria and Albert Museum, acquired in 1856 and described as 'modern' at the time. The *Magasin des Demoiselles* of 1864 states that it was then exceedingly smart to have hangings of embossed leather but recommends an embossed form of canvas 'leathercloth' (*la toile cuir*) as an excellent substitute. Desiré Guilmard, in the Album of *Le Garde-Meuble* in which he describes the exhibits at the Paris *Exposition* of 1844, states that stamped ornaments of waterproof canvas (*chanvre imperméable*) are a new invention applicable to interior decoration; he groups them with decoration formed of stamped copper (he illustrates several examples of these), *carton pierre*, and metallic paste – and maintains that they are all rather nasty.

When Cowtan's hung a 'copy of French leather paper' at Dunraven Castle in 1871 they may have been referring to a *toile cuir*, although it may have been an embossed paper. In England, at any rate, a similar effect could be achieved by using an embossed canvas known as 'Tynecastle' (after the site of the Morton factory which produced it); this became very popular in this period for rendering overall patterns in shallow relief. It was used on ceilings as well as walls. Hitherto such effects had been contrived by painting over patterned flock paper.[41]

If you were sufficiently rich you could commission a 'private paper', made specially for your own use. For example, Cowtan's supplied a 'lily of the valley' paper for Kimbolton Hall in 1863 which was so described. In an age of mass-production, the fastidious and wealthy customer liked to have a personal pattern made exclusively for him. Much the same idea lay behind breaking up the moulds after a casting had been made of a decorative bronze; Balzac mentions this practice in connection with some figurines in the luxuriously appointed residence of the singer Josepha Mirah in *La Cousine Bette* (1846).

Stencilling repeating patterns as borders and corner ornaments on walls and ceilings was common during this period (Pl.343). It had been useful during the Grecian phase, but came to assume enormous importance as a means of decoration once polychromy became fashionable, when rich patterns in bold colours began to cover every surface. Nevertheless, particularly delicate or elaborate painted decoration still had to be executed free-hand. Nathaniel Whittock's *The Decorative Painters' and Glaziers' Guide* (London, 1827) contains a great deal of information about the state of this art at the beginning of the period.

'Little advantage has hitherto been taken by our modern architects, of *Stained Glass*', writes John Britton in his description of Sir John Soane's house (1827), and credits Soane with its re-introduction. Whatever the case, stained glass began to come back into fashion during the second quarter of the century. This revival of an old art-form was noted by Nathaniel Whittock, and he claims that the art 'is but approaching perfection' in 1841. It was of course primarily associated with Neo-Gothic buildings, but glass that was painted and glass that was tinted in the process of manufacture must also be considered in this connection (stained glass proper has its colours fused into the surface), and such glass was certainly to be seen in Italianate and Renaissance revival buildings. It is interesting to note that when glass was needed for some windows in Glasgow Cathedral in 1857, an authority claimed that 'the best artists are unquestionably the Munich glass-painters', although the work of Hedgeland at Norwich and Nixon in Bloomsbury was 'more glass-like'.[42] What is presumably a French painted-glass window of about 1820 is to be seen in Pl.296.

The chimneypiece came back into its own in the 1830s after having been played down as a feature for a generation. When it had been at all prominent during that period, it was usually in Neo-Gothic or 'Elizabethan' and *Style Troubadour* interiors, and it was in describing an 'Elizabethan' library that the

Arrowsmiths said that 'too much labour cannot be bestowed on the decoration of the chimneypiece, as it is the part of the room to which the attention is chiefly drawn'. They intended this as a general statement, and it becomes increasingly true towards the middle of the century, chimneypieces in the 'Renaissance' and *Beaux-Arts* styles often being huge (Pls.385, 367, 284 and 418).

From about 1840, and right to the end of the century (in 'un-reformed' interiors), chimneypieces were often swathed in material which could totally change their appearance. 'A good mantel-shelf is improved by a velvet hanging, and a bad one is rendered endurable', *Cassell's Household Guide* of the early 1860s tells us, and explains how to make this curious contraption which was all but omnipresent by that time. It consisted of a board laid on the shelf, covered with material and with a flounce hanging down like a pelmet (Pls.387 and 388). The material of these 'mantel-boards' normally matched the rest of the upholstery in the room. Elaborate versions were taken even further, and actually had curtains which were drawn back when the fire was lit but could hide the fireplace entirely the rest of the time (Pl.394). *Cassell's* illustrates a fireplace draped with fine lace and silk, the hearth inside the fender being filled with potted plants, while another scheme is made to look exactly like a muslin-draped dressing-table complete with looking-glass, also draped. 'Curtains to chimney-pieces are much used in France, and are seen in England in many good old-fashioned houses', we learn. In the 1840s and 1850s the frame of the overmantel-glass sometimes had a velvet ground trimmed with gilded mouldings, and this could seem like an extension of the whole composition if the pelmet and curtains below were of the same material. In the 1860s a similar unity was achieved, at any rate in Parisian schemes, by also framing the overmantel-glass with a complete system of curtains like those of the windows. *Cassell's* also explains how to make chimney-boards to fit into the aperture, and how to contrive 'fire papers', which were fancy ornaments of tissue paper or fine wood-shavings placed so as to hide the empty grate in summer. It is when one sees such arrangements that one appreciates why a reaction was imminent, a reaction that would sweep away all these stifling ornaments. Nevertheless *some* chimney-decorations of this class could look charming and it needs to be remembered that they contributed substantially to the look of the general run of later Victorian interiors.[43]

An excellent survey of the various kinds of grate and stove is provided by Frederick Edwards' *Our Domestic Fire-Places*, a new edition of which appeared in 1870. After having shown how the Franklin stove worked, it explains Dr Sylvester's model (which Loudon in 1833 had found unsatisfactory) and illustrates various 'modern grates'. Every kind of permutation with air-ducts and vents seems to have been thought of by this time, which makes one suspect that the claims made by some modern manufacturers are perhaps exaggerated. One popular grate of the period was Dr Arnott's, which had a controllable butterfly-valve in the flue; it was apparently devised in the 1850s, and can be recognized by the control-knob set centrally above the opening. Edwards even illustrates an early 'Gas Asbestos Fire', which looks dangerous. Cast-iron stoves became increasingly popular on the Continent and America; the English as a nation preferred their coal fires. Gervase Wheeler, the English architect who had a large American practice, was a keen advocate of 'Heating by means of hot-water apparatus', which he said he had installed with great success in a house in Connecticut, presumably in the 1840s (his book, *Rural Homes...*, was published in 1851). He claims that the heat, 'though capable of increase to almost any degree, is yet so soft as neither to warp the wood-work of the building nor the furniture'. There must be many heating-engineers who would like to know his secret!

Loudon's *Villa Companion* of 1838 recommends that the chimney-surround in the dining-room should be of 'dove-coloured, black, or black and yellow, marble', while that in the 'modern drawing-room should be of statuary marble, the purer in its whiteness and the freer of veins of stains, the better', and 'Polished steel and cut steel should be reserved for the drawing-room [i.e. for fenders and fire-irons], which should always be a step higher in every article... than the dining-room'. He includes a rather pretty illustration of a Grecian chimneypiece with its grate and fender, the latter having tall stands at the corners arranged as supports for the fire-irons.

Loudon (1838) suggests that a 2 ft-(60 cm-)wide space be left round a fitted carpet, and this area of bare floor lent itself to decoration of various kinds. One might lay felt over it, one could stain it or even marble it with paintwork. In grand houses, the floor which was to be exposed could be decorated with parquetry, an art-form which had been revived in Paris around 1770, and spread to Germany (Pls.190 and 191) and England. Eastlake, who was normally critical of most existing practices when he published his *Hints on Household Taste* in 1868, praised the parquetry patterns produced by the Arrowsmiths, 'whose name has long been associated with the revival of this art'. He illustrates several Arrowsmith patterns, making it clear that these were obtainable ready to lay. A French architect describing himself as 'P. Champonnois the Elder' published a series of designs for parquet at Lyons in 1845. The Arrowsmiths and Champonnois offered both borders and fields.

Maybe the adoption of such bold patterns reflected the new interest in polychrome effects. This was certainly the reason for the popularity of encaustic tiles, which now came to be much used for halls and public places. Eastlake also approved of them, drawing special attention to those of Messrs Maw and of Minton's. In his *Encyclopedia* of 1833, Loudon tries to encourage his countrymen to adopt scagliola floors which, he reminds them, are common on the Continent and especially in Italy. He also discusses parquet and illustrates a pattern that was exhibited in London in 1829. Downing, addressing his American audience in 1850 in his *The Architecture of Country Houses*, recommends that a pleasing floor in an elegant cottage was achieved 'by using narrow matched floor-plank, of good quality, and staining every other plank of a dark colour, like black walnut'.

## Loose furnishings

'Window curtains', states Loudon in his *Encyclopedia*, 'give the mistress of the house an excellent opportunity for exercising her taste in their arrangement; and it is but doing justice to the French and the Germans, to state that they are far in advance of the British, or, indeed, of any other people of Europe, in this particular.' Downing (1850) says much the same: 'The French, among all people, have the best taste in the management of curtains, because they have both a natural and a cultivated taste for dress and the arrangement of drapery.' This being the case, it is worth studying French designs for window-curtains, of which a great number were published (Pls.311, 325, 347 and 394), and certainly the designs published in other countries were largely based on French examples.[44]

The wealth of information is confusing, but the general development was as follows. The late-*Empire* system of curtaining with heavy effects of drapery thrown (*jeter* was the French term used) over an eye-catching pole, of brass or wood with elaborate finials, remained in favour until well into the 1830s (Pls.311 and 312). It was then still usual to have a main colourful curtain of silk or worsted, sometimes with its lining showing where the material was reversed for contrasting effect. Underneath was a 'sub-curtain' of muslin or lace. 'Continued drapery' (see p.154) was used for situations where there were two or more windows side by side and, in these, asymmetrical dispositions could be balanced within the complete scheme. 'Continued' arrangements were less common after the mid-1830s, although they enjoyed a revival in Paris in the 1850s and 1860s and again at the end of the century. After 1830 or so, however, each window was usually treated individually and symmetry was re-established as the norm. Asymmetry only gained the upper hand again for a while at the end of the century. The fixed arrangements of festoons and swags of material at the head of the window gave way around 1840 to the *lambrequin*,[45] which was essentially a flat pelmet of fancy outline reaching far down at the sides (sometimes even to the floor) and forming a sort of arched effect round the head of the window (Pls.394, 397 and 400).[46] It cut out a great deal of light, but no one seemed to mind at first. The *lambrequin* was used with symmetrical main curtains, and with sub-curtains of muslin or lace which, however, were not invariably treated symmetrically. By varying the ornaments of the cornice, which was often elaborate at this stage (e.g. Pl.397), the shape of the *lambrequin*, and its trimming, the whole gamut of styles could be expressed; but the basic formula with all these permutations was always the same. In reaction to all this upholstery, there was a simple form of window-treatment that enjoyed favour on and off throughout our period; this had no pelmet or *lambrequin* and consisted solely of an unadorned but often rather bold pole from which hung a pair of curtains that were looped up at the sides in the usual way when not drawn (Pls.336, 354, 370 and 415). In some cases a purely decorative shallow pelmet or a deep fringe was hung *behind* the curtains and pole.

Some idea of how these arrangements looked can be gained from surveying the illustrations here, but it takes careful study of contemporary pattern-books to appreciate the many subtleties of this important branch of the upholsterer's art. Particularly helpful in this connection is Jules Verdellet's *Manuel géométrique du Tapissier* (Paris, 1864; see Pl.394), which includes cutting-diagrams and, where necessary, detail sketches.

Other interesting points are raised by various writers. Loudon (1833), for example, says that the purpose of the muslin sub-curtains is 'to exclude insects, and in some degree to soften the light of the sun', and that in dealing with a Gothic window you should have transparent curtains 'in order that they may not hide the Architecture'. James Arrowsmith (*c.*1830) tells us that 'The mode of looping up window curtains [at the sides] should be rather low than high' and that such curtains should 'hang gracefully upon the floor'. He also tells us of 'a mode of trimming which has a good effect, viz., turning over the lining upon the chintz to the breadth of an inch or more, and cording the edge where they meet'. Miss Leslie, who published in Philadelphia in 1854 her useful *Lady's House Book. A manual of Domestic Economy*, lays down that 'The curtains, etc., should always be darker than the walls; otherwise the effect will be dull and insipid, for want of contrast'. She informs us that 'silk and worsted damask, figured satin, and merino cloth' were the most usual materials in fashionable houses, but 'chintz curtains are now seldom seen in America, except for bed-rooms'. The English *Cassell's Household Guide* of the early 1860s takes up the same theme (proving that Philadelphia knew very well what was happening in London): 'All kinds of damask, moreen, and rep will, for wear and effect, be preferable to chintz'. *Cassell's* then adds that 'an excellent stout kind of curtain, very general in Paris, has lately been introduced [to England]. It wears well, looks well, and needs no trimming. It is striped horizontally in white, scarlet, black, and yellow, on a green, red or blue ground. The name is Timbuctoo.' *Le Magasin de Meubles* shows a smart bathroom with *portières* with horizontal stripes in the years 1865 to 1867 (Pl.400), but they were not, it seems, all that common until the 1880s. Eastlake admired horizontal stripes and must have had 'Timbuctoo' in mind when he wrote (in *Hints on Household Taste*, 1868) 'To the French we are

indebted for a heavy ribbed material decorated with broad bands or stripes of colour running transversely to its length, and resembling the pattern of a Roman scarf. This stuff has been much in vogue of late years, particularly among artists and people of good, independent taste' – people like himself, in fact. He also admired a German material named '*Cotelan*', which was a mixture of silk, wool and cotton with a diaper pattern; and he quite approved of the new material '*Cretonne*', which was a heavy printed cotton, unglazed and, he felt, preferable to chintz. It was soon to become very popular. As for how curtains should be made up, he wanted them simple, no 'heavy and artificial folds', just hanging straight and, when not in use, 'simply tied back'. What he really despised, as he made plain in his article in the *Cornhill Magazine* in 1864, was the then current fashion for a 'a huge brass pole, which blossoms out in a gigantic fuchsia at each end, with rings as large as a man's arm', or the alternative 'gilt cornice ... of which no mortal man has ever been able to divine the object', and the way curtains are made 'about a yard too long, in order that they may be looped up on either side, and thus afford receptacles for dust ...'. His own simple form of curtain should clear the ground by about two or three inches, he explained.

Roller-blinds were fitted to fashionable windows throughout this period; they were particularly in favour during the later *Empire* phase, 1820–35, and again from the 1850s onwards. They were not the boring, plain, practical fittings we have today. They could bear ambitious painted or printed designs, they could be of woven material with a fancy pattern, and they could be trimmed with fringe or openwork borders. In short, they formed an important and attractive feature of the window to which they were fitted (Pl.323).

Nathaniel Whittock includes a long section on painting 'Transparent Blinds' in his *The Decorative Painters' ... Guide* (London, 1827) and illustrates seven designs, all landscapes. He explains that 'fine Scotch cambric or lawn' is best for such blinds. Chenavard shows several '*transparents*' for windows in his *Recueil* of 1828, and charming blinds appear in the compositions of Le Bouteiller in his *Journal de l'Industrie et des Arts utiles* (Paris, 1840: Pl.347). However, Downing was not too happy about the blinds that were available in America in 1850. He thought the best blinds were 'of plain brown or drab linen. Nothing can be more vulgar and tawdry for a country house than most of the transparencies and painted curtains. ... If they are badly painted, as is generally the case, they are an offence to cultivated taste; if they are well painted with copies of landscapes, etc., they are not good, in the sense of pictures, while they only hide, nine times out of ten, a more interesting view of the real landscape without.' Reluctantly, he admitted they might be tolerated in towns. Miss Leslie of Philadelphia disagreed with her compatriot in New York; she felt that 'brown holland blinds darken the room too much', and says 'It is best to have them of fine white linen'. She says nothing about a pattern, so presumably hers were plain white. She also speaks of cheap roller blinds made of wallpaper pasted on to linen. Alfred Standage, who published in London some *Practical Illustrations of Upholstery Work* designed by himself in about 1865, shows what he describes as '*Diaphane*' blinds, noting that they are obtainable from Messrs Caley Brothers. According to Garnier-Audiger's *Manuel du Tapissier* of 1869, this material was a shiny, very white taffeta on which one painted or printed a pattern – suitable for blinds and screens.

'Glass-curtains', those small hangings of muslin or net fitted just inside the glass in the lower part of the windows, were common enough during this period, but rarely appeared in elegant surroundings (Pl.408). Miss Leslie called them 'short blinds'.

Beds were dressed in much the same way as windows throughout this period. Indeed, when glancing through contemporary pattern-books it can sometimes take a moment to tell whether a design is for a bed or a window-drapery, if the design is presented face-on (compare, for example Pls.311 and 325; and see also 394). In fashionable bedrooms the decoration of the windows was supposed to match that of the bed, so there was a particularly close resemblance. In any case the similarity was much greater than it had been in the past – largely because window-curtains were now invariably divided, like those of the bed; they were not of the pull-up variety, as they had been from the time window-curtains became important decorative features around 1680 until late in the eighteenth century.

*Cassell's Household Guide* tells us how 'Medical men considered it the more healthy plan to sleep on beds with as few draperies as possible'. For this reason the 'Arabian bedstead' was introduced, 'which they call the "half-tester", "canopy", according to the pattern'. It was in fact usually a half-tester (*Cassell's* illustrates one) with curtains that reached half-way down the sides but no further (Pl.357). Such beds 'admit of curtains without entirely excluding the air'. However, the Speaker's Bed, designed for the House of Commons in 1858 and described in the original accounts also as an 'Arabian bedstead', has a full tester the same size as the sleeping-surface and curtains that pull right round. Neither the half- nor the full-tester form had posts at the foot end, and these were now becoming rare for fashionable beds, although 'Four-post beds . . . are even now by many persons preferred', according to *Cassell's*.

The term 'French bed' was rather variously used at this period, in the sense of a class of bed rather than merely one from France. The Nicholsons, writing in the 1820s in *The Practical Cabinet Maker, Upholsterer and Complete Decorator*, illustrate one so described, which has its head to the wall and a crown-like canopy or tester. Loudon (*Encyclopedia*, 1833) on the other hand shows a 'French bed' as placed with its side to the wall but with a similar crown-like tester, and this is what one would expect the term to denote since the form had been much favoured in France during the eighteenth century and the *Empire* period (Pl.324). However, Loudon also shows a simple iron bedstead without any hangings and calls it 'French'. Eastlake, in the late 1860s, agrees with Loudon in saying of the French bedstead (and speaking of the past) that 'the head and foot-piece were in shape and size alike' and that its curtains fell 'from a circular canopy attached to the ceiling'.

*Cassell's* was keen on white dimity or its equivalent, and on chintz; the latter should be glazed as it lasts 'three time as long'. Instead of having iron rods for the curtains, 'handsome-looking rods or poles of the same wood as the bedstead' are now used. On these are slid wooden rings with brass eyelets through which the hooks in the curtains are passed. One great disadvantage of these wooden rings is, that 'with a slight motion, even that caused by a person walking overhead, the rings, if close together, rattle, which is an annoyance even to the ordinary sleeper . . .'. The answer was to have rings of india-rubber. 'Metal rings should never be used.' Loudon (1833) explains how springs were used in beds and mattresses, and illustrates a waisted spiral spring. He also describes a water-bed; these, he says, are 'in general use in the London hospitals'. It consisted of a large trough of lead, 1 ft (30 cm) deep and filled with water, with a sheet of india-rubber stretched over the top and sealed round the edge. Such beds were obtainable from Messrs Mackintosh & Co., Charing Cross, London.

Loudon illustrates several iron and brass bedsteads. Eastlake (1868) says these 'are fast displacing' beds of mahogany and rosewood, but adds that the design of these metal beds 'is generally very poor, especially where anything in the shape of decoration is introduced. For instance, it is usual to conceal the joint which occurs where the tie-rods intersect each other with a small boss.' A rosette would be appropriate but 'the iron-bedstead maker insists on inventing a little lumpy bit of ornament, which . . . resembles a friendly association of

garden slugs'. He supposes that they are intended to be clusters of leaves. Eastlake approves of white dimity curtains if the walls are 'decided in tone'; if the walls are light, a cretonne, chintz or damask would be preferable – but always hung simply, as with window-curtains (see p. 225). But 'Many people now-a-days prefer, on sanitary grounds, to sleep, through winter as well as summer, in beds without hangings of any kind'.

The basic form for side-chairs and their bigger brothers, the ordinary armchairs, had been established during the eighteenth century and was now adapted to meet the successive fashions in all the various styles. Moreover, when such chairs formed part of a 'parlour suite', the sofa would merely be an extended version of the chairs. Here is not the place to trace the development of this basic formula.[47] A fundamental change, however, took place in the design of seat-furniture that was primarily meant to be comfortable. This change reflected the spread of a more relaxed and informal way of life which permitted people increasingly to seek forms of seating in which they could recline. The *'crapaud'*, that toad-like armchair with its deep padding and accommodating form, first made its appearance in the 1840s; as with the more formal types of seating just mentioned, the related sofas were simply elongated versions of the same formula (see p. 216 and Pls.289 and 359). However much Eastlake and the other reformers might inveigh against it, this truly comfortable type of seating remained popular throughout the second half of the century and set the standard by which comfort in seating has been judged ever since. Whether we think the *crapaud* hideous or not, its essential form is the same as that which underlies all seating designed for relaxation, even today.

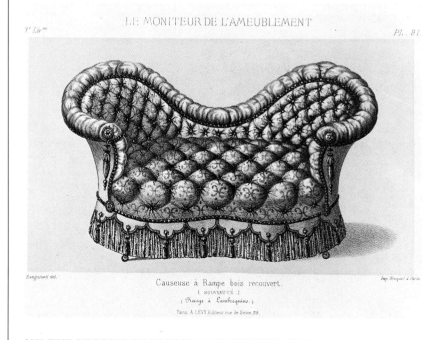

**289] THE HEIGHT OF PARISIAN COMFORT  1864**

This voluptuous *causeuse* epitomizes the unrivalled skills and inventiveness of the Parisian upholsterer at this period. Note the elaborate tassels at the fronts of the arms, and the combined fringe and apron-pieces (*frange à lambrequins*) forming a valance. (From A. Sanguineti, *Le Moniteur de l'Ameublement*, which very appropriately had the sub-title *Journal du Confort*.)
*Victoria and Albert Museum, London*

The ancestry of the *crapaud* and its relations can be traced back to the eighteenth-century *bergère*, which had been devised for relaxation in a polite way, and to the voluptuous resilience of the down cushions that went with the day-beds to be found in Parisian boudoirs of the second half of that century. The skill of the leading upholsterers had now also reached a very high level indeed, a fact that must be admitted whether one approves of their confections or not. They had improved enormously the techniques for effectively securing the stuffing of chairs during the first half of the century. They learned how to dispose the various materials brilliantly – which became very important when deep-buttoning came into fashion around 1840. And they adopted springing.

The English and the Americans had been using visible 'tufting' for the securing of the stuffing of chairs since the 1760s at any rate, but it was rarely used in France until well into the nineteenth century (see pp. 58, 102 and 156). (The French did, however, use tufting on mattresses and squabs, so the technique was perfectly familiar to them. Until the rectilinear lines of Neo-Classicism came in and affected the shape of seat-stuffing, they did not use it actually on seat-furniture.) By that time the tufts had turned into buttons, which were easier to fit and were more effective.[48] Tufts were all right so long as stuffing remained thin; but, once it was thick so that far greater strains were put on the securing-system, something stronger was required and buttons provided the answer. Wilhelm Kimbel's *Journal für Möbelschreiner und Tapezierer*, which covers the crucial years, shows sofas and easy chairs with thin stuffing and no buttoning right through the 1830s, until an easy chair with shallow buttons is illustrated in 1839. The development is thereafter very rapid. A sofa with deep-buttoning is shown in 1841 and there are plenty by the mid-1840s, including a sofa with star-shaped blue buttons on a yellow material in 1845. Deep-buttoning is also to be seen on several extremely comfortable chairs illustrated by Le Bouteiller (*L'Exposition. Journal de l'Industrie et des Arts utiles*, Paris, 1840) and quickly becomes general in the 1840s.

It was not essential to have springs with deep-buttoning, but they normally went together. Le Bouteiller shows a deeply buttoned chair (of which the Académie Française had apparently just ordered forty from the upholsterer Maigret) which is specifically described as having springs, as if this were exceptional. It seems that spiral springs had been adopted by upholsterers experimentally in the 1820s in London and probably in Paris and Vienna (see p. 155).[49] Loudon, in his *Encyclopedia* of 1833, mentions that spiral springs were now being used for seating by upholsterers who imagined they were a new invention. The English firm of Gillows was certainly using them by 1834 and, at the Paris Exposition in that same year, the Parisian upholsterer Dervilliers exhibited a '*fauteuil élastique*', as such sprung chairs were then called.[50] One of the sofas shown in Pl.290 has springing; the illustration was published before 1833. Springs were by no means universally welcomed straight away. Le Bouteiller (1840) speaks of a well-stuffed easy chair which 'possesses all the qualities of a sprung chair without having its drawbacks; this is not one of your mechanical contraptions with entrails of iron'.

Webster's *Encyclopedia of Domestic Economy* of 1844 illustrates a chair made of coiled ropes of straw. This 'beehive chair', we are told, 'has long been used in Wales and Scotland, as well as in some places in the north of England; but it is only of late that they have appeared among our fashionable furniture'. Be that as it may, cane furniture became popular during the second half of the century, being light in colour and weight, sometimes elegant and mostly inexpensive.[51] Gervase Wheeler, in his *Rural Homes . . . suited to American Life* (New York, 1851) mentions 'A material now in very general use in this country, the rattan or cane of the East Indies. . . . The principal excellencies of cane as a material of chairs, sofas . . . are its durability, elasticity, and great facility of being turned

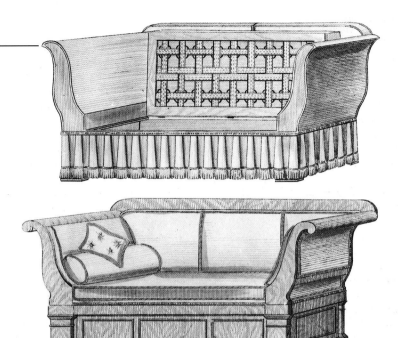

290] EARLY SPRINGING, BERLIN   before 1833
The hinged seat of one of these convertible sofas is shown pushed up to reveal the webbing and springs – a very early representation of this innovation, which was not widely adopted until about 1840. (From Wittich's *Magazin für Freunde eines geschmackvollen Ameublements*, Berlin, before 1833.)
*Metropolitan Museum of Art, New York; Jacob S. Rogers Fund, 1932*

and twisted into an almost endless variety of shapes' from which could be made 'that greatest of all luxuries – an easy seat and a springy back'.[52] The illustrations Wheeler reproduces show this furniture to have been as elegant and structurally ingenious as the Viennese bentwood furniture of Thonet and his rivals, and those who like to study the pioneers of modern design should perhaps cast a glance at early cane furniture. The manner in which the strength of such chair-backs is carried solely by a single peripheral member is similar (but in fact the back of the fully upholstered *crapaud*-type chair was also often simply built on a peripheral wire frame). The manufacture of cane furniture was by no means confined to America; it was made in all the main European countries and a Swedish basket-weaver named Carl Wilhelm Steneberg gained a reputation for his intricate wicker chairs, made first in Hanover, then in Copenhagen, and finally in 1853 in Lund in Southern Sweden.[53]

It is amusing to see that Webster (1844), after describing chairs in various styles, says: 'We omit chairs in the Gothic style, as they are never used, except the house itself be in the same style; and we may observe that this style is, in general, very ill adapted for domestic furniture, and except it be designed by artists of great taste, and who are very well acquainted with Gothic architecture, and what little remains of ancient furniture, attempts at imitation are generally very miserable, besides being extremely expensive.' But was knowing your Gothic architecture really going to produce the answer? The architect A.J. Downing, writing in New York in about 1850, did not think it was that simple: 'The radical objection to Gothic furniture, as generally seen, is, that it is too elaborately Gothic – with the same high-pointed arches, crochets, and carving usually seen in the front of some cathedral. Elaborate exhibition of style gives it too ostentatious and stately a character [see Pls.349 and 369]. Hence, in many of the finest Gothic mansions abroad, Elizabethan or Flemish [i.e. Northern

227

Renaissance] furniture has long been used in preference to Gothic furniture, as combining the picturesque and the domestic far more successfully than the latter' (*Country Houses*: see Pls.385 and 327). He had come to much the same conclusion about Gothic architecture for interior use (see p. 216), but he believed that one *could* create a style of interior architecture combining Gothic with modern forms 'expressive of our modern domestic life'.

When rockers were first put on chairs has long been debated,[54] but they are still very much with us today, especially in the United States. It is therefore curious that Miss Leslie, in her *Lady's House Book* (1854), could then write that 'The practice of swaying backwards and forwards in a parlour rocking-chair, is considered obsolete in genteel society; ... it is a most ungraceful recreation, particularly for a lady (to say nothing of its tendency to cause dizziness in the head) and very annoying to spectators, who may happen to be a little nervous'. Rocking-chairs are all right for 'reclining in ease and convenience ... [when] the chair can be tilted and kept stationary in any position desired ...', however, and for this purpose a foot-stool was of course essential. Rocking-chairs of various kinds may be seen in Pls.381, 409, 411 and 415.

The title-page of Chenavard's *Recueil des dessins de Tapisseries, Tapis et autres objets d'ameublement*, which came out in Paris in 1828, gives us some idea of what French carpets and carpeting were like at this stage. A wide loom with three operators is depicted, and on the floor lie rolled-up runners and widths. Garnier (*Manuel du Tapissier*) states that 'after the Orientals, it is the English and the Dutch who have done most' to further carpet-weaving, and that carpets were now widely used in France. 'Among the many recent improvements in Paris which evidently owe their origin to England, those which strike the eye first are the almost universal introduction of carpets within doors, and the frequent blessing of a *trottoir* without', wrote Fanny Trollope in 1835.[55]

Loudon (*Encyclopedia*, 1833) has little to say about floor-coverings but notes that one can use green baize or drugget as substitutes for carpets. This is cheap but looks good, especially if a black border is applied inset about 2 in. (5 cm) from the edge. He also mentions paper carpets which one applied to the floor like wallpaper. In his *Villa Companion* of 1838 he expands a little. He says Brussels carpeting is much used, 'but the Axminster carpet, thick and without a seam, is the most splendid article of the sort made in England'. It is Webster's *Encyclopedia of Domestic Economy* (1844) which gives most information, however. Observing that 'In America carpets are universally used as in Britain', it continues: 'Our Brussels carpets are made chiefly at Kidderminster. What are called Kidderminster carpets are mostly made in Scotland and Yorkshire; and it is not known that what we call Venetian carpeting was ever made in Venice.' After an explanation that 'Royal Wilton' has a deeper cut-pile surface than ordinary Wilton, we are told that 'Velvet pile carpets are a kind lately introduced. ... Nothing can surpass their beauty and rich effect, and they are of English manufacture.' This is presumably a reference to Templeton's new factory in Glasgow, where 'Patent Chenille Axminster' had been woven since 1839. Proper Axminster carpets, as opposed to carpeting, were not much woven any longer, according to Webster. Kidderminster carpets (normally a double-weave) had lately been made with a 'three-ply' weave and they were now 'made in squares, to suit rooms of various sizes'. Scotch carpeting is 'often confounded with the Kidderminster', but 'The three imperial Scotch carpet, which is coming much into vogue, is reckoned by many to be little inferior in texture, look, and wear, to the Brussels, though much cheaper. It is made at Kilmarnock.' Then mention is made of 'Dutch carpet', a cheap but strong yard-wide carpeting 'lately introduced' which only came in stripes and checkers. 'Venetian carpets are of the simple kind' and are striped along their length; they are chiefly used 'in bedrooms and on stairs'.

Nothing much is added to this by *Cassell's Household Guide*. For stairs 'The hard Dutch carpets wear out directly. The real Venetian is the best, but is now rarely to be obtained.' *Cassell's* considered Brussels by far the best if one could afford it, but Kidderminster carpets 'are almost indestructable' although 'rarely ever suitable for parlours, the green moss or small green-and-black coral pattern excepted', which are 'in good taste'. Samuel J. Dornsife, who has charted the technical and commercial development,[56] states that Kidderminster was exporting a great quantity of carpeting to the United States in the 1840s, and that Halifax became at that period the main centre for weaving Brussels. The American Erastus Bigelow was busy perfecting a power-loom to weave carpeting, and exhibited a loom at the Great Exhibition in London in 1851; the jury declared that Brussels carpets woven on this machine were better than those woven by hand. Crossley's in Halifax bought the United Kingdom rights to Bigelow's power-loom and soon the manufacture of carpeting was transformed, both in England and America. A great many hand-loom weavers lost their jobs at first, but more looms were constantly being added so the workforce soon increased again. The distinction between carpets proper, woven in one piece, and carpeting, woven in strips, fell away with the introduction of the power-loom because the strips could now be woven as wide as a large carpet.

According to Eastlake (*Hints on Household Taste*, 1868), European carpets were dreadful and he only found the simplest patterns acceptable: 'it not unfrequently happens that the commonest material is invested with the best form and colour'. It was all 'a matter of mere chance' and had nothing to do with 'pecuniary considerations'.

Floor-cloth was much used in England and America, but Garnier's *Manuel du Tapissier* shows that this '*toile ciré*' or oilcloth ('painted canvas' would be more correct) was also used in France, especially in summer, for dining-rooms, antechambers and rooms of lesser importance – as indeed was the case in England and America. Yet even if this material played a secondary role in furnishing, floor-cloths with very ambitious patterns were made. A supplement to the *Penny Magazine* of 1842 carries a report on 'A day at a Floor-Cloth Factory' and shows a huge cloth being prepared. It has a pattern resembling a Roman mosaic floor. Another 'carpet' of floor-cloth is also illustrated, as is the technique of manufacture. The canvas came from Dundee or Kirkcaldy and was up to 24 ft (7.3 m) wide. The paint was as thick as treacle and was plastered on to the stretched canvas, first on the back, then on the front (four coats); after which it was decorated with block-printed colours. Because the paint was oil-bound, it was said to be inadvisable to wash the floor-cloth with soap. Warm water was sufficient. In the 1880s, however, quite contrary advice was given (see p. 323).

The period from 1820 to 1870 saw extremely important developments take place in the field of domestic illumination. The Argand principle (see p. 157) was improved upon, the petroleum lamp was introduced, and gas-lighting was perfected and became common. The introduction of gas-lighting, whereby one could perform the astonishing feat of illuminating a room with several sources of light at the turn of a small tap, raised people's expectations and provided a challenge to the makers of other lighting devices, and so the level of illumination in rooms after dark was generally increased. This in itself had a profound effect on interior decoration; one could now see properly after dark. Decorators had to take this into account and had to consider the effect the different forms of light had on various colours and materials. One of the drawbacks of gas-light was that it made some colours look sickly; and it was not all that flattering to the complexion!

Webster's *Encyclopedia of Domestic Economy* of 1844 has a great deal to say on the various devices then available and explains how each functioned, with diagrams. Among the devices described are 'Palmer's candles', which had a double wick soaked in 'bismuth in a finely metallic state' (Loudon had mentioned something similar in 1838). Webster explains the original Argand system; he then goes on to describe and illustrate the French annular lamp with its flattened ring-shaped reservoir that reduced the size of the shadow cast by this obstruction. This will have been the 'Astral' lamp. He speaks of the latter in the past tense because a replacement was now in use, Parker's 'Sinumbra' lamp, which was patented in 1820 and had its annular reservoir sloping so as to cast even less of a shadow (Pls.302 and 336 show Argands; 297 and 334 'Astrals'; Pl.309 may be a 'Sinumbra'). A variant known as the 'Isis' lamp 'is now most generally seen in the shops'. The Argand-type lamps burned colza oil, which was derived from rape-seed. It was viscous and there was difficulty in getting the oil to the point of combustion. This was why reservoirs had at first been set above the flame so as to take advantage of gravity, but experiments continued with springs and clockwork that forced the oil up from a reservoir below. The 'Carcel' lamp, first patented in 1800, had a clockwork system but was 'little used in England' by Webster's time and could not be entrusted to 'the hands of ordinary servants, for, when it gets deranged, it must be sent to its constructor in Paris to be repaired'.

The 'Solar' lamp is then described, a recent 'improvement of considerable importance'. This clever but simple device made it possible to burn a wide variety of oils, including lard-oil, which was readily available, particularly in America – this led to the widespread use of this lamp there. Next comes the 'Young's Vesta' lamp, which burned 'Camphen', but this was such a new invention that Webster could only quote the opinion of others. The extremely dangerous nature of the 'rectified turpentine' used in these lamps was only hinted at by implication.

*Cassell's Household Guide*, published some fifteen years later, rounds out the picture. The 'Carcel' lamp had in the meantime been modified as the 'Moderator' lamp and although this was 'now well known' – the last major modification of the Argand lamp – Cassell's still felt it 'liable to get out of order'.[57] It had a key set in its base for winding up the clockwork mechanism that forced the oil upwards. The major rival of the 'Moderator' in the second half of the century was to be the petroleum lamp, which was an invention 'of comparatively recent date' when *Cassell's* was written. It had its genesis in the discovery in 1859 at Oil Creek in Pennsylvania of mineral oil, the substance that is so vital to the world's economy today. The petroleum lamp was still being perfected when *Cassell's* was coming out. By the mid-1860s it had virtually captured the market, although many people still preferred the 'Moderator'. But the 'Camphene' (the Americans added an 'e') or 'Burning Fluid' lamps went out of fashion quite rapidly; they really were too dangerous.[58]

An excellent survey of the use of gas for domestic lighting is provided by Myers' *Gaslighting in America*.[59] Gas was first used in factories and for street-lights, but was to be seen in domestic use in London by about 1815. In that year Frederick Accum's *Practical Treatise on Gas-Light* was published by Rudolph Ackermann (see p. 210); it illustrated several chandeliers and branches which look as if they could be used domestically; though they are simply described as 'already in use in this Metropolis', i.e. in London. Other fixtures shown by Accum were installed in Ackermann's shop and warehouse. Sir John Soane had 'erected a dining-room which is lighted by gas, concealed in a dome' at a house in St James's Square by 1824[60] and Sir Walter Scott had his house in Scotland, the famous Abbotsford, lit by gas by 1823.[61] Scott and other country-house owners after him could enjoy such illumination only if they had their own gas-producing plant, but in cities one could expect, as time went on, to have the benefit of gas coming through mains from a central gas-works. A gas-light company was established in London in 1812. A similar company was operating

in Philadelphia by 1836, while the citizens of Copenhagen had to wait until 1857 for such a utility to be established there. By the middle of the century, at any rate, gas-lighting was common indoors in cities all over the Western world (Pls.382, 407 and 413).

Long before this time the main features of the early gas lamps had been established. These relied on the flame itself for illumination; the gas-mantle had not yet been invented. It was found that a slit produced a fan-shaped, or 'bat's-wing' flame which was more efficient than a mere hole which made a straight jet or 'rat-tail'. A modification of the 'bat's-wing' was the 'fish-tail'. All were best inside a glass bowl. Although it is by no means easy to distinguish the various forms of oil-lamp at a glance, gas-lights from the middle of the century onwards are clearly recognizable, since they invariably have individual taps to each branch. By 1830 gas chandeliers that could be lowered or raised had been invented; they had a counterbalance system and the gas-supply came through telescopic tubes sealed with water at the joints (Pl.407). By the 1840s some chandeliers had an additional lamp hanging down below, connected by a rubber tube, so one could read while the general level of illumination was maintained. And by the middle of the century table-lamps connected by a rubber tube to the chandelier had been introduced. These and similar arrangements must surely have been dangerous (Pl.382).

The illustrations in this book reveal much about the way pictures were hung. During this period it was common to hang pictures in several tiers, the uppermost being set high on the wall. Pictures were often grouped in arrangements which, though quite carefully balanced, differed from the more architectural groupings favoured in the eighteenth century in seeming less rigid, with less attention being paid to matching the frames. Eastlake (*Hints on Household Taste*) abhorred this 'crowding [the walls of a room] almost from its wainscot [i.e. dado] to the ceiling. . . . To see pictures in anything like comfort or attention, they should be disposed in one row only.' the centre should be about 5 ft 6 in. (1.68 m) from the floor, with full-length life-size portraits hung higher. Pictures were usually hung canted forward but this, while 'sometimes advantageous in the highest row of the crowded gallery, is useless when every picture is hung "on the line"'. He preferred rings screwed to the upper edge of the frame, with two nails driven into the wall just below the cornice, and he advised using cord rather than wire. He has a lot to say about picture-framing and makes a special plea for gilding applied direct to oak frames so the grain shows through: 'the sense of *texture* thus produced is infinitely more interesting than the smooth monotony of gilt "compo"'.

In all the 300 years surveyed in this book, there was no period in which flowers and pot-plants were so greatly in evidence as the second quarter of the nineteenth century (Pls.316, 323, 334, 354, 367, 378, 386, 413 and frontispiece). Flower-vases were placed everywhere, pot plants stood on window sills and on special stands (the *jardinière* was a characteristic of the 1820s as the cocktail-cabinet was of the 1930s – only even more prevalent), and great screens of foliage were erected – what the Germans called *Zimmerlaube* ('room-foliage'). Flowers were often shown in association with an aquarium. Fanny Trollope, attending a party in Paris one hot summer evening in 1835, noted how 'deliciously cool and agreeable' the rooms were. 'The first was surrounded and decorated in all possible ways with a profusion of the most beautiful flowers, intermixed with so many large glass vases for gold fish, that I am sure the air was much cooled by evaporation from the water they contained.'[62] A delightful book full of illustrations of floral arrangements, aquaria, ferneries and the rest, Shirley Hibberd's *Rustic Ornaments for Homes of Taste, and Recreation for Town Folk in the Study and Imitation of Nature*, appeared in London in 1856 and was reissued the next year.

◁ 291

## A *salon* near Munich
### 1820

This room is in one of the wings of Schloss Nymphenburg, built about 1705, and the architecture of that period has only been partially disguised by the *Empire* decoration. The room was occupied by the twin sisters, the Princesses Sophie and Marie of Bavaria (b. 1805), one of whom is here seen at the piano. The windows have the new form of curtain with festoons thrown over a pole which is here still fairly discreet. The muslin may soften the daylight, but these curtains have no other function than being decorative (the door has a *portière en suite* to balance). Roller-blinds were probably fitted although they are not shown, but the room was done up in a rather Spartan manner. There is a striking French scenic wallpaper of romantic Swiss landscapes, with a framing of *trompe l'oeil* columns and *Empire* borders. Note how the stripes on the chairs run across the seats. (By Wilhelm Rehlen.)
*Wittelsbacher Ausgleichsfonds Inventarverwaltung, Munich*

292 ▷

## A Viennese drawing-room
### c.1820

The furniture is all in the same general style but does not appear to be *en suite* and the covers do not match. The room appears to be recently built, with its shallow segmental vault. There is no dado, and simplified *Empire* or Grecian painted decoration is confined to borders. Note the interior shutters, the lack of curtains (there may be a blind), and the two bell-pulls with cranks. The fitted carpeting was probably woven at Linz. Note the white earthenware stove and the *jardinière* in the window. The seat-furniture has covers trimmed with gimp and the stool has aprons at the sides, a rather common feature at this time. The picture-hanging is noteworthy, with single cords depending from studs in the frieze. The small desk has a built-in fire-screen which was presumably deployed, together with the larger screen, when the stove on the left was used with its door open. (By Johann Nepomuk Ender.)
*Historisches Museum der Stadt Wien, Vienna*

*Cabinet de la Princesse Royale à Stockholm*

### 293
## A picture-closet
## in the Stockholm Palace
#### mid-1820s

This shows the Swedish Crown Princess Josefina (Eugène de Beauharnais' daughter, who had arrived from France with her husband in 1823) writing at her desk, which was presumably made in Stockholm, although the elaborate clock and probably the candlesticks are likely to be Parisian. The large painting shows the Princess being delivered to the 'Land of the Sagas' by Zephyrs and swans. The cushions, with their inside covers bursting out (intentionally), are typical of contemporary French upholstery practice. Note the divided *portière*, the silk sleeves and rosettes hiding the cords holding up the pictures, and the fitted carpet. The covered sofa-table with piled books and adjustable candlestick is also noteworthy, as are the two disparate foot-stools.

*Swedish Royal Collection, Stockholm*

## ◁ 294
## Said to be Prince Eugène's bedchamber, Munich
*c*. 1820

Pl.297 shows the rather plain bedchamber in which Eugène de Beauharnais, Duke of Leuchtenberg, died in 1824. This much more splendid room could be his state bedchamber. The bed seems to owe much to the designs of Percier and Fontaine and the cabinet on the left must be Parisian. Even if this room was in the Leuchtenberg Palace, designed by Leo von Klenze in 1816, the impression given is that one is in a Parisian *Empire* room of the very early years of the century.

*Swedish Royal Collection, Stockholm*

## ◁ 295
## A Field-Marshal's study in Silesia
*c*. 1820

The room of the famous Prussian soldier Count von Gneisenau, who had led England's German auxiliaries in America and had fought at Jena, Leipzig and Waterloo. This shows his study at Schloss Erdmannsdorf which was done over about 1819, although here much of the old architecture is still visible. This is a military man's simple work-room, with several desks and other practical furniture. Chairs of two sorts are present. The handsome cast-iron stove is placed on a circular stone with a metal fender all round. The small vase of flowers on top of the filing-cabinet is rather touching. The two rooms beyond are not much more richly decorated. (Lithograph, after a painting perhaps by Karl Raabe.)

*Museum für Kunsthandwerk, Frankfurt-am-Main*

296

## The Duchesse de Berry's private drawing-room at the Tuileries

### early 1820s

The Duchesse occupied the Pavillon de Marsan, overlooking the Seine and now part of the Musée du Louvre. This unfinished watercolour sketch shows only one motif of the carpet fitted overall. The extreme simplicity of the wall-decoration is surprising. Beyond the silk and the muslin curtains may be seen painted glass of a Classical character. The two Argand sconces have globes of silk and wire to soften the light, while the lamp on the table (which stands *behind* the sofa) has a transparency of a vaguely Gothic form. One of the pictures has a Neo-Gothic frame. The pictures are suspended by two different methods. There is a hearth-rug, and the fire-screen is protected by a green silk cover. This room has a relaxed atmosphere; it is not on parade. The L-shaped ottoman or divan makes an English-type cosy encirclement round the fireplace. The enormous number of small objects on the tables is noteworthy. (By J.F. or A. Garnerey.)
*French private collection; photograph from Studio Lourmel, Paris*

## 297 ▽
## Bedroom in the Leuchtenberg Palace, Munich
*c.* 1824

The Palace was built by the famous architect Leo von Klenze in 1816. He was presumably responsible for the decoration of the ceiling in a cool Classical style. The room is that of Eugène de Beauharnais, Duke of Leuchtenberg, who had been Viceroy of Italy under Napoleon and was married to Auguste Amalia of Bavaria, whose full-length portrait by Gérard hangs on the far wall. On the stove is a bust of Queen Hortense, the Duke's sister. He died in this room and the scene was painted after his death; the bed-warmer lying on the floor may be intended to suggest a sick-room. The silk wall-hangings probably come from Lyons. The console table was no doubt a prized possession and is probably by Jacob-Desmalter. Two 'Astral' lamps stand on it. The chairs have loose covers.

*Swedish Royal Collection, Stockholm*

◁ 298
## King Max Joseph's rooms in the Munich Residenz
### 1820–21

This is a view through the doorway from his bedchamber (the bordered wallpaper of which forms a frame to this scene) into the closet and study beyond. The strong colours of the full-blown *Empire* style are here very evident. Note the porcelain on display on the small table, and the hooks for watches above. The muslin under-curtain has a pink edge and fringe echoing that on the main, dark blue curtain. A pile carpet almost covers the whole floor. The study has fitted carpeting with a pattern of naturalistic roses. (By Ernst Bandel.)
*Wittelsbacher Ausgleichsfonds Inventarverwaltung, Munich*

299 ▷
## A dressing-room in the Munich Residenz
### early 1820s

This is in the apartment of the Crown Princess Therese of Bavaria, who married the future Ludwig I in 1810. She may be seen at her writing-desk in the room beyond, through the glazed door; glazing was at that date a most unusual feature for an interior door. The amazing wallpaper, with its long festoons, simulated dado, the frieze of banners and festoons, is echoed by the drapery of the windows. The cornice may possibly also be of paper. There is a green 'glass-curtain', and because the room faced south it was found necessary to fit the large looking-glass opposite with a roller-blind. Presumably this glass, with its accompanying console table, was originally placed between the windows, but the Princess preferred to have her divan there where the light fell conveniently on whatever she was reading – and the number of books on her nest of tables suggests she was a great reader. The parquet floor presumably dates from the Baroque period. Note the squirrel in the cage standing on the showcase full of porcelain by the window. A silver dressing-set is set out on the console table which here serves as a dressing-table; there is a full-length dressing-glass in the far corner – a so-called '*Psyche*'. This is an early example of the cluttered room. (By Franz Xaver Nachtmann.)
*Wittelsbacher Ausgleichsfonds Inventarverwaltung, Munich*

◁ 300, 301
# Rooms in the Hofburg, Vienna
## 1826

From an album of watercolours belonging to Marie d'Orléans (daughter of Louis-Philippe), executed by Johann Stephan Decker in about 1825–6, showing the apartment of the Emperor Franz. Pl.300 (above) shows the rather overpowering nature of late-*Empire* as taken up for palatial décor all over Europe. The bold pattern of the green and mauve fitted carpeting continues into the next room. The wallpaper is of two shades of green. Chairs such as these were to be imitated in Austria around 1900. Pl.301 (below) shows the dining-room with a vast porcelain stove in the *Louis Seize* style which is probably the date of the décor, although the stools may be even earlier. Note the inset Gobelins tapestry. Although the room is here set for dining *en famille*, there are few concessions to modern fashion. Dining-rooms were usually decorated in a conservative manner, but this is a rather extreme instance.

*Metropolitan Museum of Art, New York;*
*Elisha Whittelsey Fund, 1950*

302
## An English library
*c.*1825

This shows a library serving as a pleasant drawing-room used by the whole family, with huge sofas, tables for playing chess, and so on. This room was added to Syston Hall in Lincolnshire by the architect Lewis Vulliamy in 1822–4 in a heavy Grecian style. Note the Classical busts and urns, the numerous sources of light, and the diagonal pattern of the carpeting. The elaborate cornices of the window, over which the drapery is flung, are an early expression of a style that was to become widespread in the 1830s. A heavy fringe forms a pelmet. (Engraved after T. Kearman.)

*By kind permission of*
*Captain Sir Anthony Thorold Bt, R.N. Ret'd*

◁ 303
## A Roman palazzo
### 1825

From an album of drawings made for the Polish Count Artur Potocki showing places visited during his travels (see Pls.304, 309, 315, 344 and 364). This is the *salon* of the palazzo Gregorio, in the via dei Due Macelli, which the Count presumably rented while in the Holy City.

The flounced capping of the striped wall-hangings is a characteristic Italian feature, but it may be that these effects were by this time carried out entirely in wallpaper. Note the fitted carpet.

*Jagiellonian University, Cracow*

◁ 304
## A rented room in Florence
### 1824

Presumably a room taken by Count Artur Potocki on one of his visits to Italy (see Pl.303). The strange motif painted on the ceiling appears to be an urn with a wreath of flowers round its middle; it is not a Madonna or an angel. The panels of wallpaper are unusual. The seat-furniture is stained dark green and has white covers *en suite* with the window curtains. A Persian shawl serves as a coverlet on the bed with its simple striped hangings. The floor is covered with flat-woven carpeting, perhaps what was known as 'Scotch carpet' in the English-speaking world.

*Jagiellonian University, Cracow*

## 305 ▽
## A Copenhagen drawing-room
### 1828

Here we see one corner of the room; there must have been a second window with curtains arranged on the opposite side, to balance. They seem to be of red taffeta. The pelmet-board has a curved front edge. The cords rising from a brass button show that a blind was fitted, hidden behind all the fixed drapery. Against the pier stands a pedestal surmounted by a statue (probably a cast). Note the bare floor and the pot-plant. The furniture is in the Danish *Empire* style, owing much to Sheraton's designs but with a character very much its own. (By Emilius Baerentzen; probably of his parents.)

*By courtesy of Herr Ole Mauritzen; photograph from Kunstforeningen, Copenhagen*

## 306 △
## A living-room in Copenhagen
### 1831

The artist here shows his parents at home, probably in the afternoon, as his mother reads a report in the newspaper to her husband. She has the characteristic *Biedermeier* vantage-point on a platform in the window-embrasure where stands a typical Danish late-*Empire* chair. The walls have a dado and the room is probably of the late eighteenth century, although the furnishings are up-to-date. Note the piece of carpeting, perhaps 'Scotch carpet', on the otherwise bare boards. (By Adam Müller.)

*By kind permission of Mrs Karen Müller; photograph from Ole Woldbye*

◁ 307
## A room in the Lubomirski residence, Lańcut, Poland
### 1826

The Princess Isabella Lubomirska's state bed-chamber, which was hung with *chiné* silk. Note the curious placing of the pair of Hepplewhite-style chairs, which were bought in London in 1787. The room would appear to have been decorated around 1790 but the Argand chandelier (with a large glass anti-drip dish below), the *étagères*, the dwarf cabinet and the window-curtains seem to date from about 1820. (By Willibald Richter.)
*Jagiellonian University, Cracow*

308 ▷
## The Countess Potocka's bedchamber in Cracow
### 1827

This room in the Potocki family's Pod Baranami Palace must have been decorated not long before this drawing was made. Most of the furniture seems to be Polish of the 1820s, but the commode of about 1770 on the right must be Parisian and was perhaps made by Foullet. The placing of the sofa between the windows is noteworthy – a sensible arrangement as it allowed daylight to fall on the table and on books a sitter may have been reading. The parquet floor is uncarpeted. What looks like a shawl serves as a coverlet on the bed, which has an interesting form of canopy.
*Jagiellonian University, Cracow*

◁ 309
## A *salon* in the Ukraine, Aleksandria
### 1828

The *salon* of the Countess Branicka, the wife of the Grand Crown Hetman of the Ukraine, Francis Xavier Branicki. Here, within a simple framework, quite elaborate effects have been contrived with up-to-date curtains and other items. The stand with twin Argand burners is curious, but on the oval table stands a new 'Astral' or 'Sinumbra' lamp. The card-tables seem to date from the late eighteenth century.

*Jagiellonian University, Cracow*

310 ▷
## A closet at Lańcut, Poland
### 1829

All the furniture shown here is listed in an inventory of 1802; the decoration dates from the 1790s. Incorporated in the painted decoration are coloured engravings of Raphael's *Stanze*, and in the ceiling is inset a portrait of the child Count Henryk Lubomirski as Cupid, by Mary Cosway and executed while the family were in England in 1787. The work-table and the low cabinets came from Paris; the chairs at the back are English. The rest of the furniture was made in Poland under English influence. The room is in one of the corner-towers; the tower at the opposite end of the façade may be seen through the window. The curtains are of the fixed variety, but there is an awning outside one window and there are likely to have been blinds. Note the Gothic garden bench. (By Willibald Richter.) See also Pl. 307.

*Jagiellonian University, Cracow*

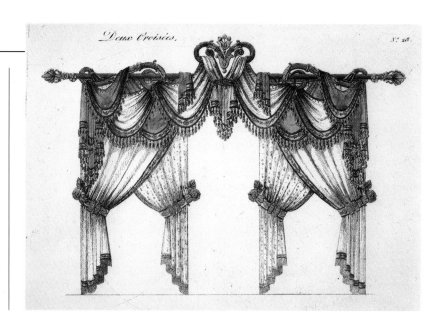

### 311 ▷
## From a Parisian upholsterer's pattern-book
#### *c.*1830

This suggests how one might curtain windows with 'continued drapery'. The style is late-*Empire*. (From *Recueil des Draperies d'Hallevant mis au jour et augmenté par Osmond et Dezon, Cahier* v.)
*Samuel J. Dornsife Collection*

313, 314 ▷
# French curtain-treatment
### late 1830s

The first, of 1837 (above), shows patterns for curtains with a 'piped' effect (*à pente tuyotée*) with ornaments that have a Renaissance character, and for curtains '*à la grecque*' with 'glass-curtains' of painted wire mesh. The second, two years later (below), shows a style very different from the late-*Empire* compositions so greatly favoured until the mid-1830s. Here called '*Louis Quinze*', it would now often be called '*Louis Quartorze*' as it has the heaviness of Baroque rather than the lighter feeling of Rococo. (From C. Muidebled, *La Pandore du Tapissier*, Paris, 1837; and La Pinsonnière, *Recueil des Draperies d'Hallevant . . .*, Paris, 1839, *Cahier* VII.)

*Metropolitan Museum of Art, New York,*
*Harris Brisbane Dick Fund, 1939;*
*and Samuel J. Dornsife Collection*

◁ 312
# German late-*Empire*
### 1837

From Wilhelm Kimbel's influential furnishing-journal published between 1835 and 1853. The style here may be called late-*Biedermeier*; it embodies much derived from French *Empire* but owes something to English Regency and adds a flavour of its own – especially in the plant-stand and the positioning of a chair and work-table in the window. (From W. Kimbel, *Journal für Möbel-schreiner und Tapezierer*, Mainz/Frankfurt, 1835–53.)

*Victoria and Albert Museum, London*

No. 14. *Croisé à pente tuyotée.*
Echelle.

No. 15. *Croisé à la grecque, avec transparents métalliques peints.*

## ◁ 315
## A house at Bad Ischl
### 1831

A room 'at Schmidt's' taken by Count Artur Potocki on a visit to this Austrian watering-place; this room was that of the artist's father. Note the painted 'finger-plates' on the door. The windows have delicate grilles of ironwork; each has a single curtain under a festooned pelmet. The house itself must date from the Baroque period, judging by the ceiling. Some of the furniture is eighteenth-century.

*Jagiellonian University, Cracow*

## ◁ 316
## An Italian drawing-room
### spring, 1838

The simple 'Grecian' fireplace-surround is fitted with a curious register-grate for coal, with bevelled cheeks of polished metal. The walls are papered bright blue but have gold fillets. The floor is fully carpeted. On the round table is a printed velvet cloth which was designed for the circular form. On the table is a candlestick with a transparency serving as a shade. The two lamps on the mantel-shelf are perhaps 'Solar' lamps (this is too early for petroleum). Some sort of standard lamp is in the corner. On the pedestal is a large alabaster bowl filled with growing hyacinths. The seat-furniture bears a resemblance to chairs of the 1920s. Behind one of the fire-screens is a stand for fire-irons and a pair of bellows. (By A. Tacce?)

*Metropolitan Museum of Art, New York;*
*Elisha Whittelsey Fund, 1954*

## 317, 318
# Two rooms in Coburg
### 1832

Prince Friedrich of Coburg had a small town residence – his *Schlösschen* or little palace – done over in 1794, from which time the inlaid floor and the stove must date. He died in 1815, after which the rooms were presumably re-decorated. Much of the furniture is stated in an inventory of 1816 to have come from Vienna (including a round table bought in March of that year from the famous Viennese upholsterer Josef Danhauser), and items were being added in the succeeding years. The general appearance of the rooms shown here is therefore that of 1815–25. It is interesting that the green *salon* was called the 'Carpeted Room', showing that none of the other rooms had carpeting. (By Heinrich Krüppel.)

*Kunstsammlungen der Veste Coburg*

◁ 319
## A bed with a difference, Berlin
### *c.*1830

This amazing confection disguising a conventional *Biedermeier*-style bed must, if ever constructed, have relied not only on exceptional skill from an upholsterer but on the craft of the papier-mâché maker, for the columns are stated to be of '*Pappe*'. The rigid coverlet must be formed on a removable frame, a so-called *Couvertrahme*. Note the valances between the legs of the bed. (From L.W. Wittich, *Magazin für Freunde eines geschmackvollen Ameublements*, Berlin, before 1833.)
*Metropolitan Museum of Art, New York;*
*Jacob S. Rogers Fund, 1932*

◁ 320
## A Berlin bathroom
### *c.*1830

The whole room is draped, even the 'pilasters' being contrived with drapery. This engraving shows a popularized version of the kind of décor devised by Schinkel earlier in the century (see Pl.252). The bath-niche could equally well serve as a bed-alcove, the accompanying text explains, and the total effect is particularly delicate if one executes it in a white material with a pink lining. However it can also be carried out entirely in *trompe l'oeil* paintwork; and we know that such effects could also be rendered on wallpaper (see Pl.337). (From L.W. Wittich, *Magazin für Freunde eines geschmackvollen Ameublements*, Berlin, before 1833.)
*Metropolitan Museum of Art, New York;*
*Jacob S. Rogers Fund, 1932*

## 321, 322
# Decorating a four-poster
### 1826 and 1835

Such beds were fast going out of fashion but were still wanted in grand houses, particularly Neo-Gothic buildings, when P. and M.A. Nicholson brought out their *Practical Cabinet Maker, Upholsterer and Complete Decorator* in 1826. This was presumably why they included a 'Four Post Bed' and also the 'Gothic Bed' reproduced here. There was no great difference between the two designs. However, being strong advocates of Classical taste created 'when the arts and sciences were in the very zenith of perfection', they felt it desirable to add a bed 'in the Grecian style', which was included in a later edition where the engraving bears the date 1835. Classicism still had plenty of mileage, but, since the ancient Greeks had not had four-posters, the Nicholsons simply took the standard formula and added different details.

*Victoria and Albert Museum, London*

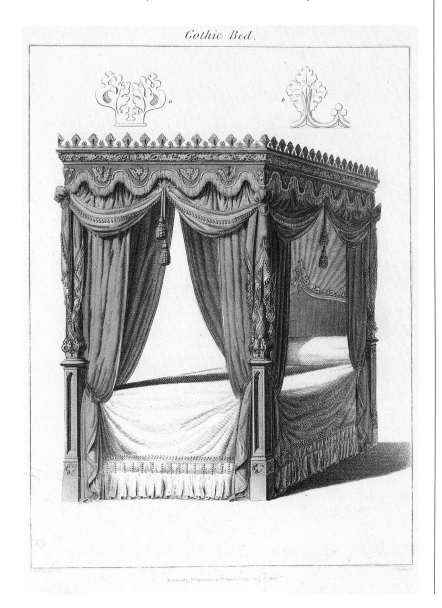

*Gothic Bed.*

*Bed in the Grecian Style.*

## 325, 326 ▷
# A Parisian bedroom and boudoir
### c.1835

Two plates from La Pinsonnière's *Recueil des Draperies d'Hallevant . . .*, which appeared in Paris before 1839 and is unusual because human figures are included in some of the proposals for complete schemes of decoration, as here. La Pinsonnière stated that he was Osmont's successor.

*Samuel J. Dornsife Collection*

## ◁ 323
# Princess Augusta's 'Muslin Closet' in Berlin
### 1829

The Princess had been married in June of that year. The picture shows her study in the Prince Wilhelm Residenz on Unter den Linden, with a view of the University, Zeughaus and Opera. The house had then just been done up by the famous Prussian architect Carl Friedrich Schinkel. This corner room was entirely draped in white muslin which seems to have had embroidered borders. Blinds are fitted to the windows; that on the right is fully down and displays a motif, probably painted, in the middle. The lower edges of the other two blinds are visible. Note the potted plants on the window-sill. In the corner stands a screen on the back of which there will have been a small desk with a hinged writing-leaf.

*Verwaltung der staatlichen Schlösser und Gärten, Berlin*

## ◁ 324
# From a Parisian upholsterer's pattern-book
### c.1830

The often rather strident colours of the 1830s are well illustrated by this proposal for a bedchamber in the late-*Empire* or Grecian taste. (From Théodore Pasquier, *Dessins d'ameublement*, Paris, c.1830.)

*Bibliothèque Forney, Paris*

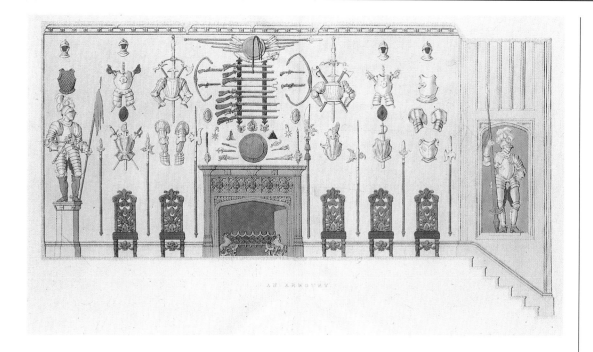

AN ARMOURY

◁ 327

## How to arrange your armour
### before 1833

A plate from Richard Bridgens' *Furniture with Candelabra and Interior Decoration* (London, 1838), a first edition of which had appeared before 1833, and the plates for which may go back to the early 1820s. Bridgens seems to have been a gentleman designer with strong antiquarian leanings and his book is an important source of information on the 'Elizabethan' style as practised in England in the 1820s. In 1818 he showed at the Royal Academy a design for 'an armoury at Abbotsford, the seat of Sir Walter Scott', and there was probably a connection between the decoration of that celebrated house and the present composition.

*Victoria and Albert Museum, London*

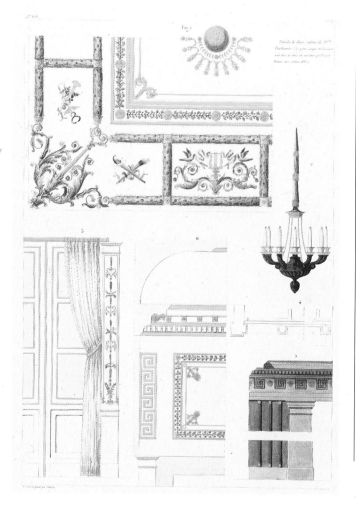

◁ 328

## Ornaments in the magnificent apartment of Mlle Duchenois, Paris
### *c.* 1830

Details of these celebrated rooms had already been published in 1835. The architect was Auguste Constantin. Fig. 1 shows the ceiling of the *salon* with its chandelier (Fig. 2); note the silk sleeve hiding the chain. Fig. 3 is a glazed door with gilt ornaments which could be hidden by a *portière*. Fig. 4 shows the plan of a chimneypiece. Figs. 5 and 6 give details of two other rooms. (From Thiollet and Roux, *Nouveau Recueil de Menuiserie et de Décorations intérieures . . .* , Paris, 1837.)

*Victoria and Albert Museum, London*

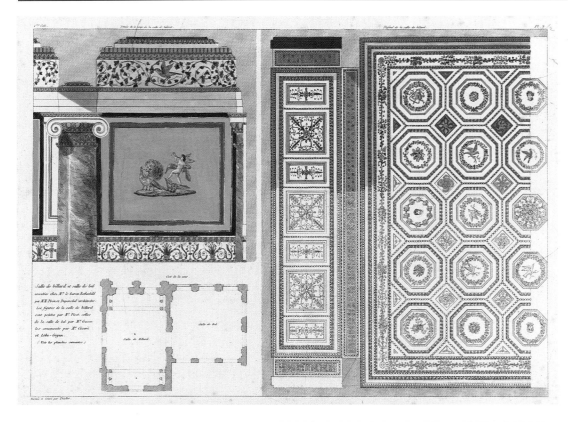

## Decoration of the Rothschild mansion in Paris
### 1820

From the same work as Pl.328. This splendid house was built for Baron James de Rothschild; its decoration was greatly admired. The architects were Piron and Duponchel, who employed four top-flight specialists to carry out the decorative paintwork shown here – two executing the figures and two the arabesques and formal elements. (From Thiollet and Roux, *Nouveau Recueil ...*, Paris, 1837.)

*Victoria and Albert Museum, London*

## Berlin Classicism
### 1840s

The Grecian style had a particularly long innings in Germany, enjoying fresh favour in its late, florid phase which is admirably exemplified by this design for 'the upper part of a richly-decorated wall', included in a pattern-book for architects and art schools. (From *Neue Ornamente von Heinrich Asmus*, Berlin, 1844.)

*Victoria and Albert Museum, London*

◁ 331

### A doctor's drawing-room in Yorkshire
*c.*1838

The strident wallpaper reaches down to the straw-coloured skirting. The room dates from the mid eighteenth century, so there must have been a dado before. In the fireplace is a hob-grate. The curtains are arranged in a rather amateur manner. The sofa has matching loose covers. The armchair must be modern as it has shallow buttoning. The carpeting seems not to have a pile so it may be a 'Scotch carpet' or 'Kidderminster' flat-weave. This water-colour shows the drawing-room at Elmswell House, the home near Langton in Yorkshire of the Best family, who were members of the landed gentry. (By Mary Ellen Best; see also Pls.332, 333, 351, 352 and 353.)
*By courtesy of Messrs Sotheby Parke Bernet, New York*

### Dinner laid, Yorkshire
332 ▷
1838

From the same source as Pl.331 and of the same house. Here the nineteenth-century dado has been preserved and the brightly striped wallpaper has a narrow fillet of dark green paper. All but one of the dining-chairs has been pulled up to the table, the family being just about to enter. Note the seats of black horsehair, still the preferred material for dining-chairs. A printed Staffordshire-ware service is on the table. Each place has a bread-roll lying on a napkin, flanked by a green-handled knife and a fork. Wine-glasses are placed on the left of each place-setting. Spoons are inverted. (By Mary Ellen Best.)
*By courtesy of Messrs Sotheby Parke Bernet, New York*

### 333
# A drawing-room in Nuremberg
### 1841

In 1840 Mary Ellen Best married the son of a German hotel-owner named Johann Anton Sang; they are here seen with their first-born in 'Our own drawing room in Platner's House' in Nuremberg. Platner was a prominent businessman and city dignitary at the time. The Renaissance ceiling and window embrasures indicate that the house dates from the late sixteenth or early seventeenth century, but it must have been done over in the early nineteenth century when new windows and a dado were fitted. The eye-catching wallpaper was presumably put up when the couple moved in. 'Continued drapery' like this would soon go out of fashion, to be revived again at the end of the century. The furniture is all late-*Empire/ Biedermeier*, except for the looking-glass which has a Neo-Rococo frame, and the armchair which she had brought with her from York. Note the stool on the platform by the window. The paintings are probably all by Mary Ellen, but none of the items in the room seem to have come from England.

*By courtesy of Messrs Sotheby Parke Bernet,
New York*

## 334
# Afternoon in Berlin
### 1830

Tea is served on a sofa-table in this typical *Biedermeier* room. The furniture is characteristic of the reticent North German version of late-*Empire* – the fall-front *secrétaire*, the flat looking-glass of architectural form, the sofa with mahogany veneer much in evidence. The window has divided cur-tains with a very deep pelmet. A straw mat lies in front of the sofa. Note the flowers in a vase – an almost obligatory form of decoration at the time. An 'Astral' lamp stands on the card-table at the side. The man is Carl Wilhelm Gropius, painter of dioramas and theatre scenery. His wife sits in the window at her work-table, her foot on a small stool. Her shawl is neatly folded on a chair.

*Märkisches Museum, East Berlin*

◁ 335
## An American bishop's study, Philadelphia(?)
### 1836

A thoroughly functional room. On the writing-desk lies a fat book-pillow on which a heavy Bible could conveniently be opened. The curious small stand next to the desk may be a home-made lectern. The armchair is new but seems to have cushions tied on. Bookcases have been added in a random arrangement as extra shelving came to be needed. Some Chippendale-style mahogany chairs of the 1770s stand at the walls alongside some modern green-stained 'half-Windsors'. A handsome older Windsor-type armchair fitted with a squab stands by the fireplace. The fireplace-surround must date from the same period as the mahogany chairs. The commode between the windows in the far room (perhaps the bedchamber) is covered with a linen cloth and probably serves as a dressing-table. In fact Protestant Episcopal Bishop William White, the occupier of these rooms, inhabits an eighteenth-century house which still contains many of its old furnishings. The lack of curtains and the matting on the floor show that it is summertime. (By John Sartain.)

*Independence National Historical Park, Philadelphia*

◁ 336
## A drawing-room in Stockholm
### c.1825

Outside may be seen the Swedish royal palace with an early steamboat in the harbour. The room dates from the late eighteenth century but the furnishings seem to be of about 1820. The sofa-arm disguised as two superimposed bolsters is typical of that period. Note the Argand lamp on the table, which has a woollen cloth with a printed border. Most curious is the late-seventeenth-century walnut chair which seems to be English (many were exported to the Continent). The caned back has been filled in and the seat is now stuffed. Presumably the sitter had antiquarian interests, explaining why he would have had such an antiquated chair in his drawing-room. (By C.S. Bennet.)

*By kind permission of Baron Sten Ramel; photograph from Kulturen, Lund*

## 337
## A *salon* at Nice
### 1833

This room would appear to have been decorated in the 1820s, but it is arranged in the old manner with the seat-furniture still standing by the walls. However, one sofa has been drawn out (probably from this end of the room) and placed with its back to one of the two fireplaces in which stand fire-screens, suggesting that it is a warm time of the year. Rather modern is the idea of placing a round table out in the middle of the floor. An occasional chair with a rush seat stands by one window. Another rather more elegant chair, which does not belong to the suite, stands by the door. The vases with artificial flowers, and the clocks, all have glass hoods on small wooden plinths. The striking feature of the room, however, is the mural decoration. This *trompe l'oeil* wallpaper is by Dufour of 1815–20.

*Swedish Royal Collection, Stockholm*

## 338
## A Russian drawing-room
### 1838

The room probably dates from the late eighteenth century, judging by the ceiling and parquet floor. The cast-iron stove is presumably of that date, as will be the oval table piled with books and the small table against the far wall. The rest of the furnishings are in the late-*Empire* taste, and so were fairly new when this charming picture was painted. The round table by the sofa may be an eighteenth-century tea-table in the English style, originally intended for occasional use but now pressed into service as a sofa-table. A more modern round table supports a pot-plant in the forefront. On the floor lies a small Persian carpet. Note the ornaments on the cord of the chandelier. As well as 'continued drapery' of muslin there are 'glass-curtains', suggesting that this room was on the ground floor. The blue walls are covered with pictures, the smallest mostly being low down.

*Museum of the Institute of Russian Literature, Moscow*

## 339 ▷
## An English dining-room
### 1835

A room at Aynhoe Park in Northamptonshire, decorated by John Soane in about 1800–2 for William Cartwright MP. Most of the furnishings seem to be of that date. The large carpet has a brown ground, which was a much favoured colour for carpets in England during the eighteenth century. The chairs are in a style influenced by French designs of the 1790s. It is curious that there are no pier-glasses above the dwarf cupboards between the windows. On one stands a bronze of a Giambologna subject which is still in the family, as are some of the chimney ornaments. The picture over the fireplace is a Rembrandt now in the Rijksmuseum, Amsterdam. Note the log-basket. Although the curtains may have been renewed since Soane's time, very little seems otherwise to have been changed. (By Elizabeth Cartwright, wife of William's son Sir Thomas, who was the British Ambassador in Stockholm; she was Bavarian.)

*English private collection*

◁ 340

## A dressing-room in Austria
### 1820s

This picture is unfinished. A small section of the carpet (probably made at Linz) has its colours filled in. The covers of the dressing-table and stools *may* have been of white muslin, but there are indications that the wall-hangings had a spotted pattern and were probably not white at all. The shawl over the arm of the sofa was certainly colourful. The hangings form a tent with a pleated roof; the material on the walls is gathered at a series of coronets to form 'pilasters' with heavy drapery between. Note the brass ring of the bell-pull. On top of the *Biedermeier* mahogany *chiffonier* is a tray with a carafe and glasses, perhaps for a cordial. A clock stands on the wardrobe beyond. This delightful dressing-room must have been exceptionally well illuminated when all the candles were lit. Not only is there a chandelier with six or seven branches; there are sconces flanking the pier-glass that is framed by the hangings, there are candlesticks on the dressing-table alongside the dressing-mirror, and there are multiple branches at two levels on the big dressing-glass at the far end of the room. The sofa-table is here seen to be a strictly functional object. (By Johann Stephan Decker.)
*Historisches Museum der Stadt Wien, Vienna*

◁ 341

## A Viennese bourgeois library
### 1839

Glazed bookcases occupy much of one wall and a large writing-desk stands in front. The elegant Classicism of this room derives from the late-eighteenth-century model; the tendency towards chubbiness so often seen in contemporary *Biedermeier* is here totally absent. (By Franz Barberini.)
*Historisches Museum der Stadt Wien, Vienna*

### 342
## 'While the Sunday lunch is laid', Stockholm
*c.*1835

The main living-room in the house of an architect living in Stockholm. The maid is about to place a table in the centre of the room and lay it for Sunday lunch, as an inscription on this amusing water-colour explains. The family wait at the side, on chairs which will soon be brought forward round the dining-table. The old formal arrangement of the seat-furniture is still used in the dining-room. The three tables all have flaps with gate-leg supports and can be added together to form an extensive table if necessary. The décor dates from the late Rococo period and the furniture from the early nineteenth century. The runners of carpeting are interesting; they will be of a flat-weave. Note the striped roller-blinds. Two chandeliers for candles hang from the ceiling, but on the walls are two modern sconces with Argand burners. A huge white-tiled stove dominates the far corner.

*City Museum, Stockholm*

### 343 ▷
## A Danish lady's boudoir
### 1838

Almost certainly the closet of the mother of the future Christian IX of Denmark, a lady with the resounding name of Louise of Slesvig-Holsten-Sønderborg-Glyksborg, perhaps in one of the family castles at Glyksborg or Gottorp. The astonishingly strong patterns widely favoured at this time are here very evident. The lady was obviously fond of needlework; every possible vehicle for such work has been commandeered, including the huge squab under the desk. The furniture is mostly in the late-*Empire* style (exceptions are the Neo-Gothic brackets above the sofa), the exceptionally tall pier-glass being characteristic of North Germany and Scandinavia at this period. The seemingly insubstantial folding chair is of a type that was to enjoy wide popularity in the 1840s. On the pedestal-cupboard is a bust of Frederik VI by Thorvaldsen. Note the closely packed ornaments on the desk. (By J. Willing.)

*Danish Royal Collection; photograph from the National Museum, Copenhagen*

### 344 ▷
## A London drawing-room
### 1839

Another of the rooms in houses taken by Count Potocki on his travels (see Pl.303). This was in a house in Dover Street and is said to have been used by the Countess as a dressing-room, although there is not much evidence that this is a woman's room. The décor is Grecian, with rather heavily draped but simple window-curtains. The sofas are tucked into the recesses on either side of the fireplace, where stand a pair of pole fire-screens. A four-branch Argand chandelier is suspended in the middle of the room. The Countess' brother Adam is seated by the window.

*Jagiellonian University, Cracow*

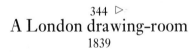

345 ▷
## A royal love-nest, Berlin
*c*.1840

One of the rooms occupied by Countess Liegnitz, the morganatic wife of King Friedrich Wilhelm III who was established in this apartment in 1824. The house was much altered in 1811, and the basic décor must date from this period. The curtains and the carpet could be of the 1820s. The very dense picture-hanging may not be an expression of any particular fashion, but may have evolved as more paintings were acquired. The carpet laid over the fitted carpet must also be an addition, as will be some of the embroidered cushions. This illustration is introduced among other pictures of around 1840 because, even if it shows the décor of an earlier date, it includes many small features of its own time. Note the stained glass and the plants in the window. (By F.W. Kloss.)
*Schlossmuseum, Darmstadt*

346, 347
## Two plates from a Parisian journal
1840

The almost overpowering effect contrived with upholstery that was to become such a feature of mid-nineteenth-century decoration is already in evidence here in these views of a boudoir (right) and a '*Divan Turc*' (above) published in 1840. The 'Turkish Divan' was a smoking-room which had evidently been created in the rue Richelieu for a club known as the *Cercle des Deux-Mondes*. The glass over the fireplace was un-silvered and actually a window, giving a view of the garden. Note the painted blind in the boudoir, which must surely be *à la chinoise*. Although well-stuffed, the *crapaud*-type chair still has no buttoning. (From Le Bouteiller, *Journal de l'Industrie et des Arts utiles*, Paris, 1840.)

*Victoria and Albert Museum, London*

## 348 ▷
## A Swedish major-general in his house
### 1840s

The wallpaper seems to have a pattern very similar to that of the muslin(?) curtains while that of the chair-covers is not a bad match. The floor is covered with carpeting of a flat-weave, perhaps 'Scotch carpet'. A full-length 'glass-curtain' of striped muslin (or it could be pleated) is fitted to the window; the room was presumably in the middle of Stockholm. The bookcase is curious. Two Chinese jars stand on it. The General was obviously interested in phrenology. (By C.S. Bennet.)

*By courtesy of Baron Gustaf Lagerfelt ; photograph from Linköpings Museum*

◁ 349

## An artist's room in Vienna
### 1841

There are several signs that this is the room of an artist: the easel, the pictures standing about, the screened window, and the exceptional interest in reflections in mirrors. It was probably the room of Ludwig Hild, who painted this scene. The room is basically decorated in the Neo-Rococo taste but the furniture is mostly in a light-hearted Neo-Gothic style. There is a low *vitrine* at the far end of the room containing porcelain, and another most curious showcase on a tall stand which seems rather precarious. The seat-furniture has shallow-buttoning, which was being widely adopted at this time. The carpet was perhaps woven at Linz. Among the many ornaments are alabaster vases, a skull in a glass dome, a globe, and a peacock's feather wedged under the frame of the looking-glass.

*Historisches Museum der Stadt Wien, Vienna*

350 △

## Drawing-room in a modest English country house
### 1842

This would appear to be a mid-eighteenth-century room re-decorated around 1830. The walls seem to be painted a stone colour while the ceiling is white. Much of the furniture is old. The desk must date from the eighteenth century, as probably do the armchairs now disguised by striped loose covers. The same material is used on the Grecian couch and the sofa, as well as on the ottoman in the far corner and the box-seat by the central sofa-table. The fire-screens and various occasional tables were presumably introduced when the room was last re-decorated. The black and gold dwarf cabinet is one of those Regency exercises in nostalgia for the time of Louis XIV, and is meant to conjure up images of the rather more substantial furniture of Boulle and his contemporaries (see. p. 157). The house, Cock-enache near Barkway in Hertfordshire, was the home of Sir William Clinton, a relative of Charlotte Bosanquet, the amateur artist who executed this watercolour.

*Ashmolean Museum, Oxford*

### 351, 352, 353
# Three adjacent rooms
# of an apartment in Frankfurt
#### Late 1841 or early 1842

Each strip shows the four sides of a room and can be folded so as to form a hollow rectangle. The apartment was that of Mary Ellen Best (see Pl.331) and her husband. The room with the plain yellow walls trimmed only with a narrow frieze (top) must be the family parlour; while the room with the boldly patterned blue-green wallpaper (centre) is the principal reception room. It contains a grand piano, a handsome sofa and – most curiously – a Franconian Baroque bureau-bookcase. The room with three windows (below) contains a bookcase but also chairs in a row and two sideboard-tables, suggesting that it doubled as a study and as a dining-room. This room has *lambrequins* at the window-heads, an early example of a form that was to become widely fashionable. What looks like 'Scotch carpeting' is on the floor in the first room; the other floors are left bare. On the wall in the yellow room is the same portrait as that to be seen in Pl.333. The house stood on the Bockenheimer Landstrasse. (By Mary Ellen Best.)

*By kind permission of Mr Francis Taylor*

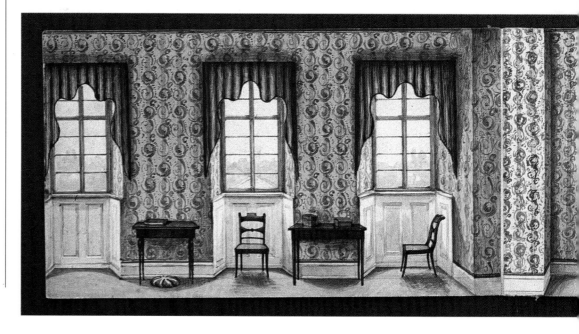

## 354

### A Viennese drawing-room
early 1840s

Not all wallpapers were decorated with bold patterns. Here is a room without a dado where the entire wall is covered with a small-patterned paper reaching from the deep skirting up to an applied paper frieze and cornice. A paper border has also been used on the ceiling. Broad tie-backs are used on the curtains which run on an undisguised rod. The use of striking accents of colour, such as the blue table-cloth and the red hanging lamp, is typical of the 1840s, as are the *jardinières* or plant-stands which are much in evidence. There are two furniture groupings in this room, one for daily use with a sofa and elongated oval table (a favourite Viennese form at the time) where someone has just had coffee; and the more formal suite on the right where albums and picture-books lie stacked on another table. There is no carpet, possibly because it is summer but more likely because the parquet was considered rather smart. (By M. Grösser.)
*Historisches Museum der Stadt Wien, Vienna*

## 355 (right, above)

### Furnishing with flowers, Austria
1843

Banks of flowering pot-plants form major features of the furnishing of this late-*Biedermeier* room. Two of the *jardinières* have naturalistic supports. The chandelier is decorated with artificial flowers, and more are painted (stencilled?) on the ceiling. Note the cloth on the parquet floor. Very shallow pelmets hide the rolled-up sun-blinds outside the windows. (By M. Grösser.)
*Historisches Museum der Stadt Wien, Vienna*

## 356 ▷

### Blondwood *Biedermeier*, Austria
1843

The furniture in this room is all veneered with birchwood, which was much favoured as an alternative to mahogany in central Europe and Scandinavia right through the first half of the century. It is curious how the contents of the vitrines are hidden from view by printed cotton curtains fitted inside the glass. Note the printed velvet table-cover. (By M. Greser – ? Grösser.)
*Historisches Museum der Stadt Wien, Vienna*

W. Kimbel in Mainz gez.                                                                                                Lith u Streng u Schneider.

*Bett mit Himmel und Leibstuhl,*
*zugleich auch als spanische Wand zu gebrauchen.*
Neue Folge II Band No. 16.
Frankfurt ⁹⁄ M, bei J. P. Streng.

## 358 ▷
### Two arm-chairs shown at the Paris Exhibition
#### 1855

Exhibited by the important Parisian upholsterer Langlois, who described one as '*Louis Quinze*' and the other as '*Louis Quatorze*'. They were not buttoned, but probably had springing in the seat. (From Victor Quetin, album of '*Ameublements Riches*' shown at the Exhibition, published in his *Le Magasin de Meubles*, Paris.)
*Victoria and Albert Museum, London*

## ◁ 357
### The spread of information

From W. Kimbel, *Journal für Möbelschreiner und Tapizierer*, Mainz/Frankfurt, 1835–53. This design for a half-tester bed (what was called an 'Arabian bedstead' in England) was published by Kimbel in an 1845 issue. Within a year this design had been copied by an architect decorating a royal residence in Oslo, although he omitted the *putti* on the tester and on the head- and foot-boards.
*Victoria and Albert Museum, London*

## 359 ▷
### Deep-buttoned comfort in Paris
#### c.1840

The development of deep-buttoning, by means of which thicker layers of stuffing could be secured, changed the shape of seat-furniture, as did the contemporaneous advent of springing. The sofa shown here represents an early attempt to incorporate the new techniques in a stylish manner. Note the strong and rather dark colouring that was much favoured during the 1840s. (From the section added to M. Santi, *Modèles de Meubles et Décorations intérieures, pour l'Ameublement...*, in the new edition published in 1841; apparently by Michel Jansen, then a leading Parisian upholsterer.)
*Victoria and Albert Museum, London*

360 △
## A Hampshire drawing-room
1843

Comfortable without being ostentatious, this shows a well-to-do middle-class house in the English countryside. The Classical chimneypiece has the usual Regency simplicity but the Neo-Rococo scrollwork of the cast-iron register-grate suggests this was fitted later. The firescreen is also in the Neo-Rococo style. The bobbin-turned chairs are characteristic of the 1840s and are fitted with squabs. Many of the other pieces are of earlier date. What may be a genuine late-seventeenth-century caned chair stands behind the round table which has a fitted carpet. (Hollington House, East Woodhay; by Charlotte Bosanquet.)

*Ashmolean Museum, Oxford*

361 ▷
## A palatial English country house
*c.*1845

The morning-room at Leigh Court in Somerset, built for the son of a banker and begun in 1814. It would appear that this room was decorated in the 1820s. It is couched in a very heavy version of the Grecian taste embodying much of the character of *Louis Quatorze*, the style which was taken up by the rich during that decade. Not only is there much reliance on white and gold, but there is a strong Baroque flavour about many of the pieces of furniture – in some cases Grecian forms have Baroque ornament while the gilt console tables in the background (only one is visible) seem to be actual late-seventeenth-century Italian. The fire-irons, grate and fire-screen also have a Baroque character. The candle-stands may be genuine English Baroque of about 1740, but could be from the 1820s. The same applies to the armchair on the left. A hearth-rug lies on the large carpet, which is not fitted and is therefore likely to be an Axminster.

*City of Bristol Museum and Art Gallery*

## 362 △
## A lady's sitting-room in Germany
### 1844

This very charming scene is among the water-colours collected by Queen Victoria during her visits to Germany, most of which show places where she stayed with her husband, Prince Albert of Saxe-Coburg and Gotha. This may be a room in one of his family's many small castles and residences in and around Coburg. The portrait may even be of Victoria; anyway, the costume makes it clear that it was new when this scene was depicted. A bonnet, shawl and parasol have been deposited on one of the two easy-chairs which are of a transitional form, on the way to acquiring the rounded forms of the typical Victorian easy chair – the so-called '*crapaud*'. On the right is a work-table perched on a platform in the window; it is carpeted *en suite* with the main floor. There is also a separate carpet in front of the sofa. Note the bell-pull. The liberal use of cords and tassels for decorating window-curtains, which was to become a feature of many schemes in the third quarter of the century, is to be seen here at an early stage in its development. (Signed W. Pätz.)

*By gracious permission of Her Majesty the Queen; Windsor Castle Library*

## 363 △
## 'My closet.
## The Palace on the Plein.
## July 1839 – May 1849',
## The Hague
### 1849

Princess Sophie of Württemberg had married the Crown Prince of Orange in 1839 and lived in a town residence (now the Dutch Home Office) until his accession as William III of the Netherlands in the year this picture was painted. The Princess had brought some of her furniture with her from Stuttgart, including the late-*Empire* rosewood desk with a gallery which dates from 1830; the Gothic chair, here largely hidden by a unifying loose cover, seems to have come from the rooms she occupied in Stuttgart as a girl. The folding table in front has an inset Sèvres plaque and is Parisian of about 1840. The *prie-dieu*-type chair next to the bust was an entirely new form in the 1840s, and folio-stands now became fashionable as polite furniture for the next few decades. Wastepaper-baskets were still by no means common at this stage. (By H.F.C. ten Kate.)

*Rijksmuseum Palais Het Loo, Apeldoorn*

## 364
# Princely lodgings in Edinburgh
### 1840

Another of the rooms in houses taken by Count Artur Potocki on one of his journeys – this time to Scotland (see Pl.303). The building seems to date from about 1810 and must have been re-decorated in the 1830s with a Neo-Rococo overmantel glass, mahogany furniture in the late-Regency taste, and a four-branch Argand chandelier. Note how the wallpaper reaches right down to the floor, there being no dado. The seat-furniture is all protected with chintz loose covers. The Countess' shawl and embroidery frame lie on the square ottoman which has no central back-rest.

*Jagiellonian University, Cracow*

1840 Edinburg w Szkocii salon Hrabiny Arturowej Potockiej malowala Aleksandra Augustowa Potocka.

366 ▷

## A music-teacher's room in Stockholm
### probably *c.*1847

Josabeth Sjöberg taught the piano and probably also the guitar. She lived in a series of rented rooms in Stockholm and recorded each in naïve water-colours, which provide a wonderful survey of the modest surroundings in which this spinster lived from 1838. In the 1880s she moved into an old people's home, which she also illustrated and which seems to have been a remarkably jolly place, judging by her sketches. In the scene reproduced here she is seen ill in bed, being visited by Doctor Levin. In the niche of the tall tiled stove is a glass of red wine being gently mulled. Her best dress hangs on the control-key for the damper. The base of her bed is partly pulled out; pushed back, the bed served as a sofa during the day. Overhead is an engraving of Uppsala Cathedral hanging on a ribbon. Most of her furniture, which she took with her when she moved, dates from the 1820s, but the white chairs are of the late eighteenth century. The curtains are simple (they accompanied her as well), and the wallpaper was no doubt cheap. Between the double windows are laid everlasting flowers.

*City Museum, Stockholm*

## 365 △
# A school-teacher's apartment in Stockholm
### 1843

His wife sits in the window on the platform so frequently placed in that position at this period all over Germany and Scandinavia. She can look out on the street, but green 'glass-curtains' screen her from view. She is doing her embroidery on a portable frame. The room is in an old house which seems to have been done over in about 1830 when the doors, cornice and new windows were installed. None of the furniture is new, on the other hand; the grey-painted chairs must date from the late eighteenth century, while the sofa-bed is rather less old. A measure of unity is imparted to the seat-furniture by the striped loose covers. The walls are colour-washed. Many ladies took up the guitar during the 1830s and 1840s, and such instruments are often to be seen in illustrations of rooms from that period. (By the teacher, whose name was Johan Gustaf Köhler.)

*City Museum, Stockholm*

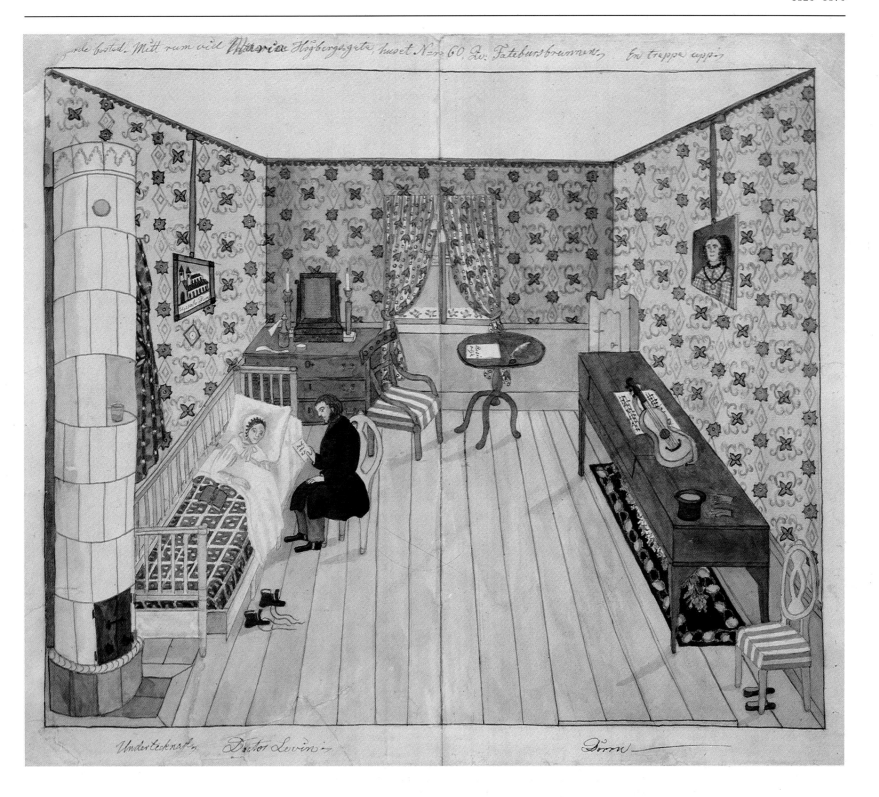

◁ 367

## Drawing-room in a small German princely residence
### 1847

This is another memento of Queen Victoria's stay in Germany with Prince Albert (see Pl.362) and shows a room at Rosenau near Coburg, a *maison de plaisance* built by the architect Carl von Heideloff for the Duke Wilhelm of Württemberg in the 1830s. The charming Neo-Gothic décor in yellow and blue is playful – the sort of thing that met with such profound disapproval from Pugin and the other advocates of 'muscular Gothic'. This romantic veneer blends very prettily with the Grecian furniture; it is not to be taken seriously. Presumably the Gothic arcading is a *trompe l'oeil* executed on wallpaper; the ceiling-ornaments are probably of papier mâché. Note the very comfortable piano-stool with a back-support. Heideloff later carried out important restoration work on famous buildings at Coburg and Nuremberg. (By Ferdinand Rothbart.)

*By gracious permisson of Her Majesty the Queen ;*
*Windsor Castle Library*

◁ 368

## Late *Biedermeier* Gothic
### *c.* 1860

Another illustration of rooms in a small courtly residence where Queen Victoria and her consort Albert stayed during visits to his homeland. A veneer of Gothic has here been applied to a plain room in what was in fact an old fortress, no doubt with the aid of a good deal of papier mâché ornament. Large vitrines filled with porcelain and coloured glass were popular as decoration in the *Biedermeier* interior. This room was in the castle at Kallenberg near Coburg and, although the décor probably dates from the 1840s, this picture was presumably painted during the royal couple's visit to Coburg in 1860. See also Pl.389. (By Ferdinand Rothbart.)

*By gracious permission of Her Majesty the Queen ;*
*Windsor Castle Library*

## 369
## Serious Gothic as décor, Germany
### 1847

This comes from the same source as Pl.367 but shows an interior of which Pugin and his friends would surely have approved. These rooms are at Stolzenfels, a castle near Koblenz, begun in 1836 on the basis of a sketch-plan by Schinkel himself but completed by two of his pupils who were undoubtedly familar with Pugin's publications. They must have provided designs for the furn-iture, which survives and was made by leading joiners in Munich and at nearby Neuwied in the early 1840s, a few years before this illustration was executed. The 'muscularity' of the throne-like armchair is anyway unmistakable, as is the clear-cut construction of the table. The chimneypiece is a most satisfactory piece of Neo-Gothic, and the splendid chandelier could not have been based on principles that were more correct – and what a splendid example of German metalworking skills it is! But the room shows few signs of human occupancy. Maybe the castle was in fact not being lived in when this picture was made; or perhaps it reflects the rather dry approach of the artist, Graeb; or it may even be that people did not spend all that much time in such rooms if they could help it. If this really is the drawing-room, as an inscription in the album claims, one has to admit that few concessions have been made to comfort. (By Carl Anton Graeb.)

*By gracious permission of Her Majesty the Queen; Windsor Castle Library*

### 370
## A fairly modest Copenhagen drawing-room
*c.*1845

This can be dated by the cipher on the façade opposite, which is of King Christian VIII who reigned from 1839 to 1848. The room seems to be that of an amateur artist, judging by the pictures leaning against the back of the sofa. The curtains are simple and presumably of printed cotton, a loose cover on a chair being *en suite*. Although there is a piano (rather an old model) and a piano-stool, there are no lamps – merely the chandelier with four candle-sockets. The furniture is of the sort obtainable ready-made in Copenhagen in the 1830s or early 1840s. A cast-iron stove probably stands in the corner alongside the log-basket on the right. The two curious objects rising up behind the sofa may possibly be to protect the wall from greased hair. In the central window are two plant-screens incorporating transparencies.

*National Museum, Copenhagen*

371 ▷
## Inexpensive lodgings in Austria
### 1847

'Our room in Tulbing', it says. One may think this is a characteristic *Biedermeier* interior but its simplicity springs from poverty rather than choice. The furnishings are of the simplest kind; dresses hang on a clothes-rack instead of in a cupboard, the windows are screened with cloths hooked up at the top corners, the wooden furniture is virtually unadorned. Only the chairs have a certain style. It is therefore curious that, in such surroundings, one should have bothered to have *Couvertrahmen* fitted to the beds (see also Pl.319).
*Historisches Museum der Stadt Wien, Vienna*

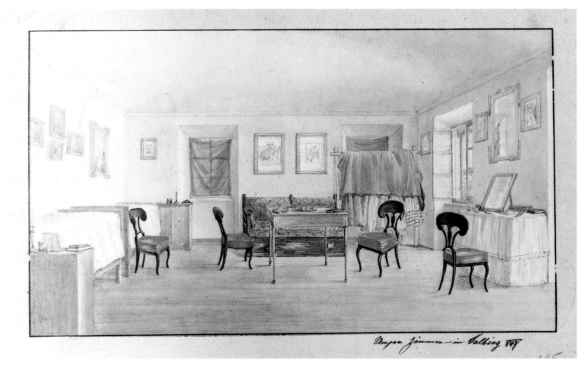

372 ▷
## A small German country house
### c.1850

This sketch is included chiefly because it is pretty and because it shows a simple interior that was old-fashioned when it was executed. Much of the furniture must date from the early years of the century or even before that. The grand piano is not old, and the hanging *étagère* is a typical decorative item of the 1840s. Note how the small carpet has been placed where it was most needed; the soles of women's shoes were at this time so thin that extra insulation had to be provided to protect their feet against the cold. At the piano is the Freiin von Welden. (By Ludwig Voltz.)
*City Archives, Nördlingen*

### 373, 374, 375
# A Parisian collector's apartment
## 1848

These must all be views of the same apartment; the style of decoration is essentially the same in each room, relying as it does on a dense arrangement of antiques (genuine or spurious) and *objets d'art* scattered among ultra-fashionable furnishings of the 1840s which include several *crapauds*, the new fully upholstered, deep-buttoned easy-chairs, and their matching sofas. Although the hangings contribute a background unity, the furniture does not match. What is more, in each room the odd chair has been given a striped loose cover that sets it apart from the rest. Such disparate schemes went well with antiques, which so rarely come in sets. Note, for example, how the two large eighteenth-century looking-glasses do not match although set up as a 'pair'. With antiques it is simpler to avoid unity. The collector obviously liked boullework, as there is some in each room – a table here, a casket, a dressing-mirror, a cabinet or two. He also liked Venetian eighteenth-century sconces; there are three in the drawing-room. There is a splendid pile carpet in the bedroom. In the dressing-room, with its tent-like and gathered hangings, the carpet is flat-woven of the Kidderminster type; while the drawing-room seems to have a tapestry-woven carpet of the sort associated principally with Beauvais. There are lacy painted borders on the ceiling. Curious ornaments are the two domes of artificial flowers mounted, framed on the wall. The fireplaces are all swathed in velvet. (By François-Etienne Villeret.)

*By courtesy of Messrs Hazlitt, Gooden and Fox, London*

### 376, 377
## Rooms in the Berlin Stadtschloss
### 1848 and 1852

Two rooms in the apartment of the Crown Prince Wilhelm and his wife Marianne, depicted by Eduard Gaertner to record their appearance for their daughter Elisabeth who became a Princess of Hesse. Her mother had died in 1846, two years before the view of her dressing-room was painted, while that of the Green Room (opposite), which must have served as a general living-room, was made soon after her father died in 1851. The couple had moved into these rooms after their marriage in 1804, when the rooms had just been done over. The painted ceilings are of that date. The slat-back chairs and the commode in the dressing-room seem also to be of the period. The dressing-glass by the window ought to date from about 1820, as surely does the curtain-arrangement. The tall-backed wing-chair looks as if it belongs to the 1840s and will have been introduced for the Princess Marianne's use in old age; it was covered with a cotton material, and the inventory of 1851 states that it came from Cologne. Also given as being from Cologne are the two screens in the window. In the right-hand foreground is a tall openwork stand described as a *Toilettenkorb* (dressing-basket); presumably one put small articles of clothing and other belongings on it as one undressed at night. The large mahogany desk (with Gothic gallery) in the middle of the Green Room was shared by the couple, each having a side with a writing-chair. In the foreground we see the corner of a great concave ottoman of the sort much favoured by Schinkel, but now deep-buttoned in the new fashion of the 1840s. In the window are set fragments of antique stained glass which are described as being 'valuable'. The carpet was apparently presented to the Prince by the City of Cologne, so presumably it was made there. On the wall hangs a Holbein *Madonna and Child*; its frame cannot have been very old when this view was executed.

*Schlossmuseum, Darmstadt*

## 378
### An artist's quarters in the Winter Palace, St Petersburg
#### 1852–3

By Luigi Premazzi, a Milanese artist who moved to St Petersburg where he set up a drawing-school, later becoming a professor at the Academy. He inscribed this picture (in German) 'My salon in the Winter Palace in Petersburg in the winter of 1852 to 1853'. The room has not been identified, but the vaulting suggests it was in the basement, as does the presence of 'glass-curtains' which are mostly needed at ground-level. There was a serious fire at the Palace in 1837 and the painted decoration here looks as if it was executed subsequently. The room seems to have served several purposes on an 'open plan' divided by screening of various kinds. On the left, beyond the screen of wrought iron(?) and foliage is a sitting-area; behind the huge jar is a writing-desk; and in the background is a space with an easel. On the console table stands a twin-burner Argand lamp of the old type, but the burners of the chandelier are of the newer 'Astral' or 'Sinumbra' form. Note how the carpet is taken up the wall under the window. The pleated screen with cords and tassels is a decorative item.

*By courtesy of Messrs Hazlitt, Gooden and Fox, London*

379, 380 ▷

## Two rooms in the old house at Balmoral, Scotland
### 1855

This was the house where Queen Victoria had been so blissfully happy with Prince Albert. It was too small for their many children and entourage, and the present 'Scottish Baronial' building was being erected when these watercolours were painted. It will be seen that the old house was a modest residence of the kind that could then be found all over the British Isles. There was nothing regal about it. The dining-room stands ready for the table to be laid, with the chairs pulled up round the table. Perhaps, in the relaxed régime that we know was the rule at Balmoral in those years, the table always remained like that between meals. The arrangement of ornaments on the mantel-shelf and the way the paintings are hung are noteworthy. Two double Argand lamps stand on the late-Regency sideboard. A handsome Turkey carpet covers the entire floor. What may be Kidderminster carpeting is used in the bedroom, where there stands an 'Arabian bedstead' with chintz hangings, the same material being used on the seat-furniture. It is rather touching that over the fireplace hangs an engraving of the Queen opening the Great Exhibition of 1851.

*By gracious permission of Her Majesty the Queen;*
*Windsor Castle Library*

## 381 ▷
## A Swedish country parsonage
### 1852

Sunne parsonage in Värmland lies far out in the Swedish countryside and it is not surprising that the décor is rather old-fashioned, echoing modes of the 1830s. The well-upholstered chair by the table, with its huge antimacassar, may have been brought in more recently, as must have been the rocking-chair. Huge numbers of Swedes went to seek their fortune – or at least a livelihood – in the United States at this period and one of the results was that the rocking-chair became popular in Sweden; one sees them in many contemporary illustrations. They were imported from America in large quantities. The floor may be covered with felt; whatever it is, runners have been laid along tracks where people were most likely to tread. Note the muslin covers of the chandeliers protecting them against the flies of summertime. The daughter is being taught the piano; her father seems deeply moved, or perhaps he is merely pained. (By John Rosendahl.)

*Swedish private collection; photograph from Nordiska Museet, Stockholm*

## 382 ▷
## The parlour in a Philadelphia boarding-house(?)
### 1853

This shows the main room in Mrs A.W. Smith's house at the corner of Broad and Spruce Streets in Philadelphia, and it is assumed that this was a private hotel or boarding-house because of the way the two men are not speaking to each other and the other groups seem unrelated. This is a late illustration of a Grecian interior. The room has a wallpaper with a deep frieze and a false dado. One of the outside slatted shutters is closed. There are no pictures and few ornaments. What looks like an antimacassar lies over one chair-back. In fact, there is nothing very remarkable about this room except the astonishing standard lamp burning gas, the metal pipe for which projects far out from the wall before turning down at right-angles to meet the lamp. This must have been a most hazardous arrangement. Anyway it was just as well that the table was a steady one, with a marble top and a heavy cast-iron stand. (By Joseph S. Russell.)

*By kind permission of Bertram K. and Nina Fletcher Little*

## 383 ▷
## Taking a bath, Paris
### 1842

This charming sketch shows how most people took baths before bathrooms became general. The vessel was carried into a living-room and placed in front of the fire. It may have been brought in by the servants, or it may have been hired from a dealer in such equipment. Filling it and later emptying it was obviously tedious. It has casters so one can move it about when empty. The bather clutches a glass of champagne while her companion commiserates with her. The caption that went with this magazine illustration could be translated: 'Our feelings? What are they, anyway? When you look into it, they're a bit of a farce – pretty impenetrable, really, don't you think?' Garvarni's girls are mostly out to enjoy themselves on the fringes of *le monde galant*. It is very odd that the candlestick has to be kept under a glass dome. It cannot have been used very often, anyway. (By Paul Garvarni; from *Charivari*, 7 October 1842.)

*Victoria and Albert Museum, London*

## 384 ▷
## A bedroom in East Coast America
### 1857

The presence on the bed of a London newspaper suggests that this shows the room of an English family who have recently arrived in America. This might account for the way two trunks are piled in the corner, and perhaps this is a rented room taken until a more permanent arrangement could be made. A map of the Eastern States hangs over the (1840s?) fireplace, but it is not known where this room was located. The fact that gas is installed should narrow down the possibilities. On the articulated gas-bracket hangs a small censer which seems to be burning. This might have been against mosquitoes. A sofa-table of the 1820s is by the window. The chest-of-drawers is probably of about the same date. In the niche is a small bookshelf in the Neo-Gothic style. On top of the trunks stands a layette basket for the baby-clothes, while the basket behind the mother is probably for soiled clothes or nappies. The baby's name was Thomas Carew Hunt Martin, but the artist's name is not known.

*Museum of Fine Arts, Boston; M. and M. Karolik Collection*

## 385, 386
## The Villa Berg near Stuttgart
### probably 1855

This Italianate country residence was built for Crown Prince Karl of Württemberg and his wife Olga during the late 1840s by the architect von Leins. In its day it was regarded as one of the most successful princely residences in the 'Renaissance' taste, and when the Crown Princess' mother, the Tsarina Alexandra Feodorowna, saw it she sent a telegram to her husband in St Petersburg reading '*Olga wohnt himmlisch*' (Olga's house is heavenly).

One of the views reproduced here (below) shows the closet. Much of the furniture was bought specially in Paris in 1848, but the house only became habitable in 1853. Among the furnishings brought from Paris were papier mâché ornaments of all sorts, and the ceiling and frieze seen here are probably decorated with this material. The pretty wallpaper and curtains must also be Parisian. Note the *Zimmerlaube*, the huge arrangement of plants in the far corner, and the huge chandelier. A lidded wastepaper-basket stands by the desk. The other view is of the library which was stated to be in the 'Old English taste' (the style more often called 'Elizabethan' in England but in this case embodying a strong element of a purer 'Renaissance' idiom), the ceiling having the pendant bosses 'so characteristic of old English country houses in this style'. It is curious that the enormous wooden chandelier is stated to be 'Rococo', although in fact it seems to be in a style fairly consonant with the rest of the décor. The chairs will have been based on English Neo-Gothic pattern-books. (View of the closet by A. Kappis; of the library by C. Obach.)
*Graphische Sammlung, Staatsgalerie, Stuttgart*

◁ 387

## A drawing-room in an Aberdeenshire country house
*c.*1860

The chimneypiece at Mar Lodge, near Braemar, would seem to date from the 1840s. Note how the brass curtain-rods are curved to conform to the bow-windows. The curtains are yellow with a green pattern, with under-curtains of a patterned Swiss net. The scattered, scarcely grouped, seat-furniture has matching loose covers. A stencilled floral border forms a frieze and a surround to the inset chimneypiece. A border also seems to run above the very deep skirting. To echo the velvet mantel-shelves, a buffet-like structure has been created at this end of the room. With all those trophies of red deer on the walls, one hardly needs the reminder provided by the music-sheet that 'My Heart's in the Highlands'.

*Metropolitan Museum of Art, New York; Elisha Whittelsey Fund, 1962*

◁ 388

## A drawing-room at The Hague
*c.*1860

The scattered arrangement of the furniture being adopted in fashionable circles all over Europe late in the 1850s is again seen here in a Dutch interior. The floor is fairly evenly covered. There is now also a tendency to arrange the curtains so as to exclude much of the daylight. Note the way the pictures and ornaments form a group over the glass-fronted cupboard. This room was in a house on the Lange Vyverberg. (From an album that belonged to the de la Bassecour Caan family.)

*Gemeente Archief, The Hague*

## 389
## A drawing-room near Coburg
### 1860

Another of Queen Victoria's mementoes of her visits to Germany (see also Pls. 362, 367 and 368), this shows the Duke's sitting-room at Kallenberg. The late-*Empire* and the Neo-Gothic furniture must date from about 1820, but the amazing chairs made of antlers cannot have been all that old when this painting was executed. There is a Schinkelesque ottoman in the far room. The Neo-Gothic carpet looks handsome and in no way matches the *Empire* covers on the chairs and sofa. Note the bell-pull. (By Ferdinand Rothbart.)

*By gracious permission of Her Majesty The Queen;*
*Windsor Castle Library*

◁ 390
## A bourgeois drawing-room in St Petersburg
### 1859(?)

By Edward Hau, a German artist who had moved to St Petersburg in about 1840 and specialized in interior views of the Imperial palaces and residences, becoming a member of the St Petersburg Academy in 1854. An inscription explains that this shows his *salon* in an old building on the banks of the Neva. The furnishings are all Neo-Rococo, the style commonly adopted for drawing-rooms in the middle decades of the century. Although set in Russia, this room could very well be in mid-century Paris and some of the furniture (e.g. the desk, writing-chair, and the small table of boulle-work) is likely to be French. The main group of furniture centred round a table is beginning to break up to form subsidiary groupings. The large branch supporting a lamp over the left-hand sofa is curious. Note that there are also candles.

*By courtesy of Messrs Hazlitt, Gooden and Fox, London*

◁ 391
## The cluttered look: an early example, Vienna
### 1844

The *Biedermeier/*late-*Empire* fashion for having arrays of ornaments on a single table or *étagère* (see also Pls.296, 299, 292, 343 and 349), and also for having plant-stands and *jardinières* scattered about the room, has here been carried to an extreme for this period and presages the almost suffocating density of furniture and ornaments admired later in the century (see Pls.445 and 481). Austere arrangements were nevertheless still quite common in the early 1840s. The seat-furniture has buttoning, some of it quite deep, but the seats are not buttoned on the *chaise-longue* and the *bergère* beyond (its fancily shaped back must have been built round a steel-wire frame). Note the large engravings in matching frames. (By M. Grösser.)

*Historisches Museum der Stadt Wien, Vienna*

## 392 ▷
## A North Italian drawing-room
### 1859

Painted by Luigi Premazzi (see also Pl.378), so this is probably the room of a Russian family in Italy. The frames of the looking-glasses and pictures are North Italian Baroque and Rococo, and the spindly chairs were probably made at Chiavari. Otherwise the furnishings have no obvious national characteristics.

*Messrs Sotheby, London*

## 393 ▷
## An English country-house dining-room
### *c.*1855

The house of a man who had made his money in the service of the East India Company, Longford Hall in Shropshire was begun in 1789 and the architectural features of this room belong to the late eighteenth century, as must the handsome hobgrate, fender and trivet. Moreover, the large Turkey carpet was probably that known to have been ordered from a leading London upholsterer at that time. Otherwise the furnishings seem to date from the 1840s, when presumably a new generation had taken over. It is interesting that at this late date the formal arrangement of chairs set against the wall still existed in dining-rooms when all sense of formality had long been banished from drawing-rooms. The various tables placed round the sides of the room can be used as serving-tables, but several seem to be parts of a large dining-table which could be made up in different permutations to whatever size was required. Note the child's chair, and the three-tier 'dumb-waiter' visible behind the central table, which is laid for breakfast. (By Lady Hester Leeke.)

*Photograph from Angelo Hornak Archives*

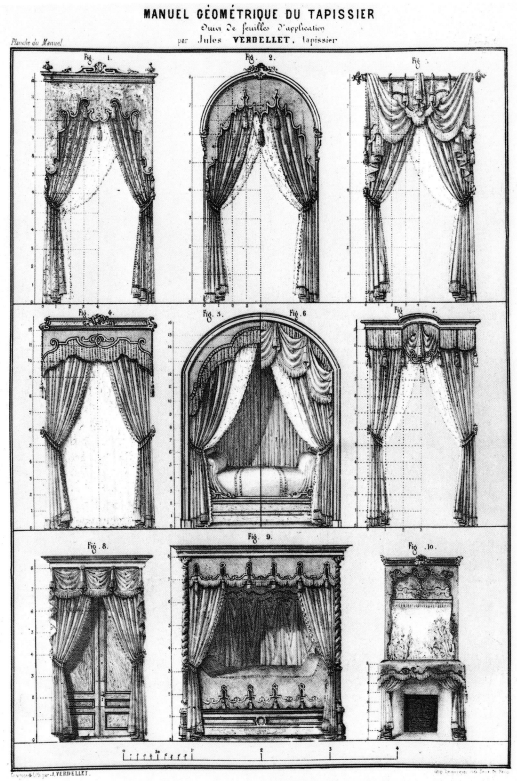

# MANUEL GÉOMÉTRIQUE DU TAPISSIER

Ouvr de feuilles d'application

par Jules VERDELLET, Tapissier

*Planche du Manuel*

Fig. 1. Fig. 2. Fig. 3.

Fig. 4. Fig. 5. Fig. 6. Fig. 7.

Fig. 8. Fig. 9. Fig. 10.

Composé & Lith par J. VERDELLET.

*Proportions à donner aux principaux genres de décor*

LE MAGASIN DE MEUBLES.

DÉCOR DE FENÊTRE GENRE NÉO-GREC

Paris. Publié & dessiné par V^te QUETIN, rue du faub^g St Antoine, 55, au IV^e

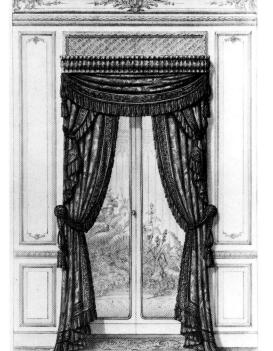

## 394 (*opposite, far left*)
# Recommended proportions for hangings, Paris
### 1864

From that most explicit of all Parisian upholstery manuals, Jules Verdellet's huge *Manuel géométrique du Tapissier* (Paris, 1864). He was an upholsterer, designer, and instructor in the art of cutting out drapery in Paris at a time when the upholsterer's art had never stood higher. Flat *lambrequins* with their fancy outline were now in vogue, as several of these drawings show. Note that the hooks for the tie-backs are always set at half the overall height. The draped chimneypiece (Fig.10) has a window above, framed with a *lambrequin* and furnished with a blind.
*Victoria and Albert Museum, London*

## 397 ▷
# German curtain-arrangement
### 1860s

The international character of fashions in upholstery is demonstrated by this plate from a German pattern-book for craftsmen. Although perhaps more pedantic (because drawn by an architect and not an upholsterer), there is not much difference stylistically between this and the contemporary Parisian design shown in Pl.394. (From *Muster-Zeichnungen für die Gewerbe*, published in series in Karlsruhe between 1863 and 1866 by a Munich-based Society for Instruction in Handicraft; this design was by Adolf Guggenberger.)
*Victoria and Albert Museum, London*

## 395, 396 (*opposite, above and below*)
# Parisian drapery
### late 1860s

The earlier plate (*above*) shows window-treatment in the 'Néo-Grec' style, with the cords and bobbins fashionable at this date; it has under-curtains *and* glass-curtains. The later design has a heading '*à gobelets*'. (From V. Quetin, *Le Magasin de Meubles*, Paris, 1865–7 and 1868–72.)
*Victoria and Albert Museum, London*

Entwürfen von Adolf Guggenberger.

Fenster- und Thürverzierungen.

gez J.Rheinberger

Kunst-Industrie № 145

Carlsruhe Verlag v J.Veith

◁ 398

## A country house on the Hudson River, New York State
### 1863

A Neo-Gothic house with a bay-window overlooking the river. The height of the room is exaggerated by the figures being shown rather too small. An armchair in the 'Elizabethan' style features prominently, as do a pair of black boullework pedestals which are also meant to conjure up images of an ideal past. The late-Regency work-table is something of an anachronism. This probably shows the room in summer. Heavier curtains and a carpet covering the complete floor would probably have been introduced in wintertime. (By Thomas Worthington Whittridge.)
*New York Historical Society*

399 ▷

## A German princely hunting-lodge
### 1857

Fürst Karl zu Leiningen had this small *Jagdschloss* built at Waldleiningen, near Frankfurt, between 1828 and 1847, the work being executed for him by an architect named Karl Brenner. After his father's death when the Fürst was still a child, his mother had married the Duke of Kent, so the young man had spent many of his formative years in England. He often visited England to stay with Queen Victoria, his half-sister. He was anyway familiar with the English Neo-Gothic style, and his *Jagdschloss* reflects this. The large desk and some of the chairs are English in taste but seem to be made of a light-coloured timber rather than of oak. Not typically English is the standing-desk at the back and the huge wastepaper-basket. (By Theodore Reifenstein.)
*Fürstlich Leiningensche Verwaltung, Amorbach*

### 400 △
## A Parisian bathroom
### 1860s

It is couched in a real mixture of styles, an exotic note being provided by the striped upholstery and the leopard-skin, as well as the pavilion-like shape of the room with its top-lighting. (From V. Quetin, *Le Magasin de Meubles*, Paris, 1865–7.)
*Victoria and Albert Museum, London*

### 401, 402, 403, 404 ▷
## Mid-century Classicism in Berlin
### 1850s

The illustrations are from Titz's 1864 collection of 'Designs for executed public and private buildings'; i.e., this had been built. It shows a reception room in the house of a Herr Rudolph Hertzog. Although it is couched in a late version of Grecian, or what would in Paris have been called '*Néo-Grec*' at this time, Titz describes this décor as one of the most perfect expressions of the Renaissance style – which shows how confused was the nomenclature in the realms of Classicism. Opposite the entrance door are the windows, one of which has its blind half-down. On the left of the windows is the chimneypiece flanked by sofas, and on the right a Schinkelesque semi-circular niche with a banquette. The furnishings are all in the same style. (From E. Titz, *Entwürfe zu ausgeführten öffentlichen und Privat-Gebäuden*, Berlin, 1864.)
*Victoria and Albert Museum, London*

Fig.3. Durchschnitt nach E.F. und Ansicht der Fensterseite B.

Fig.4. Durchschnitt nach G.H. und Ansicht der Nischenseite C.

Fr. Nicolaische Verlagsbuchhandlung in Berlin.

Fig.5. Durchschnitt nach F.E. und Ansicht der Thürseite D.

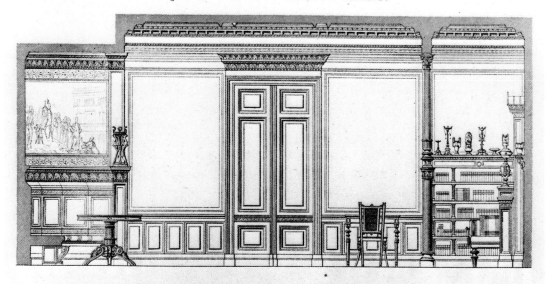

Fig.6. Durchschnitt nach H.G. und Ansicht der Kaminseite A.

Fr. Nicolaische Verlagsbuchhandlung in Berlin.

405 △
## The height of the
## upholsterer's skills
### 1860s

A Parisian boudoir largely decorated with upholstery. The back of the niche and even the cove of
the ceiling are quilted to match the opulent, deep-
buttoned stuffing of the seat-furniture. Presumably the garlands in the cove are of silk artificial
flowers. Note the tassels at strategic points on the
chairs and sofa. Upholstery was never more skil-
fully handled than at this period. (From V. Quetin,
*Le Magasin de Meubles*, Paris, 1865–7.)
*Victoria and Albert Museum, London*

## ◁ 406
## An artist's room in Berlin
### *c.*1860

This humble room seems both to serve as a living-room and as a studio. The sofa and sofa-table are old-fashioned; so are the chairs, one of which stands on a viewing-platform – a feature no longer regarded as smart, although built-in versions were to become fashionable late in the century. The embroidered net *lambrequins* are a modern feature, on the other hand. The piano is also modern. (By Wilhelm Streckfuss.)
*Stadtgeschichtliche Sammlungen, Berlin Museum*

## 407 ▷
## A middle-class dining-room in New York
### 1866

This view shows admirably how rooms acquired a rather more sombre appearance in the 1860s, as windows came to be increasingly heavily curtained. A buffet in the 'Renaissance' taste forms a focal point for an extensive grouping of pictures. Note the handsome antlers behind the gas-chandelier, which is of the kind that may be raised or lowered. On the floor is a fine Turkey carpet. This painting shows the wife and children of Robert Gordon, an Englishman who had business associations with Pierpont Morgan and was involved in the founding of the Metropolitan Museum of Art in New York. (By Seymour Joseph Guy.)
*English private collection*

## 408 ▷
## A middle-class Italian sitting-room
### 1863

These admirers of Garibaldi are sewing red shirts for his irregulars, who at this time were engaged in the siege of Rome. A portrait of their hero hangs on the wall. The curtains are still arranged in the *Empire* manner and two of the chairs are in that style. The tall-backed chair in the foreground, with its loose cover, may date from the 1840s. A 'Moderator' lamp stands on the desk. Note the 'glass-curtains'. (By Odoardo Borrani.)
*Archivio dei Macchiaioli, Rome*

Oct. 1869.

*Augusta Dardels rum No 14 Rörstrand gata*

1875.

*Augustas rum*

◁ 409, 410

# A fashionable artist's home in Stockholm
### 1869 and 1875

It is interesting to note the change in character between the still essentially *Biedermeier* arrangement of the 1860s (left, above) and the much heavier style of the 1870s (below) – even when some of the same pieces of furniture are present. The quite modest dressing-table with its oval glass is very different from the quite grand (muslin-covered) table with large glass in the arrangement of 1875. The Neo-Gothic bookcase also carried a more sober-minded message than the neat, late-*Empire* vitrine to be seen in the earlier picture. The earlier scene apparently shows the wife Augusta's drawing-room, with her two children present. The elder was also called Augusta, and it is she who sits having her hair dressed as a young woman in her own room, where some of the furniture from the other room has been placed. Presumably the mother had by this time acquired some rather more up-to-date furniture. (By Fritz von Dardel.)

*Swedish private collection; photographs from Nordiska Museet, Stockholm*

FRONT PARLOR IN ABRAHAM LINCOLN'S HOUSE, SPRINGFIELD, ILL.—SKETCHED BY OUR SPECIAL ARTIST.

### 411
# Abraham Lincoln's front parlour
### 1860

From a contemporary magazine, this rather crude sketch nevertheless seems to give a faithful impression of the room in Springfield, Illinois, where Lincoln resided just before he became President of the United States. Described as his 'Front Parlour', this must be where he and his wife received company formally – which accounts for the stiff arrangement of the ornaments. Note how much is made of the cords of the pictures. The furniture looks as if it dates from the 1840s or even earlier, but the cast-iron stove is of a pattern known as a 'Temple Parlor' stove patented in 1854 by Vose & Co. of Albany, New York. (From *Frank Leslie's Illustrated Newspaper.*)

*Library of Congress, Washington D.C.*

◁ 412, 413

## A middle-class house in Boston(?)
### 1860s

Two stereoscopic views from a group taken by the photographers Holton & Robinson of Winter Street in Boston between 1861 and 1870. They show the parlour and a bedroom. The latter might have been anywhere in the English-speaking world at this date, but it can be seen that the parlour was in the United States because of the cast-iron stove (perhaps made in Albany, New York) and the buffalo-horns. Plants are much in evidence in the parlour, which also contains a grand piano. Both rooms have gas-chandeliers, but the one in the parlour has been converted to support petroleum lamps (one can see the control knob); this suggests that the photographs were taken shortly before 1870, because petroleum only became available as a fuel in the 1860s.

*Society for the Preservation of New England Antiquities, Boston, Massachusetts*

414 ▽

## A clergyman's house in Boston
### c.1860

The library of the Reverend R.C. Watterson, probably in his house in Chester Square. It is one of those bow-fronted houses so typical of Boston residential building in the first half of the century. The decorations on the ceiling (papier mâché?) seem to date from the 1840s. A reminder of the extensive trade with China being carried on by the cities on the Massachusetts coast in the middle of the last century are the two hardwood tables in the centre of the room. The chandeliers are not for gas, nor are they for petroleum. Could they be for 'Camphene' or 'Burning Fluid'? The two book-cases have pediments and are early expressions of a revived interest in the American Colonial past. The armchair in the window is in the Adam or *Louis Seize* style. (By a local photographer, Alten.)

*Society for the Preservation of New England Antiquities, Boston, Massachusetts*

## 415 ▷
## A bourgeois Copenhagen
## drawing-room
*c.*1870

This shows a room in the apartment of J.M. Thiele, who was Keeper of the Royal Library and Secretary to the Danish Royal Academy. It lay on the ground floor of the Academy's building in the main square, and from the vantage-points provided by the platforms in the windows the family could keep an eye on who was passing in the street. In a city where pretty well everyone knew each other, such an arrangement had its attractions, especially as the pot-plants would have screened the viewers quite effectively! The room seems to have been decorated in the late-*Empire* taste of about 1830, but of later date are the grand piano and the Neo-Baroque chairs which in England would have been called 'Elizabethan'. Note that all the illumination is provided by candles. The presence of a Chinese rattan chair is curious. Surely the two tables would normally have been covered with cloths and loaded with books. Perhaps the photograph was taken just after Thiele died in 1874.

*National Museum, Copenhagen*

## 416 ▷
## A young girl's room
## in an Irish country house
*c.*1860

One of two views of a room in an album of early photographs of the manors of Muckross and Adare, respectively in County Killarney and County Limerick. This probably shows the room of a daughter of the house at Muckross. The décor seems to date from around 1850. Note the paper fillet forming a border round the small-patterned wallpaper, which may be gold on white. There are pot-plants everywhere but they are more reticent than their German equivalents. A 'fire-paper' is in the grate. Symmetry is imparted to the two figures perched on brackets by providing them with cut-out backings. This is one of the earliest clear representations of a room by photographic means.

*Victoria and Albert Museum, London*

# 1870-1920

THE ART and architecture of these fifty years have received an enormous amount of attention from historians and a vast literature on these subjects exists. As a result the general outline of developments in this field is well understood. However, it has mostly been the progressive aspects of the story which have been studied. Much less has been written about the main tradition that dominated the European scene throughout these five decades – the tradition against which the progressive people were mostly reacting.

While everyone knows something about William Morris, the Aesthetic Movement, Arts and Crafts, Art Nouveau, the Viennese *Secession*, Hoffmann, Frank Lloyd Wright, and the Bauhaus, few can name a single architect who worked in this main tradition – indeed, this central tradition has not even got an agreed name. Nevertheless, delightful, extremely comfortable, and in no way despicable interiors were created in this widely accepted mode right into the 1920s. The reason for their having received so little attention from the historians is presumably that they could not be seen as paving the way towards the Modern Movement. Failing the test of progressiveness, such interiors were good for a sneer or a scoffing remark; little heed was taken of the undeniable fact that many people lived in such surroundings. But these people can scarcely all have been wrong, or have all lacked taste and discrimination. Now, in the 1980s, when the Modern Movement itself is coming to be judged more critically, it may well be that a rather more balanced assessment of the alternatives will emerge.

The central tradition in question developed during the middle decades of the nineteenth century, springing from Neo-Classicism; it evolved within the academic framework of the Ecole des Beaux-Arts in Paris, from which it spread all over the Western world. The style is sometimes given the name of 'Free Renaissance', but in fact it embraced much more than variations of the Renaissance styles: it took in all shades of Classicism, including '*Louis Quinze*' Rococo which was seen as an extension of '*Louis Quatorze*' Baroque, and it could happily assimilate fresh revivals of Pompeian, Grecian and *Empire*. It could even encompass Turkish and Egyptian. As Jacob von Falke observed in connection with the International Exhibition held in Vienna in 1873, 'In so far as style is concerned the modern Frenchman dwells in the eighteenth century, he sleeps in that century likewise, but he dines in the sixteenth, then on occasion he smokes his cigar and enjoys his coffee in the Orient, while he takes his bath in Pompeii, in Ancient Greece' (see Pls.472, 473 and 346).[1]

Von Falke's claim remained true wherever main-line Parisian fashion was followed. 'Romantic Classicism', to give it another of its rather inadequate titles, in fact provided the essential framework for a great deal of well-mannered architecture, some of it distinguished, most of it merely comfortable, which was put up all over Europe and in America in these years. When, in 1862, James Fergusson claimed, in his *History of the Modern Styles of Architecture*, that

'There is yet one other style within whose limits progress still seems possible.... The Renaissance Italian is by no means worked out', he was not exaggerating, for this seam in the architectural mine was still capable of being worked well into the 1890s (Pl.418). Robert Kerr, author of *The Gentleman's House* (1864; see p.216), in 1884 wrote an essay, 'English architecture thirty years hence',[2] in which he insisted that architecture was always bound to return 'to the universal European Renaissance' which, while created long before in Italy, was also 'a Modern European style ... a universally accepted mode of building ... that ... has been maintained in use ever since, and is still maintained for all ordinary purposes without a question being raised ...'. The New York architects Arnold W. Brunner and Thomas Tryon, in their *Interior Decoration* (New York, 1887), noted that 'The various periods of French Renaissance have long been favorites for parlor decoration.... The Italian Renaissance ... is, perhaps, the better for inspiration, and certainly less hackneyed.' However, an interest in Post-Renaissance styles, notably the Baroque in its various guises (e.g. Pl.468), began to arise about 1875 and finally triumphed over the Renaissance modes. Neo-Georgian and, in America, the Colonial Revival were but aspects of this.

Jacob von Falke wrote a very important book, first published in Vienna in 1871, which appeared in English translation in Boston in 1878 under the title *Art in the House*. He, too, clearly believed that one could not improve on the Renaissance style, and his illustration of a 'Modern Interior' (Pl.428) shows a drawing-room decorated in this very manner, which was particularly favoured in Germany around 1870. It may well be that the enthusiasm which the Italian Renaissance style enjoyed among rich Americans in the 1880s was given a boost by the publication of this work on that side of the Atlantic. Whatever the case, a year later in 1879 a certain A. J. Bloor was remarking that 'Our merchant princes, our large manufacturers, our money-coining miners, railway magnates, and financiers of all kinds are much more disposed to emulate the expenditures of the Medici of the old Italian republics than to conform to the habits of their thrifty forefathers.'[3] In this spirit was created a novel form of building, the great American urban palace. Already by 1883 a book appeared containing numerous photographs of rooms in some of these splendid, if not always very tasteful and certainly far from reticent, residences. This was *Artistic Houses* (New York, 1883) with its 'Interior Views of a number of the Most Beautiful and Celebrated Homes in the United States, with a Description of the Art Treasures contained therein' (Pls.440, 441, 442 and 443).

Although the monochrome photographs inevitably iron out all differences in the colour-schemes, one cannot help being struck by the homogeneity of the styles adopted by all these rich people. Renaissance is certainly well to the fore, but the general effect of multiple ornamentation often seems to us confusing and oppressive (the Pierpont Morgan room shown in Pl.441 is relatively chaste). Even the rooms decorated by Louis Tiffany, who was highly regarded by the

## 417] EARLY NEO-GEORGIAN, LONDON 1874

Neo-Georgian is usually believed to have evolved from the so-called 'Queen Anne' style, mostly being a Classical variant of that comfortable idiom with much of the Picturesque element left out. But it could also spring from the wish to render what has been called the '*tous-les-Louis*' style (i.e. *Louis Quatorze, Quinze* and *Seize*) with increasing correctness, so that Baroque Classical came to look fairly plausible – as here in Lord Cadogan's house in Chelsea, designed by William Young and completed in 1875. The exterior was in 'Dwelling-house Italian', according to *The Builder* for October 1874, but the dining-room at least was in pastiche Palladian crossed with Adam, with furnishings to match (the architect himself claimed that it was 'in the Adams style'). The ceiling was executed in papier mâché, the frieze in plaster and the walls in Parian cement which was painted. There would seem to have been no intention to furnish with antiques. (From William Young, *Town and Country Mansions and Suburban Houses*, London, 1874.)
*Victoria and Albert Museum, London*

editor of *Artistic Houses* (Tiffany's own house is dealt with first of all), seem to suffer from this defect, although here the lack of colour in these early photographs may mislead us to some extent. It is only in his dining-room done up for Dr William Lusk in New York that one sees how much more intelligibly he has organized the decoration than was the norm in these palatial dwellings (Pl.443). It is refreshing, amid all this overpowering opulence, to come across the clean-cut and bold work of H.H. Richardson (e.g. the Washington house of General Anderson, 'Easily the most interesting private residence in the capital'), and the distinguished interiors created by the firm of McKim, Mead and White, like that of the Newcomb summer residence at Elberon in New Jersey which the editor regarded as 'an honor at once to American taste and to American wealth' (Pl.442). As this shows, the distinguished quality of their work was quickly recognized, and their influence was to be considerable in the 1890s.

Palatial building in a Renaissance vein continued in America, the most notable expressions being Richard Morris Hunt's amazing châteaux at Newport (Rhode Island) of the late 1880s and early 1890s. Such building could not fail to influence American taste right across the continent well into this century. However, a more reticent style came to prevail after 1900. 'The reaction against building palaces has won a complete triumph, and the good American, no matter how wealthy he may be, is now content to live in a comparatively modest and unpretentious house . . .', wrote a commentator in 1915; 'the feeling for style has . . . become very much finer and more delicate . . . and at the same time more distinguished. . . . The gibe, which had a certain measure of truth in it twenty years ago, that American architecture was either bizarre or Beaux-Arts, is no longer true.'[4]

Rich Americans tended to be richer than rich Europeans, but not a few opulent buildings were erected in Europe at this period and the character of their decoration was not essentially very different from the American palaces we have been discussing. Since Paris set the tone in this traditional vein, it is worth glancing at the main French publications of the period on this subject. The position around 1870 is neatly covered by Th. Vacquer's *Maisons les plus remarquables de Paris construites dans les trois dernières années* which came out actually in 1870 and, as its title indicates, deals with significant buildings, constructed during the previous three years. César Daly's series on *L'Architectur privée au XIXe siècle* continued into the 1870s and shows us many details of the interiors of houses in the dominant taste. He had close connections with England, and plates from his publications were sometimes reproduced in contemporary English journals.[5] Daly concentrates on new work in Paris and its surroundings; Eugène Viollet-le-Duc, in his *Habitations Modernes* of 1877, embraces houses in other countries as well and, although there are several essays in Gothic, most of his offerings have a Renaissance character (Pl. 284).

INNERE ARCHITECTUR & DECORATION

HERAUSGEGEBEN VON L. CASPAR.

*Taf. 25.*

KAMIN AUS NUSSHOLZ.

Ludwig Caspar, Architect, entw.    E. Seeger, Mannheim ausgeführt.

Lichtdruck von Joh. Nöhring, Lübeck.

VERLAG VON HEINRICH KELLER IN FRANKFURT A. M.

**418] NEO-RENAISSANCE IN GERMANY**   late nineteenth century

The Germans tended to take their Renaissance more seriously than other people and their renderings of the style were often rather accurate in their details, as here in this imposing chimneypiece. This composition is given in Ludwig Caspar's *Innere Architectur und Decoration der Neuzeit* (Frankfurt, 1888) which comprised schemes based on recently executed work.
*Victoria and Albert Museum, London*

These works are supported by the later issues of Victor Quetin's *Magasin de Meubles* which continued into the 1870s his survey of modern decoration with illustrations of upholstery work as well as complete rooms (Pl.400; see also p. 212). The first section of P. Planat's *Habitations particulières*, a work devoted to private houses, carries through into the 1880s but, while it shows mainly new Parisian houses, it also mentions briefly buildings in Cologne, Chicago and England. Once again the favoured style is Renaissance, with a glance or two at Gothic and a few exercises in eighteenth-century Classicism (Pls.471, 472 and 473). All this in turn can be backed up by E. Maincent's *La Disposition des Appartements* of 1886–7, which shows the upholsterer's side of the story (Pls.462, 463 and 464), as does Felix Lenoir's handsome great volume on upholstery (with cutting diagrams etc.) that came out in French, German and English in 1890 under the title *Practical and Theoretical Treatise on Decorative Hangings, or the Guide to Upholstery* (Pl.470). It was published in Brussels and London, not in Paris; but it was most definitely French, showing the fussy, overloaded style of drapery of the late 1880s and early 1890s which it is still difficult for us, a century later, to admire. Ernest Foussier's *Nouveaux Modèles de Tentures* of about 1892 already gives indication of a wish to tidy up these riotous effects, and indeed this had taken place to some extent by 1900 when he brought out a work on *Décorations de Fenêtres* (Pl.425). *La Décoration intérieure* of about 1900, with designs by Andien Simeneton, shows the tail-end of the ornate French tradition.

This tradition was echoed in other countries particularly in works on upholstery – in the widest sense – where this main line of variations on the Classical repertoire continues to dominate. Carl Hettwig's *Journal für Tapezierer und Decorateure* carried the same message via Berlin and then Dresden in the 1870s and 1880s (Pls.430, 431, 432, 433 and 424). So did Ludwig Caspar's *Innere Architectur und Decoration der Neuzeit nach ausgeführten Arbeiten* ('Recent schemes for interior planning and decoration based on executed works'), which came out at Frankfurt in 1888 (Pl.469); the works of the Streitenfelds in Berlin (Pl.426); and F. A. Moreland's *Practical Decorative Upholstery* of 1889, which was published in Boston. The last states that 'The tendency is toward the French drapery in loosely hanging festoons and folds', which must be the style advocated by Lenoir, since Moreland explains that in some cases it 'descends to actual slovenliness by overcrowding with material', which is precisely how the style of Lenoir would look unless handled by a master.

While the European tradition was essentially Classical and was developed within an academic framework dominated by the Parisian Ecole des Beaux-Arts, it embraced many sub-styles and was infinitely variable. Nicholas Cooper's book *The Opulent Eye* (London, 1976), which is devoted to the late Victorian and Edwardian interior, shows how varied were the effects that could be contrived within this mode in England alone, and it will surely be agreed that many of the rooms illustrated in the contemporary photographs he reproduces are very comfortable indeed.[6]

In 1902 the famous English architect Norman Shaw gave an interview and is recorded as saying that 'The Gothic Revival, for all practical purposes, is dead, and the tendency of late years has been to return to the English Renaissance. I was trained on the older Gothic lines, I am personally devoted to it, admire it in the abstract, and think it superb; but it is totally unsuited to modern requirements. . . .' He then goes on to explain 'There was no Gothic Revival in France [this is an over-simplification] . . . the French stuck to their own traditions'.[7] Robert Kerr, in his essay of 1884, said much the same: secular Gothic 'has surrendered its claims for ever'. Yet the Gothic Revival had paved the way, paradoxically, to the most creative and original interior architecture of the last decades of the century. 'Our Gothic Revival . . . has enriched the crafts by impetus and imitation. It has imbued two generations of art-workers with passion. It has been the health-giving spark – the ozone of modern art', wrote William Morris' pupil John Sedding in 1893.[8] This progressive creativity tended to be at the hands of men and women with a radical tendency, so it was not merely on account of the novelty of what they proposed that their ideas met with resistance in more conservative circles.

It had been in the 1860s that a spirit of reform began to affect taste, especially with the publication in 1868 of Eastlake's book, *Hints on Household Taste* (see p. 217). The foundation in 1861 of the firm of [William] Morris, Marshall, Faulkner and Company, described as 'a company of historical artists', was also to have great significance, but neither event bore much fruit until the 1870s. During that decade, however, the so-called Aesthetic Movement gained a firm foothold and offered an alternative mode of decoration to that of the dominant Classical tradition already discussed. At first it offered simplicity or a lack of fussiness greatly in contrast to the prevailing fashion. But very soon the reforming simplicity was itself overlaid with ornament – first by the Aesthetes themselves, who fell for Japanese art and began to cover their own creations with exotic motifs and rich effects including a great deal of gold; and second by commercial manufacturers of furniture who, striving to keep abreast of this new fashion, eagerly adopted features like turned members (spindles and balusters) and multiplied them *ad nauseam* (Pls.427, 449, 443, 447, 453 and 454). Machinery, by now readily available to the furnishing trades, made this all too easy. The result was inevitably a travesty of what the pioneering reformers had intended. This so-called 'Art Furniture' was as fussy as its 'traditional' counterpart. It also tended to be spindly and flimsy. Much of it was stained black – 'black polished wood with spidery lines of conventional flowers incised in the wood and then gilt', as Roger Fry described it dismissively in 1920.[9] The developed form of the style was admirably enshrined in B. J. Talbert's *Examples of Ancient and Modern Furniture, Metal Work, Tapestry, Decoration, etc.* which appeared in London in 1876 (Pl. 427) and in *Designs of Furniture, illustrative of Cabinet Furniture and Interior Decoration specially designed for James Shoolbred & Company* of the same year (Pl. 447). As this catalogue of a major London upholstery firm shows, they could provide decoration both in Aesthetic and traditional styles. The designs of Edward Godwin for the Art Furniture Warehouse (published in 1877 but apparently drawn in 1871) embody a rather more distinguished rendering of the same taste. It is noteworthy that a drawing-room illustrated by Godwin is said to be in 'Japanese form adapted to modern English wants'. Very similar designs were labelled 'Jacobean', however.

The precepts of Morris and Eastlake seem not to have been heeded in Continental Europe until well into the 1880s; but in the United States they were quickly accepted with enthusiasm, and the message was passed on by several of the American writers who now began to publish guides to the mysteries of interior decoration for the benefit of their countrymen: notably, Clarence Cook in his *The House Beautiful* (New York, 1881; Pl.449); Hudson Holly in his *Modern Dwellings in Town and Country* (New York, 1878), and Harriet Prescott Spofford in her *Art Decoration Applied to Furniture* (New York, 1878). The last, who was also a writer of romantic novels, claimed that Eastlake had launched 'a movement seldom, if ever before, effected by a single person; he has succeeded in inaugurating a new régime, which bears the same relation to the loose and wanton Quatorze and Quinze régimes that virtue bears to vice'. By *Louis Quatorze* and *Louis Quinze* she presumably meant current Parisian taste of the traditional kind.

Eastlake's teachings were sometimes misunderstood and often misapplied, and the 'Eastlake' style eventually acquired a bad name. Already by 1876 the Londoners Rhoda and Agnes Garrett, in their *Suggestions for House Decorating . . .* (a much more readable book than most in this genre; Rhoda Garrett was a close friend of the young Ethel Smythe), could speak of 'What is commonly called Gothic furniture, with gables and chamferings and gashes here and there to indicate carving, [which] is for the most part a gross libel upon the sketches given by Mr Eastlake . . .'. Brunner and Tryon (New York, 1887) condemn the poor copies of Eastlake's designs made in America, while Clarence Cook (New York, 1881) actually states that 'The "Eastlake" furniture must not . . . be judged by what is made in this country, and sold under that name'.

The influential handbook by the English architect Robert Edis entitled *Decoration and Furniture of Town Houses*, which came out in London in 1881 and was based on a series of lectures given the year before, offered a more accommodating version of the Eastlake style (Pl.429). It is both less rugged than true Eastlake and less fussy than the general run of imitations, and it suited well the so-called 'Queen Anne' style of architecture which by this time had secured a firm grip on the English critical public's imagination.[10]

The 'Queen Anne' episode has been admirably chronicled by Mark Girouard in his *Sweetness and Light* (Oxford, 1977). Kerr, in his informative essay of 1884, explains how 'A popular successor to the style of secular Gothic has . . . been growing up of late years . . . somewhat inexpressively and arbitrarily called by the name of the Queen Anne style'. The style, he says, evolved to meet 'the public demand, now being satisfied by means of an infinitude of charming picturesque detail, chiefly appearing, however, in the design of small works' – not least in the decoration of the interior, he might have added. Kerr states that the merits of this new 'artistic manifestation . . . are becoming very considerable' but even he would be surprised to see how profound has been its influence. 'Queen Anne' was really more an attitude of mind than a style, since it could embrace the features of almost any style that happened to appeal to the architect concerned. As the architect William Burges uncharitably put it, the recipe for 'Queen Anne' was 'to take an ordinary red brick house and to put [on it] as many gables and dormers and bow windows as possible – in fact to cut up the outlines; the great object being to get the picturesque by any and every means. The windows should be long and narrow and filled with lead glazing or with small frames divided by straight bars painted white – the ornamental parts consist of a few scrolls in the brickwork and coarse woodwork occasionally verging on the Jacobean.'[11] The haphazard, irregular arrangements of the Picturesque were fundamental to the 'style'; Jacobean elements were prominent but so were elements culled from more recent styles – including actual Queen Anne[12] – and the study of vernacular architecture of no very certain date. Frequently added to all this, moreover, was a liberal dressing of Anglo-Japanese ornament.

'Queen Anne' answered a need particularly among the English middle classes, who tended to be less thrusting, less earnest, more relaxed than their parents. The style quickly found favour in the United States, most notably in the work of McKim, Mead and White, and gave impetus to the nascent 'Shingle' style with its Picturesque planning and detailing. This last had 'old Colonial' connotations as well; indeed, Americans sometimes equate their Colonial Revival style with 'Queen Anne'. The illustrations in Robert Edis' *Decoration and Furniture . . .* (London, 1881) convey very well the spirit of 'Queen Anne'. Brunner and Tryon were speaking the same language in their *Interior Decoration*, which came out in New York in 1887.

Antique furniture had long been sought by men with antiquarian leanings, especially if they lived in Neo-Gothic or Neo-Elizabethan surroundings (see p. 157). Old furniture (other than exceptionally elaborate cabinets and the odd table) had otherwise never held much appeal for those building 'modern houses' in the past. In a modern house everything had to look smart, un-worn and un-

faded. Tattered covers, signs of repair and patina were not at all desirable in such surroundings. But with the advent in the 1870s of the 'Queen Anne' fashion, with its stress on informality, its love of irregularity and asymmetrical arrangements, antiques came into widespread demand. If they were faded, they blended nicely with the un-strident colour-schemes that were now admired. If the chair-seats were worn, this did not matter because no one now wanted a row of chairs lined up in the old manner, all spick and span. Scattered about the room, such blemishes no longer caught the eye. Wear and tear now came to be admired! From the 1870s, houses began actually to be furnished with antiques in preference to new items (Pls.435, 439, 444, 460, 467 and 475).

Clarence Cook (New York, 1881) declared that the interest in 'old furniture' was 'a fashion, that has been for twenty years working its way down from a circle of rich, cultivated people [he was one himself], to a wider circle of people who are educated, who have natural good taste, but who have not so much money as they could wish' (see, for example, Pl.436). He maintained it was not simply a result of 'Centennial mania' arising from the celebrations that surrounded the centenary of Independence in 1876, when national pride naturally came especially to the fore in the United States. Be that as it may, most of the rooms shown in *Artistic Houses* (New York, 1883) contain numerous antiques – including, in one case, a copy of a very primitive early Colonial turned chair – and in the same year Laura C. Holloway was urging her countrywomen to acquire a 'Shaker sewing chair' for their drawing-rooms (*The Hearthstone, or Life at Home. A household manual*, Philadelphia, 1883).

Naturally there were soon not enough antiques to go round. Ella Rodman Church in *How to Furnish a Home* (New York, 1882) wanted her readers to fill the many shelves of their artistic chimneypieces with bric-à-brac including 'one's own or some one else's great-grandmother's candlesticks', and she spoke

**419] FURNISHING WITH ANTIQUES, BOSTON  1900**

A scheme by Ogden Codman, who was one of the foremost creators of accurately detailed rooms in historic styles, particularly in the Classical vein. Although among drawings labelled as being for F.W. Vanderbilt's house Hyde Park, it may have been for the Boston residence of Eban Howard Gay, who wrote a book entitled *A Chippendale Romance* (New York, 1915) in which what looks like this room and much of the furniture are separately illustrated. Gay's house on Beacon Street dated from the 1880s. It was re-decorated by Codman in 1900. Where an owner did not already possess old furniture in the required style, Codman was quite prepared to have accurate reproductions specially made. Furniture in such a setting (as in the eighteenth century) had to be in mint condition, especially where a whole set of chairs was required, and in many cases it was more satisfactory to use copies.
*Metropolitan Museum of Art, New York; gift of the Estate of Ogden Codman, Jr, 1951*

of how 'every one's eyes are [now] opened to the advantages of having had great-grandfathers' on account of the 'treasures' that had in many cases come down from them. If these were lacking, one had to visit 'the Broadway bazaar, filled with antiques and supercilious clerks, with fabulous prices for the simplest articles...'. When the dealers in turn could not produce the genuine article, ingenuity was needed. By 1884 the American magazine *Cabinet-Making and Upholstery* told its readers that 'there is little doubt but the manufacture of antiques has become a modern industry',[13] and the writer of *Artistic Houses* (1883) quoted an English commentator on how one can no longer be certain of anything 'when even the authentic Chippendale may err, and sometimes has erred'.

This demand for antiques for furnishing one's house was primarily a British and North American phenomenon. A few very rich people on the Continent, as well as a number of more or less antiquarian-minded collectors, surrounded themselves with old objects; but it does not seem to have been the norm there in the 1870s and 1880s (but see Pl.475). Europeans on the whole preferred furniture in the old styles, which one might loosely call reproductions (Pl.469); they were not particularly concerned with actual old pieces although many, especially in artistic circles, did not object to them if they were easy to come by. It was anyway far more profitable for the growing antique trade to sell such things to the Americans!

In his *Habitations Modernes* of 1877, the well-known French architect Viollet-le-Duc stated that his own countrymen were best at designing public buildings but, when it came to comfort in the domestic field, it was the English and the Scandinavians who excelled. It is not yet too clear what the Scandinavians had to offer at that stage, although illustrations are reproduced here of quite a few very comfortable Scandinavian rooms.[14] As for the English contribution, he probably had in mind buildings in the 'Queen Anne' style which, it must be admitted, were very comfortable, whatever their artistic merits. It was certainly this style which Hermann Muthesius greatly admired when he praised English domestic building, and the way its peculiarities led to such great comfort, in his *Das Englische Haus* which was published in Berlin in 1904 (Pl.484). What he had to say in this excellent survey of English building, decoration and furnishing of the late nineteenth century had a considerable influence in Germany – and therefore in other parts of northern and central Europe – where numerous houses in variants of the comfortable, Picturesque English mode sprang up during the first decades of this century (Pls.503 and 511).

Such an indefinite style naturally developed in several directions. On the one hand it grew into what we know as Neo-Georgian, which was more formal and Classical than pure 'Queen Anne' (Pls. 521, 522 and 523) and thus converged stylistically with the main Classical tradition; this was even more apparent when a more monumental scale was adopted for large buildings. On the other hand there evolved a style yet more firmly based on the vernacular, which produced the 'English Cottage' style. This was immensely popular as a form of decoration, not only with the new weekenders temporarily living the rural life in actual cottages and farmhouses, but also for the thousands of houses that were built in the first part of this century in a style derived from 'Queen Anne' which W.R. Lethaby called 'Free English' (Pl.503).

But 'Queen Anne', with its long windows, its asymmetry and anti-Classical conformations, also acted in a liberating manner on those progressive architects who were still busy trying to devise a style suitable for modern times, and who were still trying to get away from elaborate ornament, heavy drapery and stylistic eclecticism. C.A. Voysey, who is usually seen as one of founding fathers of the Modern Movement, apparently regarded himself as an architect working in the English vernacular style, and, indeed, his work of the 1890s can be seen as a rendering of this: 'Queen Anne' in spirit but pared to the bone. The clean lines of his neat interiors were a source of great inspiration to the younger progressive architects (Pl.420), but the proportions of Voysey's interiors were in fact not very different from those already underlying many rooms in the 'Queen Anne' taste. Once moving in the new direction, it was not long before the process of eschewing ornament was taken to its logical conclusion and, already by the turn of the century, stark schemes were being drawn and in a few cases executed (Pls.505 and 507). This is not the place to explore the links between Mackintosh working in Glasgow but exhibiting in Germany and Austria,[15] Baillie Scott and his work in Darmstadt and Mannheim (Pls.494 and 497), Hoffmann and his colleagues in the *Secession* group in Vienna, their link with Darmstadt, the 1904 Exhibition in St Louis, Frank Lloyd Wright in Illinois, and William Bradley in

New York (Pls.488, 505, 506 and 501).[16] The fact is that out of this ferment of novel ideas came a stark new style, developed primarily in Germany and Austria, which could be very elegant indeed (Pls.504 and 509), but which was by no means to everyone's taste; and it is important to realize that expressions of these advanced ideas were not immediately to be seen on every hand. Indeed, they made very little impression on the domestic interior until after 1920. The majority of people of taste lived in more conventional surroundings based either on the great Classical tradition, or on the picturesque 'Queen Anne' or 'Free English' formula, and this applied all over Europe and America.

Yet not all the people who were not progressive were perfectly content with the way interior decoration was developing in the 1880s and early 1890s, for it was apparent to many that the fashionable decorator's aim was to pile on ever more ornament and to fill rooms with yet more knick-knacks. These were the years which saw the cluttered look reach its zenith, but it is quite evident that informed yet conventional taste also revolted in the 1890s. The 'great clean-up' may be seen taking place not only under the progressives; it is discernible in 'traditional' surroundings as well, although on a much less dramatic scale. Drapery returns to simpler forms, flounces become less pronounced, the knick-knacks are thinned out, and there is a general lightening of the load which may be seen in 'Edwardian' rooms everywhere (Pls.483, 495, 497 and 517). H.P. Shapland, who wrote a book entitled *Style Schemes in Antique Furnishing. Interiors and their Treatment*, published in London in 1909 (Pl.521), illustrated a drawing-room in a comfortable, antiques-based style as one of the 'style schemes' he was recommending, and commented that 'there is in this interior an absence of that over-crowded effect which is the bane of the modern living-room'. Not a few people were echoing such sentiments by 1910.

A lighter atmosphere could also be achieved in rooms by using colours that were of a lighter shade (Pls.494 and 496) than those popular in the 1870s and 1880s, when played-down and often downright sombre colour-schemes had been in favour as a reaction against the often rather virulent schemes of the 1850s and 1860s. In progressive circles in the late 1880s light colours were re-adopted, and soon this fashion was taken up by people of a more conservative tendency as well (Pl.483). White in particular was to be seen everywhere, often tending towards the creamy. It was not simply Voysey and Mackintosh and progressives of that generation who made use of white, however; it was to be seen, for example, in Queen Alexandra's Sandringham where some of the furniture was painted white (albeit lightly picked out with gilding), while white-painted 'Louis Seize' and 'Adam' furniture was in fact much in evidence at the end of the century (Pl.495). As the Bostonian F.A. Moreland explains in his *Practical Decorative Upholstery* of 1889, 'The tendency at present is toward light furnishing, suggesting more or less the styles of the First Empire, and the times of Louis XIV and XV' (he should really have added 'XVI'). Woodwork in white or '"old ivory", relieved by gold' is now the fashion, and the associated drapery should be of a colour 'to suit the airy tone'. Not all white-painted furniture was picked out in gold, it should be noted. If it was antique, or purported to be, it was sometimes painted plain white; in progressive circles it might also be painted green or red, but always plain. Already by 1883 a parlour in a resplendent house on Long Island had white-painted furniture 'modelled on Colonial antiques',[17] and white antique furniture may also be seen in Carl Larsson's delightful views of his family house in Sweden dating from the 1880s and 1890s (Pls.467 and 496). White-painted woodwork was almost *de rigueur* for all tasteful interiors during the first two decades of the twentieth century (Pls.493, 497, 500, 507, 526 and 531).

Moreland mentioned a revival of the 'First Empire' style. This is a very early reference to such a revival, but by November 1893 the American magazine *The*

420] THE VOYSEY STYLE, ENGLAND 1893

This design, dated January 1893, is by Walter Cave, a member of C.A. Voysey's circle, and incorporates the main elements of Voysey's style. The derivation from English vernacular building and craftsmanship is evident, but so is the rationalizing of the elements and their elegant proportions. Striking also is the colouring with the green-stained woodwork, red brick, and the wall-filling faced with brown paper. (From an album of drawings submitted by members of the Quarto Imperial Club.)
*Royal Institute of British Architects, London, Drawings Collection*

*Decorator and Furnisher* could illustrate a design for a 'Modern Empire Interior' which embodied wreaths and other more or less *Empire* motifs.[18] As Mario Praz has shown,[19] the Parisian Ernest Chesneau was already writing in 1881 about the Napoleonic architect Charles Percier (see p. 141) and the *Empire* style, 'which amateurs and artists take pleasure in reviving today, as though in protest against the voluptuous stuffings and paddings . . . of contemporary furniture'. The important Parisian firm of Jeanselme showed a bedroom in pure *Empire* at the Paris Exhibition of 1889, and in 1891 there opened in Paris an exhibition of 'The Arts at the Beginning of the Century' which included a reconstructed *Empire* room. Likewise the times of the Congress of Vienna and Schubert were celebrated in exhibitions in Vienna in 1896 and 1897.[20] A parallel development was taking place in England.[21] The plain forms, clean lines and sturdiness of the styles fashionable from about 1790 to 1830 in all but the grandest circles were in obvious contrast to current European modes. *Biedermeier* in particular, with its simplicity and virtual suppression of ornament, appealed greatly to Austrian and German progressives who, seeing in the style aspirations seemingly parallel to their own, borrowed not a few of its forms (Pls.526 and 506). As a result of all this interest it also became fashionable, at the end of the century, to collect

Regency, *Empire* and *Biedermeier* antiques – both in progressive and in traditionalist circles (Pl.499).

Architects, designers and patrons of a less extreme persuasion also found these essentially Classical styles appealing, and by 1910 a new style which owed much to that of a century earlier had become firmly established in fashionable circles; indeed, it became the dominant style among all but the most conservative. So Neo-*Biedermeier* or *Biedermeier*-inspired interiors were common in Germany before the Great War (Pl.524), while *Empire* was the basis for much French interior design at the same time and continued as a basic source of inspiration for Parisian designers in the 1920s (Pl.514).

The late 1880s also brought the sinuous style known as Art Nouveau. Charming as many of its manifestations could be (especially in small items of decorative art), comparatively few domestic rooms were couched entirely in this style. The writhing three-dimensional forms were not easy to render in wood, which immediately limited the scope of application of the style, especially in its most extreme forms. Victor Horta managed it early in the 1890s in Belgium, and Henri van de Velde also handled it successfully. A handful of cabinetmakers managed to create marvels in wood, notably at Nancy, and the Parisian architect Georges Rémon designed some delightful rooms in this idiom (Pls.485, 486 and 487), but it is not evident that they were executed. The interiors where the style came to be most in evidence were those of shops and restaurants – the most famous of which was Maxim's (1899). Otherwise, paradoxically, the style affected flat ornament, in two dimensions only, such as wallpaper, marquetry, stencilling, embroidery, etc.; and in this respect its origins in English designs of the 1880s, especially in wallpaper, at the hands of men like Voysey, Crane and Mackmurdo, become more obvious (Pl.454). Indeed, a Frenchman in 1901 explained that it was at first called 'Modern Style' in France 'in order to remind oneself of its British origin'.[22] Of course many small decorative objects – lamps, fire-irons, door-handles – were couched in full-blown Art Nouveau and such things were to be found in most houses, but the style rarely took over the room as a whole.

If Art Nouveau was short-lived and did not in itself come to constitute a new style suited to modern times, it did liberate the eye. It helped to open the way for novel forms and, perhaps even more important, novel proportions, so that a truly new style *could* be evolved: the style of the Modern Movement, the genesis of which took place in Austria and in Germany in the early years of the twentieth century.

The proto-Modern style, that almost totally unadorned style which relied for its aesthetic qualities on elegant proportions and skilful disposition, grew up in Vienna in the years around 1900 in the shadow of that giant on the European architectural scene, Otto Wagner, and in the hands principally of architect-decorators like Josef Hoffmann, Koloman Moser and other members of the *Secession* group (Pls.504, 505 and 507). The devising of such uncompromising forms represented an enormous intellectual leap but, while the style was eagerly adopted in certain circles in Germany (notably in Munich, Berlin and Darmstadt; Pl.509), it was not until after 1920 that the precepts of the Vienna School came to be at all widely assimilated. A rather more moderate version was evolved for general consumption (Pls.510 and 517), and it was from this more gentle background that was developed the style which eventually became the 'Art Deco' of the 1920s. Indeed, many of the features current in the dominant fashions of the 1920s could be found in German interior architecture by 1910. The lavishly illustrated pages of journals like *Innen-Dekoration* (published in Darmstadt by Alexander Koch) and *Moderne Bauformen* (by I. Gradl in Stuttgart) show numerous elegant rooms in this moderately advanced style; particular attention should be paid to the work of Karl Witzmann and of Otto

Prutscher in Vienna, of Bruno Paul and of Paul Renner in Berlin, of Curjel & Moser in Karlsruhe, and of Paul Würzler-Klopsch in Leipzig (Pls.517, 526 and 525). The excitement which seems to have animated the architectural scene in Germany before the Great War is readily discernible in the pages of these magazines.

These same journals carried not a few articles on English and Scottish architecture, and quite often brought news of developments in Finland (Eliel Saarinen was much admired in Germany; Pls.512 and 515), Hungary, Bulgaria and Denmark. What is noteworthy, therefore, is the almost total absence of any reference in the German publications to what was happening in France. At first sight it seems incredible that recent developments in France could be of so little interest. The French, who had dominated the field of interior decoration throughout the years from about 1620 up to the end of the nineteenth century, suddenly seemed to have nothing to offer other nations during the first two decades of the twentieth. Yet this really was the case, with few exceptions. The French themselves spoke of a loss of nerve, a lack of inventiveness, a confused sense of direction. Whatever the case and whatever the reason – and one can speculate about a delayed acknowledgement of the defeat of 1871 and the body-blow that the Dreyfus case and its squalid aftermath delivered to French self-esteem in the 1890s – French decorators and architects continued to favour Art Nouveau forms well into the second decade of the new century, and mostly worked in a rather tame style derived from *Empire* and *Louis Seize* embellished with sub-Art Nouveau ornament (Pl.518). Of course, much of this could be elegant and it was undoubtedly comfortable (Pl.520); but the Germans were probably correct in considering it nothing like as innovative as what was being created in their own country. At any rate they largely ignored it.

The English also seem to have found little of interest going on in pre-War France. In the *Studio Yearbooks* no mention is made of French architecture and interior decoration until 1914, although each year long articles had been devoted to new developments in Germany and Austria, even Hungary. When finally in 1914 an article on French architecture and decoration did appear, the author claimed that 'The part which France has played in modern design has, perhaps, been less prominent than that of other nations'. The author praises the work of Francis Jourdain, Jacques Ruhlmann and André Groult. He also illustrates a very advanced scheme by Robert Mallet-Stevens. He does not mention Dufrène or Tony Selmersheim, both of whom were creating distinguished interiors before the War. Nevertheless, it does seem to have been difficult to find much in France that was worthy of emulation between 1900 and 1914.

Naturally enough little creative work was carried out during the four years of war (although a certain amount of innovative building took place in neutral Holland and Finland), and after 1918 the exhausted combatants mostly wanted to return to the quiet pleasures of peace. They wanted security and comfort; stark arrangements were not for them, and schemes were created that were pretty or safe and traditional – nothing daring or unconventional (Pls.530 and 531). Meanwhile, a handful of disillusioned young Germans gathered at the newly formed Bauhaus and started to try to devise what was virtually a new way of living; but they were not noticed by many as yet. After the few startling expressions of a truly Modern idiom had appeared around 1900, very little of this sort was to be seen anywhere until well into the 1920s.

In England, where the Modern idiom had found virtually no welcome whatsoever before 1920, the preferred styles were the vernacular-inspired 'Free English', with its Picturesque features and its cosy Arts and Crafts 'honesty', and – if you wanted something more elegant – one of the many variants of Neo-Georgian (Pl.522). Moreover, these styles also continued to have validity on the Continent right into the 1920s, for English influence was still considerable.

Already in 1919, a few months after the Armistice, an English scheme for a drawing-room was reproduced in a German journal.

The position in America was slightly different. It is described in *The Practical Book of Interior Decoration* by H.D. Eberlein, A. McClure and E.S. Holloway, which appeared in both Philadelphia and London in 1919. Among the choices available to Americans at this point they mention the 'Peasant or English Cottage' style, which was presumably the equivalent of 'Free English'; and they speak of the 'International Inter-period' style, by which they mean a harmonious amalgam of old styles that borrowed from the great *Beaux-Arts* tradition, from the nostalgic Colonial, and from the *Empire* revival which was the dominant non-progressive style on the European Continent. Eberlein and his associates had no time for the Viennese proto-Modern *Secession* style with its 'extravagant gaucheries'. They believed that what little had been done in the United States in this direction 'has probably been by way of an interesting experiment'.

Although the seeds of the Modern Movement and of Art Deco had been sown before 1914, the world was a different place after the Great War. Indeed, Willa Cather claimed in her memoirs that 'The world broke in two in 1922 or thereabouts', which may be an exaggeration; but the growing emancipation of women, longer office-hours, the new lack of domestic servants, the now widespread ownership of motor-cars, and many other factors undermined the whole concept of the home as a haven within which a family could live most of its life. With progressive architects dabbling in social engineering, not always with complete humility, people were encouraged to get out of the house, to live in their cities, to enjoy the centralized amenities – and in consequence domestic quarters tended to be made less spacious and became the 'little boxes' of the folk-song. The domestic interior no longer occupied quite the same central position in people's lives as it had done for so many centuries before. Even if this situation were not to last, and even if there were plenty of exceptions, there was a definite break in the tradition around 1920 – which is why it seems a good place to end this survey.

## Planning and arrangement

The planning of houses for the convenience of the upper classes had more or less been worked out by 1870. There was very little else to be tried, and successful planning in the grander sort of house was merely a question of varying in small ways what had been done before. The ingenuity of architects now went increasingly into devising compact arrangements in flats and in housing for workers. There had of course been apartment-houses before 1870, where the main floors were designed for occupation by people of standing while the basement, top floors and attics provided lodging for all manner of people. But blocks of flats, where the apartments on *all* the floors were for people of more or less the same status, were a new phenomenon, and their planning required new skills.

The day of the detached house embodying a degree of magnificence was by no means over, however, and a number of guides to its planning and decoration appeared during the years that now concern us. Ris-Paquot's *L'Art de Bâtir, Meubler et Entretenir sa Maison*, published in Paris in 1890, is particularly informative and follows the pattern laid down in the eighteenth century by such authors as Blondel and Le Camus de Mézieres. Ris-Paquot lists the sort of thing one could expect to find in each room. For example, the *antichambre* is a sort of vestibule with some chairs and an umbrella-stand, he explains; it should be decorated in Gothic or Renaissance. The *salon* is the principal reception room and should be expensively done up in one of the 'Louis' styles (Pl.472); apart from the usual furniture there should be card-tables, but he suggests that one should avoid having a piano there. The *serre-salon* was evidently a conservatory, but he insists it is also suitable for smoking. The *salle à manger* should be in Gothic, Renaissance, '*Henri Deux*' or '*Louis Quatorze*', and should have furniture of carved oak or what he calls 'modern black' by which he presumably means stained; for this room he also advocates stained glass, a handsome garniture for the mantel-shelf, and faience plates hanging on the walls. He recommends that one should avoid having an alcove in the bedroom, as it 'confines the air', which is bad for the health. By the same token one should never draw bed-curtains round one when retiring at night. The bedroom furniture ought to be of rosewood with marquetry decoration, or of satinwood or maple set with Sèvres plaques. Such furniture was more costly than the white and gold kind, he informs us. He urges that the master of the household should have a separate bedroom because, as he claims, married couples expect to live separate lives these days. (Nevertheless, Parisian designs for twin bedchambers are by no means uncommon at this period.) The *boudoir* is the lady's study, he continues, and her *cabinet de toilette* is an absolutely private room. There should, incidentally, be a *chaise-longue* in the bedroom. Ella Rodman Church (New York, 1882; see p. 312) also calls this 'a necessity' but wants as well 'a low easy-chair ... in which one can lounge in wrapper and unbound hair before the fire and think over the events of the day that is past, or build air-castles for the one to come'.

French practice is praised by Edith Wharton and Ogden Codman in their excellent and eminently readable *The Decoration of Houses*, which appeared in New York in 1897 and in London the year after.[23] They explain how the French arrangement for bedchambers is both luxurious and practical. It was in fact the old Baroque 'apartment' (see p. 18), but now intended entirely for private use. Ideally there should be an antechamber, followed by a sitting-room or boudoir, after which comes the bedroom, beyond which lie a dressing-room and bathroom. There are only two entrances to this apartment, one from the corridor into the antechamber and one at the back for use by the servants. 'This arrangement, besides giving greater privacy, preserves much wall-space, which would be sacrificed in America to the supposed necessity of making every room in a house open upon one of the main passageways.'

Wharton and Codman also remind their readers about the difference, which existed already in the eighteenth century, between the '*salon de famille* or meeting-place for the whole family' and the '*salon de compagnie*' which is 'part of the gala suite used exclusively for entertaining'. They then explain that 'In houses of average size, where there are but two living-rooms – the master's library or "den", and the lady's drawing-room – it is obvious that the latter ought to be used as a *salon de famille* ... and it is usually regarded as such in England, where common sense usually prevails in matters of material comfort and convenience.' They infer that modern English drawing-rooms are furnished with comparative simplicity, and that this pattern is followed in some American houses.[24] In others the drawing-room is 'considered sacred to gilding and discomfort, the best room in the house ... the convenience of all its inmates, being sacrificed to a vague feeling that no drawing-room is worthy of the name unless it is uninhabitable'. This is partly, they claim, because the large American house is often simply a bigger version of the *maison bourgeoise*, where it was hoped that 'the mere enlargement of each room' of the old middle-class formula for a detached house would 'turn it into a gentleman's seat or town residence'. The huge drawing-rooms that resulted then had to serve both as gala rooms and as *salons de famille*. 'Nothing can be more cheerless than the state of a handful of people sitting after dinner in an immense ball-room with gilded ceiling, bare floors, and a few pieces of monumental furniture ranged round the walls.... A gala room is never meant to be seen except when crowded; the crowd takes the place of furniture.... The hostess feels this [emptiness], and tries, by setting chairs and tables askew, and introducing palms, screens and knick-knacks, to produce an effect of informality. As a result the room dwarfs the furniture, loses the air of state, and gains little in real comfort....'

They are also far from impressed by 'the tendency of recent English and American decoration ... to treat the hall, not as a hall, but as a living-room'. This development they criticize as 'an unreasoning imitation of a past style ... the sacrifice of convenience to archaism' (Pls.480 and 442). 'In most modern houses the hall, in spite of its studied resemblance to a living-room, soon reverts to its original use as a passageway.' The inconvenience of these 'living halls' is increased in America, they tell us, by there commonly being 'a yawning gap, giving on the hall' from the drawing-room, which thus loses its privacy. They deplore 'the indifference to privacy which has sprung up in modern times, and which in France, for instance, has given rise to the grotesque conceit of putting sheets of plate-glass between the rooms, and by replacing doorways by openings fifteen feet [4.6 m] wide ...'. The French fashion for large areas of glass everywhere went with the Art Nouveau, or 'Modern Style' as they called it. It is ridiculed in an amusing article in the Parisian journal *L'Illustration* of 21 February 1903. Through the glazed doors one sees the family having its tea, the maid laying the table for dinner, and a seamstress busy sewing in her bedroom. Have the architects working in the 'Modern Style' taken Auguste Comte too literally when he urged us to 'live more openly?' the author asks.

Ris-Paquot suggested that one could smoke in the conservatory. Brunner and Tryon (New York, 1887; see p. 308) wanted some easy chairs placed in the dining-room for smokers where 'if their presence in the room is permitted, [they] may enjoy their after-dinner cigars'. By 1897 Wharton and Codman are saying that 'The smoking-room proper, with its *mise en scène* of Turkish divans, narghilehs, brass coffee-trays, and other Oriental properties is no longer considered a necessity in a modern house'.

Clarence Cook (New York, 1881; see p. 311) wanted to see books introduced to the drawing-room, but conceded that 'Hardly any piece of furniture is more troublesome to bring in harmony with the conditions of our modern room than the bookcase'. If a large house had a library it would by this period have become so much of a general living-room, one suspects, that anyone wanting a place to read or study would have had to retire elsewhere – the man to his 'den', perhaps, and the lady to her boudoir. In 1905 Edith Wharton, now a novelist, describes in *The House of Mirth* an old house where the library was 'in fact never used for reading, though it had a certain popularity as a smoking-room or a quiet retreat for flirtation'. In many large houses the 'library' was simply a drawing-room lined with bookcases (Pl.460). By 1900, many drawing-rooms were in any case book-lined (Pl.502).

The Picturesque tradition of building made it easy to contrive window-bays and other niches with comfortable seating-arrangements; the inglenook flanking the fireplace was another Picturesque device much beloved during the 'Queen Anne' phase. These niches formed what amounted almost to separate small rooms off the drawing-room or hall. In England and America such retreats were often called 'cosy corners' (Pl.455). They were plentiful in England, and were taken up in Germany around 1900 under the influence of architects such as Baillie Scott (Pls.494 and 515). These small areas often had raised floors with steps, reminiscent of the platforms by the windows beloved in central and northern Europe during the *Biedermeier* phase.

Old photographs of rooms in the 1880s and 1890s make it look as if no one could cross the room without knocking things over – especially if wearing full skirts. However, experiments made in Copenhagen (see Pls.3–6) show that the apparent clutter of furniture and ornaments was in fact organized on principles that must have been perfectly clear to people at the time. Passageways were left through the minefield, as it were; furniture was best 'arranged in groups [and] must be so disposed about the room as to offer attractive conversational centres ... care must be taken that one side of the apartment does not look crowded, while the other remains bare' (Pls.462, 463 and 464).[25] This dictum comes from Jacob von Falke's book of 1871/8 (see p. 308). He also recommends that, in 'a rich assemblage of objects ... separate objects may be united into groups' (Pls.445, 467 and 471). The reformers of course wanted simplicity and tended to disapprove of clutter. 'Do not have too much furniture, but let each article be complete in itself, and necessary to the harmony of the rest', advises William Watt in the catalogue of the Art Furniture Warehouse of 1877, for which E.W. Godwin drew the illustrations. Nevertheless, even Aesthetes seem to have been able to tolerate a far higher level of visual fussiness than we can today – it is largely a question of what the eye is used to (Pls.449, 447 and 453).

From the Renaissance period onwards it had usually been thought desirable to have the furnishings of a room matching, either in design or in colour, or both. In the 1870s and 1880s this was not always so. Ella Rodman Church (New York, 1882; see p. 312) states that '"Sets" ordered of an upholsterer, besides being expensive, are seldom satisfactory to a person with an eye for simple beauty'. This we can well believe, but it is then surprising to read that such 'sets' 'quite destroy the charm of interest and variety that is produced by having few things alike' (Pl.439). Mrs Church's countryman Clarence Cook, writing the year before, suggested that 'having everything "in keeping", as the phrase is, [is] not necessary at all'. Earlier, in 1873, the May issue of the London journal *The House Furnisher and Decorator* was telling its readers that, in decorating the drawing-room, 'care must be taken not to follow a system which in large rooms, as drawing-rooms, would be as indefensible as in small rooms, such as boudoirs, it would be correct and desirable; we refer to the employment of the same material ... for hangings and for furniture coverings'. Such unity is 'generally adopted in smaller rooms ... for the purpose of increasing the feeling of "snugness"'. That is to say, unity was not thought desirable at this time in large rooms, although there were exceptions (Pl.488). In traditional circles this fashion seems to have lasted into the 1890s. Lack of unity was usually also a feature of rooms furnished with antiques. Reformers, and their successors the progressives at the turn of the century, on the other hand, tended to admire unity of style (Pls.494, 506, 485 and 515).

## The architectural shell

'Some years ago', states the London publication *Artistic Homes* in 1880, 'the fashion of making the whole side of a room into a gigantic panel, by placing a paper border round it, was very general. ... The practice ... tends to dwarf the room. ... But the revival of dados and friezes is decidedly a step in the right direction.' Dados 3 or 4 ft (0.9–1.2 m) high are recommended, but other writers suggested going higher. The frieze now became deeper and more prominent as well – sometimes 3 or 4 ft down from the ceiling – all of which tended to leave the so-called 'filling' of the wall as quite a narrow band. In fact the relative proportions of these three components (dado, filling, frieze) varied greatly, as Pl.421 shows. Sometimes, with a very deep frieze, there would be no dado at all. This fashion was to be seen in rooms affected by Aesthetic tastes during the 1870s and 1880s (but not in traditional interiors of the *Beaux-Arts* class), and the high degree of latitude allowed in the proportions was heavily exploited subsequently by architects and decorators working in the Art Nouveau style and in the progressive circles in Vienna and elsewhere around 1900 (Pls.427, 429,

443, 448 and 454; and 486, 501, 506, 507, 510 and 511).

Such bold divisions of the wall-surface tended to make rooms look less high, and it may well be that this was an aim in Aesthetic circles in the 1870s – springing from a wish for informality and cosiness. The Garretts (London, 1876; see p. 311) actually state that 'most modern rooms are too high for their area', and go on to describe how to create what they mockingly call 'the dado style'.

The Garretts stress that 'the lower part of the wall [i.e. the dado and skirting] should be heavier and more solid in colour than the upper portion', and a whole range of materials was introduced for facing dados, many of them bearing patterns in shallow relief. Edis (1881; see p. 311) mentions embossed leather, but this was very expensive. Simulations in stamped paper, often gilded, were produced in large quantities in Europe (by Messrs Jeffrey in England, for example, and by Desfossé in France; see Pl.461) and in Japan. Tiffany made great use of such gilt Japanese paper (Pl.453). Edis tells us that 'Mr. Walton of Sunbury, has invented a new kind of material for wall decoration, which he calls "Muralis". ... It is practically a linoleum ... a mixture of linseed oil and fibre rolled onto a fabric [canvas], and afterwards stamped ...'. 'Lincrusta', invented in 1877, was a similar material. Other relief-patterned wall-coverings were 'Anaglypta' and 'Cordelova'. Parquetry and 'wood tapestry' were also used; they came mounted on canvas, ready for application. Inexpensive but attractive were 'India or Manilla matting', which could also be used for this purpose. Viollet-le-Duc (*How to Build a House*, Paris, 1873/4) wanted the drawing-room of the imaginary house he was building in a vaguely Renaissance style to have walls hung with painted canvas above a 5 ft- (1.5 m-) high dado painted white. Hung walls were otherwise out of style during the 1870s and 1880s, and red flock wallpaper was no longer *de rigueur* in the dining-room; but there was a revival of wall-hangings in progressive circles at the turn of the century, mostly decorated with embroidery. Candace Wheeler, who was for a while associated with Louis Tiffany and who in 1903 published her *Principles of Home Decoration*, remarked that 'Coarse and carefully woven linens ... are really far better than old tapestries for modern houses'. Free-flowing designs executed in silk or crewels on such canvas became popular for a while; these embroidery designs could of course be adapted to suit spaces of different sizes and shapes.

Revealing, but to some extent biased, is the survey of wall-coverings provided by the wallpaper manufacturers Messrs Cowtan to their wealthy clients, as described by M. Cowtan in 1914 (see Pl.461). In the 1870s the firm was evidently producing a very wide variety of papers, but was also importing especially elaborate papers from France, as well as Chinese and Japanese papers. In 1875 they 'began to use the oil canvasses in imitation of old tapestries', and Cowtan claims that 'he brought into use at the Palace at Darmstadt the so-called Morris style of papers'. In that same year they painted a ceiling 'absolutely black'. Cowtan notes that in 1883 they started to do a lot of graining: maple for drawing-rooms, and oak or walnut for libraries; sometimes pine or chestnut were desired. In this period they seem to have done much stencilling as well. Cornices, he says, could be very elaborate, with the various components often tinted or otherwise picked out. Designs for paintwork published in Paris and Berlin at this time seem to confirm what he says; polychromy was still very much to the fore among traditionalists (Pl.422) and, in a rather different way, among Aesthetes and their successors.

In 1883 'Cretonne [a thick printed cotton material] and papers to match began to be used'. Cretonne became a favourite upholstery material at this time. In 1889 Cowtans supplied Japanese papers to the residence of the British Ambassador in Potsdam, to be trimmed with split-bamboo mouldings. The

JAMES SHOOLBRED & COMP?, TOTTENHAM HOUSE, TOTTENHAM COURT ROAD, W.

421] AESTHETIC MURAL PROPORTIONS, LONDON   1876

A page with four designs for wallpaper showing how greatly the proportions between the three main elements of the wall – dado, filling and frieze – could vary at this period. In examples 6 and 8 the filling is exceptionally narrow. (From James Shoolbred & Co.'s catalogue of 1876.)

*Victoria and Albert Museum, London*

firm sent quite a few papers abroad – to the Russian Embassy in Vienna, a Prussian baron's villa at Florence, the Viceregal Lodge at Simla, the actress Rejane in Paris, and houses on Long Island and in New York. In 1895 they began to use some French enamelled-zinc imitation tiles of a kind which had been used 'with great success in many houses in Paris', and a year later we find them installing asbestos tiles, 'the Ely pattern', on the ceiling of an office in Threadneedle Street! The boudoir in a house in Park Lane hung with 'plain metal paper' in 1896 would seem to have been unusual. Adam designs came in during the late 1890s, while a heliotrope-striped flock of 1903 probably reflects the same fashion for late-eighteenth-century styles. Cowtan specifically notes how the Adam patterns and Wedgwood colours of 1904 were reminiscent of 'the style of decoration my father used a great deal' in London houses when he himself joined the business in 1863. In 1905 he is using 'an American paper, made at Buffalo, one of the cleverest imitations of old Spanish leather that I have ever seen'. 'From this time [1903] onwards we seem to have done everything flatted white or enamelled white paint. The question of whether it was suitable or not with the decoration was entirely lost sight of.' He emphasizes how 'plain painting' had returned into fashion when he gave his talk in March 1914.

The Aesthetic Movement had tended to stress the horizontal lines on a wall, with their deep friezes and dados (Pls.427 and 447). Art Nouveau designers, on the other hand, commonly accentuated the verticals and not infrequently introduced additional vertical elements to help divide up the wall surface: pilasters, mouldings and borders of all kinds (Pls.486 and 488). This verticality was picked up by the German and Austrian progressives and became a cardinal

feature of the proto-Modern interior (Pls.506, 507, 512, 517 and 519).

It should be added, when considering wall-decoration, that much ornament of walls and ceilings was still being executed in papier mâché. When Egerton Winthrop did up his grand New York drawing-room, presumably in the late 1870s, he proclaimed that he intended to have 'created a Louis Seize room that shall produce the impression of an absolute original'. The result is illustrated in *Artistic Houses* (New York, 1883) and looks entirely plausible. The effects were achieved entirely by means of papier mâché mouldings brought over from Paris. Fibrous plaster eventually replaced papier mâché for such purposes.

The chimneypiece had fully come back into its own as the most prominent feature of a room by 1870. All the same, Ella Rodman Church (New York, 1882) was still recommending that it 'be covered up with embroidery or simply trimmed drapery'; but by 1890, when almost everything else could be smothered in drapery, the chimneypiece was no longer covered, and Wharton and Codman (1897) imagine that one could only possibly want to introduce such a drapery if one had an absolutely hideous mantelpiece (they do not recommend this solution, of course). Incidentally, they abhorred screens in the form of large brass fans or a 'stuffed bird spread out in a broiled attitude against a plush background'. They suggest that the use of chimneyboards ought to be revived as it was a pleasant feature which, they say, was still in use 'thirty or forty years ago' (i.e. in the 1860s and 1870s). Messrs Jordan & Marsh, the important Boston furnishers, who published a guide for their customers in 1889 – the *Home Decorative Art Souvenir* – recommended filling the fire-opening with 'a fine dog or tiger skin, suspended from the upper bar of a brass frame, the head resting on a carpet or rug'. It would be a very brave man who suggested hanging a dog-skin in the fireplace today!

J.J. Stevenson, in his *House Architecture* of 1880, surveys contemporary heating-systems and arrangements. He explains how 'The modern Gothic revival has caused a return again to the old open fireplace, with a basket-grate standing loose in it', and how 'Hob grates came lately into fashion again with the "Queen Anne" movement'; but he notes that they are not very efficient, being liable to smoke while giving out little heat.[26] He discusses heating by means of hot air, which is popular in America but which he considers unnatural, unwholesome, and disagreeable 'because the circulating air is so dry'. Central heating by means of large-bore pipes is better, but it is advisable simply to use the system for heating the hall and staircase because it is almost impossible, with this method, to get the heat to spread evenly through all the rooms. Low-pressure piped steam heating was also used in America and was becoming commoner in England, he claimed. All these devices affected the way life was lived in a house, and the apparatus was difficult to disguise entirely.

Much use was made of stained glass in windows during the last three decades of the nineteenth century, and some of it was very good (Pls.441 and 451). Leaded windows with plain or coloured glass were also much in evidence in Aesthetic interiors (Pls.427, 443, 453 and 494). William Morris, around 1879, was saying that 'windows are much too big' in most houses, and Mrs Orrinsmith, who wrote a rather tiresome book about *The Drawing Room* in 1878, actually recommends reducing the apparent size of windows by introducing small leaded quarry-panes.[27] The heavy curtaining of windows, so general in the 1870s and 1880s, indicates that this wish to reduce the amount of daylight in rooms was widespread. 'A room liberally hung with curtains and *portières* seems to my imagination to have shut out the disagreeable conditions of the world, and to have enclosed within itself the peaceful serenities of home', wrote a Mr O.B. Bunce in what must have been a recent essay that is quoted in *Artistic Houses* (New York, 1883). But the reaction was just round the corner, especially in Scandinavia where daylight and sunlight have always been eagerly sought. A Swede, writing in 1890, insisted that light and air must always be present in a room. 'Take away the dark wallpaper and the dark curtains that current fashion regards as elegant.... Let the sun shine unhindered in through the windows and on to the light-coloured walls. Hang up light curtains and place below them a couple of flowering green pot-plants....'[28] Scandinavian artists around the turn of the century were particularly fascinated by the effects of sunlight (Pls.477 and 495), and the Swedish artist Carl Larsson, whose views of rooms bathed in light were so influential, called one of his books of such views *Åt Solsiden* ('On the sunny side') and gave to the German edition the title *Lasst Licht Hinein* ('Let in more light'!). This work was published in 1910, but reflected Larsson's views already formulated in the 1890s.

Built-in furniture made its appearance during this period (Pl.493). Fixed seats were to be seen in the niches and inglenooks commonly associated with the 'Queen Anne' style and its derivatives. Cupboards began to be built in, particularly in bedrooms – *The Lady's World* (London, 1887), for example, illustrated what it called 'A Fitment Bedroom' where there were panelled cupboards across one whole wall. This development was no doubt partly due to the wish to reduce fussiness and clutter – an aspect of the 'great clean-up' which began to take place in the late nineteenth century – and partly to the fact that space was now quite often at a premium in fashionable surroundings, not merely among the less affluent. The fact that the well-to-do now often wanted to live in houses of moderate size or in flats must have been a powerful stimulus to this development. Paradoxically, the interest in designing flats for working-class people, which sprang up particularly in Germany and Scandinavia about 1900, also produced solutions in this direction which could have wider application.[29]

Lighting by gas had become widespread by 1870, and electricity became practicable for domestic lighting purposes in the 1880s. Since both forms of lighting required devices actually installed in the fabric of the room, it is now logical to consider lighting when surveying the architectural shell.

There was much criticism of gas-lighting in the 1870s and 1880s. Not only did the quality of the actual gas produced by the gas companies in different cities vary considerably, 'but nothing can compete with the gaselier in tawdry deformity', as Mrs Loftie insists in *The Dining Room* (London, 1878). Clarence Cook (New York, 1881), while claiming that 'candle-light is the only artificial light by which beauty shows all its beauty – it even makes the plain less plain', admitted that 'gas has also its poetry'. Nevertheless he lived 'in the blessed hope that gas will one day be superseded by something better'. Gas had many drawbacks (including the fact that it made diamonds look dull!) so that 'many people have learned to use either the German student-lamp or the French moderator [see p. 229], while some . . . have frankly gone back to candles'.

In 1879 Thomas Edison succeeded in making an incandescent electric light-bulb that burned for over forty hours. By 1882 a central dynamo was supplying electric current direct to users in New York. J. Pierpont Morgan's house was 'the first private house in New York City into which the Edison electric light has been successfully introduced.... You have simply to turn a knob as you enter' (*Artistic Houses*, New York, 1883; see Pl.441). Pierpont Morgan in fact had his own steam-driven generator in the stables. Electric lighting did not become a major competitor of gas until the 1890s, but gas fought a rear-guard action which for a while seemed likely to win the battle. The weapon that first came to hand was the incandescent gas-mantle or 'Welsbach burner' invented in Vienna, where a factory was established for its manufacture in 1887. 'Electricians will have to wake up,' wrote a commentator in the *Machinery Market* on 1 April 1887; 'within the last few days a new light has made its appearance in [London] which rivals in brilliance the best they have yet produced....'[30] The gas lobby was, however, routed by about 1910, although

**422]** HIGH VICTORIAN POLYCHROMY, PARIS   *c.*1875

Polychromy, a notable feature of much mid-nineteenth-century decoration, entered a sombre phase in the 1870s which lasted through the 1880s. It is admirably exemplified by this detail of a painted ceiling published in César Daly's *Décorations intérieures peintes* of 1877. This elaborate ceiling, with its rich 'Free Renaissance' ornament, was executed in the private study of the architect H. Parent in the house he designed for himself in the avenue Breteuil. The doors were painted *en suite* with the ceiling; the walls were brick-red and the woodwork was stained black. Colours generally became lighter in tone during the 1890s.
*Victoria and Albert Museum, London*

it fired a Parthian shot in the form of lighting by means of acetylene gas. Lawrence Weaver (see p. 322) devotes a chapter to this invention which became more or less practical in the 1890s, although its installation was 'by no means the sort of thing that the local plumber can satisfactorily carry out'. Acetylene gives 'a pure white light without any noxious fumes' but, as a form of domestic lighting, it came too late to offer serious competition to electricity.

Edith Wharton and Ogden Codman (New York, 1897; see p. 316) write that 'Electric light, with its harsh white glare, which no expedients have as yet overcome, has taken from our drawing-rooms all air of privacy and distinction. . . . That such light is not needful . . . is shown by the fact that electric bulbs are usually covered by shades of some deep color, in order that the glare may be made as inoffensive as possible.' These shades were usually of silk on wire frames, but shades of stained glass became popular early in the new century. What Edith Wharton would have felt about much of today's lighting in living-rooms, with 100- or 150-watt bulbs and even spotlights being now quite normal, can scarcely be imagined. Light-bulbs at the turn of the century were run at a far lower wattage, so their light cannot have been at all intense by modern standards. Charles Edward Hooper (*The Country House*, London, 1906) states that 'The electric light, although quite powerful, is readily subdued. Using a low-power lamp with an enclosing bulb of fairly thick semi-opaque glass, which can be tinted if desired, some excellent results are obtainable.' Eberlein, McClure and Holloway (Philadelphia and London, 1919; see p. 315) recommend using 'a number of dim or subdued lights' as they are 'preferable to one or two powerful, glaring lights'. They observe that 'it is indefensible to mount electric bulbs atop of imitation candles'; sham candles, they say, ought to be fitted with shades 'large enough and of such shape as to hide the offensive deception' (Pl.530). H.P. Shapland (London, 1909; see p. 313) likewise felt that 'The fault of artificial lighting at the present day is . . . that it is too brilliant'. Mention is made of hidden lighting, and even of cornice-lighting, as remedies. The illustrations will show some of the solutions put forward for lighting by electricity early in this century. Several schemes involving lamps sunk into the ceiling date from around 1910, but most light-fittings were being modelled on ancient lighting equipment right up to 1920. It was certainly possible to buy Adam-style brackets for electric candles by 1902, for example. Some Art Nouveau designers devised charming light-holders in the shape of plants where the light-bulbs took the place of flowers.

Almost all the writers on these matters during this period admit that, when it comes to dining, candle-light is infinitely preferable. If placed on the dining-table, the candles should be well above eye-level so as not to dazzle the diners and prevent them from seeing those sitting opposite.

## Loose furnishings

The characteristic Victorian look, it is commonly believed, was one of clutter, bold patterns, suffocating drapery and a proliferation of ornaments. This is partly true but needs qualifying. In the first place the 'cluttered' look lasted a rather shorter time than is generally supposed. It made its appearance in some fashionable circles in Paris in the 1850s but did not become widespread until the 1860s and did not reach full strength until the 1870s. In spite of determined onslaughts by the reformers, which had already begun in the 1860s, it then reigned supreme until the late 1890s and was at its absolute height around 1885–90. One can therefore say that this seemingly characteristic look was only paramount over a period of twenty years or so. One also needs to remember that most Victorians liked it: it did not seem cluttered to them. Clearly, the Victorian eye – or rather, the Western eye between 1865 and 1895 – was exceptionally ready to assimilate complex patterns, whether in the form of ornament or as combinations of objects. The reformers tried hard to simplify everything – the arrangement, the shapes, the patterns – but, as they were also children of their time, they found it difficult to adhere to their own precepts and 'clutter' soon crept into their schemes, with the result that the Aesthetic interior could be at least as fussy as an interior of the more traditional kind. Reformist thinking took over twenty years to work through, to allow the communal perception to alter, and it was only in the 1890s that what may be called the 'great clean-up' really became possible. By then the communal eye was ready.

The development of drapery during this period epitomizes these changes. The high point of fussiness was reached in the late 1880s, and this stage is admirably reflected in Felix Lenoir's great tome, his *Practical and Theoretical Treatise on Decorative Hangings, or the Guide to Upholstery*, which appeared in Brussels and London in 1890 with texts in French, German and English (Pl.470). There was scarcely anything which could not be swathed in drapery at this time, as Lenoir's illustrations show.

A simpler guide to these matters is F.A. Moreland's *Practical Decorative Upholstery* (Boston, 1889). He recognized that the current fashion was part of a long tradition which had suffered a temporary setback at the hands of the reformist movement but had now returned to favour. Reformers must have shuddered to read how 'If not sufficiently elaborate, an over-valance may be added' to curtain-arrangements. Moreland advocates a return to the old *Empire* device then called 'continued drapery' (Pl.470), which is a form also shown by Lenoir. Having created a main set of curtains with an elaborate valance, he reminds his readers that the task is not complete. 'Lace curtains should be added, of course, and also short laces or glass-curtains, hung on rods next to the glass.' He then illustrates the principal forms, which do in fact range from fairly simple curtaining, divided and with a flat, lappeted valance hanging from a bold pole with visible rings, to very complex arrangements. The latter include 'irregular drapery', which means asymmetrical arrangements with an element thrown over the pole (Pl.426); and 'raised drapery', which has its drapery flung up over an additional short length of rod set above the main pole. Several intricate schemes have 'flat valances', which were in fact only moderately flat, as they could have festooning, or one end could be thrown over the pole. He illustrates a form of net sub-curtain which became popular at this time but remained in favour long after simpler forms of curtaining had become fashionable – the so-called 'Austrian shade' (Pl.527). This could be raised or lowered and was arranged so as to form close-set festoons. It sometimes had a rod set in a sleeve along its lower end but, unlike eighteenth-century festoon curtains, did not have a straight bottom edge when lowered but retained its festooning when fully dropped (Pl.530). For the long, horizontal windows, often leaded, that went with 'Queen Anne' buildings, a very plain curtain was used. He shows one hanging down straight; at the most it had a simple tie-back. Such simple curtains were of course the norm in reformist circles and were naturally taken up by the progressives at the turn of the century.

The *lambrequin*, so beloved during the third quarter of the century, was totally out of fashion by 1890. As Brunner and Tryon said (New York, 1887), 'Lambrequins draped over the curtains are generally ugly and are worse than useless, as they cannot be drawn aside'.

By the time Edith Wharton and Ogden Codman were writing (New York, 1897) the reaction had truly set in. They criticize 'the heavy stuff curtains, so draped as to cut off the upper light of the windows by day, while it is impossible to drop them at night'. They also consider ridiculous 'the two sets of muslin curtains, one hanging against the panes, the other fulfilling the superrogatory duty of hanging against the former'.

THE HOUSE-FURNISHER & DECORATOR, MAR. 1ST 1872

BEDSTEAD, &C. BY E. EASTLAKE

**423] HALF-TESTER BED IN A NORTHERN RENAISSANCE PASTICHE** *c.*1870

Furniture designed by Edmund Eastlake (not to be confused with Charles Eastlake) in the Flemish Renaissance style and executed 'for Mr. Sandford, formerly the American Minister at the Court of Brussels who has now returned to America'. This Eastlake had spent many years in Brussels, 'where he was actively engaged in designing and controlling the principal works connected with furniture and interior decoration in the essentially art-producing kingdom of Belgium'. The valances of the bed are unlike any sixteenth-century forms but owe much to contemporary *lambrequins*. Eastlake had had to devise a bedside table in the Renaissance style, such objects having been quite unknown in the sixteenth century. (From *The House Furnisher and Decorator*, London, March 1872.)
*Victoria and Albert Museum, London*

Twenty years later the 'great clean-up' was complete. Eberlein, McClure and Holloway (Philadelphia and London, 1919) state that 'The most sensible treatment for the usual double-sash window is that of simple curtains of white or ivory white on rings, suspended on a simple brass rod'. Eastlake would have been delighted, but it had taken fifty years. However, the three authors are not able to maintain their ascetic stance and go on later to say that 'valances are not only a strong decorative asset but often seem required as a finish', not with white curtains, to be sure, but with other materials. 'Valances may be plain, shaped or pleated.'

The Garretts (London, 1876; see p. 311) mentioned 'the new-fashioned wicker screens, sometimes plain, sometimes gilded, but always ugly'. This view was shared by Edis (1881) who instead advocated fitting a second sheet of glass, suitably decorated, fixed against the lower portion of the window to act as a screen. The Garretts also spoke of 'the everlasting drab or yellow venetian blinds, which are constantly out of order, and always draw up crooked . . . invariably used in modern rooms', but Eberlein and his colleagues disagreed: 'the good old Venetian blind is unsurpassed . . . it may be painted any tint to agree with its surroundings'. Ordinary roller-blinds were common during the last decades of the nineteenth century (Pls.430, 425 and 491). They were mostly of buff-coloured cloth, but they could be striped and some had *lambrequins* (or

**424] THE CONTRASTING ROLL;** *FIN-DE-SIECLE* **UPHOLSTERY**

The rolled edge, often made in a contrasting material, had been used back in the 1870s but became extremely common on elaborate seat-furniture at the end of the century. Buttoning went out of fashion in the 1880s, however, leaving the main surfaces smooth. (From C. Hettwig, *Journal für Tapezierer und Decorateure* (new series), Dresden, *c.*1883.)
*Victoria and Albert Museum, London*

425] THE SIMPLER STYLE OF AROUND 1900

From Ernest Foussier's *Nouveaux Modèles de Tentures, Décorations de Fenétres*
(new series), Paris, 1900. The blind is of embroidered taffeta. The green paint of the
panelling is in two shades.
*Victoria and Albert Museum, London*

lappets) along their lower edge. Constance Harrison (*Woman's Handiwork in Modern Homes*, New York, 1881) speaks of 'the present mania for red Holland window-shades' (using the American term for blinds) which, she says, has been compared to 'a descent into the Inferno at every afternoon tea'. She, incidentally, greatly praises the effects achieved by Tiffany with the aid of exotic textiles, including 'India mulls' which were 'used as scarfs by native dancing-girls'.

As in earlier periods, the hangings of beds followed closely the current styles in window-curtains. With regard to the beds themselves, 'Brass or iron bedsteads are unquestionably best, although there seems something of an inclination to return to those of wood in the French and Arabian forms', one reads in *Artistic Homes* (London, 1880), and this indicates that the hung bed was returning to favour. Moreland (Boston, 1889) claims that 'The full canopy covering the entire bed is seldom used. . . . The usual method is to use the half-canopy . . . attached to the wall . . . kept in place by an iron rod or chain with a turn buckle' (Pl.423). Ella Rodman Church (New York, 1882) said that canopies were inviting but should only project about half a yard (45 cm). Favoured materials were 'dotted or plain Swiss' and cretonne. It is a curious fact that the hung bed found favour with progressive designers around 1900 (Pls.505, 488 and 500); it is less surprising that it also continued to be used in 'traditional' interiors of the grander sort right up to 1920 (Pl.503).

The deep-buttoning of seat-furniture went out of fashion in the late 1880s. This was perhaps a sign of the times, but any reduction in fussiness that this might have entailed was often cancelled by the addition of scarves and festoons draped between the legs and over backs (Pl.471). Comfortable seat-furniture remained heavily stuffed during the 1890s, even when buttoning was dispensed with (Pl.424 shows an early example). Squared seats (and backs, where padded) of course went with the strictly Classical styles.

From the 1870s and through the 1880s, upholsterers achieved an especially elaborate effect by making the edge of the back distinct from the main area of the back, which would usually be deep-buttoned. This edge (or *contrefonds*, as the French called it) was formed like a long roll and was often bound criss-cross with cord – like some forms of salami sausage. The roll was sometimes covered with a contrasting material (Pl.424). The effect was undeniably rich.

Brunner and Tryon (1887) recommend stamped leather or 'close-woven tapestry' for dining-chairs, but seek to discourage the use of plush or velvet. Edis (1881) likewise urges his readers to use leather and to avoid velvet, 'which is liable to hold dust and to drag the laces of ladies' dresses'. Antimacassars should also be 'fixed securely to the chair of sofa-backs, so as not to be liable to be carried off as pendants to the fringe of a lady's dress or to the buttons of a gentleman's coat'.

'As regard the floor,' writes Edis, 'the practice of covering the whole with carpets . . . answers no purpose but to increase the upholsterer's bill, and to keep up a dust trap. . . .' Edith Wharton and Ogden Codman in 1897 also urged their readers to have carpets 'laid in the middle of the room, and not cut to follow the ins and outs of the floor . . . [which] not only narrows the room but emphasizes any irregularity in its plan'. On the whole they preferred marble or parquet floors, noting that 'Modern dancers prefer a polished floor'. By 1910 one could state that 'the fitted carpet now is seldom seen outside a dressmaker's showroom' (L. Weaver, *The House and its Equipment*).

Until they were totally banned, however, carpets (or carpeting made up into rectangular carpets) were laid so as to leave exposed an area of floor all round; this area could be stained and varnished (a practice said to have come in with the Gothic revival), wax-polished, or covered with 'plain felt . . . India matting, or floorcloth printed in tile patterns' (*Artistic Homes*, 1880). Matting came plain or in bright colours, the bright checks of Canton matting being very popular. Some authorities felt that coloured mats did not wear well, however, because the dye did not penetrate the fibres. Jordan & Marsh (Boston, 1889), commenting on their design of a 'Fashionable New England Spare Room', done up with Colonial furniture and cretonne overall, advocate 'English matting, stained a delicate grey-green and a tiger skin in front of the dressing-table' as being 'a great addition to the artistic and quaint effect'. Animal skins were an extremely popular form of decoration in the 1880s (Pls.438 and 442).

Shoolbred's give a list of the carpets and other forms of floor-covering they could provide in their catalogue of 1876 (see p. 311), but the most informative statement comes in the Bostonian upholsterer Moreland's publication of 1889 (see p. 310). 'The principal varieties sold, and named in order according to their grade, are as follows: Turkish, French Moquette, Scotch and English Axminsters, English and American Wiltons and Brussels, English and American Velvets and Tapestries, and "Woollens", as all Ingrain carpets are called by the trade; also Venetian . . . cheap stair carpeting; and several lower grades. . . .' He amplifies this considerably, but the general distinction between these classes has already been explained (see pp. 101, 155 and 228). All were by this time woven on power-looms, with the exception of the Turkish carpets which were of course hand-woven. The latter could be made to fit specific rooms, 'plans of which are made and sent to the native manufacturers'. The Near-Eastern carpet industry was revived during the second half of the nineteenth century, largely with European and American capital and organization, and the use of Turkish and Persian carpets in the West increased greatly as a result. *Artistic Homes* (London, 1880) explains that 'Turkey carpets are made from six feet [1.8 m] square upwards – Persian carpets . . . [come from] Khurdestan, Khorasson, Feragan, and Serabend . . . [and are] especially adapted for boudoirs and ladies' rooms. . . . Amongst other Oriental carpets and rugs may be specified the India fabrics from Mirzapore, Ellore, Jubbalpore, Hyderabad, and the Kurd rugs and antique prayer carpets of Daghestan; also so-called Persian rugs and mats from Khoola and Ghordes.' (The spelling of 1880 is here retained.)

Moreland also mentions floor-cloths, which he calls 'oilcloths, or painted carpets'; he recommends they should be washed with warm water and Castile soap, and every year given 'a heavy coat of copal varnish'. He then goes on to explain that 'Linoleums are similar to oilcloths and in some respects are better, being softer and less noisy to walk over, and are neither cold nor slippery as the oilcloths are apt to be. They are made of cork ground with oil, with a cloth foundation, and otherwise are similar to oils. These should not be varnished.' Ella Rodman Church (New York, 1882) calls linoleum 'a new substance' and says it 'will wear as well probably as the best English oilcloth'. In fact floor-cloth very quickly faded from the scene once linoleum had been introduced. Like floor-cloth, linoleum came plain or patterned; the latter type was thought hideous by many reformers. By 1910, however, Lawrence Weaver could report that 'So far as linoleum is concerned, there has of late been a distinct improvement . . . the plain-coloured cork carpets . . . being very useful floor coverings . . . [which] do not pretend to be other than they are. . . . Linoleum, then, has a great future before it. It is cheap and very hygienic, in that it can be easily washed.'

There is no room here to discuss fully the various types of secondary furniture – foot-stools, screens, stands and so on – or the enormous variety of ornaments which were to be found in houses before the 'great clean-up' began to take place at the turn of the century. One of the most noticeable was the palm-leaf fan which first made its appearance in Aesthetic interiors and was soon

426] ELABORATE WINDOW-DRAPERY, BERLIN  *c.*1888

Asymmetrical effects like this were fashionable in the late 1880s, with thrown drapery much in favour for the more ambitious schemes. The glazing of the window and the balustrade suggest that the décor was Renaissance, still very popular in Germany. Banded materials (advocated by Eastlake and others back in the late 1860s and 1870s) were thought particularly suitable for the earlier historic styles. It was apparently almost impossible to exclude Japanese fans and dried grasses from decorative schemes at this time, however incongruous the effect. (From A. and L. Streitenfeld, *Die Praxis des Tapezierers und Decorateurs*, Berlin, *c.*1888.)
*Victoria and Albert Museum, London*

ubiquitous (Pls.447 and 426).[31] Easels, often draped, were used in the 1880s and 1890s as stands for showing paintings (Pl.450). Plates of porcelain or faience came to be used as wall-decoration in the 1870s, either hanging from a nail in a wire frame or standing on edge on a cornice at the top of tall panelling in the seventeenth-century manner (Pls.438, 443 and 460). Potted plants, especially palms, began to make their appearance in the late 1870s as an almost obligatory feature, and were soon to be seen everywhere right into the 1890s (Pls.439, 451, 472 and 480). Arrangements of dried flowers and grasses also became very fashionable in the 1870s and remained so through the 1880s (Pls.426 and 478). In Germany the latter were known as '*Makart-Blumen*' because the painter Hans Makart made them popular (Pl.444).

The illustrations here show how ornaments of all kinds were often grouped to form more or less coherent patterns. Heavily loaded with ornament as the characteristic late-nineteenth-century interior may have been, this does not mean that confusion reigned. It is very difficult for us, having come through the era of the Modern Movement, to discern the principles which underlay these arrangements; but they existed nevertheless and were understood at the time, sometimes intellectually but more often purely subconsciously – as interior arrangements have in fact always been.

## Early Aesthetic, London

427 △

1870

B.J. Talbert's influential *Examples of Ancient and Modern Furniture, Metal Work, Tapestry, Decoration, etc.*, appeared in London in 1876 but included earlier designs of his, such as this which was shown at the Royal Academy in 1870. This rather chunky style bridges the gap between 'muscular' Gothic and the fussier phase of Aestheticism which made its appearance in the mid-1870s (see Pl.447). Note the deep frieze, and the raised floor in the bay window.

*Victoria and Albert Museum, London*

**429 ▷**

## The drawing-room in Robert Edis' own house in London
*c.* 1870(?)

Drawn by the architect himself and reproduced in his influential book *Decoration and Furniture of Town Houses* which appeared in 1881. He describes the room as having been done up ten years before, but it is likely that a number of features were introduced subsequently. The ceiling was 'slightly toned in colour' and had stencilled decoration. The very deep frieze was painted by the artist Stacey Marks. Edis used gas-piping for a picture-rail which may be seen beneath the frieze. The walls are papered with a pomegranate pattern provided by William Morris' firm. The cabinet is ebonized and has painted heads representing the seasons; note the curtains in front of the shelves – a formula much loved by reformers and Aesthetes at this period.

*Victoria and Albert Museum, London*

**◁ 428**

## Recommended Renaissance
1870s

Reproduced from Jacob von Falke's influential *Art in the House*, which first appeared in German in 1871, and then in English translation in Boston in 1878. Von Falke strongly advocated the Renaissance style, using this illustration of a 'Modern Interior' to support his case. Although especially popular in Germany and America, the style was adopted internationally in the 1870s and 1880s. In Germany it lasted through the 1890s as well. The lady seen here sitting comfortably in the middle of this tasteful composition was intended to underline the central role Woman was supposed to play in the home, and therefore in the field of decoration – a theme to which von Falke devotes his whole last chapter.

*Victoria and Albert Museum, London*

Lith Anst v. Leopold Kraatz in Berlin.

◁ 431
## Quilted conjugal bliss, Berlin
*c. 1871*

Twin beds united under a single tester supported by posts, with a ruched headcloth. Much use is made of quilting with decorative buttons of a contrasting colour. There are no pot-cupboards; chairs still stand alongside the bed. (From C. Hettwig, *Journal für Tapezierer und Decorateure*, Berlin, *c.* 1871.)

*Victoria and Albert Museum, London*

◁ 430, 432 ▷

## Two German schemes in the traditional vein
### early 1870s

Both from Carl Hettwig's *Journal für Tapezierer und Decorateure*, a magazine which at that time was being published in Berlin (it later came out in Dresden) with a middle-class public in mind. In both these schemes, which date from about 1870 and 1871, the style is basically Classical with motifs taken from Renaissance and *Louis Seize*. Variants of such 'Free Renaissance' décor were to be found all over Europe and America. 'Continued drapery', to be seen in the scheme on the left, had largely gone out of fashion by this time but was to be revived in the 1890s. Note the painted blinds.
*Victoria and Albert Museum, London*

ERKER.

433 ▷

## Corner sofa, Berlin
### *c.* 1871

It took exceptional skill on the part of a first-class upholsterer to create such an ambitious design. Once completed, there can rarely have been a more comfortable form of seating. (From C. Hettwig, *Journal für Tapezierer und Decorateure*, Berlin, *c.* 1871.)
*Victoria and Albert Museum, London*

◁ 434
## A Copenhagen drawing-room
### 1872

This shows the businessman Frederik Dithmer and his family in a room that is characteristic of the main tradition of European interior architecture and decoration of the time. An iron rocking-chair similar to that in which he reclines was shown by an English manufacturer at the Great Exhibition of 1851. It is late winter. Bulb-vases stand on the window-sill. The heavy curtains are still in position and so is the fitted carpet; both would probably be removed in summer. The gasolier has a 'water-slide' to seal the pipe when it is raised or lowered. A handsome pair of Neo-Rococo console tables with their pier-glasses form striking features and conform to the convention that '*Louis Quinze*' was particularly suitable for drawing-rooms. A cast-iron stove may be seen reflected in one of the glasses. The carpeting is taken up the wall under the windows. The curtains run on rods hidden behind the frieze, so the fancily 'thrown' valance at the corner window must be entirely false.

*National Museum, Copenhagen*

◁ 435
## Early Neo-Colonial taste, New York
### 1873

This picture, by Jonathan Eastman Johnson, the well-known East Coast painter, is evidence that the interest in America's Colonial and early Federal past actually sprang up some time before the Centennial of 1876 (see p. 312). Here a Sheraton-style sideboard of the late eighteenth century with an early Georgian looking-glass and a Georgian mahogany box containing flasks all form a prominent group in a fairly modest room. The vaguely Gothic wallpaper further reflects antiquarian interests and also reformist tendencies (the lady wears 'reformed' dress), while the sketch pinned on the wall suggests that this painting shows the artist's own house. Artists moving in reformist circles were among the first to recognize the attractions of furnishing homes with antiques. Note the very simple *portière* and the window curtained only with a deep valance and a slatted roller-blind.

*Corcoran Gallery of Art, Washington D.C.; gift of Captain A.S. Hickey, U.S.N., in memory of his wife, Caryl Crawford Hickey*

436 ▷
## A New York interior
### mid-1870s

A view from the hall into the drawing-room through the wide opening characteristic of nineteenth-century American houses. This arrangement did not make for any high degree of privacy. Entitled *Not at Home*, this picture shows the lady of the house creeping away upstairs to avoid a caller. The open view of the drawing-room meant that she could not have hidden herself in there. The room is furnished with reproduction furniture in the Northern Renaissance style, but an eighteenth-century long-case clock stands in the hall. Eastman Johnson, who painted this picture between 1872 and 1880, was evidently interested in antiques (see Pl.435).

*Brooklyn Museum, New York*

◁ 437

# Artistic exoticism, London
### *c.*1877

The room of a painter (note the picture on an easel) who liked exotic furnishings. Handsome Persian rugs lie scattered on the floor, there are a tiger-skin and other furs cast over the comfortable seat-furniture, a painted screen is in the window-bay, and an Indian brass vessel stands on a Chinese table along with an oil-lamp mounted on a porcelain vase. Note the white holland blinds and the conservatory beyond. This is by J.J. Tissot and probably shows his own house in Grove End Road, St John's Wood, where he lived from 1873 and into the 1880s. The picture is entitled *Hide and Seek*. *National Gallery, Washington D.C.; Chester Dale Fund, 1978*

## ◁ 438
## Exoticism in Italy
### 1878

The lady has dropped off while reclining *en negligée* in her boudoir, where she has a pile of novels. The décor basically conforms to the main European tradition (the cupboard and table are Renaissance in style) but a strong element of exoticism has been introduced – a bamboo stand, fans, a (pseudo?) Oriental ewer and basin, and one of the large Chinese porcelain vases which became so fashionable at this period, here filled with peacock-feathers. And then there is the lion-skin with its huge head and glass eyes, all too easy to trip over. (By Adolpho Belinbau.)

*Palazzo Pitti, Florence*

## 439 ▽
## Parisian interior
### 1877

Mihály Munkácsy, who painted this picture, was a rich Hungarian who lived in Paris, and this is a view of his apartment. The seemingly rather advanced taste of the décor can indeed probably be explained by the fact that this is the home of people moving in artistic circles. The heavy reliance on antique and/or exotic textiles, and the fondness for palms, were to be characteristic of the fashionable interior in the 1880s. These rooms are decorated in a free rendering of the French Renaissance taste, which fell within the central Classicized tradition favoured in France. The furnishings will mostly have been reproductions and range in style from the '*Henri Deux*' cabinet to the armchair in what was, and still often is, called '*Louis Treize*' – although it is actually in the style of about 1685, which would make it '*Louis Quatorze*', strictly speaking.

*National Gallery, Budapest; photograph from the Corvina Archives, taken by Alfréd Schiller*

◁ 440

### A celebrated Philadelphia drawing-room
#### 1870s

In 1877 Longfellow visited the house of which this room was a principal feature. Among the many other famous people who came there were Dickens, the Duke of Sutherland, J.A. Froude and the Emperor of Brazil. This view is of George W. Child's drawing-room, seen from the music-room. It was panelled in aramanth-wood with fields of crimson satin and chimneypieces of satinwood. The ceiling was formed of papier mâché. In the description of this photograph, particular attention was drawn to the 'superb mirrors', the Aubusson carpet and the 'Byzantine clock', which has a huge figure holding its pendulum. It is noteworthy that amid all this magnificence stands a wickerwork chair. The architecture owes much to the Parisian *Beaux-Arts* tradition. (From *Artistic Houses*, New York, 1883.)

*The Collection of American Literature, The Beinecke Rare Book and Manuscript Library, Yale University*

◁ 441

### An American millionaire's palace, New York
#### 1883

J. Pierpont Morgan's drawing-room at his residence on Madison Avenue at 36th Street was decorated throughout by the distinguished firm of Christian Herter in a style 'of Pompeiian inspiration' embodying 'no slavish copying . . . a mild gayety of expression amid the aroma of perfect taste'. The ivory-white woodwork was sprinkled with gold (called 'modest' in the description). The deep cove was painted to resemble mosaics. The frieze was Pompeian red with touches of gold. The upholstery was contrived with embroidered Japanese silks and Persian appliqué work. This was the first private house in America to be lit by electricity; numerous bulbs can be seen hanging in a row from the ceiling, forming an ornamental feature. No shades were necessary as the wattage was very low. (From *Artistic Houses*, New York, 1883.)

*The Collection of American Literature, The Beinecke Rare Book and Manuscript Library, Yale University*

## Advanced taste in New Jersey
### early 1880s

The 'extraordinarily spacious hall' (it was 50 × 25 ft, 15.2 × 7.6 m) of H.V. Newcomb's house at Elberon in New Jersey, built by the celebrated firm of McKim, Mead and White. They mostly worked in an American variant of the so-called 'Queen Anne' style at this time but exhibited considerable innovative powers – as here where the bold horizontality presages the proto-Modern forms evolved by Frank Lloyd Wright in the 1890s. The grilles, which constitute such a dominant feature, and may be seen as looking forward to the quadrilateral ornament admired by progressive designers around 1900, must in fact be an abstraction from the Oriental wooden-grille screens much favoured by contemporary decorators like Tiffany. The 'chaste finishing of darkened American oak' was noteworthy, according to the description. (From *Artistic Houses*, New York, 1883.)

*The Collection of American Literature,*
*The Beinecke Rare Book and Manuscript Library,*
*Yale University*

## An Aesthetic interior in New York
### *c.*1880

This shows a dining-room decorated by Messrs Louis C. Tiffany & Co. for Dr William T. Lusk. The description of 1883 calls it 'mainly a study of delicate and charming tones'. Some idea of the colouring used by Tiffany can be gleaned from Pl.453. The woodwork of stained pine included a dado 4 ft (1.2 m) high. What looks like a plain Japanese paper is on the walls, and above is a frieze painted with simulations of Japanese enamels. The exotic curtains over the lower part of the windows, and the 'light amber tones' of the stained glass above, all added to the colourful effect contrived by this skilful decorator. (From *Artistic Houses*, New York, 1883.)

*The Collection of American Literature,*
*The Beinecke Rare Book and Manuscript Library,*
*Yale University*

## 444
## A prominent artist's studio in Vienna
### 1885

The hangar-like atelier of Hans Makart, who tended to paint enormous pictures. Makart had started to decorate the room in 1872 and it could be visited at publicized hours. This view, executed in 1885, shows the flamboyant décor that Makart favoured, in which Baroque works of art played an important role. Particularly striking is the vegetal decoration comprising a huge palm-tree and large arrangements of dried grasses and feathers. In Germany and Austria such decorations were often called 'Makart-Blumen'. The style embodied in the décor was extremely influential in central and northern Europe. In the roof is a 'Sunburner' which was a form of chimney, around the lower end of which was a ring of gas-burners. These were intended to remove stale air from the room by convection. (By Rudolph von Alt.)

*Historisches Museum der Stadt Wien, Vienna*

445 ▷

## An intellectual lady's study, New York
### 1878

The bookcases are purely functional. Both the desk and the cabinet are piled with books, and more lie on the floor. The desk is fairly sturdy, as is the throne-like armchair on the left, possibly an antique; but the vaguely '*Louis Quatorze*' chair by the desk seems out of place, and so does the *guéridon* with its two-tier flower-stand which must surely have got horribly in the way. The ornaments on the walls form groups. The lady is Martha Lamb, writer and historian, author of the celebrated *History of the City of New York*. Married to Charles A. Lamb of Ohio and Chicago, she took up residence in New York in 1866. (By Cornelia Adele Fassett.)

*New York Historical Society, New York City*

446 ▷

## Princely comfort in Darmstadt
### 1878

This shows the *salon* in the New Palace, which was built in the mid-1860s. The architecture is strictly Classical, without any Renaissance features, and is a reflection of the revived interest in eighteenth-century Classicism that arose in the late 1870s (see Pl.417). The supremely comfortable manner in which this room, completed in 1877, is decorated would surely have been considered entirely up to date in contemporary Paris. In the centre of the window-bay is a four-sided ottoman surrounding a statue of Venus. The curtains have the new simplicity which goes well with the Classical décor. The *chaise-longue* is exceptionally well arranged for reading the novels lying on the velvet-covered occasional table. Music is piled high on a stool next to the upright piano. Over the central round table is cast a blue cloth with a richly worked gold border trailing to the ground. Mosque-type oil-lamps hang in the corners of the bay. An anti-macassar is draped over the chair on the right. Although much use is made of textiles and there are numerous ornaments, this room remains light and airy.

*Schlossmuseum, Darmstadt*

DRAWING ROOM FURNISHED & DECORATED IN THE OLD ENGLISH STYLE.

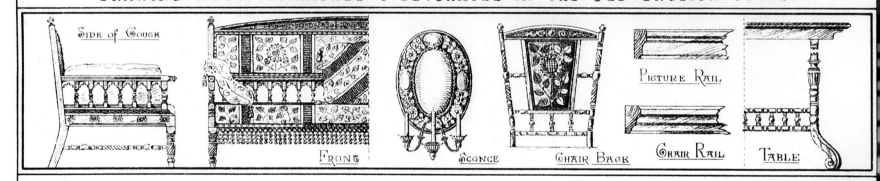

SIDE OF COUCH · FRONT · SCONCE · CHAIR BACK · PICTURE RAIL · CHAIR RAIL · TABLE

JAMES SHOOLBRED & COMPY, TOTTENHAM HOUSE, TOTTENHAM COURT ROAD, W.

Centennial Exhibition 1876. A. KIMBEL & J. CABUS, 7 & 9 east 20. St. New York.

### ◁ 447
## Commercial Aestheticism, London
### 1876

From the trade catalogue of the important firm of Shoolbred & Co. in the Tottenham Court Road. Although combining late-Mediaeval, Northern Renaissance, Japanese and entirely modern motifs, the design shown here is called 'Old English'. Other very similar schemes were called 'Jacobean'. The total effect is Aesthetic, and it is contrived with the aid of 'Art Furniture'. The terms are confusing but the style is unmistakable. See Pl.421 for another subject from this catalogue.

*Victoria and Albert Museum, London*

### 448 △
## A late expression of the Gothic Revival, New York
### 1876

This reformed Gothic interior was shown by the well-known New York upholsterers Kimbel & Cabus at the Centennial Exhibition held in Philadelphia in 1876. The 'muscular' style is beginning to drift into Aestheticism, with its multiple balusters, and its deep frieze and high dado. From Harriet Prescott Spofford's *Art Decoration Applied to Furniture* (New York, 1878), where the style is described as 'Modern Gothic'.

*Victoria and Albert Museum, London*

### 449 ▽
## The Anglo-American link
### 1870s

This is the frontispiece to Clarence Cook's *The House Beautiful*, which came out in New York in 1881. It is by the Englishman Walter Crane and shows how charming the Aesthetic interior could sometimes be. In this artist's hands the style is clear-cut and does not suffer from the confusion so often associated with it, especially in its late version. Crane's influence was not only considerable in America; he was also greatly admired in Germany, especially for his wallpaper designs.

*Victoria and Albert Museum, London*

### What 'brass' could buy in Yorkshire
##### 450
###### c.1880

The suite of reception rooms at Cliffe Castle, Keighley, in Yorkshire. The house was begun in 1878 and the rooms were completed by 1883, when the *Bradford Weekly Telegraph* described the house with its magnificent accoutrements including the 'very luxurious French carpet specially manufactured for the purpose'. The owner, Henry Isaac Butterfield, was a successful manufacturer who had spent some time in Paris and it may well be that many of the furnishings were sent over from France. At any rate the result was a *tour de force* of the upholsterer's art. Note the several paintings displayed on easels.

*Cliffe Castle Museum, Keighley, Yorkshire*

## 451 ▷
# A lady's sitting-room, Leipzig
### 1879–80

Like the Parisian rooms shown in Pl.439, this probably also shows an interior in an advanced taste, for the illustration comes from a book of interiors described as being 'artistically decorated' (*in künstlerischer Ausstattung*). The text implies that it was based on an actual room and there is no cause to doubt this. The room is described as a '*Damenzimmer*', meaning an enlarged boudoir of the type sometimes to be found, in the mid nineteenth century, alongside the drawing-room (i.e. not the kind of boudoir that was simply a closet associated with the bedroom); it thus became a small drawing-room for the lady of the house and her female friends. If the Renaissance style was popular in France at this period, it was, if possible, even more so in Germany. Palms were allowed to become increasingly dominant in the 1880s. Note how little daylight came into fashionable rooms at this period (but compare with Pl.446, which shows an exception). (From O. Mothes, *Unser Heim im Schmuck der Kunst*, Leipzig, 1880.)
*Victoria and Albert Museum, London*

## 452 ▷
# An American lady's boudoir
### c.1880

An illustration from Ella Rodman Church's *How to Furnish a Home* (New York, 1882) which was one of a spate of books on such subjects that appeared in America at this time. The décor shown here follows the main tradition, which was essentially Classical and often a free rendering of Renaissance, coupled with much stress on showy effects contrived by the upholsterer. The density of the scattered arrangement is characteristic of the 1880s.

*The Athenaeum, Philadelphia*

### 453 △
# The Tiffany look, New York
## 1881

Louis C. Tiffany was probably the most talented American decorator working in the Aesthetic style, and he was famed for the colourful schemes he contrived. Unfortunately only black and white photographs of his interiors exist (such as Pl.443), so it is not easy for us to see quite why his work was so greatly admired. Some slight inkling can be obtained from this colour frontispiece to a contemporary book, however. At this stage he relied greatly on Japanese gilt papers, coloured glass, and exotic textiles – all set off by dark woodwork. (From Constance Harrison, *Woman's Handiwork in Modern Homes*, New York, 1881.)

*Victoria and Albert Museum, London*

### 454 ▽
# An Artistic drawing-room in Boston
## 1882(?)

This shows a room in an unknown house decorated in a manner that would surely have met with the approval of reformers such as Eastlake, Bruce Talbert and Edis. They would have liked the striped cloth on the table, the rugged 'reformed Gothic' chairs, and the handsomely inlaid and carved chimneypiece. On the walls is a wallpaper with attenuated floral ornament of the kind taken up in the 1890s by artists working in the Art Nouveau vein. If the date ascribed to this photograph is correct, this shows a very early use of such motifs; but this would have been perfectly plausible, especially if the wallpaper were English. Note the petroleum-lamps mounted in porcelain vases. This is a stereoscopic view. The photographer was J.A. Williams.

*Society for the Preservation of New England Antiquities, Boston, Massachusetts*

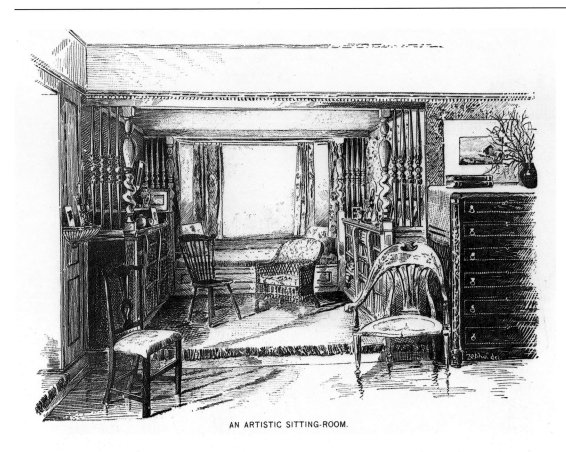

AN ARTISTIC SITTING-ROOM.

### 455 △
## 'An Artistic Sitting-Room', Boston
### 1889

From the catalogue of a local firm of furnishers. The text draws attention to the low ceiling in this 'pleasant country home' where the 'tired business or professional man, overwrought with the cares and trials of business life, finds rest and quiet . . .', to the 'quaint low book-cases', the walls in two shades of olive-green, the upholstery of an Indian silk, and the 'cosey little corner . . . deserving of special notice'. The last is the central feature in this view. It was apparently finished in white and gold, unlike the rest of the room. We are told that this design 'is a happy blending of Louis VI [*sic*] and Colonial'. (From Messrs Jordan, Marsh & Co.'s catalogue, the *Home Decorative Art Souvenir*.)
*Victoria and Albert Museum, London*

### 456 △
## 'Post-dado' mural decoration, England
### 1887

The tall dados and deep friezes of the Aesthetic phase in the 1870s and early 1880s tended to give way to an overall treatment of the wall area at the end of the century – mostly in traditionalist circles but also among ultra-progressives. Adherents of the Arts and Crafts Movement, on the other hand, mostly clung to their beloved dados. Olive or grey-green was much favoured at this period. The way the border of the wallpaper is here taken up round the door-frame is noteworthy. Painting flowers in panels was to become a favourite decorative device during the Art Nouveau phase.
*Bodleian Library, Oxford ; John Johnson Collection*

◁ 457
## A bourgeois drawing-room, Copenhagen
### 1883–5

The father of the lady seen here sitting in her drawing-room was a glover in Hälsingborg, across the Sound in Sweden, a city that is very much closer to Copenhagen than to Stockholm. In fact his daughter married a Dane, a master tanner; and it will have seemed entirely natural for the father to order from the most prominent upholsterer in Copenhagen, C.B. Hansen, the entire furnishings for the rooms in this, the young couple's first home. The bride was allowed to choose the materials for covering the chairs and for the curtains. One suspects she may also have added the Japanese parasol – the only exotic note in an otherwise conventional interior that follows Parisian main-line taste. A petroleum-lamp stands on the table. The chandelier comprises a petroleum-lamp with candles all round.

*National Museum, Copenhagen*

◁ 458
## A steamship captain's house, Copenhagen
### c. 1887

This shows his wife with their two children (note the doll's house on the floor) in the drawing-room which was probably furnished when they were married in 1877. The English engraving over the sofa is, however, known to have been acquired in the 1880s and the profusion of plants is character-istic of that decade. There is a vase on the table and an array of greenery growing in pots stands by the window. Note the stencilled ornament on the ceiling. Through the heavily draped opening, which probably had double doors, one can see the captain's desk. Stress was laid in his title that he was captain of a *steam* ship.

*National Museum, Copenhagen*

## 459
## Opulence with discrimination, New York

*c.*1885

The reception rooms of a well-to-do New York lady, Mrs George Frederic Jones, mother of the future novelist Edith Wharton. The latter's first book was in fact a work on interior decoration, published in 1897, in which she criticizes the taste of her countrymen (see p. 316). The daughter cannot, however, have disapproved totally of her mother's own arrangements, for the unities are at least preserved by the upholstery and by the *boiseries* which adhere more or less to the *Louis Seize* style. Indeed, if the fleurs-de-lys above the door are anything to go by, the daughter's love for everything French seems to stem from her mother. The room beyond seems to be couched in the Renaissance taste. The pleated shade on the petroleum-lamp is of a form that became popular in the 1890s, and was then adopted for use with electric light.

*Yale University Library, Yale Station, Connecticut*

◁ 460
## A reception room in a large English country house, Cheshire
### early 1880s

This room at Eaton Hall, the country seat of the Duke of Westminster, was entirely re-decorated by Alfred Waterhouse in 1882. He took the early-nineteenth-century Neo-Gothic room and transformed it into a rather overblown Aesthetic interior, where Gothic was laced with Japanese. Like other members of his class at the time, the Duke habitually entertained large house-parties. The arrangement of the furniture in clusters facilitated conversation when the company broke up into groups. The room is ostensibly a library but it was clearly intended to serve primarily as a drawing-room. Note the fixed standards supporting gas-lamps which form decorative features. Waterhouse does not seem to have been able to exert any influence over the furnishings otherwise; the furniture is mostly of patterns standard at the period but some antiques are present – notable being some mid-eighteenth-century armchairs, two of which are in the foreground. These have been re-stuffed, and probably furnished with springs, so their lines are quite different from those originally intended. The bloated effect is enhanced by the use of two materials, a woollen velvet at the sides and a rich silk with the Westminster arms applied. The chairs are still in the family's possession but are now trimmed to something like their original conformation.

*Victoria and Albert Museum, London*

461 △
## Samples from the furnishing-materials used in the Library at Eaton Hall, Cheshire
### 1882

Two of the '24 Chippendale chairs' may be seen in the foreground of the old photograph of the room reproduced in Pl.460, where the 'lampas bordered with plush' is evident. (From the pattern-books of Messrs Cowtan.)

*Victoria and Albert Museum, London*

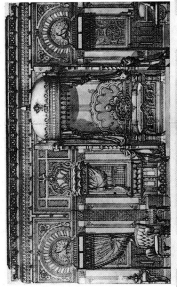

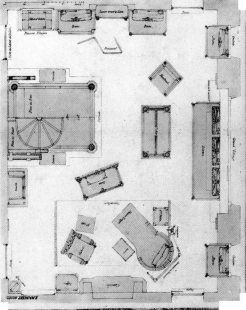

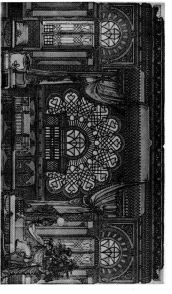

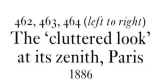

## 462, 463, 464 (*left to right*)
## The 'cluttered look' at its zenith, Paris
### 1886

Three Parisian room-plans showing the disposition of the furniture during the phase when the density was at its most extreme. These fascinating plans, with their exploded elevations, repay close inspection. They come from the Parisian upholsterer E. Maincent's *La Disposition des Appartements* (Paris, 1886). Maincent very generously recommends on where to obtain the various components, but also states that he could co-ordinate the complete enterprise. For instance, for

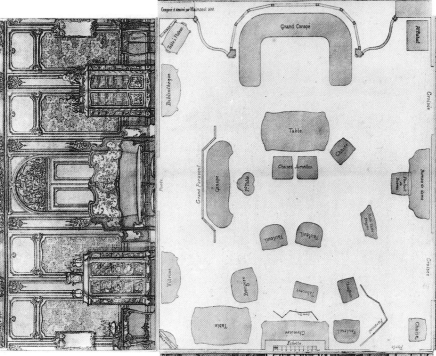

the 'Salon genre Moderne', where the central feature in front of the window was to be a bronze statuette, one should 'ask for Christopher Columbus as a Child' – presumably from Messrs Roussel & Laverlochère, whose name is given in the text. The furniture forms groups which would facilitate the functioning of the rooms, making conversation easier in the two *salons* and repose more enjoyable on the day-bed, or on the bed itself in the 'Moorish Bedroom', but also leaving pathways through the apparent clutter. The arrangement in fact follows a more or less axial basis, and asymmetry on the ground is always carefully balanced to form a harmonious symmetry in effect.

*Victoria and Albert Museum, London*

## A Liverpool interior
### 1885

This gives a good idea of the sombre colour-schemes admired in the 1880s, but also shows how accents of bright colours shone in the general murkiness. Dull gold wallpaper likewise produced a glowing effect. Note the prevalence of Oriental porcelain. On the table is a material from Morris & Co. (By John Atkinson Grimshaw.)

*By courtesy of Messrs Sotheby Parke Bernet, New York*

467 ▷
## A provincial house in Sweden
### 1885

The charming views by Carl Larsson of his country cottage on the outskirts of Falun, a mining town in Dalcarlia, executed in the late 1890s and early 1900s, are familiar to many (see Pls.496 and 516), but this shows a room in the same house when it was occupied by his wife's aunt. It is furnished with antiques, some of which may have been in the family since they were new; but it is noteworthy that Larsson has here depicted them with such loving care. The simple muslin valance, used in conjunction with a roller-blind (the cord is on the right of the window) is characteristically Swedish, as is the arrangement of the rag-woven runner in a square to form a walkway that saves the floor itself.

*By courtesy of Messrs Hazlitt, Gooden and Fox, London*

◁ 466
## A bourgeois Parisian bedroom
### 1883

This may be the artist's own room (there are drawings pinned on the wall and an old-fashioned desk placed on the writing-table which would have been useful for a watercolourist). The room is pleasant but not very distinctive and is certainly not in an advanced taste; it conforms to the main conventions current since the 1850s. The bed stands in the corner and has a tester fixed to the ceiling which subtends the corner and does not extend over the whole bed. Designs for such corner-placed beds were commonly given in French upholsterers' pattern-books in the third quarter of the century. On the right is what looks like a Dutch marquetry commode, mid-eighteenth-century in style. (By Marcel Blairet.)

*By courtesy of Messrs Hazlitt, Gooden and Fox, London*

## 468
## A fashionable London
## drawing-room
### 1887

This drawing is from a magazine edited by Oscar Wilde that carried a series of articles on 'London Drawing Rooms and their Châtelaines'. It shows the drawing-room of Lady Seton, who lived at Durham House overlooking Chelsea Hospital. She not only held a regular salon in these rooms; she was also a novelist, although no one seems to remember her today. The room is in a *Louis Quatorze* or Neo-Palladian style. The window-curtains 'of amber brocade' are remarkably plain, but the billowing drapery (said to be bluish-green) in the doorway is in contrast to this simplicity. The wallpaper had scrollwork in two tones of grey. Judging from this drawing, the room was extremely comfortable and seems to have been well suited to entertaining. (From *The Lady's World*, London, 1887.)

*Victoria and Albert Museum, London*

## 470 ▷
# The heavily draped style
### late 1880s

A page from Felix Lenoir's *Practical and Theoretical Treatise on Decorative Hangings, or the Guide to Upholstery* (Brussels and London, 1890). This shows the stage when almost everything had to be draped. However, buttoning was going out and simpler forms were being introduced for the stuffed seat-furniture. The double effects used in the covering of the *chaise-longue* are typical of the rich upholstery at this period. In the face of such tumultuous confections it is hardly surprising that the 'great clean-up' was soon widely welcomed. Nevertheless, in the hands of a really skilled and sensitive upholsterer, such schemes could have their charms.

*Victoria and Albert Museum, London*

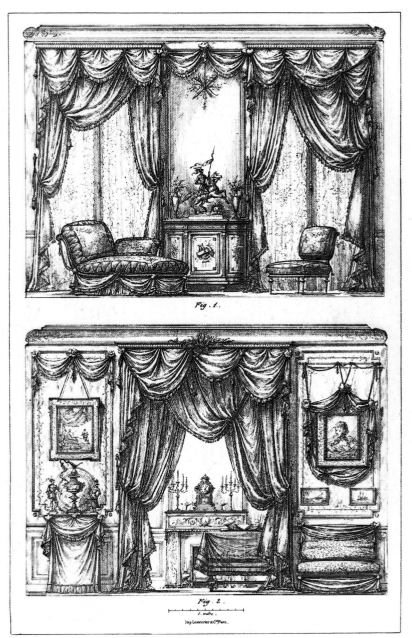

## 469 △
# A reception room for V.I.P.s at Heidelberg
### 1886

This room at Heidelberg University was done up to receive some important visitors, as a temporary measure, in 1886. The result was thought sufficiently distinguished by Ludwig Caspar for him to illustrate the room in his *Innere Architectur und Decoration der Neuzeit*, which appeared in Frankfurt in 1888. The book comprised illustrations of rooms '*nach ausgeführten Arbeiten*' ('based on executed works'), and the caption to this drawing indicates that this room existed even if the odd detail has been omitted. The stress on drapery and fancy effects on the seat-furniture, the huge vases with dried grasses, and the stained glass are all characteristic of the period. The general style is Renaissance, as favoured by all serious-minded Germans during the second half of the century.

*Victoria and Albert Museum, London*

## ◁ 471
## A fashionable Parisian artist's drawing-room
### c.1887

An illustration from P. Planat's *Habitations particulières*, which deals with private houses in Paris and was published in about 1887. It shows a room in the house of 'a painter of military scenes named N[euville]'. Pictures by this artist were avidly bought by, among others, several of the rich Americans whose houses were depicted in *Artistic Houses* (New York, 1883; see Pls.440 and 441). This house stood in the rue Brémontier and was by the architect M. Gerhardt. The room shown here is done up in a *François Premier* or *Henri Deux* style, much use being made of old embroideries. On the walls is a gold paper. The hanging of plates on the wall (in a group, be it noted) is a modern feature and the draped *chaise-longue* with its parasol (frilly and *not* Japanese) are very much of the period. The scattered Oriental carpets lie on a red (felt?) ground.

*Victoria and Albert Museum, London*

## 473 ▷
## A stylish Parisian dining-room
### c.1887

This shows the dining-room of the 'Comtesse de F . . .', whose cipher is carved into the ornament of the chimneypiece. The elaborate woodwork was executed by the celebrated firm of Fourdinois, and there can be no doubt that this house was exceptionally well appointed. The architect was M. Feine and the house was in the rue Scheffer. The style, as was proper for dining-rooms in France, was Renaissance – rendered rather freely. Note the lined-up chairs; formality lingered on in dining-rooms long after it had been banned from the drawing-room. The chandelier comprises a petroleum-lamp with candle-branches around it. (From P. Planat, *Habitations particulières*, Paris, c.1887.)

*Victoria and Albert Museum, London*

472 △
## A smart Parisian drawing-room
*c*.1887

This shows a house by the architect Thévin on the avenue Malakoff. The painted décor was by Gruz (see Pl.288) and some of the ornaments were executed in Lincrusta Walton. The style is *Louis Seize*, the preferred style for fashionable drawing-rooms in the 'traditional mode' at this period. Unlike in a real Louis XVI room, the furniture is here scattered across the floor in the normal late-nineteenth-century manner. The garden-room beyond is decorated with trelliswork. Lighting is by candles. Note how the pictures are canted forward. The edge of the floor round the carpet is covered with blue felt. (From P. Planat, *Habitations particulières*, Paris, *c*.1887.)

*Victoria and Albert Museum, London*

◁ 474
## An English middle-class house
### 1885

The seated young man wears spurs, so this scene is set in a country house, apparently not a large one. Edith Hayllar, who painted this picture, lived at Castle Priory, a medium-sized Georgian house on the Thames near Wallingford in Berkshire. She tended to depict scenes of her family in their home. The panelling could just possibly have been made in the provinces during the eighteenth century; but the family acquired many antiques, some obviously spurious Neo-Jacobean confections, so it is more likely that the panelling had been installed not long before this picture was painted. The Sheraton chairs are also likely to be reproductions. A Charles II gate-leg table, once again probably not genuine, serves as a dining-table. Note the very large Persian carpet, and the Japanese painted-paper screen – a highly decorative feature of a type popular at this period. Behind it hang framed lithographic prints.

*From the Hayllar family photograph album; by courtesy of the Christopher Wood Gallery, London*

◁ 475
## Furnishing with antiques, Belgium
### 1886

This probably shows the artist's own house, perhaps with his wife as model. Artists were particularly keen on antiques as furniture, but the owner of this room has obviously tried to re-create a seventeenth-century interior – even down to having the model dressed in the style of that period. There is gilt leather on the walls and much use is made of old textiles, but not all the furniture is likely to be as old as the owner imagined and the candlesticks are unlikely to be antiques. Mantelboards were not known in the seventeenth century; the one to be seen here is made up with Baroque bed-valances. (By H. de Braekeleer.)

*Koninklijk Museum voor Schone Kunsten, Antwerp*

### 476
## American late Aesthetic, New York(?)
### 1887

The vaguely Jacobean chimney-surround, the high panelled dado and the gilt-leather panels above follow the general precepts of the Aesthetic Movement, but in a moderate manner. This is a very pleasant middle-class room of the period, displaying no extremes; it would surely have been acceptable both to Aesthetes and traditionalists.

Note the now almost obligatory potted palm in its huge container, the plates hanging on the wall, and the chandelier which comprises a petroleum-lamp as well as candle-branches. A pair of petroleum-lamps stands on the mantel-shelf. There is a Persian carpet on the floor, lying on some plain floor-covering. (By. W.H. Lippincott, a Philadelphia artist who had spent eight years in Paris before settling in New York in 1882.)

*Pennsylvania Academy of the Fine Arts, Philadelphia; gift of Homer Evans and Francis Jones*

## ◁ 477
### *Sunlight in the dining-room,* Copenhagen(?)
#### 1889

Viollet-le-Duc insisted that the Scandinavians were clever at contriving pleasant interiors. Little heed has been paid to stylistic unity here but the mixture seems to blend very happily. In northern countries, where the winters are long and dark, daylight is at a premium, and one gets the impression that Scandinavians were quick to drop the fashion for excluding light by the heavy swathing of windows: light was too precious. At any rate, this artist (and it may have been a tendency that arose in artistic circles) painted many views of interiors where the play of daylight was his evident preoccupation – as indeed the title of this painting indicates. A late-*Biedermeier* (the Danes would say late-*Empire*) pier-glass and console table have been removed from their traditional position and placed across the interior corner of the room. (By Viggo Johansen.)

*Swedish private collection; photograph from National Museum, Stockholm*

## 478 ▽
### A Swedish bishop's residence, Växjö
#### 1889

This shows the Bishop of Växjö's wife Elise reading while sitting in a huge throne of Gothic inspiration, using a fat cushion, apparently covered with tapestry, as a foot-rest. This may be an early bishop's throne of perhaps 1840 or so, now used as an armchair with romantic overtones in a less earnest age. Although details are not easy to discern, this watercolour shows an interior at the very height of the 'cluttered phase' around 1890 when to our eyes, and to those of progressives at the time, rooms had become suffocating with their overload of ornament. In fact, the palms, the *portières*, the dried grasses, the fussy wallpaper, the picture on an easel and all the other standard trappings of the time are present; but somehow this delightful sketch manages to convey the fact that, in the eyes of contemporaries, such rooms could seem charming.

*Stiftelsen Smålands Museum, Växjö*

## 479 △
### A Swedish middle-class home
#### *c.*1890

As in Pl.477, old-fashioned furniture is combined to produce an attractive, airy and harmonious effect. It is noteworthy that relatively few loose ornaments are present. This could be due to conservatism prolonging *Biedermeier* simplicity in a provincial setting, or it could just be that we here see early signs of the 'great clean-up' when the burden of ornaments that had become so monstrous in the 1880s was beginning to be reduced. Scandinavians were on the whole rather keen to let in more light, but they do not seem to have been among the first to banish clutter. (Painted by Josefina Holmlund.)

*Östergötlands Länsmuseum, Linköping*

## 480 ▷
## The great English living-hall
### 1891

This impressive room at Shiplake Hall in Oxfordshire had been built only the year before this photograph was taken. It was one of the last of its kind. These 'living-halls' were actually rather difficult to live in; they were not comfortable rooms in which to settle down. Apart from being draughty and often cold, it was almost impossible to prevent them serving as passageways for people passing from one part of the house to the other. They were also difficult to furnish because only objects on a large scale could avoid being dwarfed in such a vast space. Ernest George and Harold Peto, the distinguished architects responsible, were among the foremost of those who sought to furnish interiors with antiques. While real objects could often be secured, they were not averse to advising their clients to acquire good reproductions – like that of a famous seventeenth-century couch at Knole which may be seen here. The amazing electric-light chandeliers, mediaeval in spirit, are noteworthy. The photograph was taken by H. Bedford Lemere.

*Royal Commission on Historical Monuments;*
*National Monuments Record, London*

### 481 ▽
## A Dutch middle-class drawing-room at The Hague
### 1890

The basic décor and some of the furnishings are probably earlier than 1890, but the general density and the arrangement of the furniture is characteristic of that time; and rooms such as this were then to be seen in every city in the Western world. Except to the very discerning, the only item that identifies this room as Dutch is the *vitrine* which carries echoes of a well-known class of eighteenth-century Dutch cabinet. Otherwise this old photograph depicts an international style of decoration following the main-line tradition. Note the adjustable gasolier and an early example of a standard lamp (petroleum-burning) on the right. It seems incredible that the palm could really be *growing* in that bronze vase held by a maiden, standing on the round table. The house was in Anna Pavlownastraat.

*Gemeente Archief, The Hague*

◁ 482
## 'Arts and Crafts' par excellence, Baltimore (Maryland)
### *c.*1900

The teachings of Philip Webb, William Morris and Charles Eastlake which had inspired the Arts and Crafts Movement in England were heeded in America with enthusiasm by Gustav Stickley in the 1890s. He evolved an extreme variant of the honest Arts and Crafts manner, the so-called 'Craftsman' style. This room in Baltimore, the residence of Martin Hawley in Eutaw Place, epitomizes Stickley's creations. When Stickley in 1909 claimed that furniture in this style should reveal 'just what it is, how it is made and what it is made for' he was merely echoing English Arts and Crafts sentiments, but he liked to think that it also expressed 'the fundamental sturdiness and direct-ness of the American point of view'. As 'we have no monarchs and no aristocracy', he explained, 'the life of the plain people is the life of the nation'. Whether so or not, his version of Arts and Crafts had a profound influence in America.
*Maryland Historical Society, Baltimore*

◁ 483
## An actress' room in New York
### 1898

The library in the apartment of Elsie de Wolfe and her friend Elisabeth Marbury at 122 East 17th Street, a house previously occupied by Washington Irving. She re-decorated it several times and was later to become a celebrated interior decorator herself, one of the first women to do so. She is usually credited with introducing the vogue for ivory-white to New York, although she can in fact only have given this fashion fresh impetus. This view of one of her rooms was taken while she was still on the stage. It shows that her own tastes were simple but quite stylish, and that she already had an eye for antiques. Her flair caught the attention of the fashionable architect Stanford White who, the year before he was murdered in 1906, invited her to decorate the Colony Club on Madison Avenue. Here, for one room, she adopted trellis-work very similar to that shown in Pl.472. There-after she took up decorating as a business, and even wrote a book on the subject. She enjoyed enormous success but it is no longer easy for us to perceive quite why, because the style she helped to evolve has been so widely imitated ever since and is still with us today. (Photographed by Joseph Byron.)
*Museum of the City of New York, Byron Collection*

## 484
## Admired in Germany:
## an English room
### 1895

Hermann Muthesius admired this room greatly and reproduced this actual photograph in his *Das Englische Haus*, which was published in Berlin in 1904. Through Muthesius particularly, such English interior architecture was to have a profound effect in Germany. The house is Great Tangley Manor in Sussex, built late in his life by Philip Webb, one of the original reformers of the 1860s. Less rugged than his early work, and not overlaid with ornament like so much subsequent reformist decoration, this represents the breakthrough of the English reform movement when the world was finally ready to receive it. Unassuming, simple in its lineaments and without much ornament, it offered a new style that had wide appeal to those nurtured on the Picturesque or to those who were weary of traditional Classicism. It was a style that ran entirely counter to the progressive taste that was shortly to be expressed so trenchantly in Vienna and in Germany. The photograph was taken by H. Bedford Lemere.

*Royal Commission on Historical Monuments;*
*National Monuments Record, London*

### 485, 486, 487
# Parisian Art Nouveau
### 1900

Most Art Nouveau decoration was a good deal more sober than is generally supposed, and most of the features in the style tended to be two-dimensional. Grey-green with a salmon colour formed an alternative colour-scheme at this time to the ubiquitous white. The *portière* on the right (from the room shown on the left) bears characteristic Art Nouveau embroidery. (From *Intérieurs modernes* (Paris, 1900) by Georges Rémon, who called himself '*architecte-décorateur*'.)
*Victoria and Albert Museum, London*

BREND'S.& Cº

488 △
### German proto-Modern, Munich
1898

Design for a bedroom 'in modernem Karakter' by the Munich architect Patriz Huber, who was shortly afterwards to join the progressive Artists' Colony at Darmstadt (see Pl. 506). The layout seems to owe something to English designs by such men as Baillie Scott, and the flat ornament clearly derives from Art Nouveau; but the resulting amalgam nevertheless looks forward to the clean lines and stylishness of the Modern Movement. Unfortunately Huber, a designer who has probably been under-rated, committed suicide in 1902. Note the plan, bottom left. (From A. Koch, *Moderne Innen-Architektur und innerer Ausbau*, Darmstadt, 1899.)

*Victoria and Albert Museum, London*

491, 492 ▷
### Art Nouveau curtains, Berlin
1904

From a suite of attractive designs in this style by the architect J.H. Biegler, simply entitled *Neue Vorhänge* ('new curtains'). The simplicity of the general conformation, in such contrast to the complex drapery of a decade earlier, counterbalances the bold ornament. The Art Nouveau style lent itself particularly well to such two-dimensional ornament. Note the blind and what must be panels of coloured glass.

*Victoria and Albert Museum, London*

**LXXVI STUDEERKAMER**

**LVI BADKAMER**

489, 490 (*above, left and right*)
## Advanced Dutch, Amsterdam
### 1903

These striking illustrations come from the Dutch monthly *Het Huis* during its first year of publication. All the designs there published were by an architect named E. Cuypers, a man of reformist tendencies. The windows of the study have an Aesthetic character and the frieze clearly springs from Art Nouveau, but the curtains and the rug are entirely up-to-date and the lineaments of the furniture are advanced in style. The built-in furnishing of the bathroom is neat and functional. This house was apparently built in Jan Luyken Straat in Amsterdam.

*Victoria and Albert Museum, London*

493 ▷
## A Roman bedroom
*c.*1900–05

This painting, entitled *Late*, shows the white-painted décor that was internationally fashionable during the first decade of this century. Note the fitted cupboards occupying the whole of one wall. This interior seems to owe something to Voysey. It is modern without being extreme; nevertheless there can be no mistaking the fact that ornament has largely been suppressed. (By Camillo Innocenti.)

*Museo Nazionale d'Arte Moderna, Rome*

494 (*right, below*)
## A 'tree-top' retreat for a princess, Roumania
1897–8

This shows *Le Nid*, a small house built on stilts formed by tree trunks in a pine-wood at Sinaia, a fashionable summer resort in Roumania, for the young Crown Princess Marie. The Manxman M.H. Baillie Scott designed and built it in 1897–8, and this is his own sketch which he subsequently published in his *Houses and Gardens* (London, 1906). The Crown Princess was a sister-in-law of the Grand Duke of Hesse for whom Baillie Scott also worked (see Pl.497). The main room is decorated with stylized representations of the sun (on the ceiling, seen through foliage!) and sunflowers. In the raised section, where there is a small oratory, lilies are the decorative motif. Next door was a bedroom 'where the drowsy poppy prevails'. Baillie Scott's schemes were widely admired on the Continent, especially in Germany (where *Houses and Gardens* was subsequently published in 1912), and his influence on early-twentieth-century interior decoration must not be under-estimated (see also Pl.515). He borrowed much from Voysey and a little from Mackintosh, but added a freshness that is admirably conveyed by his own pretty watercolours. The distribution of rooms in his ground-plans was often ingenious.

*By courtesy of Clive Wainwright; photograph from Victoria and Albert Museum, London*

◁ 495
## The birthday table, Sweden
### 1902

This delightful picture by Fanny Brate once again shows the Scandinavian preoccupation with light and especially sunlight. Northerners can never get enough, and they are particularly adept at depicting it. Note the white-painted chairs, which are probably reproductions, and the sofa (it could pull out to form a bed) which may be a genuine late-eighteenth-century antique; also the very simple muslin curtains, which are purely decorative and cut out very little light indeed. On the floor lies a rag-weave runner forming a runway round the room in the traditional manner. The scene is set in her husband's old home in the country, hence the dog-daisies and other wild flowers in the vase. The wall-paintings were executed in 1790. (The actual title is *The Name Day*.)
*National Museum, Stockholm*

496 (*left, below*)
## An artist's country cottage in Sweden
### 1899

One of the many delightful pictures by Carl Larsson of the house he and his wife Karin occupied when they retired to the country for the summer. They were published in Sweden, notably in *Ett Hem* ('A Home') which appeared in Stockholm in 1899, and in *Larssons* ('At the Larssons') of 1902 which included this charming picture of Karin in her white bedroom. Other books followed in Sweden, but the influence of Larsson and his wife's ideas on decoration (she was at least as creative as he) was greatly increased when a German publisher put together a small volume of Larsson's views of the house under the title *Das Haus in der Sonne* (Düsseldorf and Leipzig, 1909) from which this illustration is reproduced. By 1912, 10,000 copies had been printed. Already by 1904 *The Studio* had included an article on Larsson and his scenes and in 1907 a big exhibition of his work was held in Vienna which was widely noticed. The style the Larssons actively advocated was light, bright, simple, colourful and picturesque. Both were artists, much travelled and widely read; they were familiar with recent developments in Europe but also cherished the local vernacular handicrafts. They added to all this a significant artistic contribution of their own. See also Pls.467 and 516.

*(Author's photograph)*

◁ 497
### An ultra-modern apartment at Mannheim
*c.*1898

Designed by M.H. Baillie Scott (see Pl.494) for the Grand Duke of Hesse. The architect was particularly pleased with this commission because he was invited not only to decorate the room but also to design the furniture. This view is of the music-room from the boudoir. The music-room is all white; the ceiling and frieze are decorated with stylized renderings of trees between which are wreaths of mountain-ash and roses – all modelled in relief and painted. (From M.H. Baillie Scott, *Houses and Gardens*, London, 1906; his work also came out in German in 1912.)
*Victoria and Albert Museum, London*

499 ▷
### A handsome New York drawing-room
1903

This room was presumably decorated in the 1890s when the admiration for *Empire* furniture was at its height. The chairs are of fine quality and could be actually of that period rather than reproductions. Indeed the room is apparently furnished throughout with antiques and with exotic textiles, plus a polar-bear skin which would probably have been more at home in the 1880s. Particularly striking are the *lambrequins*, which are made up from Chinese hangings. The curious relief roundels in the ceiling and on the far wall may be meant to be in the *Empire* taste. This was the drawing-room of Mrs R.E. Schroeder. (Photographed by Joseph Byron.)
*Museum of the City of New York; Byron Collection*

◁ 498
### A Harvard undergraduate's room
*c.*1903(?)

The Art Nouveau poster is for the Pan-American Exposition held in Buffalo in 1901, so this photograph probably dates from soon afterwards. Gas-lighting is still fitted, and the 'style' is vaguely Aesthetic. The lighting has been supplemented by a standing petroleum-lamp supported by a figure in fancy dress. The numerous photographs, the exotic bed-cover, the many cushions (two decorated with Red Indian images) all presumably belong to the room's temporary occupant.
*By courtesy of Stewart Johnson, New York*

# A Glasgow School interior

*c*.1903

This design by George Logan, a member of the Mackintosh circle in Glasgow at the turn of the century, was published in 1904 in the Parisian journal *Documents d'Architecture moderne*. The colour-plates in this publication almost all came from the Stuttgart journal, *Moderne Bauformen*. Logan favoured a slightly less attenuated style than Mackintosh; but the rose motif, the ovoid shapes and the white paint are all characteristic of the Glasgow School, which was astonishingly influential at this period, especially in Germany and Austria. Logan was employed by the Glasgow cabinetmaking firm of Wylie & Lockhead, who commissioned this design.

*Victoria and Albert Museum, London*

## The 'English Cottage' style in Germany; Stuttgart
### 1902

This design by an architect named MacLachlan was published in a French journal in 1902, but the colour-plates used in the publication had previously appeared in Stuttgart, where MacLachlan apparently worked. Several British interior architects and designers were working in Germany at this time: John A. Campbell was another, working in Berlin. They brought with them an intimate knowledge of the cosy – or quaint, as it would have been called – English pseudo-vernacular style which enjoyed much favour on the Continent, especially in Germany. Many of MacLachlan's designs appeared in German magazines in these years. When this design was published, Muthesius' influential work on English domestic houses (see p. 313) had not yet been brought out. (From *Documents d'Architecture moderne*, Paris, 1902.)

*Victoria and Albert Museum, London*

◁ 501
## American proto-Modern, New York
### 1901(?)

This is probably one of several designs in an advanced vein composed by Will Bradley for publication in *The Ladies Home Journal* in 1901. It was subsequently included in an article on Bradley that appeared in the German journal *Moderne Bauformen* in 1906. Carrying echoes of Baillie Scott's planning and frieze-patterns, and of Mackintosh's affected attenuation, not to mention the sturdy constructivism of the young Frank Lloyd Wright, this composition has grace and charm. A few cushions would make this a very comfortable room. The electric-light fitting is rather bizarre.

*Victoria and Albert Museum, London*

502 △
## A flat in Budapest
### c.1905

The furnishings were made by the Guild of Handicrafts at Chipping Campden in Gloucestershire, to the designs of C.R. Ashbee, and then installed in this flat in Budapest. The electric-light fittings were of hammered copper and the woodwork was of mahogany inlaid with holly, which is almost white when fresh. English modernism was never as extreme as its Austrian and German counterparts at this time (see Pls.504–510). In fact it never advanced beyond this tradition-based stage until well into the 1920s. (From *Flats, Urban Houses and Cottage Homes* (ed. W. Shaw Sparrow), London, 1906.)

*Victoria and Albert Museum, London*

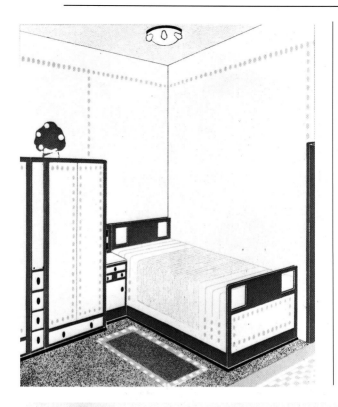

## ◁▽ 504, 505
## Viennese ultra-progressive, the *Secession* style
### 1901–2

The hung bed, with its rectilinear conformation, displays admirably the extremely severe style advocated by Josef Hoffmann in Vienna around 1900. The leap forward that he and his associates suddenly made at this time was enormous. The elimination of all but the simplest geometric ornament was brought about quite suddenly. The other scheme is in fact for a twin-bedded arrangement with a wardrobe between. The vertical divisions of the walls favoured by progressive designers at this stage are very noticeable. Apart from the affected tier of drawers in the wardrobe this design would not have seemed out of place in an architectural journal of the 1930s. (Both from supplements to *Das Interieur*, Vols II and III, Vienna, *c.*1901 and 1902; the first by Hans Scharfen, the second by Josef Hoffmann.)

*By courtesy of Christian Witt-Döring*

## 506 ▷
## A German lady's sitting-room, Darmstadt
### 1901

This was in a house designed together with all its furnishings by the architect Peter Behrens for the seminally important exhibition of modern building and decoration held in the Artists' Colony at Darmstadt in 1901. It was his first house. Although designed as a show room, it is said that the entire furnishings of the room were subsequently bought by a rich lady as a wedding-present for her daughter, who then had them built into her own house. The room, anyway, betrays an intimate awareness of the progressive experiments being carried out in Vienna at this time, with the stress on vertical divisions, the bold patterns of textiles and the general simplicity of line. A strong Classical character is also present, however, and this reflects the great attraction that the *Biedermeier* style had for German and Austrian designers at this time. Note the elegant electric-light fittings designed by this brilliant architect, who was soon to make a name for himself in the field of industrial design, particularly for his pioneering work with the giant German electricity company A.E.G.

*Germanisches Nationalmuseum, Nürnberg*

DAS INTERIEUR II

85

WANDKÄSTCHEN
BETTANORDNVNG

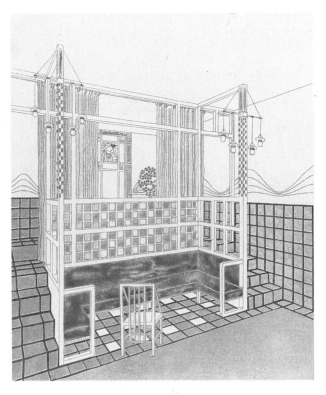

## The elegance of proto-Modern, Darmstadt
### 1906

Design for a living-hall by Valentin Mink. This style depended largely on subtle proportions. Ornament is fairly reticent and the colours are cool. The bow-shaped line of the grate suggests that Mink was a pupil of Olbrich, who had come to Darmstadt in 1899 from Vienna where he had been one of the originators of the ultra-progressive *Secession* style. (From *Moderne Bauformen*, Stuttgart, 1906.)

*Victoria and Albert Museum, London*

### 507, 508 (*above, left and right*)
## Viennese ultra-progressive in colour
### *c.*1900

These stylish designs exemplify perfectly the uncompromising compositions being drawn by progressive architects and decorators in Vienna at the turn of the century. They show the *Secession* style *par excellence*. Although such schemes had their roots in Art Nouveau and in the work of the Glasgow School of architects (Pl.500), they were also the result of a giant intellectual stride: shedding ornament, refining and paring down the elements, reducing the whole to a rigid geometric formula. One room (above, left) was for children and was to have washable surfaces; the other is a guest-room. They form part of a portfolio of designs by Leopold Bauer, one of Professor Otto Wagner's most radical pupils, which were submitted by Bauer to a competition for a 'Connoisseur's House' (*Das Haus eines Kunstfreundes*) which was held in 1901. Other competitors included Baillie Scott and Mackintosh; all three won prizes. (All these submissions were published by Alexander Koch, Darmstadt, 1902, with Hermann Muthesius as editor.)

*Victoria and Albert Museum, London*

## 510
# A young girl's room, Hamburg
### 1908

The style is clearly based on that evolved in Vienna around 1900 by architects such as Olbrich and Hoffmann. The elegant white chairs, with their vertical backs, do not look all that comfortable. The rather cool colouring is typical of progressive architectural schemes at this period. This design is by Otto Struck, who seems to have been an architectural student at this time. (From *Moderne Bauformen*, Stuttgart, 1908.)

*Victoria and Albert Museum, London*

### 511 ▽
## 'Free English' in a villa in Hamburg
### 1912

A German interpretation of the English vernacular style, which was apparently executed. It is by Paul Stosseck of Berlin. This is the complete antithesis of the Viennese progressive style. Rooms in this taste were to be found all over Europe and America. (From *Moderne Bauformen*, Stuttgart, 1912.)

*Victoria and Albert Museum, London*

### 512 △
## Progressive Finnish, Alt Ruppin, near Berlin
### 1909

This elegant design for a lady's sitting-room was apparently executed at a house in a Berlin suburb. It is by the distinguished Finnish architect Eliel Saarinen, whose work was greatly admired in Germany at this stage. This composition clearly has affinities with designs by progressive Viennese architects, and one appreciates why contemporary critics thought it would be difficult to live in such severe surroundings where few concessions were made to bodily comfort. To introduce a cushion into such a room would surely be unpardonable. However, this way the future lay, or part of it: as is well known, Saarinen emigrated to the United States in 1923 and there became a much respected pioneer of the Modern Movement. The columns of the screen in this room owe much to Mackintosh, but in other schemes Saarinen apparently derived inspiration from Baillie Scott (see Pl.515). He was a far greater architect than either. (From *Moderne Bauformen*, Stuttgart, 1909.)

*Victoria and Albert Museum, London*

513
## German Neo-Sheraton, Munich
*c*.1910

The link between fashionable modern and the style of about 1800 is here once again very apparent. The furniture clearly owes much to the designs of Sheraton and of his followers in Germany, but the accentuated verticality and details such as the rectangular lattice of the candlesticks reflect an acute awareness of recent progressive developments in Vienna. This proposal for a dining-room was designed by Paul Ludwig Troost of Munich. (From C.H. Baer, *Farbige Raumkunst*, Stuttgart, 1911.)

*Victoria and Albert Museum, London*

## 514
# Fashionable Neo-*Empire*, Paris
### 1911

This fashion-plate by Georges Lepape shows a fur-trimmed gown designed by Paul Poiret, but it is the setting that really dominates this charming illustration. The dependence of both the gown and the décor on the *Empire* style is not hard to discern. Both in traditionalist and in progressive circles at this period, the *Empire* (and likewise the coeval Regency and *Biedermeier*) provided potent inspiration for architects and decorators. A room decorated in this manner would not have looked wildly out of fashion in Paris in the mid-1920s. Poiret in fact launched an interior decoration workshop under the name 'Martine' in 1911, the year this illustration was published. (From *Les Choses de Paul Poiret*, Paris, 1911.)
*Victoria and Albert Museum, London*

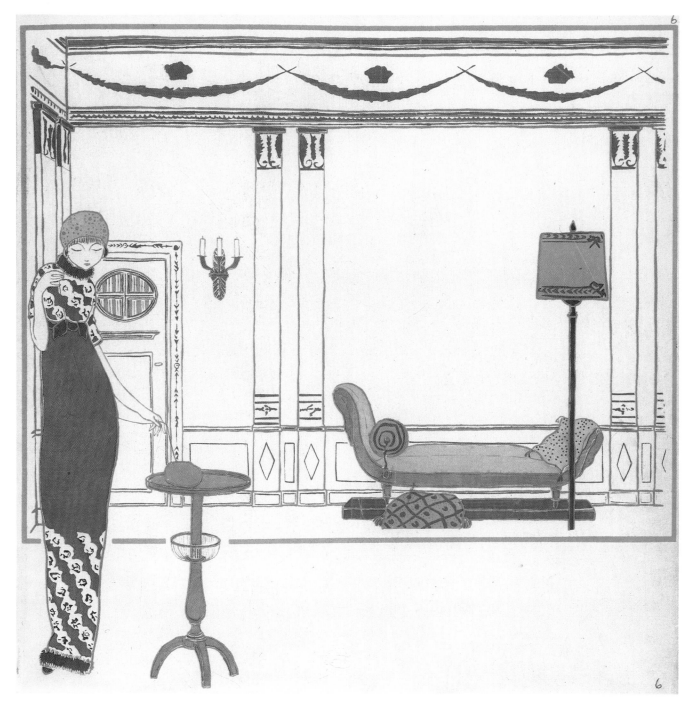

515 ▷
## A country house on the Rhine
### 1907

A design by the distinguished Finnish partnership of Gesellius, Lindgren and Saarinen. The Germans came to admire Eliel Saarinen's work greatly, and he was to build a number of houses in an advanced taste in Germany before the Great War (see Pl.512). This design shows the firm still under the influence of Mackintosh and Baillie Scott, and not yet free from Art Nouveau. But one can see that the seeds of the Modern Movement have been sown. Unity has been neatly contrived in this pretty scheme. (From *Moderne Bauformen*, Stuttgart, 1907.)

*Victoria and Albert Museum, London*

516 (*right, below*)
## Moderate modernism in Sweden
### 1909

Another view by Carl Larsson of his house (see also Pls.467 and 496), showing a more advanced stage in the evolution of its décor. The Larssons read *The Studio* and were aware of the developments taking place in Austria and Germany. This picturesque wooden country cottage is here still furnished with antiques (the green chair is Swedish mid-eighteenth-century even if the colour has been enhanced) and with vernacular pieces, but the new bed owes much to fresh Germanic inspiration, as do its hangings, embroidered so decoratively by Karin Larsson herself. The name of the book in which this was published, *Åt Solsiden* ('On the sunny side', Stockholm, 1910) reflects the perennial Scandinavian demand for more light. This book was only slightly less influential than *Ett Hem* and the German anthology *Das Haus in der Sonne*. It was also published in German soon afterwards under the title *Lasst Licht hinein* ('Let in more light'). No other house in the world can have been so widely publicized, and the influence of these pictures was enormous. Larsson consciously intended them to be propagandist, setting forth a new ideal.

*Victoria and Albert Museum, London*

◁ 517

## Viennese modern in Bucharest
### 1913

The Assan Haus was the first in the modern Viennese style to be erected in Roumania. The architect was Marcell Kammerer but the interiors were decorated by the distinguished Viennese professor of architecture Karl Witzmann, a pupil of Otto Wagner and an adherent of the modern style in an elegant but muted form. This photograph of the 'living-hall' comes from an article on the house by Mme Assan which appeared in the Darmstadt journal *Innen-Dekoration* in 1913, soon after the house had been finished. Note the 'boxed-in' fireplace with small showcases for *objets d'art* above. The walls were white with a green pattern; the furniture was executed in satinwood by the Viennese firm of J. Soulek.

*Victoria and Albert Museum, London*

518 ▷

## Art Nouveau drags on, Paris
### before 1913

The Parisian journal *Art et Décoration* carried a report in 1913 on the interior decoration of the house of the designer Charles Stern, who had employed various artists to decorate it. The paintings by Maurice Denis here seen in the ceiling were shown at the Salon d'Automne in 1910, by which time the room they were to fit must also have been designed – a task given to the firm of Jallot, who also designed the furniture. It will be seen how Art Nouveau features remained fashionable in Paris rather longer than in discriminating circles elsewhere. Indeed, the report speaks of the slow rejuvenation of French design at this period. The carpet was designed by Stern himself.

*Victoria and Albert Museum, London*

◁ 519

## Advanced stylishness in Aachen
### before 1910

Another example of the modern idiom in its moderate guise as practised by quite a few German architects just before the Great War. The rectilinear style, almost unadorned, owes something to the Viennese originality of about 1900, but also looks forward to the characteristic taste of the 1920s. The Haus Hupertz was designed by Professor Carl Sieben of Aachen but the elaborate joinery, executed in American birchwood, was carried out by the Munich firm of A. Pössenbacher. It is curious to find in such reticent surroundings a chandelier of such a heavy, almost Romanesque form; it was made by Wilhelm & Co. of Munich. (From *Innen-Dekoration*, Darmstadt, 1910.)

*Victoria and Albert Museum, London*

520 ▷

## Advanced Parisian taste
### 1912

This room was shown at the 1912 exhibition of the Salon d'Automne. It was designed by Maurice Dufrène, one of the best Parisian architect-designers of the period. In an article in *Art et Décoration* on the Salon of 1912 the room is described as 'Louis-Philippe with lacquer-paint', but the writer praises the sense of discreet and elegant intimacy that Dufrène has conjured up in this '*cabinet de travail*', where 'the deluge of cushions reminds us that not all the hours of the day are given over to work'. In style this room was about as advanced as any to be seen in France at that date.

*Victoria and Albert Museum, London*

◁ 521
## A very different ideal, England
### 1909

Very few people wanted to live *à la Hoffmann* (see Pls.505 and 509), all stiff and rectangular. Something like the room shown here had a very much wider appeal both in established circles and among the aspiring who could afford such things. Neo-Georgian rooms of this kind were widely admired in England and America, in all the Dominions and Colonies (at that time constituting in all not an inconsiderable portion of the world), and the equivalent was admired in many places on the Continent. It was definitely not progressive but it was comfortable, it had grace, and it reminded people of past glories. A few rooms of this sort were furnished with real antiques but most people had to make do with reproductions, and this composition shows pieces that do not quite ring true. That was not the primary concern. It was the effect that mattered. The arrangement is of course quite unlike that which would have been seen in a real Georgian room. The density of the scattered arrangement is unmistakably 'thinned-out late-Victorian' – the Edwardian ideal. (This 'late 18th Century Dining Room' was one of the *Style Schemes in Antique Furnishing* that H.P. Shapland published in London in 1909 with the sub-title *Interiors and their Treatment*.)
*Victoria and Albert Museum, London*

◁ 522
## Another Neo-Georgian room, Newcastle
### *c.*1910

From the catalogue of '*Interior Woodwork*' of Robson & Sons, 'The North Country Firm', as they proudly called themselves. They could provide complete schemes of interior decoration, and had executed work for the S.S. *Mauretania* which was launched in 1909. They had extensive showrooms in Newcastle which included 'Retiring and Tea Rooms for Ladies'. All the illustrations in the catalogue had been 'accomplished for our customers', and, although the purist will shudder while glancing through the booklet, one cannot help feeling that many of the rooms must have been rather comfortable. This drawing-room had panels of silk damask.
*Victoria and Albert Museum, London*

## 523 ▷
## The German equivalent of Neo-Georgian, Berlin
### 1912

This shows a room decked out in the Baroque taste with a Classical structure. As with the English schemes shown in Pls.521 and 522, the furnishings might be genuine but were probably expected to be reproductions. This design by the architect Walther Rathenau was for his own house at Grunewald, on the outskirts of Berlin. Rathenau admired the styles of Gilly and Schinkel and created for himself an unashamed pastiche of their late-Classical taste in this building, which was published in detail in *Moderne Bauformen* in 1912, although this view is from C.H. Baer's *Farbige Raumkunst* (Stuttgart, 1914). Many schemes in this entirely anti-progressive spirit are included in Baer's two volumes.

*Victoria and Albert Museum, London*

## 524 ▷
## Pre-war *Biedermeier* revival, Cologne
### before 1914

*Biedermeier* returned to favour in the 1890s and remained highly acceptable during the early decades of the new century. This pretty scheme by the firm of Rath & Balbach in Cologne has charm and must have been comfortable. Although a certain escapism may imbue this particular composition, which was sketched as war loomed, one gets the impression that such schemes were by no means rare in Germany in the pre-war years. For the many who felt comfortable in such surroundings, the unadorned functionalist rooms that were to be seen here and there held no appeal whatsoever: one could admire their elegance, perhaps, but one could hardly *live* in them. The world was not yet ready for the new architecture. The Modern Movement could not really be established before the 1920s. (From C.H. Baer, *Farbige Raumkunst*, Stuttgart, 1914.)

*Victoria and Albert Museum, London*

## ◁ 525
# Ultra-modern in Leipzig
### 1913

This elegant music-room embodies most of the characteristics of fashionable décor in the 1920s, and few people would be surprised if this caption had read 'Paris, 1925'. This 'proto Art Deco' style had in fact been evolved in Germany by 1910, even if it was not then widespread. The panelling is of rosewood and ebony. Designed by the architect Paul Würzler-Klopsch and shown at an exhibition in Leipzig in 1913. Reproduced from Alexander Koch's survey of recently completed German interiors, *Handbuch neuzeitlicher Wohnungskultur* (Darmstadt, 1914). Würzler-Klopsch also designed the stand at the 1913 Leipzig Exhibition for Koch's influential publishing house.

*Victoria and Albert Museum, London*

## 527 △
# Elegant comfort in Berlin
### before 1914

A further illustration from Koch's *Handbuch neuzeitlicher Wohnungskultur* of 1914. This shows a modernistic interior of a moderate kind, furnished in an immensely comfortable manner with seat-furniture of forms that go back deep into the nineteenth century. Stylistic dash and complete unity of style may be lacking, but this would be an easy room to live in. The architect was Dr Otto March, who held what was no doubt an influential appointment as *Geheim-Baurat* – a privy counsellor on architectural matters. This lady's sitting-room was in the suburb of Charlottenburg.

*Victoria and Albert Museum, London*

## ◁ 526
# A Viennese lady's dressing-room
### before 1914

From Koch's *Handbuch neuzeitlicher Wohnungskultur* of 1914, this room also reflects an advanced taste which looks forward to the 1920s. It is not so uncompromisingly modern, however, and the style of the furniture evidently derives from late Neo-Classical and *Biedermeier*. The source of inspiration for much French Art Deco furniture also of course lay in that general style. The room was designed by Professor Otto Prutscher. The woodwork is white (once again!) and the material a blue satin.

*Victoria and Albert Museum, London*

## 528 ▽
## Comfort in Boston
### 1915

This room is comfortable and not cluttered with a mass of small objects. The general effect is restful. The scattered arrangement still follows the nineteenth-century formula, but there are fewer elements. This room admirably shows the characteristic 'watered-down Victorian' style favoured all over the Western world from the early part of the century and still to a large extent with us today.

This is the music-room in Isabella Stewart Gardner's house in the Boston suburb of Brookline. She had moved here when quite old, but the décor is entirely up-to-date, although the antiques with which she surrounded herself were rather grander than those of most other people at the time. (By Martin Mower.)

*Isabella Stewart Gardner Museum, Boston, Massachusetts*

## 529 ▷
## Neo-*Louis Seize*, Munich
### 1914

Clearly, much here derives from the style of *Louis Seize*; but the elegant linear division of the walls into panels of full height without a dado springs from the early *Modernismus* of around 1900. Designed by Theodor Veil and Gerhard Herms. (From A. Koch, *Handbuch neuzeitlicher Wohnungskultur: Empfangs- und Wohnräume*, Darmstadt, 1914.)

*Victoria and Albert Museum, London*

## 530 △
## Post-war romanticism, Munich
### 1919

During the war years the Modern Movement evolved in neutral Holland. The combatant nations were too preoccupied to contribute much, on the other hand, and when the Great War was over most people wanted to return as quickly as possible to the pleasures and feelings of safety associated with peace. This illustration from a German publication of 1919 exemplifies such nostalgia, the widespread longing for conventional comfort. In the miserable chaos springing from defeat and revolution some young Germans were eagerly seeking to rejuvenate architecture and industrial design, notably at the newly formed Bauhaus, but their efforts did not have any widely noted result until well into the 1920s. This photograph shows a lady's bedroom designed by the Munich architect Ferdinand Götz. (From A. Koch, *Handbuch neuzeitlicher Wohnungskultur*, new series (Bedrooms), Darmstadt, 1919.)

*Victoria and Albert Museum, London*

## 531 △
## Post-war prettiness, Cologne
### 1919

The Cologne firm of Rath & Balbach were renowned for their charming designs which, however, sometimes bordered on the sugary (see Pl.524). After the War such escapist schemes found great favour with the public. This nostalgic composition is essentially Neo-Sheraton or *Louis Seize* in taste, but is also an early example of the numerous chinoiserie rooms in such a pastiche style that were to appear everywhere in the next two decades. This room could well have been created in New York, Paris or London in 1935. (From *Moderne Bauformen*, Stuttgart, 1920.)

*Victoria and Albert Museum, London*

## 532 △
## Munich Classicism
### 1920

This *Festsaal* is couched in a Classical idiom that embodies many of the features of Art Deco, for example the reeded panels and the decoration of the pier-glass. Something very like this was to be the fashionable style for grand rooms in the 1920s and early 1930s. The design is by the versatile Munich architect Franz Gebhard who could work equally well in the 'English Cottage' style. It must be one of the first schemes embodying a true sense of grandeur to appear in Germany after the War. (From *Moderne Bauformen*, Stuttgart, 1920.)

*Victoria and Albert Museum, London*

Opposite: a bedroom-design by Ruhlmann from *Art et Décoration*, a Parisian journal of 1920.
*Victoria and Albert Museum, London*

# NOTES

## Introduction

1  T.B. Macaulay, *History of England from the Accession of James II*, London, 1848, Vol. I, Ch. III.

2  Praz's book first came out in Italian with the title *La filosofia dell'arredamento*, although he did not say all that much about the actual philosophy of furnishing and decoration.

3  Hugh Honour, 'From the House of Life', *The New York Review of Books*, 3 March 1983.

4  Even a photograph may be edited in the sense that items may be removed or shifted around by the photographer before he takes the picture.

5  Harold L. Peterson, *American Interiors from Colonial Times to the late Victorians. A pictorial source book of American domestic interiors . . .*, New York, 1971, p. xii. This book offers a further wide selection of views of interiors and has excellent commentaries.

6  See *Les relations artistiques entre la France et la Suède, 1693–1718. Nicodème Tessin le jeune et Daniel Cronström, Correspondance*, Stockholm, 1964.

7  I owe this piece of information to a discussion I had with Dr Bozenna Majewska-Maszkowska of Warsaw, who has written at length about the Princess and her residences.

8  See Svend Eriksen, *Early Neo-Classicism in France*, London, 1974.

9  Le Camus de Mézieres, *Le Génie de l'Architecture*, Paris, 1780, pp. 111–13.

10  Charles Percier and P.F.L. Fontaine, *Recueil de Décorations intérieures*, the first suite of designs for which was published in Paris in 1801, the whole series coming out together in 1812 (p. 15).

11  John Britton, *The Union of Architecture, Sculpture and Painting . . .*, London, 1827, p. 23.

12  William Mitford, *Principles of Design in Architecture . . .*, 2nd edn., London, 1824, pp. 249–55.

13  Robert Kerr, *The Gentleman's House*, London, 1864, p. 111.

14  Jacob von Falke, *Die Kunst im Hause*, first published in Vienna in 1871 and then in English translation (*Art in the House*) in Boston in 1878, p. 335.

15  Charles Eastlake, *Hints on Household Taste . . .*, London, 1868, p. 173.

16  e.g. P. and M.A. Nicholson, *The Practical Cabinet Maker, Upholsterer and Complete Decorator*, London, 1826; A. Garnier, *Manuel du Tapissier Décorateur*, Paris, 1830; H.W. and A. Arrowsmith, *The House Decorator's and Painter's Guide*, London, 1840 (the Arrowsmiths called themselves 'Decorators to Her Majesty', incidentally).

17  An excellent but all too short survey of early-twentieth-century interior decorating businesses is given in the first pages of John Fowler and John Cornforth's *English Decoration in the 18th Century*, London, 1974.

## 1620–1670

1  Peter Thornton, *Seventeenth-Century Interior Decoration in England, France and Holland*, New Haven and London, 1978, p. 104. The rather immodest number of references in this section to this previous work by the author stems from the fact that it deals in much greater detail with many of the subjects surveyed in the present volume and includes many additional references which it would not be possible to give here.

2  The House of Orange Inventories (*Inventarissen van de Inboedels in de verblijven van de Oranjes . . . 1567–1795*), ed. S.W.A. Drossaers and Th.H. Lunsingh Scheurleer, The Hague, 1974–6. Inventory of the Stadholder's Residence at the Noordeinde, The Hague, 1632, p. 190. In store at the same palace were several more matching suites of furnishings for rooms.

3  The Ham House Inventories (P.K. Thornton and M.F. Tomlin, *The Furnishing and Decoration of Ham House*, The Furniture History Society, London, 1980), invt. of *c*.1654, p. 23.

4  See Thornton, *op. cit.*, pp. 8 and 9, for a more complete evaluation of Mme de Rambouillet's contribution to French interior decoration and planning.

5  The Ham Invts., *op cit.*, *c*.1654, pp. 25–6 and 127–37.

6  Henri Sauval, *Antiquités de Paris*, II, p. 169. This work was published in 1724 but Sauval died in 1670 and was probably writing in the 1650s and 1660s.

7  *Inventaire des Merveilles du Monde rencrontrées dans le Palais du Cardinal Mazarin*, Paris, 1649; published by Le Comte de Laborde, *Le Palais Mazarin . . .*, Paris 1846.

8  Sauval, *op. cit.*, VII, p. 173.

9  *Parentalia : or Memoirs of the Family of Wrens . . . but chiefly of Sir Christopher Wren . . . Compiled by his Son Christopher ; Now published by his grandson, Stephen Wren . . .*, London, 1750, p. 261.

10  Sauval, *op. cit.*, VII, p. 34.

11  Thornton, *op. cit.*, p. 36. A collection of French designs for interior decoration dating from the 1630s to the early 1650s, which is in the Ashmolean Museum, may have belonged to Inigo Jones or to his assistant John Webb. The collection was certainly on the shelves in the Offices of Works, the organization that superintended all royal architectural undertakings, by the late seventeenth century. Most are by Jean Cotelle; three are illustrated here (see Pls.9, 23 and 24). See K.T. Parker, *Catalogue of Drawings in the Ashmolean Museum*, Oxford, 1938, No. 395.

12  The Orange Invts., *op. cit.*, I, p. 196.

13  'Travels in Holland . . . of Sir William Brereton, Bt', *Chetham Society*, London, 1844, p. 33. See also Thornton, *op. cit.*, pp. 38–40.

14  Thornton, *op. cit.*, Pls.65–67.

15  *Parentalia, loc. cit.*

16  See Alfred Marie, *Naissance de Versailles*, Paris, 1968, I, Ch. III.

17  Francis Bacon, *Essays*, 1625, XLV, 'Of Building'.

18  Sauval, *op. cit.*, VII, p. 201.

19  'Travels in Holland . . . of Sir William Brereton, Bt', *Chetham Society, op. cit.* Pepys had several fireplaces 'done with Dutch tiles' (*Diary*, 19 January 1666).

20  Apparently nut-shells glow pleasantly without a flame and produce a certain amount of warmth.

21  An important study of plasterwork ceilings is in Geoffrey Beard's *Stucco in Europe*, London, 1983. It has an excellent bibliography.

22  The French designs at the Ashmolean can have influenced English practice since they seem to have been in the possession of someone in the Office of Works, perhaps already by the middle of the century (see note 11, and John Harris, 'Inigo Jones and his French sources', *Bulletin of the Metropolitan Museum*, New York, May 1961). The Office of Works handled all royal building enterprises and its drawing-office was the principal training centre for architects in England at the time.

23  See note 21.

24  See notes 11 and 22.

25  T. Clemmensen and M. Mackeprang, *Kina og Danmark . . .*, Copenhagen, 1980, pp. 52–60.

26  The Orange Invts., *op. cit.*, p. xxv.

27  See Thornton, *op. cit.*, pp. 75–80.

28  Most astonishing must have been the *Cabinet des Miroirs* in Louis XIV's private apartment at Versailles, begun in 1664 and completed the next year. The walls were totally faced with mirror-glass up to the frieze (see A. Marie, *op. cit.*, Pl.CXLVI). Of the circular *Cabinet aux Miroirs* at the Château de Maisons (about 1650) a visitor in 1664 said that 'whatsoever way you turn yourself you see an army of your owne selfe' (Thornton, *op. cit.*, Pl.97).

29  Elphège Frémy, *Histoire de la Manufacture royale des glaces au 17è et 18è siècle*, Paris, 1909, p. 16. All large plates of glass came from Venice before about 1670.

30  Henry Havard, *Dictionnaire de l'Ameublement . . .*, Paris, 1888–90, 'Miroir'.

31  H.J. Louw, 'The Origin and Development of the Sash-Window . . .', D.Phil. thesis, Oxford University, 1981, cites references to 'making holis for pinns to hold up the shasses in the Queen's Bedchamber' at Whitehall in 1665, for instance, and to rings by means of which one could 'heave up ye shashes' as well as to wooden screws to 'fasten the shashes'. He discusses the invention of counterbalanced sashes in about 1670 in England. His work has now been published as 'The origin of the sash-window' in *Architectural History*, Vol. 26, 1983.

32  R.T. Gunther, *The architecture of Sir Roger Pratt*, Oxford, 1982, p. 66.

33 See Thornton, *op cit.*, p. 89; also H. Kier, *Schmuckfussböden in Renaissance und Barock*, Munich, *c*.1977.

34 See S. Jervis, 'A tortoiseshell cabinet and its precursors', *Victoria and Albert Museum Bulletin*, IV. 4, October 1968; also Thornton, *op. cit.*, pp. 244–7.

35 John Webb, for instance, designed the alcove for Charles II's bedchamber at Greenwich in 1665 and showed the bed in some detail (Thornton, *op. cit.*, Pl.45). His proposal was probably based on French engravings like that reproduced in Pl.12 here. Le Brun was probably designing furniture for the main rooms at Vaux in 1660; he was certainly designing furniture for royal buildings by 1670.

36 Engraved designs for cabinets, beds, tables and other classes of furniture were available during the early part of our period but they were often rather old-fashioned (e.g. those published by Paul Vredeman de Vries in 1630; see S. Jervis, *Printed Furniture Designs before 1650*, The Furniture History Society, London, 1974). When the engravings of Jean Le Pautre appeared, mostly in the 1660s apparently, they must have been welcomed with enthusiasm as revealing something fresh and exciting. Nevertheless an architect wanting to produce a truly coordinated effect cannot have relied solely on these; a contemporary said Le Pautre's designs were 'ideas gauged to fire the imagination' rather than to serve as direct models (see R.A. Weigert, introduction to catalogue of the exhibition *Louis XIV: faste et décors*, Musée des Arts Décoratifs, Paris, 1960).

37 Le Comte de Cosnac, *Les Riches du Palais Mazarin*, Paris, 1884, e.g. p. 787.

38 The term 'dornix' is derived from Doornik, otherwise called Tournai, a city in which great quantities of woollen upholstery materials were produced.

39 Very little work has been done on this class of material. It is admittedly not very glamorous but it can be extraordinarily decorative (see Thornton, *op. cit.*, pp. 108–9 and notes).

40 A diagram showing the components of a typical seventeenth-century bed is given in Thornton, *op. cit.*, p. 150.

41 Historical Manuscripts Commission, VI, p. 275 (De L'Isle and Dudley, 1955).

42 See The Ham Invts., *op. cit.*, e.g. pp. 10, 12 and 20.

43 A variation of this formula had a loop at one end only; the other end of the rod was plain and was pushed first into a fixture like a modern screw-eye, after which the looped end was dropped on to its hook.

44 Turkeywork was technically similar to the knotted pile rugs and carpets of Anatolia but from 1620, at any rate, the patterns used for turkeywork were European in character and were closer to the traditions of needlework than of carpet-weaving.

45 The term 'back-stool' is apt, for it was essentially a square stool with a back formed by extending the legs and adding a back-rest. While this type of chair remained popular, this was how it was usually designated – or one called it simply a 'chair'. In France it was called a '*chaise*', sometimes with the additional designations '*à demoiselle*' (i.e. for women, so this may have had a lower seat), '*à caquetoire*' ('nattering chair', also implying use by women) and '*à vertugadin*' (for farthingales, implying that women wearing these monstrous ring-pads round their waist – see Pl.19 – could nevertheless easily sit on such chairs. The term 'farthingale chair' is not found in English inventories, it seems, but the term has been adopted for this class of chair by some modern writers).

46 Thornton, *op. cit.*, Pl.103.

47 It should be noted that the term '*dais*' in French refers to the canopy or 'cloth of estate' which was normally suspended over such a platform of honour.

48 William Karlson, *Ebba Brahe's Hem*, Lund 1943, note 10. For *Ebba Brahe's Hem* see note 51 in the next section.

49 Thornton, *op. cit.*, p. 118.

50 Thornton, *op. cit.*, p. 109.

51 P. Verlet, *The Savonnerie, Its History. The Waddesdon Collection*, London (The National Trust) and Fribourg, 1982.

52 See Henri d'Orléans, *Inventaire de tous les Meubles du Cardinal Mazarin* (1653), London, 1861.

53 Laborde, *op. cit.*, p. 301.

54 Tallemant de Réaux, *Historiettes*, Paris, 1834–40, III, p. 69 (written 1657–9).

55 'The Inventory and Valuation of The King's [Charles I's] goods, 1649–51', ed. Oliver Millar; *Walpole Society Journal*, Vol. XLII, 1973.

56 Francis Bacon, *The Historie of Life and Death*, London, 1638, pp. 249–50 (Bacon died in 1626). He also advocated anointing the body 'with oyles and salve' after which one sat in the bath for two hours. According to Aubrey, writing at the end of the century, Bacon had at the house he built near St Albans 'two Bathingrooms or Stuffes [from the Italian '*stufa*', a steam bath], whither his Lordship retired afternoons as he saw cause'.

57 When some unhygienic occurrence is described by a seventeenth-century writer it was usually in the knowledge that the reader would agree that what had happened was indeed disgusting.

58 Rush-lights (stripped rushes soaked in fat) only lasted about half an hour: they could not effectively be used for illuminating a grand room.

59 For instance at Somerset House in 1650 there was 'a chest of yellow wax lights' (Charles I Invt.; see note 55).

60 Laborde, *op. cit.*

61 Havard, *op. cit.*, 'Plaques'.

62 Havard, *op. cit.*, 'Carton pierre', and Thornton, *op. cit.*, Pl.262.

63 *Dictionary of English Furniture*, 'Chandelier', London, 1954.

64 'A Memoriall of all the Roomes and the Household Stuffe at Tart-Hall; an Inventory of all the goods there belonging to the Rt. Hon. The Countess of Arundel ... 1641', *The Burlington Magazine*, 1911, pp. 97–100, 233–6 and 341–3.

65 Havard, *op. cit.*, 'Guéridon'.

66 William Sanderson, *Graphice, the use of penn and pensill ...*, London, 1658.

## 1670–1720

1 See Alfred Marie, *Naissance de Versailles*, Paris, 1968, pp. 197–226.

2 See Alfred and Jeanne Marie, *Mansart à Versailles*, Paris, 1972, pp. 3–72.

3 Le Camus de Mézières, *Le Génie de l'Architecture ...*, Paris, 1780.

4 *Letters from Liselotte*, ed. Maria Kroll, London, 1970, letter of 11 August 1716.

5 See Fiske Kimball, *Le Style Louis XV. Origine et évolution du Rococo*, Paris 1949. This was published after the war when the author had had the opportunity of correcting various points in his *Creation of the Rococo* of 1942.

6 Editions appeared in 1694, 1710, 1738 and 1760. That of 1710 is discussed on p. 50.

7 *Les Relations artistiques entre la France et la Suède 1693–1718. Extraits d'une correspondance entre l'architecte Nicodème Tessin et Daniel Cronström*, ed. R.A. Weigert and C. Hernmarck, Stockholm, 1964, letter of 3 January 1694.

8 In Stockholm, for example, and in various German cities.

9 See Peter Thornton, *Seventeenth-Century Interior Decoration ...*, New Haven and London, 1978, p. 342.

10 Information kindly supplied by Reinier Baarsen.

11 Jean Courtonne, *Traité de la Perspective*, Paris, 1725. He also noted how the character of interior decoration in important French houses had changed completely over the previous thirty years or so. He thought the modern forms were altogether too restless, perhaps all right for furniture and carriages but not for architectural features.

12 The additional pages are all marked with a star against the page-number.

13 Henry Havard, *Dictionnaire de l'Ameublement*, Paris, 1888–90, 'Lit'.

14 *The Travels of Cosmo the Third, Grand Duke of Tuscany, through England during the reign of Charles II* [1669], London, 1821.

15 John Evelyn described a fashionable dressing-room entertainingly in his *Mundus Muliebris, or the Ladies Dressing-Room unlock'd and her toilette spread*, London, 1690.

16 See Thornton, *op. cit.*, Pl.22. Cronström, reporting to Tessin in 1695 (see note 7 above), stated that sofas should be 'covered like the chairs' (letter of 7 January 1695).

17 Havard, *op. cit.*, 'Sopha'. To the writer a sofa must have resembled what he knew about the Near Eastern *divan*, which was in fact to become the 'ottoman' of the early 1800s. Cronström (see the previous note) also claimed in 1695 that 'There is now no room here [in Paris] where there is not one'.

18 See Thornton, *op. cit.*, pp. 172–4 and 210–17.

19 G. Eland, *Shardeloes Papers*, London, 1947, p. 11.

20 *Letters from Liselotte* (see note 4), letter from Paris of 24 March 1718. She added that 'the top is very fine' and was presumably inlaid or faced with marquetry. It has 'gilt ornaments', probably of brass or bronze.

21 *Ibid.*, letter of 25 February 1706.

22 See Thornton, *op. cit.*, pp. 78–9 and the associated notes.

23 Celia Fiennes saw a wall of composite mirror-glass at Chippenham in the late seventeenth century and noted particularly that 'it shows one from top to toe' (*The Journeys of Celia Fiennes*, ed. Christopher Morris, London, 1947).

24 *Portes à placard et lambris dessinez par le Sr. Mansard et nouvellement executez dans quelques Maisons Royales*, about 1690; *Livres de Cheminées executées dans les apartemens de Versailles sur les desseins de Monsieur Mansart surintendant*;

*Livre de Cheminées executées à Marly sur les desseins de Monsr. Mansart surintendant*, 1699; *Cheminées à la Royalle à grand miroir et tablette*, about 1698; *Cheminées et Lambris à la mode executez dans les nouveaux bâtimens de Paris*, 1690s. See Fiske Kimball, 'The development of the "Cheminée à la Royale"', *Studies*, Metropolitan Museum, New York, 1934.

25 Jean Bérain, *Desseins de cheminées dediez à Monsieur Jules Hardouin Mansart*, 1699; *Nouvelles Cheminées gravé sur les desseins de M. Francard, Architecte du Roi*, 1690s.

26 H. Kreisel, *Deutsche Spiegelkabinette*, Darmstadt, c.1953.

27 Daniel Marot, *Nouvelle Cheminées à panneaux de glace à la manière de France*, Amsterdam, c.1695; *Nouveaux lievre de Cheminées à la Hollandoise*; *Nouvelles Cheminées faittes en plusieur en droits de la Hollande et autres provinces*, n.d.

28 See P. K. Thornton and M. F. Tomlin, *The Furnishing and Decoration of Ham House*, London, 1980, Ch. III.

29 For further information see Kimball, *op. cit.*; F. Lenygon, *Decoration in England from 1660 to 1770*, London, 1914; Nathaniel Lloyd, *A History of the English House*, London, 1931; John Fowler and John Cornforth, *English Decoration in the 18th century*, London, 1974.

30 Eagerly awaited at the time of writing is Ian Bristow's study of ancient paintwork, which is based on extensive research carried out over the last few years in Britain.

31 See Thornton, *op. cit.*, pp. 90–2.

32 See Fiske Kimball, *op. cit.*, Fig. 119.

33 Tessin Correspondence (see note 7); letters of 29 November 1694 and 7 January 1695.

34 *Ibid.*, 7 January 1695. Gilt leather was also not considered suitable for all seasons, he indicates. Anyway, it hardly seems a practical material to use if one intends to exchange it with summer hangings every six months, since it was usually mounted on a framework that was then fitted to the wall.

35 Some authorities insist that mohair was a worsted material. The arguments are set out in Thornton, *op. cit.*, p. 116.

36 Tessin Correspondence (see note 7), letter of 24 February 1702.

37 This was probably what was meant by a 'rising tester', a term met with in inventories of the period.

38 G. Jackson-Stops, 'William III and French Furniture', *Furniture History*, VII, 1971.

39 Thornton, *op. cit.*, p. 168. Nicodemus Tessin, during a visit in 1687, describes the bed: 'Le lict est en forme de lict d'ange et admirablement beau . . . le pavillon est suspendu du toict avec cordons et houppes d'or . . .'.

40 Havard, *op. cit.*, 'Lit'.

41 At Augsburg in 1581 the saddlers were permitted to make the woodwork for chairs, which shows they were in the business of padding chairs, for they would be unlikely to have any other reason to enter the woodworking field. They were not allowed to train apprentices, however. The coffer-makers (*Kistler*) were also permitted to cover chairs at this time (see F. Hellwag, *Die Geschichte des Deutschen Tischlerhandwerks*, Berlin, 1924, p. 78). The future Karl X of Sweden, who came to the throne in 1654, had some stuffed chairs provided by his Court Saddler. They were stuffed with reindeer-hair (see W. Karlson, *Stât och Vardag i Stormaktstidens herremanshem*, Lund, 1945).

42 Savary des Bruslons, in his *Dictionnaire de Commerce* of 1723, under the heading 'Rotin' (cane), refers to caned chairs 'of which one makes such great use and so extensive a commerce in England and in Holland, and which begin to be adopted in France'.

43 See Thornton, *op. cit.*, pp. 206–7.

44 A French tariff of import duties in 1664 refers to '*tapis d'Angleterre*' which was 'for chairs and furnishing' (Havard, *op. cit.*, 'Tapis'). Chair-covers of what looks like English turkeywork are to be found in Scandinavia although how long they have been there is not known; seat-furniture with this covering was also known on the East Coast of North America. See also Jonathan L. Fairbanks and Elisabeth Bidwell Bates, *American Furniture, 1620 to the Present*, London, 1981, p. 39, portrait dated 1674 from Boston, Mass.

45 This is a big subject and cannot be treated at length here. The reader will find more information in Thornton, *op. cit.*, pp. 217–25.

46 Unpublished inventory in the archives of the Duke of Northumberland at Alnwick Castle; information kindly communicated by his daughter, The Lady Victoria. There were, incidentally, three 'Beaver carpetts' in the house. In a related inventory of Syon House, reference is made to a carpet of Yorkshire turkeywork; most turkeywork came from Norwich at that date.

47 Inventory of Dr Thomas Lockey, Canon of Christ Church, Oxford, and erstwhile Bodley's Librarian, *Bodleian Library Record*, V, 1954–6.

48 The Lockey inventory (see previous note) also makes mention of three striped carpets in a room with striped hangings. They can hardly have been table-carpets and are more likely to have been of a woollen cloth of some kind, like 'Scotch carpeting'. At the beginning of the eighteenth century, a room at Dyrham had a complete *ameublement* of 'Scots Plodd' or plaid which presumably also had a tartan effect; the walls were hung with it, the window-curtains were made of it, and the chairs were covered in this material.

49 However, Voltaire, in his *Dictionnaire Philosophique*, claimed that the night-table, as it was first called, was invented in 1717. He gives no further information. Night-tables as a new phenomenon are discussed on p. 147; see also Pls.160 and 161.

50 Havard, *op. cit.*, 'Tapis'.

51 A particularly revealing series of inventories is those of Ebba Brahe, a powerful Swedish lady who owned several houses both in Stockholm and out in the country (William Karlson, *Ebba Brahe's Hem*, Lund, 1943). They range from 1665 through the 1670s. She had shellwork pictures in silver frames, glass flower-pots with glass flowers, glass pictures with glazed frames, gilt repoussé copper pictures with gilded frames, pictures executed in straw-work, some vases with silk lilies, wax fruit in a basket of beadwork, 'Indian pictures' on paper (presumably Chinese paintings) in frames, engravings in blue frames, and a plaster figure on a chimneypiece.

52 Celia Fiennes, *op. cit.*

53 Geoffrey Wills, *English Looking-glasses*, London, 1965, p. 140.

54 Jean de la Bruyère, *Caractères*, 1688.

55 Celia Fiennes, *op. cit.*

## 1720–1770

1 The Venetian architect Giacomo Leoni, who was practising in England, published a translation of Palladio's *Quatro Libri del Architettura* in two volumes in 1715 and 1716.

2 Daniel Neal, *History of New England*, 1720. Neal was a Londoner. Much the same could no doubt be said of Philadelphia, Charleston and Williamsburg.

3 For general information about the background to the English Palladian style the reader is referred to Sir John Summerson, *Architecture in Britain, 1530–1830*, London, 1969 (5th edn.); Geoffrey Beard, *Craftsmen and Interior Decoration in England, 1660–1820*, Edinburgh, 1981; and John Fowler and John Cornforth, *English Decoration in the 18th Century*, London, 1974.

4 Houghton was the subject of a special monograph: Isaac Ware and William Kent, *The Plans, Elevations and Sections; Chimney-Pieces, and Ceilings of Houghton in Norfolk*, 1735.

5 Fowler and Cornforth, *op. cit.*, p. 45.

6 G. Smith, *Laboratory, or School of Arts*, London, 1756 edn.

7 Another work which complements Blondel's seminal treatise is Charles-Etienne Briseux's *L'Art de bâtir des Maisons de Campagne . . . de leur distribution, de leur construction, & de leur décoration*, Paris, 1743.

8 Blondel, *Architecture françoise*, Paris, 1752, Vol. I, pp. 117, 26, 35, 122.

9 These matters are treated by Fiske Kimball, *Le Style Louis XV. Origine et évolution du Rococo*, Paris, 1949, the French revised version of *The Creation of the Rococo*, Philadelphia, 1943; Blondel also makes reference to these buildings in his *Traité* and *Cours*.

10 Good examples of such a veneer are to be seen in the publications of Abraham Swan which enjoyed great popularity for, as he informed his readers, his designs were 'for much General Use than the grand and Pompous Designs published by others'. He was aiming primarily at 'Gentlemen of moderate Fortunes [rather] than of Great Estates' (*A Collection of Designs in Architecture*, 1757; see also *The British Architect: or Builder's Treasury . . .*, 1745). When the Classical foundation is discarded, English Rococo often goes completely out of control, as in many of the designs of Thomas Johnson and of Chippendale.

11 For further information see Svend Eriksen, *Early Neo-Classicism in France*, London, 1974; Michel Gallet, *Demeures parisiennes, l'époque de Louis XVI*, Paris, 1964; Allan Braham, *The Architecture of the French Enlightenment*, London, 1980.

12 It was originally to be entitled *Livre d'Architecture contenant différens desseins de la Décoration intérieure*.

13 Eriksen, *op. cit.*, p. 205.

14 *Recueil d'antiquités égyptiennes, étrusques, grecques et romaines*. Caylus had been taught the art of engraving by Watteau and engraved all the plates in his great publication.

15 See Eileen Harris, *The Furniture of Robert Adam*, London, 1963 (a new edition is in preparation); Damie Stillman, *The Decorative Work of Robert Adam*, London, 1966; Geoffrey Beard, *The Work of Robert Adam*, London, 1978.

16 See Thomas Chippendale, *The Gentleman and Cabinet-Maker's Director*, London, 1754, but more especially the third edition of 1762.

17 Some idea of the sort of preposterous compositions Chambers had in mind may be gained from a glance at Edwards and Matthew Darly's *A New Book of Chinese Designs* of 1754.

18 'My Gothick Building is now completed', wrote William Shenstone in July 1749 (*Letters*, ed. Marjorie Williams, Oxford, 1939) of his house at Leassowes.

19 As Clive Wainwright has observed, Strawberry Hill is 'one of the best-documented eighteenth-century houses in the country'. Apart from all Walpole's letters to his friends recording progress and consulting them about details, the *Description* he published in 1774 and then (revised and illustrated) in 1784 provides a wealth of information.

20 The huge plates of mirror-glass inset in the piers of the drawing-room at Osterley, dating from about 1773, must be French, from Saint-Gobain, because no English factory could perform the feat of producing sheets of this size. Indeed, the glass in the chimneypiece in the bedchamber, which must date from about 1778, is recorded in the inventory of 1782 as being '1st plate made in England'.

21 L.S. Mercier, *Tableau de Paris*, 1782–3; also Shenstone, *op. cit.*, letter of 6 June 1749.

22 J.F. Blondel, *Discours sur la Nécessité de l'étude de l'Architecture*, Paris, 1754.

23 J.F. Blondel, *Traité d'Architecture dans le goût moderne*, Paris, 1737/8.

24 The following analysis springs from Blondel's *Maisons de Plaisance* (1737–8) and *Architecture française* (1752). C.E. Briseux's *L'Art de bâtir des Maisons de Campagne* (1743) provides supplementary comments.

25 Le Blond (1710, see p. 50) had proposed that the *second* antechamber be used as a dining-room.

26 The myth that the French did not have dining-rooms is once again contradicted by Blondel, for the term is used in the title of this plate.

27 Henry Havard, *Dictionnaire de l'Ameublement*, Paris, 1888–90, 'Lit'.

28 See Eriksen, *op. cit.*, p. 55.

29 Victor, Marquis de Mirabeau, *L'Ami des hommes*, 1759.

30 Mercier de Compiègne, *Manuel des boudoirs, ou Essais érotiques sur les Demoiselles d'Athènes*, published at 'Cythère' (Paris), 1727.

31 Le Blond mentioned such arrangements in 1710 (see p. 50) but seemed rather unclear about the way they functioned – as if they were still very rare in France.

32 Havard, *op. cit.*, 'Garderobe'.

33 'The chimney-piece being the first thing designed, and the fixed point from which the architect is to direct his work in the rest' of the room (Isaac Ware, *A Complete Body of Architecture*, London, 1756).

34 W. & J. Welldon, *The Smith's Right Hand ... containing Near Forty genteel, new, and beautiful Designs for ... Stoves*, London, 1765. Franklin stoves were also known in France. A certain J.F. Desnarod published a *Mémoire sur les Foyers* in Paris in 1789, illustrating '*foyers de Docteur Franklin*' in three sizes, as if they were available for sale. He states that the Chevalier Fossé had further developed the stove in 1786.

35 Letter of 17 December, 1716. See R. Halsband, *The Selected Letters*, London, 1970, and *The Life*, 1956.

36 Mercier, *op. cit.*

37 Havard, *op. cit.*, 'Poêle'.

38 E.g. Fiske Kimball, *op. cit.*; Svend Eriksen, *op. cit.*; G. Beard, *op. cit.*; Francis Lenygon (M. Jourdain) *Decoration in England from 1660 to 1770*, London, 1914, and revised edn., 1927, covering 1640 to 1766.

39 Isaac Ware, *op. cit.*, p. 469.

40 See note 30 in the previous section.

41 See note 18. Letters of 14 July 1751; 14 March and 6 June 1752. According to Mayhew and Myers (see note 48), papier mâché ceiling-ornaments were reaching America

from London by the 1760s.

42 See *Historic Paper Hangings from Temple Newsam and other English Houses*, catalogue of an exhibition held at Temple Newsam, Leeds, in 1983.

43 See C.C. Oman and J. Hamilton, *Wallpapers*, Victoria and Albert Museum, London, 1982, p. 47. This work contains an excellent survey of the subject.

44 Havard, *op. cit.*, 'Papier peint'. See below for further information on wallpaper.

45 In 1765 and 1766 the fall in the export of these goods to France from England was dramatic, as the Customs records show.

46 *London Evening Post*, 15–18 October 1737.

47 Chippendale's bill covering the period 1767–8 refers to 'cutting out the prints, borders & ornaments & hanging them' in a dressing-room. The ornaments included 'bustos', festoons, knots, vases, pedestals and 'sayters'. See P. Thornton, 'The Furnishing of Mersham-le-Hatch', *Apollo*, April and June 1970.

48 Edgar Mayhew and Minor Myers, *A Documentary History of American Interiors ...*, New York, 1980, p. 68.

49 Havard, *op. cit.*, 'Glace'.

50 See Hiltrud Kier, *Schmuckfussböden in Renaissance und Barock*, Munich, 1976.

51 Also see Praz, *An Illustrated History of Interior Decoration*, London, 1964, Pls. 116 and 117.

52 Isaac Ware, *op. cit.*

53 P. Thornton, *Baroque and Rococo Silks*, London, 1965, p. 135. This was embodied in the Regulations of 1787, but will have reflected the then existing position.

54 Havard, *op. cit.*, 'Pékin', says they were imitated in France, notably at Valence. The French variety could be decorated either with chinoiseries or with European designs.

55 *Ibid.*

56 *Colonial Williamsburg Today*, special edition on the Governor's Palace, Vol. III, No. 3, 1981. On this subject, see also Fowler and Cornforth, *op. cit.*, pp. 125–7.

57 Annabel Westman has a paper on this subject awaiting publication, which she has very kindly allowed me to see. It clarifies the terminology, which is confusing.

58 *The Public Advertiser*, 8 July 1754.

59 Havard, *op. cit.*, 'Rideau'.

60 Burney Newspaper Collection, British Museum, *The Craftsman*, 15 February 1735 and 1 August 1741.

61 Havard, *op. cit.*, 'Store'.

62 Havard, *op. cit.*, 'Jalousie'.

63 Havard, *op. cit.*, 'Rideau'. He says they were of cotton at this early date.

64 Charles F. Hummel, 'Floor coverings used in eighteenth-century America', *Proceedings, Irene Emery Round Table on Museum Textiles*, ed. Patricia Fiske, The Textile Museum, Washington, D.C., 1976.

65 'The Travels through England of Dr Richard Pococke', ed. J.J. Cartwright, *The Camden Society*, London, 1888.

66 Havard, *op. cit.*, 'Tapis'.

67 Hummel, *op. cit.*; see also Margaret Swain, 'A Note on Scotch carpets', *Furniture History*, XIV, 1978.

68 Havard, *op. cit.*, 'Tapis'.

69 Hummel, *op. cit.*

70 *Ibid.*

71 See C.F.C. Tattersall, *A History of British Carpets*, London, 1934. Much fresh information on the English carpet-weaving establishments and the French artisans who came over to work in them is contained in Pierre Verlet's recent work on *The Savonnerie* (a Waddesdon Manor catalogue), London and Fribourg, 1982.

72 Susan H. Anderson, *The Most Splendid Carpet*,

Philadelphia, 1978.

73 Sarah B. Sherrill, 'Oriental carpets in seventeenth- and eighteenth-century America', *Antiques Magazine*, January 1976. Smyrna was the chief port for this trade from Turkey and here implies a large carpet; 'segiadya' was a corruption of the Arabic word for a prayer-rug.

74 Nina Fletcher Little, *Floor Coverings in New England before 1750*, Sturbridge, 1967.

75 Eriksen, *op. cit.*, pp. 83–93. He can only firmly establish the presence of straight legs by the mid-1760s in France, although he suggests they were to be seen earlier. In England the fact that Kent and the Neo-Palladians favoured straight-legged chairs with Classical details confuses the issue somewhat, but Chambers designed a chair with straight legs for the Society of Arts in 1759 which still exists, and Stuart designed chairs for Kedleston in 1757 with straight legs.

76 W. Stengel, *Alte Wohnkultur*, Berlin, 1958, p. 144. He also claims he has seen a mention of a sprung sofa in 1766 but gives no reference. He cites a reference to an English bed with steel springs in 1738, incidentally.

77 Christopher Gilbert, 'The Temple Newsam furniture bills', *Furniture History*, 1967.

78 Adam Smith, *The Theory of Moral Sentiments*, 1759.

79 This was in 1760. See Geoffrey de Bellaigue, *Preferences in French Furniture*, Wallace Collection Monograph No. 2, London, 1979.

80 Anthony Coleridge, *Chippendale Furniture ...*, London, 1968, p. 166.

81 Except in a few rather eccentric English arrangements (e.g. at Hinton House and at Corsham).

82 Havard, *op. cit.*, 'Lampe', 'Garderobe', and 'Veilleuse'.

# 1770–1820

1 For further information about this and other important Parisian houses of the period, see the works of Gallet, Braham, and Eriksen mentioned in note 11 in the previous section.

2 See Michel Gallet, 'La Maison de Madame Vigée-Lebrun . . .', *Gazette des Beaux-Arts*, LVI, 1960.

3 R. and J. Adam, *The Works in Architecture*, London, Vol. II, 1779, and Vol. I, 1773–8.

4 The architect Bélanger designed three carpets to go in the luxuriously appointed mansion of the Duchesse de Mazarin (Pl.205). One was to be woven at the Savonnerie workshops on the edge of Paris. Another was to be produced at Beauvais. But the third was to be made in England, maybe at Moorfields. Admittedly Bélanger had been to England and will have seen fine English carpets. Nevertheless it betokens considerable respect for the English product – or great trust in her architect – that this fastidious lady considered placing this order *outre-Manche*.

5 An interesting article in this connection is that by Hedvig Szabolcsi, 'English influence on Hungarian furniture at the end of the eighteenth century', *Furniture History*, 1973.

6 Mention should here also be made of George Richardson's *Book of Ceilings composed in the style of the antique grotesque* which appeared in 1776 and must have helped to spread further the 'Adam style'.

7 See Svend Eriksen, *Early Neo-Classicism in France*, London, 1974, Pl.82.

8 Juste-François Boucher brought out several suites of 'arabesques' in the mid-1770s, which no doubt also helped spread the style.

9 The upholsterer Sherringham had working for him Louis Delabrière, a painter who had probably worked for the Comte d'Artois, the future King Charles X of France and a friend of the Prince of Wales. Artois' pavilion, the Bagatelle, was one of the most admired creations in its day. Most of the loose furnishings at Carlton House came from Paris, supplied by Daguerre, and included chairs by Jacob and tables believed to be by Weisweiler.

10 It is doubtful whether Sheraton's book would have been so readily welcomed abroad if George Hepplewhite's *The Cabinet-Maker and Upholsterer's Guide* (1788) had not previously aroused interest in English furniture. The style Hepplewhite promulgated was a simplified version of that of Robert Adam and architects working in the same general Neo-Classical idiom (e.g. James Wyatt, Thomas Leverton and John Carr), which placed it within reach of middle-class clients.

11 For example, an edition of Percier and Fontaine's famous *Recueil de Décorations intérieures* (1801–12) was published in Venice in 1843. See also p. 210.

12 I am much indebted to Hans Ottomeyer for information on the work of Percier and his contemporaries which is so admirably set out in Herr Ottomeyer's doctoral thesis on *Das frühe Oeuvre Charles Perciers* (Ludwig-Maximilians University, Munich, 1976); published by D. Gräbner, Altendorf, 1981). Apparently the *Recueil* appeared in *cahiers* from 1801, fifty-four plates having been published by 1805 and all seventy-two by 1812.

13 Like Percier and Fontaine's *Recueil* (see previous note), the first *cahier* was published in 1804 with all twenty-four *cahiers* appearing in book form in 1820. Its first title made specific mention of interior decoration.

14 La Mésangère was a publisher who in 1799 took over the *Journal des Dames et des Modes*, from the office of which he then also subsequently published his *Meubles* which kept his readers informed on matters of taste in furnishings and reached a wide public in France and abroad. About 100 plates appeared in the first year of publication (1802–3) and some 450 were out by 1814, after which they came out at the rate of eighteen a year.

15 E.g. *Magazin für Freunde eines geschmackvollen Ameublements*, Berlin; *Journal des Luxus und der Moden* and its successors, Weimar; *Magazin für Industrie und Literatur*, Leipzig; *Konst och Nyhetsmagazin*, Stockholm (from 1818); and Rudolph Ackermann's (note the German connection) *Repository of Arts, Literature, Commerce, Manufactures, Fashions, and Politics*, London, 1809–28.

16 Quoted by Ottomeyer, *op. cit.*, p. 195.

17 C.R. Cockerell's diary; see D. Watkin, *The Life and Work of C.R. Cockerell*, 1974.

18 Sir Robert Smirke, unpublished treatise on architecture: about 1815–20 (MS. in R.I.B.A. Library, London).

19 Nathaniel Whitlock (*The Decorative Painters' and Glaziers' Guide* . . ., London, 1827) states that 'Only large apartments look well' in the Egyptian style while the Chinese taste 'is best adapted to small fancy apartments'. The reader may also like to refer to *The Inspiration of Egypt*, the catalogue of an exhibition held at the Brighton Museum in 1983.

20 Chinoiserie is of course very different from japonnerie. The latter played an important role in the late nineteenth century (see p. 311).

21 N. Pevsner, *Some Architectural Writers of the Nineteenth Century*, Oxford, 1972, p. 61.

22 *Ibid.*, p. 26. *Specimens* . . . was the famous work illustrated by Auguste Pugin, father of A.W.N. Pugin.

23 R. and J. Adam, *op. cit.*, Vol. I, pp. 9 and 10.

24 *Ibid.*, Vol. II, in his discussion of Derby House.

25 Stéphanie-Félicité Brulat de Genlis, *Dictionnaire critique et raisonné des Étiquettes de la Cour, ou l'Esprit des Étiquettes et des Usages anciens comparés aux modernes*, Paris, 1818.

26 Antoine Caillot, *Vie publique des Français*, Paris, 1788, II.

27 *Moderne i Kiøbenhavn for begge Kiøn og Vaerelsers Møblering efter Moden for Aar 1777*. I am indebted to Dr Tove Clemmensen for providing me with a photocopy of this rare work.

28 Louis Simond, *Journal of a Tour and Residence in Great Britain during the years 1810 and 1811*, Edinburgh, 1817. Simond was a resident of New York City at this time.

29 'Will it be credited, that, in a corner of the very dining-room, there is a certain convenient piece of furniture, to be used by any body who wants it.' The article could be kept in a small closet, but not a few sideboards in the Sheraton style of the 1790s and a bit later have a small cupboard at the side for the purpose. Sheraton, indeed, explains how the left-hand drawer of a sideboard is 'sometimes made very short, to give place to a pot-cupboard behind' (T. Sheraton, *Drawing-Book*, 1793, p. 364).

30 *Mémoirs de la Reine Hortense publiés par le Prince Napoléon, avec notes par Jean Hanoteau*, Paris, 1836, Vol. II, p. 107.

31 *Mémoirs de Madame de Chastenay, 1771–1815*, Paris, 1897, p. 160. Pierre Verlet most generously sent me this quotation.

32 See F.J.B. Watson, *Louis XVI Furniture*, London, 1960, p. 35, where is illustrated a plan of the *salon* at the Hôtel de Nivernais about 1780 where the two banks of chairs are shown very clearly. This drawing was made by a Swedish royal architect. Why he should have drawn it is difficult to explain. The formal arrangement of *chaises meublantes* cannot have been unknown in Sweden at that date. There may have been something unusual about the arrangement, perhaps the placing of the *chaises courantes* (movable chairs), or that the other chairs were placed curiously, slightly overlapping into the window-embrasures, that is, not precisely aligned on the pilasters. The plan is also reproduced by P. Verlet, *French Furniture and Interior Decoration of the 18th century*, London, 1967, Fig. 88.

33 M. Girouard, *Life in the English Country House*, London, 1978. See pp. 236–8 in the present connection.

34 *The Diary of Fanny Burney*, ed. L. Gibbs, London, 1940, pp. 79–85.

35 See Girouard, *op. cit.*, p. 237 (illus.).

36 Sale of stock of Matthew Gregson, Upholder, Liverpool, 1814. Information kindly communicated by June Dean through Simon Jervis.

37 The Christie's sale was held on 25 November 1825. There had been two auctions of ancient stained glass already in 1761, according to Edmund Bartell, *Hints for Picturesque Improvements in Ornamental Cottages*, London, 1804, p. 24.

38 Geoffrey Beard, *The Work of Robert Adam*, Edinburgh, 1978, includes excellent colour illustrations of designs for painted ceilings, for example.

39 See E. Croft-Murray, *Decorative Painting in England, 1537–1837*, Vol. II, London, 1970, Figs. 117 and 118.

40 T. Sheraton, *The Cabinet-Maker, Upholsterer and General Artist's Encyclopaedia*, London, 1804.

41 Mme de Genlis, *op. cit.*, 'Manufactures'. The Weimar *Journal* also mentioned a rival manufactory in Leipzig. A complete room, made of far more costly materials, was designed and created in Paris by the most celebrated artisans and then exported in sections to Madrid where it was erected at the royal palace as a closet for the King of Spain. It is illustrated in the 1812 edition of Percier and Fontaine's *Recueil*. The walls were of mahogany and the ornaments 'of platinum', the *Recueil* states.

42 See C.C. Oman and J. Hamilton, *Wallpapers*, London, 1982, which includes an excellent survey of the history of wallpaper and a catalogue of the extensive collection in the Victoria and Albert Museum. For information on the use of wallpaper in England, see A. Wells-Cole, *Historic Paper Hangings from Temple Newsam and other English Houses*, Leeds, 1983.

43 Mme de Genlis, *op. cit.*, 'Ameublements'.

44 Smith's book was much inspired by Thomas Hope's publication but the plates are of poor quality. One of them is dated 1 January 1807 so must have been drawn already in 1806.

45 E. Bartell, *op. cit.*

46 The looking-glass at Osterley specified as being '1st plate made in England' in an inventory of the house made in 1782 must date from about 1775, and came either from Southwark or the then recently established works at Ravenshead in Lancashire. However, the making of plate-glass in England was not of much consequence until French competition was held back by hostilities in the Napoleonic War.

47 Nina Fletcher Little, *Floor Coverings in New England before 1850*, Old Sturbridge Village, 1967.

48 See Hermann Schmitz, *Schloss Paretz* . . ., Berlin, c.1920.

49 James Malton, *An Essay on British Cottage Architecture*, London, 1798, p. 58.

50 Bartell, *op. cit.*, p. 40.

51 Mme de Genlis, *op. cit.*, 'Ameublements'.

52 Harold L. Peterson, *American Interiors* . . ., New York, 1971, Pl.17.

53 George Smith, *Household Furniture*, London, 1808, p. 2.

54 An excellent essay on this subject is Samuel J. Dornsife's 'Design Sources for Nineteenth-Century Window Hangings', *Winterthur Portfolio*, No. 11, 1975.

55 H. Havard, *Dictionnaire de l' Ameublement*, Paris, 1888–90, 'Store'.

56 Susan H. Anderson, *The Most Splendid Carpet*, Philadelphia, 1978. See also. W. Hefford, 'Thomas Moore of Moorfields', *Burlington Magazine*, CXXIX, December 1977.

57 Audrey Michie, 'The Fashion for Carpets in South Carolina', 1735–1820, *Journal of Early Southern Decorative Arts*, May 1982.

58 L. Boynton, 'Sir Richard Worsley's Furniture at Appuldurcombe Park', *Furniture History*, Vol. I, 1965.

59 Charles Hummel, 'Floor coverings used in eighteenth-century America', *Proceedings, Irene Emery Round Table on Museum Textiles*, ed. Patricia Fiske, The Textile Museum, Washington, D.C., 1976.

60 Michie, *op. cit.*

61 *Ibid.*

62 W. Stengel, *Alte Wohnkultur*, Berlin, 1958, p. 145; Havard, *op. cit.*, 'Matelas'.

63 Mme de Genlis, *op. cit.*, 'Manufactures'.

64 Stengel, *loc. cit.*

65 Dorothy Holley, 'Upholstery Springs', *Furniture History*, XVII, 1981.

66 Scottish Record Office GD1/377/40, bundle 1, item 23 and National Library of Scotland, Acc. 4796/26/2. My attention was kindly drawn to these documents by Ian Gow.

67 Mme de Genlis, *op. cit.*, 'Couches'.

68 Caillot, *op. cit.*

69 Stengel, *op. cit.*, p. 135.

70 Bartell, *op. cit.*, 1804.

71 This statement needs qualifying. Red boullework (the red being contrived with pigment under a layer of tortoiseshell) was also popular at this period, but it probably did not carry the same haughty message. Red boullework was relatively uncommon in the seventeenth century; it was probably mostly intended for use in pretty rather than grand settings.

72 Between ten and twenty times that of a candle. Sir Benjamin Thompson (Count Rumford) claimed in 1811 that 'no decayed beauty ought ever to expose her face to the direct rays of the Argand lamp'. See Jane S. Shadel, 'Glass Lighting Devices', in *Lighting in America*, ed. L.S. Cooke, New York, 1975, a useful collection of articles on lighting first published in *Antiques Magazine*.

73 Havard, *op. cit.*, 'Lampe'.

74 Shadel, *op. cit.*

75 Havard, *op. cit.*, 'Lampe'; also E. Mayhew and M. Myers, *A Documentary History of American Interiors . . .*, New York, 1980, p. 94.

76 Orme, see p. 155 here.

77 I am indebted to Peter Scott of the Science Museum in London for information about this and other lighting devices.

78 See Schadel, *op. cit.*

# 1820–1870

1 See Garnier-Audiger, *Tapissier Décorateur*, Paris, edition of 1869. Anastase Garnier had worked at the French Royal Wardrobe (*Garde-Meuble de la Couronne*) where Percier was naturally much revered. His work first appeared in 1830 as the *Nouveau Manuel complet du Tapissier Décorateur*. Presumably Audiger revised the work for the 1869 edition.

2 Mark Girouard, *The Victorian Country House*, Oxford, 1971, p. 15. This informative work has much to offer those studying the subject with which we are here concerned. Jill Franklin's *The Gentleman's Country House and its Plan, 1835–1914*, London, 1981, is also most helpful.

3 Garnier-Audiger (see note 1 above) actually states this.

4 Osmont was a Parisian upholsterer and '*Editeur de dessins*'. His first *cahier* encompassed the designs of d'Hallevant (see Pl. 311) and augmented them with some of his own. A new style is to be seen in *Cahier v*, and the next *cahier* was published by Pinsonnière who claimed to be Osmont's successor. *Cahier VII* was published in 1839. A new series in the '*Style Renaissance*' was brought out by a man named Bordeaux who also claimed to be Osmont's successor. Bordeaux exhibited at the Paris Exhibition of 1844. To confuse matters further a C. Muidebled, also '*Editeur à Paris*', issued *La Pandore du Tapissier* with similar designs in 1837 and again in 1839. A helpful guide through this territory is provided by Samuel J. Dornsife (see note 54 in the previous section).

5 Quoted by Hans Ottomeyer in his doctoral thesis on Percier (Ludwig-Maximilians University, Munich, 1976; published by D. Gräbner, Altendorf, 1981). This contains a section on Percier's influence on French Historicism.

6 See *The Second Empire, 1852–1870*; catalogue of the exhibition held at the Philadelphia Museum of Art in 1978 and at the Grand Palais in Paris the year after. See also the relevant chapters of H.R. Hitchcock's *Architecture; Nineteenth and Twentieth Centuries*, Pelican History of Art, London, 1958.

7 Henry Havard, *Dictionnaire de l' Ameublement*, Paris, 1888–90, 'Boudoir'.

8 Havard, *op. cit.*, 'Boudoir', 'Salle', 'Salon'.

9 H.W. and A. Arrowsmith, *The House Decorator's and Painter's Guide*, London, 1840.

10 H. Kreisel and G. Himmelheber, *Die Kunst des Deutschen Möbels*, Vol. III, Munich, 1973, p. 157.

11 J.C. Loudon, *An Encyclopedia of Cottage, Farm and Villa Architecture and Furniture*, London, 1833.

12 Arrowsmiths, *op. cit.* As they were 'Decorators to the Queen' they can hardly have been trying to be democratic in making this statement.

13 A.J. Downing, *The Architecture of Country Houses*, New York, 1850, p. 380.

14 'Perhaps no other mode so wide-spread in its acceptance and so prolific in its production has ever received so little attention from posterity', wrote Hitchcock (*op. cit.*, p. 172) in 1958. This situation is now gradually being rectified. See, e.g., *The Beaux-Arts and Nineteenth Century French Architecture*, ed. R.D. Middleton, London, 1982; R. Middleton and D. Watkin, *Neoclassical and 19th Century Architecture*, New York, 1977; the Catalogue of the *Second Empire* exhibition, see note 6 above; and *Buildings on Paper: Rhode Island Architectural Drawings 1825–1945*, ed. W.H. Jordy and C. Monkhouse, Rhode Island School of Design, 1982, especially the introduction.

15 Downing, *op. cit.*, p. 392.

16 *Buildings on Paper, op. cit.*, p. 12.

17 See C. Wainwright, 'Specimens of Ancient Furniture', *The Connoisseur*, October 1973.

18 Robert Kerr, *The Gentleman's House*, London, 1864, pp. 366–7.

19 Moreover Gothenburg (Göteborg) means the 'Castle of the Goths'. When the Crown Prince Oskar was honoured by Uppsala University in 1819 the students called him 'Beloved of the Goths' (*Göternas Älskling*) as if these were mystical beings looking down on the Swedish nation.

20 Much has been written in the past forty years about Neo-Gothic, but a particularly fascinating survey is Charles Eastlake's *A History of the Gothic Revival. An attempt to show how the taste for mediaeval architecture which lingered in England during the two last centuries has since been encouraged and developed*, London, 1872, which was written by someone who had lived through the period of revival although it had still not quite run its full course. All subsequent essays on the subject inevitably rely largely on this source, which was reprinted in 1970 with a thoughtful introduction by J. Mordant Crook setting the work into its historical perspective. A new edition with a revised introduction appeared in 1978.

21 Downing, *op. cit.*, pp. 383 and 387.

22 'The Louis Quinze style . . . is often, from careless inspection, confounded with that of the Louis Quatorze', insisted the Arrowsmiths (*op. cit.*), but the designs they themselves show to illustrate the two styles make the distinction very far from clear.

23 Arrowsmiths, *op. cit.*

24 Kreisel and Himmelheber, *op. cit.*, p. 153; and J. Braund, *Illustration of Furniture . . . from the Great Exhibition of London and Paris . . .*, London, 1858.

25 See the interesting essay on *Hittorff's polychrome campaign* by R.D. Middleton (see note 14 above).

26 Kreisel and Himmelheber, *op. cit.*, p. 175.

27 *Second Empire Catalogue*, p. 31.

28 Editions appeared in Boston in 1872, 1874, 1875, 1876 and twice in 1879, while the fourth revised edition of the book appeared in New York in 1878. The book was based on articles that had previously appeared in *The Queen* and *The London Review*. It is not widely known that there was also a French edition. A useful essay on manuals of interior decoration available in America is Martha C. McClaugherty, 'Household Art. Creating the Artistic Home, 1868–1893', *The Winterthur Portfolio*, XVIII, No. 1, 1983.

29 I am grateful to Clive Wainwright for drawing my attention to this important essay which is discussed by J. Mordant Crook in his introduction to the 1978 reprint of Eastlake's *A History of the Gothic Revival*.

30 Bruce Talbert's work was also popular in America, editions coming out in Boston in 1873 and 1877.

31 'Cutting out a lot of rooms in cards and throwing them together anyhow is the way to plan a Gothic house', wrote a scathing commentator in 1876, but what he said could apply to any house planned on Picturesque lines (M. Girouard, *op. cit.*, p. 37).

32 Gervase Wheeler, *Rural Homes, or sketches of Houses suited to American Life . . .*, New York, 1851; and *A Practical Handbook of Useful Information on all points concerned with . . . building a House*, London, 1872. See also A.J. Downing, *op. cit.*; Robert Kerr, *op. cit.*; Girouard, *op. cit.* and *Life in the English Country House*, New Haven and London, 1978; Jill Franklin, *op. cit.*; and H.R. Hitchcock, *op. cit.*

33 Wheeler, *Handbook, op. cit.*, pp. 134–44.

34 Loudon, *op. cit.*, pp. 795–6.

35 Loudon (*op. cit.*, p. 1051) went so far as to claim that a

certain form of dining-table was 'a luxury worth the attention of bachelors: but unworthy of any family who do not prefer wine to the rational conversation of women'.

36 B. Disraeli, *Coningsby*, London, 1844.

37 E. Mayhew and M. Myers, *A Documentary History of American Interiors . . .*, New York, 1980, p. 375.

38 Frances Trollope, *Paris and the Parisians in 1835*, London, 1836, Vol. I, p. 231.

39 Garnier here contrasts the modest boudoir, dedicated to work and relaxation, with that of a lady-about-town (*petite maîtresse*) or *élégante* who is in no way embarrassed by pecuniary considerations, where everything is luxurious and soft.

40 M.C. Cowtan, *Reminiscences and Changes in Taste in House Decoration. A paper read before the Incorporated Institute of British Decorators . . . March 6th, 1914* (V. & A. Library). The essay on 'Papier Peint' in Havard, *op. cit.*, is informative on the history of this trade in Paris during his lifetime. See also A. Wells-Cole, *Historic Paper Hangings from Temple Newsam and other English Houses*, Leeds, 1983.

41 Cowtan, *op. cit.*

42 Charles Winston, *Memoirs Illustrative of the Art of Glass-Painting*, London, 1865.

43 Eastlake (1868) picked on just this feature in his criticism of the typical Victorian interior he wanted to get rid of. 'I firmly believe that if the West End upholsterers took it into their heads that . . . the drawing-room fender ought in summer time to be planted with mignonette, there are people who would repose implicit confidence in such advice.'

44 The manner in which Stockholm upholsterers copied French patterns in this way is demonstrated by E. Stavenow-Hidemark, 'Möbelförlagor och mönsterböcker från 1840-talet', *Fataburen*, 1975.

45 'Or, as they are called, *lamberkins*', as Harriet Beecher Stowe and her sister Catherine Beecher say in their *The American Woman's Home*, New York, 1864.

46 In a pattern-book entitled *Practical Illustrations of Upholstery Work. Being new designs . . .* by Alfred Standage, London, n.d., the plates of which are dated 1864, one plate with festoons at the head is described as having 'the old "swag hangings"' which were so very different from the *lambrequins* then in fashion.

47 Two helpful surveys of nineteenth-century furniture are E.T. Joy, *Pictorial Dictionary of British 19th Century Furniture Designs*, Woodbridge, Suffolk, 1977, and Christopher Payne, *The Price Guide to 19th Century European Furniture*, Woodbridge, Suffolk, 1981.

48 Referring to the leather-covered seats of dining-chairs, Loudon (*Encyclopedia*, 1833) states that 'instead of tufts, small rings are used, covered with the same leather as the chair [i.e. matching buttons]; these rings being found to look as well as, and wear better than, tufts of silk; at the same time they do not harbour dust'. The last was surely not true!

49 See Dorothy Holley, 'Upholstery springs', *Furniture History*, London, 1981; Havard, *op. cit.*, 'Elastique'; and S. Giedion, *Mechanisation takes Command*, Oxford, 1948, p. 376.

50 The name '*confortable*' was probably also used specifically for chairs with sprung seats.

51 See Gillian Walkling, *Antique Bamboo Furniture*, London, 1979.

52 According to Wheeler the best cane furniture in America came from Messrs Berrian of Broadway, New York, while 'a number of Germans have in their employment at least

two thousand girls occupied in this manufacture' in the New York suburbs and in Bloomingdale.

53 *Svenskt Möbellexikon*, Malmö, 1961, 'Steneberg'. The best cane apparently came from Galicia.

54 Benjamin Franklin is often credited with the invention of the rocking-chair. It seems anyway to have been invented by the late eighteenth century. *op. cit.*

55 Frances Trollope, *op. cit.* Taking a dig at the Parisian tendency to riot in the streets, she adds that 'in a few years, unless all paving-stone should be torn up in search of more immortality, there can be no doubt that it will be almost as easy to walk in Paris as in London' (Vol. I, p. 347).

56 Samuel J. Dornsife, 'Timetable of Carpet Technology', *Nineteenth Century*, Victorian Society of America, Autumn 1981. See also in the present connection C.E.C. Tatersall, *A History of British Carpets*, London, 1934.

57 A Frenchman named Franchot invented the 'Moderator' lamp in 1836, though Havard, *op. cit.*, 'Lampe', says it was 1837 and that it was perfected by Hadrot and Neuburger. It was, Havard adds, still by far the most practical lamp available in his time (1888–90).

58 See *Lamps & Other Lighting Devices, 1850–1906*, Princeton University, 1972, American Historical Catalog Collection.

59 Denys Peter Myers, *Gaslighting in America. A Guide for Historic Preservation* (U.S. Dept. of the Interior), Washington D.C., 1978. Miss Leslie's *Lady's Household Book* (Philadelphia, 1854) devotes much space to the cleaning and management of lamps.

60 John Britton, *The Union of Architecture . . .; Descriptive Accounts of the House . . . of John Soane*, London, 1827.

61 I am grateful to Clive Wainwright for this information. In his thesis on 'The Antiquarian Interior in Britain 1780–1850' he throws interesting light on Sir Walter's arrangements. One visitor describes how, after dinner, 'at the turning of a screw, the room was filled with a gush of splendour worthy of Aladdin'. However, while 'Jewelry sparkled . . . cheeks and lips looked cold and wan in this fierce illumination, and the eye wearied, and the brow ached, if the sitting was at all protracted'.

62 Frances Trollope, *op. cit.*, Vol. II, p. 302.

## 1870–1920

1 Quoted by Tove Clemmensen, 'Et Klunkehjem, Møbelstudier paa Herregaarden Broløkke', *Fra Nationalmuseets Arbejdsmark*, Copenhagen, 1942. This, incidentally, is a very interesting and early study of nineteenth-century furnishing arrangements.

2 Quoted in full as an appendix in N. Pevsner, *Some Architectural Writers of the Nineteenth Century*, Oxford, 1972. It gives a most admirable, if biased, survey of English architecture during the third quarter of the century.

3 Quoted by H.W. Desmond and H. Croly, *Stately Homes in America*, London and New York, 1903. These authors make a rather cruel gibe that 'one is inclined to believe that a palatial residence is sometimes the rich American girl's compensation for the absence of a "palatial" husband'.

4 Herbert Croly, *Architectural Record*, September 1915. Quoted in the excellent introduction to the catalogue of the exhibition *Buildings on Paper* held at the Rhode Island School of Design in 1982.

5 E.g. in *The House Furnisher and Decorator*, 10 April 1873.

6 The learned introduction to this admirable book throws much additional light on this subject as regards England. William Seale, *The Tasteful Interlude*, New York, 1975, covers much the same ground for the United States. See also A. Service, *Edwardian Interiors*, London, 1982, which includes many relevant illustrations as well.

7 W.R. Lethaby, *Philip Webb and his Work*, Oxford, 1935 (reprinted Ramsbury, 1979). This biography first appeared as a series of articles in *The Builder* in 1925.

8 J.D. Sedding, 'Our Art and Industries', *Art and Handicraft*, London, 1893.

9 Elisabeth Aslin, *The Aesthetic Movement*, London, 1969, p. 35. This work provides a helpful survey and has a chapter on the Aesthetic interior.

10 Nikolaus Pevsner has perhaps been too severe in his judgement of Edis (see 'Art Furniture of the 1870s', *Studies in Art, Architecture and Design*, London, 1968; the original essay was published in 1952).

11 Aslin, *op. cit.*, p. 46.

12 *Artistic Homes*, published in London in 1880, spoke vaguely of 'the forms adopted by Chippendale, and Sheraton, and other cabinet makers of the Queen Anne period'.

13 See Jonathan L. Fairbanks and Elizabeth Bidwell Bates, *American Furniture. 1620 to the Present*, London, 1981.

14 The main Scandinavian contributions were to come in the 1930s, although the illustrations by Carl Larsson had a certain influence in Germany in the early years of the century (see Pls.467, 496 and 516).

15 Exhibitions played a very important part in the dissemination of new ideas on interior decoration at this period, notably where complete rooms in a new style were shown. Not only were these exhibitions visited by other architects and by potential patrons, but the displays were commonly photographed and criticized in contemporary journals.

16 There are many books on the subject. The best guide remains Nikolaus Pevsner's *Pioneers of Modern Design*, London, 1936 (re-issued many times). See also Reyner Banham, *Theory and Design in the First Machine Age*, London, 1960.

17 *Artistic Houses*, New York, 1883, Vol. II, p. 91. The house of Samuel Hinckley.

18 E. de N. Mayhew and M. Myers, *A Documentary History of American Interiors*, New York, 1980, Fig. 125. This

well-illustrated book is especially informative about the period 1870–1915.

19 M. Praz, 'Resurrection of the Empire Style', *On Neoclassicism*, London, 1969.

20 Catalogue of the exhibition *Moderne Vergangenheit. Wien 1800–1900*, Künstlerhaus, Vienna, 1981, p. 18.

21 Frances Collard, 'The Regency and Empire Revival', *Decorative Arts Society Journal*, Vol. VII, 1984.

22 Stefan Tschudi Madsen, *Art Nouveau*, London, 1967, p. 27. The same author's *Sources of Art Nouveau* (London, 1957) is of seminal importance to an understanding of this interesting phase of modern art history.

23 It was in fact Edith Wharton's first book; her first stories were published the year after. The historical survey of architecture was probably by Codman, who was an excellent architect working in close imitations of the actual styles of the Louis XIV period, the eighteenth century and the *Empire* (see Pl.419). The book is a pleasure to read;

apparently they submitted the text to their friend Walter Berry who, they insist, improved it.

24 Edith Wharton and Ogden Codman praise the way Italians have always managed these things, and it is interesting to note that Archimede Sacchi, in his *Le habitazioni . . .* (Milan and Naples, 1874), a guide to building gentlemen's houses modelled on Robert Kerr's work of 1864 (see p. 216), makes clear the old distinction between *stanze per ricevere* (reception rooms) and *stanze dei abitazione* (rooms inhabited by the family only).

25 'The secret of a pretty room is to break up the straightness of the walls and to arrange the chairs as if a merry party of gossips had only just vacated them', stated *The Lady* in 1894.

26 C.H.B. Quennell's article on fireplaces in Lawrence Weaver's *The House and its Equipment*, London, *c*.1910, provides an interesting survey of developments of this feature from the time of Norman Shaw to that of Lutyens.

27 Pevsner, *op. cit.*, p. 128.

28 See Elisabet Stavenow-Hidemark, *Villabebyggelse i Sverige, 1900–1925* (Nordiska museets Handlinger No. 74, Stockholm), Lund, 1971, p. 100. Quoted from the weekly journal *Idun*, 1890.

29 The fact that dust could not collect under fitted wardrobes made them desirable on hygienic grounds. Very early examples were to be seen at the International Health Exhibition of 1884 (see N. Cooper, *The Opulent Eye*, London, 1976).

30 See D.P. Myers' excellent *Gaslighting in America*, Washington, D.C., 1978, p. 207. Apart from the Welsbach burner, the downward-turned gas-jet was an improvement that helped to prolong the popularity of gas-lighting.

31 The Japanese cult is 'more than a fashion, it is a craze', wrote W.E. Henley in 1882; 'the Japanese dado has become almost a household word and the Japanese fan a household essential'.

## BIBLIOGRAPHY OF USEFUL BOOKS PUBLISHED SINCE THE FIRST EDITION OF *AUTHENTIC DECOR*

John Adamson, *The Princely Courts of Europe 1500–1750*, Weidenfeld & Nicolson, London, 1999, ISBN 0297836536

Pauline Agius, *Ackerman's Regency Furniture & Interiors*, The Crowood Press, Marlborough, 1984, ISBN 0946284504

Geoffrey Beard, *Upholsterers and Interior Furnishing in England 1530–1840*, Yale University Press, New Haven and London, 1997, ISBN 0300071353

Ian Bristow, *Architectural Colour in British Interiors 1615–1840*, Yale University Press, New Haven and London, 1996, ISBN 0300038666

Frances Collard, *Regency Furniture*, The Antique Collector's Club, Woodbridge, Suffolk, 1985, ISBN 0907462510

John Cornforth, *The Inspiration of the Past: Country House Taste in the Twentieth Century*, Viking, New York and Penguin Books, Middlesex, 1985, ISBN 0670801801

Caroline Davidson, *The World of Mary Ellen Best*, Chatto and Windus, London, 1985, ISBN 0701129050

Elisabeth Donaghy Garrett, *At Home, The American Family 1750–1870*, Harry N. Abrams Inc, New York, 1989, ISBN 0810918943

Mark Girouard, *Life in the French Country House*, Cassell & Co., London, 2000, ISBN 0304354007

The National Museum, Stockholm, *Hemma i Konsten*, N.M. Exhibition No.502, 1987

Elisabeth Stavenow-Hidemark, *Nytt tyg på gamla stolar, Stoppning och Klädsel Förr och Nu* [*New Cloth on Old Chairs, Upholstery Then and Now*], Nordiska Museet, Stockholm, 1993, ISBN 9153415582

Patricia Waddy, *Seventeenth-Century Roman Palaces: Use and the Art of the Plan*, MIT Press, Cambridge, Mass., 1990, ISBN 0262231565

Clive Wainwright, *The Romantic Interior: The British Collector at Home, 1750–1850*, Yale University Press, New Haven and London, 1989, ISBN 0300042256

John Whitehead, *The French Interior in the Eighteenth Century*, Laurence King Publishing, London, 1992, ISBN 1856690180

# INDEX